Lecture Notes in Computer Science 10296

Commenced Publication in 1973
Founding and Former Series Editors:
Gerhard Goos, Juris Hartmanis, and Jan van Leeuwen

More information about this series at http://www.springer.com/series/7409

Panayiotis Zaphiris · Andri Ioannou (Eds.)

Learning and Collaboration Technologies

Technology in Education

4th International Conference, LCT 2017
Held as Part of HCI International 2017
Vancouver, BC, Canada, July 9–14, 2017
Proceedings, Part II

 Springer

Editors
Panayiotis Zaphiris
Cyprus University of Technology
Limassol
Cyprus

Andri Ioannou
Cyprus University of Technology
Limassol
Cyprus

ISSN 0302-9743   ISSN 1611-3349   (electronic)
Lecture Notes in Computer Science
ISBN 978-3-319-58514-7   ISBN 978-3-319-58515-4   (eBook)
DOI 10.1007/978-3-319-58515-4

Library of Congress Control Number: 2017939725

LNCS Sublibrary: SL3 – Information Systems and Applications, incl. Internet/Web, and HCI

Printed on acid-free paper

This Springer imprint is published by Springer Nature
The registered company is Springer International Publishing AG
The registered company address is: Gewerbestrasse 11, 6330 Cham, Switzerland

Foreword

The 19th International Conference on Human–Computer Interaction, HCI International 2017, was held in Vancouver, Canada, during July 9–14, 2017. The event incorporated the 15 conferences/thematic areas listed on the following page.

A total of 4,340 individuals from academia, research institutes, industry, and governmental agencies from 70 countries submitted contributions, and 1,228 papers have been included in the proceedings. These papers address the latest research and development efforts and highlight the human aspects of design and use of computing systems. The papers thoroughly cover the entire field of human–computer interaction, addressing major advances in knowledge and effective use of computers in a variety of application areas. The volumes constituting the full set of the conference proceedings are listed on the following pages.

I would like to thank the program board chairs and the members of the program boards of all thematic areas and affiliated conferences for their contribution to the highest scientific quality and the overall success of the HCI International 2017 conference.

This conference would not have been possible without the continuous and unwavering support and advice of the founder, Conference General Chair Emeritus and Conference Scientific Advisor Prof. Gavriel Salvendy. For his outstanding efforts, I would like to express my appreciation to the communications chair and editor of *HCI International News*, Dr. Abbas Moallem.

April 2017   Constantine Stephanidis

HCI International 2017 Thematic Areas and Affiliated Conferences

Thematic areas:

- Human–Computer Interaction (HCI 2017)
- Human Interface and the Management of Information (HIMI 2017)

Affiliated conferences:

- 17th International Conference on Engineering Psychology and Cognitive Ergonomics (EPCE 2017)
- 11th International Conference on Universal Access in Human–Computer Interaction (UAHCI 2017)
- 9th International Conference on Virtual, Augmented and Mixed Reality (VAMR 2017)
- 9th International Conference on Cross-Cultural Design (CCD 2017)
- 9th International Conference on Social Computing and Social Media (SCSM 2017)
- 11th International Conference on Augmented Cognition (AC 2017)
- 8th International Conference on Digital Human Modeling and Applications in Health, Safety, Ergonomics and Risk Management (DHM 2017)
- 6th International Conference on Design, User Experience and Usability (DUXU 2017)
- 5th International Conference on Distributed, Ambient and Pervasive Interactions (DAPI 2017)
- 5th International Conference on Human Aspects of Information Security, Privacy and Trust (HAS 2017)
- 4th International Conference on HCI in Business, Government and Organizations (HCIBGO 2017)
- 4th International Conference on Learning and Collaboration Technologies (LCT 2017)
- Third International Conference on Human Aspects of IT for the Aged Population (ITAP 2017)

Conference Proceedings Volumes Full List

Learning and Collaboration Technologies

Program Board Chair(s): **Panayiotis Zaphiris and Andri Ioannou, Cyprus**

- Ruthi Aladjem, Israel
- Mike Brayshaw, UK
- Jitender Kumar Chhabra, India
- Anastasios A. Economides, Greece
- Maka Eradze, Estonia
- Mikhail Fominykh, Norway
- David Fonseca, Spain
- Francisco J. García Peñalvo, Spain
- Evangelos Kapros, Ireland
- Tomaž Klobučar, Slovenia
- Efi Nisiforou, Cyprus
- Antigoni Parmaxi, Cyprus
- Marcos Roman Gonzalez, Spain
- Telmo Zarraonandia, Spain
- Maria Zenios, Cyprus

The full list with the Program Board Chairs and the members of the Program Boards of all thematic areas and affiliated conferences is available online at:

http://www.hci.international/board-members-2017.php

HCI International 2018

The 20th International Conference on Human–Computer Interaction, HCI International 2018, will be held jointly with the affiliated conferences in Las Vegas, NV, USA, at Caesars Palace, July 15–20, 2018. It will cover a broad spectrum of themes related to human–computer interaction, including theoretical issues, methods, tools, processes, and case studies in HCI design, as well as novel interaction techniques, interfaces, and applications. The proceedings will be published by Springer. More information is available on the conference website: http://2018.hci.international/.

General Chair
Prof. Constantine Stephanidis
University of Crete and ICS-FORTH
Heraklion, Crete, Greece
E-mail: general_chair@hcii2018.org

http://2018.hci.international/

Contents – Part II

Diversity in Learning

Learning Analytics

Improving the Learning and Collaboration Experience

Contents – Part I

e-Learning, Social Media and MOOCs

Beyond the Classroom

Games and Gamification for Learning

STEM Education

Using Augmented Reality Interactive System to Support Digital Electronics Learning

Poonpong Boonbrahm[✉], Charlee Kaewrat, and Salin Boonbrahm

School of Informatics, Walailak University, Nakorn si Thammarat, 80160 Tha Sala, Thailand
poonpong@gmail.com, Charlee.qq@gmail.com,
salil.boonbrahm@gmail.com

Abstract. The fundamental theories and concepts of digital electronics which usually being taught at entry level electronics courses is designed to help the students develop solid underlying knowledge of how computer works. The topics usually covered Boolean algebra, Logic Gates and etc. Beside Theory, which are being taught in the lectures, practical skill is required by doing the experiments. In the past the digital electronics laboratory is needed for this purpose, but recently, it was replaced by the software that can simulate the digital circuits. The advantage of this software is that, the students can study the behavior of a systems without building them which save a lot of time and expense. The drawback of these simulators is that, it lacks real charisma in performing the experiments and difficult to interpret. In this research, we have applied interactive marker-based augmented reality (AR) to solve these problems. The advantage of using this marker based techniques in this research is that we can implant the functions of each logic gates in the marker and program these markers to interact with others just like in the real logic gates laboratory. The other advantage is that, markers can be in any shape or have any pictures or symbol on it which make user recognize them easily. In this research, we have created 9 markers which represent 7 basic Logic gates i.e. AND gate, OR gate, NOT gate, NAND gate, NOR gate, XOR gate and XNOR gate. Since we can implant the functions of each logic gates in the marker, the output from these markers will represent the function of each logic gate. By adding them together, the output will be the same as adding the logic gates together. The advantage of using this marker based AR techniques is that we can construct the digital circuit using these markers and the output will be just the same as using the real logic gates, except there is no need for power supply and can be done anywhere and anytime.

Keywords: Augmented reality · Interactive · Logic gate · Boolean algebra · Marker

1 Introduction

Most students who took the courses related to computer or electronics must understand the basic of digital system. Digital systems are constructed by using logic gates such as AND, OR, NOT, NAND, NOR, EXOR and EXNOR gates. The basic operations can be described by using the truth table, which is a logically-based mathematical table that

© Springer International Publishing AG 2017
P. Zaphiris and A. Ioannou (Eds.): LCT 2017, Part II, LNCS 10296, pp. 3–11, 2017.
DOI: 10.1007/978-3-319-58515-4_1

shows all the possible outcomes of the scenario. Beside theory, usually practical work is required by doing the experiments. In the past the digital electronics laboratory is required and all the equipment such as IC chips, breadboards, IC Testers, power supplies and etc. should be provided in the laboratory. Even though, the cost for setting up the lab is not so high but there must be at least one technician to take care of the setup. Recently, there are some software that can simulate the digital circuits, so they can replace the real hardware experiments. The advantage of these software are that, the students can study the behavior of the systems without building them. Besides that, the results are quite accurate compared to analytic model and it is also easy to perform "what if" analysis. The drawback of these simulators, beside the cost, is that, it lacks real charisma in performing the experiments and sometimes it is difficult to interpret the simulation results.

In this research, we have applied interactive augmented reality to solve these problems. Augmented Reality or AR is the technology that integrated the computer's generated information or object into the user's environment in the real world. Unlike virtual reality which creates the whole virtual environment, AR uses real environment and overlay virtual environment on top of it. There are two types of AR, i.e. marker based AR and marker-less AR. In marker based AR, computer will generated the virtual environment related to the marker but in marker-less AR, the generated environment that the computer generated are related to information provided such as GPS location. The advantage of using this marker based technique in this research is that, we can implant the functions of each logic gate in the marker and program each marker to interact with others easily just like in the real logic gates. The other advantage is that is marker can be in any shape or have any picture or logo on it which make user recognize it easily.

2   Background

2.1   Overview of Augmented Reality

Augmented Reality (AR) is the integration of computer generated objects and the real world environment, in which the virtual object is overlaid on top of existing space. The computer generated objects that were projected on the real surface can be in any forms such as 2D image, 3D model, text, video or sound. Unlike virtual reality (VR) in which users are immerged into the computer generated virtual environment, AR let users experience virtual environment in their real space. To make it simple, in VR, users can see only virtual environment while in AR, users can see both virtual and real environment at the same time.

There are two types of AR application in terms of development i.e. marker based AR and marker-less AR. In marker-less AR, the coordinates or locations of the virtual objects were assigned by GPS, while in marker based AR, the position of the virtual objects placed on the real environment come from the marker. There are many type of 2D graphics that can be used as a markers in marker based AR such as, templates marker, 2D barcode marker, imperceptible markers, frame marker and etc. Template marker is black and white marker that has a simple image inside a black border. 2D barcode markers are markers that consist of black and white data cells. Imperceptible markers

Fig. 1. 2D markers; (1) templates (2) 2D barcode (3) Imperceptible (4) Frame marker

or image marker is the marker that uses natural color images as marker. Frame marker is the marker developed by Qualcomm that are transparent with the black border and black-white marker. Summarize of these markers are shown in Fig. 1. Today, 3D marker is also available.

2.2 Logic Gate and Its Truth Table

A logic gate is a basic building block of a digital circuit, which performs a logical operation on one or more binary inputs, and produces a single binary output. Most logic gates, except NOT gate, have two inputs and one output. The status of the terminal at one time is either "0" or "1". The status of the terminal will change as the circuit process the data. There are seven basic logic gates: AND, OR, XOR, NOT, NAND, NOR, and XNOR. The AND gate, is the logic gate that acts as the logical "and" operator, which mean that the output will be "1" or "high" only when both input terminals are "1", otherwise it is "0" or "low". When the output is "0", it is called "false" and when it is "1", then it is called "true", that is why the name "truth table" comes from. The "truth table" is a table that lists all the truth value of the outcome for each of the possible combinations. The OR gate is the logic gate that behave as a logical inclusive "or". The output is "true" if either or both of the inputs are "1". The **XOR (exclusive-OR)** gate behaves like the logical "either/or." The output is "true" if either, but not both, of the input is "true". The NOT gate or inverter, which has only one input, has the function that reverses the logic state. The NAND gate operates as an AND gate followed by a NOT gate. In other word, the output from AND gate will be the input of the NOT gate and the output of the NOT gate will be the output of the NAND gate. For the NOR gate which is a combination OR gate followed by an inverter. Its output will be "true", only if both inputs to the OR gate are "false". The XNOR (exclusive-NOR) gate is a combination XOR gate followed by an inverter. Its output is "true" if the inputs to the XOR gate are the same. The gate symbols, Boolean Algebra and truth table of seven basic logic gates (NOT, AND, NAND, OR, NOR and XNOR) are shown in Fig. 2. By using combinations of these logic gates, complex operations can be performed.

Logic Gates

Name	NOT	AND	NAND	OR	NOR	XOR	XNOR
Alg. Expr.	$\bar{A}$	AB	$\overline{AB}$	$A+B$	$\overline{A+B}$	$A\oplus B$	$\overline{A\oplus B}$
Symbol							

Truth Table

NOT		AND			NAND			OR			NOR			XOR			XNOR		
A	X	B	A	X	B	A	X	B	A	X	B	A	X	B	A	X	B	A	X
0	1	0	0	0	0	0	1	0	0	0	0	0	1	0	0	0	0	0	1
1	0	0	1	0	0	1	1	0	1	1	0	1	0	0	1	1	0	1	0
		1	0	0	1	0	1	1	0	1	1	0	0	1	0	1	1	0	0
		1	1	1	1	1	0	1	1	1	1	1	0	1	1	0	1	1	1

Fig. 2. Logic gate symbols, boolean algebra expression and its' truth table

3   Related Work

Augmented Reality Technology has been applied in many areas ranging from manufacturing, architecture, arts, entertainment and education. Since the unique capabilities of augmented reality to display information in almost any form of media, the potential for learning process is very promising. Many researchers have studied about how to use AR in education. Chen et al. [1], review more than 55 papers related to applying Augmented Reality in education that published between 2011–2016 and mentioned about the trend, future and opportunities in using augmented reality for education. Boonbrahm et al. [2], investigate on how to use AR to motivate children in learning English. Different AR techniques were used for this purpose i.e. marker-marker interaction and user-defined target. The results agree with the prediction that children really enjoy and eager to learn more. Fan et al. [3] indicates the significance of AR based experiment in education and mentioned that this technology will bring lots of new features for experimental education. Aquirregoitia Martinez et al. [4] presented the results of using AR applications for preschool education. The area of applications covers reading, numbers and etc. The conclusion indicated that the applications encourage interaction, content adaptability, multisensory stimulus and can be successfully adopted for learning and development in Preschool education. In the area of using AR Interface for Laboratory Experiments, Onime et al. [5], presented an application of Augmented Reality (AR) technology for hands-on practical laboratory experiments for Science and Engineering students and confirmed that the students found the AR technology easy to use, and they were satisfied with the simulation and rendering quality of the implemented AR applications. Boonbrahm et al. [6], show that adding physical properties to the virtual object in AR experiment will make interaction between virtual objects feel more realistic. Srivastava et al. [7] use Augmented Reality based Instructions for Electronics Lab (ARIEL) and tested amongst undergraduate students of Basic Electronic Engineering Laboratory course. This paper discusses the methodologies utilized for the design process. Even though, there are many AR applications being used in many fields of education but very few are available for replacing the real laboratory experiment, so there still be the opportunity to research into this area.

4 System Development

The virtual Digital electronics system development can be broken down into two parts i.e. AR applications for mobile and system setup.

4.1 Application Development

In this research, Unity3D game engine was used on Qualcomm's Vulforia platform. Unity is a fully integrated development engine for creating games and other interactives 3D content. Qualcomm's Vulforia platform made it possible to write a single native application that run on almost all smartphone and tablets. This application is designed for iOS system but can be modified to be used on Android as well. For the marker, frame marker was selected for this purpose since it is easy to detect.

4.2 System Setup

In the real setup of digital electronics experiment, all the equipment must connected to each other via wires or cables, but for virtual experiment, connection via wire is impossible. The only connecting path between each virtual parts i.e. logic gate markers, input/output markers, can be done through vision only. By placing logic gate marker on spot, the applications program in the smartphone will scan for the marker on the left sides which is the input and get the data for processing by logic gate markers' function and then send the output to the marker which is located on the right side (output marker). Since almost all the logic gate has two inputs, the program will scan for two markers and get the data from both inputs before transfer the data for processing. After processing, the output data will be processed by next logic gate's markers or displayed as the output.

4.3 Virtual Configuration

Since the markers in marker-based AR can be programmed to represent the virtual objects in both location of the object and mathematical functions, then the interaction between markers is possible. For example, if we have three markers that represent alphabet "D", "O" and "G" and put them in that consecutive order, the program will process and interpret them as a word "DOG" and with the AR application, the 3D model of the dog will be displayed on top of the marker as shown in Fig. 3. The same concept can be applied to the logic gate as well.

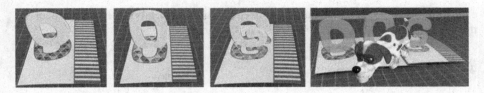

Fig. 3. Marker-marker interaction

4.4 Mapping AR and Logic Gate

In order to make a virtual logic gate circuit work just like the real logic gate circuit, the function that it performs should follow the truth table of that logic gate. In real logic gate, the input of the logic gate should be connected to the input source and the output should be connected to the display device or to another input of the next logic gate. To duplicate this process for virtual setup, there will be at least four AR markers, two for the input which can be either "0" or "1", one logic gate marker and one output marker. Each of the markers can have the picture or symbol that show their function. For example, markers that have the number "0" and "1" are the input source and will give the value either "0" and "1". Marker that shows the symbol of the logic gate should perform as that logic gate. Marker that has the bulb symbol is the display marker and it will perform as a light bulb, i.e. it is dark if the signal is "0" and bright if the signal is "1". Example of the virtual setup for different logic gate are shown in Figs. 4, 5 and 6.

B	A
0	0
0	1
1	0
1	1

Fig. 4. Truth table, setup for AND gate and its operation

B	A	X
0	0	0
0	1	1
1	0	1
1	1	1

Fig. 5. Truth table, setup for OR gate and its operation

A	X
0	1
1	0

input   process   output

Fig. 6. Truth table, setup for NOT gate or inverter and its operation

5   Implementation

In real digital electronics circuit, there are many logic gates connected to each other, so in the virtual circuit, the virtual logic gate should be able to do the same thing. In order to make this AR logic gate replace the real one in the lab, these AR logic gates must be able to interact with each other, giving a larger circuits that is useful in construct parts of the computer. As mentioned before, the markers in marker-based AR can be programmed to represent the virtual objects with mathematical functions, then the interaction between markers is possible. To demonstrate the possibility, we have constructed larger circuits consisted of many logic gate as shown in Figs. 7, 8 and 9.

Fig. 7. Output from AND gate and NOT gate were used as an input to the OR gate.

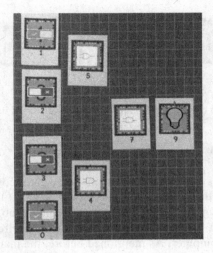

Fig. 8. Output from OR gate and AND gate were used as an input to the NAND gate.

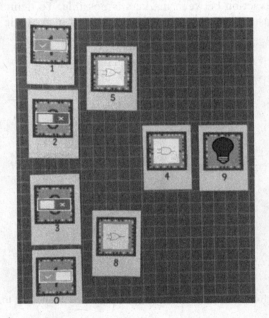

Fig. 9. Output from OR gate and NOR gate were used as an input to the AND gate.

6   Summary and Conclusion

From this research, we have found that, virtual Logic gate can replace real Logic gate for the laboratory experiment. The advantage of using the virtual experiment is that, the experiment can be done anywhere, anytime without using using the facilities in the laboratory. The only device needed is the smartphone or tablet with AR application program and paper markers. The disadvantage is the limitation of the space that can be clearly detected by the mobile phone camera. The suitable area that the mobile phone camera can detect nicely is A4 paper with the distance between camera and markers is around 12 to 20 inches. This concept can be adapted to cover other areas of experiments such as basic electronics, Physics, Chemistry and etc.

References

1. Chen, P., Liu, X., Cheng, W., Huang, R.: A Review of Using Augmented Reality in Education from 2011 to 2016. Lecture Notes in Educational Technology, pp. 13–18 (2016)
2. Boonbrahm, S., Kaewrat, C., Boonbrahm, P.: Using augmented reality technology in assisting english learning for primary school students. In: Zaphiris, P., Ioannou, A. (eds.) LCT 2015. LNCS, vol. 9192, pp. 24–32. Springer, Cham (2015). doi:10.1007/978-3-319-20609-7_3
3. Fan, P., Zhou, M., Wang, X.: The significance and effectiveness of augmented reality in experimental education. In: 2011 International Conference on e-Business and e-Government (ICEE), pp. 1–4. IEEE (2011)
4. Aquirregoitia Martinez, A., Allende Lopez, I., Lopez Benito, J.R., Artetxe Gonzalez, E.: Leihoa: a window to augmented reality in early childhood education. In: 2016 International Symposium on Computer in Education (2016)
5. Onime, C., Abiona, O.: 3D mobile augmented reality interface for laboratory experiments. Int. J. Commun. Netw. Syst. Sci. **9**, 67–76 (2016)
6. Boonbrahm, P., Imbert, M., Vignat, F., Kaewrat, C.: Adding physical properties to 3D model in augmented reality for realistic interactions experiments. Procedia Comput. Sci. **25**(2013), 364–369 (2013)
7. Srivastava, A., Yammiyanvar, P.: ARIEL: Augmented Reality based Instruction for Electronic Laboratory in Engineering Education. Working Paper (2016)

An AI System for Coaching Novice Programmers

Gilbert Cruz, Jacob Jones, Meagan Morrow, Andres Gonzalez,
and Bruce Gooch$^{(\boxtimes)}$

Texas A&M University, College Station, USA
{gilbertcruz,meagmccright,agonzalez95,
Gooch}@tamu.edu, jtjonesjt@gmail.com

Abstract. We inhabit a century where every job will be technical. In the 21st century, learning to program a computer is empowerment. Programming instruction teaches procedural and functional thinking, project management and time management, skills that are essential components of an empowered individual. Programming is the power to create, the power to change and the power to influence. Today's students regardless of their field of study or need this fundamental knowledge.

Rapidly giving students meaningful feedback is a fundamental component of an effective educational experience. A common problem in modern education is scalability, as class size increases an instructor's ability to provide meaningful feedback decreases. We report on an online Artificial Intelligence (AI) system capable of providing insightful narrative based coaching to beginning programmers. We document system tests to ensure that: it generates a unique response to every input, makes responses in real time, and is deployable online.

Keywords: Feedback · Coaching · Programming · Education

1 Introduction

Statistics show that number of students pursuing computer science as a major in American colleges and universities has dropped by as much as 60% [1, 2]. These statistics indicate decreasing interest of college freshmen in computer science at a time when industry advertises employment opportunities in computer related fields. Several misconceptions deter college students from pursing computer science as a major, one being that computer scientists are males who lack social skills and whose lives revolve around sitting in front of the computer all day long; such misconceptions deter college students from pursing computer science as a major [3–5]. Industry has voiced its concern about the decreasing supply of qualified employees in computer related fields, deciding to partner with academia to find solutions to address the issue of recruitment and retention of computer science majors. One solution involves invigorating traditional core computer science curriculum with pedagogical strategies that leverage the use of digital media as a means to generate interest in courses perceived to be designed exclusively for techies, geeks and programming gurus.

© Springer International Publishing AG 2017
P. Zaphiris and A. Ioannou (Eds.): LCT 2017, Part II, LNCS 10296, pp. 12–21, 2017.
DOI: 10.1007/978-3-319-58515-4_2

2 Curriculum

Teachers often struggle with creative and meaningful ways to assist students in developing their programming skills and provide ample support for beginning programmers [6]. In addition, first year Computer Science carries the highest cognitive load of any academic disciple [1–6]. Students have to learn the problem the solving skills of Engineers and a new form of language. Compounding this problem is the widespread use of Mathematics pedagogy. Exercises and tests use a "fill in the blank" model. Students receive nonworking computer code or a specification and expected to generate a solution.

We have found more practical methods of teaching introductory computer science by incorporating cognitive linguistics research [13–18]. The most useful result is changing the Exercise format from "fill in the blank" to creative writing. Students receive working code and educational scaffolding based on industry practice. Students extend the starter code to increase functionality or efficiency. Then test their code using data they are responsible for creating (Fig. 1).

Fig. 1. Students must Credit their source not Plagiarize. Students may Transform the work of others, not Imitate. Students may Remix the work of others, not Rip-Off. Banksy by Information of New Orleans used under Creative Commons Attribution 2.0 http://commons.wikimedia.org/wiki/File:Banksy_NOLA_SimpsonsA.jpg Jan. 15 2015.

To support this effort, we develop an infrastructure that accommodates novice programmers. The infrastructure includes:

- Sixty creative writing style programming assignments.
- Laboratory programming assignments that emphasize team based enquiry and learning.
- Built-in software evaluation tools to assist students with developing good programming skills.

2.1   Assignments

For each assignment students will be shown how to write Java code that solves a well defined and interesting problem using a programing topic that is the learning objective for that assignment. Students will be responsible for modifying and extending the code to solve a similar problem that interests them. Examples will be provided.

This is a Studio course all assignment code will be posted in an open forum. Grading will be based on three factors; is an individuals code different from the code provided by the instructor, is the code different from that of all the other students, and the instructor may award bonus points for innovation, novelty, and coolness.

Students are not only encouraged they are required to use, modify and communicate with others about computer code they did not write. Students may include copyright free code in their assignments so long as they provide the source of the code and the date in a comment. Assignments must contain 25% original code. Changing variable names and values does not constitute "original code."

2.2   Team Based Learning

Traditional computer science curriculum emphasizes individual achievement, discouraging students from working together for fear of unethical practices such as cheating. In contrast, industry values teamwork as a necessary practice. To facilitate students' ability to work with others and strengthen their interpersonal skills, we incorporate teamwork as an essential component of computer science curriculum and present a team-based learning model applicable to programming assignments. The team-based learning model promotes collaborative learning among students, dividing them into groups for the purpose of completing a programming assignment that is virtually impossible for one student to do given specific time constraints.

We define the process of team-based programming according to the following steps:

Students review the rubric for each programming assignment.

We equate rubric to the course requirements, providing a framework for assignments, learning objectives and methods for student assessment. A well-defined rubric serves as a guide for students' learning and communicates the teacher's expectations for each programming assignment [5]. Therefore, we post the rubric for each module on the course wiki so that the information is available in a public place.

Teams participate in a top-down design approach to derive a solution for the programming assignment, breaking down the design of the game module into manageable pieces (e.g. background scenery, user interface, etc.). Team members negotiate the portions of the assignment that each student will complete; member assignments are posted on the wiki for review. The act of negotiating engages team members in supportive communicative practices such as sharing information that builds group knowledge, acknowledging peers' ideas, mediating conflict when group members disagree, and asking for assistance.

These social interactions form the basis for building a high performance team that works together to accomplish the common goal of designing a game module.

Individual students write code and complete assessment. Although team-based learning emphasizes collaboration among group members to acquire object-oriented design skills, it is not a substitute for individual students mastering these skills. Students write code for their portion of the team programming assignment. Each student then uploads individual submitted code segments to the course wiki and completes an online quiz. The quiz lists open-ended questions and the answers are available only to the instructor (Fig. 2).

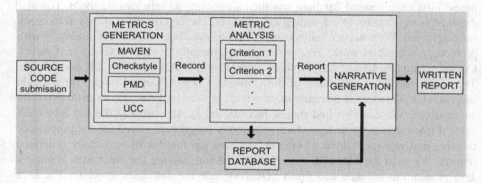

Fig. 2. A Diagram of the system. Code is submitted by students, if the code passes the compile and copy process it moves to metric generation and metric record is generated. The record is stored in a report database that tracks individual student progress and may be used to enhance the compile and copy process. The metric analysis system creates a report that is passed to the narrative generation process. The narrative generation software builds a written report from the code metrics. The report aids in coaching a student based on their personal improvement rather than in comparison to fellow students.

3 Software Evaluation Tools

We used a bottom-up design process shown to be useful in Computational Linguistics [24], Applied Computing [23] and Machine Learning [22]. We first built components. We linked them together to form subsystems. Finally we connected subsystems to develop the top-level system. Our top-level system requires three subsystems; advanced metrics, pattern matching, and narrative generation. The pattern matching subsystem finds similarities, while the advanced metrics subsystem finds differences. Their output forms the input to the narrative generation subsystem. In order to reach multiple goals and manage our project development, our team implemented a project management task known as scrum. This allowed for the building and testing of the AI system to have a designated timeline. Our team also used our personal past assignments as a sample material. These assignments were used as a testing aid when implementing the system.

Current auto-grading software uses a Compile, Correct, Copied model [19]. The software checks that submissions compile, run, produce correct output, and are not plagiarized. Such software is not enough to provide meaningful feedback [20]. Our Coaching AI first performs the standard Compile, Correct, Copied checks. If the submission passes, we compare with a database of the student's previous work. We generate Feedback in the form of a unique narrative. The story details the effects of the student's modifications (speed, functionality, memory usage, etc.). It also contains, tips on improving the functionality and readability of their code. A story may go on to detail how their work is novel compared with their peers. An evaluation of how their coding ability is improving is always included.

The advanced metrics subsystem classifies code and compares it with two databases. First are a general database and then a personal submissions database. The first database is a collection of old coding assignments. The first database allows us to check for plagiarism. We compare submissions with this database to check for similarity with previously submitted work. We wrote a Java program to make a Compile, Correct, Copied part using CCCC [25], Unified Code Count [26], and RSM [27] and Maven. The second database composed of the Compile, Correct, Copied output for a single individual. It allows us to compute metrics such as increased complexity from two code submissions. We can also find trends, records, deltas, and streaks. We use it to track student improvement over time. Every student's progress is stored for the purpose of creating new reports without making them sound too familiar to previously generated reports. We used the MariaDB system to create and manage the databases. We use a Java program to accesses and inject SQL code into the databases remotely. The Java code is included as metadata in the report. The report uses the Java code to access the tables in individual students information.

The pattern matching subsystem performs lexical analysis to generate an abstract a syntax tree. Abstract syntax trees are analogous to sentence diagrams with parts of speech labeled. Machine learning methods find correlations between the abstract syntax tree of a submission and those stored in a database. These allow us to find improvements like repeated errors, best practice use, or readability.

The narrative subsystem uses natural language generation to tell a story around insights obtained by the advanced metrics and pattern matching subsystems [37]. We used the KPML system from the University of Bremen [28]. The KPML system offers a robust, mature platform for large-scale grammar engineering. Both flexibilities of expression and speed of generation are issues for us. KPML is particularly useful in applications like ours. The finalized report is designed in an easy to read manner that will hold specific detail that is relevant to the students as individuals.

4 Development Plan

Design and development planning culminated in a plan that identifies necessary tasks, procedures for anomaly reporting and resolution, resource requirements, and design review requirements. A software life cycle model and associated activities will be determined, as well as those tasks necessary for each software life cycle activity. We used a test first iterative waterfall software life cycle model.

The student's software creation plan identified the personnel, the facility and equipment resources for each task, and the role that risk (hazard) management will play. A configuration management plan was developed to guide and control development activities and ensure proper communication and documentation. Version control software is necessary to provide active and correct correspondence among all approved versions of the specifications documents, source code, object code, and test suites that comprise the software system. The project used controlled release system software (CVS) to ensure exact correspondence between software versions. The CVS software will also provide accurate identification of, and access to, the currently approved versions. Procedures were be created for reporting and resolve software anomalies found through validation or other activities. Throughout the software development process the International Organization for Standardization (ISO) software creation, documentation, and testing standards were met.

We tested and evaluated the software using the HP software evaluation tools [39]. We ensured that our software; it meets the design and development requirements. It responds to input correctly. It performs in real-time. It is sufficiently usable and can be installed and run online.

Requirements development includes the identification, analysis, and documentation of information about the device and its intended use. Areas of special importance include allocation of system functions to hardware/software, operating conditions, user characteristics, potential hazards, and anticipated tasks. In addition, the requirements will clearly state the intended use of the software. The software requirements specification document will contain a written definition of the software functions. Typical software requirements specify the following: All software system inputs; All software system outputs; All functions that the software system will perform; All performance requirements that the software will meet, (e.g., data throughput, reliability, and timing); The definition of all external and user interfaces, as well as any internal software-to-system interfaces; How users will interact with the system; What constitutes an error and how errors should be handled; Required response times; The intended operating environment for the software, if this is a design constraint (e.g., hardware platform, operating system); All ranges, limits, defaults, and specific values that the software will accept; and All safety related requirements, specifications, features, or functions that will be implemented in software. We will develop the requirements for the software in the first months of working on the project and post them on the project webpage.

Software safety requirements were derived from a technical risk management process that is closely integrated with the system requirements development process. Software requirement specifications will identify clearly the potential hazards that can result from a software failure in the system as well as any safety requirements to be implemented in software. The consequences of software failure will be evaluated, along with means of mitigating such failures (e.g., hardware mitigation, defensive programming, etc.).

In the design process, the software requirements specification is translated into a logical and physical representation of the software to be implemented. The software design specification is a description of what the software should do and how it should do it. The completed software design specification constrains the programmer/coder to stay within the intent of the agreed upon requirements and design.

The activities that occur during software design have several purposes. Software design evaluations are conducted to determine if the design is complete, correct, consistent, unambiguous, feasible, and maintainable. Software design evaluations will include analyses of control flow, data flow, complexity, timing, sizing, memory allocation, criticality analysis, and other aspects of the design. A traceability analysis will be conducted to verify that the software design implements all of the software requirements. The traceability analysis should also verify that all aspects of the design are traceable to software requirements. An analysis of communication links will be conducted to evaluate the proposed design with respect to hardware, user, and related software requirements. The software risk analysis will be re-examined to determine whether any new hazards have been introduced by the design.

At the end of the software design process, a Formal Design Review was conducted to verify that the design is correct, consistent, complete, accurate, and testable, before moving to the coding phase of the project.

Software may be constructed either by coding (i.e., programming) or by assembling together previously coded software components (e.g., from code libraries, off-the-shelf software, etc.) for use in a new application. Coding is the software activity where the detailed design specification is implemented as source code. Coding is the last stage in decomposition of the software requirements where module specifications are translated into a programming language. The project will be coded in the Java programming language using off the shelf OpenGL libraries to drive the graphics accelerator cards. The system will be run on the Linux operating system.

The project used the TogetherJ development environment. The TogetherJ tool from TogetherSoft is a development environment for building object-based systems using the Java software language. It combines design and coding, letting developers effortlessly switch between the two, and facilitating an iterative style of software development. TogetherJ supports and promotes, a "design, code, test" approach to object-oriented design.

Software testing entails running software products under known conditions with defined inputs and documented outcomes that can be compared to their predefined expectations. Throughout the project we will followed the testing guidelines put forth in NUREG/CR-6293, Verification and Validation Guidelines for High Integrity Systems.

Testing at the user site is an essential part of software validation. Project site testing took place at a user's site with the actual hardware and software that will form an installed system configuration. User site testing followed a pre-defined written plan with a formal summary of testing and a record of formal acceptance. The testing plan specified testing throughout the full range of operating conditions and should specify continuation for a sufficient time to allow the system to encounter a wide spectrum of conditions and events in an effort to detect any latent faults that are not apparent during more normal activities. All testing procedures such as test input data, and test results will be documented and retained. In addition to an evaluation of the system's ability to properly perform its intended functions, there was an evaluation of the ability of the users of the system to understand and correctly interface with the workstation (Fig. 3).

Metrics

Lines	20
Comemnts	5
Cyclomatic Complexity (CC)	2
Whitespace	27

Criteria

	Great	Good	Neutral	Bad
Comments/Lines	X < .25	.25 <= X<= .30	.30 < X <= .35	X > .35
CC	X < 3	3 <= X <= 6	6 < X <= 9	X > 9
Whitespace	X < 5	5<= X <= 15	15 < X <= 25	X >25

*These values are for illustrative purposes only.

Example Report: This week you did very well in commenting your code, you have greatly improved your commenting skills in the past 3 weeks! In the past, you've had trouble with the amount of nested loops, but this week there was great improvement. You seem to have a little trouble with whitespace in your code. Additional whitespace is being put in unnecessary places; removing this whitespace will give your code a cleaner look. Overall, this week you have improved a lot more than any other week. Keep up great work!

Fig. 3. Shows some of the possible metrics and criteria that are generated in the statistical analysis programs and an example report based on the illustrative metrics and criteria.

5 Program Evaluation

We performed both formative and summative evaluation of the assignments and team based learning laboratories. Formative evaluation metrics included pre-tests administered to students prior to participation in the project, and baseline attitude surveys administered to student participants. The surveys were repeated at the end of the course and six months after the course.

The evaluation instruments were designed to answer the following questions:

- Has the students' knowledge, of java programming, increased since the pre-test.
- Have their attitudes toward studies and careers changed since learning to program?

Over the past two years we have evaluated six cohorts in all six cases the answers we received are yes and yes. Student knowledge of Java programming has increased and tends to increase after the course. We found that students tend to write small, less than one thousand lines of code, programs to solve homework problems in other classes. We have also found that students who listed Java programming experience on resumes were more likely to receive internships. We have anecdotal evidence that a significant number of students have transferred into the CS major, but at this time we lack a rigorous longitudinal study. The most telling statistic is the fact that over three years we have less that 1% dropout from the course and a less 1% failure rate. This compares to the traditionally taught course with a 30% dropout rate over the same time period.

6 Future Work

To determine the effectiveness of our platform we are currently conducting a multiyear longitudinal study. We will compare students' performance in our course to students who enroll in a traditional object oriented programming class. In phase one groups of students will complete a pre and post assessment that measures their understanding of object-oriented programming concepts and ability. The assessment will help us to recognize factors that contribute to learning outcomes for each group. In phase two we are tracking the student performance in second year of programming courses. We also plan to compare fan-in and fan-out. (i.e. do non-majors who take this class change their major to Computer Science and what proportion of Computer Science majors change after taking this class versus a standard class.)

7 Conclusion

The computer's role in culture has expanded from a calculating machine used by governments to the iPod as a fashion accessory, the Smart Phone as a companion, and the Internet as a medium of self-expression. In the 1950s, the idea of dedicating a computer to entertainment was unthinkable; today revenues from the computer game industry exceed Hollywood. More humans own a computer than own a toothbrush and Apple is the worlds largest company having overtaken Oil, Agriculture and Manufacturing. From if conditionals to for loops, knowing the basics of programming allows one to understand the way the modern world works.

References

1. Snyder, N.: Universities see a sharp drop in computer science majors
2. Vesgo, J.: Interest in CS as a major drops among incoming freshman
3. Guzdial, M., Forte, A.: Design process for a non-majors computing course
4. Guzdial, M., Soloway, E.: Teaching the Nintendo generation to program: preparing a new strategy for teaching introductory programming. Commun. ACM **45**, 17–21 (2002)
5. Margolis, J., Fisher, A.: Unlocking the Clubhouse: Women in Computing. MIT Press, Cambridge (2002)
6. Layman, L., Williams, L., Slaten, K.: Note to self: make assignments meaningful. In: Proceedings of the Thirty-Eighth SIGCSE Technical Symposium on Computer Science Education, pp. 459–463. ACM Press (2006)
7. Tuovinen, J., Sweller, J.: A comparison of cognitive load associated with discovery learning and worked examples. J. Educ. Psychol. **91**(2), 334–341 (1999)
8. Sweller, J.: Cognitive load theory learning difficulty, and instructional design. Learn. Instr. **4**(4), 295–312 (1994)
9. Pea, R.D.: Midian Kurland, D.: On the cognitive effects of learning computer programming. New Ideas Psychol. **2**(2), 137–168 (1984)
10. Jenkins, T.: On the difficulty of learning to program. In: Proceedings of the 3rd Annual Conference of the LTSN Centre for Information and Computer Sciences, vol. 4 (2002)

11. Pennington, N.: Stimulus structures and mental representations in expert comprehension of computer programs. Cogn. Psychol. **19**(3), 295–341 (1987)
12. Mayer, R.E.: Different problem-solving competencies established in learning computer programming with and without meaningful models. J. Educ. Psychol. **67**(6), 725 (1975)
13. Soloway, E., Spohrer, J.C.: Studying the Novice Programmer. Psychology Press, Hove (2013)
14. Gomes, A., José Mendes, A.: Learning to program-difficulties and solutions. In: International Conference on Engineering Education–ICEE, vol. 2007 (2007)
15. Du Benedict, B.: Some difficulties of learning to program. J. Educ. Comput. Res. **2**(1), 57–73 (1986)
16. Lahtinen, E., Ala-Mutka, K., Järvinen, H.-M.: A study of the difficulties of novice programmers. ACM SIGCSE Bull. **37**(3), 14–18 (2005). ACM
17. Mayer, R.E.: Teaching and learning
18. Tan, P.-H., Ting, C.-Y., Ling, S.-W.: Learning difficulties in programming courses: undergraduates' perspective and perception. In: International Conference on Computer Technology and Development, ICCTD 2009, vol. 1. IEEE (2009)
19. Ala-Mutka, K.: A survey of automated assessment approaches for programming assignments. Comput. Sci. Educ. **15**(2), 83–102 (2005)
20. Ihantola, P., et al.: Review of recent systems for automatic assessment of programming assignments. In: Proceedings of the 10th Koli Calling International Conference on Computing Education Research. ACM (2010)
21. Morris, D.S.: Automatic grading of student's programming assignments: an interactive process and suite of programs. In: Proceedings of 33rd Annual Frontiers in Education, FIE 2003, vol. 3. IEEE (2003)
22. Califf, E.: M., Mooney, R.J.: Bottom-up relational learning of pattern matching rules for information extraction. J. Mach. Learn. Res. **4**, 177–210 (2003)
23. Chang, B.-M., Choe, K.-M., Giacobazzi, R.: Abstract filters: improving bottom-up execution of logic programs by two-phase abstract interpretation. In: Proceedings of the 1994 ACM Symposium on Applied Computing, pp. 388–393. ACM Press (1994)
24. Erbach, G.: Bottom-up early deduction. In: Proceedings of the 15th Conference on Computational Linguistics, pp. 796–802. Association for Computational Linguistics (1994)
25. http://sourceforge.net/projects/cccc/
26. http://sunset.usc.edu/ucc_wp/
27. http://msquaredtechnologies.com/m2rsm/rsm_demo.php
28. http://www.fb10.unibremen.de/anglistik/langpro/kpml/readme.html
29. The Boyer Commission on Educating Undergraduates: Reinventing undergraduate education: a blueprint for America's research universities (1998)

Affective Walkthroughs and Heuristics: Evaluating Minecraft Hour of Code

Reza GhasemAghaei[✉], Ali Arya, and Robert Biddle

School of Computer Science, Carleton University, Ottawa, Canada
{Reza.GhasemAghaei,Ali.Arya,Robert.Biddle}@carleton.ca
https://hotsoft.carleton.ca/

Abstract. This paper presents an evaluation of Code.org's Minecraft Hour of Code that was created to encourage and support people initial learning of computer programming. In particular, this web-based software uses a spatial model world, where the learner's programs manipulate the world. We applied the Affective Walkthrough and the Affective Heuristic Evaluation, proposed evaluation methods for affective learning in multimodal educational software. Our findings provided illumination about the Minecraft Hour of Code approach, highlighting some aspects that are successful, and others where improvement appears necessary. We also gained insight about the evaluation methods and their effectiveness.

Keywords: Education software · Evaluation · Affective learning · Spatial environments

1 Introduction

This paper presents an evaluation of Code.org's Minecraft Hour of Code. The software was created to encourage and support people initial learning of computer programming. In particular, this web-based software uses a spatial model world, where the learner's programs manipulates the world. We applied the *Affective Walkthrough* and the *Affective Heuristic Evaluation* proposed earlier [4] and refined with the previous case studies [5,6]. Our previous studies were conducted with participants to refine our methods, and inform us about the collaborative processes. In this new study, we simply applied this knowledge and conducted the evaluations ourselves. Our findings provided illumination about the Minecraft Hour of Code approach, highlighting some aspects that are successful, and others where improvement appears necessary. We also gained insight about the evaluation methods and their effectiveness.

Code.org is a non-profit organization that encourages learning of computer science, especially programming and computation thinking. It's "Hour of Code" is an initiative that emphasizes short introductory tutorials aimed at total beginners, and has been widely used, claiming almost 100 million learners, including US President Barack Obama [14].

The Hour of Code approach is strongly visual in nature, both for the program itself, and for what the program does. This is reasonable, as it is established

P. Zaphiris and A. Ioannou (Eds.): LCT 2017, Part II, LNCS 10296, pp. 22–40, 2017.
DOI: 10.1007/978-3-319-58515-4_3

that such visual environments might assist in novice engagement, and also support them demonstrate skills and strategies in a familiar or easily understood context [1].

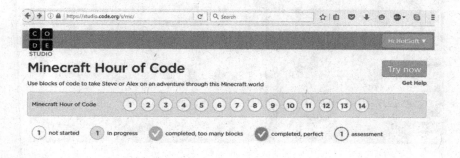

Fig. 1. The initial interface of the Minecraft Hour of Code tutorials.

One aspect of Hour of Code's visual nature relates to the program itself, and it uses a variant of the "jigsaw" or "block" approach used in Scratch [11], Alice [2] and other learning systems. The other aspect is the spatial model world, where such worlds include graphical elements that serve as integral parts of a computational context, problem, and solution. The Hour of Code tutorials include many variants of this, for example including ones resembling many popular games, e.g. "Angry Birds", "Plants vs. Zombies". In this paper we focus on the "Minecraft" variant — see Figs. 1 and 2. This is of special interest because Minecraft itself involves programming as a core part of the appeal of the "game".

Our interest is in *affective* learning in multimodal educational software, focusing on the emotional elements in the software. This reflects calls for more attention to emotion in the domain of Human-Computer Interaction (HCI) and education [15]. In this paper we present our application of two such methods, the affective walkthrough and the affective heuristic evaluation proposed earlier to the Hour of Code Minecraft software.

2   Overview of Hour of Code Minecraft

The Hour of Code Minecraft tutorial was developed to engage students in learning programming. It introduces players to basic programming concepts, allowing them to navigate, mine, craft, manipulate and explore in a 2D Minecraft world by plugging together blocks to complete all actions and generate computer code.

The system provides a sequence of tutorials, illustrated by a horizontal line with nodes representing each tutorial step, as shown in Fig. 1.

For each tutorial, the learner uses an interface such as shown in Fig. 2. On the left top is the model world ("play space"), resembling the rectilinear blocks as used in the full Minecraft game, representing objects such as grass, trees,

Fig. 2. The Hour of Code Minecraft interface, with model world on the left, and the program on the right.

sheep, etc. On the left bottom is a panel with instructions to the learner. When a learner begins the tutorials, they select an avatar, either "Alex" or "Steve". The chosen avatar then appears in the model world, and the program controls their actions within the world.

On the right is an area consisting of a "toolbox" of jigsaw-like pieces, and a "workspace". The pieces in the toolbox are for simple statements or commands, as well as loop ("repeat") and conditional ("if") statements, and the shape of the pieces shows how they connect with other pieces. These can be copied and dragged into the workspace, and assembled in sequence to form programs.

When assembled, the jigsaw pieces do resemble traditional (textual) code, and in most Hour of Code this is the only code shown. In the Minecraft tutorial, however, whenever a tutorial step is completed satisfactorily, a pop-up window shows the equivalent code in JavaScript, which is what is actually used to program Minecraft.

In Hour of Code Minecraft, the tutorial steps reflect teaching and learning goals, in sequence. The sequence is fairly traditional, beginning with sequences of commands, moving on to loops, and then conditional structures. At first, the introduction is strongly guided, and then more freedom allowed to encourage a program solving approach.

In the interface and the tutorial steps, several modalities are involved. Firstly, the interface is graphical and spatial, with the model world and the jigsaw piece program. The character of the graphics is appealing, with a coarse lo-fi and fun game-like appearance that might help engagement. Secondly, the model world suggests a "world of action", like a board game, where the blocks might be moved and interact. Thirdly, and related, is that the tutorial instructions build narrative elements where the player's avatar should accomplish goals by moving and acting in the model world. Over the sequence of the steps, these build into an overall story. This approach would appear to help learner motivation, understanding, and possibly supporting reflection and creativity about what other possibilities might be programmed. Finally, there are audio elements with calm background music and occasional effects to emphasize events.

3 Minecraft Hour of Code and Affective Walkthrough

The affective walkthrough proposed earlier [4] was based on Wharton et al.'s cognitive walkthrough [13], and Dormann and Biddle's affective walkthrough [3]. Following case studies, it was refined [6] to de-emphasize normal usability issues, and to acknowledge the contextual role of teaching goals and potential modality benefits. It follows Kort et al.'s affective model [7]. This identifies four phases of learning and the affective character of each. The first phase is encouraging exploration with positive affect. The second phase introduces challenges, and negative affect is expected. The third phase is to support overcoming challenges and reduce the negative affect, and the fourth phase is to affirm learning and restore positive affect.

3.1 Method

As with the earlier cognitive walkthrough by Wharton et al., the main idea is to select user tasks and then step through the software considering key questions, and making notes and observations, as shown in Table 1. The walkthrough was conducted by us, role-playing evaluators. We used a large screen display to collaborate in the same manner as done by participants described in [6].

Table 1. The affective walkthrough (version 3).

The affective walkthrough (version 3)	
1	What is the learning goal of this task?
2	Where in the affective cycle of learning is this task? (i.e. exploring, challenging, overcoming, and affirmation)
3	Is the appropriate affective support provided?
4	Does the affective support work as intended?

The objective of our study was to evaluate affective learning in Hour of Code Minecraft tutorials, with special attention to the supporting modalities involved. We presented, above, the basic design of the tutorials and the interfaces, and identified the modalities involved and their potential benefits. We then outlined the basis of the affective walkthrough, and the steps involved.

To select the tasks, we simply used the Hour of Code Minecraft tutorial steps, although we grouped the 14 steps into 4 larger tasks, bringing together steps that had strongly related educational purposes.

We then followed the walkthough as shown in Table 1, and considered each question in turn. We made Walkthrough Evaluation Sheets to record our answers and related observations. In the section below, we review the nature of the taskes, and the results of our walkthroughs.

3.2 Findings

First Task. To begin, we select a character. We have two choices, e.g. we can pick either Alex or Steve. The first task is about "commands". The steps are shown in Table 2 and the results of the walkthrough are shown is Table 3.

Table 2. First task: walk around.

First task: command sequences	
1	Add a second "move forward" command to reach the sheep
2	Then walk to the tree and use the "destroy block" command to chop it down
3	Use the "shear" command to gather wool from both sheep
4	Cut down all trees

By completing the first part of Task 1, the software gave emotional feedback such as happy sounds, a jumping character, green highlight on the achievement bar and a pop-up window providing feedback. Figure 3 shows the pop-up window with the achievement bar and our character reaction at the bottom. If we were not able to complete the step with the minimum lines of code, the software will let us know with a challenging part, but it does not help us to complete the step with the minimum lines of code (see Fig. 4). But if it was really going to encourage exploration, it should allow the user to see all of the options he/she could select and do, but it does not.

For every task, the software only provides us with the number of blocks we need. Therefore, they are not encouraging exploration all that much. They are not providing us with other alternatives. That is a bit of a criticism if we are encouraging people to explore. If we want to encourage exploration, we do not constrain people. We give them a bunch of different things, so that they explore to see what happens. We are surprised they did not give all the blocks that are relevant to let us explore a bit (e.g. *shear* sheep and *cut down* tree). We were a bit confused that we did not know all the possible things or at least some small subset of the possible things.

In the second part of the first task, the software took away *cut down*, and added *shear*.

It provides the user with more information about the reason of doing the task, e.g. "wood is a very important resource. Many things are made from it." The third part of the first task uses "shear" command instead of "destroy block".

As we are not using repeat loops in this task, the last part of task one needed lots of "moveForward()" blocks. It would be easier if we could just tell

Table 3. First task walkthrough results: walk around.

Walkthrough— First task: command sequences
1	What is the learning goal of this task? About learning programming and being engaged. In this task we used commands and add them in the work space to help the character move around the screen. we were able to see the code that we created with using blocks. It can be done, but there were no motivation to it, and considering the role of narrative, which could be better *Summary: The learning goal of this task was understood to learn how to add new commands in the program, but no motivation*
2	Where in the affective cycle of learning is this task? (i.e. exploring, challenging, overcoming, and affirmation) It cover exploring and gives feedback through sound and text if I did wrong and otherwise an affirmation sound with jumping character and the character being happy *Summary: The affective cycle of learning was exploring and affirmation*
3	Is the appropriate affective support provided? Yes, by adding blocks from toolbox in the work space, we can see how our character moves in the play space, and receiving positive feedback or negative that is still encouraging by providing how to try again with character's emotional reaction *Summary: appropriate affective support is provided with different multimodal support*
4	Does the affective support work as intended? No, affective support did not work as intended. The emotional support was well provided, but the task did not provide reasons of using the commands *Summary: even with the affective support provided, the purpose of the task was not clear*

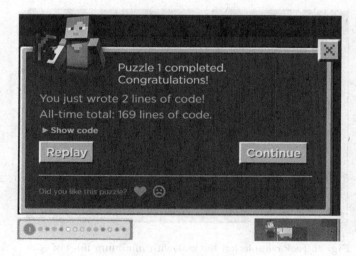

Fig. 3. Task 1 - Step one.

Table 4. Second task walkthrough results: build a house.

Second task: repeat loop and commands — Simple task
1	What is the learning goal of this task? The learning goal of this task was to help you learning about repeat loops and commands in programming *Summary: learning about repeat loops and commands*
2	Where in the affective cycle of learning is this task? (i.e. exploring, challenging, overcoming, and affirmation) The affective cycle of learning in this task covers all the four cycles. The Minecraft let us explore, and provide us with three different easy to medium, and hard questions covering the challenging cycle. Then it helps us to overcome with popup windows. And at the end it gives us affirmation *Summary: it has exploring, challenging, overcoming, and affirmation*
3	Is the appropriate affective support provided? Yes, it starts with a question and a hint, i.e. "We need to build a house before the sun goes down. House requires a lot of wood. Cut down all the 3 trees" *Summary: affective support was provided*
4	Does the affective support work as intended? No, it does not work as intended. It really does not help us to build a house, just create some walls. Other issue with the software it tells us the task should be done before the sun goes down, but it does not work as intended, and we do not have a time limit or a change in the background *Summary: the purpose of this task is to build a house, which it did not help us to do so*

Fig. 4. Task completion but not with minimum lines of code.

the computer to perform the move forward command the number of times we needed. It would be much easier to transition to repeat loops, if we had told the computer to "move forward" a specific number of times. We will need thousands and thousands of blocks to create a new world in Minecraft.

Second Task. The second task is about building the rest of a house from the material available. The "repeat" command will come in handy. For the last part of the task we can select "Easy", "Medium" or "Hard". The steps are shown in Table 5 and the results of the walkthrough are shown is Table 4.

Table 5. Second task: build a house.

Second task: repeat loop and commands — Simple task
1	Build the first part of your house by putting the "place" and "move forward" commands inside the repeat loop
2	Let's build a house. Choose the floor plan (easy, medium or hard) for your house

The second and third tasks are about how to come up with algorithms, giving a problem and solve it using repeat loops. For the first part of task two, the software provides the reason and time to complete this part by saying: "We need to build a house before the sun goes down. Houses require a lot of wood." For the second part of this task it suggests: "Every house starts with a wall."

This part of the software is not telling the user how much wood he/she gets, and why we need to chop down all the trees. We do not have variables. We do not have any idea how much wood we have. Also we can not really build a house; we can just build some walls, so the story is not correct.

Third Task. This task is again about using "Repeat loops" and "commands", but in a more challenging way using some creativity and freedom. It has four steps and each step takes you to different interactive spaces including: 1. Plant crops on both sides of water, 2. Move past the Creepers and reach safety at home, 3. Move underground placing torches and mine coal, 4. Avoid walking into molten and place cobblestone to create a bridge, and mine iron blocks. The steps are shown in Table 6 and the results of the walkthrough are shown is Table 7. This task has gamification steps to bring more engagement to the user.

Forth Task. Finally, the last task is about "commands", "repeat loops", and learning about "if" statements; a fundamental part of learning to program. It introduces us to a concept, which requires more problem solving. "if" statements help all computers make decisions. We are able to use "if" statement in the code to make our character react to what they see in the world, e.g. if there is rock in front of her, she can turn left or right and watch her steps. It has two steps; first step is simple and second step is more challenging, which are including: 1. Lava is hiding beneath some of these blocks, which you'll need to cover up

Table 6. Third task: plan some crops.

Third task: repeat loop and commands — Challenging task commands
1	Plant crops on both sides of the water so you don't get hungry later on (It's good to plan ahead.)
2	Running into a Creeper is a bad idea. Carefully move past the Creepers and reach the safety of your home
3	You'll find the most valuable resources underground, but it can get dark. Place at least 2 torches and mine at least 2 coal
4	Walking into molten lava is a bad idea. Place cobblestone to create a bridge, then mine at least two of the iron blocks

before moving forward, 2. Mine redstone but don't fall in the lava by placing cobblestone over any lava you uncover. The steps are shown in Table 8 and the results of the walkthrough are shown is Table 9. This task has gamification steps to bring more engagement to the user.

3.3   Discussion

Reviewing the results of our walkthroughs, we are able to make several general observations. Most simply, we were pleased with several strengths: good visual effects and artwork, and sensible audio. Beyond those, however, we found more insight, described in sections below.

Table 7. Third task walkthrough results: plan some crops.

Third task: repeat loop and commands — Challenging task commands
1	What is the learning goal of this task? The learning goal of this task was to practice using different commands with repeat loops bringing challenging steps *Summary: providing challenging steps*
2	Where in the affective cycle of learning is this task? (i.e. exploring, challenging, overcoming, and affirmation) This task only covers affirmation and somehow challenging cycles, the steps are not encouraging enough and there is no clear help to overcome the challenges *Summary: it covers challenging and affirmation cycles*
3	Is the appropriate affective support provided? Yes, there are similar affective support provided that are: giving a short story about the task and then emotionally trying to engage us in the space *Summary: it was provided*
4	Does the affective support work as intended? There was a story at the beginning of each step, but narrative is not considered well to make it an exciting experience *Summary: even with bringing challenge in this task it was not motivating and good story is missing*

Table 8. Fourth task: "if" statement.

Fourth task: "if" statement
1	Lava is hiding beneath some of these blocks, which you'll need to cover up before moving forward. An "if" command will come in handy here. Add a "move forward" command in the correct place to mine these blocks
2	Now things are getting tricky. Mine 3 redstone, but don't fall in the lava. Use an "If" command to place cobblestone over any lava you uncover

Table 9. Fourth task walkthrough results: "if" statement.

Walkthrough — Fourth task: "if" statement
1	What is the learning goal of this task? The learning goal of this task was to use command, repeat loop, and "if" statement *Summary: learning about "if" statement*
2	Where in the affective cycle of learning is this task? (i.e. exploring, challenging, overcoming, and affirmation) This task covers the challenging (providing two steps: simple and challenging) and affirmation, but does not encourage in exploration or help to overcome *Summary: covers challenging and affirmation, but exploring and overcoming is not very well done*
3	Is the appropriate affective support provided? Yes, we saw different affective support during the task *Summary: there is appropriate affective support provided*
4	Does the affective support work as intended? No, the affective support did not provide a clear narrative to engage us in doing this task *Summary: no, the affective support did not provide a clear narrative*

World and Story. Perhaps our main positive finding was the interplay between the model world of the "playspace" and the narrative aspects of the programming tasks given in the instructions. We felt it was clear and motivating when the learn was asked to create programs to move the avatar, chop down the tree, build a wall, and so on. The world and the story seemed to go together well, almost the way that narratives often work in computer games. This worked very well here, and showed some limitations in tutorials in Scratch, for example, which typically start with a blank canvas, rather than a world ready for a story.

While acclaiming this aspect, we found two weakness. One is that there was often little motivation for the actions requested in the instructions. The learner is asked to chop down trees, for example, before any mention of building walls for a house. Second is that there was no overall story, no eventual goal to accomplish, despite this being so common in computer games. Even in Mario, the player knows they are not done until the princess is saved.

Challenge but Not Overcome. We very much appreciate the way in which the tutorials helped the learner get started, offering a clear narrative goal, exactly the right tools to accomplish it, and providing affirming feedback when done. In several places, however, it seemed that this limited exploration: it encouraged simple constrained programming, but did not add the context of a large number of possibilities in the "toolbox". Learning to choose a strategy in the presence of many possibilities, with different strengths, is essential to learning about problem-solving.

We also liked the ideas of greater challenge by suggesting it might be done with fewer steps: we felt it really would make the learner try to do better. But whereas a real teacher might monitor and provide hints when the learner gets frustrated, the tutorial offered nothing equivalent. Considering Kort's cycle, there was support to challenge, but not to overcome. As we show in Fig. 5, we see the support for the cycle strong in some places (Challenge, Affirm) but weak in others (Explore, Overcome).

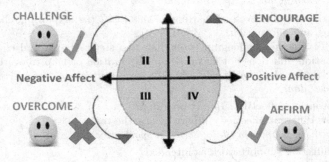

Fig. 5. Minecraft and Kort et al. [7] steps.

Simple Programming. As the name "Hour of Code" suggests, the tutorial only addresses the simple beginnings of programming — "First Hour of Code" might be more appropriate. We noticed no real introduction to variables, for example, despite the potential of having them associated with objects in the model world. There was also no lead-in to object orientation, the most common practical paradigm for programming, again despite the potential of objects in a model world — this is exploited well in Alice, for example. In reviewing comments on official videos about the Hour of Code tutorial, this was a common criticism, that it wasn't introducing "real" programming:

> I'm not convinced that this kind of a tutorial could help anybody in understanding of programming paradigms. Modern programming is mostly object-oriented, and this film could at most give a little of vision, how sequential programming should look alike. IMO it's not proper to teach only sequential programming, without any code and without even telling, that another styles of programming exists. Moreover, I think that beginning learning of programming with sequential programming instead of object-oriented programming could make OOP harder to understand
> *Youtube Comment*

However it is still an open question as to whether OOP or sequential programming is best for absolute beginners. Similarly, other programming paradigms are also not addressed. These issues are beyond our limited scope in this study.

One last point is perhaps more relevant. By basing the tutorial on Minecraft, many beginners might hope to get started with actually programming in Minecraft, which is done in JavaScript. The tutorials do show pop-up windows showing JavaScript code equivalent to the jigsaw blocks, but go no further. We understand that the complexities and dependences in real JavaScript would present great difficulties to address within the Hour of Code framework, but we also anticipate that some beginners might find this disappointing.

Table 10. The affective heuristics (version 3).

Affective heuristics (version 3)
H1: Design elements and modalities should support the affective learning strategy
H2: Ensure help and documentation is provided where needed but does not distract from affective learning strategy
H3: Maintain visibility of progress, affirming challenges already overcome, and those remaining
H4: Allow the user freedom to explore but also to return to the previous step
H5: Avoid or prevent actions with neither feedback to help overcome, nor affirmation when success
H6: Visualize options clearly to encourage exploration
H7: Tailor actions to be encouraging at first and efficient later, while learners are attempting to overcome challenges
H8: Challenge learners and provide constructive feedback if they fail, and affirming success when they succeed
H9: Match the learners world view in affective strategy and multimodal support
H10: Maintain interface cohesion to support affective strategy

4   Minecraft Hour of Code and Affective Heuristic Evaluation

This section addresses the use of the affective heuristic evaluation [5] to evaluate affect in the user interface, educational design, and content of Minecraft Hour of Code to see if the software supports the educational objectives, narrative and persuasion to make the learners more engaged in learning programming. The affective heuristic evaluation is based on Nielsen and Molich [9], and adapted with affect supported by Norman [10] and Kort et al.'s emotional cycle of learning model [7] as well as multimodal design based on Sankey [12]. We have explained the full rational in more detail earlier [4].

4.1   Method

The study was performed in the same laboratory as earlier. In this study, we applied the evaluation method as discussed earlier. We reviewed the heuristics, explored, and then reflected on the software. We then wrote comments about the environment filling in a table with respect to the different heuristics. For heuristic severity we adapted Nielsen's severity ratings for usability problems [8], changing their emphasis to reflect emotional educational impact. We explicitly emphasized on the learning objective and the modality that was employed.

For the learning objective we considered the following. This system was designed to be fun for a student working alone or in a classroom where the instructor has minimal preparation or computer science background. It has fourteen tutorials to learn the basics of JavaScript programming concepts that are: use of commands, repeat loops and if statements. It aims to create a quick and enjoyable experience for students and instructors who are new to computer science.

The modality involved a 2D block world with programming using jigsaw pieces. There is also an avatar to represent the user, animation of the block world, and engaging audio samples. Moreover, it used a narrative and persuasion quasi-modalities.

We went through the interface systematically. For example we added blocks to the workspace, trying to think of the intended user. We checked in each step if the system state to consider the learning objective and the modality employed. At the end of the suggested tasks, we filled in a table with issues based on the ten heuristics. Table 10 shows the affective heuristic evaluation. This is the set of heuristics following revisions discussed in [5].

4.2   Findings

In this study, the evaluators read the heuristics, explored, and then reflected on the environment. They then wrote comments including the interface element that was violated, problems that illustrated poor considering of affect and modality, suggestions and recommendations for solutions, and the severity based on Jakob Nielsen's five-step rating scale [8]. Tables 11 and 12 show the affective heuristic evaluation results. Each of the ten heuristics led to a useful comment at least once.

4.3   Discussion

The heuristics invited reflection on modality as well as affect. Our findings show that the affective heuristic evaluation led to identification of many problems and potential solutions as shown in the tables. By reviewing these results, we can make some general observations.

Narrative and Continuity. There was no clear continuity between the steps. One of the tutorial steps was to chop down trees (Fig. 6 top left), and the next one

Table 11. The affective heuristic evaluation H1 to H5.

Affective heuristic evaluation involved	Interface element	Problems not considering affect and modality	Suggestions for Solution/ Comments/ Recommendations	Sev (0 to 4)
H1: Design elements and modalities should support the affective learning strategy	Show code	The JavaScript code is provided but without affective support	Have it be more interactive Some kind of interaction to get them more engaged Use more physical/material design elements	4
H2: Ensure help and documentation is provided where needed but does not distract from affective learning strategy	Affirmation pop-up window	It does not provide all the possible things or at least some small subset of possible things	Give hints and use affective persuasion	3
	Tasks, command sequences	Reasons of using commands not provided	There can be a multimedia content e.g. video and providing the purpose and goals of using commands	3
H3: Maintain visibility of progress, affirming challenges already overcome, and those remaining	Entire environment	Pretty good job for this part	Progress timeline can also show the steps	0
H4: Allow the user freedom to explore but also to return to the previous step	Tool Box	Software only provides us with number of blocks we need, and it is not encouraging exploration all that much	It should provide us with other alternatives	3
	Minecraft Hour of Code tutorials list	No label next to each task in the timeline	Better to have label	4
H5: Avoid or prevent actions with neither feedback to help overcome, nor affirmation when success	Affirmation pop-up window	To overcome the challenge with minimum lines of code there is no feedback to help overcome	Provide some feedback to how to be able to get to minimum lines of code	3

Table 12. The affective heuristic evaluation H6 to H10.

Affective heuristic evaluation involved	Interface element	Problems not considering affect and modality	Suggestions for Solution/ Comments/ Recommendations	Sev (0 to 4)
H6: Visualize options clearly to encourage exploration	Tasks, command sequences	No motivation and role of narrative could be better	Provide a good narrative about using command sequences in this task	2
	Tasks, repeat loops	Narrative is not considered well to make it an exciting experience	Provide a good narrative about using repeat loops in this task	2
	Tasks, "if" statement	No clear narrative	Provide a good narrative about using "if" statement in this task	2
H7: Tailor actions to be encouraging at first and efficient later, while learners are attempting to overcome challenges	All tasks	No clear narrative and connection between the steps	Easier tasks are earlier but there is no clear connection between the steps	2
H8: Challenge learners and provide constructive feedback if they fail, and affirming success when they succeed	Puzzle 2 to 3	No challenge	add some challenge to puzzle 3	0
H9: Match the learners world view in affective strategy and multimodal support	Puzzle 4	Starts well, but then give examples, and then does not continue well, e.g. not building a house. Sun does not go down. Story is not correct	It is not complete but it is pretty good at creating a child world	1
H10: Maintain interface cohesion to support affective strategy	Tool box	No learning to choose a strategy in presence of many possibilities with different strengths	Add more affective strategies	3
	Show Code	Also JavaScript not bringing engagement and motivation	Using affective strategies to have interaction with users	4
	All steps	Narrative is not well done	Have a better storytelling and continuity	2

was to *shear* sheep (Fig. 6 top right). The wool that resulted from shearing was never used or mentioned again. It did say that wood was useful for building and later steps did build walls for a house, but there was no indication of the wood came from chopping down the trees. It could have been made more continuous making it clear that the trees were used to build the house and also by using the wool to make carpets etc. They are building a house without using the wood or the wool, and therefore, there is no strong continuity and storytelling between the steps (Fig. 6 bottom). This might also have been a useful opportunity to introduce quantities of wood or wool as variables.

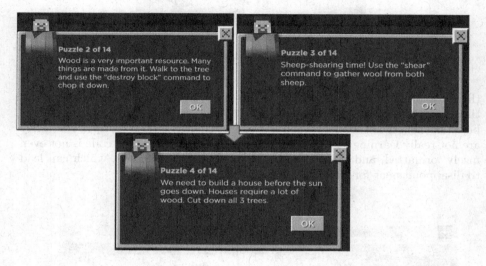

Fig. 6. Narrative and continuity.

Encouraging Exploration. There was not enough encouraging to explore at each step, and no clear story for exploration. The commands provided were specific to each step, meaning there were not all commands provided in each tutorial e.g. *shear* was provided in the sheep-shearing task but not in other tasks. The commands were changed for every tutorial, which is a real limit to learning as it restricts exploration, and people would expect specific commands for each programming situation. Figure 7 shows the command blocks for tutorials two and three. They can use "destroy block" in the second tutorial step but it is not seen in the third tutorial step where they have to use "shear" instead.

JavaScript Code. As we mentioned, the real Minecraft software is programmed using JavaScript. Minecraft Hour of Code uses the jigsaw command blocks. But when the task is complete, is shows the real JavaScript code. But a learner would not know what they have to do with this code; there is a poor connection between

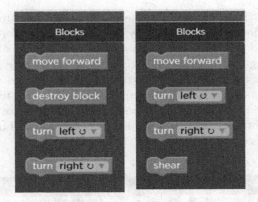

Fig. 7. Encouraging exploration.

the JavaScript code and the block commands that represents that code, and there is no affective feedback provided to the learners. Therefore, the connection between them is not made; we can not edit or change the JavaScript code. They are not really learning the JavaScript language. The JavaScript code is not even nicely formatted, and there is no interaction with the learners, which can lead to disappointment for them (see Fig. 8).

Fig. 8. Blocks with the generated code.

5   Conclusions

In this paper, we presented our evaluation of the multimodal affective learning support in Code.org's Hour of Code tutorial set based on the popular game

Minecraft. We applied our two proposed evaluation methods called the affective walkthrough and the affective heuristic evaluation, modeled on the widely used cognitive walkthrough and heuristic evaluation. The new methods keep the procedural framework of the cognitive walkthrough and heuristic evaluation, but as the evaluator steps through, the questions and heuristics are about emotional support in education.

The Hour of Code Minecraft software applies various modalities to support learning, talking a visual approach with a engaging game-like graphics, a model world, and a programming language using jigsaw-like pieces (as do Scratch and Alice). The tutorial instructions add a narrative aspect, whereby the programming tasks involve acting out a story in the model world.

Our experience in conducting the evaluation was positive and enlightening. We recognized elements in the Hour of Code design that we would not otherwise have noticed, and also identified ways in which the design might be improved. We see as especially valuable the interplay between the spatial model world, and the narrative stemming from the instructions. On the other hand, we felt that some extra freedom in command choice might in several places be helpful. Also, where challenges were provided by suggesting shorter solutions were possible, it would be helpful to add a capability for the learner get hints so they can overcome the challenges if they are stuck. We also recognized the limits of the tutorials, which really only learners with the very early steps in learning to program.

We appreciated the focus of the affective walkthrough and affective heuristic evaluation focus on modality benefits and teaching goals, and most importantly its use of Kort's model of the affective cycle in learning. We feel they offer a helpful and systematic approach to evaluating affective learning in multimodal software.

References

1. Chao, P.Y.: Exploring students' computational practice, design and performance of problem-solving through a visual programming environment. Comput. Educ. **95**, 202–215 (2016) .
2. Dann, W.P., Cooper, S., Pausch, R.: Learning to Program with Alice (w/CD ROM). Prentice Hall Press, Upper Saddle River (2011)
3. Dormann, C., Biddle, R.: Understanding game design for affective learning. In: Proceedings of the 2008 Conference on Future Play: Research, Play, Share, pp. 41–48. ACM (2008)
4. GhasemAghaei, R., Arya, A., Biddle, R.: Multimodal software for affective education: UI evaluation. In: EdMedia: World Conference on Educational Media and Technology, vol. 2015, pp. 1851–1860 (2015)
5. GhasemAghaei, R., Arya, A., Biddle, R.: Evaluating software for affective education: a case study of affective heuristics. In: EdMedia: World Conference on Educational Media and Technology, vol. 2016, pp. 573–580 (2016)
6. GhasemAghaei, R., Arya, A., Biddle, R.: Evaluating software for affective education: a case study of the affective walkthrough. In: Stephanidis, C. (ed.) HCI 2016. CCIS, vol. 618, pp. 226–231. Springer, Cham (2016). doi:10.1007/978-3-319-40542-1_36

7. Kort, B., Reilly, R., Picard, R.W.: An affective model of interplay between emotions and learning: reengineering educational pedagogy-building a learning companion. In: ICALT, p. 43. IEEE (2001)

8. Nielsen, J.: Severity ratings for usability problems. Pap. Essays **54**, 1–2 (1995)

9. Nielsen, J., Molich, R.: Heuristic evaluation of user interfaces. In: Proceedings of the SIGCHI Conference on Human Factors in Computing Systems, pp. 249–256. ACM (1990)

10. Norman, D.A.: Emotion design: why we love (or hate) everyday things (2004)

11. Resnick, M., Maloney, J., Monroy-Hernández, A., Rusk, N., Eastmond, E., Brennan, K., Millner, A., Rosenbaum, E., Silver, J., Silverman, B., et al.: Scratch: programming for all. Commun. ACM **52**(11), 60–67 (2009)

12. Sankey, M.D.: How to develop 15 multimodal design heuristics in 3 easy (not) lessons. Int. J. Pedagogies Learn. **3**(2), 60–73 (2007)

13. Wharton, C., Rieman, J., Lewis, C., Polson, P.: The cognitive walkthrough method: a practitioner's guide. In: Usability Inspection Methods. pp. 105–140. John Wiley Inc. (1994)

14. Wilson, C.: Hour of code–a record year for computer science. ACM Inroads **6**(1), 22 (2015)

15. Woolf, B., Burleson, W., Arroyo, I., Dragon, T., Cooper, D., Picard, R.: Affect-aware tutors: recognising and responding to student affect. Int. J. Learn. Technol. **4**(3–4), 129–164 (2009)

Fairy Houses:
A Creative Engineering Experience

Andres Gonzalez, Robert Fowler, Harrison Froeschke, Sabra Leong,
and Bruce Gooch(✉)

Texas A&M, College Station, USA
gooch@cse.tamu.edu

Abstract. A common misconception is that neither Engineers nor their projects are creative. We report on a laboratory program for creating educational displays like those in Museums. The program enables students to (1) design and build an edutainment product, (2) gather data to test their product, and (3) interpret their data. The objective of the project is to create an educational experience for users that shows the potential for creativity within the field of Computer Science. The undergraduate participants created an interactive display that teaches two Computer Science concepts. They created an interactive experience for via a Bluetooth connection to an Arduino powered "Fairy House." Users unravel a story that involves solving riddles via interpreting Morse code. The display has two learning goals. First, players gain an understanding of how to turn code into text. The second is players discover how binary trees speed search tasks. We also had two design goals, any number of people can play, and players can join or leave without interrupting others. Through in-house testing and trial runs, the students determined that this method of interactive learning is useful for teaching new concepts.

Keywords: Fairy house · Chat-bot

1 Introduction

Most people know about Morse code. Yet, few understand it. The task of decoding streaming Morse code using a table is involved. One must search the entire table for every dot or dash. Decoding streaming Morse code using a binary tree is simple. One traverses the tree by following the pattern of dots and dashes to find a letter. So, learning Morse code fits both of our educational goals. We now needed a compelling story to engage users.

We decided that a light display is a good way for users to learn Morse code. During World War 1, the Allies used Begbie Lamps to relay messages on the battlefield. After World War 1, photos of the Cottingley Fairies arose. The photos show two girls with what appears to be fairies. We came up with a story of English Fairies who pledged to defend the Empire. King George assigned them to the Royal Signal Corps. They learned Morse code to send messages to humans. Following the war, our fairies left the violent world of men for 100 years and have now just returned.

© Springer International Publishing AG 2017
P. Zaphiris and A. Ioannou (Eds.): LCT 2017, Part II, LNCS 10296, pp. 41–49, 2017.
DOI: 10.1007/978-3-319-58515-4_4

The story gave us the idea of creating a fairy village with the houses made from signal lanterns. The fairy houses flash at one another as if talking. When a person approaches, the community falls silent as if to see whom the new person is. One fairy house has a sign explaining how to communicate with fairies. The houses send simple Morse code questions via LED lights. The Fairy Village display provides two charts to aid users in deciphering Morse code, a Morse code table and a Morse code tree. The user can send text messages to the fairies using a Bluetooth-enabled mobile device. This simple communication enables people to learn about Morse code and binary trees.

2   Related Work

There have been other projects that have tried to implement Computer Science to engage users in a mix of the virtual and physical environment. Chit Chat Club [3] attempts to this by creating human-sized avatars that attempt to engage users, both present and remote, using facial expression. Our project however takes this ideology a step further as there is communication via the messages sent by the house and the light flashes to give the user feedback on different levels.

Another similar idea to our project is Architales, an interactive story table that creates an interactive environment for users to give users an enjoyable engagement with applications. This project is very similar to what we aimed to do, as the table creates an interactive environment that allows users to be immersed and learn about the story and see computer science in action.

In 2015, The Harmonic Walk was developed at the University of Padova in the Department of Information Engineering to create an "interactive physical environment designed for learning and practicing the accompaniment of a tonal melody." This project, in a similar way to the Fairy House, presents a method of interaction for the user to learn about something new to them. In the case of music for the researchers at Padova, users learned about tonal melody as well as chord progressions, melody accompaniment, and improvisation. An important distinction made in this project that is also made in the Fairy House Project is the distinction of skill level by the users of the interactive environment.

3   Methods

3.1   Hardware

Each fairy house contains an Arduino Uno and Rasberry Pi to provide computation and I/O control. Their small form factor allows us to hide the hardware inside the houses. Also, in order to update the output future programmers need no knowledge of Arduino. We used Arduino HC-05 Bluetooth modules to send messages to participant's mobile phones. An RGB LED serves as the Morse code output (Fig. 1).

The original idea for our fairy houses was to retrofit solar powered lanterns with proximity and light sensors. Users would interact with the lanterns by moving near them and shining or flashing lights at them. Multiple lanterns would be connected via a

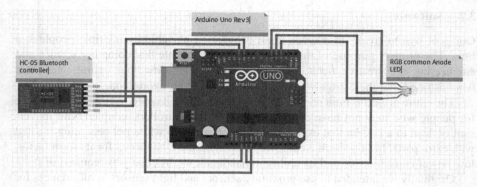

Fig. 1. Diagram of the Arduino hardware.

network and would communicate and interact with each other based on the actions of the users. The program for this networking would run on Raspberry Pi's installed in the bottom of every lantern.

The first major change to the project was the use of Arduino's instead of Raspberry Pi's. The reason for this change was the design simplicity Arduino possessed compared to the Raspberry Pi. Arduino's capability to run small machines such as sensors or servos using a small amount of RAM was much more appropriate than the more advance Raspberry Pi. Since we intend to create a large number of these lanterns, it would also be cheaper to use the Arduino's. However, as we began to work with Arduino's in the houses, we found that the networking capabilities were a challenge for us to effectively set up. We decided to drop this feature, as it would also allow more people to play the game separately in an area containing many lanterns instead of one person or group using the entire network (Fig. 2).

Fig. 2. The internal hardware of a fairy house.

3.2   Software

Our goal was to create an interactive art installation playable by multiple people at a time. The primary purpose of this project is to demonstrate that computer science and engineering are creative fields. We wanted to create something entirely new that demonstrated that there are always new forms of art and expression.

The entire project is built on the Arduino platform. We have found that its ease of use for people who may not have experience with microcontrollers, coupled with its versatility, lead to a system that everyone could contribute to while not becoming bloated with extra parts. In this specific case, we decided on the UNO Rev3 for its form factor, low power consumption, and its ability to handle all the I/O that was required of it.

Originally we intended to use proximity sensors and light sensors as affordances for interaction with the lanterns. However testing demonstrated that users found only Morse code interaction to be to slow and cumbersome. Users became rapidly bored.

These results lead the team to consider text communication. We installed a HC-05 Bluetooth module into the lantern. The UNO is currently using a HC-05 Bluetooth module as its primary means of input which also doubles as an output source. This way, a user can connect to the lantern via Bluetooth and send it messages just by texting it. The lantern would now more effectively communicate with the user and use Morse code for certain messages. Since we knew how the lanterns could communicate, we needed to figure out what specifically they would say to the users (Fig. 3).

Participants can use any Bluetooth terminal app to connect to a fairy house. This allowed us to have an input source that is in the participant's hands and makes them all that much more engaged in the exercise, while also allowing us to have a standardized way of giving instructions, hints, etc., via printing out to the participants terminal screen.

The hardware level code is straightforward. A nested for loop converts words to characters. Characters are mapped to a corresponding series of dots and dashes using a switch statement. If no input from the participant is detected the message will simply repeat until it detects new information, then depending on the input either a new message will start to be broadcast or the encoded message will repeat but the Bluetooth terminal will display a reason why the message has not changed.

Our first idea was to install a chat-bot into the lantern for the user to converse with. However this presented a problem because if the user wanted to communicate any complicated sentences, then the user would have to have a complete mastery of Morse code. As a result, we decided upon another idea that reduced the amount of Morse code needing to be interpreted. This idea would have the user begin the game by connecting to the fairy house and texting it "Hello". The fairy in a house would ask the user riddles. By solving the riddles users gain trust of the fairy and unlock further dialogue into the fairies' backstory.

As the user is reading the riddle, the lantern that they are connected to would flash the answer in Morse code. We found that most users were not familiar with interpreting Morse code. We made it easier to distinguish between dashes and dots by making dashes a blue light and dot a red light. We found that coloring the lights significantly lowered the cognitive load of Morse code translation for novices. They were able to solve the fairy's riddle, and send a text with the answer.

Fig. 3. A completed fairy house.

A portion of the project was designing the look and feel of the lantern to give the appearance of a Fairy house. We spray painted the lantern brown, covered it in twigs, rocks, and left a window in the side to show an image of a fairy. Inside the lantern, along with all of the electronic components, is a circular piece of paper with a scene of magical fairies drawn on it. When the lantern flashes, the scene is illuminated and can be easily seen in the dark.

To tell the fairy's story we developed a text-based adventure. We used the ADRIFT software package. It allowed us to map the story with response paths based on user/fairy questions and answers. The text-based adventure allows players have a different set of interactions with the fairies. While the users may traverse different paths, the final story is always complete. Users are able to "find their spot" once they return to a Fairy House for a new session at a new time and even new location by giving key words to the fairies that trigger a response.

4   Evaluation

4.1   Interactive Display

We evaluated the fairy village using a practice-oriented model developed by Nacke. The Nacke standard calls for separate testing of the technology, gameplay, and social quality. We used Arduino TestSuite to unit test the hardware for correct input and output. We tested the text-based adventure software using the HP software evaluation tools. We tested that; software is installable on the RasberryPi, runs in real-time, and responses are correct for given input. Gameplay analysis proceeded in three phases. First by expert evaluation, second a usability study. Third, we measured learning outcomes in players with a survey.

The testing that has been completed about the interactivity and ability to learn from the communication with the house shows that this medium is optimal for teaching and showing the creativity that can be found in Computer Science. High School students and college students alike are able to interact and learn about the creativity that engineering has to offer in a world where technology is so prevalent and only becoming increasing so. With Fairy Houses set up in various locations, users will be able to stumble upon an world hidden in plain sight, akin to the world of programming and engineering. With this information, we hope that readers will use the findings in this paper to implement teaching strategies to educate while creating a fun environment and experience for users.

4.2   Student Team

Learning is a multi-faceted activity, and almost everyone has a learning style preference. Most of us use components from many styles when we try to learn something. Since there are so many ways to learn, it follows that there should be many ways to evaluate how effectively learning, and the corresponding teaching, are taking place. Therefore, we used a multi-dimensional evaluation strategy to determine if the learning goals of the project were met.

We conducted evaluation along three axes: the student, a neutral observer, and the instructor. Results from each evaluation axis were analyzed individually, and then triangulated against the results of the others.

Student Provided Data. Research method: Qualitative design journal, Quantitative questionnaire. Each student created a design blog. The design blog gave the instructor an opportunity to assess students' knowledge of HCI concepts as well as enable students to develop critical thinking skills applicable to software and hardware design. We evaluated student learning via lab reports, project documentation, and a project presentation. We also used a novel method of documenting student learning. The undergraduate students developed a second "making of" text-based adventure. It tells the story of a creative team of engineers bringing a fairy village to life.

The second method for collecting student data was a questionnaire to establish baseline information about the learners. The following list of questions is examples; How do they rate themselves as programmers? How experienced are they with Arduino? How "interested" are they game design? How experienced are they with a research and reporting. The questionnaire allowed us to answer the following questions:

Did the students with more experience do better than those without? In the case of hardware the answer was yes team members who were previously Arduino hobbyists were able to answer questions and suggest solutions that other team members were not. In the case of software all students were evenly matched and all were able to make contributions. In the case of game design two students had far more experience, however all team members were able to make significant contributions to the final product.

How long does it take for learners to consider themselves "experienced"? By the end of a one-semester course all of the students considered themselves experienced in system design and reporting. All of the students started the course believe that they were experienced in software design and programming. All of them admitted at the end that their initial assessment was in error as they had learned a great deal about software engineering and programming. Students universally remarked on the post course questionnaire that they learned a great deal about programming that is, "not in the books."

System Provided Data. Research method: Quantitative data collection from within the software development system. We tracked GitHub commits and changes as well as user communication statics during project development. Initially extroverted students contributed more to discussions. After three weeks of meeting and talking in a round table fashion all students were comfortable enough to contribute to online and face-to-face. GitHub commits showed no significant change over the course of the project. This may be due to the tight scheduling and oversight that the students enforced upon them.

Observational Data. Research method: Qualitative observation. Looking for things that learners enjoy and find frustrating can quickly lead instructors to enhance certain areas of the project while fixing others. Trained observers can quickly see patterns and suggest modifications. Moreover, the observers can quickly see if their suggestions were effective. Learners consistently identify responsiveness as one of the most important dimensions of instructor "service" to students. Close observation of potential problems will let us respond in a very timely manner. We employed a neutral observer of the project who observed team meetings and reviewed the team's research blogs. The observations were shared with the instructor and team during the project. The observer documented their observations on the following: How do the students interact with one another? How do the students interact with the instructor? Where does most of the "enjoyment" seem to be coming from? Where is most of the frustration coming from?

Student interaction with the instructor evolved over the course of the project. Initially students assumed that they would be given an assignment. By the end of the project they were able to interact with the instructor as a research peer. The enjoyment came from interaction in the laboratory and from exceeding the expectations that the students had of them. Student frustration in the beginning of the project was due to the open-ended nature of the project. During the reporting portion of the project some of the students were dismayed by the fact that their writing was not like that of the research papers they were reading.

Instructor Data. Research method: Qualitative structured anecdotal recording. Reflective practice is a way in which educators can "develop a greater level of self-awareness about the nature and impact of their performance". This practice involves looking critically at our own work as instructors. Questions that we pose to ourselves can start this process such as: What "worked" and why?

5 Conclusion

Computer Science is typically viewed as a field that lacks creativity due to the prevalent stigma of the field being boring. As a result, many creative minds are off put by the field that they believe to be inhospitable to their creativity. Changing this stigma is vital for the future of the field, so that a variety of thoughts and ideals are able to help shape the future and drive innovation. This is an important issue to address because as we move towards increasingly difficult challenges, varied ways of thinking will be crucial for finding different approaches to the problems of tomorrow. Many typical approaches to this issue fail miserably as looking at the creative side of computer science and exemplifying this side to students is forgotten. Some previous approaches have tried to show this creativity through programs, having a tangible object to interact with and receive visual feedback from engages people and sparks interests. Our project shows the creativity that is found in Computer Science by generating critical thinking, engagement, learning a tangible skill, and having a visually stimulating object to interact with.

6 Future Work

In the future, we would like to look into other methods of creating entertaining environments for users to learn about not only an interesting topic, but also the creativity of computer science. One way that this could be done is evolving the Fairy House system into an experience that includes motion detection and light detection to make the houses even more interactive. The motion detection will have the lights projected by the fairy house intensify as users draw near to the houses, and have the lights fade when no motion is detected. The light detection will allow the users to use a light source to communicate back to the fairies in Morse code, making the act of learning Morse code even more interactive. In this way, a more immersive experience for the user can encourage repeated interactions as well as spread of the popularity and bring more users to the Project to learn about Computer Science and Engineering.

In addition to advancements with the Fairy Houses, we will also begin development on a teaching platform based on the experience we gained from working with the users of the Fairy House Project. The new project will implement an interactive achievement system for students so that they will have constant positive feedback and response to make an otherwise menial task more engaging.

References

1. https://cfacaa.human.cornell.edu/dea.arl/linked%20docs/Green_DIS2014%20.pdf
2. http://mf.media.mit.edu/pubs/conference/TangibleNavigation.pdf
3. Karahalios, K.G., Dobson, K.: Chat club: bridging virtual and physical space for social interaction. In: Proceedings of 2005 Extended Abstracts on Human Factors in Computing Systems (2005)
4. Karahalios, K., Bergstrom, T., Yapchaian, M.: The ISEA chit chat club. Ginger - an installation. ISEA c4f3 2006, San Jose, CA (2006)
5. http://social.cs.uiuc.edu/projects/Ginger/index.html
6. http://social.cs.uiuc.edu/people/karriekarahalios.html
7. Mazalek, A., Winegarden, C., Al-Haddad, T., Robinson, S.J., Wu, C.-S.: Architales: physical/digital co-design of an interactive story table. In: Proceedings of the 3rd International Conference on Tangible and Embedded Interaction 2009, Cambridge, UK (2009)
8. http://synlab.gatech.edu/data/papers/mazalek_tei2009_architales.pdf

Make World, A Collaborative Platform to Develop Computational Thinking and STEAM

Mariluz Guenaga[1]([⊠]), Iratxe Mentxaka[1], Pablo Garaizar[1],
Andoni Eguiluz[1], Sergi Villagrasa[2], and Isidro Navarro[2]

[1] Faculty of Engineering, University of Deusto, Bilbao, Spain
{mlguenaga, iratxe.mentxaka, garaizar,
andoni.eguiluz}@deusto.es
[2] La Salle, Universitat Ramon Llull, Barcelona, Spain
{sergiv, inavarro}@salle.url.edu

Abstract. The demand for computer programming professionals in STEAM-related areas has rocketed in the last decade. Initiatives such as the Hour of Code or CodeWeek take advantage of online platforms like Code.org to reach millions of students through a one-hour introduction to computer science and computer programming. Despite the excellent curricular design of Code.org courses, we believe that learners could benefit from a platform where they can create their own programming challenges that can be shared, assessed and remixed by the rest of the users. We named this platform Make World (http://makeworld.eu). After more than one year of use, we studied how students and teachers used this tool to propose and solve learning activities where computational thinking and STEAM skills are developed at the same time. This paper describes the main characteristics of Make World and analyses the use and piloting phase where more than 500 students of primary education have participated to measure the impact of Make World in their learning. The result of this analysis provides a better understanding of the difficulties students face when using a technological platform for STEAM and computational thinking education.

Keywords: Computer-supported collaborative learning · Serious games and gamification · Technology-enhanced learning · Computational Thinking · STEAM

1 Introduction

STEM (Science, Technology, Engineering, and Mathematics) is a priority area in education in Europe, and basic skills in numeracy, mathematics and sciences are considered key foundations for further learning [1]. Similarly, increasing academic achievements in mathematics and science is also a critical goal for the education reform in the United States [2]. Recently, Arts was also included in this set of key competences. Therefore, STEM replaced STEM as a broader vision of the needed skills for the future.

One of the main reasons to promote STEAM vocations is to cover the lack of workforce in these areas foreseen for the coming decades. Compared to the estimated

© Springer International Publishing AG 2017
P. Zaphiris and A. Ioannou (Eds.): LCT 2017, Part II, LNCS 10296, pp. 50–59, 2017.
DOI: 10.1007/978-3-319-58515-4_5

rise in overall employment of 3% by 2020, it is estimated that employment in STEAM related professions will increase by 14% in Europe [3], very similar to the rise of 14.8% for all Science and Engineering occupations in the United States by 2022. What is more, it is estimated that 80% of jobs will need some type of scientific or mathematical skill.

But working to improve STEAM education is not just about making money. As Gago [4] pointed out, "in many countries the profit motive for choosing a STEM career was over-emphasized and this was actually driving young people away from science and technology". Conversely, we should focus on the human and ethical values of science, on the development of critical citizens who understand the technology around us with a positive attitude.

In order to achieve good results, engagement and a positive attitude towards STEM, children have to feel attracted to these subjects at school [5]. Tai found that the aspirations for STEM before 14 yr. is a good indicator of choosing STEM studies in the future [6], so interventions have to be at early stages and maintained over time.

1.1   Programming and Computational Thinking

Computer programming is a process that involves the analysis of the problem, the design and verification of the algorithm, and its implementation in a programming language. Though related, Computational Thinking (henceforth CT) goes beyond programming to include solving problems, designing systems, and understanding human behavior [7]. CT also helps to understand today's digitalized society and foster 21st century skills like creativity and logical thinking.

Initiatives such as the Hour of Code or CodeWeek take advantage of online platforms like Code.org to reach millions of students through a one-hour introduction to computer science and computer programming. Of 21 countries analyzed in Europe, 16 have already integrated coding in the curriculum, mainly at secondary level but increasingly in primary school [8].

According to the NMC Horizon Report K12 [9], "honing these skills in learners can lead to deeply engaging learning experiences in which students become the authorities on subjects through investigation, storytelling, and production. Other components include game development, and access to programming instruction that nurtures learners as inventors". Teachers and students require new methodologies and tools providing opportunities for communication, co-creation and collective assessment in a social environment that leverages the positive reinforcement techniques and personalized assessment of games, story-telling and CT to improve the understanding and assimilation of complex ideas.

Despite the excellent curricular design of Code.org and similar courses, and in line with the Horizon Report, we believe that learners could benefit from a platform where they can create their own programming challenges that can be shared, assessed and remixed by the rest of the users. We named this platform Make World (http:// makeworld.eu). It aims at offering a tool where both STEAM and CT are addressed in the same activity, it is oriented to primary school and extensible to secondary when students become authors of their own learning resources.

During the development of the project, we have tested the platform with 524 students in the three partner countries (Spain, Greece and Poland). This internal piloting has provided valuable feedback from students in the classroom using developed resources and tools. The result of this analysis provides a better understanding of the difficulties novice programmers in primary education face when they are challenged with a computational thinking challenge integrated with STEM concepts.

2   Make World Platform Overview

MW is a free and open online platform that includes ready-to-use educational resources and teacher's guides in English, Spanish, Greek, Polish and Basque. The Spanish, Polish and Greek collaboration was possible thanks to the support of the Erasmus + program of the European Commission, within the Strategic Partnership category. One primary school in each country, a university and a research institution jointly designed and developed the platform and educational resources that were recognized as best practice by the Spanish national agency in December 2015. According to the EC rules and the consortium policy, all resources are released under Affero General Public License (AGPL).

Make World (MW henceforth) aims at creating a symbiotic relationship between CT and STEAM areas. Accordingly, activities in the platform should challenge students both in computer programming and in STEAM related concepts. But, is any scientific concept suitable to be addressed in a MW activity? The answer is no. In order to naturally merge programming and STEAM we have to consider the programming flow of actions, in our case the sequence of movements triggered by events. This makes concepts that involve cycles and systematic procedures the best topics to design a MW activity, e.g. the water cycle, food chain or digestive system.

The main concepts of the platform are worlds, stories and characters. A world is a two dimensional grid where characters interact (see Fig. 1). Each world has a set of goals the player has to meet by building the characters' programs with the set of instructions provided for each character. The student is who combines the available instructions to create the program, this is, the character behavior. Goals can be achieved when a given event occurs or when the user gets a number of points. Events are the rules of the game and trigger actions that change the state of the game.

Within Make World, a story is a sequence of worlds that may be intertwined by text explanations or multiple choice questions to create a learning track. The sequence is not necessarily linear. Depending on the score obtained in the previous world or the answer to the question of the previous explanation, the learning path may vary. This enables retrying the activity, providing extra content or reinforcing the learning concept. Figure 2 shows the way stories are built. On the right side, the sequence of explanations, worlds and jumps that form the story can be seen. The element highlighted on the right panel marks the step within the story that is being edited currently on the left. Editing a jump requires a description, the score range that will trigger the jump and the destination point within the story (the author has to point out where the jump will direct the program execution, it can be a world or an explanation included in the story).

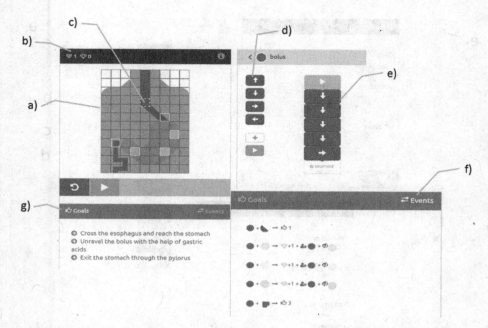

Fig. 1. Make World interface to solve a challenge, the key sections are: (a) world, (b) points and lives, (c) character, (d) available instructions, (e) program, (f) events, (g) goals.

The social nature and flexibility of the platform are some of its biggest assets. In addition to the ready-to-use worlds and stories provided by project partners in the official gallery, users can remix existing resources to modify, adapt and create new versions. Users that get skillful in MW can also create activities from scratch. Players can follow the activities performed by other players, and also comment and like their creations. This social interaction enables gamification dynamics within MW. Players get bronze to ruby badges for several activities in the platform, such as playing worlds and stories, getting their creations remixed by other players, being followed, or creating new resources.

Target users' involvement in the consortium is key to guarantee the success of MW, both in terms of utility for teachers and students learning, and concerning usability in a tool oriented to primary school boys and girls. Fatima school in Spain, Doukas school in Greece and Warsaw Bilingual school in Poland represented the final users during the whole project development. They participated in the initial design, as well as in interim testing and final piloting. The result is a simple and clear interface, with the minimum elements to interact with (i.e. one character is in one tile, one action represents one movement) that shows only the actions needed to complete the activities. Unlike other tools designed for novice programmers, no reading or writing skills are needed to code in MW, and only sequences and procedures are included as computer programming concepts. The little time (less than one hour) needed to train more than 750 teachers and students in the use of the platform is an indication of its usability.

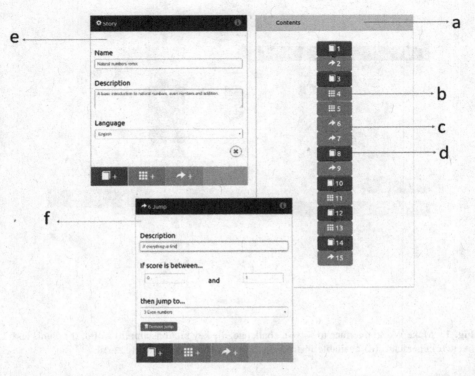

Fig. 2. Story editing interface, where you can see the story sequence (a), with worlds (b), jumps (c) and explanations (d); as well as the story description options (e) and the jumps options (f).

Ethics and privacy issues regarding under-13 users was a big concern for project partners. As a consequence, no personal data has to be provided to use the platform. The sign up process only requires a username and a password. In order to avoid privacy and copyright related issues, image uploading is not permitted. Therefore, users have to use images provided in the MW gallery to define their avatars and create new learning resources.

2.1   The Community

MW success relies on its community. MW users play, remix and create worlds and stories, interact with other users, and therefore enrich their learning experiences. We have expanded this community organizing several workshops with educators and students in Spain, Greece, and Poland (167 educators took part in the workshops: 52 in Spain, 70 in Greece, and 45 in Poland). We also piloted the platform (524 primary students participated in the piloting, aged from 10 to 12 years old: 255 in Spain, 200 in Greece, and 69 in Poland); and held an international conference with more than 80 education experts and practitioners.

These dissemination activities result in an active community of 1,330 users, 670 of whom have created at least one world, and a total of 3,656 worlds created in one year. Without considering users from the project consortium, the community is made up of 669 males (51%) and 649 female users, the average age is 18 (33% adults and 54% aged between 10 and 14), and their preferred languages are: Spanish (48%), English (16%), Basque (15%), Greek (14%) and Polish (7%).

There have been a total of 8,000 accesses to the platform during the last year, with an average duration of 31.5 min for each session. Users have played with 6,959 worlds and successfully finished 58% of them. Their social activity can be measured in terms of the number of comments made (473); the average number of followers of each user (8.24), and average number of followees (10.24).

3   The Piloting of Make World

The piloting of MW took place between January and April 2016 in three primary schools: ESC Fatima in Bilbao and Santander (Spain), Doukas (Athens, Greece) and Warsaw Bilingual School (Warsaw, Poland). Following we describe the steps followed during the piloting phase.

3.1   Approval of the Ethics Committee of the University of Deusto

Before contacting the legal tutors of students, the consortium obtained the approval of the ethics committee of the University of Deusto. This is especially relevant as the project deals with data registered automatically by the platform from the interaction of under aged students. However, it does not register any personal data that may harm participants' privacy, such as email, personal identification number, name or address. The only data needed to access the platform is a username and a password, which do not identify the user. In this stage the informed consent for legal tutors was also developed.

The platform also complies with data privacy and legal issues regarding working with minors. In this sense, the coordinators developed with the support of their legal department the Terms of Service of the platform.

3.2   Pre-piloting Process

The informed consent previously mentioned was distributed among families, and the school collected those who accepted to get involved. In parallel, teachers provide a unique code to each student, so only they knew the identity of students who took part on the experiment, but researchers were able to match the answer to questionnaires with the activity in the platform. This way we ensured the anonymization of data gathered.

Teachers responsible for each participating group were trained for two hours in the basis of Make World, the objectives, approach, computational thinking and STEAM concepts; and they played with the platform as users. Project members also explained them the whole piloting process and tools.

3.3   Experimentation with Students

Groups were randomly distributed in control and experimental groups. 524 students took part in the whole process (255-Spain, 200-Greece and 69-Poland), aged between 10 and 12 years old.

During the first session the experimental group (E-group) was introduced to the MW platform. They played worlds and stories, accessed their profile and stuff, and also used the social features, such as comments, likes followers and followees relations. Meanwhile, the control group (C-group) was introduced to the piloting process and talked about STEM and computational thinking skills.

In the next class, both groups answered a knowledge questionnaire about Recycling, the topic selected for the piloting. They also filled a questionnaire about their Attitudes towards STEM and the Flow of their traditional STEM classes, based on previously validated studies [11–13].

Students have two or three days with no intervention in which those of the E-group could use MW at home. During the next class session, the E-group worked the recycling topic using a story developed in Make World, while the C-group followed a traditional learning process.

In the last intervention session, both groups answered a knowledge questionnaire about recycling, different from the first one but similar in structure and content. They also filled the questionnaire about their Attitudes towards STEM and the E-group filled a questionnaire about their Flow using MW, with more than 80 indicators of other measures from the literature related to the satisfaction of using technology.

4   Results

Since the platform was made public in January 2016, it has more than 2,200 users (51% men and 49% women), who have accessed in more than 8,000 occasions, and they have created more than 3,000 worlds. Users have played almost 7,000 worlds, and have successfully completed 58% of them. These data give evidence of the great user activity. In addition, the system registry allows us to verify that users repeatedly enter the platform, which indicates that they explore its use beyond the action that has developed during dissemination or piloting actions.

More than 500 students who have participated in the piloting have shown a high degree of satisfaction. They have answered several questionnaires that provide information about their attitude towards STEM areas, their opinion on the subjects and method of learning related subjects and on the use of MW as an innovative STEAM learning tool. We have collected more than 80 indicators, and the first analyzes allow us to conclude that the short-term impact on students has been positive. The results of the most relevant questions are show in Table 1, related to the use of the platform.

Table 2 shows some of the items in the questionnaires related to the learning process using Make World. You can see a high level of acceptance of the platform as a STEAM learning tool, since close to 80% of participants find it suitable for learning science.

Table 1. Feeling about the use of MW

	Strongly disagree	Disagree	Neither agree nor disagree	Agree	Strongly agree
It is easy for me to become skillful at using MW	1%	4%	18%	34%	44%
MW is fun for me to use	2%	5%	14%	30%	50%
I find MW easy to use	0%	3%	10%	37%	50%
My interaction with MW is clear and understandable	1%	4%	12%	29%	54%

Table 2. Learning with MW

	Strongly disagree	Disagree	Neither agree nor disagree	Agree	Strongly agree
Using MW improves my learning	1%	7%	11%	38%	44%
Using MW makes it easier to learn science	3%	4%	15%	38%	41%
I find MW useful in my learning	1%	2%	14%	33%	50%
Using MW enhances my learning effectiveness	1%	3%	20%	42%	35%

Satisfaction questionnaires completed by teachers after training show a high level of satisfaction. Bearing in mind that several of these workshops were offered when the platform and resources were not yet complete (January and February 2016), we consider the responses to be very positive. Here are some of the data collected:

- +85% consider Make World "interesting", "funny", "useful for teaching" and "easy to use", with answers in degree "yes" and "yes, a lot".
- +60% have come up with new ideas to promote STEM in primary school.
- +50% declare their intention to use it in their class. Those who have indicated that they will not, mostly are high school teachers or non-academic staff.

Moreover, MW has had a positive impact in their attitude towards STEM. Comparing the attitudes questionnaire filled before and after using MW, you can appreciate an increase in some items, such as:

- Technology is fascinating: +1.06 points
- A career in STEM is interesting: +0.81 pts.
- Mathematics are attractive: +0.80 pts.

5   Conclusions

Increasing the interest on STEAM fields and improving the way they are learned is a priority at international level. Not only due to the current demand for STEAM professionals, but also because there is a need for critical and literate citizens able to understand the 21st century world. Over recent years, policy makers, the educational community, and other related initiatives have been promoting computational thinking skills among young people. It helps them to understand the technology they use every day and involves the development of crucial skills to deal with unforeseen challenges such as problem solving, logical thinking and creativity. The piloting performed with Make World and data collected through several questionnaires shows the positive feeling of students towards MW as an attractive and effective tool for STEAM education.

Considering the cognitive categories defined in the Bloom's taxonomy [10] regarding the skills involved in the learning process, we find that synthesis and assessment are at the top level of the taxonomy. Even in the new approach used in the revision of this taxonomy made by Anderson, et al. [14] "evaluating" and "creating" are also the learning skills that involve the highest level of development. This is the main reason for the development of MW.

The online platform presented here not only tries to address computational thinking issues but also fosters the creation and assessment of new user-generated learning activities. We need STEAM professionals not only able to appropriately use what others have developed before, but also capable of creating their own tools (either remixing existing solutions or from scratch), debugging and solving their errors, and sharing them with the community.

Acknowledgement. The current paper is based on "Make World: learning Science through Computational Thinking", project developed thanks to the funding of the Erasmus + Programme of the European Union (Ref. Num. 2014-1-ES01-KA201-004966). This research is being carried out through the Second ACM – Aristos Campus Mundus Research Grants Call – 2016 to fund the association's best projects of the ACM network. Project Code: ACM2016_07.

References

1. Anderson, L.W., Krathwohl, D.R., Airasian, P.W., Cruikshank, K.A., Mayer, R.E., Pintrich, P.R., Raths, J., Wittrock, M.C.: A Taxonomy for Learning, Teaching, and Assessing: A Revision of Bloom's Taxonomy of Educational Objectives. Pearson, Allyn & Bacon, New York (2001)
2. Bloom, B.S., Engelhart, M.D., Furst, E.J., Hill, W.H., Krathwohl, D.R. (eds.): Taxonomy of Educational Objectives, Handbook I: The Cognitive Domain. David McKay Co Inc., New York (1956)
3. Balanskat, A., Engelhardt, K.: Computing Our Future: Computer Programming and Coding-Priorities, School Curricula and Initiatives Across Europe (2014)
4. DeWitt, J., Archer, L., Osborne, J.: Science-related aspirations across the primary–secondary divide: evidence from two surveys in England. Int. J. Sci. Educ. **36**(10), 1609–1629 (2014)

5. Kier, M.W., Blanchard, M.R., Osborne, J.W., Albert, J.L.: The development of the stem career interest survey (StemCis). Res. Sci. Educ. **44**, 461–481 (2014)
6. Mahoney, M.P.: Students' attitudes toward stem: development of an instrument for high school stembased programs. J. Technol. Stud. **36**(1), 24–34 (2010)
7. Tyler Wood, T., Knezek, G., Christensen, R.: Instruments for assessing interest in stem content and careers. J. Technol. Teache **18**, 341–363 (2010)
8. European Commission: Rethinking education: investing in skills for better socio-economic outcomes (2012)
9. European Commission: EU Skills Panorama Analytical Highlight Science, technology, engineering and mathematics (STEM) skills (2012a)
10. Gago, M.: How ministries of education should uptake STEM challenges? In: 2nd Scientix Conference, Brussels, 24–26 October 2014
11. National Science Board: Science and Engineering Indicators 2016, National Science Foundation (NSB-2016-1), Arlington, VA (2016)
12. New Media Consortium: NMC Horizon Report K12 (2015)
13. Tai, R.H., Liu, C.Q., Maltese, A.V., Fan, X.: Planning early for careers in science. Life Sci. **1**, 0–2 (2006)
14. Wing, J.M.: Computational thinking. Commun. ACM **49**(3), 33–35 (2006)

Manipulation of Mathematical Expressions in Collaborative Environments

Marco Pollanen[1(✉)], Sohee Kang[2], and Bruce Cater[1]

[1] Trent University, Peterborough, Canada
{marcopollanen,bcater}@trentu.ca
[2] University of Toronto Scarborough, Toronto, Canada
soheekang@utsc.utoronto.ca

Abstract. Recent decades have seen phenomenal growth in the use of communication and collaborative technologies in many academic disciplines. There has, however, been little adoption of tools for online collaboration in post-secondary mathematics education. In this paper, we argue both that this may be due to limitations of mathematical interfaces and that the adoption of collaborative tools may provide significant pedagogical benefits. To date, mathematical user-interface research has focused primarily on mathematical expression input, and mostly from a perceptive of document creation or computer algebra system use by expert users. Little work has been done on the specific needs of novice users, including students, and even less work has considered the manipulation of mathematical expressions. In this paper, we outline some user-interface challenges of current input systems with respect to entry and manipulation of mathematical expressions by novice users, and we introduce a model that makes entry and manipulation easier for those users.

Keywords: Mathematical collaboration · Novice user interfaces · Mathematical formula input · Mathematical software · Post-secondary mathematics education

1 Introduction

Most Internet communication tools are text-based messaging applications that also allow for the transmission of useful videos, photos, and voice notes. Perhaps 25% of academic subjects, however, rely heavily on symbolic and diagrammatic content for knowledge transference – content that cannot be conveyed electronically in a form that allows for the rich interaction that occurs, say, between classmates or between a student and a professor at a blackboard during an office hour. This puts online students of these subjects at a particular disadvantage, relative to their counterparts in a traditional learning environment..

Ideally, the level of interaction between students and instructors should be based on what is pedagogically best. Consider a student in an online chemistry course, who may wish to seek clarification from their instructor as to the structure of a particular chemical (see Fig. 1). The structure should be communicated

© Springer International Publishing AG 2017
P. Zaphiris and A. Ioannou (Eds.): LCT 2017, Part II, LNCS 10296, pp. 60–70, 2017.
DOI: 10.1007/978-3-319-58515-4_6

in a way that is easy to manipulate in order to demonstrate a process. A Psychology student may similarly wish to collaborate online with other students on a lab project, and to be able to communicate and manipulate a basic statistical formula. Moreover, a large number of studies, largely based on face-to-face classroom applications, extol the benefits of new interactive pedagogical models, such as peer-based learning [6]. Others have shown that out-of-class student-teacher interaction (e.g., office hour attendance) leads to improvements in many key academic measures, including student performance, retention, and satisfaction, while students themselves overwhelmingly show an interest in greater online communication with their professor [2].

Interaction and communication in courses rich in quantitative content is particularly important, as evidenced by the significant supporting resources universities allocate to such courses. Quantitative service courses, for example, are typically assigned a disproportionate level of tutorial and teaching assistant resources. There are usually counselling and academic skills programs in place to deal with general numeracy skills, and there are almost always mathematics and statistics tutorial centres available to deal with specific course content.

Rarely, however, are these supports replicated for online learners. Unfortunately, the level of interaction between students and instructors in online symbolic and diagrammatic-rich courses is more constrained by what is technologically possible, than it is based on what is pedagogically best. Intuitive technologies for interacting with symbolic and diagrammatic course content are not currently available, and given the online paradigm shift to mobile devices, it has only become more difficult to create symbolically rich content due to the interface limitations of smartphones and tablets. As a result of these technological limitations, there has been very little adoption of online communication tools in the quantitative sciences [1].

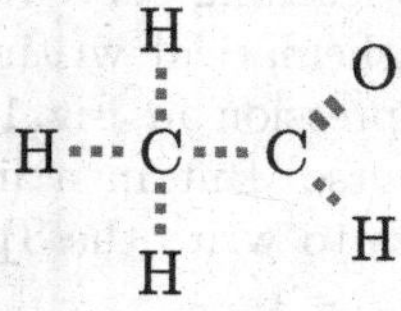

$$r_{xy} = \frac{n\sum_{i=1}^{n} x_i y_i - \sum_{i=1}^{n} x_i \sum_{i=1}^{n} y_i}{\sqrt{n\sum_{i=1}^{n} x_i^2 - \left(\sum_{i=1}^{n} x_i\right)^2}\sqrt{n\sum_{i=1}^{n} y_i^2 - \left(\sum_{i=1}^{n} y_i\right)^2}}$$

Ethanal

Fig. 1. Simple molecular structure (left) and an elementary statistical formula (right)

New tools that allow for non-text-based communication may lead to new pedagogical approaches that would be of particular value to online students. These tools may also lead to the ability to better engage students who are underrepresented in the academic discourse in quantitative courses. It has, for example, long been known that women are less likely to engage in classroom dialogue than their male peers in post-secondary mathematics [4]. Moreover, because English language learners, such as recently-arrived immigrants and international students, may be shy to engage in classroom conversation, new communication tools for the technologically-enhanced class may create a more inclusive student-centred environment leading to further democratization of learning.

1.1 Online Tools for Communication of Symbolic Academic Content

Teaching introductory quantitative service courses to a wide range of students presents a number of challenges and opportunities. In a first-year statistics course, for example, although some students will be statistics majors, the majority may be seeking only a single statistics requirement and may suffer from some "math anxiety". One symptom of this anxiety, which affects up to 85% of students [9], is that it prevents students from visiting their instructor's office hours, thereby undermining their rates of student success, retention, and satisfaction [7]. The anxiety may also represent a barrier for specific groups, including women and English language learners.

In [3], we explored the use of anonymity in online communication and found it to have dramatically improved participation rates for office hours from less than 10% of students in the class attending a traditional office hour, to over 80% attending via online delivery. Despite the potential of anonymity, our experience is that students in completely online courses have particularly low-levels of help-seeking behaviour due in large part to technological limitations.

While other areas of Internet communication have evolved at an astonishing pace, mathematical collaboration online remains a formidable challenge [12]. There are at least two reasons for this. First, a given piece of hardware must somehow allow for the inputting of hundreds of mathematical symbols. Second, the inherently two-dimensional structure of mathematical notation (see Fig. 2B) requires that spatial relationships between those symbols be accurately conveyed. There are, of course, current standards that allow for the text-based entry of mathematical expressions. But those standards have a steep learning curve and low human readability. The predominant standard for mathematical writing, TEX could be used to express, for example, the simple expression in Fig. 1 – a standard equation in any first-year Statistics service course. But in a live conversation, how realistic is it to expect first-year students to write the TEX representation of that equation, shown in Fig. 2C? Namely,

```
r_{xy} = \frac{n \sum_{i=1}^{n} x_{i} y_{i} - \sum_{i=1}^{n} x_{i}
\sum_{i=1}^{n} y_{i} }{ \sqrt{n \sum_{i=1}^{n} x_{i} ^{2} - \left(
\sum_{i=1}^{n} x_{i} \right)^{2} }  \sqrt{n \sum_{i=1}^{n}
y_{i}^{2} - \left( \sum_{i=1}^{n} y_{i} \right)^{2} } }
```

The main alternative to text-based input is a structure-based editor, such as that which is found in Microsoft Word. In such an editor, the user inserts individual symbols and mathematical structures, separately selecting them by clicking through tabs of buttons (see Fig. 2A). As with text editors, however, structure-based editors suffer from severe usability problems [8]. For example, in an observational study [1], we argued that structure-based editors usually force a user to write a formula in a manner that is different from how he or she would write it out by hand. To see this, consider the expression $\sqrt{x}/y$. The default behaviour of a structure-based editor forces the user to input the fraction first, followed by the root, and then the x and y. Intuitively, though, a person writing this expression using a pen and paper would likely write the root of x first, followed by the fraction bar, and then the y. In essence, then, the user of a structure-based editor must use an unintuitive order to input the expression, requiring the user to have the ability to mentally parse the mathematical expression into valid sub-expressions. This too may be an unrealistic expectation for students and other novice users who are struggling to understand complex expressions.

A completely different approach is handwriting recognition of mathematics, which uses the intuitive pen and paper paradigm for input. But that approach too has many limitations. Pen-computing hardware is still far from ubiquitous, and robust recognition of mathematical writing is still a formidable task [13]. Moreover, this paradigm is limited to the intuitive input of mathematics, and does not create a form that can be edited or modified [5].

A further and fundamental problem with all mathematical input systems to date is that they have been designed largely for document creation or interaction with a computer algebra software system, and not for collaboration.

We argue that real-time collaboration and communication has unique interface requirements. An instructor, while chatting online with a student, might, for example, want to ask the student to simplify the expression $\sqrt{\sqrt[3]{\left(\frac{x^2+x}{x}\right)^3}}$ to $\sqrt{x+1}$ in a step-by-step fashion. With any one of the traditional formula editor models, it is very difficult to accomplish this type of rich interaction, for they were designed only to create expressions, and it is often easier to create a new formula from scratch than it is modify an existing formula. To overcome this problem, we introduce a user interface model that, much like the pen-based system, is based on drawing a representation of the expression, but that is also based on a diagram-editor UI model in which symbols are selected from palettes (or other shortcuts). And again like a pen-based approach, this follows a well-known UI model, so there is little learning curve, but expression recognition rates are dramatically better and the model is consistent with most hardware interfaces from keyboard/mouse to touch-based interactions. Moreover, modifications of expressions can occur under the same UI model, unlike pen-based systems where input and modifications occur under different interaction models. Usability results suggest that not only that this allows for faster and more intuitive input from novice users, but also that mathematical expressions can be easily interacted with and modified, making it well-suited for collaborative environments.

2 Input and Manipulation of Mathematical Expressions

There are a variety of mathematical input methods: handwriting-based, palette-based or text-based. In addition, these methods use various combinations of

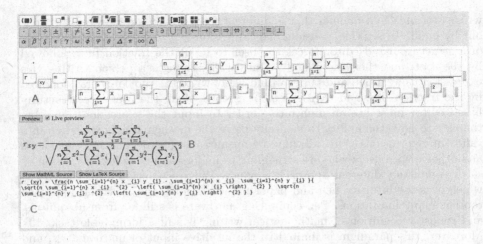

Fig. 2. A common elementary statistics formula (B) along with its representation in a structure-based editor (A) and in TeX code (C).

stylus, keyboard, mouse or touch input over a variety of hardware form factors – computers, tablets, and smartphones. Despite a plethora of different mathematical input technologies, computer input of mathematics remains slow and cumbersome, relative to handwriting mathematics on a chalkboard. So, handwritten mathematics is thought of as the *gold-standard* for mathematical input.

However, mathematics written on a chalkboard is only a visual representation of mathematics. There is a dichotomy between the input of mathematics for visual presentation of mathematics, such as produced by software packages such as TeX, and the input of mathematics for semantic purposes, through the use of software packages such as Mathematica.

From a presentation standpoint, it is quick and easy for mathematics to be written on a chalkboard and for corrections, such as changing a plus to a minus sign, to be made. Great potential does, however, lie in striving to go beyond this model. Handwritten mathematics cannot be easily reused, searched, and edited. For example, when working on a step-by-step calculation, it might be more efficient to copy a line and edit it than to rewrite the expression each time. Likewise, an instructor conducting virtual office hours might gain efficiency by being able to search through old questions and reusing parts of explanations and expressions from common questions.

From a semantic standpoint, there is potential to create user interfaces that go far beyond just being able to replicate the efficiency of handwritten mathematics. Mathematical communication has always relied on a facilitating medium, such as a chalkboard. Even mathematical thought requires one to work out ideas on paper. However, if one were able to write mathematics that is semantically understood by a machine, perhaps an interactive interface can be designed to handle routine calculations though the use of a computer algebra system.

For example, something simple like grabbing a sub-expression and moving it from one side of an equation to another might result in the sign being automatically changed. By reducing the cognitive load associated with more mundane elements of calculation, it might be possible to have a writing environment that frees the mind, allowing one to think more deeply about core concepts.

Since there has not been much focus in the literature on the ability to edit and manipulate mathematical expression, we will briefly review palette-based and pen-based input systems from the perspective of entry and manipulation by a novice user – say, a student. From a user interface point of view, text-based entry interfaces for mathematics mimic that of text-editors, however, as pointed out before they require advanced knowledge to input mathematics properly and are inappropriate for novice users and so we will not discuss them further.

2.1   Structure-Based Editors

Structure-based models typically allow users to select structures from palettes and separately populate them with symbols. Structure-based editors make it easy to find symbols and structures, and guarantee well-formed expressions that could make it easier for inputting semantically into a computer algebra system. From a usability perspective, however, they tend to suffer from a number of difficulties and due to these there is recognition that these types of editors have a reputation of being unattractive to both inexperienced and advanced users [8].

One problem is that entry of an expression typically requires users to navigate menus of symbols and templates as well as enter characters, causing the user to frequently switch between the keyboard and mouse.

A much larger problem is that structure-based editors take the two-dimensional visual representation of an equation and represent it as a series of nested structures, usually represented by nested boxes (see Fig. 2A). To interact with, and navigate though, this structure requires the use of interface interactions that a novice user might not be familiar with. In [8], it was shown that there was a lack of consistency between editors and that navigation can defy WYSIWYG principles. Pressing the cursor key, for example, may cause the cursor to jump from one structure to the next in an unpredictable way, as the two-dimensional structure is navigated.

[1] has shown that novice users, who don't have experience with a structure-based editor, have greater difficulty in inputting mathematics, and often get stuck and cannot even complete their expression, let alone manipulate it. It was also shown that users are forced to write expressions in a different order than they would on a piece of paper, forcing them to mentally parse the expression. This could be particularly challenging for students who don't have a great deal of mathematical training.

2.2   Pen-Based Input

The allure of pen-based input is that it is natural, effectively mimicking the experience of using a piece of paper, allowing input with little effort, and requiring no ability to mentally parse an expression beyond that required to writing the expression on paper [14].

The first obstacle encountered is that pen-based systems are not yet commonly used. And even if they were widely used, a second obstacle is that pen-based input in its most basic use just creates a digital image of what is written onto the screen, making it no different from writing on paper. To move beyond this point, we must be able to recognize the handwritten mathematics.

Robust recognition of handwritten mathematics is still a challenge. It is typically done in two phases, the recognition of symbols and the recognition of structures. Recognizing symbols, alone, is a difficult task. With handwritten recognition of text clues, such as dictionary matches, or in cases of languages such as Chinese, where there are a great many characters, stroke order can give many clues. However, in mathematics many symbols are very similar (e.g., $\cdot, 0, O, o, \bullet, {}^\circ, \circ, \odot, \oplus, \otimes, \oslash, \emptyset, \phi, \ominus, \theta, \Theta, \cdots$). And even once the symbols have been correctly identified, knowing precisely where the user intended to put those symbols makes structural identification difficult. For example, $4 \cdot 5$ and 4.5 could be hard to differentiate.

So, while writing mathematics by pen is an intuitive and effortless task, even for novice users, corrections will inevitably need to be made for mis-recognized input. This necessarily requires a change in interface model. For example, do you delete things with a lasso or by crossing out? Do you select the correct symbol from a pop-up menu of symbols? Such switching of user interface models can interfere with completing the task. Furthermore, is writing converted to typeset text as it is written, or are only full expressions? In either case, the user might find the sudden transformation jarring. Editing of already entered expressions would face the same sorts of challenges, but on a larger scale.

In the next section, we discuss a user interface model that is a hybrid of the palette and pen-based models that we have shown to be more intuitive for novice users and that has the potential to make the editing and manipulation of expressions more natural.

3   An Alternative Hybrid Input Method

As an alternative to the restrictive input approach of a structure-based editor and pen-based input, we proposed a collaborative environment based on a diagram editor user-interface model [13] – an open-source Web-application called iCE: interface for Collaborative Equations (see Fig. 3). Further in [12], we argued that this model is consistent with smartphone and tablet touch-based user-interface principles, and a mobile version of iCE was subsequently developed (see Fig. 4).

The advantage of the diagram-editor model for novice users is its familiarity to most users who have used office software that allows for the drawing of vector-based diagrams. In the case of mathematics, however, instead of just including resizable diagrammatic elements, such as lines and rectangles, the diagrammatic elements include re-sizable mathematical symbols, such as summation signs and brackets.

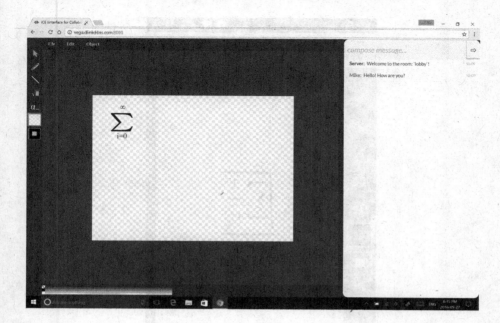

Fig. 3. Screenshot of the desktop version of the iCE: interface for Collaborative Equations. On the left side is a shared workspace that allows for mathematical writing, and the right side is a chat window for conversation.

This approach is a hybrid of a palette-based editor and pen-based input – the user is able to select symbols from palettes, but is free to place the symbols anywhere they want on a canvas in order to create a 'picture' of their expression in a similar way to a pen-based system. One advantage over the pen-based system is that there is a subtle snapping of symbols to baselines, and so a baseline structural analysis algorithm [15] can be used to identify the expression. Unlike with handwriting, where the recognition failure rate is high, this approach allows for even very complicated mathematical expressions to be easily recognized [10]. The success is since, unlike handwriting analysis, the symbol was chosen from a palette it is known with certainty as well as is the location the user intended to place the symbol.

In an observational study [1], we compared how university students with no experience in inputting mathematics in a computer entered expressions with this model, with a structure-based editor, and by handwriting. It was shown that, unlike a structure-based editor, users had no difficulty quickly grasping the diagram-editor user-interface model, and they wrote expressions in the same order with it as they did by hand.

In terms of manipulation of mathematical expressions, because the expressions are diagrammatic, they can easily be modified, copied, and pasted, just as is the case with diagrams in a vector-based editor. For example (see Fig. 5), if a user clicks on a re-sizeable symbol, draggable resize widgets are added to

Fig. 4. Screenshot of the smartphone version of the iCE: interface for Collaborative Equations

the element. But if a selection is dragged out, all elements within that selection are temporary grouped together. That grouping could then easily be deleted or dragged to another location.

While the structure-based and pen-based input of mathematics involves a dichotomy between entry and manipulation of expressions, entry and manipulation with the diagram editor uses the same model. It has been shown that users are quickly able to grasp this and manipulate expression with relative ease. To invert a fraction, for example, users could select the numerator by dragging a selection box and then moving it to a new location temporarily. At this point, the denominator is moved to the numerator and the old numerator is moved into the denominator position. Unlike with a structure-based editor, each symbol is at the same layer level, so even deeply nested structures can be modified by clicking on or dragging components.

One weakness of this model is that users have been observed [11] to spend about 25% of their time making the diagram look 'prettier', which, of course,

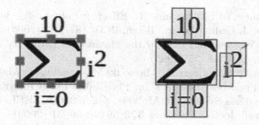

Fig. 5. Screenshot of a diagram-editor based mathematical input model showing a single selected symbol (right) and selection of multiple symbols (right).

benefits the structural analysis algorithm in no way. So, the model could perhaps be improved by incorporating more structural analysis as the user is creating or modifying an expression. When symbols are in a correct position, for example, they could become 'stickier', just as with the snap-to-baseline that is already used. So, while users would always have the freedom to place symbols anywhere they want, symbols would tend to be attracted to their 'correct' location. This would likely speed up the input process.

4 Conclusion

While the computer input of mathematical expressions is a well-studied topic, few studies have focused on the manipulation of mathematical expressions. This is an important topic, given the pedagogical potential of building online tools for mathematical communication and collaboration, particularly for students who are novice users. In this paper, we have discussed existing input models and showed that they are limited in their ability to allow for easy editing and manipulation of mathematical expressions. And we have argued that a diagram-editor model for mathematical expression entry allows not only for easier input, but also for an intuitive approach to manipulation. This is an avenue of research that would benefit from further study.

Acknowledgments. The work of the authors was partially supported by a research grant from eCampus Ontario.

References

1. Gozli, D.G., Pollanen, M., Reynolds, M.: The characteristics of writing environments for mathematics: behavioral consequences and implications for software design and usability. In: Carette, J., Dixon, L., Coen, C.S., Watt, S.M. (eds.) CICM 2009. LNCS (LNAI), vol. 5625, pp. 310–324. Springer, Heidelberg (2009). doi:10.1007/978-3-642-02614-0_26
2. Helvie-Mason, L.: Office hours: 'there's an app. for that?!': student perceptions of faculty channels for out-of-class communication. Int. J. Instr. Technol. Distance Learn. **9**, 31–38 (2012)

3. Hooper, J., Pollanen, M., Teismann, H.: Effective online office hours in the mathematical sciences. J. Online Learn. Teach. **2**(3), 187–194 (2006)
4. Krupnick, C.G.: Women and men in the classroom: inequality and its remedies. On Teach. Learn. **1**(1), 18–25 (1985)
5. Labahn, G., Lank, E., MacLean, S., Marzouk, M., Tausky, D.: Mathbrush: a system for doing math on pen-based devices. In: The Eighth IAPR International Workshop on Document Analysis Systems, DAS 2008, pp. 599–606. IEEE, September 2008
6. Mazur, E.: Farewell, lecture? Science **323**(5910), 50–51 (2009)
7. Nadler, M.K., Nadler, L.B.: Out-of-class communications between faculty and students: a faculty perspective. Commun. Stud. **51**(2), 176–188 (2000)
8. Padovani, L., Solmi, R.: An investigation on the dynamics of direct-manipulation editors for mathematics. In: Asperti, A., Bancerek, G., Trybulec, A. (eds.) MKM 2004. LNCS, vol. 3119, pp. 302–316. Springer, Heidelberg (2004). doi:10.1007/978-3-540-27818-4_22
9. Perry, A.P.: Decreasing math anxiety in college students. Coll. Student J. **38**, 321–325 (2004)
10. Pollanen, M., Wisniewski, T., Yu, X.: XPRESS: a novice interface for the real-time communication of mathematical expressions. In: Proceedings of MathUI , 8 pages (2007)
11. Pollanen, M., Reynolds, M.: A model for effective real-time entry of mathematical expressions. Res. Reflections Innovations Integr. ICT Educ. **3**, 1235–1512 (2009). Formatex
12. Pollanen, M., Hooper, J., Cater, B., Kang, S.: A tablet-compatible web-interface for mathematical collaboration. In: Hong, H., Yap, C. (eds.) ICMS 2014. LNCS, vol. 8592, pp. 614–620. Springer, Heidelberg (2014). doi:10.1007/978-3-662-44199-2_92
13. Pollanen, M., Hooper, J., Cater, B., Kang, S.: Towards a universal interface for real-time mathematical communication. In: Proceedings of MathUI 2014: CICM-WS-WiP 2014, vol. 1186, 12 pages (2014)
14. Smithies, S., Novins, K., Arvo, J.: A handwriting-based equation editor. In: Graphics Interface, vol. 99, pp. 84-91, June 1999
15. Zanibbi, R., Blostein, D., Cordy, J.R.: Recognizing mathematical expressions using tree transformation. IEEE Trans. Pattern Anal. Mach. Intell. **24**(11), 1455–1467 (2002)

Designing Tools that Allows Children in the Early Childhood to Program Robots

Kryscia Ramírez-Benavides[(✉)], Gustavo López,
and Luis A. Guerrero

Universidad de Costa Rica, San José, Costa Rica
{kryscia.ramirez,gustavo.lopez_h}@ucr.ac.cr,
luis.guerrero@ecci.ucr.ac.cr

Abstract. This paper describes the design and evaluation process of two mobile programming assistance tools that allow children in the early childhood to develop programs and execute them using robots. The tools are called TITIBOTS and TITIBOTS Colab which incorporates collaboration. The tools have icon-based interfaces and integrate visual programming, robotics, and mobile devices as one tool. The main issues and lessons learned during the design process are described. The methodology used in this project was User-Centered Design (UCD) process. The tools were developed and evaluated applying participatory-design, experience prototyping, and usability testing. The final product are two simple, intuitive, and easy to use tools, for children between 4 and 6 years old. The results were promising: children liked the applications and were willing to continue using it to program robots for solving specific tasks.

Keywords: User interfaces and Human computer interaction · Interaction design · User-Centered Design · Early childhood education · Programming tool · Programming robots

1 Introduction

Children born during Information Age are digital natives, i.e., the constant use of technology transformed them into expert users [1]. This characteristic could be exploited to improve the learning process through the use of technology. Science, technology, engineering, and math (STEM) concepts proved to be complex. However teaching these subjects during foundational early childhood years (preschool to grade two) can be engaging and rewarding to young learners, especially if the topics are addressed through robotics and basic programming [2].

Incorporating activities that promote the 21st century skills (Binkley et al. 2012) in the learning process will help digital natives to develop abstract thinking abilities and apply them in an organized way [3].

For many years robotics allowed to ease learning process based on STEM concepts [4, 5]. Moreover, the abilities obtained while programming and using robots are a key aspect in the development of children and their future professional life [6].

Many authors have discussed the importance of programming as a capability for digital natives. For instance, Resnick [7], considers programming the new literacy.

© Springer International Publishing AG 2017
P. Zaphiris and A. Ioannou (Eds.): LCT 2017, Part II, LNCS 10296, pp. 71–89, 2017.
DOI: 10.1007/978-3-319-58515-4_7

He states that, "in addition to writing and reading, programming helps organize thoughts and express ideas". Furthermore, the skills gained with programming and using robots are key aspects in the development of children and their future careers [6].

This paper describes the design process of two mobile programming assistance tools that allow children in the early childhood to develop programs and execute them using robots. The tools are called TITIBOTS and TITIBOTS Colab which incorporates collaboration. The main issues and lessons learned during the design process are described.

The main research question driving this work was to assess the possibility of designing a tool based on mobile interfaces and robots that children aged between 4 and 6 years can use. Similar works have been conducted in recent years, but focused mainly in older children.

The methodology used in this project was the User-Centered Design (UCD) process. Particularly, we used the ISO standard 13407. Moreover, the tools were developed and evaluated applying participatory-design, experience prototyping, and usability testing.

This research involved 12 experts within areas such as education, informatics, and robotics, 11 researchers and 15 preschool teachers. Approximately 100 children in the early childhood participate during the different evaluation phrases. The evaluation results showed that children in the early childhood are capable of program robots using our mobile applications tools.

2   User-Centered Design

The User-Centered Design (UCD) is defined by the Usability Professionals Association (UPA) as a process outlines the phases throughout a design and development life-cycle all while focusing on gaining a deep understanding of who will be using the product [8, 9]. The international standard 13407 is the basis for many UCD methodologies. It's important to note that the UCD process does not specify exact methods for each phase.

It should be clear that usability is not the same as UCD, since usability is a quality attribute final design, while the UCD is the way to reach and improve the usability of the product. So, usability is why, while the UCD is how; designing usable objects is something laudable but not necessarily means that has been achieved using UCD [10].

According to the ISO 13407 standard, the following are the general phases of the UCD process (the iterative nature of these activities is illustrated in Fig. 1) [11]:

- **Specify the context of use.** Identify the people who will use the product, what they will use it for, and under what conditions they will use it.
- **Specify requirements.** Identify any business requirements or user goals that must be met for the product to be successful.
- **Create design solutions.** This part of the process may be done in stages, building from a rough concept to a complete design.
- **Evaluate designs.** Evaluation, ideally through usability testing with actual users, is as integral as quality testing is to good software development.

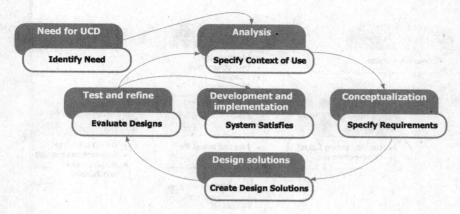

Fig. 1. UCD process.

There are many variations of the UCD process. It can be incorporated into waterfall, agile, and other approaches. Depending on your needs, the UCD process is composed of several methods and tasks. What you are developing, your requirements, team, timeline, and the environment in which you are developing will all help determine the tasks you perform and the order in which you perform them [8].

3   Design Process of Programming Tools for Early Childhood

Since the design process is iterative, seven iterations of the UCD process were made. Now, the final version of the tools is simple, intuitive, and easy to use for children between 4 and 6 years old. During the first interaction, we prove the technical feasibility of the tool. Four interactions were necessary to create TITIBOTS, and two more interactions for creating TITIBOTS Colab. The results were promising: children liked the applications and were willing to continue using it to program robots for solving specific tasks.

Figure 2 shows the iterative UCD process with the main techniques applied in each phase. Table 1 describes these techniques. The used techniques were taken from the ISO standard TR-18529.

Each iteration had the need to solve the research problem and, two public pilots were developed with the two functional and usable prototypes. Each of these iterations is described in this chapter below.

3.1   First Iteration

The iteration focused on verify the technical feasibility of the programming tools that were created. A programming tool (individual, without collaboration) was developed where effective communication was established between the mobile device and the robot.

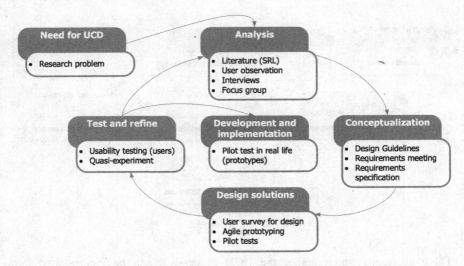

Fig. 2. Techniques used in each UCD phases.

The techniques used in each phase were (see Fig. 3) [12, 13]:

- **Analysis.** Literature review and specification of the context of use.
- **Conceptualization.** Identification and documentation of the technical environment.
- **Design solutions.** Prototype development.
- **Test and refine.** Functionality testing.

The first prototype is very simple and it was developed with the aim of solving technical problems regarding Bluetooth communication between the mobile device and the NXT intelligent brick (see Fig. 4). For this reason, a communication protocol with the commands was created as well as a language interpreted for the communication of the commands was implemented, both from the mobile device to the NXT intelligent brick, therefore a one to one connection was established. The programming tool was named MODEBOTS (Mobile Development Environment for Robots).

This prototype includes the commands for the robot to carry out locomotion and manipulation in the environment; in other words, control the actuators and effectors of the robot. Command controls were included to indicate the beginning and end of the instructions sequence. Actions can be executed sequentially and loops or conditionals are not included.

The commands were tested on this iteration prototype to verify they were functional, resulting that all commands were usable. Also, the response times of communication between the tablet and the robot as well as the times of interpretation and execution of the program resulted acceptable in the initial tests.

The result of this iteration was to start generating design solutions aimed at pre-school children by checking the technical feasibility with the first prototype, in search of public pilots.

Table 1. Description of the techniques used at each UCD phase.

Phase of the UCD process	Techniques used
Analysis Understand and specify the context of use	• **Literature.** A literature review to understand and specify the context of use was used. • **User observation.** Researchers observe users working in the field of study, and take notes on every activity. • **Interviews.** A set of questions was used by experts to gather information for improving the design: opinions, motivations and experiences of final users. • **Focus group.** An informal assembly of users probes the tool. The goal was to elicit perceptions, feelings, attitudes, and ideas of participants about design solutions.
Conceptualization Specify user and organizational requirements	• **Design guidelines.** Usability requirements were monitored during the whole project. • **Requirements meeting.** We use workshops attended by users and developers for identify usability requirements. • **Requirements specification.** Description of features, requirements and restrictions of the tool and its context of use were created.
Design solutions Produce design solutions	• **User survey for design.** Surveys were used to find out how the tool is used by a specific set of end users. • **Agile prototyping.** A preliminary validation was carry out with various institutions. The tool interface was evaluated and accepted. • **Pilot tests.** Testing was applied to functional prototypes. Several pilots were performed using few users (5 users recommended).
Test and refine Evaluate designs against requirements	• **Usability testing.** Tests were applied based on observation of how a group of users perform a series of tasks. • **Quasi-experiment.** Design of experimental research in which subjects or groups of study subjects are not randomly assigned, working with natural groups. The quasi-experimental design is a form of experimental research widely used in social sciences and psychology.
Development and implementation System satisfies specified user and organizational requirements	• **Pilot test in real life.** A final prototype was tested with real users in a real environment.

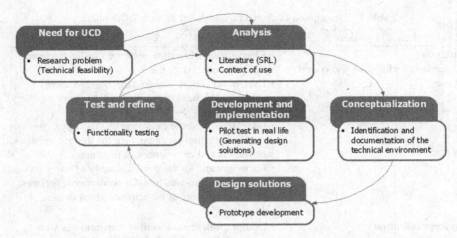

Fig. 3. Techniques used in the first iteration of UCD phases.

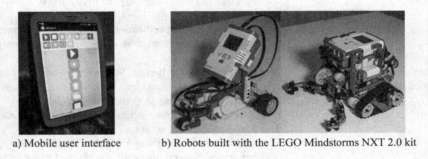

a) Mobile user interface   b) Robots built with the LEGO Mindstorms NXT 2.0 kit

Fig. 4. First prototype: MODEBOTS.

3.2 Second Iteration

The second iteration focused on generating design solutions for the programming tool (individual, without collaboration) aimed at preschool children, and validating them with 12 experts from Omar Dengo Foundation[1] (FOD) and 6 preschool teachers, who validated iconography and interaction. In order to validate the interface design, iconography, and interaction, a set of instruments were created to validate the form, color, and possible interaction [14].

The techniques used in each phase were (see Fig. 5) [12, 13, 15, 16]:

- **Analysis.** Literature review, user observation, scenarios of use and interviews.
- **Conceptualization.** Requirements meeting and requirements specification.
- **Design solutions.** Group sketching and paper prototype.
- **Test and refine.** Validation with experts and preschool teachers.

---

[1] *Fundación Omar Dengo* (FOD), San José, Costa Rica. URL: http://fod.ac.cr/.

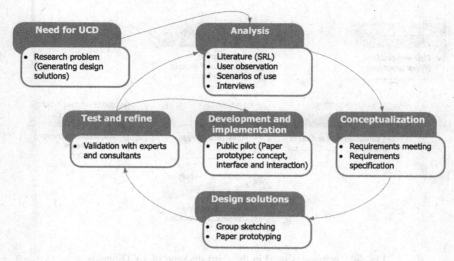

Fig. 5. Techniques used in the second iteration of UCD phases.

A group sketching and paper prototyping activities were conducted to design a preliminary version of TITIBOTS. When a consensus was achieved, design validations begun with the best interaction proposals.

The result of this iteration was to develop a paper prototype (concept, interface and interaction), see Fig. 7, to validate it with preschool children, in search of public pilots.

3.3 Third Iteration

The third iteration focused on validating the paper prototype developed in the previous iteration with 40 preschool children. This iteration has the best proposal of the concept, the iconography and the interaction resulting from the consensus of experts and pre-school teachers to carry out the validation with the children.

The techniques used in each phase were (see Fig. 6) [12, 13]:

- **Analysis.** Brainstorming and consensus of experts and preschool teachers.
- **Conceptualization.** Requirements meeting and requirements specification.
- **Design solutions.** Paper prototyping (concept, interface e interaction).
- **Test and refine.** Validation with end users (preschool children).

A sketch that represents the interface, iconography and interaction patterns were created (see Fig. 7). Using the results of validation several changes in the design of the tool were implemented, the most significant changes were:

- Reducing graphical load of the interface (i.e., decreasing background colors and figures, removing visual distractions to allow focus on the relevant elements).
- Perform visual closures (for attention), and use primary and secondary colors.
- Enlarge icon size.

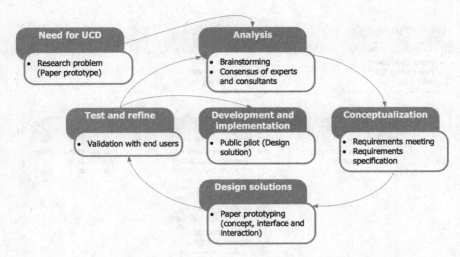

Fig. 6. Techniques used in the third iteration of UCD phases.

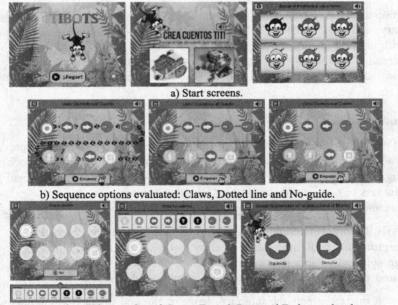

a) Start screens.

b) Sequence options evaluated: Claws, Dotted line and No-guide.

c) Interaction options evaluated: Insert, Drag & Drop and Task completed.

Fig. 7. Paper prototyping TITIBOTS.

The result of this iteration was to obtain a design solution (concept, interface and interaction) to begin with the implementation, in search of public pilots. With the information gathered we developed the first functional prototype of TITIBOTS.

3.4   Fourth Iteration

The fourth iteration focused on implementing the design solution resulting from the previous iteration. In this iteration, TITIBOTS functionality was evaluated with 7 preschool children [14].

The techniques used in each phase were (see Fig. 8) [12, 13, 16]:

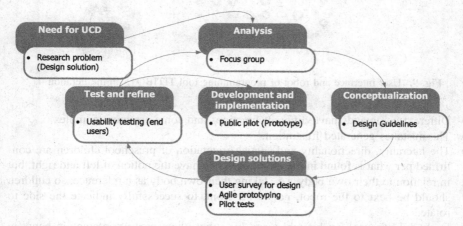

Fig. 8. Techniques used in the fourth iteration of UCD phases.

- **Analysis.** Focus group with preschool teachers. In addition, literature review focused on guidelines for learning tools aimed at preschool children.
- **Conceptualization.** Design guidelines.
- **Design solutions.** User survey for design, agile prototyping and pilot test.
- **Test and refine.** Usability testing with end users (preschool children).

The design of the user interface was minimalist, a programming tool as simple as possible and removing graphic overhead due to the target audience (see Fig. 9). In relation to the evaluation, a set of challenges were created for the children and used observations to evaluate their behavior. The main goal of this evaluation was to see the children's reaction with the tool and to find difficulties.

Observations were performed in order to evaluate the usability of the software [17], to determine the necessity of a teacher's intervention when using TITIBOTS, and whether it helps or not in the learning process to have a strong guidance.

In this evaluation, we observed the following:

- The usability of the prototype was considered successful, the interface showed to be simple and intuitive.
- All the participants (preschool children) showed interest in the application and want to keep using it after the activity.
- The use of play in learning with children is important.
- The teacher mediation has a strong influence in the use of the tool and the level of achievement in the challenges.

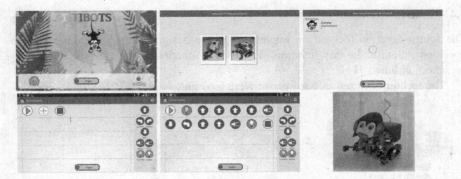

Fig. 9. User interface and robot of programming tool TITIBOTS in the iteration 4.

- Different commands have different functions and some are more complex.
- The mistakes generated frustration.
- The laterality, directionality and spatial orientation of preschool children are confirmed per what is found in the literature. They have the notion of left and right, but in relation to their own body, i.e., taking their own body as a reference, so children should be next to the robot, not to the front, to successfully indicate the side to rotate.
- Each child focused on his tablet and his robot, there was no interaction between them. Sometimes it was just curiosity.

Several problems were found in the system during the evaluation:

- Robot's claws smashed easily. This forced a redesign in the software to avoid an open command if the claw was already opened.
- Bluetooth connection was unstable. The software was redesign to reconnect automatically.
- Commands placed in pairs (for instance: on and off, catch and release) were easier to understand by the children than those in the form of keyboard (Forward and Backward, Left and Right). The software interface was redesigned to allocate all the commands in pairs.
- Real time feedback is required from the application to let the user know what is happening.
- The tablets would go out if they were unused for a few minutes. The software was redesigned so that the tablets were kept on while the tool was active.

In addition, functionalities were added on the recommendation of experts and evaluators:

- Levels to the tool, by level shows a new pair of commands: Level 1. forward/backward, Level 2. left/right, Level 3. on/off, Level 4. grab/release.
- Clean button, to clear the command screen and execute a script that restarts the robot in the initial state (open claw) when you want to create a new program.
- Load button, to open a previous program created (the tool saves the last program created).

The result of this iteration was to obtain a functional and usable preliminary prototype to continue evaluations with end users, in search of public pilots.

3.5   Fifth Iteration

The fifth iteration focused on improving the prototype of the previous iteration, correcting the problems encountered and following the suggestions of the consultants (10 preschool teachers).

The techniques used in each phase were (see Fig. 10) [12, 13, 16]:

- **Analysis.** User observation (field study) and focus group with experts and preschool teachers. In addition, literature review focused on guidelines for learning tools aimed at preschool children.
- **Conceptualization.** Design guidelines and refinement process.
- **Design solutions.** User survey for design, prototyping and pilot test.
- **Test and refine.** Usability testing with end users (preschool children).

The improved prototype of TITIBOTS was evaluated in a real scenario, our testing scenario was a workshop at FOD with 6 preschool children [14]. The methodology proposed by Nielsen was followed to conduct a usability test with users [9].

In the robotic workshop the children use the tool to be introduced with programming concepts. During the workshop, the teacher played with the children, and each game introduced the instructions that TITIBOTS tool allowed each day. Figure 11 shows some pictures of the workshop during different activities.

In this evaluation, the following was observed:

- Usability and functionality of the prototype were considered successful.

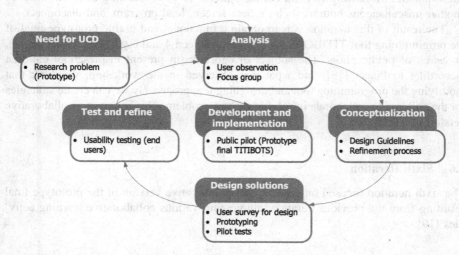

Fig. 10. Techniques used in the fifth iteration of UCD phases.

Fig. 11. Preschool children using TITIBOTS.

- All the participants (preschool children) achieved the basic knowledge intended for the activity.
- The activities in which each child mimicked the robot and acted the commands were crucial to the learning process.
- At the beginning, each child focused on his tablet and his robot, there was no interaction between them. As the workshop progressed, children began to help others, explaining what to do and indicating what was wrong.

In addition, experts and preschool teachers recommended the following:

- The time of each workshop session should be one and a half hours, since the maximum possible limit is considered to have the attention of the children. Consideration should be given to reducing the duration or raising breaks.
- The workshop should have the presence of an assistant to support the mediator in the activities, as the task is extremely absorbing for a single person.

The most important result of the workshop (obtained from evaluator's report, recordings and usability metrics) was that the children were always happy and attentive with the prototype. They found it easy to use and fun, according to the satisfaction questionnaire. Moreover, they did not have problems understanding the commands or another miscellaneous buttons such as clear screen, load program, and disconnect.

The result of this iteration was to obtain a functional and usable prototype final of the programming tool TITIBOTS for children between 4 and 6 years old (see Fig. 12), in search of public pilots. The subject of egocentrism present in preschool children (according to Piaget [18]) and what was observed in the workshop, we think that modifying the programming tool and designing it appropriately we can create strategies for the children to collaborate in solving a given problem. This is part of a collaborative version of TITIBOTS.

3.6 Sixth Iteration

The sixth iteration focused on creating the collaborative version of the prototype final resulting from the previous iteration, automating various collaborative learning activities [19].

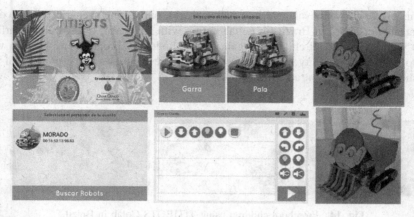

Fig. 12. User interface and robot of programming tool TITIBOTS in the iteration 5.

The techniques used in each phase were (see Fig. 13) [12, 13, 16]:

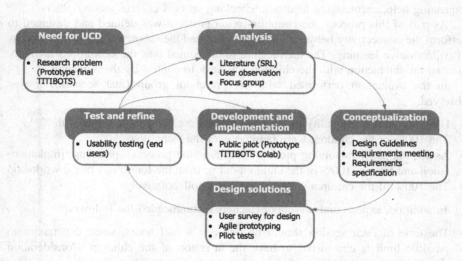

Fig. 13. Techniques used in the sixth iteration of UCD phases.

- **Analysis.** Literature review, user observation (field study) and focus group with RExLab's researchers and preschool teachers.
- **Conceptualization.** Design guidelines, requirements meeting and requirements specification.
- **Design solutions.** User survey for design, agile prototyping and pilot test.
- **Test and refine.** Usability testing with end users (preschool children).

This prototype was evaluated in a real scenario, our testing scenario was a workshop at public school in Brazil (in collaboration with RExLab[2], 6 researchers participated) with 16 preschool children. Again the methodology proposed by Nielsen was used to conduct a usability test with users [9]. Figure 14 shows some pictures of the workshop during different activities.

Fig. 14. Preschool children using TITIBOTS Colab in Brazil.

The collaboration process was implemented through the distribution of resources (commands divided among the children that formed the group). The automated activities were: size of groups, formation of groups and assignment roles, monitoring, requesting help, encouraging feedback, checking success criteria, among others.

As part of this process, the communication protocol was defined and designed to perform the connectivity between mobile devices and the robot, to support the process of collaborative learning. The architecture implemented was the centralized architecture, so the interaction with the children was easy to control by the mediator.

In the evaluation performed with the preschool group (real scenario) it was observed:

- Usability and functionality of the application were considered successful.
- The 100% of the children were familiar with the technology.
- As for the problem-solving process (programming process): planning, implementation and testing, 100% of the children did so from the fourth day of the workshop
- The 100% of the children were able to work collaboratively.

In addition, experts and preschool teachers recommended the following:

- The time of each session should be one and a half hours, since the maximum possible limit is considered to have the attention of the children. Consideration should be given to reducing the duration or raising breaks.
- The workshop must be attended by one or two assistants who support the mediator in the activities, as the task is extremely absorbing for a single person.

The result of this iteration was to obtain a functional and usable prototype of the TITIBOTS Colab for children between 4 and 6 years old (see Fig. 17), in search of public pilots.

---

[2] *Laboratório de Experimentação Remota* (RExLab), *Universidade Federal de Santa Catarina*, Araranguá, SC, Brazil. URL: http://rexlab.ufsc.br/.

3.7   Seventh Iteration

The seventh iteration focused on improving the prototype of the previous iteration and performing a second evaluation in a real scenario in Costa Rica to evaluate the impact of the collaborative programming tool on the collaboration process in children between the ages of 4 and 6.

The techniques used in each phase were (see Fig. 15) [12, 13, 20]:

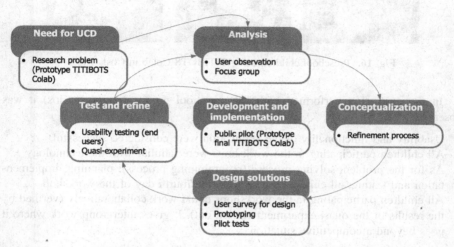

Fig. 15. Techniques used in the seventh iteration of UCD phases.

- **Analysis.** User observation (field study) and focus group with FOD's experts and preschool teachers.
- **Conceptualization.** Refinement process.
- **Design solutions.** User survey for design, prototyping and pilot test.
- **Test and refine.** Usability testing with end users (preschool children) and quasi-experiment (to evaluate the impact of the collaborative programming tool on the collaboration process in children between the ages of 4 and 6).

This prototype was evaluated in two workshops in two different schools in Costa Rica (in collaboration with FOD) with 30 preschool children (15 children in each school). The methodology proposed by Nielsen was used to conduct a usability test with users [9]. Figure 16 shows some pictures of the workshop during different activities.

With the results obtained in the quasi-experiment, it was verified that in the experimental group there was a statistically significant difference in the components of collaborative learning in the post-test in relation to the collaborative groups of the control group. The difference between the natural groups was the application of the treatment in the experimental group, since the initial comparability of both groups was verified. Therefore, it is concluded that the use of TITIBOTS Colab encourages collaboration in children between the ages of 4 and 6 years.

Fig. 16. Preschool children using TITIBOTS Colab in Costa Rica.

In the evaluation performed with the preschool groups (real scenarios) it was observed:

- Usability and functionality of the application were considered successful.
- All children participating in the workshops were familiar with the technology.
- As for the problem-solving process (programming process): planning, implementation and testing, all children did so from the fourth day of the workshop.
- All children participating in the workshops could work collaboratively (verified by the results of the quasi-experiment carried out). It gives intergroup work where it goes beyond a competitive situation.

The most significant result was that all the children participating in the workshops could work collaboratively, where two situations can be highlighted. The first situation was the communication between members of a team to discuss the solution of a challenge, since this dialogue is surprising for children of this age. The second situation was the intergroup work that arose, where the competitive situation was left behind and certain children, when they finished their contribution in the equipment, were going to help other teams. The observed phases that children go through during their interaction with TITIBOTS Colab:

- **Phase 1.** The first contact with the collaborative tool causes a stage of discovery and experimentation.
- **Phase 2.** When the collaborative tool was mastered a little more, the feeling of collaboration within the team and competitive between teams appears.
- **Phase 3.** Having the collaborative tool dominated gives the intergroup work, where the competitive situation disappears.

The result of this iteration was to obtain a functional and usable collaborative programming tool TITIBOTS Colab (final prototype) for children between 4 and 6 years old (see Fig. 17), which encourages the collaboration process, in search of public pilots. With the collaborative programming tool TITIBOTS Colab, public pilots were carried out with children of preschool age.

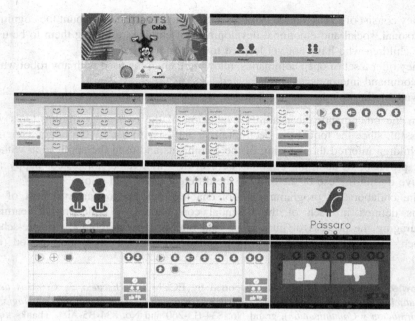

Fig. 17. User interface of programming tool TITIBOTS Colab.

4 Conclusion

Programming tools allowed early childhood children to create programs using tablets and run them with robots (allowing any robot to implement a command interpreter). What promotes the development of computational thinking from an early age through the programming of robots.

One of the principal challenges presented in the research was to design applications for preschool children, since the design of the tools should capture the visual attention of the children and motivate them and, at the same time, easy to use by them. This was achieved using the user-centered design process, which was useful for achieving the usability of the tools. Since it was necessary to identify and specify the context of use, and characterize the target audience. Then, a refinement process was carried out in relation to its design and functionality, based on the different pilots performed. Finally, they were evaluated in real environments. In this refinement process we evaluate usability through prototypes and usability tests.

In this process the guideline was generated to build programming tools aimed at pre-school children. This guide was generated from studies carried out by different authors and evaluations carried out in the research, fulfilling the criteria of the Cognitive Dimensions of Notations framework [21, 22].

The two programming tools created have a unique set of features:

- They have a simple, intuitive and easy-to-use user interface for children in early childhood.

- They consist of iconographic symbols and sounds taking into account the cognitive, personal, social and emotional development of children, allowing them to be used by children who have not yet learned to read and write.
- They offer a set of open commands, allowing them to be used with any robot where a command interpreter is implemented.
- Available in three languages: Spanish, Portuguese and English.

On the other hand, the usability evaluation of the two programming tools was successful, since the tools have been intuitive and easy to use by the target audience. The children inferred the meaning of the commands and used the application without major problem. In addition, children were always motivated, interested, happy and attentive during the use of the tools in the different developed pilots.

The collaborative programming tool enabled children to perform most of the actions defined in each of the essential components of collaborative learning; Encouraging the process of intra-group and inter-group collaboration in pre-school children, making them leave aside their initial egocentrism, in a short period (one week).

Acknowledgments. This work was supported by ECCI-UCR (*Escuela de Ciencias de la Computación e Informática*) and by CITIC-UCR (*Centro de Investigaciones en Tecnologías de la Información y Comunicación*), grand No. 834-B3-260 and No. 834-B5-A04. Thanks to the FOD (*Fundación Omar Dengo*) and RExLab for helping us in the validation and evaluation of programming tools. Thanks to Mariana López (designer and usability expert) and to Franklin Garcia (designer and system developer).

References

1. Prensky, M.: Digital natives, digital immigrants part 1. Horiz. **9**(5), 1–6 (2001)
2. Bers, M.U.: Blocks to Robots: Learning with Technology in the Early Childhood Classroom. Teachers College Press, New York (2008)
3. Hsin, C.-T., Li, M.-C., Tsai, C.-C.: The influence of young childrens use of technology on their learning: a review. Educ. Technol. Soc. **17**(4), 85–99 (2014)
4. Bers, M., Rogers, C., Beals, L., Portsmore, M., Staszowski, K., Cejka, E., Carberry, A., Gravel, B., Anderson, J., Barnett, M.: Innovative session: early childhood robotics for learning. In: Proceedings of the 7th International Conference on Learning Sciences, ICLS 2006, pp. 1036–1042 (2006)
5. Bers, M.U.: Programming in Kindergarten: A Playground Experience. Comput. Sci. K–8 Build. A Strong Found., no. Special, 7–8 (2012)
6. Binkley, M., Erstad, O., Herman, J., Raizen, S., Ripley, M., Miller-Ricci, M., Rumble, M.: Defining twenty-first century skills. In: Griffin, P., McGaw, B., Care, E. (eds.) Assessment and Teaching of 21st Century Skills, pp. 17–66. Springer, Netherlands (2012)
7. Resnick, M.: Learn to Code, Code to Learn. EdSurge (2013)
8. Usability.gov Staff Writer, "With Measurable Usability Goals – We All Score," Usability.gov Staff Writer (2013). http://www.usability.gov/get-involved/blog/2013/09/measurable-usability-goals.html. [Accessed: 14 Jun 2014]
9. Nielsen, J.: Usability Engineering, 1st edn. Elsevier, Cambridge (1993)

10. Hassan-Montero, Y., Ortega-Santamaría, S.: Informe APEI sobre usabilidad, Informes A. APEI Asociación Profesional de Especialistas en Información (2009)
11. International Organization for Standardization, ISO 13407:1999 Human-centred design processes for interactive systems (1999)
12. International Organization for Standardization, ISO TR-18529:2000 Human-centred lifecycle process descriptions (2000)
13. Ferre, X., Bevan, N., Escobar, T.A.: UCD method selection with usability planner. In: NordiCHI 2010 Proceedings of the 6th Nordic Conference on Human-Computer Interaction: Extending Boundaries, pp. 829–830 (2010)
14. Ramírez-Benavides, K., López, G., Guerrero, L.A.: A mobile application that allows children in the early childhood to program robots. Mob. Inf. Syst. **2016**, 1–12 (2016)
15. Greenberg, S., Bohnet, R., Roseman, M., Webster, D.: GroupSketch, vol. 87 (1992)
16. Nielsen, J.: Usability inspection methods. In: Conference companion on Human Factors in Computing Systems, CHI 1994, pp. 413–414 (1994)
17. Bekker, M., Barendregt, W., Crombeen, S., Biesheuvel, M.: Evaluating usability and challenge during initial and extended use of children's computer games. In: Fincher, S., Markopoulos, P., Moore, D., Ruddle, R. (eds.) People and Computers XVIII — Design for Life, pp. 331–345. Springer-Verlag London Limited, London (2005)
18. Piaget, J.: Seis Estudios de Psicología. Origen/Planeta, México (1985)
19. Collazos, C., Muñoz, J., Hernández, Y.: Aprendizaje Colaborativo Apoyado por Computador, 1st edn. Iniciativa Latinoamericana de Libros de Texto Abiertos (LATIn) (2014)
20. Nielsen, J.: Heuristic evaluation: how to conduct a heuristic evaluation. In: Nielsen, J., Mack, R.L. (eds.) Usability Inspection Methods. Wiley, New York (1994)
21. Blackwell, A.F., Green, T.R.G.: A cognitive dimensions questionnaire optimised for users. In: 12th Workshop of the Psychology of Programming Interest Group, pp. 137–154 (2000)
22. Green, T.R.G., Petre, M.: Usability analysis of visual programming environments: a 'cognitive dimensions' framework. J. Vis. Lang. Comput. **7**(2), 131–174 (1996)

Decision-Making for Interactive Systems: A Case Study for Teaching and Learning in Bioinformatics

Vanessa Stangherlin Machado[⊠], Walter Ritzel Paixão-Cortes,
Osmar Norberto de Souza, and Márcia de Borba Campos

Faculty of Informatics (FACIN), Pontifical Catholic University of Rio
Grande do Sul (PUCRS), Porto Alegre, Brazil
{vanessa.stangherlin,
walter.paixao-cortes}@acad.pucrs.br,
{osmar.norberto,marcia.campos}@pucrs.br

Abstract. This paper presents the partial results of an evaluation procedure study in which satisfaction of use is a key factor in the selection of software aimed at Bioinformatics teaching and learning strategies. The objective of this research is to understand the attitudes, feelings, preferences and values that are involved in the selection of Bioinformatics resources with similar features and compare the results with usability and ergonomics criteria. To this end, we conducted a case study applying the following methods: user observation, questionnaire, interview and documental research. In this paper, we present the results of the analysis for two (2) types of tools: biological databases and sequences and macromolecule structures viewers.

Keywords: User experience · Usability · Ergonomics · Evaluation · Bioinformatics · Case study

1 Introduction

The Bioinformatics comprises the use of technology for retrieval, storage, mathematical, physical-chemical and statistical analyses, and interpretation and integration of data to solve biological problems [1]. With the advancement of technology and its increasing ease of use, Bioinformatics computational resources have become popular, especially in the academic sphere. However, for an easier understanding and manipulation of molecular structures accessed by these tools, it is indispensable that they meet Human-Computer Interaction (HCI) criteria. Usability and Ergonomics should be persistent concerns in Bioinformatics systems given the amount of information they need to handle and visualize using several tools with various choices each.

On Bioinformatics, in an educational context, there are difficulties faced by both teachers and students. Teachers may have difficulties related to the selection of available resources, biological databases, and tools to manipulate and analyze data such as DNA and protein sequences and structures. There are a variety of tools [1–4], with different interfaces and interactions. The selection of features may require extra time to

P. Zaphiris and A. Ioannou (Eds.): LCT 2017, Part II, LNCS 10296, pp. 90–109, 2017.
DOI: 10.1007/978-3-319-58515-4_8

learn new tools as well as to select them and evaluate their use in different teaching contexts. For students in the learning process, these issues are aggravated because many tools use Bioinformatics technical terms, with which students are still unfamiliar or do not have adequate background to understand them. Some tools do not have friendly interfaces when compared to others used on a day-to-day basis [5]. Studies indicate that problems with Bioinformatics tools usage satisfaction are related to high workload associated with access to information [6], interactions via command line, navigation and tasks' execution [7, 8] and usability limitations [7, 9–12]. For a better user experience, some evidences point towards measures that can be adopted to call the user's attention, such as reducing cognitive and perceptive overload, being agile, intuitive, consistent, efficient, accessible and that can be easily learned [7, 8, 12–15]. Furthermore, Bioinformatics tools are usually developed or designed by scientists who have little or no experience in user interface design issues, or even by software developers, who often have little understanding of the Bioinformatics users' needs [14, 16]. These, however, are challenges common to interdisciplinary areas of teaching and research. In short, as emphasized in [17], it is not uncommon for Bioinformatics software users to experience a steep learning curve to perform their tasks.

The work presented here is the partial result of an evaluation process that involved satisfaction of use criteria as a determining factor in the choice of computational resources, considering different teaching and learning strategies in Bioinformatics. From the analysis of various proposals for syllabi and tools available, a case study was conducted in the Bioinformatics discipline, part of the curriculum of an undergraduate degree in Biological Sciences at PUCRS University in Brazil. The goal was to list Bioinformatics computational resources, analyze how they are used, and understand the factors that influence the selection of these resources by the teacher. Thus, it was possible to understand attitudes, feelings, preferences and values that were involved in the selection of Bioinformatics resources, and to compare them with usability and ergonomics criteria.

Data collection was conducted through observation, questionnaire, interview, and documental research. The interview, documental research, and observation sought to identify the tools and methodology used in the classroom for teaching Bioinformatics, as well as to participate in the teaching process in the classroom. The questionnaire aimed to extract the reasons behind the teacher's selection of tools. It included usability and ergonomics questions so the teacher could compare different tools, some already known but not always used by him/her. The evaluation instrument was based on the questionnaires SUPRQ[1], SUS[2], SUMI[3], WAMMI[4], and QUIS[5], which are standards in the scientific community to evaluate HCI criteria, and intended to maximize the identification of interface problems, interaction, and satisfaction of use. We also considered the ergonomic criteria [15, 18–21]. The instrument contained 74 questions

---

[1] http://www.suprq.com/.

[2] http://www.measuringu.com/sus.php.

[3] http://sumi.ucc.ie/whatis.html.

[4] http://www.wammi.com/questionnaire.html.

[5] http://www.lap.umd.edu/quis/.

directed at the assessment of biological databases (40 questions) and sequences and macromolecule structures viewers (34 questions). These are the tools evaluated:

- Biological databases: Protein Data Bank Japan (PDBj) [22], Protein Data Bank Europe (PDBe) [23], and The Protein Data Bank (RCSB PDB) [24].
- Sequences and macromolecular structures viewers: Swiss-PdbViewer (Swiss) [25], VMD - Visual Molecular Dynamics [26], and PyMOL - Molecular Graphics System [27].

The final work discusses reflections on the use of technological resources to support the teaching of Bioinformatics, assessment on the satisfaction of use, usability and ergonomics, aimed at Bioinformatics tools, as well as a discussion of the adopted assessment procedures and the results of the data gathering. The article also presents recommendations for interface design and interaction for Bioinformatics tools.

2   Background

Despite the growth in the area of Bioinformatics since the mid-1950s, due to the exponential increase in computer data generation and processing capacity and advances in the area by the union of computational and experimental information on biological macromolecules [28], it was only in 2001 that Education in Bioinformatics begins to be more prominent. The International Society for Computational Biology (ISCB) has organized the Workshop on Education in Bioinformatics (WEB), which deals with educational and pedagogical issues to determine the nature, extent and content, and the tools available for undergraduate and training programs in Bioinformatics [29]. However, only in 2005 did Bioinformatics education receive more formal recognition when, for the first time, the ISCB includes Bioinformatics Education as a session at the conference [29].

The ISCB, through the Education Committee (EduComm), promotes education and training in Computational Biology and Bioinformatics, offering resources and advice to organizations interested in the development of educational programs [30, 31]. Edu-Comm was responsible for organizing a pilot project that resulted in the creation of a core curriculum for Bioinformatics, called the Task Force Curriculum [30, 32]. In 2012, [30] presented a set of curricular guidelines for education in Bioinformatics. From these, the Global Organization of Bioinformatics Learning, Education and Training (GOBLET) was created, which aims to provide global and sustainable support in Bioinformatics for teachers and apprentices [33].

Some papers deal with perspectives and challenges in the Bioinformatics area [9, 29, 34–37], and its interdisciplinary nature [31, 38]. There are also different systems that can be used to support the teaching of Bioinformatics. In order to organize these features in terms of use and functionality, the classifications of [39, 40] were used.

Portals such as ExPASy[6] and the National Center for Biotechnology Information[7] (NCBI) are online resources that provide access to a variety of sources of information (biological databases and computational tools) in different areas of Bioinformatics (proteomics, genomics, transcriptomics, phylogeny, others). Biological databases, such as GenBank [41] and RCSB PDB, for example, involve both storage and methods of maintenance, extraction and visualization of information [42] for nucleotide, amino acid sequences or three-dimensional (3D) protein structures. There are also online applications and tools for sequence analysis, such as FASTA [43], BLAST [44], ClustalW [45], which involves sequences of macromolecules (nucleic acids and proteins) and perform alignment of these sequences to identify similar regions between biological sequences. Applications such as Swiss-PdbViewer and PyMOL, are sequence and macromolecule structure viewers, which encode atomic coordinates of PDB data files [46] into three-dimensional (3D) structures, obtained from biological databases. There are also offline tools for analysis of 3D structures, which allow to verify the chemical accuracy of a protein structure, such as PROCHECK [47], and online tools, applications and simulators for prediction of 3D protein structures, such as Modeller [48], I-TASSER [49], which generate 3D structures from a sequence of amino acids.

In view of this large number of tools, it is important to evaluate HCI criteria to alleviate possible usability and ergonomic barriers, which are obstacles in the use of interactive systems. This question becomes more complex when there is a wider range of user profiles such as in Bioinformatics area.

With this orientation, some researches have evaluated the usability in Bioinformatics tools using different methods. The papers of [5–7, 17, 50, 51] describe end-user evaluation while papers like [7, 12, 17, 52] describe the use of inspection evaluation. In this way, the objectives of the evaluations were varied. There were studies that analyzed the criteria of efficiency, usability and user preferences regarding the navigation control in tools for navigation in genetic sequences [17], evaluated layout and navigation [51], ease of use [5, 6]. Other studies proposed user-centered design criteria, considering both novice and experienced users [5] and another adapted the Nielsen heuristics [53] to evaluate Bioinformatics tools [52]. We used different tools such as BLAST [6, 17], Varsifter [51], KGGSeq [51], CATH [7], BioCarta [7], Swiss-Prot [7], NCBI [5, 7, 17], Ensembl [17], MEGA [17], among others.

There are also researches that apply user-centered design techniques (personas, interviews, card sorting, usability testing, etc.) in the development of software for the area of Bioinformatics [54, 55]. Overall, these papers argue that the Bioinformatics community knows that there are many resources to access information and visualize it. However, they also agree that there are many interface problems that make it difficult to use such systems.

---

[6] https://www.expasy.org/.

[7] https://www.ncbi.nlm.nih.gov/.

3 Case Study: Methodological Course

Considering different proposals of Bioinformatics curricula and the experience in the use of tools available for teaching contents of this area, the question of this research was related to the reasons that make a teacher select certain tools to use in the classroom. To that end, the focus of this study was the discipline of Bioinformatics, which integrates the curricular structure of the undergraduate course in Biological Sciences of the Pontifical Catholic University of Rio Grande do Sul (PUCRS). It has a weekly workload of 4 h and a total of 60 classroom hours, being offered in the 4th period of said course. The discipline of Molecular Biology is a prerequisite for this one.

The discipline's objective is to give the student conditions to know and understand the Bioinformatics main concepts, how to use computational resources for visualization and manipulation of sequences and macromolecular structures, how to locate and use the main Bioinformatics tools available on the Internet, to recognize important problems in the area of Bioinformatics, being able to discuss them with scientists from other areas, and to develop a perception about Bioinformatics literature.

3.1 Subject Matter Expert (SME)

The SME has 26 years of experience in Bioinformatics research, working for 15 years as a Professor in the area both in undergraduate (G) courses in Biological Sciences, Computer Science, Nursing and Pharmacy as in post-graduate (PG) courses in Cellular and Molecular Biology, Computer Science, Science and Mathematics Education and in a Master's degree in Pharmaceutical Biotechnology. The subjects taught were Bioinformatics (G, PG), Programming for Biological Sciences (G), Scientific Methodology (G), Information Technology Applied to Biological Sciences (G), Informatics for Pharmacy (G), Structural Bioinformatics, Introduction to Bioinformatics (PG), Design of Drugs and Molecular Modeling (PG), Comparative Bioinformatics (PG), Special Topics in Bioinformatics and Computational Modeling (PG), among others.

3.2 Data Gathering Process

To had better understand on what guides the teacher's choices, data were gathered through different instruments. The study was as follows:

- **Preparation I:** analysis of the discipline plan, preparation of the interview script and logbook structure.
- **Data Gathering I:** interviews were conducted to identify the Bioinformatics tools used in class, their usage and what guided the choice of the teacher to use them. It also occurred by the researcher participating in classes as an observer, registering entries in a logbook.
- **Interpretation I:** transcription of interviews and data recorded in the diary. As an outcome, it was chosen to include, in this study, biological databases and visualizers of sequences and macromolecular structures.

- **Preparation II:** an online questionnaire was developed with criteria for usability and satisfaction of use. The instrument was based on the SUPRQ, SUS (System Usability Scale), SUMI (Software Usability Measurement Inventory), WAMMI questionnaire and QUIS (Questionnaire for User Interface Satisfaction) question-naires. The final version of the questionnaire contained 40 questions applicable to biological databases: 35 closed (using Likert scale) and 5 open. There were 2 questions of identification, 21 of usability, 6 of satisfaction of use and 11 related to use as a resource for teaching and learning process. For sequence and macro-molecule structures viewers, there were 34 questions (31 closed and 3 open), of which 2 were of identification, 14 of usability, 6 of satisfaction of use and 12 related to learning.
- **Data Gathering II:** the professor answered the questionnaire online and did not present doubts in the interpretation of the questions.
- **Interpretation II:** the results were discussed and compared with an analysis of the tools according to HCI criteria: usability, satisfaction of use and ergonomics.

4   Results

4.1   Data Gathering I

The data gathering was carried out to indicate what is taught in the case study discipline and the tools that are used in the classroom, for later identification of the reason for choosing these tools based on HCI criteria.

The discipline content is split in units, per the syllabus: I - Molecular Biology and Informatics; II - Visualization and Computational Manipulation of Three-Dimensional Structures of Biological Macromolecules; III - Pairwise Biological Sequence Align-ments; IV - Methods for Multiple Alignments of Biological Sequences; V - Compu-tational Methods for the Prediction of the Secondary and Tertiary Structure of Proteins.

The textbooks used are [39, 40, 56]. Access to the genome and protein data files, tools that have been developed to work with these files and types of questions that these data and tools can answer can be seen in [40]. The reference [39] has a more focused approach on tools that are used in Bioinformatics and [56] provides a critical and comprehensive analysis of the computational methods necessary for the analysis of DNA, RNA and protein data, with basic explanations about the Algorithms, compu-tational methods and strategies for their application to biological problems. The stu-dents are also exposed to scientific papers from recent publications of database [41], tools [57], computational methods [58] and special volumes of Nucleic Acids Research[8, 9, 10].

It was observed the methodology used in classes is theoretical and practical, since students need to know the concepts necessary to solve biological problems and learn to

---

[8] https://nar.oxfordjournals.org/.

[9] http://nar.oxfordjournals.org/content/44/W1.toc.

[10] https://nar.oxfordjournals.org/content/44/D1.toc.

use the computational resources in practice effectively. In theoretical classes, biological contents are presented together with the computational resources used to manipulate information, in a systematic way, linking content and the tool used in practice. The criteria used by the professor to select the resources adopted are:

- **Self-contained tools:** it tries to identify the most complete tools, that do not have dependencies of other tools in the execution of a specific functionality.
- **Origin of tools:** seeks to value the origin of knowledge, using tools well established in the scientific and academic environment, that are authoritative and keep up to date and with good performance.
- **Ease of learning:** the main features of the tools should be clear and easily accessible, so that students can assimilate their content and use it quickly.
- **Tool updates:** because Bioinformatics tools are updated frequently, teachers and students need to be aware of content and interface updates.
- **Offline and online tools:** offline tools must be accessible to students (free software) and easy to install. As for sequencing tools and biological databases, online tools are preferred, for the convenience of access and the most up-to-date information.
- **Integrated tools:** tools that integrate and are validated by others, so that the output of one tool can serve as input to another are preferred. This clearly demonstrates how the workflow of a Bioinformatics researcher looks like.
- **Content filtering:** because of the large amount of information it is important that the tools have filters to customize their searches and preferences.
- **Interface standards**: familiar to users, like other classic interfaces, such as word processors, for greater ease of use and memory recall.
- **Operating system:** applications with Windows interfaces are preferred, for their ease of use, opposed to Linux command-line interfaces, common in these tools.

Considering these criteria and his pedagogical experience as a teacher, he mentioned that he uses: portals - NCBI and ExPASy; biological databases - GenBank, RCSB PDB, CATH - Class, Architecture, Topology, Homology [59] and SCOPe - Structural Classification of Proteins – extended [60]; sequence and macromolecule structures viewers - Swiss-PdbViewer (Swiss); tools for sequence analysis - BLAST and ClustalW; tools for predicting 3D structures - Swiss-Model [61] and Modeller. In addition to all these tools, he uses the educational portal of RCSB PDB, the PDB-101 [24].

From the tools above mentioned, two types are used in more than one learning unit, complementing the use of other tools, constantly participating in theoretical/practical classes and are essential, according to the professor, for the progress of the discipline: biological databases and sequence and macromolecular structures viewers.

During the discipline, the professor uses the RCSB PDB database, which was compared to PDBe and PDBj databases, chosen for having the same type of deposited data, in equal quantity, but that are presented differently in their interfaces. He also adopts the Swiss viewer, compared to VMD and PyMOL, chosen for having interfaces with similar features for the visualization of the structures, to be free and accessed offline. For all the tools, the teacher was asked to examine their interface and answer the questionnaire, the results of which are described in the following subsection.

4.2   Data Gathering II - Results - Part 1: Biological Databases

The professor has already used all the RCSB databases: PDB, PDBe and PDBj, having more experience in RCSB PDB. On his view, all three databases meet usability criteria such as ease of use, ease of navigation, user help and efficiency, and fast response to queries. Icons are intuitive and menus are organized properly.

He further agrees the three databases have a logical structure for biological databases, with easily identified search fields, search filters, and the possibility of querying from different input fields. He also pointed out that the functionalities of the three databases are well integrated. It considers the usefulness of the information to be adequate, with easily understandable and clearly demonstrated results. Information is reliable and up to date. When it comes to satisfaction of use, he agrees that he are comfortable using them, that they look simple and clean, and that he can customize the information that is displayed. However, he stated that PDBj interface could be improved because it is very textual. With the exception of the eight (8) questions listed in Table 1, the feedback provided was very positive.

Table 1. Questions with mixed feedback for RCSB PDB, PDBe and PDBj

Questions	RCSB	PDBe	PDBj
I can quickly find what I want	A	SA	SA
The database does some error handling in case it does not locate the requested information	**NA**	A	**NAD**
The database does not require technical knowledge to perform a search	**D**	**D**	**D**
The needs of inexperienced and experienced users are taken into consideration	**NAD**	SA	SA
It is possible search the database using logical operators	SA	**NAD**	SA
The database is visually appealing	SA	SA	A
Working with this database is satisfactory	SA	**NAD**	SA
I would like to use this database every day	SA	**NAD**	SA

Legend: SA - Strongly agree, A - Agree, NAD - Neither agree nor disagree,
D - Disagree, SD - Strongly disagree, NA - Not applicable.

The professor uses RCSB PDB as an educational tool and as a researcher. He mentioned he uses this database because data files are updated weekly, its interface receives constant improvements and does not need to perform error handling. He strongly recommends this database for teaching Bioinformatics, but has a neutral opinion when comes to PDBe and would not recommend PDBj. In his opinion, the greatest difficulty in using these databases in the classroom is the English language, universal for scientific research, but not accessible to users who do not understand the language.

4.3   Data Gathering II - Results - Part 2: Sequences and Macromolecular Structures Viewers

The Swiss and VMD viewers have been used by the professor since 1998, and PyMOL since 2006. Swiss is adopted in the classroom and as a researcher, at the frequency of more than once a week. The others are used in scientific research once a week.

In the usability criteria, it has evaluated that the three viewers have simple and clean appearance, help options to understand the functionalities and allow the user to control the updates of the tool. He also said that he feels completely comfortable in visualizing a protein in Swiss and PyMol, and that they present information about the structure in a clear and comprehensible way.

He agrees that Swiss-PdbViewer is easy to use and has useful interface components, intuitive icons, and well-integrated features. The other viewers partially meet these features. The preference for Swiss as a viewer can also be noted in Table 2, which brings the issues that have had a negative and neutral feedback.

Table 2. Questions with neutral and negative feedback

Questions	Swiss	VMD	PyMol
I can quickly find the tasks I want	A	**D**	**D**
The menus or lists organization seems quite logical	A	**D**	**NAD**
Tasks can be performed in a simple way	SA	**D**	**D**
The response time in performing the tasks is adequate	SA	**D**	SA
The viewer does some error handling in case I make an unwanted change in the protein	SA	**NAD**	**NAD**
The needs of inexperienced and experienced users are taken into consideration	SA	**D**	**D**
The viewer features are performed directly on the interface (no command line)	SA	SA	**D**
I would like to use this viewer daily	SA	**D**	SA
Working with this viewer is satisfactory	SA	**D**	SA
I can customize what information the viewer presents to me	SA	**NAD**	SA
Learning to operate the viewer is easy	SA	**D**	**D**
I can use this viewer without previous knowledge about it	SA	**D**	**D**
Remembering names and using commands is easy	SA	**D**	**NAD**

Legend: SA - Strongly agree, A - Agree, NAD - Neither agree nor disagree,
D - Disagree, SD - Strongly disagree, NA - Not applicable.

In this sense, he considers that Swiss is a sophisticated, free, and easy-to-learn viewer and manipulator. He also mentioned criteria such as ease of use, portability, and speed in handling structure files. However, he says its interface is partially attractive. He recommends its use as a teaching resource for Bioinformatics, as well as PyMOL to create images for published papers, due to the good quality of rendered visualizations and generated images.

In his opinion improvements could be made to each of the viewers. Swiss could undergo a graphical rendering of different types of protein structure representation, the VMD menu might be clearer and have easier access options, and the suggestion for PyMOL would be a control panel similar to Swiss.

4.4   Interpretation II

The analysis performed by the professor on the databases and viewers was compared to ergonomics and usability criteria, to verify the reasoning behind the professor's choice. The criteria were based on - article [18]; Set of criteria for interface ergonomics and user experience of Cybis [15], based on Nielsen's Heuristics, Shneiderman Gold Rules, Android Design Principles, Principles of ISO/ABNT 92: 41: 110 and Bastien and Scapin ergonomic criteria.

These criteria were translated into recommendations for design and interaction for biological databases and sequence and protein viewers, which are desirable in a good interface and therefore represent principles of good practice that can be adopted by the Bioinformatics interactive systems. The criteria used for evaluation are identified by number, which are followed in subsequent discussions.

Criteria for biological databases

CBD1 - Interaction experience: The interface should be pleasant and beautiful for the user, motivating a good experience of use, without forgetting to consider aspects such as effectiveness and efficiency to carry out the tasks.

CBD2 - Good use of the screen: The database must have a logical organization to access information, to simplify access and to aid learning. Components with similar features should be close and non-related should be further away without over-loading the interface with many elements. The groups can be distributed according to the actions that they apply, for example, in chronological order or importance of the task.

CBD3 - Ease of access to information: Key information must be in evidence, clearly available and easily retrieved. The user should not perform multiple inter-actions to access them. It should be clear where the search field is, search filters, information retrieved at the database, external resources, database statistics, and help and documentation.

CBD4 - Visibility of the information and of the system: The database must keep the user informed about the location that is in the interface of the database. Input information and results must be visible, clear, and legible. Buttons and shortcuts of user interest (download, save and refine the search) need to be visible and close to the query field. You should also flag the tools built into the database.

CBD5 - Consistency and Interface Standards: Users feel more comfortable and are more efficient if database features maintain a pattern throughout the interface. Menus, search components, filters, query result fields must have the same color pattern, location, and configuration, to facilitate the identification of the resources in the interaction and the user's learning, so that the user can use it quickly.

CBD6 - Data entry made easy: The search field for data search should preferably be at the top of the screen and highlighted, the standard commonly adopted in biological databases. This field should differentiate itself from other search fields, such as from search engines on the internet, for example. In addition, the user must be informed about possible input types, without any ambiguities or doubts. It should have the possibility of refinement of the search (advanced search), and clearly present help and examples of submissions.

CBD7- Clarity of information on components and functionalities: The components should be related to their use, without any ambiguities or doubts as to their functions. Metaphors must be clear and easily understood.

CBD8 - Accessibility of information: The database must be prepared for assistive technology resources, such as screen readers, magnifiers, auto-contrast, to facilitate access to users who have some type of information access barrier. Accessibility design patterns in database design, such as description of the images and shortcuts by keyboard commands should be observed.

CBD9 - Database resource adaptability: The database must be prepared to serve different user profiles, be flexible so tasks can be performed in different ways, and allow customization of the interface for less experienced users. The interface may not display complex information, embedded software, links, and other resources.

CBD10 - The Database User Experience: The database should provide the means for experienced users to perform tasks more quickly, through shortcuts and tools that can assist in their work. Similarly, for non-expert users, systematic demonstrations, quick help buttons, input field samples, and data download types, should be made available.

CBD11 - Legibility: Because a database has a lot of textual information, it must be legible so that it is accessible to different types of users, such as elderly people, for example. Features to facilitate reading, such as font size, letter/ background contrast, line spacing, line length, should be respected.

CBD12 - Decreased workload: This criterion advocates that the user should be spared cognitively and perceptually. It should save you having to perform repeated actions, such as database entries, and save the user unnecessary readings of information. Inputs and outputs must be concise, providing adequate default values.

CBD13 - Information Density: The density of information displayed on the screen must be taken care of, so that beginning users do not have difficulty in finding what they need in the database interface. In this way, we recommend that only items related to the user search are presented, and there may be information filters, hidden panels, and menus for accessing other information.

CBD14 - Updates to the database: The databases must clearly display in the interface to the user data about their updates, such as the date of the last update, the amount of data deposited, and how long the database is updated.

CBD15 - Ease of access to results: The results of a query should be easily accessible, objective, and clear. They should be arranged in a prominent place on the interface and allow customization with filters. Tools that facilitate access to these results can be made available, such as the adequacy of tools to visualize these data directly in the interface and tools for the analysis of this data.

CBD16 - Management, protection, and prevention of errors: The database must have a secure interface to the user. You should be prepared to detect and prevent data entry or command errors. User input can be suggested from the character typing.

CBD17 - Tolerance to errors: A database with tolerance minimizes risks and negative consequences due to accidental or involuntary actions.

In the evaluation of the database, a search of information was carried out and the initial pages, the search field, the result page of the query, the page displaying the selected result, statistics and documentation were checked. Additional tools such as visualizers, among others, were also observed. The three databases met CBD5, CBD10 and CBD15 criteria. Table 3 shows the criteria that the databases did not meet or partially met, along with the justification.

Criteria for sequence and macromolecular structures viewers

CV1 - Interaction Experience: it is related to the interface to have a good aesthetic, but keeping the application working properly, for an effective and pleasant experience. In addition, the viewer should be simple to the point where the user does not require intensive learning and read extensive documentation before using.

CV2 - Message and Functionality Adequacy: The viewer functionality should provide instructions for its use. These should be clear, objective, and easy to understand. The language should be simple and speak the language of the user. Technical terms should be avoided. However, when necessary add quick help buttons and active help, with explanation of terms and suggestions of actions for the user.

CV3 - Immediate feedback of actions: When the user performs an action in the viewer the result should be presented quickly and be easy to be noticed. If the action is in progress, the user must be informed that the processing is being performed. Progress indicators should be visible and have the option to cancel, or allow another activity to be performed during its execution.

CV4 - Functions with easy access and grouped by type of interaction: The interface must be functional, keeping key tasks at a rapid range and grouped by the type of data they manipulate through.

CV5 - Viewer's Feature Adaptability: The viewer should allow its functions and screens to be customizable, flexible, and adaptable to inexperienced and experienced users. Different paths can be made available for a feature that is accessed frequently, such as the same function in an icon in the toolbar, in the menu, and by keyboard shortcut.

CV6 - Error handling, protection, and prevention: This criterion recommends that the viewer interface must be safe for the user to manipulate their protein without worrying about losing the changes made or overwriting manipulated PDB files without due warning.

CV7 - Interface homogeneity: the interface must respect the standards and styles of the operating system platform to which it was developed. Consistency is important because a novice user can repeat previously used strategies in interaction with other known applications. Commonly used commands, menus, and icons

Table 3. Evaluation of ergonomic and usability criteria for biological databases.

	RCSB PDB	PDBe	PDBj	Justification
CBD1	M	M	P	Although PDBj maintains a standard in the interface, it brings the interface elements very similar, which can increase the user's cognitive load and hinder access to information
CBD2	M	M	P	PDBj brings components logically split according to the actions they apply, but they are similar and overload the interface
CBD3	M	M	P	Although the main PDBj information is centered on the interface, they are not in evidence. Again, the menus and the refinements are very similar
CBD4	M	M	P	In PDBj the 3D structure of the protein on the results page is small, having the same prominence as the download and 3D visualization icons
CBD6	M	P	P	PDBe does not indicate that the search performed in the upper field occurs inside the database and does not indicate which input types are accepted. PDBe provides only the example of the query that can be performed
CBD7	M	M	P	PDBj has few icons, displaying most of its features as links
CBD8	N	N	N	The automatic validation through W3C web validators (HTML[a] and CSS[b]) and HERA[c] have presented errors and warnings (see Footnote 2), which can mean accessibility barriers on all databases
CBD9	P	P	M	RCSB PDB and PDBe, despite having filters and advanced searches for experienced users, do not allow customization and change of location of menus and tasks
CBD11	P	P	N	The three databases presented small fonts and no clear font increase options were found. PDBj also features a lot of text content and too many menus, which can make reading tiring and discouraging
CBD12	M	P	N	PDBj and PDBe have no option to save search history and search results. However, PDBe has the option of downloading the input parameters
CBD13	M	P	P	PDBj displays a large number of menus on the sides of the screen, which can divert attention and focus on results. In PDBe, the division of information is subtle, making it difficult to distinguish content, and information filters could be presented more clearly, along with main information, in the form of hidden panels instead of menus

(continued)

Table 3. (*continued*)

	RCSB PDB	PDBe	PDBj	Justification
CBD14	P	P	P	Although the databases display the last update date, they do not report on the homepage the time for next update
CBD16	M	P	M	As for data entry, PDBe does not issue warning if the search field is blank
CBD17	M	P	P	PDBj and PDBe does not disregard typing error and perform search providing results with the correct terminology

Legend: M = Met, P = Partially Met, N = Not Met
[a] https://validator.w3.org
[b] http://jigsaw.w3.org/css-validato
[c] http://www.sidar.org/hera

should be easily recognized, located, and stable on the same screen location. This facilitates learning because the system becomes predictable, intuitive, and more easily remembered.

CV8 - Decreased workload: The user should be spared from cognitive and perceptive overload, simplifying the actions to be performed in the viewer. The interaction should be as simple as possible, avoiding to require many actions to complete it. For manipulation of a macromolecule, the commands should be minimized to the maximum, avoiding that the user needs to go through several menus or screens, or having to perform actions through the command line.

CV9 - User control and freedom: The user must be able to control the interactions with the viewer, having commands to undo and redo a certain task, control decreases the probability of errors and favors learning. This is important for the user to explore the interface by applying different commands on the protein and verifying the actions they perform.

CV10 - Help and documentation: Refers to user support in learning and helping you to do an activity. It can present the user with help in contextual, conceptual, systematic, tutorial style and quick help buttons. The application should also bring informational and technical documentation, which assist users with possible doubts.

The three viewers analyzed have interfaces that are similar, with a large viewing area and additional windows with some commands and main menu. These components were analyzed and the results are shown in Table 4.

Based on what was presented in the results it was observed that it is possible to establish relations between the software choices used by the professor and ergonomic and usability criteria. The following are some of the most obvious relationships.

According to the professor's assessment, Swiss did not have any negative feedback, while for VMD it was registered 10 negative questions (related to usability, satisfaction of use and learning) and to PyMOL, 6 negative questions (related to menu organization and memorizing commands). He did not know how to comment on the error handling criteria and interface customization in VMD's case.

Table 4. Evaluation of ergonomic and usability criteria for sequence and macromolecular biological viewers.

	Swiss	VMD	PyMoL	Justification
CV1	M	P	P	VMD and PyMol, by default, open windows without graphical user interface, for script and status information, next to the desktop, creating an environment with excess of screens and that can confuse the user. Only Swiss brings icons of its main features
CV2	P	P	P	Viewers bring help to their functionalities through the Help button, tutorials and FAQ, but no aid was found directly in the functionalities, besides that they present many Bioinformatics technical terms
CV4	M	P	M	Despite grouping its features, VMD does not have a desktop with buttons and quick access icons for the main features
CV5	M	P	M	No keyboard shortcuts were found in VMD
CV6	P	A	P	Both in Swiss and PyMol we can close the application without confirming the closure of the work and the changes made in the protein. Doing so may result in errors and data loss
CV7	M	N	N	Swiss have an aspect more familiar to Windows users, with the menu layout and icons that can be more easily remembered
CV8	M	N	M	The interactions with VMD could be simplified. To perform some activities the user needs to scroll through several menus, checklists, and windows with different (non-standardized) interfaces, increasing the user's cognitive overload
CV9	M	N	M	No undo and redo options were found
CV10	M	P	P	All viewers contain Help and informational and technical documentation, but in PyMol and VMD they are not accessed directly in the interface, the content is web-oriented. Quick help buttons could also be included

Legend: M = Met, P = Partially Met, N = Not Met

In the evaluation performed according to 10 HCI criteria for viewers, the CV3 criterion, immediate feedback of the actions, was the only one that was attended in equality in the three applications. Swiss assessment was positive, partially meeting the CV2 and CV6 criteria and in full to the others. This is in agreement with the professor's positive assessment. VMD met only two criteria: management, protection and prevention of errors and immediate feedback of actions, which may suggest why the professor's negative evaluation. PyMOL obtained 5 positive criteria: CV3, CV4, CV5, CV8 and CV9, presenting only one negative barrier regarding interface homogeneity - CV7.

In the evaluation of the 17 criteria of HCI for biological database all the database attended CBD5, CBD10 and CBD15 criteria. RCSB PDB met 13 criteria and 3 partially, PDBe met 8 criteria and 8 partially and PDBj met 6 criteria and 8 partially. Criterion CBD8, accessibility of information, was not met in all three databases. It should be remembered that this evaluation was automatic, being recommended a manual revision, essential to prove the accessibility of the page, verification that will be dealt with in future works. PDBj also had a negative assessment of readability and decreased workload (CBD11, CBD12), and the professor also pointed out the excess of textual information in an open question related to interface improvements.

Despite these differences, the professor evaluated most of the database instrument issues positively. The downside of his assessment is that database users need technical knowledge to be able to consult the database, which can make access difficult for non-expert users. He adopts the RSCB PDB by its weekly updates for interface improvements, and does not require error handling. He has also recognized the authority of the database, since RCSB PDB was the first primary database of 3D structures for biological macromolecules.

5   Conclusion

This work is part of a doctoral research that aims to contribute knowledge about the use of tools in teaching Bioinformatics, based on the analysis of the practical experiences of a teacher. The objective of the doctoral study is to propose and validate a teaching method and analyze how we can represent specific information in the field of Bioinformatics and molecular biology, targeting people with visual impairment. It also proposes to observe which characteristics should be contemplated in the development of accessible/ inclusive interfaces for teaching in this area.

In this part of the study, we sought to analyze the perceptions of a university professor about the teaching-learning process with the use of services and tools in Bioinformatics, providing a set of HCI criteria that can be used to evaluate usability, satisfaction of use and ergonomics of biological databases and visualizers of sequences and biological macromolecules, and which translate into recommendations for interface design and interaction for applications in the Bioinformatics field.

For future work, we suggest extending the case study, carried out in the discipline of bioinformatics of PUCRS, to other institutions and compare the tools used to the criteria described in this study. In addition, the results of the evaluations were measured qualitatively only. We could improve these results with a quantitative evaluation, where we could measure usability, satisfaction of use, and ergonomics of these applications in a less subjective way.

Acknowledgments. This work was supported in part by grants ONS (CNPq, 308124/2015-4; FAPERGS, TO2054-2551/13-0). ONS is a CNPq Research Fellow. VSM is supported by CAPES/PROSUP PhD scholarships. WRPC is supported by a DELL scholarship.

References

1. Magana, A.J., Taleyarkhan, M., Alvarado, D.R., Kane, M., Springer, J., Clase, K.: A survey of scholarly literature describing the field of bioinformatics education and bioinformatics educational research. CBE Life Sci. Educ. **13**, 607–623 (2014)
2. Rigden, D.J., Fernández-Suárez, X.M., Galperin, M.Y.: The 2016 database issue of Nucleic Acids Research and an updated molecular biology database collection. Nucleic Acids Res. **44**, D1–D6 (2016)
3. Pavlopoulos, G.A., Malliarakis, D., Papanikolaou, N., Theodosiou, T., Enright, A.J., Iliopoulos, I.: Visualizing genome and systems biology: technologies, tools, implementation techniques and trends, past, present and future. GigaScience **4**, 38 (2015)
4. NCBI Resource Coordinators: Database resources of the National Center for Biotechnology Information. Nucleic Acids Res. **41**, D8–D20 (2013)
5. Javahery, H., Seffah, A., Radhakrishnan, T.: Beyond power: making bioinformatics tools user-centered. Commun. ACM **47**, 58–63 (2004)
6. Shaer, O., Kol, G., Strait, M., Fan, C., Grevet, C., Elfenbein, S.: G-nome surfer: a tabletop interface for collaborative exploration of genomic data. In: Proceedings of the SIGCHI Conference on Human Factors in Computing Systems, pp. 1427–1436. ACM (2010)
7. Bolchini, D., Finkelstein, A., Perrone, V., Nagl, S.: Better bioinformatics through usability analysis. Bioinformatics **25**, 406–412 (2009)
8. Bolchini, D., Finkestein, A., Paolini, P.: Designing usable bio-information architectures. In: Jacko, J.A. (ed.) HCI 2009. LNCS, vol. 5613, pp. 653–662. Springer, Heidelberg (2009). doi:10.1007/978-3-642-02583-9_71
9. Bishop, Ö.T., Adebiyi, E.F., Alzohairy, A.M., Everett, D., Ghedira, K., Ghouila, A., Kumuthini, J., Mulder, N.J., Panji, S., Patterton, H.-G., H3ABioNet Consortium, H3Africa Consortium: Bioinformatics education—perspectives and challenges out of africa. Brief. Bioinform. **16**(2), 355–364 (2014). doi:10.1093/bib/bbu022
10. Veretnik, S., Fink, J.L., Bourne, P.E.: Computational biology resources lack persistence and usability. PLoS Comput. Biol. **4**, e1000136 (2008)
11. Mirel, B.: Supporting cognition in systems biology analysis: findings on users' processes and design implications. J. Biomed. Discov. Collab. **4**, 2 (2009)
12. Al-Ageel, N., Al-Wabil, A., Badr, G., AlOmar, N.: Human factors in the design and evaluation of bioinformatics tools. Procedia Manuf. **3**, 2003–2010 (2015)
13. Douglas, C., Goulding, R., Farris, L., Atkinson-Grosjean, J.: Socio-cultural characteristics of usability of bioinformatics databases and tools. Interdiscip. Sci. Rev. **36**, 55–71 (2011)
14. Mirel, B.: Usability and usefulness in bioinformatics: Evaluating a tool for querying and analyzing protein interactions based on scientists' actual research questions. In: 2007 IEEE International Professional Communication Conference, pp. 1–8. IEEE (2007)
15. Cybis, W.A., Betiol, A.H., Faust, R.: Ergonomia e Usabilidade: Conhecimentos, Métodos e Aplicações. Novatec, São Paulo (2007)
16. Macaulay, C., Sloan, D., Jiang, X., Forbes, P., Loynton, S., Swedlow, J.R., Gregor, P.: Usability and user-centered design in scientific software development. IEEE Softw. **26**, 96 (2009)
17. Rutherford, P., Abell, W., Churcher, C., McKinnon, A., McCallum, J.: Usability of navigation tools for browsing genetic sequences. In: Proceedings of the Eleventh Australasian Conference on User Interface, vol. 106, pp. 33–41. Australian Computer Society, Inc. (2010)
18. Rocha, L.C., Andrade, R.M., Sampaio, A.L.: Heurísticas para avaliar a usabilidade de aplicações móveis: estudo de caso para aulas de campo em Geologia. TISE (2014)

19. Nielsen, J.: Usability Engineering. Elsevier (1994)
20. ABNT, A.B.D.N.T.: NBR ISO 9241: ergonomia da interação humano-sistema. Parte 110: princípios de diálogo (2012)
21. Shneiderman, B.: Designing the User Interface: Strategies for Effective Human-Computer Interaction. Addison-Wesley Longman Publishing Co., Inc., Boston (1997)
22. Kinjo, A.R., Yamashita, R., Nakamura, H.: PDBj Mine: design and implementation of relational database interface for Protein Data Bank Japan. Database 2010, baq021 (2010)
23. Velankar, S., Best, C., Beuth, B., Boutselakis, C.H., Cobley, N., Sousa Da Silva, A.W., Dimitropoulos, D., Golovin, A., Hirshberg, M., John, M., Krissinel, E.B., Newman, R., Oldfield, T., Pajon, A., Penkett, C.J., Pineda-Castillo, J., Sahni, G., Sen, S., Slowley, R., Suarez-Uruena, A., Swaminathan, J., van Ginkel, G., Vranken, W.F., Henrick, K., Kleywegt, G.J.: PDBe: protein data bank in Europe. Nucleic Acids Res. 38, 308–317 (2010)
24. Zardecki, C., Dutta, S., Goodsell, D.S., Voigt, M., Burley, S.K.: RCSB protein data bank: a resource for chemical, biochemical, and structural explorations of large and small biomolecules. J. Chem. Educ. 93, 569–575 (2016)
25. Guex, N.: Swiss-PdbViewer: A new fast and easy to use PDB viewer for the Macintosh. Experientia 52, A26 (1996)
26. Humphrey, W., Dalke, A., Schulten, K.: VMD: Visual molecular dynamics. J. Mol. Graph. 14, 33–38 (1996)
27. Schrödinger, LLC: The PyMOL Molecular Graphics System, Version 1.3r1 (2010)
28. Ouzounis, C.A., Valencia, A.: Early bioinformatics: the birth of a discipline—a personal view. Bioinformatics 19, 2176–2190 (2003)
29. Ranganathan, S.: Bioinformatics education—perspectives and challenges. PLoS Comput. Biol. 1, e52 (2005)
30. Welch, L.R., Schwartz, R., Lewitter, F.: A report of the curriculum task force of the ISCB education committee. PLoS Comput. Biol. 8, e1002570 (2012)
31. Welch, L., Lewitter, F., Schwartz, R., Brooksbank, C., Radivojac, P., Gaeta, B., Schneider, M.V.: Bioinformatics curriculum guidelines: toward a definition of core competencies. PLoS Comput. Biol. 10, e1003496 (2014)
32. Welch, L.R., Schwartz, R., Lewitter, F.: Report from the ISCB Education Committee: a draft curriculum for bioinformatics [abstract]. In: Third annual RECOMB Conference on Bioinformatics Education (RECOMB-BE), An ISMB/ECCB 2011 (2011)
33. Atwood, T.K., Bongcam-Rudloff, E., Brazas, M.E., Corpas, M., Gaudet, P., Lewitter, F., Mulder, N., Palagi, P.M., Schneider, M.V., van Gelder, C.W., GOBLET Consortium: GOBLET: the global organisation for bioinformatics learning, education and training. PLoS Comput. Biol. 11, e1004143 (2015)
34. Buttigieg, P.L.: Perspectives on presentation and pedagogy in aid of bioinformatics education. Brief. Bioinform. 11, 587–597 (2010)
35. Cummings, M.P., Temple, G.G.: Broader incorporation of bioinformatics in education: opportunities and challenges. Brief. Bioinform. 11, 537–543 (2010)
36. Ojo, O.O., Omabe, M.: Incorporating bioinformatics into biological science education in Nigeria: Prospects and challenges. Infect. Genet. Evol. 11, 784–787 (2011)
37. Dimitrov, R.A., Gouliamova, D.E.: Bioinformatics education: perspectives and challenges. Biotechnol. Biotechnol. Equip. 23, 40–42 (2009)
38. Bruhn, R., Jennings, S.F.: A multidisciplinary bioinformatics minor. ACM SIGCSE Bull. 39, 348–352 (2007)
39. Gibas, C., Jambeck, P.: Desenvolvendo Bioinformática: ferramentas de software para aplicações em biologia. Campus (2001)
40. Lesk, A.M.: Introdução à Bioinformática. Tradução de Ardala Elisa Breda Andrade et al. LABIO, FACIN, PUCRS (2008)

41. Benson, D.A., Clark, K., Karsch-Mizrachi, I., Lipman, D.J., Ostell, J., Sayers, E.W.: GenBank. Nucleic Acids Res. **43**, D30–D35 (2015)
42. Wiley Encyclopedia of Computer Science and Engineering: Wiley Encyclopedia of Computer Science and Engineering (2008)
43. McWilliam, H., Li, W., Uludag, M., Squizzato, S., Park, Y.M., Buso, N., Cowley, A.P., Lopez, R.: Analysis Tool Web Services from the EMBL-EBI. Nucleic Acids Res. **41**, W597–W600 (2013)
44. Johnson, M., Zaretskaya, I., Raytselis, Y., Merezhuk, Y., McGinnis, S., Madden, T.L.: NCBI BLAST: a better web interface. Nucleic Acids Res. 36, W5–9 (2008)
45. Larkin, M.A., Blackshields, G., Brown, N.P., Chenna, R., McGettigan, P.A., McWilliam, H., Valentin, F., Wallace, I.M., Wilm, A., Lopez, R., Thompson, J.D., Gibson, T.J., Higgins, D. G.: Clustal W and Clustal X version 2.0. Bioinforma. Oxf. Engl. 23, 2947–2948 (2007)
46. Ansari, S.N., Iliyas, S.: A Comparative Study of Protein Structure Visualization Tools for Various Display Capabilities. Biosci. Discov. Int. J. Life Sci. 2, P222–P226 (2011)
47. Laskowski, R.A., MacArthur, M.W., Moss, D.S., Thornton, J.M.: PROCHECK: a program to check the stereochemical quality of protein structures. J. Appl. Crystallogr. **26**, 283–291 (1993)
48. Fiser, A., Šali, A.: Modeller: generation and refinement of homology-based protein structure models. In: Carter Jr., C.W., Sweet, R.M. (ed.) Methods in Enzymology, pp. 461–491. Academic Press (2003)
49. Yang, J., Zhang, Y.: I-TASSER server: new development for protein structure and function predictions. Nucleic Acids Res. **43**, 174–181 (2015). doi:10.1093/nar/gkv342
50. Néron, B., Ménager, H., Maufrais, C., Joly, N., Maupetit, J., Letort, S., Carrere, S., Tuffery, P., Letondal, C.: Mobyle: a new full web bioinformatics framework. Bioinformatics **25**, 3005–3011 (2009)
51. Shyr, C., Kushniruk, A., Wasserman, W.W.: Usability study of clinical exome analysis software: top lessons learned and recommendations. J. Biomed. Inform. **51**, 129–136 (2014)
52. Mirel, B., Wright, Z.: Heuristic evaluations of bioinformatics tools: a development case. In: Jacko, Julie A. (ed.) HCI 2009. LNCS, vol. 5610, pp. 329–338. Springer, Heidelberg (2009). doi:10.1007/978-3-642-02574-7_37
53. Nielsen, J., Molich, R.: Heuristic evaluation of user interfaces. In: Proceedings of the SIGCHI Conference on Human Factors in Computing Systems, pp. 249–256. ACM, New York (1990)
54. de Matos, P., Cham, J.A., Cao, H., Alcántara, R., Rowland, F., Lopez, R., Steinbeck, C.: The Enzyme Portal: a case study in applying user-centred design methods in bioinformatics. BMC Bioinform. **14**, 103 (2013)
55. Pavelin, K., Cham, J.A., de Matos, P., Brooksbank, C., Cameron, G., Steinbeck, C.: Bioinformatics meets user-centred design: a perspective. PLoS Comput. Biol. **8**, e1002554 (2012)
56. Mount, D.W.: Bioinformatics: sequence and genome analysis. Cold Spring Harbor Laboratory Press, Cold Spring Harbor (2004)
57. Martí-Renom, M.A., Stuart, A.C., Fiser, A., Sánchez, R., Melo, F., Sali, A.: Comparative protein structure modeling of genes and genomes. Ann. Rev. Biophys. Biomol. Struct. **29**, 291–325 (2000)
58. Santos Filho, O.A., de Alencastro, R.B.: Modelagem de proteínas por homologia. Quím. Nova **26**, 253–259 (2003)
59. Sillitoe, I., Lewis, T.E., Cuff, A., Das, S., Ashford, P., Dawson, N.L., Furnham, N., Laskowski, R.A., Lee, D., Lees, J.G., Lehtinen, S., Studer, R.A., Thornton, J., Orengo, C.A.: CATH: comprehensive structural and functional annotations for genome sequences. Nucleic Acids Res. **43**, D376–D381 (2015)

60. Fox, N.K., Brenner, S.E., Chandonia, J.-M.: The value of protein structure classification information—Surveying the scientific literature. Proteins Struct. Funct. Bioinform. **83**, 2025–2038 (2015)

61. Guex, N., Peitsch, M.C.: SWISS-MODEL and the Swiss-PdbViewer: an environment for comparative protein modeling. Electrophoresis **18**, 2714–2723 (1997)

Preschool Learning with a Fingertip

Concept of a Tablet-Based Training Program to Support Emergent Literacy and Mathematical Skills

Sabine Völkel(✉), Madlen Wuttke, and Peter Ohler

Media-Psychology, Faculty of Humanities, Chemnitz University of Technology,
Thüringer Weg 11, 09126 Chemnitz, Germany
{sabine.voelkel,madlen.wuttke,
peter.ohler}@phil.tu-chemnitz.de

Abstract. Emergent literacy in preschool and the understanding of numbers and quantities has a positive impact on the later school success of children. Research studies have shown a close connection between preschool achievements in phonological awareness or numerical-quantity understanding and later school performance. New interactive and mobile media like tablets have the potential for educators and children to deal with preschool content in a playful way. Why do we not use the potential of new media technologies to support future school success? A research group of the Chemnitz University of Technology wants to make use of the potential and will concept, develop and evaluate a training program with different building blocks to support skills in phonological awareness, in alphabetic awareness and in understanding of numbers and quantities. The concept of preschool learning with a fingertip is presented and discussed.

Keywords: Training program · Emergent literacy · Media literacy · Proactivity · Learning · Children · Preschool learning · Tablet learning · Mobile learning

1 Introduction

In politics, society and science prevails that preschool education has a high priority [1, 2]. There is broad agreement that it is necessary to improve the quality of educational processes in kindergartens, but how this can be implemented is less the subject. Normative proposals are made, but there are generally less practical offers for systematic preschool education programs. In Germany, some institutions place more emphasis on the emergent literacy or other school-related skills and other institutions focuses more on the general education. In the kindergarten laws of the federal states of Germany, a central goal of preschool education is to support children in linguistic abilities and create equal opportunities for all children. Some federal states such as Bavaria use scientific tests and training programs to promote preschool competences (e.g. [3, 4]). But this approach is rather an exception and is less practiced in other federal states in Germany. Across borders of Germany, the states are implementing different forms of preschool education. Countries such as Great Britain or Finland

© Springer International Publishing AG 2017
P. Zaphiris and A. Ioannou (Eds.): LCT 2017, Part II, LNCS 10296, pp. 110–119, 2017.
DOI: 10.1007/978-3-319-58515-4_9

attach great importance to preschool education, which is organised in day-care centres and schools and offers children and their families a systematic education and instruction [5, 6]. Other European countries like Germany or Poland focus more in their preschool education on the promotion of social skills or self-employment and less on school-related skills such as emergent literacy or mathematical competencies.

Tablet computers and their possibility of app-based learning provide kindergarten and day-care centres with the opportunity to create a systematic preschool education for all children. Tablet computers seem to have the capability to influence cognitive or social skills positively. Potential positive effects of computer use by children include enhanced cognitive development and school achievement, reduced barriers to social interaction, enhanced fine motor skills and visual processing. Potentially negative effects are more likely to be found in later childhood and adolescence, with the risk of child safety, inadequate content, violence, and bullying. Other negative influences are also to be observed in the early childhood, such as, sleeplessness, displacement of physical activity, as well as muscular problems [7]. But taking into account the knowledge about the negative influences, a tablet-based training program with the aim to support school relevant skills in preschool age offers the possibility for all children to participate in a standardized development program, which is inspirational, playful and matched to the individual level of development. In addition, a tablet-based training program provides the opportunity for all preschool children to acquire rudimentary skills in dealing with new media. The children would get to know the tablet as a learning medium as early as in kindergarten.

2   Emergent Literacy and Quantity-Number Competencies in Preschool Education

Children have a lot of experience language and numbers before they are going into school. Already the time before school entrance appears to be an important developmental stage for children, which can be co-determining for the success in school [8]. It is generally accepted that these early experiences are important for the subsequent school success in reading, writing and spelling. Several studies emphasize the importance of phonological awareness and quantity-number competencies for predicting later school achievement in literacy and mathematics [8–11].

Emergent Literacy
The term *emergent literacy* describes the developmental process of reading and writing in childhood. It means that children do not start with the reading and writing process at the beginning of school, rather the roots will already be laid in the preschool age [12, 13]. The precursor abilities of reading and writing are summarized under the concept of *phonological awareness*. The phonological awareness refers to the ability of a child to gain insight into the phonetic structure of the language [4, 11]. Phonological awareness describes an understanding of syllables, onsets, phonemes and rhymes. Children between 3 and 4 years are able to determine the number of syllables of a word and are interested in rhymes [14]. After this, they are able to identify different units of syllables. At the age of 4 and 5 years children indicate rhymes and onsets in words [15].

The development of phonological awareness is an ongoing process that begins early in childhood. Children benefit from an active promotion of awareness for language already before school start and so the phonological awareness could be found as a predictor of later reading success in various research [11, 16, 17]. In addition, the combination of training of phonological awareness and letter knowledge turned out to be particularly effective [16]. Literacy skills are also positively influenced through home literacy environment like story book reading or writing with parents [18]. The exploration of digital tools has also a positive influence on emergent literacy skills [18, 19]. For example, E-books can foster word recognition and writing [20] and phonological awareness [21].

Phonological awareness is the foundation of learning to read and also it has long-term effects on children's success in school. And as such, a tablet-based learning concept with a playful environment while learning has the potential to promote these competences even more effectively.

Quantity-Number Competencies

Many people believe that math is about numbers. But there is more to understand for children behind the numbers: the quantities [10]. The competence to understand numerical quantities develops early in life [10, 22]. Infants after birth are able to distinguish a set of two objects from a set of three objects [23]. They have a small set of quantity-number competence, which is expanded, when infants become toddlers. By the age of 4 years, children have two schemas: one for quantity comparison and another for counting and at the age of 5 or 6, they connect both schemas together. These conceptual structures provide the basis for all higher-level mathematics learning [10]. The formation of early mathematical competences seems to depend not only on the general cognitive development but also on the educational environment of the children. Children who living in low-income communities showed less advanced mathematical abilities as children of higher-income communities [24]. These differences in children's early quantity-number competencies have long term implications for their school success [10, 25].

Children benefit above all in their mathematical skills in preschool age from the support of three basic abilities: combining number and quantity, counting and knowledge about the symbolic representation of numbers. The *Number Sense* intervention from Griffin, Case and Siegler [24] could show that a well-designed program is able to support mathematical competencies.

The early promotion of phonological and letter awareness as well as of numbers and quantities can bring a decisive advantage in learning in school and thus tablet-based learning should be an effective tool inside a comprehensive preschool education.

3 Media Literacy in Preschool Education

Media are involved in processes of permanent dynamic change in different areas of society. In a mediatised society, it is therefore indispensable to deal with media competently and to promote media literacy.

Development of Media Literacy in Childhood

However, since children are not competent media users from the beginning, over the course of their development, they acquire an ever more differentiated competence for the understanding and active use of media. The development towards a competent media user is continuous and is determined by a large number of dimensions. Some dimensions are determined by natural maturation processes and develop more universally in mediated societies than others. Some basic dimensions in the handling of media develop parallel to cognitive maturity and other dimensions are more strongly characterized by individual experiences and learning processes. For example, children have to learn the functions and objectives of different media offerings through external instructions (e.g. the intentions of advertising) but they are able to understand the representational function of pictures [26] without any instruction.

Media Literacy represents a coherent network of skills and knowledge, which firstly changes as a result of cognitive maturity in the course of development and secondly which can be actively influenced by experience and instruction.

Media Literacy – Development of Skills and Knowledge Structures

Media literacy expands the literacy concept by the media aspect and describes how to deal with media and understand media on different dimensions [27]. According to Potter, different skills have to be developed when dealing with media. These skills are increasingly evolved during the developmental process on the basis of cognitive maturation, experience in handling media and explanations. The aim of media literacy lies on "adapting to our new world by being skilled at assessing the meaning in any kind of messages, organizing that meaning so that it is useful, and then constructing messages to convey that meaning to others" [27, p. 15]. In order to deal adequately with news and information in all media forms, people have to develop different skills. Potter describes these skills in building blocks, which enables people to develop "a set of perspectives that we actively use to expose ourselves to the mass media to interpret the meaning of the messages we encounter" [27, p. 22]. Children have to build out three building blocks of media literacy: personal locus, knowledge structures and skills. The skills represent the prerequisites for building knowledge structures. Subskills of media literacy are the capability to analyse, evaluate, to inductive and deductive thinking as well as to synthesis and abstractive thinking and are prerequisites for knowledge structures and personal locus. The knowledge structures are formed in the fields of media effects, media content, the media industry, the real world and their own self in the media environment. And the personal locus includes the individual motivation of the media user to deal with the content, functions, intentions [27].

Media Literacy Programs in Preschool

The concept of media literacy is much discussed and implemented very differently in various countries such as the preschool education in the linguistic and mathematical field in general. Media education has a high priority in schools and preschools in countries like Canada, Great Britain or Australia by integrating media education into the school curriculum. In most countries as well as in Germany, media literacy is regarded as particularly important for children and adolescence, but there is a lack of concrete implementation in school and preschool. In Germany, media-educational projects such as the creation of films, school newspapers or school radio are sometimes available as full-day care services after school. For the children in preschool age there are less programs for the promotion of media literacy. Besides the programs for media education in Canada, Great Britain or Australia there are currently in these countries also less systematic training programs for media literacy.

In most mediatised societies, preschool education and media literacy represent a central societal tasks. How this central tasks can be implemented is much discussed, but there are currently less practical implementations. An application-based tool, which focuses on the support of phonological and the letter awareness as well as on the number and quantity understanding, is automatically actively promoting media literacy. A tablet-based preschool program has the potential to provide first building blocks for closing the gap between societal challenge and implementation in development of media literacy.

4   Concept of Tablet-Based Training Program in Preschool

New media technologies are increasingly offering the possibility of active participation to people without reading and writing skills. Today, children can already intuitively deal with tablet computers, since a touchscreen replaces the input via a mouse and keyboard. Thus tablet computers are also interesting as learning tools for preschool children. For children and educators, these new tools present new opportunities as well as challenges [25]. But which features of a tablet computer are suitable for use as a learning tool?

Touch Screen

Tablet computers combine the keyboard of a laptop with a touch screen [28]. Young children without any reading and writing skills are able to use touch screen devices due to the simple and intuitive handling of manual gestures on the screen. Even the youngest can quickly learn touching, swiping and pinching with only one or two fingers (Fig. 1). Touch screens make the handling cognitively simpler than computers and thus manageable for younger children. Touch screens on tablet computers respond to multitouch inputs, which provides a natural means of input.

Children between 3 and 6 years quickly learn the handling with touch screen devices and are engaged and interested in these digital tools [29]. Already 3-year-old

Fig. 1. Intuitive touch screen for children

children can learn with touch screen devices and also 24-month-old children learn with it, but the younger group has to be interactively involved in the learning situation [30]. Younger children benefit most from traditional books and the interaction with parents compared to tablet-based stories. From the age of 4 years, children benefit from both forms of media [31]. Therefore, the touch-screen-based tool for children in preschool age offers a comparable potential as traditional media forms such as books, pens and paper.

Multimodality, Interactivity and Proactivity

Tablet-based learning combines two different modes to represent knowledge: verbal and pictorial information [32]. By addressing two senses, the processing capacities of two different pathways are utilized. Both modes have to be optimally coordinated in *multimodal learning environments* in order to optimize the learning success. Above all, multimodality offers an ideal learning environment for children to use both visual as well as auditive learning types.

Children learn mainly about *interactivity*. They imitate their caregivers, learn by talking to them, and need constant exchanges. Parents and educators, on the basis of the continuous exchange, are able to promote children optimally at the respective developmental stage. By answering questions and giving food for thought, they enable the children to reach the next level of development (*Zone of proximal development*, [33]). An interactive multimodal learning environment can also give children answers and ideas, to assist them in climbing the next level of development. An interactive approach with addressing of the learner motivates children to learn and give them information in an individual pace and adapted to the individual action of the learner. The tablet-based material should offer children the opportunity to interact with the content and to direct their own exploration. The children can determine what they look at and how long they look at something. Focusing attention based on the children's own interests motivates them to learn [34].

Proactive Elements of a Training Program

As it has been previously described [35] human-machine-interfaces are currently limited to traditional forms of input devices. We already mentioned the beneficial aspects of a touch interface presenting an intuitive form of input, especially for young children at a pre-school-age and without the literacy skills of reading and writing. But besides the possibility of touching and pinching, modern day tablet computers also possess the hardware capabilities for detecting non-verbal cues. Since this paper is focused on the utilization of tablet computers in teaching young children, proactive elements like gaze detection via webcam and the observation of auditory noise levels appear to be important aspects.

If a child would avert their gaze from the tablet computer, the system could detect this and react to it by stopping a current presentation and by re-establishing a connection, for example by addressing the child verbally. Once the attention has been restored, the training program would be able to recommence, while assuring that critical elements of the information conveyance will not be lost due to distractions.

Mobility, Motivation and Active Engagement

The smaller sizes of new technologies allow for increased mobility. Tablet computers can be used anytime and anywhere and support independent learning. The mobile handling of tablets makes the use for learning so simple and ideally suited for the nursery school day. Mobile technologies are motivating and more attractive for children engaging than traditional learning tools [36]. With the multi-touch devices, children are motivated to discover content in a new form and in new environments. Preschool time is a particularly important time because the motivation to learn is especially high. Engagement in learning processes is connected with motivation. Children were intrinsically motivated, when they were allowed to use computers for learning [29]. Discussed in dealing with new media is always the novelty effect, which Couse and Chen [29] could slightly invalidate. Even after a two-month daily use of the tablet, the interest of the children remained very high in this new technology.

Tablet-Based Training Program

A tablet-based learning tool for the development of relevant reading and literacy skills as well as the understanding of numbers and quantities is to be designed, developed with all termed learning features of mobility, multi-touch-screen, multimodality, interactivity and in addition proactivity. Based on scientific test methods for phonological awareness [4, 37], as well as for number and quantity comprehension [3] an app-based, interactive and proactive learning tool is created.

Three cognitive abilities are to be addressed through the app: Literacy, Mathematics and Media Literacy (Table 1).

Table 1. Learning modules and subtask of the tablet-based training program

Learning modules	Subtasks in learning module				
Literacy	Letters	Letter-sound	Syllables	Rhymes	Onsets
Mathematics	Numbers	Quantities	Counting	Connection: numbers and quantities	
Media literacy	Media content: tablet as learning tool	Technical literacy in dealing with the tablet	Participation		

As an example, the task type designed for the number and quantities module will be presented (Fig. 2). The training program is intended to systematically build up a number-to-quantity understanding through playful allocation, search and reordering tasks. It promotes awareness that ascending numbers correspond to increasing numbers, volumes, and lengths, as well as that numbers can be split into other numbers.

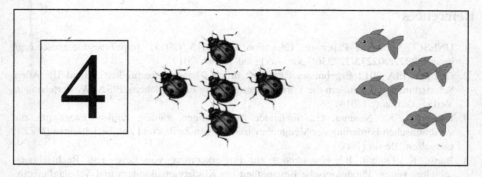

Fig. 2. Example for a number and quantity task

5   Conclusion

A tablet-based training supports the development of children on three central dimensions:

(1) *Emergent literacy* is supported by an active intervention of the phonological awareness. The children learn in the intervention rhymes, onsets and elaborate words according to their syllables. All levels of phonological awareness are supported by playful, multimodal, interactive and proactive tasks. The multi-modal, interactive and proactive design of the learning environment via a multi-touch operation ensures fun and information in one application. This ensures a high level of commitment and high motivation for the children and thus a high learning success. An evaluation design with a pretest post-test and follow-up measurement will test this assumption.

(2) The *understanding of numbers and quantities* is to be promoted centrally on a second dimension. The children explore through the app-based tablet usage the number space up to ten. They become familiar with the symbols of numbers and their quantities as well as learn which numbers are larger or smaller in the number space up to ten.

(3) A tablet-based training of preschool skills promotes media literacy on a third dimension. Children learn something about the technical side of a tablet and use it as an information tool with some entertaining elements.

The promotion of three relevant development dimensions, which can be viewed as a predictor of success in society, can be achieved via a tablet-based learning tool. A research group in Chemnitz has set itself to the task of designing, developing and evaluating such a tablet-based tool for use in kindergartens. With such a tablet-based learning tool, a systematic preschool education in the area of emergent literacy and numerical-quantity understanding can be ensured. Based on interactivity and proactivity, the learning content can be optimally adapted to the characteristics of the learner in order to optimize the learning sequence.

References

1. UNESCO: Position Paper on Education Post-2015 (2015). http://unesdoc.unesco.org/images/0022/002273/227336E.pdf. Accessed 15 Feb 2017
2. OECD: PISA 2012 Ergebnisse: Exzellenz durch Chancengerechtigkeit. (Band II): Allen Schülerinnen und Schülern die Voraussetzungen zum Erfolg sichern, PISA, W. Bertelsmann Verlag, Germany (2014)
3. Krajewski, K., Nieding, G., Schneider, W.: Mengen, zählen, Zahlen: Programm zur vorschulischen Förderung der Mengenbewusstheit von Zahlen und Zahlbeziehungen (MZZ). Cornelsen, Berlin (2007)
4. Barth, K., Gomm, B.: *Gruppentest* zur Früherkennung von Lese- und Rechtschreib-schwierigkeiten. Phonologische Bewusstheit bei Kindergartenkindern und Schulanfängern. Ernst Reinhardt Verlag, München (2014)
5. Finish National Agency for Education: Early childhood education and care (2017). http://www.oph.fi/english/education_system/early_childhood_education. Accessed 15 Feb 2017
6. Government UK: Education system in the UK (2017). https://www.gov.uk/government/uploads/system/uploads/attachment_data/file/219167/v01-2012ukes.pdf. Accessed 15 Feb 2017
7. Straker, L., Pollock, C., Maslen, B.: Principles for the wise use of computer by children. Egonomics **52**(11), 1386–1401 (2009)
8. Duncan, G.J., Dowsett, C.J., Claessens, A., Magnuson, K., Huston, A.C., Klebanov, P., Pagani, L.S., Feinstein, L., Engel, M., Brooks-Gunn, J., Sexton, H., Duckworth, K., Japel, C.: School readiness and later achievement. Dev. Psychol. **43**(6), 1428–1446 (2007)
9. Krajewski, K., Schneider, W.: Exploring the impact of phonological awareness, visual-spacial working memory, and preschool quantity-number competencies on mathe-matics achievement in elementary school: findings from a 3 year longitudinal study. J. Exp. Child Psychol. **103**(4), 516–531 (2009)
10. Griffin, S.: Teaching number sense. The cognitive science offer insights to how young children students can best learn math. Educ. Leadersh. **61**(5), 39–42 (2004)
11. Torgesen, J.K., Davis, C.: Individual difference variables that predict response to training in phonological awareness. J. Exp. Child Psychol. **63**, 1–21 (1996)
12. Gillen, J., Hall, N.: The emergence of early childhood literacy. In: Larson, J., Marsh, J. (eds.) The Sage Handbook of Early Childhood Literacy, 2nd edn., pp. 3–17. Sage Publication, London (2013)
13. Pfost, M.: Children's phonological awareness as a predictor of reading and spelling. A systematic review of longitudinal research in German-speaking countries. Zeitschrift für Entwicklungspsychologie und Pädagogische Psychologie **47**(3), 123–138 (2015)
14. Wyse, D., Goswami, U.: Early reading development. In: Larson, J., Marsh, J. (eds.) The Sage Handbook of Early Childhood Literacy, 2nd edn., pp. 379–394. Sage Publications Inc., London (2013)
15. Badley, L., Bryant, P.E.: Categorizing sounds and learning to read: a casual connection. Nature **301**, 419–421 (1983)
16. Bus, A.G., van Ijzendoorn, M.H.: Phonological awareness and early reading: a meta-analysis of experimental training. J. Educ. Psychol. **9**(3), 403–414 (1999)
17. Snow, C.E., Burns, M.S., Griffin, P.: Preventing Reading Difficulties in Young Children. National Academy Press, Washington, DC (1998)
18. Neumann, M.M.: Young children's use of touch screen tablets for writing and reading at home: relationship with emergent literacy. Comput. Educ. **97**, 61–68 (2016)

19. Van der Kooy-Hofland, V., Kegel, C.A.T., Bus, A.G.: Evidence-based computer interventions targeting phonological awareness to prevent reading problems in at-risk young children. In: Neuman, S.B., Dickinson, D. (eds.) Handbook of Early Literacy Research, vol. 3, pp. 214–227. Guilford Press, New York (2011)
20. Shamir, A., Korat, O.: Developing an educational E-book for fostering kindergarten children's emergent literacy. Comput. Schools **24**, 125–143 (2007)
21. Korat, O., Shamir, A.: Electronic books versus adult readers: effects on children's emergent literacy as a function of social class. J. Comput. Assist. Learn. **23**, 248–259 (2007)
22. Dehaene, S.: The Number Sense. Oxford University Press, New York (1997)
23. Antell, S.E., Keating, D.P.: Perception of numerical invariance in neonates. Child Dev. **54**, 695–701 (1983)
24. Griffin, S., Case, R., Siegler, R.: Rightstart: providing the central conceptual prerequisites for first formal learning of arithmetic to students at risk for school failure. In: McGilly, K. (ed.) Classroom Lessons: Integrating Cognitive Theory and Classroom Practice, pp. 24–49. MIT Press, Cambridge (1994)
25. Clements, D.H., Sarama, J.: Young children and technology: what does the research say? Young Child. **58**(6), 34–40 (2003)
26. Völkel, S., Ohler, P.: Understanding pictures in early childhood. In: Sachs-Hombach, K., Schirra, J. (eds.) Origins of Pictures. Anthropological Discourses in Image Science, pp. 378–400. Harlem, Köln (2013)
27. Potter, W.J.: Media Literacy, 6th edn. Sage Publications Inc., Los Angeles (2013)
28. Henderson, S., Yeow, J.: iPad in education: a case study of iPad adoption and use in a primary school. In: 45th Hawaii International Conference on System Science (2012)
29. Couse, L.J., Chen, D.W.: A tablet computer for young children? Exploring its viability for early childhood Education. J. Res. Technol. Educ. **43**(1), 75–98 (2010)
30. Kirkorian, H.L., Choi, K., Pempek, T.A.: Toddlers' word learning from contingent and noncontingent video on touch screens. Child Dev. **87**(2), 405–413 (2016)
31. Lauricella, A.R., Barr, R., Calvert, S.L.: Parent–child interactions during traditional and computer storybook reading for children's comprehension: implications for electronic storybook design. Int. J. Child Comput. Interact. **2**, 17–25 (2014)
32. Moreno, R., Mayer, R.: Interactive multimodal learning environments. Special issue on interactive learning environments: contemporary issues and trends. Educ. Psychol. Rev. **19**, 309–326 (2007)
33. Vygotsky, L.S.: Mind in society: The Development of Higher Psychological Processes. Harvard University Press, Cambridge (1978)
34. Ricci, C.M., Beal, C.R.: The effect of interactive media on children's story memory. J. Educ. Psychol. **94**, 138–144 (2002)
35. Wuttke, M.: Pro-active pedagogical agents. In: Fakultät für Informatik (ed.) Proceedings of International Summer Workshop Computer Science, July 2013, pp. 59–62 (2013)
36. Blackwell, C.K., Lauricella, A., Wartella, E., Robb, M., Schomburg, R.: Adoption and use of technology in early education: the interplay of extrinsic barriers and teacher attitudes. Comput. Educ. **69**, 310–319 (2013)
37. Mayer, A.: Test zur Erfassung der phonologischen Bewusstheit und der Benennungsgeschwindigkeit (TEPHOBE), 3rd edn. Ernst Reinhardt Verlag, München (2016)

Diversity in Learning

Augmentative and Alternative Communication in the Literacy Teaching for Deaf Children

Sandra Cano[1(✉)], César A. Collazos[2], Leandro Flórez Aristizábal[2,3], and Fernando Moreira[4,5]

[1] LIDIS Group, University of San Buenaventura, Cali, Colombia
sandra.cano@email.com
[2] IDIS Group, University of Cauca, Colombian, Popayan, Colombia
ccollazo@unicauca.edu.co, lxexpxe@gmail.com
[3] GRINTIC Group,
Institución Universitaria Antonio José Camacho, Cali, Colombia
learistizabal@admon.uniajc.edu.co
[4] Portucalense Institute for Legal Research – IJP, Univ Portucalense,
Rua Dr. António Bernardino Almeida, 541-619, 4200-072 Porto, Portugal
[5] IEETA, Univ Aveiro, Aveiro, Portugal
fmoreira@upt.pt

Abstract. Deaf children face various challenges in their daily life in the social, cultural and educational ambits. Therefore they must learn to communicate with society through writing and reading. However learn read and writing without sounds are major challenges, because the teacher must find another learning strategies as communication boards. Taking in account previous works, we propose a communication board for deaf children using the teaching method Fitzgerald Key's, which we make use of a physic board and technology as an alternative that the child can interact in a real environment and virtual using physic elements and augmented reality.

Keywords: Human computer interaction · Deaf children · Augmentative and Alternative Communication · Technology to assist literacy development

1 Introduction

Deaf children face various challenges in their daily life in the social, cultural and educational ambits. In addition to these challenges, they tend to acquire cognitive skills at a much slower pace than a hearing child. Deaf children therefore require a special education just in order to receive the appropriate educational development. In the educational field, they must make use of communication strategies that have been adjusted to their needs.

Hearing impairment is an obstacle preventing the processing of information linguistically through the ear. It is more generally known as deafness. A deaf child who does not use a hearing aid must communicate with society through sign language or lip-reading. As a result, these children have a better-developed visual attention span [1, 2]. Educators are therefore using tools accompanied by images and text as a channel of communication so as to convey the extraction of meaning of a concept.

P. Zaphiris and A. Ioannou (Eds.): LCT 2017, Part II, LNCS 10296, pp. 123–133, 2017.
DOI: 10.1007/978-3-319-58515-4_10

Educators consequently require play-based tools that can motivate children in their learning and that can be integrated within their educational planning.

Augmentative and alternative communication (AAC), meanwhile, is used for people with little or no functional speech, due to severe speech impairment [3]. Another definition by [4] is defined as intervention instruments destined for people with problems in communication and language, the aim of which instruments is teaching meaning in specific procedures with the use of symbols and pictures, etc., as an aid for children using alternative communication. The goal of AAC is to break the speech barrier between a child with speech difficulties and the teacher.

Research by [6] suggests that the function AAC can play in language and communication development varies depending on the child's chronological age, degree of disability, and specific environment requirements. Furthermore, it was found that children on using these AAC systems learned to communicate expressively using the skills they had explicitly been taught.

2   System Communication and Deaf Children

Deaf children are faced with major challenges in different areas such as health, education, cultural and social. A deaf child is one who has no hearing aid available and must learn to communicate through sign language.

Communication with deaf children is done using visual tools such as pictograms and pictures that can help to support them in understanding language. A communication board can be used as an alternative form of communication to replace or supplement speech that is not functional for expressing thoughts, needs, wants, and ideas in the child.

An AAC system can be used as an instrument for people with special needs who have different impairments in communication and/or language, and whose objective is to teach through other teaching methods a structured set of non-vowel but visual codes that facilitate functional communication [10]. However, it must be borne in mind that these boards are a means to communicate so as to acquire skills that make it possible to interact with the environment.

An AAC can be represented by physical or digital devices such as communication boards with drawings, charts with images or words or digital devices with or without verbal output such as Tablet or Smartphones. An AAC system called PECS (Picture Exchange Communication System) was created for people with autism spectrum, since they cannot use speech to communicate. These PECS were systems created with low technology that involve elements in paper, cards with images, to communicate graphically certain specific actions. Although PECS was developed for autistic people it has been used in a wide range of people with disabilities. Early AAC technologies quickly became more portable and less expensive and they are now being used in mobile applications. Furthermore, work proposed by Casey [9] demonstrates that communication systems can be an alternative for people who have complex communication needs and can help the development skills in reading and writing. In addition, it emphasizes that these types of work, which involve AAC systems, can be complemented collaboratively. Meanwhile, [11] states that AAC may be an important element for the development of language and communication, but this system may vary depending on the chronological age of the child. The design may further change depending on the child's disability and how they can use AAC systems and which exit channels can be enabled.

The communication system aims for deaf children to have better access to the different components of the oral language. The system consists of a series of keys to differentiate the structure of a sentence. As such, colors are often used to differentiate these keys making it possible to represent the structure of a sentence and allowing the children to use the rules in some way.

3   Literacy in Deaf Children

Deaf children who do not have hearing aid need to learn sign language, which is considered their first spoken language. However, they still have to learn to read and write in Spanish in order to communicate with society. For them, learning written Spanish takes longer, as they have to learn all the morpho-syntactic and pragmatic structure. In addition, research shows [12] that the extent of their lexicon is small and its evolution with age and schooling is slow.

The handling of syntactic structures is more deficient as they become more complex. As stated by Niederberger [13], the morpho-syntactic competence of deaf children is low, since in their partial perception of speech they confine themselves to identifying key words such as verbs and nouns in the content of sentences, but do not give much importance to prepositions or articles. For a deaf child lacking phonology, the only way available to establish connections between written word and concept is sometimes to memorize without establishing a phonology relationship with the word, so that memorizing vocabulary could almost be considered a mission impossible. For example, with a word like "casa" (house) when a consonant changes giving rise to different meanings such as "cava" (cave), "cama" (bed), and "cara" (face), among others. The task of the child with no phonology, who has to associate an orthographic detail with a particular meaning, is very difficult. It is therefore important to consider a visual strategy to consider phonology and make it available to deaf children. In addition, many spelling errors are found, such as "arina" (harina), "baca" (vaca), etc., so often to consider phonology with writing, dactylological language is used as a way for children to be able to represent each of the sounds of a word.

Deaf children usually use word complement (WC) as an option or strategy for their teaching, widely used in children with lip-facial reading. Strategies using color codes are also used for the teaching of literacy, to facilitate with the help of colors and question schemes which ones correspond to the part of a sentence, i.e. subject, verb, adjective, among others. Within these color codes lie a number of proposed learning methods, such as Fitgerald [12], Goossens, Crain & Elder [25, 26].

The strategies that teachers use are through visual and gestural codes. A major difficulty children have is memorizing visually the concepts of each word. However, it is difficult to write very long words correctly. Therefore, teachers are supported by a teaching method called Fitzgerald Key [5]. Fitzgerald Key (see Fig. 1) involves a linguistic code of visual representation, making use of color codes in the form of questions, in which the user must put the word sequence together (i.e. person + action + object). Fitzgerald works by a scheme of questions to complement the sentence, such as: when, where, who, actions, among others, and each of these schemes represents a set color according to whether it corresponds to a pronoun, object, verb, noun, adjective or adverb.

Fig. 1. Fitzgerald Key

Furthermore, technology has been integrated into AAC systems to design better tools to maximize the development of communication, language and literacy skills, hence the use human-computer interaction (HCI) to understand different factors in the children – e.g. psychological, social, cultural and educational. These factors help to determine how children operate and use the technology. A model of user centered design on the user structures of the information concerned for the end user was proposed by [6], in which different aspects of the deaf child were identified, such as behaviors, cognitive aspects, and interests, among others.

Research conducted [6–9] shows that HCI can play a part in the creation of a smart, interactive model for children with a hearing disability and could be an alternative for designing an interactive communication board oriented to literacy teaching, applying the Fitzgerald Key teaching method. Thus, when designing a communication board for mobile devices it is important to take into account such variables as color, shape, texture, size, position, and movement, which can help to optimize the design of AAC technologies.

4   Methodology

The methodology followed is a methodology called MECONESIS proposed by Cano et al. [14], which follows some stages within the process, such as: Analysis, pre-production, production and post-production. The methodology is oriented to the design of serious games for children with hearing impairment. Therefore, the first thing that should be done is an analysis of the profile of the deaf child from an educational context in the teaching of literacy. Children with whom work is done to evaluate the communication systems in literacy teaching are deaf children from the USAER program (Units of Service to Support Regular Education, in Aguascalientes, Mexico), made up of several public schools that allow access to children with Special Educational Needs (SEN) in regular education. Seven children with hearing impairment between 11 and 15 years old at USAER, Aguascalientes, México and eight children aged between 4 and 8 years from the ITES (Special Sensory Therapy of the Lions Club) in Cali, Colombia, were analyzed.

4.1 Analysis

The different aspects that have been analyzed in the deaf child are researches proposed in [17], which are: Personal Information (Age, Gender and Academic year), Competences, Disability (Cognitive, Physical), Disability level (Slight, Moderate, Profound and Severe), Learning styles, Behavior/Academic, Emotions, and Motivation.

For the Deaf children evaluated, the direct observation method was used in USAER. These children are in secondary education, however they do not have a grasp of Mexican sign language and their strategies for communicating are through the alphabet and some informal signs they themselves create to find a way to communicate faster. These children are included within the regular school, so there is a supporting teacher figure, who has one-hour sessions twice a week per group in the areas of literacy and math. Most of these children come from deaf parents and are from low-income families. On the other hand, the ITES children are only deaf children where they are taught Colombian sign language as well as the writing and reading of Spanish as their second language. Deaf children communicate through visual language, so the teachers in their teaching strategies rely on pictograms to explain the concepts and color codes for differentiating between the elements and rules that allow sentences to be constructed.

4.2 Analysis

With the support teachers of the USAER, a search was carried out for mobile applications that function as communication boards and are oriented toward the writing and reading of the deaf children.

As a result, five applications were selected for mobile devices (Smartphone) (Table 1), whose purposes were to serve as an alternative and augmentative communication tool. Thus, each of them was analyzed first with the support teacher, whose approval was given if it could serve as an educational resource and then it was evaluated with the child. The purpose is that the children, when interacting with applications should, without too much effort, understand the graphical interface, the responses to the interactions and each one of the activities, and that in turn, these would provide support to the teacher to use in their teaching strategies in the classroom.

Table 1. Communication boards in mobile devices

Application	Description	Devices
e-Mintza	This is a customizable and dynamic system of augmentative and alternative communication directed to people with autism or with oral or written communication problems [18]	iPad & Android
Tom Taps Speak	Tom Taps Speak is designed to work in collaboration with parents and speech therapists, to help people with communication problems. It is image-based and has a friendly text-to-speech function. It was done so that parents could support their child with autism and the child could communicate with people through this communication board [19]	iPad
Communication book	An application that allows an alternative or augmentative system of communication based on pictograms. It works on Fitzgerald Keys, where it associates grammatical categories with colors [15]	Android
AraBoard constructor	This is a set of tools designed for alternative and augmentative communication, whose purpose is to facilitate functional communication through the use of images and pictograms, to people who present some type of difficulty in this area [20]	Android
Pictogram	Application of augmentative and alternative communication, which is accompanied by images and text [16]	Android
Araword, Adapro	Free Word processor Text Editor of augmentative and alternative communication to convert text to pictogram. These processors help towards individuals with learning difficulty like dyslexia or a developmental disorder such as autism [27, 28]	PC

Of the five applications selected that meet the function of communication boards, most are oriented for children with serious communication problems. In addition, these applications have a very basic vocabulary and do not give importance to the rules of the sentence using color keys. It is quite the reverse with the communication book application developed for Android, which has a set of categories grouped by color, and each color represents a structure of the sentence. However, it does not handle questionnaires and pictograms, while navigation through the categories is not very clear. Taking as a background the design and development of the communication board, Literacy with Fitzgerald [9] is proposed, a serious game where game mechanics are taken into account and punctuation, challenges and levels of difficulty are created using questionnaires and grouping by color categories (see Fig. 2). Each category that has been created is accompanied by icons representative of the group of vocabulary in which it is contained. In addition each questionnaire is subject to the level of difficulty, where three levels of difficulty have been created (basic, intermediate and advanced).

This application was developed for Android Tablets in such a way that this educational resource was able to be carried around by teachers, and at the same time being

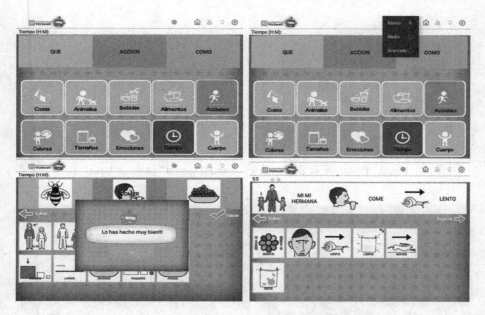

Fig. 2. Literacy with Fitzgerald, mobile application [21]. (Color figure online)

affordable. However, it is important to realize that the great majority of these children are of low economic resources and in the center they attend depend on donations or external aid. So, not everyone can have a mobile application so easily, in which only the interaction is digital.

4.3 Pre-production

Analyzing the information obtained in the previous stage, the development is purely digital, a continuation of the work proposed by [6], which seeks to interact with a real environment and a digital one at the same time, giving very favorable results. Therefore a physical board is proposed that makes it possible to interact with the child in a real environment and at the same time to link information technologies by means of augmented reality (Fig. 3).

For the design of the physical board, it is taken into account that it can have the number of times for a board where the correct sequence can be constructed according to the scheme of questions, which is presented in each activity by learning level (Fig. 4). Therefore, it is very important that the teacher is a moderator in the development of this activity. The activity revolves around a set of cards, where each card is grouped according to a learning level (basic, intermediate, or advanced) that is associated with a color (blue, yellow, and orange). The different tasks to be performed are on activity cards that are included in the physical game, where the teacher should take control of the game to indicate to the student the activities to be performed. Technology has been included to be part of this physical board game integrating each card of vocabulary in text to be visualized in a 3D model relating to the corresponding pictogram.

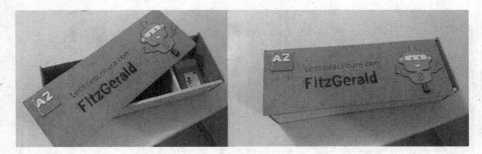

Fig. 3. Prototype of the "Literacy with Fitzgerald" physical board

Fig. 4. Managing the physical board (Color figure online)

Augmented reality is used to define direct or indirect vision of a real-world physical environment whose elements are combined with virtual elements to create a mixed reality in real time.

With augmented reality (AR), there is a relationship between virtual and physical elements in the real world. AR also allows access to information in a different way using technology, modifying the mode of learning and improving knowledge of reality.

Authors such as Fabregat [22] and Basogain et al. [23] state that AR is a technology that complements the interaction with the real world and allows the user to be in an enhanced real environment with additional information provided by technology, which can be through a computer or mobile devices. As a result, Fabregat [22] has put forward some characteristics of AR, such as: (1) it combines the real and the virtual, (2) it works in real time and (3) it registers in three dimensions. Iulian et al. [24], meanwhile, refers to AR as the technology that allows virtual content to be included in a physical-real context, allowing students to view virtual content as it appears in the real world and control the virtual environment through the interaction of tangible objects.

AR involves a number of basic concepts, such as **Marching**, to mark the vertices in the image; **Tracking**, to locate an object that is moving in a space-time; **Target**, which are images that allow the positioning of the virtual content in the scene; and finally **Rendering**, the process of generating an image. So, for each card of the physical board it is necessary to carry out tracking so that it can generate the image corresponding to the text on each card.

4.4   Production

Each card image corresponds to a virtual content that can represent visual information for the child. The idea is to be able to relate the text and if the meaning of the text is not known, the mobile device can be used to provide visual information of the meaning of the image. The objective of this is that the child can associate the word with the pictogram (Fig. 5).

Fig. 5. Models in 3D for obtaining additional information.

5   Conclusions and Future Work

The physical board proposes to act as an alternative educational resource for Fitzgerald Keys teaching for deaf children as an augmentative communication board. Therefore, it is sought to continue measuring the impact produced when working simultaneously with real objects and virtual, augmented reality. Today, educational experiences for children come with play resources as a means of motivating them during their learning. Furthermore, interaction with real objects allows the child to have a real interaction and to associate objects more easily within their environment. As a future work it is hoped to carry out an evaluation with deaf children who use Fitzgerald Keys as a teaching method in reading and writing, as it has been observed that some schools are using the Fitzgerald Keys strategy. However, they do not use the same colors or schemes that Fitzgerald uses strictly, so a way must be found that the physical game can configure the question schemes according to the colors that the teachers handle, as the work by Cano et al. [7] does.

References

1. Grigonis, A., Narkevicienė, V.: Deaf children's visual recall and its development in school Age. Vytauro Didziojo Universitetas K, 52 (2010)
2. Marschark, M., Everhart, V.S.: Problem-solving by deaf and hearing students: twenty questions. Deafness Educ. Int. 1, 65–82 (1999)
3. Beukelman, D.R., Mirenda, P.: Augmentative and Alternative Communication: Management of Severe Communication Disorders in Children and Adults. Paul H. Bookes Publishing Co., Baltimore (2005)
4. Gómez Villa, M., Díaz Carcelén, L., Rebollo Martínez, T.: Comunicación Aumentativa y Alternativa. Notas de clase. Aula Profesora Teleformación. https://teleformacion.murciaeduca.es/pluginfile.php/4428/mod_resource/content/1/UNIDAD26.pdf. última visita 4 de diciembre del 2016
5. Fitzgerald, E.: Straight Language for the Deaf. Volta Bureau, Washington, D.C. (1954)
6. Cano, S., Muñoz, A.J., Collazos, C.A., Amador, V.: Model for analysis of serious games for literacy in deaf children from user experience approach. In: Proceedings of the XVI International Conference on Human Computer Interaction (2015)
7. Cano, S., Collazos, C.A., Manresa-Yee, C., Peñeñory, V.: Principles of design for serious games to teaching of literacy for children with hearing disabilities. In: Moreno, L., de la Rubia Cuestas, E.J., Ruiz Penichet, V.M., García-Peñalvo, F.J. (eds.) Proceedings of the XVII International Conference on Human Computer Interaction (Interacción 2016), 2 p. ACM, New York (2016). https://doi.org/10.1145/2998626.2998650. Article 6
8. Light, J., Drager, K., McCarthy, J., Mellott, S., Millar, D., Parrish, C., Welliver, M.: Performance of typically developing four- and five-year-old children with AAC systems using different language organization techniques. Augmentative Altern. Commun. 20, 63–88 (2004)
9. Casey, M.: The bridge to literacy: a literacy approach for all students including those who use augmentative and alternative communication. In: Proceedings of the 4th International Convention on Rehabilitation Engineering & Assistive Technology (iCREATe 2010), 3 p. Singapore Therapeutic, Assistive & Rehabilitative Technologies (START) Centre, Kaki Bukit TechPark II, Singapore (2010). Article 7

10. Tamarit, J.: Sistemas Alternativos de Comunicación con autismo: algo más que una alternativa. Alternativas para la comunicación, pp. 3–5 (1988)
11. Romski, M.A., Sevcik, R.A.: Augmentative and alternative communication for children with developmental disabilities. Ment. Retard. Dev. Disabil. Res. Rev. **3**, 363–368 (1997). doi:10. 1002/(SICI)1098-2779(1997)3:4<363:AID-MRDD12>3.0.CO;2-T
12. Fitzgeral, E.: Straight Language for the Deaf. Washington D.C., Volta Bureau (1954)
13. Niederberger, N.: L'apprentissage de la lecture – écriture chez les enfants sourds. Enfance **59**, 254–262 (2007)
14. Cano, S., Muñoz, J., Collazos, C., Gonzalez, C., Zapata, S.: Hacia una Metodología para la concepción de juegos serios para niños con discapacidad auditiva. IEEE Latin America Transactions **14**(5) (2016)
15. https://play.google.com/store/apps/details?id=es.geeknekodroid.librodecomunicacion &hl=es. visitado el 17 de Enero del 2017
16. https://play.google.com/store/apps/details?id=es.pictogramas.pictogramaslite. visitado el 17 de Enero del 2017
17. Cano, S., Collazos, C., Fardoun, H.M., Alghazzawi, D.M., Albarakati, A.: Model based on learning needs of children with auditory impairment. In: Meiselwitz, G. (ed.) SCSM 2016. LNCS, vol. 9742, pp. 324–334. Springer, Cham (2016). doi:10.1007/978-3-319-39910-2_30
18. https://play.google.com/store/apps/details?id=air.com.orange.emintza&hl=en. Accessed 17 Jan 2017
19. https://itunes.apple.com/us/app/tom-taps-speak-aac-for-kids/id805544185?mt=8. Accessed 17 Jan 2017
20. https://play.google.com/store/apps/details?id=air.AraBoardConstructor&hl=en. Accessed 17 Jan 2017
21. Cano, S., Muñoz, J., Collazos, C., Bustos, V.: Aplicación móvil para el aprendizaje de la lectoescritura con Fitzgerald para niños con discapacidad auditiva. In: X Conferencia Latinoamericana de Educación, Tecnologías y Objetos de Aprendizaje, LACLO 2015, Maceió, Brasil (2015)
22. Fabregat, R.: Combinando la realidad con las plataformas e-learning adaptativas. Revista Venezolana de Información, pp. 69–78 (2012)
23. Basogain, X., olabe, M., Espinosa, K., Rouèche, C., Olabe, J.C.: Realidad Aumentada en la educación "una tecnología emergente" in Online Educa Madrid, 7 Conferencia Internacional de la educación y la formación basadas en tecnologías, pp. 24–29 (2007)
24. Radu, I., Zheng, R., Golubski, G., Guzdial, M.: Augmented reality in the future of education. In: Workshop Next Generation of HCI and Education, Atlanta, Georgia, USA (2010)
25. Groossens, C.: Aided communication intervention before assessment: a case study of a child with cerebral palsy. Augmentative Altern. Commun. **5**, 14–26 (1989)
26. Grossens, C., Crain, S., Elder, P.: Communication displays for engineered preschool environments (Book 1). Mayer-Jhonson Company, Solana Beach (1994)
27. ADAPRO. http://adapro.iter.es/es.html. Accessed 17 Jan 2017
28. Araword. http://www.arasaac.org/software.php?id_software=2. Accessed 17 Jan 2017

Girls in Robot Class_Smart Textiles Interactive Tool-Kits to Enhance the Participatory of Women in Technology

Aqua Chuan-Yu Chen[1] and Yu-Cheng Lin[2(✉)]

[1] Department of Product Design, Ming Chuan University, Taipei, Taiwan
aquachen@mail.mcu.edu.tw
[2] Department of Electronic Engineering,
Ming Chung University, Taoyuan, Taiwan
yclin@mail.mcu.edu.tw

Abstract. "Girls in Robot Class" focuses on provide teaching aids and instructions to include girls in the learning of STEAM education contents, so that they could experience the so-called intelligent world, which are created by the output behavior and controlled by the input data sensing. Textiles are easy to obtain in our daily life and often used as expressions of cultural response characteristics. In the meantime, Smart Textiles are soft, intimate which you can weave, splice, fold, stretch, but are also related the concept of science and technology simultaneously. Besides, interactive kits of the Smart Textiles require different characteristics of sensing and feedback devices other than the plastic products.

The teaching case of sensor (input) and feedback (output) components must be consistent with the experience in life in order to make the teaching content actively and enhance the interest of participation. Soft robot, in terms of technology, can be simplified easily for the purpose of studying how to control the light, motor, heat and sound. On the other hands, it can also be developed into clouds data technology and the Internet of Things items.

In this paper, we describe our experience in designing and organizing a robot course but with smart textiles. We will show that (1) a set of soft robot prototype by digital printing. (2) Three interactive modules of difficult levels were developed by the use of smart textiles. (3) The study of the outcome of teaching implementations and the learning tools of Interactive components inside the toolkits and digital printing soft robot template, a robot workshop course plan were designed and held with 30 participants (15 girls and 15 boys, design background). Product designers and electronic engineers were team up to plan teaching content and plan. Participants of different genders developed their own soft robot sketches through 3D printing and digital embroidery creation sewing machine. (4) The syllabus evaluation about STEAM interest and the applicability.

Aqua Chun-Yu Chen is assistant professor (Taiwan), PhD Dong-A University (Korea), MID Pratt Institute (USA). Further developments of this research is been updated in the webpage: https://www.facebook.com/grobotroom/.

P. Zaphiris and A. Ioannou (Eds.): LCT 2017, Part II, LNCS 10296, pp. 134–147, 2017.
DOI: 10.1007/978-3-319-58515-4_11

Keywords: Technology-enhanced learning · Smart-textiles · Gender difference · STEAM interest · Teaching modules

1 Introduction

This study aims to break glass wall of genders gap of the science education by adapting smart textile (e-Textile) and interactive devices such as media to create tool-kits. We design the programs to evaluate the facilities and effectiveness of this workshop. The Maker Movement and STEAM education prevailed and gathered more different types of creators to build their original prototypes, as well as the development of new products and services. However, interactive curriculum and programs are mostly imitation of the robot, which is still being defined by the boy's activities. We are facing the pressing issue of a declining birthrate and aging population. Providing the suitable subjects for women to learn science and contribute their ability for the society has become an urgent issue.

The motivation of this project is to find the preference tools for enabling non-engineers staff - especially young girls - to generate interest in science and technology. The research is to make use of the application of smart textiles and interactive elements to develop soft and flexible tool-kits to be used in interaction designed learning. 15 male and 15 female were invited to be the research subjects. There are robots made by textiles with no face and costumes, in the meantime, knowledge of circuit were digital printed on the surface of the robot and programing skills were also introduced in the interaction design workshop. In the class, students were encouraged to make their own specific face look simply by hand drawing and applied in sewing embroidery techniques. From this soft robot prototype, the circuit and programming knowledge were taught to control the behaviors by adapting the interaction tool-kits. The prototypes developed by participants were used as research materials to evaluate how interactive science and technology concepts were interpreted by the tool-kits provided. This research results help to understand the criteria of female friendly creative experience in the field of interactive science and technology.

Project is divided into three parts:

1. Case study: Evaluation of Smart textile (E-Textiles) or Wearable Technology Projects that are acceptable to apply in girls' robot classroom. 150 questionnaires were distributed which include both genders. The result shows that both girls and boys are interesting in this topic but think that the programming is the most difficult part of developing similar projects.
2. Developing of the tool-kits: Base on the result of case study, sensors (pressure, heart rate, touching, bending) and reactors of smart textiles (heating pad, heating fiber, LED yarns, sound) were used and introduced. Teaching materials were prepared and tested to facilitate the applying process.
3. Experience Modules: verification test included the benefits and disadvantages of these teaching tools, and the tendency of the function and shape adapted between both genders. A final prototype was suggested to increase the interest of women to learn science and involve in STEAM education.

2   Literature Research

Robot for the learners is mainly inspired by their concepts of programming and computing. Let them know the so-called intelligent world is by sensing the input data to create the output behavior and control. Fabrics are readily available as long as the needle and thread are on the hand. They do not need complicate machine for industrial production e.g. plastic injection. Compared to the blockish robot teaching aids such as LEGO blocks, little Bits and other types of interactive educational building blocks, textiles are closer to the concept of wearing technology, and mobility in daily life.

Smart textiles have often reminiscent those can deliver exceptional performance with light, sound, electricity, input and feedback. They were also commonly defined as detection of physiological signals, mood changes, and feedback information to the controller to determine what is the reaction on the textiles.

2.1   Smart Textiles, e-Textiles from Taiwan Textiles Industry

Smart Textiles are able to sense stimuli from the environment, to react and adapt to them by integration of functionalities in the textile structure. The stimulus as well as the response can have an electrical, thermal, chemical, magnetic or other origin. The Smart Textiles or E-Textiles usually contain both sensing and feedback components. It can sense, test and collect information about people or the environment, such as body temperature or human action. Output through the shining light, temperature changes, image display and other feedback electronic message transmission allow users to feel the situation changes. Smart Textiles, due to the characteristics of sensing and feedback, is different from the general fabric, but also because of the softness is different from electric plastic product. Specific textiles can replace the hard circuit, or show the light and temperature feedback.

The extent of intelligence can be divided in three subgroups:

- Passive smart textiles can only sense the environment, they are sensors;
- Active smart textiles can sense the stimuli from the environment and also react to them, besides the sensor function, they also have an actuator function;
- Finally, very smart textiles have the gift to adapt their behavior to the circumstances (Dadi 2010).

Basically, 5 functions can be distinguished in an intelligent suit, namely: Sensors, Data processing, Actuators, Storage, Communication (Van Langenhove and Hertleer 2004). When study wearable technology, Smart-Textiles are essential elements to be considered, which incorporates elements of design and fashion and thus it is more gender-neutral than robotics. It is also caters to a much broader range of children's social goals and desire for self-expression (Lau and Ngai 2009).

Using textiles to design a robot could be an interesting combinations of contradictions. We began by surveying the adaptable and accessible smart textiles material in Taiwan to make sure the following production without any doubt which mostly from Taiwan Textile Research Institute (TTRI 2011) and textile industry (Chen 2012). Even though those textiles are not defined as "Smart Textiles", but we found that it is quite useful in the idea development as shown in Table 1.

Table 1. Achievements and materials of Taiwan smart textiles

Conductive	Energy	Light	Heat

2.2   Robot, Puppet, and Textiles

A review of Arduino, a popular robotics toolkit, revealed female designers constituted less than 1% of users (Buechley and Hill 2010). By contrast, crafting, sewing, and other textile design communities attract disproportionate numbers of girls and women (Buechley 2013). Often, we are unaware of the subtle gendered messages that accrue in tools and materials over long histories of use. For example, LEGO bricks and robotics are marketed to and often used by boys. By contrast, crafting kits and fabrics are marketed to and often used by girls (Buchholz et al. 2014). In this study, we examined the combination of robot made by Textiles (Soft Robot as shown in this paper) and apply in a class to see the acceptability and difference between two genders.

In the gender-bending world, is it possible not to divide the gender by learning technology with bricks but textiles? This study addresses the question by developing a soft robot prototype to test three hypotheses: (i) girls like robot, (ii) boys like textile, and (iii) boys and girls have the same ability to learn technology.

Since this research aim to blend gender in one classroom, then there is a question some might ask, why puppet-like robot? Not fashion Clothes or accessory? Dr. Bromfield affiliated with Harvard Medical School mentioned, "By standing in for real people, puppets allow a child to displace feelings from the significant persons with whom they were originally connected. In doing so, puppets offer physical and psychological safety that, in turn, invites greater self-expression. For example, a child can express aggression or love toward a puppet without the risk of actual retaliation or rejection. Although a child still imagines and experiences uncomfortable psychic repercussions, she cannot be assaulted or abandoned by a puppet (Bromfield 1995).

Puppetries (finger puppets, small puppets and marionettes) are common within Waldorf schools because they are a living play imbued with inner imagination and fantasy. Puppet shows draw the child into a story, watching it unfold step by step, grow and change, and these pictures are taken right into the stream of life forces, without creating hard and fixed impressions. The draw forth from children their imagination and allow the story to take them where they need to do as far as the inner life working pictures (Homeschoolers and Waldorf 2012). Waldorf School teachers tell stories gently and use puppets without facial expression while they are leading a story-telling instrument. In order to bring up children's imagination, they seldom express their own opinions toward the stories (Fig. 1).

Fig. 1. Use puppets without facial expression. (Source: Study of this research)

2.3 Stem + Art

STEAM is an interdisciplinary structure that combines science, technology, engineering, art, and mathematics to enable students to learn on the basis of mathematical logic, engineering and art. STEAM education, such as 3D printing, Arduino micro controllers, robots and other cool technology are loved by both boys and girls. It would be helpful for them to increase their interest in science and technology learning. Kylie Peppler (Peppler 2013) mentioned to broaden STEM participation in youth communities leverage e-textiles as an alternative approach to computing education. Recent findings indicate that introducing such novel, cross-disciplinary technologies can broaden participation, particularly woman. This STEAM (STEM + art) powered approach also improves learning outcomes and thus has ramifications that extend beyond the issue of gender in computing.

The contrary between LEGO bricks and robotics and Smart-Textiles crafting kits and fabrics are like "laborsaving" V.S. "entertainment". "Much of the foundational rhetoric concerning technology portrays it in terms of saving labor, avoiding presumed drudgery through automation, or making tasks easier and faster… Another common rhetorical theme is the view of technology as a source of entertainment or distraction… Both these rhetorical traditions in turn dictate specific themes for the study of interaction: the "laborsaving" tradition stresses themes such as rapid (and error free) use, ease of learning, and improved productivity, while the "entertainment" tradition stresses (again) ease of learning, holding the user's attention, comparative preferences between different entertainment technologies, and so forth." (Buechley et al. 2008).

How to adapt 'ART' in the Robot class is an important issue during the development of the soft robot. Fabrics easily absorb pigments that facilitate the creativity. In this study, we intergrade the digital embroidery technique that allows students to draw without worrying about their sewing and embroidery skill to get beautiful result to decorate their robots' outlook.

2.4   Gender + Icon

Any agent desiring to seamlessly operate in a social manner will need to incorporate this type of core human behavior. As in human interaction, myriad aspects of a humanoid robot's appearance and behavior can significantly alter its persuasiveness this work will focus on one particular factor: gender (Siegel 2009). The signs identifying public toilets are some of the most common images existing cross-culturally in the contemporary era. More often toilets signs represent users, differentiated into men and women, which I consider to be an iconic function (Ciochetto 2003) (Fig. 2).

Fig. 2.   Toilet sign. (Source: Depositphotos.com)

For the soft robot in the Girls' Robot Class, we redesign this toilet sign to represent the gender factor.

3   Process

Preliminary research trial tested by design department students showed us that Arduino programming was too difficult as they tend to get bogged down with syntactic mistakes which got into the way of them actually learning programming concepts. Therefore, we develop the modules into three different levels.

3.1   Course Contents

One of the biggest attractions of using robotics or wearable computing in educational computing is the tangible factor. Buechley argues that the use of physical materials in a learning task enhances absorption of concepts and knowledge more readily than if purely virtual objects are used. From experience, students derive a greater sense of reward and satisfaction when successfully constructing a physical object as compared to constructing a virtual one. (Ngai et al. 2010). Table 1 presents the syllabus of our girls' robot course, which consists of five levels, with one to two set tasks per level. The set tasks serve, as mini-checkpoints to make sure that the students have understood the course contents presented in that particular level. The learning outcomes of each level are also listed in the Table 2.

Table 2. Girls Robot course contents.

1st-level module: Make it into art	
Contents:	Apply artistic personality on the robot puppet
Tasks:	Drawing it face and make by digital embroidery sewing process
Learning outcomes:	Students should give his robot a look and design its own clothes
2nd-level module: Angel in the dark robot/electronic circuit theory	
Contents:	Electricity, electrical circuits and electrical resistance
Tasks:	Create simple circuite with LED yarns and light sensors
Learning outcomes:	Basic electrical knowledge: voltage, conductivity and resistance
3rd-level module: Yoga to the extreme robot/circuit design	
Contents:	Introduction to the circuit design, sensors and reactors
Tasks:	Create complex circuits with bending sensors and vibrators
Learning outcomes:	Students should be able to write a program that reads in signals from bending sensors and send simple signals to the output devices
4th-level module: Devil's advocate robot/programming	
Contents:	Incorporate a microcontroller onto the puppet and program a circuit consisting of voice sensors and speaker
Tasks:	Use a voice sensor, DFplayer mini
Learning outcomes:	Students should be able to record the voices, write a program that reads in signals from recorder and send signals to the speakers
5th-level module: Integration	
Contents:	Development of 3 modules
Tasks:	Create complex circuits reads in signals from voice sensor and bending sensors and sending signals to vibrators and speaker
Learning outcomes:	Students should write a program that reads in signals from bending sensors and recorder and send signals to the vibrators and speakers simultaneously

3.2 Digital Printing Prototype

To support this Girl's robot course, we also designed 3 modules of circuit layout specifically for learning program in one clothes version. This clothes version was provided to the students as teaching tools to construct circuits which support the teaching tool-kits of electronics devices and the instructions already. Stripes made of conductive wire provide the backbone for the circuit. The circuit diagrams used in electronic circuit theory were drawn. This allows the students not to worry about connective and conductive issues when constructing their circuits, and makes the learning and trial-error process quicker and more enjoyable (Table 3).

Table 3. One Robot with three interactive modules to express different behaviors: (1) Angel in the dark. (2) Yoga to the extreme. (3) Devil's Advocate.

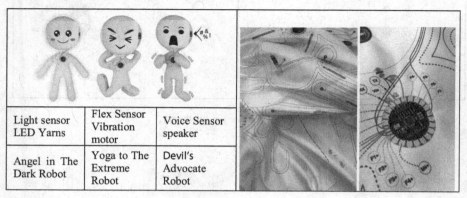

Light sensor LED Yarns	Flex Sensor Vibration motor	Voice Sensor speaker		
Angel in The Dark Robot	Yoga to The Extreme Robot	Devil's Advocate Robot		

This prototype design by the following requirements:

1. The use of electrical wires, plastic insulation, and solder are avoided or kept at a minimum.
2. To allow students to learn the basic fundamentals without having to be concerned about material imperfections (such as overly-high resistances), the performance of these materials would also need to be as close to their electrical equivalents as possible.
3. The interface would have to be usable to the beginner users without much skills in either sewing or soldering.
4. The graphic on the fabric should support active and hands-on learning and iterative construction and design.
5. It should encourage trial-and-error experiments among its users by allowing quick and iterative assembly of a diverse variety of electronic components, including different microprocessors.

3.3 Interactive Modules and Electronic Circuit Theory

The Lilypad Arduino (Doctorow 2010), is designed for wearable computing and e-textiles, being small and washable. We used the Lilypad as the "brain" of the soft robot, which provided a platform for the students to learn how to program the three different interactive robotics programs especially for beginner students (Fig. 3).

When we were making the prototype of soft robot, we felt that there needed to be easier way to attach input and output devices on the textiles and connect to the conductive wire. From the previous research, we have developed soft power switch (Chen 2014). Another suitable components of bending sensors, vibrators and speakers and microphone were re-designed for adapting on textiles. Working with this redesign devices and sensors gave students an opportunity of testing what would be possible

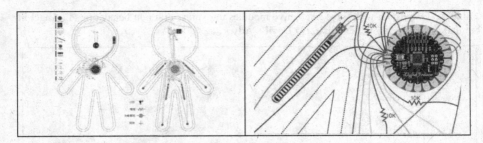

Fig. 3. Electronic circuit theory.

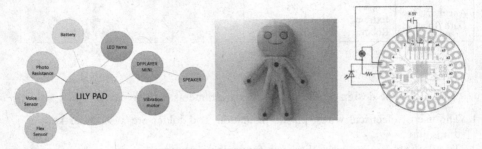

Fig. 4. Components and layout.

with the other options and also allowed them to experiment with logical problems that exercised and tested their grasp of concepts (Fig. 4).

This study found that youth who engaged in e-textile design demonstrated significant gains in their ability to diagram a working circuit, as well as significant gains in their understanding of current flow, polarity and connection (Peppler and Glosson 2013).

3.4 Digital Embroidery and Sewing Techniques

This process is about the artistic envisioning of material science. Students were asked to drawing or took a face photo to create their own robot look. The face of the robot was scanned and saved as .jpg file and applied in the software (Pre-Design for embroidery machine) that participants can digitize designs manually or use embroidery offset feature, which creates unique effect such as Auto-punch and Cross Stitch functions (Fig. 5).

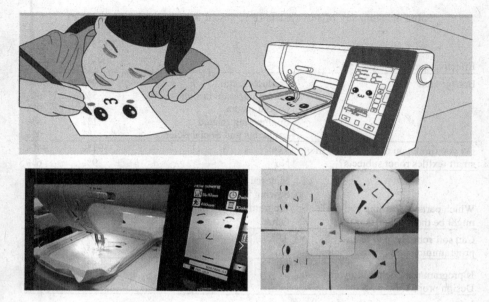

Fig. 5. The process of applying digital embroidery.

4 Evaluation

To evaluate whether our workshop and tool-kits design achieved our aims, we wants to investigate along three angles. First, we wanted to see whether this soft robot class was interesting and inspiring to both the boys and the girls. Second, we wanted to know whether the workshop had helped to simulate the student's imagination and to exercise their creativity. Third, we need to see whether they had indeed gained some knowledge about technological and programming concepts.

Our evaluations were performed using surveys and feedback from the students and instructors. To gauge the difference that the workshop created, we used both a pre-course and a post-course survey for the students. We also interviewed them as well as the instructors to get the students' feeling as to whether they were inspired by the course and how they felt about the level of difficulty of the tasks. The final project also afforded us the opportunity to see how well the workshop allowed the participants to exercise the creativity.

4.1 Surveys

The survey focuses on the interest subject of the students. Table 4 presents the survey questions. The soft robot prototype and the interaction module were presented by power point before the class. Although we had only budget for 30 participants to provide the research material (the soft robot prototype and the interactive devices), the other students are free to choose the material either with the soft robot or develop by

Table 4. Summary of survey data (F represent as Female; and M as Male)

		F123	M36
Effective questionnaires 159		77%	23%
Background	Product design	90%	86%
	Communication design	5%	6%
	Digital media	4%	0%
	Engineering related	1%	6%
	Language and Social Science	1%	0%
Do you think you are interested in smart textiles robot subjects?	Yes	91%	94%
	No	9%	6%
Which parts of learning you think might be the most difficult?	Material select	33%	22%
	Sewing Technique	18%	36%
	Program	75%	67%
	Other	1%	6%
Can soft robot help to learn programming and electronic circuit	Yes	86%	86%
	No	14%	14%
Is programming helpful to your Design project?	Yes	98%	94%
	No	2%	6%
Is learning outcome of Smart textiles robot course similar to other robot class, e.g. Lego?	Yes	86%	89%
	No	14%	11%

their own concept in this class. Finally, There are 159 respondents. Both boys and girls had high percentage interest in Smart-Textiles subjects before they applied to the workshop. However, when asked to evaluate their self-perceived programming knowledge, boys have 67% and girls have 75% feel that they did not know much about programming. It was not surprising to us that twice the number of girls showed more confidant in sewing techniques than boys, but the difficulty level are below 36%. Personal conversations further confirmed the fact that even thought the subject looks feminine, but because it is related to electronic and programming, they still feel that the subject is cool as shown in Table 4.

Table 5. Revised version of survey questionnaire (F represent as Female; and M as Male)

Effective questionnaires		F	M
1. What have learned from the course? (May have more than one answer)	(A) Design		
	(B) Circuit		
	(C) Programming		
	(D) Sewing technique		
	(E) Others		

(*continued*)

Table 5. (*continued*)

Effective questionnaires		F	M
2. Which parts of the course did you like the most?	(A) Make it into art		
	(B) Angle in the dark		
	(C) Yoga to the extreme		
	(D) Devil's advocate robot		
	(E) Integration		
3. Which parts of the course did you think is the most difficult to learn?	(A) Make it into art		
	(B) Angle in the dark		
	(C) Yoga to the extreme		
	(D) Devil's advocate robot		
	(E) Integration		
4. Which tasks of the process did you think is the most difficult to do?	(A) Drawing and embroidery		
	(B) Sewing the conductive wire		
	(C) Learning the circuit		
	(D) Learning the Arduino coding		
5. Do you think this course arouse your interests to learn science/computer Engineering?	(A) A lot		
	(B) A little		
	(C) Not at all		
5. Will you take science in the future because of your experience in this class?	(A) Certainly		
	(B) May be		
	(C) Make it into art		
6. Overall, how do you rate this course?	(A) Very good		
	(B) Good		
	(C) Neutral		
	(D) Bad		
	(E) Very bad		

5   Conclusions and Future Works

The Girls Robot Class is composed of three different workshops that took place in Ming Chuan University. From interviews with participants' opinions, we had gotten response that Level 1 (Angel in the dark) is possible for elementary students from grade

5–12, boys and girls. This is going to be the next stage of research experiment. Overall, The class has the following features:

1. Gender bending
2. Personals expression and aesthetically compelling possibilities.
3. Multidiscipline Learning

We designed another survey questionnaire as shown in Table 5 that is more specific to individual module. The factors to analyze students' works and instructors' feedback were studied as shown for the time being.

Acknowledgments. This article is based upon work supported by the National Science Council of Taiwan (MOST 105-2511-S-130-003-), awarded to the author.

References

Peppler, K., Glosson, D.: Stitching circuits: learning about circuitry through e-Textile materials. J. Sci. Educ. Technol. **22**, 751–763 (2013). Springer, Ed.

Bromfield, R.: The use of puppet in play therapy. Child Adolesc. Soc. Work J. **12**(6), 435–444 (1995)

Buchholz, B., Shively, K., Peppler, K., Wohlwend, K.: Hands on, hands off: gendered access in crafting and electronics practices. Mind Cult. Act. **21**, 278–297 (2014)

Buechley, L., Eisenberg, M., Catchen, J., Crockett, A.: The LilyPad Arduino: using computational textiles to investigate engagement, aesthetics, and diversity in computer science education. In: CHI 2008 Proceedings Aesthetics, Awareness, and Sketching, Florence, Italy, pp. 423–432 (2008)

Buechley, L., Hill, B.M.: LilyPad in the wild: how hardware's long tail is supporting new engineering and design communities. In: Proceedings of the Conference on Designing Interactive Systems, pp. 199–207. ACM Press, New York (2010)

Chen, A.C.: Designing for the daily-life applications with functional textiles. In: IASDR 2013 Proceeding (2012)

Chen, A.C.-Y.: Using smart textiles in customized product design children's drawings as example. In: Stephanidis, Constantine (ed.) HCI 2014. CCIS, vol. 434, pp. 79–84. Springer, Cham (2014). doi:10.1007/978-3-319-07857-1_14

Ciochetto, L.: Toilet signage as effective communication. Visible Lang. Spec. Issue Cult. Dimensions Commun. Des. **3**, 208–221 (2003)

Dadi, H.H.: Literature overview of smart textiles. Master thesis, University of Boras, Swedish School of Textiles (2010)

Doctorow, C.: LilyPad microcontroller's success in welcoming women to electronics (2010). Boing Boing. http://boingboing.net/2010/10/04/lilypad-microcontrol.html

Waldorf Homeschoolers: Puppetry and Story (2012). Waldorf Homeschoolers. http://www.waldorfhomeschoolers.com/puppetry

Van Langenhove, L., Hertleer, C.: Smart clothing: a new life. Int. J. Clothing Sci. Technol. **16**(1/2), 63–72 (2004)

Ngai, G., Chan, S.C., Cheung, J.C.Y., Lau, W.W.Y.: Deploying a wearable computing platform for computing education. IEEE Trans. Learn. Technol. **3**(1), 45–55 (2010)

Peppler, K.A.: STEAM-powered computing education: using e-Textiles to integrate the arts and STEM. Computer **46**, 38–43 (2013)

Siegel, M.C.: Persuasive robotics: the influence of robot gender on human behavior. In: Intelligent Robots and Systems, IEEE/RSJ International Conference (2009)

TTRI.: 2011 Annual Report_Substainable innovation: dream com true. Taiwan Textile Research Institute, Taipei (2011)

Lau, W.W.Y., Ngai, G.: Learning programming through fashion and design: a pilot summer course in wearable computing for middle school students. In: SIGCSE 2009 Proceedings of the 40th ACM Technical Symposium on Computer Science Education, pp. 504–508. ACM (2009)

A Model for Collaboration in Virtual Worlds Bringing Together Cultures in Conflict

Elaine Hoter[1,2(✉)]

[1] Talpiot College of Education, Holon, Israel
elaine@talpiot.ac.il
[2] The Mofet Institute, Tel Aviv, Israel

Abstract. This paper puts forward a pedagogical model and design for using virtual worlds to not just connect people from different cultures, but to be a center for collaboration. It demonstrates how virtual worlds have been incorporated in a nationwide project to connect between Moslem, Druze, Christian and Jewish children in Israel and follows the development of the pedagogical model through the stages of collaborative learning. The stages move from learning about one another and carrying out joint assignments through a social network to meeting in virtual worlds and designing the interior of a joint home and "living" there throughout the year.

Keywords: Virtual worlds · Collaboration · TEC Model · Opensim

1 Introduction

Collaboration is a basic skill in our society but the concept is easier said than done. Collaborative learning has been around for the last 60 years and since the 1990s collaborative online learning has been used to bring together people from different parts of the globe. Virtual online worlds are not a new phenomenon, Second Life, the most popular 3D virtual world, started in 2003. This world is open to and free for adults and has been used successfully for various online learning and collaborative ventures. However, by 2007 the idea of an open simulator began and in the last few years numerous private worlds have been made using the Opensim for educational purposes. These environments can be protected for the learners and allow the young learner to participate as well as forming a closed and safe environment for students.

These worlds allow participants from different locations to meet through their avatars and interact through voice, gestures and text. Can this environment be used not just to bring together students from diverse cultural background and even cultures in conflict but to be a place where the participants learn to collaborate, respect and understand one another?

© Springer International Publishing AG 2017
P. Zaphiris and A. Ioannou (Eds.): LCT 2017, Part II, LNCS 10296, pp. 148–157, 2017.
DOI: 10.1007/978-3-319-58515-4_12

2 Related Work

2.1 Types of Virtual Worlds

Virtual worlds come under the area of virtual reality. They are 3 dimensional worlds where the participant as an avatar feels they are part of the world. The participants can interact via voice and text as well as being able to add specific gestures. These worlds are realized in various forms or combinations. We need to distinguish between Gaming Virtual Worlds (GVWs) which are 3D environments which normally involve clearly defined quests, for example Mindcraft, and Social Virtual worlds (SVWs) where the stress is on engaging in social interaction (Vrellis et al. 2016). A recent example of a very accessible SVW Virtual world is Edorble. Here there are premade college campuses where Avatars can meet socially and also watch live presentations together. Each teacher receives their own campus which allows for blended and online learning between the students.

Open source virtual worlds (OSVWs) have an open-ended technological infrastructure and can be in different server modes (networked or standalone). In these worlds users interact and can, if permitted by the owner, create their own virtual environment (grids). In this case users can be involved alone or with others in co-creating or coordinating their activities, using programming scripting languages "open" to all users without financial cost for constructing a virtual environment. Two of the most well-known open source virtual worlds are Open Simulator (or Open Sim) and Open Wonderland.

Another category of virtual worlds are Collaborative virtual learning worlds (CVLWs): CVLWs are used in the educational world for blended (mixed online and face to face courses) or online instructional formats. Students, who are separated spatially or temporally, can work as teams and this can be done through co-existing in a common virtual environment and by interacting through synchronous communication tools. Examples of CVLWs are Active Worlds, Quest Atlantis, Multiverse and Aeroquest (Pellas et al. 2016).

Pellas et al. (2016) in their extensive review and assessment of the use of virtual worlds in the teaching of STEM present the results of various studies that show the positive impact of working in Virtual Worlds on students' learning outcomes including knowledge transfer, higher-order thinking, problem solving and social skills. They also show a large improvement in student engagement referred to as the affective learning experience.

Liou (2012) explored EFL college students' attitudes toward a computer-assisted language learning course conducted in SL. (Second Life), the research pointed to advantages of Virtual Worlds for language competence and collaboration. Overall, the students perceived SL as an optimal virtual environment for language learning due to its features, such as immersive collaboration and real-world task simulations in 3D mode. The 3D environment also facilitated real-world task delivery, which is difficult to manage in a conventional class and promoted authentic interaction. Liou also argued that an ecological language learning system should be implemented by using pedagogically sound, sense-making tasks instead of relying on the novelty value of technology alone.

Peterson in his numerous studies on using text chats for interactive sessions (Peterson 2006, 2012) using Active Worlds and SL shows that the EFL students saw their SL learning experience as beneficial, more enjoyable, and less stressful than a traditional class. Peterson's findings show that the EFL students were engaged in collaborative interaction and also used different social management strategies to their interactions. He also showed that the avatar presence improved student engagement and sense of autonomy.

The reticence to use virtual worlds to improve language skills and collaboration in the classroom is not just because of issues of technophobia for some of the teachers, but based on real technical issues. These include technical requirements to use virtual worlds which do not exist in many schools (bandwidth, compatible graphic cards etc.) The system often crashes and there is still an issue of platform stability. Users also need to invest time to master the skills required to work in a virtual world (Dawley and Dede 2014; Liou 2012). Taking into account these drawbacks, Cooke-Plagwitz (2008) argue that there is great potential for integrating SL to promote authentic target language learning simulating real-world language immersion when the use of SL is planned and constructed within the language curricula (Chen 2016).

3   Intercultural Literacy

When students from different cultures meet, the issue of intercultural literacy needs to be addressed. Hasler (2011) uses Heyward's Model of Intercultural Literacy (2002) together with the Cultural Historical Activity Theory and claims that Intercultural learning environments need to be designed so that students from different cultures will be able to participate equally. the students need to be aware of their own culture and of other foreign cultures so as to increase their understanding, develop their competencies, to increase their language proficiencies, and ultimately to form transcultural or global identities. Hasler's research using SL shows that although the cross-cultural exchanges in SL do not guarantee intercultural literacy, they provide participants with opportunities to move in that direction.

4   Collaboration in Virtual Worlds

Firstly it should be noticed that there is a great difference between presence and collaboration in a virtual world. Working together is not necessarily collaboration. Many practitioners and researchers have concluded that totally free, unguided or unstructured collaboration does not necessarily result in productive activity or learning (Kreijns et al. 2003). Some see the establishment of rules to be an important feature to support cooperation (Owens et al. 2009). Slavin took the skills for collaboration together with Allport's contact theory to show how cooperation can be used to bring diverse cultural groups together in a face to face situation. (Slavin 1985; Allport 1954)

According to the contact hypothesis, competition is destructive in trying to reduce bias between groups in conflict (Allport 1954), but most of the existing virtual worlds tend to be individualistic or competitive in nature.

The wealth of research and practice in Collaborative Learning (CL) over the past 60 years allows us to confidently claim that all students benefit from learning this way. Yet the effect of CL is not automatic. As we all know, in any context just placing students in groups does not guarantee that they will work smoothly together; all the more so when there is a potential gap between teachers; and students' expectations and behaviors in the classroom (Sharan 2010).

According to Boris and Tsiatsos (2006) a collaborative learning environment is an environment in which:

- The users participating have different roles and privileges.
- The educational interactions in the environment transform the simple virtual space into a communication space.
- The information in the environment is represented in multiple ways that can vary from simple text to three dimensional (3D) graphics.
- Students are not passive users but can interact with each other and with the virtual environment.
- The system that supports the environment integrates multiple technologies.
- The possibility of implementing multiple learning scenarios is supported.
- Recognizable elements from the real world are visualized.

Sociable computer-supported collaborative learning (CSCL) environments emphasize the social (emotional) aspects of group learning. Kreijns et al. (2007) define sociability as the extent to which a CSCL environment is seen to facilitate a social space with attributes as trust and belonging, and where there is a strong sense of community, and good working relationships.

If we combine this with the "Big Five" components for teamwork (Salas et al. 2005) which are:

1. Team Leadership: Ability to direct and coordinate the activities of other team members, assess team performance, assign tasks, develop team knowledge, skills, and abilities, motivate team members, plan and organize, and establish a positive atmosphere.
2. Mutual performance monitoring: The ability to develop common understandings of the team environment and apply appropriate task strategies to accurately monitor teammate performance.
3. Backup behavior: Ability to anticipate other team members' needs through acc-rate knowledge about their responsibilities. This includes the ability to shift workload among members to achieve balance during high periods of workload or pressure.

4. Adaptability: Ability to adjust strategies based on information gathered from the environment through the use of backup behavior and reallocation of intra-team resources. Altering a course of action or team repertoire in response to changing conditions (internal or external).

5. Team orientation: Propensity to take other's behavior into account during group interaction and the belief in the importance of team goals over individual members' goals.

Together we have the requirements to be able to build collaborative activities in a virtual world and the criteria for making this effective.

4.1 The "Six Learnings" Framework

Lim (2009) suggested a six stage model for working in virtual worlds with children. He termed it six learnings where the stages are not necessarily hierarchical or mutually exclusive, but presents the range of pedagogies that can be used while using the island as a learning experience. He recommends that interventions should target one or two of these "learnings".

- Learning by exploring within the virtual island
- Learning by collaborating with others on different tasks;
- Learning by being through understanding self and role-playing
- Learning by building through designing and building on the island
- Learning by championing; By this Lim means to "adopt, champion, and evangelize causes from Real Life" (p. 8)
- Learning by expressing this would include explaining to the "outside world" what is going on in the world using different forms of media and genres.

5 The TEC Model

The TEC (Technology, Education and cultural Diversity) model was created to form a framework for small group collaborative online learning between students from different cultures (Hoter et al. 2009, 2012). The model suggests a way for students from different cultures and religions, often in conflict, to work together online. The model has been explained in depth elsewhere, suffice it to say here that the model moves from a low level of collaboration to higher levels, from low technology use, to high technology use and from written text to hearing to verbally communicating online to real face to face meetings. The idea is to first get to know the person before meeting face to face to lessen bias and prejudice.

5.1   Project Design

One of the programs designed and implemented by the TEC Center is TEC4Schools. The pupils, grades five to nine, taking part in the TEC4schools program, study with students from 2 other schools where the pupils come from different cultures. They study in small groups of six, two from each class and culture. They have a weekly hour throughout the year in their school timetable to work together on collaborative tasks moving gradually from peer work, to eventually synergetic collaboration.

About 3000 children from 100 schools take part each year in the program. Results and feedback from this year of collaboration show the students improve their inter-cultural competencies. However, the most prevalent complaint about the year is that it finishes and the pupils want to continue studying together.

This year we opened a pilot program for 12 schools where students could continue collaborating together for an additional year. These students are technically competent after a year of online collaborative learning which integrated many new technologies. At this stage our aim is to move the students to a higher level of collaboration and intercultural understanding. How can we get the pupils to really collaborate together in this second year?

5.2   The Process

According to the TEC Model students gradually get to know one another through tasks demanding more collaboration. The environment chosen for this is a social network developed specifically for the population in three languages. This allows the pupils to work in small groups. Initial communication is intentionally text based so the students do not know how the others look (just seeing clothes, hijab, skull caps etc. cause bias before they have even met). The problems we have previously faced using the social network was the difficulty to create a sense of belonging to the small group and develop inter dependence within the small group. We also had difficulties planning meetings between the groups.

With all the advantages for using virtual worlds to enhance collaboration and intercultural competence we built a social virtual world (SVW) called TEC Island as a meeting place to understand other cultures.

The TEC island includes 4 places of worship, a Mosque, a Synagogue, a Church and a Hilwah (place of worship for the Druze religion). The Island is a place for the children and students to meet virtually and carry out joint assignments. The Island has a storytelling corner, a "dabuka" drum circle, a place to learn languages, Hebrew, Arabic and English as well as games about festivals connected to the other religions.

As creative and fun this world might be, there were a number of drawbacks. Not enough teachers used the world and aside from technical considerations we realized that many of the teachers, despite in-service training, were not confident themselves in using the island. To overcome these issues we made a training Island for everyone as a precondition to being on the TEC Island where the participants need to go through 14 stations and then they earn their wings and can proceed to the TEC Island.

Hillwah-Druze place of worship

Interactive board about faces of Jerusalem

Inside of the synagogue

Interactive maze about Christianity

The Ramadan interactive area

A drum circle

Role playing in the market

We tried to make collaborative activities in the Island for example in the virtual Jerusalem area you can add a prayer for Jerusalem onto a balloon and only when three different people write a prayer do the balloons lift off. We also have role playing activities for buying fruit. However, it was almost impossible for the children from the three classes to have their class at the same time and be able to meet online together. Last year they only managed to have one class together. Most of the activities, unless set specifically by the teachers, are individualized experience and children don't want to keep going there unless there they have new activities. As Kreijns et al. (2007) said, we needed a social space where there is feeling of trust and belonging, and where there is a strong sense of community, and good working relationships. This takes time to build and can't be done through a one hour session. We need to build a place where the pupils feel they really belong and where they will want to continually return.

Principals, teachers and students wanted to continue in the TEC project for an additional year. In this year we hoped to reach synergetic group collaboration. In order to do this we realized that we needed to build an Island that would belong to the children. As explained above there are islands where the participants can jointly build the Island, but this is specialized work belonging to a different course on building virtual worlds with different pedagogical aims. Not everyone likes to build and we can't make an Island just for the techno-minded students. As in life, some people like to buy things, they prefer ready-made items and not DIY! We wanted the students to work truly collaboratively and learn from one another.

The solution we can up with was to combine building and shopping. We built a new virtual world for the continuing pupils. The world is divided into areas, each area for a different cluster of schools (three classes work together). Each area consists of residential areas with beautiful modern houses. The small group of six pupils (two from each class) get an empty house with the number of their small group on the door. They get to live in their house throughout the year and design the interior of their home. Many items they can get from the various shops on the Island and some they can learn to build. The world is designed so that each student can only build within their own house and garden.

The project has only just begun and by the time of the conference we will be able to report back how the students managed to collaborate living together in a virtual home. We hope that the world and activities will encourage the students to join from home and feel this is a home away from home. This is surely the highest level of collaboration which comes the closest to actually living together.

References

Allport, G.: The Nature of Prejudice. Addison-Wesley, Cambridge (1954)

Bouras, C., Tsiatsos, T.: Educational virtual environments: design rationale and architecture (MTAP). Int. J. Multimedia Tools Appl. **29**, 153–173 (2006)

Chen, J.C.: The crossroads of English language learners, task-based instruction, and 3D multi-user virtual learning in Second Life. Comput. Educ. **102**, 152–171 (2016)

Cooke-Plagwitz, J.: New directions in CALL: an objective introduction to second life. CALICO J. **25**(3), 547–557 (2008). Cooke-Plagwitz

Dawley, L., Dede, C.: Situated learning in virtual worlds and immersive simulations. In: Spector, J.M., Merrill, M.D., Elen, J., Bishop, M.J. (eds.) The Handbook of Research for Educational Communications and Technology, pp. 723–734. Springer, New York (2014)

Hasler, B.S.: Intercultural collaborative learning in virtual worlds. Cutting-Edge Technol. High. Educ. **4**, 265–304 (2011)

Heyward, M.: From international to intercultural: redefining the international school for a globalized world. J. Res. Int. Educ. **1**, 9–32 (2002)

Hoter, E., Shonfeld, M., Ganayim, A.: Information and communication technology (ICT) in the service of multiculturalism. Int. Rev. Res. Open Distrib. Learn. **10**(2) (2009). http://dx.doi.org/10.19173/irrodl.v10i2.601

Hoter, E., Shonfeld, M., Ganayem, A.N.: TEC center: linking technology, education and cultural diversity. I-manager's J. Educ. Technol. **9**(1), 15 (2012)

Kreijns, K., Kirschner, P.A., Jochems, W.: Identifying the pitfalls of social interaction in computer-supported collaborative learning environments: a review of the research. Comput. Hum. Behav. **19**(3), 335–353 (2003)

Kreijns, K., Kirschner, P.A., Jochems, W., Van Buuren, H.: Measuring perceived sociability of computer-supported collaborative learning environments. Comput. Educ. **49**(2), 176–192 (2007)

Lim, K.Y.: The six learnings of second life. J. Virtual Worlds Res. **2**(1), 3–11 (2009)

Liou, H.C.: The roles of Second Life in a college computer assisted language learning (CALL) course in Taiwan, ROC. Comput. Assist. Lang. Learn. **25**(4), 365–382 (2012)

Owens, D., Davies, A., Murphy, J., Khazanchi, D., Zigurs, I.: Real-World. pp. 34–41. IT Pro, IEEE (2009)

Peterson, M.: Learner interaction management in an avatar and chat-based virtual world. Comput. Assist. Lang. Learn. **19**(1), 79–103 (2006)

Peterson, M.: EFL learner collaborative interaction in Second Life. ReCALL **24**(01), 20–39 (2012)

Salas, E., Sims, D.E., Burke, C.S.: Is there a "big five" in teamwork? Small Group Res. **36**(5), 555–599 (2005)

Sharan, Y.: Cooperative learning for academic and social gains: valued pedagogy, problematic practice. Eur. J. Educ. **45**, 300–313 (2010)

Slavin, R.E.: Cooperative learning: applying contact theory in desegregated schools. J. Soc. Issues **41**(3), 45–62 (1985)

Vrellis, I., Avouris, N., Mikropoulos, T.A.: Learning outcome, presence and satisfaction from a science activity in Second Life. Australas. J. Educ. Technol. **32**(1), 59–77 (2016)

Different Students – Different Ways: Challenges of Integrating Non-traditional Students in Higher Education and How Electronic Learning Can Support Inclusion

Verena Jahn[✉], Linda Heise, André Schneider, and Susanne Günther

Mittweida University of Applied Sciences, Mittweida, Germany
{verena.jahn,linda.heise,andre.schneider,
susanne.guenther}@hs-mittweida.de

Abstract. The inclusion of non-traditional learners is an important challenge of higher education institutions. The paper presents a research project of Mittweida University of Applied Science Mittweida which investigated the special needs and challenges of two non-traditional student groups, student top athletes and part-time students with professional background. The paper will first present the results of a qualitative study with student top-athletes and students with professional background in order to analyze the conditions and challenges of their study programs and additional commitments. Non-traditional students were asked about their learning requirements and resulting challenges as well as their media literacy and attitude towards electronic learning. Organizational, social and didactic challenges were identified. Based on the results a blended learning design – the flipped classroom approach – is introduced. This approach has been implemented and tested within the framework of a class in scientific writing. Evaluation results show evidence that the developed approach met the needs of non-traditional students and supported inclusion.

Keywords: Higher education · Inclusion · Non-traditional students · Blended learning · Flipped classroom · Qualitative study

1 Introduction

The inclusion of non-traditional students' organizational, emotional and academic needs into higher education structures has proven to be comparatively difficult. Successful academic development requires guidance, counselling and time. Non-traditional students demand clear communication of expectations, study contents as well as learning methods and individual learning commitments.

According to Wang [18] "participation in postsecondary education represents one of the most viable pathways to economic and social success" (p. 301). Attending a higher education institution seems to be a beneficial as well as logical step for high school graduates. The number of students pursuing a postsecondary degree coming from different professional backgrounds has also steadily increased throughout the past [19]. Thus, The growing numbers of individuals entering higher education result in a

© Springer International Publishing AG 2017
P. Zaphiris and A. Ioannou (Eds.): LCT 2017, Part II, LNCS 10296, pp. 158–169, 2017.
DOI: 10.1007/978-3-319-58515-4_13

diverse learning environment characterized by diverse student learners, different levels of knowledge and different expectations of teaching and learning [2].

Having a closer look on the inclusion of non-traditional students into higher education as their new habitat seems reasonable since studies have shown, that students who do not succeed in enculturating to their study environment have a higher risk of dropping out than students who successfully master the integration process [5]. Student top-athletes (as one group of non-traditional learners) seem especially vulnerable to the challenges resulting from the constant balancing of two different 'worlds' – sports and academics.

College sports have been an essential part of Mittweida University's campus life for many years. Integrating sports' infrastructure, mass participation events and physical education classes into organizational structures and practices has been a pillar of campus diversity and has also become a vital part of students' social interactions.

However, the inclusion of top-athletes' organizational needs into educational curricula has proven to be comparatively difficult. Challenges for both parties – athlete-students and teachers – are obvious. Student-Athletes have to balance demanding training routines, time-consuming out-of-class activities (e.g. tournaments, world cups) on the one hand, educational requirements, inflexible schedules and exams on the other hand. University teachers are bound within an academic framework of course work, teaching and research productivity as well as external pedagogic target evaluations. Any kind of additional academic need is regarded as labor and time intensive, thus difficult to implement.

The discourse emerging from research on the inclusion of top-athletes into academic curricula, in particular, and non-traditional students, in general, seems to neglect such educational realities. Therefore, Mittweida University started a research project ("Promoting dual carriers of elite sport students through new teaching and learning cultures") that aims at presenting how educational needs of non-traditional students can be met. It outlines how Mittweida University effectively pursues and incorporates online teaching and electronic learning methods within the framework concept of Sustainability Education fostering academic success.

2   Empirical Study

The main research objective of the project was to analyze special needs and specific challenges of student top-athletes as one group of part-time students. The aim of the present study was to investigate the special circumstances such non-traditional students face while pursuing a dual career, managing their time between curricular and extra-curricular activities. The study aimed at creating innovative and integrative approaches acknowledging the special needs of non-traditional students.

The project followed four principles: After a basic analysis, we conceptualized a suitable learning scenario which correlated the students' needs. In a third step the learning scenario was tested and evaluated. From the evaluation results we derived didactical guidelines on how to include and foster non-traditional students. Electronic learning proofed to be a teaching and learning instrument that was accepted by all actors involved – teachers and students as well as higher education administration. The research project consisted of four main steps (see Fig. 1).

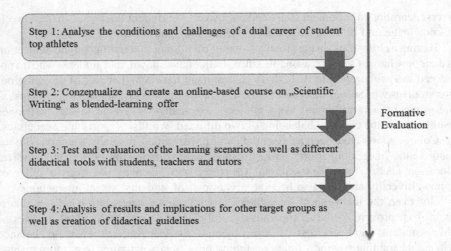

Fig. 1. 4-Step-Model of the research project

The integration of digital learning arrangements incorporates various teaching and learning methods, innovative learning environments as well as manifold learning locations. The consideration of many different key aspects that influence learning outcomes and their integration into didactic concepts and organizational processes eventually results in a higher rate of academic success of non-traditional students [8]. Due to the diversity of higher education institutions, the diversity of student and faculty bodies as well as the diversity of learning and teaching techniques, there can only be suggestions – a tool kit of instruments – that might improve certain aspects of higher education. The present study focuses on student top-athletes and their learning needs.

2.1   Research Design

In order to effectively address the complex aspects of learning needs of non-traditional students a cross-sectional research design has been chosen. The data collection has been based on qualitative research methods: the analysis of literature and existing studies as well as semi-structured interviews with student top-athletes. In order to compare the learning needs of that particular group of non-traditional students, a second group of students has been included as a case study: part-time students with a professional background. Research goals included the following scientific objectives: the identification of non-traditional students' learning expectations and needs as well as their learning and teaching preferences.

The faculty's expectations in teaching success and learning outcomes have to be taken into consideration as well since they are part of the framework requirements that influence students' academic success. We considered the following aspects as pre-conditions for the successful inclusion of non-traditional students:

(1) Students' personalities, expectations as well as experiences are considered as meaningful, thus chance for university didactic. Teachers ought to be sensitive in that regard.
(2) Diverse study groups with diverse learning and teaching knowledge require flexible curricular, e.g. learning environments, teaching methods or exam options.
(3) Flexible learning and teaching designs require transparency of expectations and their assessment.
(4) Flexible learning and teaching designs require guidance and time.

These aspects were not mentioned during the conducted interviews but served as key elements within the process of the data analysis. The interviewers focused on questions regarding study conditions and challenges, learning requirements and individual learning habits as well as individual preferences.

A rather small sample of 18 students was interviewed, however only 1% of Mittweida University's students are top-athletes. The same number of part-time students was interviewed and served as comparison group. All interviewees are currently enrolled in different study programs at Mittweida University and represent different levels of study – beginning students as well as advanced students, bachelor and master students.

The semi-structured design of the interview questions provided the necessary comparability of results [15]. The interview approach proved to have many advantages. It allowed the gathering of various general themes touching academic experiences of non-traditional students in general, and individual learning needs and preferences on particular.

The data analysis linked the advantages of quantitative content analysis (by using MAXQDA for creating thematic categories) with the qualitative-interpretative approaches of data analysis. The undertaken content analysis led to four main categories that influence academic success and learning outcomes of non-traditional students.

2.2 Results and Implications

The first subject area that could be drawn from the interviews focused on organizational challenges. 95% of all interviewed non-traditional students mentioned a lack of time for their academic obligations. Whereas student top-athletes particularly mentioned the constant struggle of balancing training, study and travelling schedules, part-time students with a professional background more often mentioned social commitments (childcare, daily routine, volunteering) as challenges to be considered next to their professional and academic obligations.

To meet the organizational needs of non-traditional students carefully structured timetables and exam schedules need to be created which should apply for the whole student body. That way, top-athletes and part-time students can take part in regular in-class activities and they can socially bond with their fellow classmates. In addition, regular students might benefit from the time management skills and high learning engagement of non-traditional students. However, the inclusion of part-time students into academic and student life has so far be proven to be easier than the integration of student top-athletes. Especially the frequent absence from university in either summer or winter semesters – depending on the sports seasonal requirements – makes it challenging to follow regular study programs. That problem is closely linked to the second subject area that included social challenges non-traditional students face in the higher education system. The lack of communication to fellow students and faculty leads to a lack of information regarding curricular as well as extracurricular activities. The interviewed student top-athletes consistently mentioned integration programs from and with fellow students as instrument in order to foster their different 'worlds of obligations'. Part-time students more often mentioned the promotion of benefits that learning within diverse study groups comprises of. The support of faculty members and individual mentoring opportunities was considered of utmost importance by both non-traditional study groups.

The third and fourth subject area focused on learning requirements from a general as well as a student perspective. The lack of flexible learning options was mentioned by all interviewed students. The curricular requirements in regard of exam dates and exam methods often times cause problems. The lack of teachers' support is also considered a major hurdle for individual learning progress. There have been two different ways of assessment. The larger group of interviewees considered the lack of support by the faculty as challenge, whereas the other group considered the special attention of teachers (especially during class) a challenge which – on the one hand, fostered their learning success – but on the other hand hindered their integration into the class and the communication with fellow students.

The lack of innovative learning methods that would enhance continuous learning processes for non-traditional students was mentioned repeatedly in all interviews. Whereas in-class learning is often accompanied by an information overload, self-learning opportunities are too scarce. The inability or missing awareness of teachers to adapt their teaching content for electronic methods was considered an aspect of frustration, especially within the group of student top-athletes.

The fourth subject area focuses on such challenges. The lack of technical support for electronic learning, the low level of instruction and feedback by teachers as well as the electronic requirements (web access, mobile access options) that are often times unrealizable when absent from university. These aspects were diversified discussed and raised a higher awareness among the group of student top-athletes who face the technical problems on training and competition sites more often than part-time students. However, part-time students more often mentioned the lack of instruction and self-assessment opportunities in order to follow individual learning progress.

Electronic learning instruments were considered the most effective tool in order to enhance individual learning opportunities. One interviewee mentioned that "for athletes there is nothing better than that. When I cannot attend regular lectures, it would be great to have videos of the lectures that I can watch when I have time. I could watch a lecture that was held in the morning in the evening after my training session. There are hardly any better solutions for athletes than that." A part-time student mentioned that it would be helpful to revise the online materials again in class: "When you prepare yourself with the learning material that is available for the course and you read everything and then you attend the lecture afterwards and discuss the learning content and ask questions. That is the best case."

The following table provides an overview of the topic areas and the related variables (see Table 1) that were mentioned by the non-traditional students.

Table 2 includes possible didactic solutions for the challenges presented before. Based on the data assessment, a blended learning scenario for non-traditional students was designed and tested by a group of non-traditional students including athletes and part-time students with professional backgrounds. The didactic chances and challenges will be elaborated on within the next chapter.

2.3   Conceptual Design of Learning Scenario

Blended Learning is a promising approach to learning and is widely recognized in educational psychology and constructive didactics. There is evidence that this learning format has positive impact on learning outcome and dropout rates as well as learning perception in general [3, 13, 14]. It can be described as thoughtful fusion of face-to-face and electronic (online) learning which combines the strengths of each learning scenario [12]. Learners do not feel isolated in an e-learning only setting but are more flexible when and where to learn. Other advantages are the individual learning pace and revision possibilities. Indeed, it is a high potential approach to support meaningful learning, especially for non-traditional students because it provides flexibility of place and time [7] – important requirements for both part-time students with a professional background and student top athletes.

However, there is a very wide range of design possibilities because there are no further limitations how to set a blended learning arrangement. There are several distinct models like the rotation model or the flex model that are well known in education and didactics [6] but the design varies despite the same underlying approach. Neither the order of the different phases nor the design with regard to content is specified. Thus, every instructional designer and teacher needs to decide how to arrange the parts [4]. The course can either start with an on-site meeting for community building reasons or the learning scenario can present the main theoretical information online followed by a traditional face-to-face meeting (see Fig. 2). Determining factors for this complex decision are for example subject of course, target group specifications and didactical approach. Therefore, blended leaning does not only change learning, it also influences teaching and organizational issues in (higher) educational institutions [10].

The described combination of traditional and online learning forms can particularly combine the advantages of both settings and compensate their drawbacks. Nevertheless, the course procedures of the hybrid scenario and the methods and approaches used in the different phases have to be taken into consideration as well.

A special content structure can be provided by the flipped classroom model. The flipped classroom model originates from traditional classroom settings in which the teacher lectures on basic information, theories and models during class time. Students primarily listen to the teacher and write down important information. At the end of the lecture students get homework to be done after the class and often by themselves [16]. In this common scenario, the teacher plays an active part, the students are more passive.

Table 1. Learning challenges of non-traditional students

Organizational challenges	Lack of time to attend classes and exams ◇ Due to overlapping training schedules ◇ Due to training camps and competitions ◇ Due to inflexibility of academic and training schedules
	Lack of time to participate in academic and student life ◇ Due to overlapping training schedules ◇ Due to training camps and competitions ◇ Due to commitments in sports related activities (representation, promotion of young talents) ◇ Due to commitments in social life (family, volunteering)
Social challenges	Lack of integration into student groups ◇ Due to times of absence ◇ Due to different approaches towards learning ◇ Due to special attendance from university teachers ◇ Due to missing attendance from university teachers
	Lack of communication within study groups ◇ Due to times of absence ◇ Due to missing contacting possibilities ◇ Due to lack of information (e.g. scheduled meetings)
Didactic challenges (student's perspective)	Lack of basic knowledge as prerequisite for study success ◇ Due to absence in classes, especially opening sessions ◇ Due to missing self-study materials ◇ Due to missing support by teachers and fellow students
	Lack of continuous learning processes ◇ Due to constant shift between academic and training commitments ◇ Due to information overload while attending classes/compact courses ◇ Due to lack of self-learning opportunities during times of absence (no lecture recordings, no online learning materials) ◇ Due to lack of test options to assess level of learning progress
Didactic challenges (framework requirements)	Lack of flexible learning options ◇ Due to administrative and curricular requirements (e.g. schedules, exam methods)
	Lack of technical support ◇ Due to learning content that is not applicable to mobile devices ◇ File size of learning materials requires premium mobile access options ◇ Electronic learning requires web access (not necessarily required in training camps or competition sites)
	Lack of didactic support ◇ Low level of instruction and feedback by teachers ◇ Lack of learning content that is adapted to online learning instruments

Table 2. Didactic approaches for non-traditional students

Methods of organizational resolution	➤ Creation of flexible curricular ➤ Promotion of flexible learning and exam schedules ➤ Promotion of innovative learning instruments (e.g. electronic learning)
Methods of social resolution	➤ Inclusion of non-traditional students through support programs (e.g. buddy programs) ➤ Promotion of communication opportunities through learning management systems ➤ Promoting benefits of learning within diverse study groups ➤ Raising awareness for challenges non-traditional students face ➤ Promotion of (virtual) team work on- and off-campus
Methods of didactic resolution (student's perspective)	➤ Creation of flexible learning frameworks ➤ Creation of flexible exam frameworks ➤ Creation and enhancement of self-learning opportunities ➤ Support by teachers and administration through lecture recordings and accompanying instructions as well as feedback ➤ Creation of micro learning units in order to promote continuous learning opportunities as well as slow-learning sessions
Methods of didactic resolution (framework requirements)	➤ Adaption of learning content to different technical requirements ➤ Download option to learn offline if necessary ➤ Reducing file size of learning content ➤ Promotion of clear instructional design in order to enhance handling of learning content ➤ Promotion of clear instructional design in order to enhance learning ➤ Promotion of flexible learning approaches ➤ Promotion of online consultations and self-assessment options

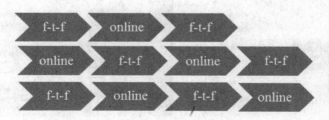

Fig. 2. Blended learning scenarios: different ways to scaffold the course

In order to increase learning outcomes, teachers shall rather promote active learning in class rather than simply transmitting information to students [11]. Flipped classroom inverts this traditional setting by delivering all basic information before and outside of the classroom. The valuable class time is only used for discussion, practice and other learning activities. These learning activities involve the application of the acquired information as well as interactive and collaborative parts in order to support the engagement of students. It is an important prerequisite for meaningful learning processes like elaboration, transfer and knowledge construction.

Furthermore, it is assumed that flipped classroom arrangements can foster learning by increasing intrinsic and extrinsic motivation and enhance the management of cognitive workloads [1]. However, there is still little empirical evidence of these assumptions and more research has to be done [1, 9]. Nonetheless, it seems to be a useful supplement to blended learning and will be implemented in the present approach. To combine the flipped classroom model with blended learning, all activities before and after the on-campus meeting will take place online. The teacher provides all necessary information in form of pre-recorded video clips, presentation slides and further reading via a learning management system. The students learn self-directed, when and where they want, skip parts they already know and repeat difficult content until they feel confident about it. By using chats, bulletin boards, and online tutorials in the self-studying phase students can interact with each other, stay in contact and collaborate virtually. Implemented online self-assessment tests and exercises help students to evaluate their individual learning progress.

2.4   Combined Approach for the Learning Module "Scientific Writing for Academic Purposes"

Within the research project we developed a blended learning course teaching basic rules of scientific writing and fostering key learning competences. Figure 3 presents the basic procedure of the approach, combining blended learning and flipped classroom.

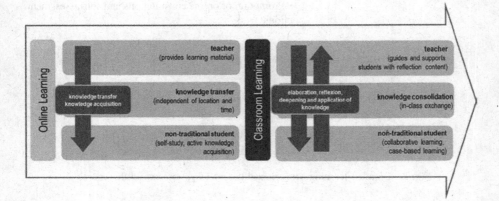

Fig. 3. Combined learning approach

The course started with a kick-off event for the participating non-traditional students. Absent student top-athletes received all necessary information via email. The course agenda, the learning objectives and the procedure were explained in order to make the learning responsibilities as transparent as possible. Another important part of this kick-off was the explanation of the teaching and learning methods, e.g. the use of the learning management system OPAL (Online Platform for Academic Teaching and Learning). The teacher introduced the training modules and the technical possibilities. The learning process consists of acquiring theoretical knowledge by reading, getting to know the subject matters and important theoretical models. These information is fundamental for the discussion during the classroom training. Subsidiary video, small course units, self-tests and a forum for discussion were supplied on OPAL. The integration of the flipped classroom into a blended learning scenario allows discussing, applying and enhancing the acquired knowledge.

As mentioned before, the exchange with fellow students is difficult for student top-athletes because of the times of absences as well as the extended study time which allowed more individual learning. That is why we involved cooperative and collaborative tools in the blended learning scenario. Besides the forum for general exchange, the learners attended a three-part peer-feedback. They had to deliver three work samples online which were discussed and assessed within the working group. They interacted with each other, applied their knowledge and learned with as well as from each other.

Exercises and discussion points have also been included into the classroom seminars which enabled the student learners to elaborate, reflect, deepen and apply their knowledge. The self-learning videos supported the knowledge transfer. In order to support the active watching of learning videos, the students had to accomplish accompanying worksheets.

2.5   Evaluation

After participating in the class, we asked the 22 participants of the group of non-traditional students about their learning experiences. The assessment contained of two steps: (1) an online questionnaire focusing on individual motivation, learning experiences and the evaluation of teaching methods and learning outcome; and (2) a group discussion on personal experiences, benefits and challenges.

Overall, the students were satisfied with the course design. Most of them appreciated the flexibility the blended learning approach offered. The learning content as well as the implementation of e-learning instruments were considered suitable for both student top-athletes and part-time students with a professional background. Framework requirements such as expenditure of time, level of difficulty and required e-learning skills were considered at an appropriate level. The provided videos and the self-assessment tests were appraised as the most significant features of the e-learning elements. Only two students mentioned usability problems while using their smartphones for learning.

Regarding motivational aspects, all non-traditional students considered themselves as motivated or very motivated throughout the class. Elite sport students' motivation was higher than those of the other non-traditional student groups. Especially the e-learning environment fostered the motivation of the student top-athletes, whereas there was no positive impact on part-time student's motivation.

All students evaluated the combination of face-to-face meetings and e-learning positively and mentioned the well-fitted interrelation between the two.

3   Conclusion

Developing learning and studying abilities of students is crucial for student's academic success. The habitat of higher education needs to be explored and tested; students need to learn how to learn and how to behave within that special setting. Subsequently, they will be able to develop individual learning techniques that are continuously to be supported by suitable teaching methods. At the end of their studies they will be able to transfer their knowledge into practice but will also be confident and aware of their expertise.

The research project proved that learning for non-traditional students not only comprises of gaining knowledge and passing exams but also includes the balancing of two different worlds: the academic and outside requirements such as training or work. A comprehensive teaching and learning approach seems to be applicable for creating 'a perfect world of higher education' for such non-traditional students.

To meet the organizational needs of student top-athletes, as well as other groups of non-traditional students, carefully structured timetables and exam schedules have to be created that apply for the whole student body. That way, top-athletes can take part in regular in-class activities and they can socially bond with their fellow class mates. In addition, non-athlete students benefit from the time management skills and high learning engagement of student-athletes that have been observed during the scientific writing class-project at Mittweida University. Blended-Learning options, especially the Online Platform for Academic Teaching and Learning (OPAL) and even simple social media tools such as Skype or Facebook learning groups are of valuable quality for Mittweida's non-traditional students in periods of time-intense tournament preparation, business obligations or travelling.

In conclusion, the research project showed that the development of a range of flexible forms of education delivery is critical to meeting the needs of non-traditional students in all types of education. Distance and electronic learning in particular may provide non-traditional students with flexibility in terms of the timing and location of their academic and 'outside' activities.

References

1. Abeysekera, L., Dawson, P.: Motivation and cognitive load in the flipped classroom: definition, rationale and a call for research. High. Educ. Res. Dev. 34(1), 1–14 (2015)
2. Chickering, A.W., Gamson Z.F.: Seven principles for good practice in undergraduate education. AAHE Bull. 39, 3–7 (1987). Accessed http://files.eric.ed.gov/fulltext/ED282491

3. Cooner, T.S.: Creating opportunities for students in large cohorts to reflect in and on practice: lessons learnt from a formative evaluation of students' experiences of a technology-enhanced blended learning design. Br. J. Educ. Technol. **41**(2), 271–286 (2010)
4. De George-Walker, L., Keeffe, M.: Self-determined blended learning: a case study of blended learning design. High. Educ. Res. Dev. **29**(1), 1–13 (2010)
5. Demoulin, D.F.: A student's credibility and personal development are essential elements for college success. Coll. Student J. **36**(3), 373 (2002)
6. Friesen, N.: Report: defining blended learning (2012). http://learningspaces.org/papers/Defining_Blended_Learning_NF.pdf. 21 February 2017
7. Garrison, D.R., Kanuka, H.: Blended learning: uncovering its transformative potential in higher education. Internet High. Educ. **7**, 95–105 (2004)
8. Georgieff, P.: Zielgruppenorientiertes eLearning – ein Angebot auch für ältere Menschen? In: Kimpeler, S., Mangold, M., Schweiger, W. (Hrsg.): Die digitale Herausforderung. Zehn Jahre Forschung zur computervermittelten Kommunikation, S. 135–146. VS Verlag für Sozialwissenschaften, Wiesbaden (2007)
9. Goodwin, B., Miller, K.: Evidence on flipped classroom is still coming in. Educ. Leadersh. **70**(6), 78–80 (2013)
10. Hicks, M., Reid, I., George, R.: Enhancing on-line teaching: designing responsive learning environments. Int. J. Acad. Dev. **6**(2), 143–151 (2001)
11. King, A.: From sage on the stage to guide on the side. Coll. Teach. **41**(1), 30–35 (1993)
12. Koop, B., Mandl, H.: Blended learning: forschungsfragen und perspektiven (blended learning: research questions and perspectives). In: Klimsa, P., Issing, L.J. (eds.) Online Lernen – Handbuch für Wissenschaft und Praxis, 2nd edn, pp. 139–150. Walter de Gruyter, Munich (2011)
13. Lim, D.H., Morris, M.L.: Learner and instructional factors influencing learning outcomes within a blended learning environment. Educ. Technol. Soc. **12**(4), 282–293 (2009)
14. López-Pérez, M.V., Pérez-López, M.C., Rodriguez-Ariza, L.: Blended learning in higher education: Students' perceptions and their relation to outcomes. Comput. Educ. **56**, 818–826 (2011)
15. Mayring, P.: Qualitative Inhaltsanalyse: Grundlagen und Techniken. 12. überarb. Auflage. Beltz-Verlag, Weinheim and Basel (2015)
16. Mok, H.N.: Teaching tip: the flipped classroom. J. Inf. Syst. Educ. **25**(1), 7–11 (2014)
17. Tinto, V.: Colleges as communities: taking research on student persistence seriously. Rev. High. Educ. 21(2), 167–177 (1998). Accessed https://muse.jhu.edu/
18. Wang, X.: Stability of educational expectations among baccalaureate aspirants beginning at community colleges. Community Coll. Rev. **49**(4), 300–319 (2012). doi:10.1177/0091552112454914
19. Wolniak, G.C., Engberg, M.E.: Academic achievement in the first year of college: evidence of the pervasive effects of the high school context. Res. High. Educ. **51**(5), 451–467 (2010). doi:10.1007/s11162-010-9165-4

"Beyond EFL Writing Anxiety": Tapping into the Individual Emotionality of Proficient EFL Writers Through Semi-structured Analysis and Wearable Sensing Technology

Luciana Lew[1] and Tiffany Y. Tang[2(✉)]

[1] Department of English, Wenzhou-Kean University, Wenzhou, China
lewl@kean.edu
[2] Media Lab, Department of Computer Science,
Wenzhou-Kean University, Wenzhou, China
yatang@kean.edu

Abstract. A high level of writing proficiency is a critical foundation for undergraduate writing performance and general academic success in an English-medium university. The present study proposes a model of "deconstruction" of the "anxiety" plaguing EFL writers by using a case study (Study one). The purpose of this qualitative single embedded case study is to explore both perceived/real challenges and positive affective factors experienced and harnessed by competent Chinese EFL writers studying at an English-medium university. In order to further objectively uncover the writers' temporal emotion change, we will conduct a second study to continuously collect their physiological data through wearable and sensing technology. Both studies aim to add depth into our understanding of the link between anxiety and writing efficacy. Gaining an understanding of what is perceived as positive affective factors by competent EFL writers, stakeholders, instructors and institutions can utilize these facts to develop/adjust writing teaching techniques, methods, or beneficial interventions, thereby increasing the potential for academic success.

Keywords: Anxiety · Emotion · Writing · EFL · Physiological data · Chinese · Wearable and sensing technology · Classroom

1 Introduction and Background

The paradigm of written discourse first shifted from being a product to a writer's recursive process, and under a further shift, is currently recognized as a merger of cognitive and affective processes. In her seminal writings, A.G. Brand stated: "Understanding the collaboration of emotion and cognition in writing is both fundamental and far-reaching. It is in cognition that ideas make sense. But it is in emotion that this sense finds value. Without such priorities we could not think" ([5], p. 442). The singular most often cited descriptive emotion associated with English as a Foreign Language (EFL) writing is anxiety [13, 41]. Krashen's introduction of the affective filter hypothesis [21] confirms that mental upsets experienced by learners inhibits

© Springer International Publishing AG 2017
P. Zaphiris and A. Ioannou (Eds.): LCT 2017, Part II, LNCS 10296, pp. 170–181, 2017.
DOI: 10.1007/978-3-319-58515-4_14

language learning. Further, agreeing with McIntyre and Gardner [27]; Horwitz et al. [19] see the imposition on EFL writers the additional socio-cultural and linguistic demands that exacerbate a complex of self-perceptions, confidence, feelings, and conduct related to classroom language learning.

Launching from this cognitive-emotive theoretical construct, a plethora of research has evolved on the EFL learning front in search of pedagogical answers to minimize negative affective states related to both oral and written performance apprehension linked to Second Language Acquisition (SLA) [28]. This body of research ranges from various constructs and models and their implications [5, 9, 23, 30], emotional intelligence and mediating role of emotional control [43], writer motivation and attitudes [26], dissection of anxiety and apprehension [3, 7, 14], self-efficacy as predictors to text production [2, 29, 48], configuration and interaction among various emotions and personality traits [14, 32, 37, 46]. Complementing these fruitful lines of enquiry are novel methodologies and analytical instruments (scales) [10, 13].

A high level of writing proficiency is a critical foundation for undergraduate writing performance and general academic success in an English-medium university. Researchers, while agreeing that EFL learners face significant challenges in the language classroom, searched for solutions by examining and identifying primarily the perceptions and emotions of EFL writers prior to and after entering English-medium university that focused on negative factors and challenges [20, 22, 40, 44]. What is crucial, however, is the direct report on experiential journey (development of cognitive-emotive states) of successful EFL writers revealing their perceptions, usage of positive affective factors [40], as well as what they believe in, and how and what was adjusted to achieve writing proficiency.

This paper proposes a model of "deconstruction" using a case study (Study one) to mine this missing data. The purpose of this qualitative single embedded case study is to explore both perceived/real challenges and positive affective factors experienced and harnessed by fluent Chinese EFL writers studying at an English-medium university. This qualitative case study is utilized to obtain information regarding how, what and why something has occurred – to explore the perceptions and affective experiences, including the moderating role of effortful control – in the words of those who have experienced it, in the setting in which it occurred, and without manipulation [12, 33, 50]. For example, what were the subjects' emotional and intellectual cues that prompted them to start writing. What in fact does happen affectively between having an idea for writing and beginning a first draft? Such research provides understanding on why certain problems occur during the writing process and the solutions of skilled writers [5, 6].

Unlike the majority of previous studies on the association between language acquisition and emotions that only rely on structured- or unstructured interviews, objective measurements of the learning outcomes (among many, [1, 11, 17, 23, 39, 49], used in our present study goes a step further to obtain writers' physiological data in order to characterize the temporal emotion change through wearable and sensing technology. The physiological data that is expected to be collected in Study two includes heart rate and skin temperature through Galvanic Skin Response (GSR) [25]. Results from affordable sensors have increasingly been adopted for understanding target users' affect in education [15, 16, 31, 38, 45]. Ertin et al. [18] also designed a multi-sensor suit (embedded with a total of six sensors) to continuously measure a user's stress level.

2   Study One: The Qualitative Single Embedded Case Study

Participants for the study are purposively selected from a large metropolitan English-medium university in China to meet predetermined criteria. Purposive sampling is considered an efficient method to ensure alignment with specific goals of the study and to provide accurate and relevant data [50]. The units of analysis and comparison are the perceptions of upperclassmen in each of the following disciplines, namely, English, Accounting/Finance, Global Business, and Computer Science. A field-tested interview guide will set parameters for the semi-structured open-ended interviews. Data from the interviews will be recorded, transcribed verbatim, and triangulated with other units of analysis (GPA's, length of study, and other esoteric personal characteristics). Special attention will be paid to ascertain if the subjects' coping mechanisms also drew from aspects of Vygotsky's Sociocultural theory [47] – mediation, the obtainment of meaning, and the zone of proximal development – and the degree of SCT effectiveness for EFL writers [8, 51].

2.1   Qualitative Case Study

Theoretical Perspective. This study is guided by Pekrun's use of modern theories on process emotions [42], by which he describes emotions as "sets of interrelated psychological processes including affective, cognitive, physiological and emotional components" ([36] p. 37).

Questions Pursued in this Case Study

- Which academic emotions do students experience in EFL writing while pursuing homework, in-class, and timed class examinations?
- What are the components within the above-named emotional experiences?
- How do these emotions affect the process of learning and student achievement within EFL writing
- What are the sources of these emotions given the students' personality traits within the context of EFL writing?
- What are effective coping mechanisms regarding negative emotions and the pedagogical lessons on avoiding emotions detrimental to academic achievement and student educational life?

2.2   Research Methods

Participants. The 8 participants are all registered for four-year full-time undergraduate study. These are comprised of 6 seniors and 2 juniors who by their advisors-instructors' account possess excellent to high intermediate writing skills in EFL. Two of them are

English majors, two Accounting majors, two Finance majors, one Computer Science major, and one in Global Business. Their GPA ranges from 3.4 (lowest) to 3.9 (highest) out of 4.0. Their commonalities in educational background are that they are tier one level of students based on their college entrance examination and are eligible to enter this same university that utilizes English as the medium of instruction. Another common exam passed by all is the CET 4 that is required at the end of the first year as a prerequisite for them to graduate. Exceptional cases, where participants took more demanding English tests and other international exams (TOEFL, IELTS, GRE, and GMAT) will be mentioned subsequently where relevant. Two of the participants spent one semester studying abroad in an English-speaking country, while one participant did receive special tutoring on English during high school. Participants include both genders with ages ranging from age 20–22.

Procedures During the Individual Interview. A simple explanation of the objective of this study was given verbally at the start. The interview was recorded. Student participation was on a voluntary basis and none of the students receive any financial returns nor feedback of the results in exchange for participating. While guided by the list of questions below, the interviews had no time constraints. Each interview lasted between 1.45 to 2 h depending on the interviewee's willingness to share his/her experiences.

The participants were guided by the following prompts in our semi-structured interviews:

1. Description by the participant of his/her existing trait predisposition and emotionality when entering freshmen year.
2. Description of initial emotions in the face of EFL writing courses as freshmen.
3. What the participant believed were his/her motivations and positive academic emotions they started with and how these were sustained.
4. Description of the various individual emotions experienced during the process of completing homework writing assignments.
5. Description of emotions experienced during timed in-class exam and in-class writing.
6. Description and explanation of effective external mediating factors and support.

Once settled comfortably in a quiet environment, the researcher would start interviewing the participants using the above questions. Questions often do not take the same sequence as the interviewer will digress where there is a belief the participant is reporting an unusual or unexpected observation that merits further exploring.

2.3   Results

Responses to self-rating (at start of freshmen year) of attitude towards writing in general (e.g., writing in Chinese), being in a English medium university, level of English writing proficiency, tendency to over worry about situations rather than not, self-confidence in starting a new undergraduate life, and so on:

- None of participants claimed they like to write.
- Participants claimed they did reach an objective in their life by being admitted into a university. While still fearful, they hoped for the best and were willing to try it out.
- Participants expressed a low level of confidence and claimed to have a low-level quality in EFL writing when entering freshmen year. When probing their reasons for selecting an English medium university, all admitted that this institution was not their first choice. Two participants indicated parental pressure in entering this university and the major to take.
- One of the participants, unlike the rest, believes he is a worrier when encountering a problem. The others seem fairly even keel.

Emotions encountered when facing required Freshmen EFL Writing Courses:

- While the participants expressed resignation in the face of potential difficulties contending with English for the next four years, they also felt hopeful that with adaptation, they would successfully acquire a Bachelor degree with good English skills.
- Without any qualifications, the participants recognize the strategic significance in the ability to use English, in this case for EFL writing.
- The participants described an all-consuming uncertainty, almost fear, that there will be no appropriate employment at the end of the four years. This feeling that spans all their undergraduate years, is ubiquitous among their peers.
- At the start, all participants found the courses worrisome as they were fearful of failure in these pass/fail courses which would then have to be repeated.

Traumatic Journey of EFL Writing under the Homework Setting:

- Completing homework was unanimously voted as the experience where "effective" writing skills were learned.
- The participants experienced the highest intensity of emotions during the daunting task of completing writing assignments.
- Upon the receipt of an assigned writing homework, the aroused feeling of "anxiety" include emotions of confusion, dislike or frustration about the topic because the student has no idea about what to write on the topic, fear, shame, or shyness about asking the instructor for clarification, and lastly the worry that the student will not be able to write 3 pages.

Common coping/mediating mechanism in the following order of popularity:

- googling in Chinese for ideas on the topic
- brainstorming with peers
- consulting with instructor.

Unconventional (within the context of the 8 participants) answers:

- Three participants mentioned having emotions that can safely be assumed to be positive innate traits for purposes of academic achievement: "curiosity", "trust" (in himself).
- One even voiced anger at China's foreign language (i.e., English) program for middle school and high school which has created the unpreparedness for entering

freshmen. He had no wish and to this day does not talk to classmates about development of essay topics. He spends time thinking and developing his own ideas which he does not wish to share with others. In the actual writing portion, he spends the most time writing his introductory paragraph which would summarize all his ideas. The interviewee trusts his own judgment and he reported he did receive outside English tutoring when attending secondary school. Perhaps that experience rendered him more familiar with writing in English.

- The participant who characterized himself as always being "curious" will spend days researching until he "believes" he has enough material. He gets progressively more excited with the material gathered and has used the word "inspiration" at least twice when he is ready to start the writing. He describes himself as agonizing over each paragraph and will not move to the next paragraph until he is satisfied with the quality and the expressions of the substance of that one paragraph. He also becomes upset when discovering he is still on paragraph 3 (his example) when he has 5 more to complete. He then describes himself as being ecstatic with a sense of satisfaction when he is near the finishing line of the assignment. He is delighted and feels a sense of accomplishment when the essay is completed to his satisfaction. He then feels so relieved after its submission.

Best pedagogical practices named in the learning process of how, what, when to write:

- The participants named the instructor's clear demonstration of every step in the building of an essay of a particular genre as the best teaching method. Aside from the general skills in the overall structure of an essay, such as the thesis statement and paragraphing, the reading and examination with the students of samples of specific pieces of writing of all genres prior to the assignment, is also very helpful.
- As reported, the participants reported disliking the holistic method used by some teachers in reviewing written essays. Correspondingly, the best feedback is the type where the instructor does comprehensive review of the essay. All participants generally agree that instructors who are empathetic and encouraging in their attitudes towards students definitely help boost students' self-confidence.
- One participant emphatically mentioned that reading English books of all types – those with topics that interested him – was his secret weapon for honing writing skills. Whenever possible he will try to cover two books in three days.
- Though without much love for the process of writing, one participant mentioned that she does write in her diary (in Chinese). She also mentioned an aversion to having her essays being read. She remarked insightfully that she has created a conflict for herself– how can she fulfill her desire to improve her writing unless her essays gets read and corrected or evaluated? This participant professes to be quiet, shy, not very talkative, and somewhat introverted.
- As a corollary, emotions of gratitude, admiration, respect, and even affection, have been expressed towards instructors who have expended extra efforts in promoting students' learning.

Emotions experienced during English classes and timed in-class exam:

- It has been reported, the participants' attention and therefore their interest in the lesson are generally captured by skilled instructors where the teaching is engaging and can be readily followed by the class. Boredom is most often mentioned when the topic is not interesting. Discomfort was experienced when individual contribution in class participation was expected.
- Although exams can be the most stressful time, as compared to homework writing assignment, the time span is limited. All participants will spend 5–10 min to develop ideas about the topic before putting pen to paper. Some of the participants believe that the feeling of time pressure can sometimes be helpful in creating stronger powers of concentration and focus to bear on the writing.
- One participant complained that he dislikes English writing exams because it prevents him from taking his time to produce a better piece of writing, or to fully develop his ideas.
- Outcomes of tests would arouse disappointment (less than expected result) and joy, surprise (better than expected result).

Self-rated proficiency level of writing and the improvement of EFL writing with passage of time:

- Most participants mentioned that after the initial two years, writing in English felt easier and less of a struggle, although one mentioned it took only one year. Some remarked that perhaps this was a sign that their writing skills have improved and this fact may also have spilled into other courses that require English writing.
- The participants self-rated their current writing levels to be between B+/A−.

2.4   Analytical Discussion

China's Domestic Marketplace that is Awaiting the New Entering Workforce.
Given its economic globalization, nowhere more than in China is it true that a bachelor's degree is a minimum requirement to secure decent employment. The sought after firms (global or internationalized domestic firms) all require proficient practical writing and speaking English skills. In this competitive market where resources are tied to individual achievement, the academic degrees and grades are premium as they also serve as the only yardsticks for entering elite graduate schools overseas or to acquire that dream position.

This is the overriding motivation, the consistently overarching achievement pressure that constitutes the highest source of arousal driving all university undergraduates. Aside from landing that professional position, there is a sizeable number of students who are destined to undertake graduate work in English speaking countries.

To help better understand this study's qualitative results and to further the purposes for studying these multiple emotions involved in EFL writing, one could analyze the data from the perspective of seminal concepts on why and how emotions influence students' cognitive processes and performance. Pekrun [34] proposes to use the term "academic emotions" to mean emotions that are directly linked to academic learning, learning in the classroom, and achievement such as enjoyment experienced in learning or the process of studying, pride in successfully completing assignments, or anxiety instigated by tests. His ideas regarding achievement emotions – emotions experienced in academic settings – can support students' motivation and influence academic performance [35] based on his concept of "appraisals of control and value" That is, these emotions arise from students' assessment of control (controlling outcomes) and value (value attributed to such outcomes [35].

There is also a dearth of empirical evidence and studies involving emotions in the academic field, focusing on the interaction of the rich diversity of academic and achievement emotions. When Pekrun [35] introduced his Control-Value Theory of Achievement Emotions, he offered an integrated system where emotions should be seen as "sets of interrelated psychological processes including affective, cognitive, physiological and motivational components" ([36] p. 37).

3 Study Two: Anxiety Elicitation Through a Wearable Sensor

3.1 Study Procedure

Following the study protocol in [15, 16, 31, 38, 45], a pilot study was conducted to correlate the heart rate and GSR data to anxiety. The subject wrote an essay (up to 10 min); the quality of the essay and the temporal emotion changes can then be used to not only characterize the temporal emotion states of the subject but hopefully also predict her anxiety. To the best of our knowledge, such a multimodal, layered analysis is rare in the literature.

3.2 Apparatus

The Microsoft Band 2 which is capable of recording both heart rate and GSR data was worn by the subject. Note that, though, Band 2 was discontinued by Microsoft in October 2016 and its SDK had been removed recently, it remains to be one of the few wearable and programmable sensors in the market that can record GSR data (Fig. 1).

Fig. 1. The Microsoft Band 2

During initial testing, we found out that Band 2 is not stable in continuously monitoring and recording the data; adjustment has to be made to ensure the band is properly pressed against the skin.

3.3 Results and Discussions

Figures 2 and 3 show the GSR and heart rate readings within five minutes while the subject was writing an essay.

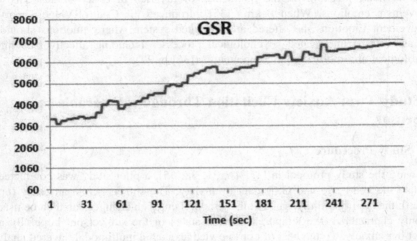

Fig. 2. GSR readings over time

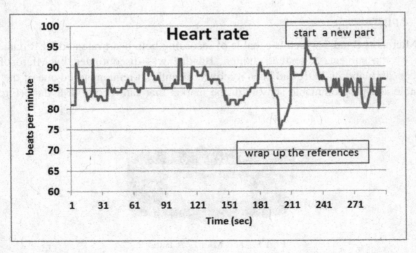

Fig. 3. Heart rate changes over time where a spike appeared when the subject starts a new part with new arguments

At odds with our prediction, the GSR data shows an increasing trend. But the heart rate readings did show two moments when the subject's heart rate dropped and increased significantly (see Fig. 3). During the interview with the subject, we found out that she expressed stress when starting the new paragraph because she has to find background sources to back her arguments up; and the anxiety was picked up by the heart rate reading only.

Plausible explanations of the lack of variability of GSR data might be related to the nature of the experiment; that is, more repeated experiments need to be conducted before a reliable link could be established between GSR and stress; in addition, the interplay of GSR and heart rate and the exterior environment might complicate the problem.

4 Concluding Remarks

Findings from the first study bring insights on how to improve current support programs such as peer mentoring, team/group collaboration, ESL courses, and intensive English writing programs. The second study aims to objectively measure the physiological measurement of the subject so as to characterize her anxiety level based on the temporal emotional changes. Plausible explanations of the lack of variability of GSR data might be related to the nature of the experiment; that is, more repeated experiments need to be conducted before a reliable link could be established between GSR and stress; in addition, the interplay of GSR and heart rate and the exterior environment might complicate the problem.

Both studies add depth into our understanding of the link between anxiety and writing efficacy. Gaining an understanding of what is perceived as positive affective factors by proficient EFL writers, stakeholders, instructors and institutions can utilize these facts to develop/adjust writing teaching techniques, methods, or beneficial interventions, thereby increasing the potential for academic success [24].

References

1. Al-Shboul, M.M., Ahmad, I.S., Nordin, M.S., Rahman, Z.A.: Foreign language reading anxiety in a Jordanian EFL context: a qualitative study. Engl. Lang. Teach. **6**(6), 38–56 (2013)
2. Bandura, A.: Self-efficacy conception of anxiety. Anxiety Res. **1**, 77–98 (1988)
3. Bline, D., Lowe, D.P., et al.: A research note on the dimensionality of daly and miller's writing apprehension scale. Written Commun. **18**, 61–79 (2001)
4. Brand, A.G.: Hot cognition: emotions and writing behavior. J. Adv. Compos. **6**, 1985–1986 (1983)
5. Brand, A.G.: The why of cognition: emotion and the writing process. Coll. Compos. Commun. **38**(4), 436–443 (1987)
6. Brand, A.G.: Social cognition, emotions, and the psychology of writing. J. Adv. Compos. **11**(2), 395–407 (1989)

7. Burgoon, J.K., Hale, J.L.: A research note on the dimensions of communication reticence. Commun. Q. **31**, 238–248 (1983)
8. Chen, X., de Sikao, D.Y. (2012). http://www.eep.com.cn/in2004/ca2605.htm
9. Cheng, Y.S.: Factors associated with foreign language writing anxiety. Foreign Lang. Annal. **35**(5), 647–656 (2002)
10. Cheng, Y.S.: A measure of second language writing anxiety: scale development and preliminary validation. J. Second Lang. Writ. **13**, 313–335 (2004)
11. Choi, J.: English speaking classroom apprehension: a study of the perceptions held by Hong Kong University students. J. Teach. Engl. Specif. Acad. Purp. **4**(2), 293–408 (2016)
12. Cozby, P.C., Bates, S.C.: Methods in Behavioral Research. McGraw-Hill, New York (2012)
13. Daly, J.A., Miller, M.D.: The empirical development of an instrument of writing apprehension. Res. Teach. Engl. **9**(3), 242–249 (1975)
14. Daly, U.A., Wilson, D.A.: Writing apprehension, self-esteem and personality. Res. Teach. Engl. **17**, 327–341 (1983)
15. de la Guía, E., Camacho, V.L., Orozco-Barbosa, L., Luján, V.M.B., Penichet, V.R.M., Pérez, M.L.: Introducing IoT and wearable technologies into task-based language learning for young children. IEEE Transl. Learn. Technol. **4**(9), 366–378 (2016)
16. D'Mello, S.K., Craig, S.D., Gholson, B., Franklin, S., Picard, R., Graesser, A.C.: Integrating affect sensors in an intelligent tutoring system. In: Affective Interactions: The Computer in the Affective Loop, Workshop in International Conference on Intelligent User Interfaces, pp. 7–13. ACM Press, New York (2005)
17. Dewaele, J.-M., MacIntyre, P.: The two faces of Janus? Anxiety and enjoyment in the foreign language classroom. Stud. Second Lang. Learn. Teach. **4**(2), 237–274 (2014)
18. Ertin, E., Raij, A., Stohs, N., al'Absi, M., Kumar, S., Shah, S.: AutoSense: unobtrusively wearable sensor suite for interring the onset, causality and consequences of stress in the field. In: Proceedings of ACM SenSys 2011, pp. 274–287. ACM Press (2011)
19. Horwitz, E.K., Horwitz, M.B., Cope, J.A.: Foreign language classroom anxiety. Mod. Lang. J. **70**, 125–132 (1986)
20. Khawaja, N.G., Stallman, H.M.: Understanding the coping strategies of international students: a qualitative approach. Aust. J. Guidance Couns. **21**(2), 203–224 (2011)
21. Krashen, S.D.: Principles and Practice in Second Language Acquisition. Pergamon, Oxford (1982)
22. Li, T.B., Moreira, G.: English language teaching in China today. J. Engl. Int. Lang. **4**, 180–194 (2009)
23. Liu, M., Ni, H.: Chinese university EFL learners' foreign language writing anxiety: pattern effect causes. Engl. Lang. Teach. **8**(3), 46–58 (2015)
24. Lobo, A., Gurney, L.: What did they expect? Exploring a link between students' expectations, attendance and attrition on English language enhancement courses. J. Further High. Educ. **38**(5), 730–754 (2014). doi:10.1080/0309877X2013.817002
25. Lykken, D.T., Venables, P.: Direct measurement of skin conductance: a proposal for standardization. Psychophysiology **8**, 656–672 (1971)
26. MacIntyre, P.D.: Motivation, anxiety and emotion in second language acquisition. In: Robinson, P. (ed.) Individual Differences and Instructed Language Learning, pp. 45–68. John Benjamins, Philadelphia/Amsterdam (2002)
27. MacIntyre, P.D., Gardner, J.C.: Language anxiety: its relation to other anxieties and processing in native and second languages language learning. Lang. Learn. **41**, 513–534 (1991)
28. MacIntyre, P., Gregersen, T.: Affect: the role of language anxiety and other emotions in language learning. In: Psychology for Language Learning: Insights from Research, Theory and Practice, pp. 103–118. Palgrave Macmillan, UK (2012)

29. Matsuda, S., Gobel, P.: Anxiety and predictors of performance in the foreign language classroom. System **32**(1), 21–36 (2004)
30. Milolajczak, M., Luminet, O.: Trait emotional intelligence and the cognitive appraisal of stressful events: an exploratory study. Study 1. Pers. Individ. Differ. **44**, 1445–1453 (2008)
31. Muller, L., Divitini, M., Mora, S., Rivera-Pelayo, V., Stork, W.: Context becomes content: sensor data for computer-supported reflective learning. IEEE Trans. Learn. Technol. **8**(1), 111–123 (2015)
32. Nelis, D., Quoidbach, J., et al.: Increasing emotional intelligence: (How) is it possible? Pers. Individ. Differ. **47**, 36–41 (2009)
33. Patton, M.Q.: Qualitative Evaluation and Research Methods. Sage, Thousand Oaks (2002)
34. Pekrun, R.: A social cognitive, control-value theory of achievement emotions. In: Motivational Psychology of Human Development. Elsevier, Oxford (2000)
35. Pekrun, R.: The control-value theory of achievement emotions: assumptions, corollaries, and implications for educational research and practice. Educ. Psychol. Rev. **18**, 315–341 (2006)
36. Pekrun, R., Frenzel, A.C., et al.: The control-value theory of achievement emotions: an integrative approach to emotions in education. In: Emotions in Education. Academic Press, San Diego (2011)
37. Petrides, D.V., Pita, R., Kokkinaki, F.: The location of trait emotional intelligence in personality factor space. Brit. J. Psychol. **98**, 273–289 (2007)
38. Petrovica, S., Ekenel, H.K.: Emotion recognition for intelligent tutoring. In: International Workshop on Intelligent Educational Systems, Technology-Enhanced Learning a Technology Transfer Models (INTEL-EDU) (2016)
39. Rahim, S.A., Hayas, K.M.: Investigating student's second language writing anxiety: a case study. In: Persidangan MICELT 2014, pp. 13–15 (2014)
40. Rawlings, M., Sue, E.: Preparedness of Chinese students for American culture and communication in English. J. Int. Stud. **3**(1), 29–40 (2013)
41. Shang, H.-F.: Factors associated with English as a foreign language university students writing anxiety. Int. J. Engl. Lang. Teach. **1**(1), 1–12 (2013)
42. Scherer, K.R.: On the nature and function of emotion: a component process approach. In: Appraisal Processes in Emotion. Erlbaum, Hillsdate (1984)
43. Shao, K.Q., Yu, W.H., Ji, Z.M.: The relationship between EFL students' emotional intelligence and writing achievement. Innov. Lang. Learn. Teach. **7**, 107–124 (2012)
44. Sherry, M., Thomas, P., Chui, W.H.: International students: a vulnerable student population. High. Educ. **60**(1), 33–46 (2010)
45. Tsiatsos, T., Apostolidis, H.: Using sensors to detect student's emotion in adaptive learning environment. In: Proceedings of the Second International Conference on Innovative Developments in ICT, INNOV, vol. 1, pp. 60–65 (2011)
46. Valiente, C., Swanson, J., Eisenberg, N.: Linking students' emotions and academic achievement: when and why emotions matter. Child Dev. Perspetives **6**(2), 129–135 (2012)
47. Vygotsky, L.S.: Mind in Society: Development of Higher Psychological Processes (1978)
48. Woodrow, L.: College English writing affect: self-efficacy and anxiety. Elsevier **39**, 510–522 (2011)
49. Yaman, H.: The relation general anxiety levels, anxiety of writing, and attitude for Turkish course of secondary school students. Educ. Sci.: Theor. Pract. **14**(3), 1117–1122 (2014)
50. Yin, R.K.: Case Study Research: Design and Methods, 5th edn. Sage, Thousand Oaks (2014)
51. Zhang, D., et al.: Sociocultural theory applied to second language learning: collaborative learning with reference to the Chinese context. Int. Educ. Stud. **6**(9), 165–174 (2013)

Training Socially Responsible Engineers by Developing Accessible Video Games

Rafael Molina-Carmona[✉], Rosana Satorre-Cuerda, Carlos Villagrá-Arnedo,
and Patricia Compañ-Rosique

Cátedra Santander-UA de Transformación Digital,
Universidad de Alicante, Alicante, Spain
{rmolina,rosana,villagra,patricia}@dccia.ua.es

Abstract. University has an active social responsibility that is addressed both by acting responsibly as institution and by transferring this ethical duty to the students. Our proposal is achieving the social inclusion of disabled people, as part of the social responsibility of future engineers, through the realization of the final degree project in collaboration with associations of disabled users, in particular through the design and development of adapted video games. This paper presents our experience in developing these projects in collaboration with an association of users with cerebral palsy. The objective is training the students in the social responsibility but also solving some problems of inclusion in the collective of disabled users (such as the access to digital entertainment) and carrying out an in-depth study about the interaction problems for users with cerebral palsy, providing concrete and practical solutions. The methodology for this experience is Action Research, with four research stages (plan, implement, evaluate and reflect) that are iteratively repeated. Following this methodology, three iterations have been carried out and a fourth one is planned. As a result, three adapted video games have been developed and a guide for adapting video games to people with cerebral palsy has been defined. This experience has served to introduce the aspects of social responsibility in the curricula of engineers in a very effective way and to study and design new ways of making video games accessible to disabled people, giving them the chance to exercise their right to entertainment.

Keywords: Social responsibility · Accessibility · Accessible video games

1 Introduction

University has an active social responsibility, that is, it has the obligation to act for the benefit of society at large. This active social responsibility must be addressed from two perspectives: acting responsibly as institution and transferring this ethical duty to the students it educates. The latter is usually tackled by introducing social and ethical aspects in the curricula to prepare the future professionals to be committed to their social environment. One important aspect

© Springer International Publishing AG 2017
P. Zaphiris and A. Ioannou (Eds.): LCT 2017, Part II, LNCS 10296, pp. 182–201, 2017.
DOI: 10.1007/978-3-319-58515-4_15

of this social commitment is actively ensuring the social inclusion of any individual, no matter his or her circumstances. A paradigmatic case is the inclusion of disabled people.

The degree of Multimedia Engineering of the University of Alicante, introduced the aspects of inclusion in its curriculum. The main objective of this degree is "to train professionals in the ICT sector who are able to direct new projects in the field of multimedia, both in the sectors of digital leisure and entertainment and of content management for its dissemination in information networks [...] This training is focused on providing students with the skills to build digital systems for the management of multimedia information, provide technical support for multimedia projects in the field of culture, telecommunications, teaching or business, and create and support the technical elements involved in the creation of image and sound related to digital leisure" [23]. It has two specialties: Digital Creation and Entertainment, mainly oriented to the design and development of video games, and Content Management, oriented to the tools for the content management and dissemination, especially through the web. The concepts of accessibility, usability, ergonomics, equality and professional responsibility are present in every subject and area of the curriculum. In this context, the aspects of accessibility for disabled people are fully justified in the curriculum of Multimedia Engineering.

For the development of a mature and fair society, it is essential the citizens to achieve a normalised vision of disabled people in all of the areas, particularly in the field of leisure. The normalized vision and the equal treatment become the key aspects to obtain the true social inclusion. Our proposal is introducing social responsibility for achieving this true social inclusion through the realization of the final degree project in collaboration with entities, institutions or associations of disabled users, in particular through the design and development of adapted video games. This paper presents our experience in developing these projects in collaboration with an association of users with cerebral palsy. The objectives of this experience are:

- Training multimedia professionals in the social responsibility they have as engineers who develop their profession in a social context and in the need to provide solutions to a diverse society.
- Solving some problems of inclusion in the collective of disabled users, including making them participants in digital entertainment, since leisure is an essential human activity and an individual right.
- At the technical level, carrying out an in-depth study of how to solve the interaction for a specific group, that of users with cerebral palsy, providing concrete and practical solutions that allow them to access technology in general and video games in particular.

The methodology that we use for this experience is Action Research [6]. In this methodology the research process is divided in four stages (plan, act, evaluate and reflect) that are iteratively repeated introducing improvements in each iteration. During the plan the activities to develop the project are established (meetings with the association, definition of objectives, requirements and limitations); during the implementation, the adapted video game is designed and developed, using incremental and agile methodologies; during the evaluation, several user tests take place and opinions are collected; during reflection, the collected data are analysed and improvements are proposed for the next iteration. Following this methodology, three iterations have been carried out and a fourth one is being developed right now.

This experience has served, on one hand, to introduce the aspects of social responsibility in the curricula of engineers in a very effective way and, on the other hand, to study and design new ways of making video games accessible to disabled people, giving them the chance to access to the right to entertainment.

The document is organised as follows: Sect. 2 presents the concepts and previous works about social responsibility in higher education, disability and cerebral palsy in particular, and adaptation of video games. Our proposal of methodology is presented in Sect. 3. Section 4 is devoted to explain in detail the iterative and incremental development of the adapted video games. Discussion is presented in Sect. 5, resulting in a list of lessons learned about adapting video games to users with cerebral palsy. Finally, the conclusions and future work are presented in Sect. 6.

2   Background

2.1   Social Responsibility and Higher Education

Within the main functions of the university (teaching, research and transfer), the social dimension is of the utmost importance [1]. The different curricula should incorporate aspects related to professional ethics, the development of key competences and entrepreneurial initiatives, as well as the impact of technologies and processes in terms of social and environmental sustainability, as a driver of change for future professionals. Among the basic principles and values of the university are social participation, through the creation of channels of communication and participation to respond to the demands of its stakeholders.

Particularly, the University of Alicante, in which this proposal is framed, is a public and socially responsible institution, whose mission is Òthe integral training and development of its students. Not only in knowledge and disciplines, but also the promotion of the critical awareness, social responsibility, health and sustainability principles, to contribute effectively to the welfare of the society where it is inserted. It should also be added the guarantee of personal dignity, the free development of persons, without any discrimination, and finally, the right to effective equality between women and men. Research is another basic principle to increase improvement of knowledge. On the one hand, by its transfer through teaching. On the other hand, the direct contribution of the University to the society through its inescapable commitment to the cultural, scientific and technological development. In this way, thanks to the collaboration with other social agents, such research can be realized in innovation for sustainable development and the improvement of the quality of life [24]. The references that guide the values of the University of Alicante are designed in order to foster the quality of a public university. Among these, it can be found solidarity and sustainability.

This initiative is part of the curriculum of Multimedia Engineering, among which the following competences stand out [23]:

- Conceive, organize, plan and develop projects in the field of multimedia engineering and the design, development or operation of multimedia systems, services and applications.
- Design, develop, evaluate and ensure the accessibility, ergonomics, usability and security of multimedia systems, services and applications, as well as the information they manage.
- Analyse and assess the social and environmental impact of technical solutions, including the ethical and professional responsibility of a Multimedia Engineer.
- Know and understand the multimedia concept, the characteristics of the multimedia language, the technologies involved, the organization and management of multimedia systems and the socio-cultural impact in the society of information and knowledge.
- Develop and direct multimedia engineering projects in an efficient and effective manner, taking into account the feasibility, sustainability, legislation, job security, regulation, standardization and accessibility and gender equality related to the information society in the development of projects.
- Create, design and evaluate personal computer interfaces that guarantee accessibility and usability.

The concepts of accessibility, usability, ergonomics, equality and professional responsibility are present in every subject and area of the curriculum. In this context, the aspects of accessibility for disabled people are fully justified in the curriculum of Multimedia Engineering. A good way to complete the training of these future professionals may be the development of final grade dissertations for entities and institutions supporting this group of users.

2.2 Disability and Cerebral Palsy

Disability is defined as the consequence of damage that may be physical, cognitive, mental, sensory, emotional, developmental, or a combination of these. It affects how the individual interacts and participates in the society and it can be present from birth or occurring during a person's life.

According to the World Health Organization [27], more than one billion people live in the world with some form of disability, of whom almost 200 million experience considerable difficulties in functioning. People with disabilities have poorer health outcomes, lower education achievements, less economic participation and higher rates of poverty than people without disabilities. In part, this is a consequence of the obstacles in accessing services that many of us take for granted, in particular health, education, employment, transportation, or information. These difficulties are exacerbated in less favoured communities. In order to achieve development goals, it is necessary to provide means to make people with disabilities independent and to remove the barriers that prevent them from being an active part of the communities, training and finding a job [27].

Cerebral palsy (CP) describes a group of permanent disorders of the development of movement and posture, causing activity limitation, that are attributed to non-progressive disturbances that occurred in the developing fetal or infant brain. The motor disorders of cerebral palsy are often accompanied by disturbances of sensation, perception, cognition, communication, and behaviour [19]. Although the main characteristic of this disability is movement disorder, of individuals affected by CP, 28% have epilepsy, 58% have communication difficulties, at least 42% have vision problems, and 23% to 56% have learning disabilities [11]. Cerebral palsy is characterized by abnormal muscle tone, reflexes, or motor development and coordination. There may be deformities and contractures of joints and bones or tight muscles and joints. The frequent symptoms are spasticity, spasms, other involuntary movements (e.g., facial gestures), unsteady gait, balance problems, or decreased muscle mass [3]. More specifically, depending on the functional effects, it is possible to distinguish between the following types of CP [17]:

- Spastic: this is the most common group; about 75% of people with CP have spasticity, that is, significant stiffness in the muscles, an inability to relax them, due to an injury to the cerebral cortex that affects motor centres.
- Athetoid: it is characterized by frequent involuntary movements that interfere with normal body movements. There are usually contortion movements of the extremities, the face and the tongue, gestures, grimaces and awkwardness when speaking. Hearing disorders are quite common in this group, which interfere with language development. Injury of the basal ganglia of the brain seems to be the cause of this condition. Less than 10% of people with CP show athetosis.
- Ataxic: the person affected in this case has poor body balance, an awkward gait and difficulties in the coordination and control of hands and eyes. Ataxic cerebral palsy is a relatively rare form of the disorder that stems from damage to the cerebellum.
- Mixed: it is not common to find pure cases of spasticity, athetosis or ataxia. Typically, cerebral palsy sufferers have a combination of the different types.

2.3   Video Games and Disability

Video games have become in the last years a mainstream form of entertainment. Their popularity may be explained, among other reasons, by the immersion produced by the continuous interaction, in contrast to other more classic forms of entertainment, such as books or cinema. Moreover, video games have transcended their role of mere outlets of entertainment, and nowadays many examples of leveraging the potential in other areas can be found. This is the case of teaching [7,9,10,12,20,25] or health [21,26]. However, there are a significant number of potential disabled players that may not be able to access video games if they are not thought of when designing the games. For this group of players, the access to video games can mean a form of leisure that they did not know, and improvements in their education [4] or rehabilitation [13,18].

From the player's perspective, the basic flow of any video game is [28]:

1. Receiving a stimulus.
2. Determining a response to the stimulus.
3. Executing the response.

Creating an accessible video game means giving support and offering options to allow this flow to run correctly to players with any limitation. There are several ways to adapt the interaction so that the flow is maintained. Particularly, in the case of functional diversity in mobility, two main aspects must be considered: the access technologies (the adapted devices that allow the interaction), and the adaptation strategies (the game design decisions that make the game accessible).

The access technologies are the intermediary devices between the player and the game. They manage to translate the functional intentions of the player into the opportune result produced by the game. In the case of motor impaired players, it is often difficult or impossible for them to interact using conventional input devices such as mouses or keyboards. There are some alternative input devices specifically designed to accommodate their abilities, such as [22,28]:

- Mechanical switches: In the simplest case, a mechanical switch consists of two or more contacts and an actuator that connects or disconnects the contacts to close or open the switch, respectively. The mechanism may respond to specific mechanical stimuli, including changes in displacement, inclination, air pressure or force. These switches are controlled with an explicit physical movement. Some examples of mechanical switches are one-button switches, mouth switches or head switches.
- Infrared sensing: these sensors consist of a source of infrared light and a receiver. Receivers detect the radiation and generate a proportional output voltage, identifying the depth of the scene from the point of view of the source. An example of infrared sensor is Kinect sensor, from Microsoft.
- Electromyography (EMG): these devices consist of a set of electromyographic electrodes placed on the skin that record the electrical activity generated by the muscles at rest and during contractions. This allows devices to be controlled by EMG patterns associated with movements of different muscles, such as facial muscles for instance.
- Oculography: gaze-based communication systems can map eye movement or point-of-gaze to cursor position. There are two main technologies: Video-oculography (VOG) and electro-oculography (EOG). VOG is based on an infrared light source and a camera, so that the view direction is calculated from the displacement between the reflection of the cornea and the centre of the pupil. EOG is based on electrodes that are placed around the eyes and measure potential changes between the cornea and the retina that occur when the user changes the direction of the gaze.

- Computer vision: these systems track the location of a facial reference point of the user (e.g. nose or pupil) through a camera and translate the position changes in cursor movements on a screen.
- Brain-Computer Interfaces: these systems directly capture the brain activity through the use of different types of electrodes. Depending on the electrodes placement, the main technologies are electroencephalography (EEG) (superficial electrodes placed on the scalp), electrocorticography (ECoG) (surgically implanted epidural or subdural electrodes) and intracortical recordings (electrodes chronically implanted in the cortex).

Beyond the devices used for the interaction, another aspect to study is how to design video games so that players with motor disabilities can easily access them. In this case, the main strategies for adaptation are [14]:

- Control with one button: it is possible to design games that are controlled only by using a button, or, at least, using the minimum number of buttons.
- Control with one hand: the controller interaction is designed to be used with one hand only.
- Non-simultaneous buttons: avoid that the accomplishment of an action entails to press more than one button at the same time.
- Configurable control sensitivity: provide the possibility of adjusting the sensitivity of controls.
- Configurable game speed: provide a possible decrement of game speed to make the game easier to be controlled.
- Various levels of difficulty: a mode of immunity or the ability to jump directly to the next episode of the game may be used to make the game easier to play.
- Control by microphone: provide the possibility of using the microphone as peripheral to control the game, either by voice recognition or simply by sounds that emulate the pulsations of a single button.

3   Methodology

The final degree projects have been developed in collaboration with APCA (*Asociación de Paralíticos Cerebrales de Alicante*, Association of Cerebral Palsy of Alicante). Its main objective is defending the rights of people affected by Cerebral Palsy, aimed at achieving normality [2]. APCA offers care, advice, education, training and leisure to affected people. The research team made contact with the association in 2013, starting collaboration, initially in an informal and voluntary way, to develop final degree projects for designing and developing accessible video games, adapted for users with cerebral palsy.

The methodology that we chose for this experience is Action Research [6]. In this methodology the research process is divided in four stages (plan, implement, evaluate and reflect) that are iteratively repeated introducing improvements in each iteration. Action research does not have an end point so it always poses new questions. Figure 1 graphically shows the stages of the methodology and the concept of iteration.

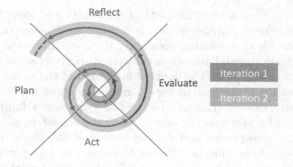

Fig. 1. Action research methodology

During the *Plan* stage, the activities to develop the project are established. In particular, there is an initial meeting with APCA, to know the users and their context; the objectives of the final degree project are defined; there is a process of requirements and restrictions identification (limitations about the users' abilities, technical requirements and limitations, and economic and resource requirements); and the video game design and development planning is set up.

The *Act* stage is devoted to the incremental design and development of the video game. Agile software development methodologies are used, with short iterations, in which different functionalities are incorporated and continuous tests are carried out with users.

The *Evaluate* stage takes place after the development of the project. Tests are carried out with the users (end users and instructors) collecting their opinions, to know their level of acceptance. The results are compared with the initial requirements to know if they have been fulfilled. The implementation plan is also monitored and evaluated.

The *Reflect* stage is based on the results obtained in the previous phases. All data are compiled and analyzed. We collect the recommendations and observations that will help us begin a new iteration with the initial Plan Stage. In short, improvements for the next iteration are proposed.

4   Results

4.1   First Iteration: Footb-all Game

In the first iteration, an adapted video game about football was developed. This first experience allowed us to understand the problem of making video games accessible to users with cerebral palsy, to identify the main strategies to reduce and adapt interaction, to use simple interaction devices such as mechanical switches, and to define the improvements for the next iteration.

Plan Stage. Once the contact with APCA was established, the first step was to meet up with them to know their needs. The participants were: the tutors of the projects, the students, the therapists of the centre and some final users. As a result, a list of general requirements was defined: simple design, configuration options, customizable user profiles, possibility to cancel an action, use of sweeps for element navigation, emphasis when the action succeeds or fails, and graphic support for textual elements. The conceptual design of the video game was the next step: by decision of the final users, the game was about football. It consisted of a series penalty throws. The scenario of the game was a football field. The interaction should be very simple, using a mechanical switch, just to click. The way to select the parameters and characteristics of the throw (direction and speed, mainly) should be through the use of circular or bar meters (sliders), so that just a click is needed to stop the needle. The speed of the needle would also be configurable. The direction of the throw would be complemented with a random variable that represents the nervousness of the player to make the throw more unpredictable. There would also be some extras: choosing different teams, players, and avatars, and including a ranking.

Act Stage. During this stage the application was built following the initial requirements. It needed an iterative refinement of the prototype. After each visit to the association, new or adapted requirements arose or it was necessary to modify some part of the game, generating new versions of the prototype. The final prototype, called *Footb-all* [8], was presented to the members of the association.

The game is played in three main stages: Configuration (the players profile about interaction, the selected team and the avatar are selected, see Fig. 2), game (the direction and speed are setup and the ball is thrown, see Fig. 3), and results (the ranking is presented, see Fig. 4).

Fig. 2. Configuration screen of Footb-all game. The profile is selected just clicking with the switch when the desired picture is highlighted during the sweep.

Fig. 3. Main game screen of Footb-all game. The sliders to select the horizontal and vertical direction and the speed are placed on the right bottom corner of the screen.

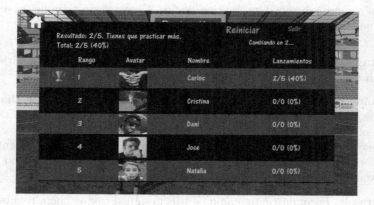

Fig. 4. Results screen of Footb-all game. It shows a ranking of the players.

Evaluate Stage. During the previous stages, many data were gathered from the users (CP patients and their therapists) but also from the development of the project. It allowed us to determine the progress and make the necessary adjustments for the project to succeed. The analysis of this information and the comparison against the design and the requirements showed us that there was little deviation during the implementation, so the plan to develop the game was appropriate and complete.

We also sounded out the final users and the therapists to obtain their opinions about the game and how to improve it. The therapists affirmed that the video game enhances the emotional well-being and the motivation for personal improvement. They also considered that playing in a continued way could favour the strategic planning and perceptual abilities, as well as spatio-temporal organization and increased physical response speed. Final users, besides, found to access new technologies very attractive, especially when they are related to leisure. They also pointed out that there had been some competition between them.

Reflect Stage. This first experience allowed us to understand the problem of making video games accessible to users with cerebral palsy, to identify the main strategies to reduce and adapt interaction and to use simple interaction devices such as mechanical switches. All the gathered information and the analysis allowed us to define an improvement plan with two main objectives:

- Explore new ways of interaction: Although the users found very easy the use of adapted switches, the interaction turned out to be too limiting in many cases.
- Introduce characters which the player could identify with: The use of disabled characters could achieve a higher level of empathy of the player.

4.2   Second Iteration: Formula Chair Game

The second iteration was devoted to design and develop a video game about wheelchair races, an adapted sport that many players do. We also introduced the use of a more advanced interaction device, Kinect, using simple movements. The evaluation phase made us detect that Kinect was a good choice.

Plan Stage. In this second iteration we proposed the following objectives, defined in the improvement plan of the previous iteration:

- Maintain the main successful elements of the interface, such as the sweep concept for the selection of profiles, the structure of the profiles and the final screen of ranking.
- Introduce a character and a context in which the users could feel identified.
- Incorporate a new interaction device that would increase the range and variety of movements, but maintaining the requirement of simplicity.

As a result, *Formula Chair* game [5] was designed taking these requirements into account. The game would consist of a character that is infinitely moving in a scenario with three lanes. Some different objects (coins, obstacles or other people) may appear and they must be avoided or collected. The score would be calculated according to the play time without losing all lives, the number of collected coins and the number of dodged obstacles and people.

The user could decide which extremity to use to interact with the game: head, right arm, left arm, right leg or left leg. The capture of the movement of the chosen extremity would be performed using the *Microsoft Kinect* device [16].

Act Stage. This stage was devoted to develop the video game. An agile and incremental methodology was also used. As a result, successive prototypes were obtained, so the work of monitoring the progress and the adaptation to the requirements were facilitated. The main milestones were:

- Start up and configure the interaction using the Kinect device.
- Determine the interaction. Each user had a profile in which he or she selected the extremity for interaction.

– Define the ranges of movement of the extremities. In particular, two configurable ranges were defined: right range (minimum movement range of the extremity to the right to change to the right lane) and left range (minimum movement range of the extremity to the left to change to the left lane).
– Calculate the score in function of collected coins and dodged obstacles and people.

During the realization of the project, we detected some aspects to be redefined: for example, it was necessary to implement a pause function. The game is paused at the beginning, until the user is ready to start, and there is also an automatic pause if the Kinect device loses the user's reference. Figure 5 shows a screenshot of the interaction configuration screen and Fig. 6 the main screen of the game.

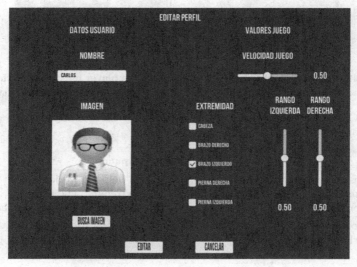

Fig. 5. Interaction configuration screen of Formula Chair game. The profile allows the selection of the extremity and the movement ranges.

Evaluate Stage. Once implemented the video game, several tests were carried out to verify the functionality of the game and to obtain the opinion of the therapists and the users. Therapists responded to three questions on a Likert scale with values between 1 (strongly disagree) and 5 (strongly agree), in addition to providing their personal opinion. An open question was also set out. These questions try to explore the possibility of using video games to complement the work of physiotherapists. Since only two therapists participated, the results are not statistically significant but they allow us to propose improvements for the next iteration. Table 1 shows the questions and answers obtained.

Eight users responded to a more general questionary about their users' experience. All of them liked the game, considered it as a good tool to be incorporated in their physiotherapy sessions and had a high opinion about developing

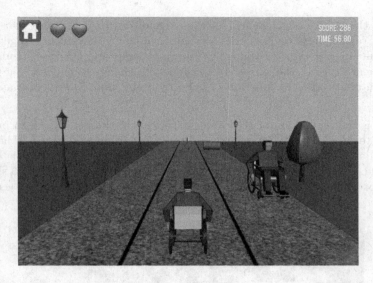

Fig. 6. Main game screen of Formula Chair game. The player must change the lane to avoid obstacles and people and collect coins by moving the selected extremity.

Table 1. Questions and answers of therapists about the use of the video game for physiotherapy

Question	Average value	Opinion
I would use this video game as a possible method of physiotherapy	5	It helps to work with an extremity. The users are motivated to improve their score
The video game can help improve the mobility of people	5	Configuration (speed, extremity and movement range) improves therapy possibilities
The video game is fun and suitable for people with cerebral palsy	4	The game is suitable and fun, but there may be other more interesting topics
What would you improve in the video game?	–	Improve user capture, especially for those who use a wheelchair

this type of collaboration between APCA and the University. Some of them, however, found the game difficult to use because of the limited movements.

Reflect Stage. This second video game allowed us to approach to the access to games from two different points of view: the interaction through new devices and the possible use of games as therapy tools. As a consequence, the new improvement plan has as main objective placing the requirements of the physiotherapists in the centre of the design process. In the previous iterations the aim was providing fun but in the following one this aim should be balanced with the use of the game as a physiotherapy tool.

4.3 Third Iteration: Fisio Run

The third iteration included the team of physiotherapists of the association in the project, developing a new game with two main objectives: serving as entertainment and helping the physiotherapists to achieve their goals with the patient. This game should use several movements to obtain different results, so that it helped the players to distinguish different movements.

Plan Stage. In this iteration the main objective was to develop a video game that, besides being fun, had a therapeutic purpose. The therapists of the centre considered that this type of applications could motivate the users to make more complex movements to achieve their goals, thus it would help in their rehabilitation. Therefore, it was decided that this new video game should include more complex movements than the previous ones.

The video game was decided to be about running while jumping and ducking to avoid the obstacles. The movement should be controlled by different parts of the player's body. The good results obtained in the other iterations led us to maintain the definition of profiles to configure the system (adding the necessary elements to incorporate a more complex interaction) and the sweep scheme for the selections.

Act Stage. The implementation used an agile methodology to carry out the successive prototypes, as in the previous iterations. These prototypes led to a final version of the game, which was called *Fisio Run* [15], which included the following features:

- The scenario was created automatically, from an infinite plane in which two types of obstacles to avoid, by jumping or crouching, were randomly incorporated.
- Two game modes were created for one and two players. This motivates users through competition between them.
- Each player created a profile to configure, among other aspects, the speed, the extremities to interact and their movement. In total, three types of actions must be configured: running, jumping and crouching.
- Each player initially had three lives (the number of lives was configurable though to help the users with higher difficulties), discounting a life each time the avatar crashed an obstacle. The final score was calculated in function of the time the player is able to stay in the game.

Figures 7 and 8 show the configuration and the game screens.

Evaluate Stage. The collection of data during the previous phases and the constant communication with the therapists allowed us to make an adequate evaluation of the development process and the opinion of the users. The main results are:

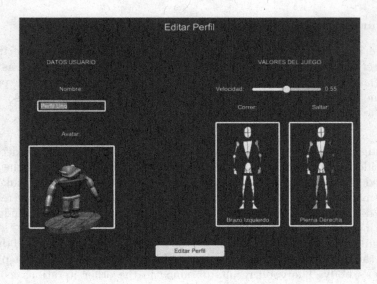

Fig. 7. Interaction configuration screen of Fisio Run game. The profile allows the selection of the extremities for each movement.

- From the point of view of the interaction, Kinect is a tool of reduced cost and quite acceptable results. However, it leaves out certain users with a very low level of mobility and it still has some problems when detecting users in a wheelchair.
- From the institutional point of view, the need to establish stronger ties between the University and APCA has been detected in order to carry out new joint actions.

Reflect Stage. The collaboration between the University and APCA is close and easy. However, we must go further to develop other projects. Moreover, the Kinect device should be complemented with other interaction devices. Therefore, the next improvement plan has as main objectives:

- Signing a formal agreement between our organization and APCA to deepen our relationship and develop new more ambitious projects.
- Explore the use of other interaction devices to widen the scope of the projects to users with very low level of mobility.

4.4 Fourth Iteration

Now, the fourth iteration is beginning. A first action has been made: signing a formal agreement between the institutions. We have planned two main objectives for this iteration:

Fig. 8. Main game screen of Fisio Run game. The player must jump or crouch to avoid the obstacles by moving the selected extremities.

- Develop new games, exploring the new interaction devices.
- Improve our dissemination actions by letting every development at the disposal of any other institution through the institutional platform of the university.

5   Discussion

Most people who suffer from cerebral palsy have movement limitations. This implies that many of them do not have the physical capacity to respond quickly to certain stimuli, to interact with precise movements or to make combinations of movements that many video games demand. Our experience in these projects tells us that the adaptation of the interaction can be done through several strategies. In the following paragraphs, these strategies, that can be combined in several ways, are compiled to serve as a guide for future developments.

Interaction Reduction. One of the most effective way of making a video game accessible is reducing the interaction so that it can be performed with a single button, by means of just a click, avoiding combinations of buttons, multiple buttons or pointing devices. In general, this is achieved by using mechanical switches that can be pressed with the hand, foot or head, or by other more specific devices.

Sweeping. Reducing the interaction to a single click can be achieved through sweeping strategies. This technique is used to navigate between several options and select one of them. All the options are highlighted, one at a time, at a certain speed, and then changed after a defined time. The user must click on the moment the desired option has the focus. Apart from the option with the focus, the other previous and future options must be displayed on the screen, so that the user can anticipate the next option and prepare to perform the action.

Sliders and Circular Meters. Sliders and circular meters allow the selection of a value within a range. They have a needle that runs the slider automatically, so that the user can stop it at the desired value with a single click. This strategy allows the selection of different values without requiring a pointing device that needs to be handled with greater precision.

Speed. The speed of each user when handling the interaction devices during the game can be very varied. Therefore, it is important to allow the configuration of the speed, both during the selection of the characteristics and the profile, and during the game action.

Interaction Devices. In addition to switches, the inclusion of other more versatile interaction devices can be very interesting. In particular, the use of Kinect in our games has given us very good results. On the one hand, not having to hold any element in the hand facilitates freedom of movement. On the other hand, it is possible to define with which part of the body we want to perform the interaction. It is necessary, therefore, that the games allow different configurations and ranges of movement.

Game Interface and Graphics. The game interface should be simple so as not to divert users' attention from the main focus. The design of the interaction elements should allow easy identification, making use of appropriate colors and sizes. As for the game scenario, we must avoid too many superfluous elements that divert attention from the main character.

6   Conclusions and Further Work

This experience has served, on one hand, to introduce the aspects of social responsibility in the curricula of engineers in a very effective way and, on the other hand, to study and design new ways of making video games accessible to disabled people, giving them the chance to access to the right to entertainment.

The use of the proposed incremental and agile methodology has been proved to be very suitable for this type of projects. It has the advantage of allowing students to gradually introduce themselves in the knowledge of adapting video games to make them accessible. In addition, in this way, the successive reunions and tests with the users of APCA allow the students to know the problems of users affected with cerebral palsy and to strengthen the bonds between students and users. This gives students an important awareness of the need to give all people, regardless of their conditions, access to digital platforms and, why not, to digital leisure.

As a result of the design and implementation of several video games, we have also obtain a guide for designing and developing adapted games. This is a preliminary version that will be completed in the future as next iterations will be performed. This guide can also be extended to other types of digital systems that must be adapted to disabled users.

This work is considered as a seed for the digital transformation of the interaction environments adapted to users with disabilities, and for the involvement of professionals of the future in this transformation. Therefore, the lines of future work are many and widely open. In particular we propose for the future:

- Widen and strengthen the links between our University and APCA and other associations of disabled users.
- Introduce this iterative and incremental methodology of work in other curricula in the context of Information Technology Engineerings.
- Improve the diffusion of the results so that it can be used for any disabled user.

Other future lines are related to other more technological objectives. In this context, our next steps will be:

- Explore other interaction devices. We are particularly interested in Brain-Computer Interfaces.
- Explore new ways of adapting the interaction to complete the guide and lessons learned about adapting video games to disabled users.

Acknowledgements. We thank the final degree project students Roberto Gómez Davó, author of Footb-all game; Aitor Font Puig, author of Formula Chair game; and Alberto Martínez Martínez, author of Fisio Run game, for their great work and their kind implication in the projects.

We also thank the Association of Cerebral Palsy of Alicante (APCA) and particularly its therapists, for their important and amazing labour with their patients, and their implication in the projects.

We specially thank the people affected of cerebral palsy, particularly those belonging to APCA, because of the enthusiasm with our projects and their valuable contributions.

This research is partially supported by *Cátedra Santander-Universidad de Alicante de Transformación Digital.*

References

1. Alcántara, O.J.G., González, I.F., López, M.A.C., Gistaín, A.R.: Responsabilidad Social en las Universidades: Del conocimiento a la acción. Pautas para su implantación - Social Responsibility at Universities: from Knowledge to Action. Guidelines for Its Implementation, May 2016
2. APCA: A.P.C.A. Asociación de Paralíticos Cerebrales de Alicante (2016). http://www.apcalicante.com

3. Disabled World: Cerebral Palsy: Types, Diagnosis & Research. https://www. disabled-world.com/health/neurology/cerebral-palsy/

4. Durkin, K., Boyle, J., Hunter, S., Conti-Ramsden, G.: Video games for children and adolescents with special educational needs. Zeitschrift für Psychologie **221**(2), 79–89 (2013). http://econtent.hogrefe.com/doi/abs/10.1027/2151-2604/a000138

5. Font Puig, A.: Proyecto Final de Grado: formula chair. Universidad de Alicante, Alicante, September 2015. http://hdl.handle.net/10045/49408, proyecto Final de Grado

6. Gay, L.R., Mills, G.E., Airasian, P.W.: Chapter 20. Action research. In: Educational Research: Competencies for Analysis and Applications, 10th edn. Pearson, Boston (2012). oCLC: ocn710045202

7. Gee, J.P.: What video games have to teach us about learning and literacy. Revised and Updated edn. Palgrave Macmillan, New York (2007). oCLC: ocn172569526

8. Gómez Davó, R.: Proyecto Final de Grado: Videojuego adaptado para personas con parálisis cerebral. Universidad de Alicante, Alicante, September 2014. http:// hdl.handle.net/10045/40272, proyecto Final de Grado

9. Jenkins, H.: Game theory. https://www.technologyreview.com/s/401394/ game-theory/

10. Kebritchi, M., Hirumi, A.: Examining the pedagogical foundations of modern educational computer games. Comput. Educ. **51**(4), 1729–1743 (2008). http://linkinghub.elsevier.com/retrieve/pii/S0360131508000778

11. Kent, R.M.: Cerebral palsy. In: Barnes, M.P., Good, D.C., Aminoff, M.J. (eds.) Neurological Rehabilitation, pp. 443–459 (2013). No. ser. ed.: Michael J. Aminoff ...; vol. 110 = 3. Ser., [vol. 32] in Handbook of clinical neurology, Elsevier, Edinburgh. oCLC: 817269354

12. Llorens-Largo, F., Gallego-Durán, F.J., Villagrá-Arnedo, C.J., Compañ Rosique, P., Satorre-Cuerda, R., Molina-Carmona, R.: Gamification of the learning process: lessons learned. IEEE Revista Iberoamericana de Tecnologias del Aprendizaje **11**(4), 227–234 (2016). http://ieeexplore.ieee.org/document/7600433/

13. Lohse, K., Shirzad, N., Verster, A., Hodges, N., Van der Loos, H.F.M.: Video games and rehabilitation: using design principles to enhance engagement in physical therapy. J. Neurol. Phys. Ther. **37**(4), 166–175 (2013)

14. Mairena, J.: Videojuegos accesibles, por qué y cómo hacerlos. In: IV Congreso de la CiberSociedad 2009. Crisis analógica, futuro digital (2009). http://www.cibersociedad.net/congres2009/es/coms/ videojuegos-%20accesibles-por-que-y-como-hacerlos/317/

15. Martínez Martínez, A.: Proyecto Final de Grado: Fisio Run. Videojuego adaptado para personas con parálisis cerebral. Universidad de Alicante, Alicante, October 2016. http://hdl.handle.net/10045/58492, proyecto Final de Grado

16. Microsoft: Meet Kinect for Windows. https://developer.microsoft.com/en-us/ windows/kinect

17. Minear, W.L.: A classification of cerebral palsy. Pediatrics **18**(5), 841–852 (1956)

18. Muñoz, J.E., Villada, J.F., Muñoz, C.D., Henao, O.A.: Multimodal system for rehabilitation aids using videogames, pp. 1–7. IEEE, November 2014. http://ieeexplore. ieee.org/document/7000395/

19. Rosenbaum, P., Paneth, N., Leviton, A., Goldstein, M., Bax, M., Damiano, D., Dan, B., Jacobsson, B.: A report: the definition and classification of cerebral palsy April 2006. Dev. Med. Child Neurol. Suppl. **109**, 8–14 (2007)

20. Squire, K., Squire, K.: Changing the game: what happens when video games enter the classroom? Innov.: J. Online Educ. **1**(6) (2005). https://www.learntechlib.org/ p/107270/

21. Street, R.L., Gold, W.R., Manning, T. (eds.): Health Promotion and Interactive Technology: Theoretical Applications and Future Directions. Lawrence Erlbaum Associates, Mahwah (1997)
22. Tai, K., Blain, S., Chau, T.: A review of emerging access technologies for individuals with severe motor impairments. Assistive Technol. **20**(4), 204–221 (2008). http://www.tandfonline.com/doi/abs/10.1080/10400435.2008.10131947
23. Universidad de Alicante: Degree in Multimedia Engineering, March 2012. https://cvnet.cpd.ua.es/toolsnet/ClasePDF/generaPDF.aspx?Cuerpo=%2fwebcvnet%2fPlanEstudio%2fplanestudioPDF.aspx%3fplan%3dC205%26caca%3d2016-17%26lengua%3dE
24. Universidad de Alicante: Plan Estratégico UA 40, February 2014. https://web.ua.es/en/peua/documentos/peua40cg.pdf
25. Villagrá-Arnedo, C., Gallego-Durán, F.J., Molina-Carmona, R., Llorens-Largo, F.: PLMan: towards a gamified learning system. In: Zaphiris, P., Ioannou, A. (eds.) LCT 2016. LNCS, vol. 9753, pp. 82–93. Springer, Cham (2016). doi:10.1007/978-3-319-39483-1_8
26. Whitehead, A., Johnston, H., Nixon, N., Welch, J.: Exergame effectiveness: what the numbers can tell us, pp. 55–62. ACM Press (2010). http://portal.acm.org/citation.cfm?doid=1836135.1836144
27. World Health Organization, World Bank (eds.): World Report on Disability. World Health Organization, Geneva, Switzerland (2011). oCLC: ocn742386216
28. Yuan, B., Folmer, E., Harris, F.C.: Game accessibility: a survey. Univ. Access Inf. Soc. **10**(1), 81–100 (2011). http://link.springer.com/10.1007/s10209-010-0189-5

The Use of a New Visual Language as a Supporting Resource for People with Intellectual Disabilities

Francisco Rodríguez-Sedano[(⊠)], Miguel A. Conde-González, Camino Fernández-Llamas, and Gonzalo Esteban-Costales

Robotics Group, Department of Mechanical, Computer Science and Aerospace Engineering, University of León, Campus de Vegazana, S/N, 24071 León, Spain
{francisco.sedano,miguel.conde,camino.fernandez, gestc}@unileon.es

Abstract. Our society is radically changing at an astonishing rate essentially, due to the fact that Information and Communication Technologies (ICT) are becoming an ever greater part of our lives. The frenetic rhythm at which the technology has evolved in recent years, has caused a significant separation between individuals who use communication technologies and those who don't. There is a technological gap, and most of the time it's because of the inadequacy both of the hardware and the software currently present for people with different levels of disability. This article discusses the use of a new visual language, known as VILA (VIsual LAnguage), to resolve the accessibility problems that people with certain types of disabilities have when they use ICTs to access to information and knowledge society and to communicate with other people under equal terms. We also present a first evaluation of a software prototype performed by a group of trainers specialized in children with Down syndrome to demonstrate their utility and the application fields of the language, as well as its advantages.

Keywords: Educational media/multimedia · Personalization and adaptation in learning technologies · Accessibility · Functional diversity · Intellectual disability · Visual language

1 Introduction

In recent years, Information and Communication Technologies (hereinafter ICT) have transformed the way in which we work, live and interact with others. There are many terms that have been coined in an attempt to identify and understand the scope of these changes. At the World Summit on the Information Society (held in a first phase in Geneva in 2003 and in a second phase in Tunis in 2005) two terms stood out among the rest: information society and knowledge society. And although the first of the two was used primarily at the meeting, the second currently seems to make more sense. In fact, the term has begun to be used in the plural form (knowledge societies) to reflect the different social, ethical and political dimensions; thus, rejecting the idea of a single model that does not reflect the cultural and linguistic diversity present in any modern society today [1].

© Springer International Publishing AG 2017
P. Zaphiris and A. Ioannou (Eds.): LCT 2017, Part II, LNCS 10296, pp. 202–214, 2017.
DOI: 10.1007/978-3-319-58515-4_16

However, from the beginning of time, knowledge control has often led to a significant series of inequalities, exclusions and gaps which increase the existing differences between the rich and poor, industrialized and developing countries and even between the citizens of the same country. It is precisely the use of new technologies that has generated what is known as a "digital divide" which can be defined as the separation that exists between the people (communities, states, countries, etc.) that use ICTs as a routine part of their daily lives and those that do not have access to them or those that have access, but do not know how to use them [2].

As a matter of fact, the group of people in our society that is most susceptible to these kinds of inequalities is made up of individuals who suffer from certain types of disabilities or functional diversity which often times prevents them from accessing and using the information under the same terms as the rest of society.

Perhaps the discrimination that most affects this group is their lack of access to the various environments, products and services; and for this reason, terms such as "breaking down barriers", "design for all" or "accessibility" have come to be commonly used in reports, rules, technical standards, etc.

But, the concept of accessibility has evolved in parallel to the progress made integrating people with disabilities. At first, these people were treated as a group requiring protection and a distinct environment (an approach known as the "medical model"). Today, this approach has changed. Now, the trend is towards their normalized inclusion without discrimination (the "social model" approach and the principle of "equal opportunities") [3].

Therefore, a need to classify accessibility arises so as to approach the study and problems that appear in each individual case. This classification could be as follows:

- Architectural and urban planning accessibility.
- Transport accessibility.
- Information and communication accessibility.

For this research work, we will focus on the latter precisely because of the importance of information in today's society as mentioned at the beginning of the article.

When analyzing the problems that people with certain types of disabilities encounter when accessing ICTs, we run into two new terms: "e-accessibility" and "e-inclusion".

The concept of "e-accessibility" may be defined as the removal of barriers that older people and/or people with disabilities encounter when they try to access ICT products, services and applications.

The concept of "e-inclusion", which is broader and includes the other, is defined on the European Knowledge Society's website [4] as the strategy aimed at ensuring that disadvantaged people are not excluded from this society due to their lack of digital literacy or Internet access. This term also involves being able to make use of the advantages offered by the new opportunities generated by new technologies in the interest of the social inclusion of disadvantaged people and underprivileged areas.

On the other hand, it is important to acknowledge that the information society can provide more independence and opportunities to people with disabilities although they can also become even more excluded from access to information and participation in society than is currently the case if a series of fundamental rights such as the right to information is not respected.

The solutions to guarantee this access to information using ICTs for people with disabilities include very diverse resources which range from software adaptations (voice recognition, graphic and non-graphic interfaces, sign language translators, etc.) to hardware adaptations (switches, adapted keyboards, pointing devices, amplifiers for sound reception, etc.). These solutions are known as technical aids or support products; and United Nations Convention 61/106 on the Rights of Persons with Disabilities, which was approved in December 2006, establishes a general obligation for the signatory States to promote research and development, the availability and use of mobility aids, technical devices and assistive technologies that are suitable for people with disabilities.

This article is organized in the following way. The second section outlines the theoretical framework by explaining the accessibility problems of people with disabilities when using ICTs and describing VILA visual language. The third section describes the methodology used to do the research and describes the software prototype developed with the research. The experiment and results section analyzes some of the advantages of using VILA language with these types of systems that make it possible to improve communication and language use for people affected by certain types of disabilities. Finally, some of the problems that arose while carrying out the research are described and their solutions are provided in the discussion section. The article ends with some conclusions on the questions and objectives set forth at the beginning of the research work.

2   Theoretical Framework

2.1   Accessibility Problems for People with Disabilities

The use of new technologies also involves disadvantages for people with some type of functional disability for whom it is more difficult to access the information and knowledge society. The new information and communication technologies must be adapted to the individual needs of all groups of people with disabilities. Just as all citizens, these people have different needs and interests and the information and knowledge society can also provide different types of information, communications, knowledge and network creation for these groups. Thus, considering people with disabilities as a homogeneous group is discriminatory and does not take into account the capacities and possibilities of some individuals who, in some cases, simply need tools that are adapted to their needs.

Moreover, producing support products so that people with disabilities may access information requires technical and functional requirements in order for the final result to be effective. These requirements must include the official authorization and standardization of suitable technologies which must be based on knowledge, experience and technological development. All of the parties must be involved in their creation: the industry, users, professionals, etc. For this reason, in order to guarantee the participation of end users in the research and development of technological products and applications, this must be done by either including people with disabilities in the process of developing the new products or in the analysis of the users' real needs and the adaptation of the existing products as people with disabilities are the ones who best know what requirements these products must meet.

Therefore, if we wanted to classify the accessibility technologies available on the market, we would have to follow standard UNE-EN ISO 9999:2007 (Assistive products for persons with disability. Classification and terminology), which offers this classification in accordance with their function and consists of three hierarchical levels (classes, subclasses and divisions). However, we believe that this may be confusing for users as this standard frequently uses cross references meaning that the interested party is constantly directed to sections that are found in various parts of the document which can make it difficult to quickly and accurately locate a desired product.

For the particular case of people who suffer from some type of intellectual disability, we believe the classification based on promoting and stimulating intellectual capacities offered in the 2008 Study on Accessibility Technologies in Spain, published by the National Accessibility Technologies Center [5] is more appropriate. It includes four types of technological solutions or support systems; namely: memory development and training systems, reading and writing learning and support systems, sensory stimulation enhancement systems and language and communication development and training systems. The four types are related to cognitive skills learning, development and training.

For this research work, we focus on systems that enable improved communication and the use of language with accessibility technologies for people affected by intellectual disabilities. All of these systems are based on the use of symbols, graphics and images that are used to support natural language. Our objective is to improve these systems by using a new two-dimensional visual language instead of natural language which will help eliminate some specific barriers encountered by people with intellectual disabilities such as a difficulty understanding complex communication structures and accessing abstract concepts or a difficulty appropriately interpreting the symbolic language used on the Internet.

In this research we have focused on children with Down syndrome and their problems to use and learn natural language. Reading is a very effective way to help these children learn the language. The ability to read opens many doors to any child, but in children with Down syndrome the advantages are even greater. Reading helps them learn the concepts of language through their visual channel, thus avoiding other difficulties. Sue Buckley of Down Syndrome Education International has discovered that learning to read has positive effects on the tasks of spoken language, receptive vocabulary and memory. It advocates the use of visual processing and visual memory skills to support all learning [6].

Some children with Down syndrome begin using spoken words at the age of two, and some use speech before that age, but many will not begin to speak until they are seven or eight years old. In addition, a small percentage will never come to use speech as the main communication system. In these cases, it is necessary to use alternative communication systems, such as communication boards, so that children can communicate with each other.

2.2 New Visual Language: VILA

The research described in this article came out of a project developed by a research group which has been working in the Knowledge Engineering field for several years. A new visual language called VILA (VIsual LAnguage) was created within the context of this project.

The basic objective of Knowledge Engineering is to represent knowledge in a way that it can be automatically processed with a computer. But, knowledge is generated in natural language by human beings and in order to be able to automate it on computers, this knowledge must be represented in formalized structures. Transforming knowledge expressed in natural language to formalized structures requires a translation process. And the problem lies precisely with this translation process. In order to formalize knowledge, the translator (normally an expert or specialist in the field of knowledge that is to be formalized) needs to eliminate the ambiguities inherent in natural language, its lack of precision, the various meanings of the terms and its structural "vagueness". There are no standards for this task. Each translator applies his/her own criteria and this leads to very subjective results. The structures formalized by one translator are not usually compatible with those completed by another [7].

After several years of reflection, we have reached the conclusion that it is necessary to eliminate the translation process that causes the aforementioned ills. Our proposal consists of generating knowledge directly in a formalized language - a language that is common to man and machine. And this represents a change in paradigm. The structure of this new language must resolve the problems of ambiguity and "vagueness" inherent in natural language. Let's see how this objective is achieved.

VILA language grammar is based on the concept of linguistic expression. There are many types of linguistic expression, but all of them are constructed by grouping together the three basic types. These are: linguistic expressions of identification, linguistic expressions to describe characteristics and linguistic expressions to describe actions. Each linguistic expression is represented inside a rectangle. The rectangles are grouped into pages and these into documents [8].

For linguistic expressions of identification, it must be kept in mind that when the words of any given language are used to identify a concept or an object, only one form of this word - the most common - is used. Plurals are not used and there is no difference between masculine and feminine; this is only done when referring to living things that are differentiated by sex (i.e.: cow, ox, etc.), but gender is not assigned to objects or concepts. There may also be cases where the concept to be represented is comprised of several words although the identifier is considered to be unique. The words are then joined with an underscore. (i.e.: tooth_brush).

The second type of basic linguistic expressions is comprised of those used to describe characteristics. These are the expressions associated in natural language to the verbs "to be", "to have" and a few others. There are many special features and major differences in these verbs between some languages and others. Verbs are not used in VILA to express the characteristics of something. Characteristics are always applied to one or more already identified elements using the corresponding linguistic expression (see Fig. 1). Characteristics are distributed into one of the following groups: adjective, value, relationship, space, time and adverb.

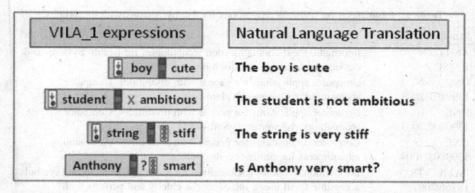

Fig. 1. Example of VILA language expressions and their translation to natural language.

The third group of basic linguistic expressions is comprised of those used to describe actions. They are expressions which are used to describe changes in the characteristics of a concept or entity. The main element of these types of expressions is the verb. The corresponding action is described with it. The verb is always expressed in the infinitive.

Both linguistic expressions that describe characteristics as well as those used to describe actions can be used to identify elements. Linguistic expressions of the same type can also be grouped together using "and" and "or" operators. This way we can easily communicate without the linguistic barriers that can be found in the use of natural language.

Furthermore, and given that the immense majority of man/machine knowledge transactions are via an electronic screen, the language must have a clear visual orientation. It is precisely this characteristic that makes this new language appropriate to be used as a support resource by people with intellectual disabilities, facilitating access to information by these types of users through the new information and communication technologies.

3 Methodological Framework

To corroborate this hypothesis, we have developed and evaluated a software prototype by adapting the linguistic structures of this new visual language to the picture communication symbols (PCS) that are often used in assistive products and are known as alternative communication systems. They have already been commercialized and tested by users with this type of functional diversity.

For the development of the prototype we have taken into account the recommendations of software engineering in terms of accessibility of computer applications for people with disabilities, especially when designing the interface. We have also taken into account the regulations concerning software adaptations that people with disabilities should use (see Table 1).

Table 1. Regulations on software adaptations for use by persons with disabilities.

Standard	Title
AEN/CTN 139/SC 8	Information and communication technologies for health. Systems and devices for later age and disability
UNE 1399801:2003	Computer applications for people with disabilities. Computer accessibility requirements. Hardware
UNE 1399802:2003	Computer applications for people with disabilities. Computer accessibility requirements. Software
UNE 1399803:2004	Computer applications for people with disabilities. Accessibility requirements for content on the web
ISO/IEC TR 19766:2007	Information technology. Guidelines for the design of icons and symbols accessible to all users, including the elderly and persons with disabilities

In the application development process, we used the methodology known as "user centered design" [9], because as indicated above, users with disabilities are the ones who best know which requirements these types of assistive products must meet. We also took into consideration the principles of quality, usability and functionality in the software design and development process as we believe that the quality of software products is an ever greater concern in the field of information technologies and that this can make a major difference in a market with similar products. But, in order to be able to offer a quality software product, the focus must be on the entire lifecycle of the product and not just on the latter part. Thus, the process must begin with a thorough compilation of the customer's requirements and then final tests and finally, acceptance of the final product by the users once the software has been developed.

Two important terms must be kept in mind when ensuring the quality of the product throughout its entire lifecycle: verification and validation [10]. Verification checks that the product meets the requirements established by the user and helps ensure that the product is being developed correctly. Validation evaluates the product based on the user's needs making sure that the product fulfills the use for which it was created. In order to achieve these two objectives, tests, analyses and inspections have been carried out always with the collaboration of the end user - which in this case were people with Down syndrome (children between the ages of 7–10).

4   Experiment and Results

In this paper, we have tried to design a prototype digital communication board that will serve, as Basil and Puig [11] point out, to cover the full range of communicative functions in people with some kind of disability, allowing him to communicate with all kinds of interlocutors.

To achieve this goal, we have consulted with several educational psychologists and professionals who work with people with some type of disability and who have problems communicating with normality. We have also evaluated different software available in the market and that allow the development of communication boards, such as, Boardmadker, Plafoons, Sicla II and TPWIN. Apart from the high cost in most cases, they are usually proprietary programs and do not allow the export or use of some modules to other systems. All this, has led us to the need to create our own software with the advantages and disadvantages that this decision supposes.

The software is still a communicator prototype where, after choosing the language (Spanish or English) and the level of language (see Fig. 2), the user goes to the main panel where he/she can choose between the different pictograms and easily communicate.

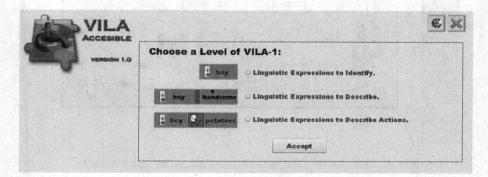

Fig. 2. Prototype software home screen.

This main screen is divided into 4 areas (see Fig. 3). The first, which is on the left side of the screen, shows the seven categories into which we have grouped the different symbols. Each one of them is represented by a color. The first five and their respective colors correspond to the standards used in augmentative and alternative communication [12]. A new category called "Social Expressions" was added which groups together a series of commonly used expressions from a pragmatic perspective of language and includes salutations and farewells, asking about wishes and basic needs, requests for attention, expressing emotions and feelings, requests for information, etc. Also was added is a new category called "Nexus" in which are grouped the symbols corresponding to those elements that serve as union between words or phrases.

The area corresponding to the sentence the user goes about building by choosing the pictograms from the corresponding category is found at the top right (zone 5 and 6 in the Fig. 3). The pictograms appear in a third central area (zone 2) on successive screens each with a maximum of 24 pictograms.

The area corresponding to the actions the user can take, which are represented by buttons, is found at zone 4.

4.1 Evaluation of Software Prototype

Although we have worked with different professionals specialized in the training and treatment of people with disabilities, we have discarded the test phase with users with

Fig. 3. Main screen of the software prototype. (Color figure online)

intellectual disability (more specifically with Down syndrome) for two main reasons. First, the assessment instruments required by these tests (Stanford-Binet intelligence scale, Wechsler intelligence scale for children, visual perception development test, auditory and phonological discrimination evaluation and psychomotricity test) and suggested by the specialists themselves, escape our scientific knowledge. The same happens with the analysis of the results of the same. Second, the tests require the written consent of the parents of users with Down syndrome, prior information about the characteristics and content of each test.

Therefore, in the test phase the evaluation of the prototype has been carried out by the educational psychologists and teachers of the AmiDown Association[1]. The test involved three teachers and two educational psychologists with extensive experience (5–15 years).

One of the ways to measure the usability of a software application is to perform these measurements using specially designed questionnaires for that purpose. The main reason for these questionnaires is that it is possible to obtain concrete answers by providing verifiable data, for example, statistical studies. The most relevant questionnaires in this area are: QUIS (Questionnaire for User Interface Satisfaction), SUMI

---

[1] Down León Amidown, founded in 1995 by parents and professionals, is a non-profit organization whose purpose and object is the search and achievement of the full social integration of people with Down syndrome, guaranteeing the safeguard of their Rights in all Aspects of life (training, psychological, legal, labor, recreational, sports, etc.), helping these people and their families and raising awareness of society. http://www.amidown.org/.

(Software Usability Measurement Inventory), WAMMI (Web Site Analysis and MeasureMent Inventory) and MUMMS (Measuring the Usability of Multi-Media Systems).

In this paper we have decided use and a SUMI questionnaire, adapted and modified according to our needs. For this, we have defined several hypotheses to validate the software prototype. Each hypothesis is accompanied by a series of statements, which users evaluate according to the Linkert Scale (Strongly Agree, Agree, Undecided, Disagree, Strongly Disagree). Let's look at these hypotheses in more detail:

Hypothesis 1: The Software has an Appropriate Level of Difficulty of Use

This hypothesis aims to identify if users have the ability to use the software, and that does not have a level of complexity that prevents its use. For this, the following statements are made:

- I had no great difficulty working with the main interface of the application.
- I had no major difficulties performing the basic operations to open, save, print and exit the application.
- Going through the different categories of pictograms and choosing each one was easy for me.
- I had no major problems creating and modifying the sentences with the application.
- Sometimes I do not understand what I have to do.
- Overall, the app was easy for me.
- The application works correctly.

Hypothesis 2: The Software Allows Functions that do not Allow Other Programs

It indicates if the user has found that the software is useful and better than others already existing, and that allows him to perform operations that he had not achieved with other applications. The following statements are made:

- When it comes to creating reading and writing exercises for my students, I prefer this tool over others.
- To develop communication boards for my students, I prefer this tool over others.
- When I used the application I managed to perform tasks I had not been able to accomplish with other tools.

Hypothesis 3: The Prototype Interface is Appropriate to this Type of Application

Indicates whether the interface designed for the application is useful and usable.

- The interface is visually appealing.
- The user interface is intuitive.
- The interface responds quickly.
- It is difficult to find some options.
- The user interface is very static and not very customizable.
- The interface needs to be improved.

Once the hypotheses and the objectives of each of them have been defined, we proceed to carry out the questionnaires with the people chosen for the test. For this, a questionnaire was designed in which the hypotheses raised previously were collected. Sixteen closed questions were defined on a five-level Likert scale and a comment was included at the end of the questionnaire.

In this research, we performed a qualitative analysis instead of a quantitative one, since the number of people who participated in the study is not enough to perform the first one. Users found it easy to manage the software. However, it was shown that at the beginning of its use, the goal was not very clear and what was the first step to be taken.

Another point to keep in mind is that there are users who were not clear using any of the buttons. However, by working more with the application, they recognized its usefulness. Therefore, the first hypothesis is met, since users could work with the software.

As for the second hypothesis, the users also find it valid, since they had not worked with other similar programs. This hypothesis is also fulfilled, since the first one is satisfied (could use it), and has not used other similar software.

The last hypothesis is also completely valid although it is perhaps the one that has generated the majority of the comments or observations.

4.2 Advantages of Using VILA

From the results obtained in the test it is deduced that the use of an alternative communication system, enable improved the learning capacity, the communication and the use of language on children with Down syndrome by replacing natural language with the use of symbols, graphics and images as support, have already been mentioned in Sect. 2.1.

Some of the advantages of using VILA language in these types of systems are based on simplifying the syntactic structures of this new language, which eliminate the ambiguity inherent to natural language.

Another of the advantages is that the new language enables expressing just one idea per sentence, thereby avoiding technical terms and abstract concepts. These are very important aspects when it comes to information access by people who have problems related to their capacity to understand and communicate either because they suffer from some type of disability or functional diversity or have limited cultural training, use a language that is not their maternal language or because they are elderly and have serious problems using new technologies to access information. These advantages are common to the European directives for generating easy-to-read information as promoted by the International League of Societies for Persons with Mental Handicap (ILSMH) [13].

5   Discussion

Using pictographic communication systems favors the visual memory process and relating words to concepts. Moreover, special motivation has been observed in children in general when using pictograms, not just those who suffer from some type of functional diversity. But, the meaning of some pictograms is complicated for them and this involves a specific sentence syntax learning process, especially for those who suffer from Down syndrome. In an attempt to solve this, we have enabled an option that allows the user to customize the symbols or graphics used by replacing the pictograms with images of real objects that the person using it is familiar with which facilitates their identification. This option has improved the functionality of the software and arose as a proposal by the users and educational psychologists themselves during the testing phase we conducted (see Fig. 4).

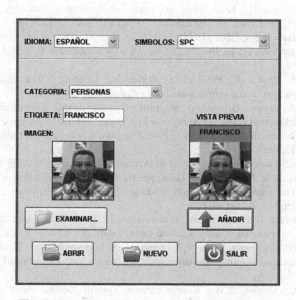

Fig. 4. Prototype file editing and customization box.

We also observed that, at first, the use of the verbs confuse children as there are no verb tenses since the pictograms do not vary for each grammatical change. The same occurs with the lack of distinction between gender and plurals in the definition of the concepts; however, they are used to using these types of communicators. In any case, the final objective, which is to achieve simple communication between people who have difficulties expressing themselves, is fulfilled quite satisfactorily.

6 Conclusions

The role of the new information and communication technologies in today's society is ever more decisive. Paradoxically, the use of these new technologies has, in some cases, generated risks of exclusion for groups such as people with certain types of disabilities or those who, because of their cultural level or advanced age, have serious problems when using ICTs to access information. This paper proposes the use of a new visual language known as VILA to resolve the accessibility problems people with certain types of disabilities have when using ICTs to access the information and knowledge society and communicate with other people under equal terms.

References

1. Mansell, R., When, U.: Knowledge Societies: Information Technology for Sustainable Development. United Nations Commission on Science and Technology for Development. Oxford University Press, USA (1998)
2. Serrano, A., Martínez, E.: La Brecha Digital: Mitos y Realidades. Editorial UABC, Mexico (2003)
3. Devlieger, J.P., Rusch, F., Pfeiffer, D.: Rethinking Disability: The Emergence of new Definition, Concepts, and Communities. Garant, Antwerp (2003)
4. Wynne, R., McAnaney, D.: Active inclusion of young people with disabilities or health problems - Background paper. In: European Foundation for the Improvement of Living and Working Conditions, Dublin, Ireland (2010). http://www.eurofound.europa.eu/publications/htmlfiles/ef1013.htm
5. INTECO: Estudio sobre las Tecnologías de Accesibilidad en España 2008. Centro Nacional de Tecnologías de la Accesibilidad, León, pp. 62–67. INTECO (2008)
6. Buckley, S.: The significance of early reading for children with down syndrome. Down Syndr. News Update 2(1), 1 (2002)
7. Alonso, A., García, I.: El conocimiento automatizado: la revolución que viene. Instituto de Automática y Fabricación, Universidad de León, León, pp. 10–12 (2006)
8. Alonso, A.: Introducción a VILA_1. El lenguaje de la accesibilidad. Hacia un mundo sin barreras lingüísticas. Instituto de Automática y Fabricación, Universidad de León, León, pp. 4–9 (2009)
9. Norman, D.A., Draper, S.W.: User Centered System Design: New Perspectives on Human-Computer Interaction. Lawrence Erlbaum Associates, Hillsdale (1986)
10. INTECO: Guía de mejores prácticas de calidad del producto. Centro Nacional de Tecnologías de la Accesibilidad, León, pp. 55–57. INTECO (2008)
11. Basil, C., Puig, R.: Comunicación aumentativa. Curso sobre sistemas y ayudas técnicas de comunicación no vocal. INSERSO, Madrid (1988)
12. Torres, S.: Sistemas alternativos de comunicación. Manual de comunicación aumentativa y alternativa: sistemas y estrategias. Aljibe, Málaga (2001)
13. Freyhoff, G., Hess, G., Kerr, L., Menzel, E., Tronbacke, B., Van Der Veken, K.: Guidelines for Easy-to-Read Materials. IFLA Headquarters, Belgium. IFLA Professional report, n. 54 (1997)

"Thinking in Pictures?" Performance of Chinese Children with Autism on Math Learning Through Eye-Tracking Technology

Pinata Winoto[✉], Tiffany Y. Tang, Zeqian Huang, and Piao Chen

Media Lab, Department of Computer Science,
Wenzhou Kean University, Wenzhou, China
{pwinoto, yatang, huangze, chenpi}@kean.edu

Abstract. Popular movies such as *Rain Man*, *A Beautiful Mind* and *The Imitation Game* often depicting the leading characters with high-functioning autism spectrum disorder (ASD) with exceptional math skills (referred to as autistic savants) which is largely inconsistent with research; in fact, only 10% of individuals with ASD have such savant skills; instead, prior studies showed that during their middle school years, students with ASD usually under-perform an average of 5 years below their neuro-typically developing (NT) peers in mathematics. Plausible explanation of such a gap is attributed to the population's impairments of memory and cognitive development which in turn might undermine their learning abilities in one or more mathematical domains. Our present study aims to compare the effects of three different presentation styles during the training for children with ASD's mathematical skills (image-based, mathematical digit-based and audio-based ones) through the behavioral analysis and eye-tracking technology. Together with their actual performance in a small-scale pilot test, these data can provide clues to the questions we raised.

Keywords: Chinese children · Autism · Math learning · Eye-tracking technology

1 Introduction and Background

Popular movies such as Rain Man, A Beautiful Mind and The Imitation Game often depicting the leading characters with high-functioning autism spectrum disorder (ASD) with exceptional math skills (referred to as autistic savants) which is largely inconsistent with research [1]; in fact, only 10% of individuals with ASD have such savant skills and is rare in the population [22]; instead, prior studies showed that during their middle school years, students with ASD usually under-perform an average of 5 years below their neuro-typically developing (NT) peers in mathematics [23]. Plausible explanations of such a gap have been attributed to the population's impairments of working memory, cognitive development, visual-spatial which in turn might undermine their learning abilities in one or more mathematical domains [5, 6, 9, 13, 16, 20]. Whitby [24] also attributed such a gap appeared in their middle school years to the increasing difficulty of this population's understanding of the abstract nature of mathematics and their impairments in generalizing acquired skills to the real-world settings.

© Springer International Publishing AG 2017
P. Zaphiris and A. Ioannou (Eds.): LCT 2017, Part II, LNCS 10296, pp. 215–226, 2017.
DOI: 10.1007/978-3-319-58515-4_17

In addition, quite a number of individuals with ASD have posited the fact that they tend to rely more on the visual mental representations instead of verbal ones in understanding abstract concepts in their daily life [7, 11]; a term referred to as 'thinking in pictures' [7, 15]. However, due to the wide variability of impairments each individual with ASD demonstrates, the bias towards the adoption of visual mental representations might be suitable to be interpreted at the group, not individual level [15], which thereby demanding avenues for further research. One of our present study goals aims to address this issue by recruiting a population of users that have not been included in previous studies: Chinese children with ASD [21].

Meanwhile, the overwhelming number of prior studies attempted to tap into the intertwined relationships among these factors, but little previous empirical evidence directly addresses the issue of how some fundamental math presentation strategies might affect the learning outcome which motivates our study. In particular, in present study, we aim to gain access to the additional information with regards to the complex interrelationship between presentation features, contexts and learning outcome afforded through the referential understanding of children's gaze.

2   Related Work

Four indirect lines of prior research are relevant to our present study which will be briefly reviewed here.

2.1   Mathematics Learning of Individuals with ASD

Popular media has portrayed individuals with high-functioning ASD with exceptional math skills (referred to as *autistic savants*), which is largely inconsistent with research [1]. However, earlier studies showed that during their middle school years, students with ASD usually under-perform an average of 5 years below their neuro-typically developing (NT) peers in mathematics [23]. Plausible explanations of such a gap have been attributed to the population's impairments of some cognitive impairment which in turn might undermine their learning abilities in one or more mathematical domains [5, 6, 9, 13, 16, 20]. Whitby [24] also attributed such a gap appeared in their middle school years to the increasing difficulty of this population's understanding of the abstract nature of mathematics and their impairments in generalizing acquired skills to the real-world settings.

In addition, quite a number of individuals with ASD have posited the fact that they tend to rely more on the visual mental representations instead of verbal ones in understanding abstract concepts in their daily life [7, 11]; a term referred to as 'thinking in pictures' [7]. However, due to the wide variability of impairments each individual with ASD demonstrates, the bias towards the adoption of visual mental representations might be suitable to be interpreted at the group, not individual level [15], which thereby demanding avenues for further research.

2.2   Eye-Tracking for Behavioral Analysis During the Decision-Making Process

Eye-tracking technology has allowed the shift from traditional outcome-based measurement of decision making (as inferred by choices and preferences, etc.) to process-tracing based methodology [4]. The achievement of the latter has relied on the traditional mouse–tracking methods [17], and eye-tracking which could examine attention, information acquisition, arousal, etc. at the cognitive and neurological level [2–4, 19, 25]. For example, Fiedler et al. [3] analyzed the dynamics of risk preferences in two gambles and verified that the visual attention to the outcome of a gamble tends to increase when the probability of winning increases. In addition, the cognitive efforts and arousal indexed by pupil dilation had also been observed to increase. Zhou et al. [25] quantitatively measured the quality of the decision-making process via physiological sensors such as GSR and an eye tracker in an attempt to alter the user interface where human and computer can augment each other's strengthens. Franco-Watkins and Johnson [4] observed increased pupil dilation during the decision making process and is influenced by presentation format.

2.3   Eye-Tracking for Behavioral Analysis in ASD Research

Eye-tracking technology has been commonly adopted in the autism research area both clinically and empirically due to a number of advantages it has provided [8, 18]: (1) it may be ideally suited to tap into many abnormalities this population are plagued with; (2) it is objective and easily implemented; (3) it is safe to be used from infancy to adulthood [10, 14, 18]. In our study, we will adopt the affordable version of eye-tracking device, Tobii EyeX^{TM1} which is marketed to develop eye-gazed based games; such an affordable eye-tracker will not comprise the quality of the collected eye-gaze data; instead, it offers us the same advantages as those of its more expensive peers (such as Tobii Eye Glass^{TM}) by providing additional information with regards to the complex interrelationship between presentation features, contexts and learning outcome. As of present, the overwhelming number of prior works on eye-tracking attempt to probe into the unusual patterns of visual preferences among the population, among many, [12, 14, 18].

2.4   Preferences of Presentation Format Among Children with ASD

One of the notable studies is the one by Kunda and Goel [15] which examined the long-standing assumption of whether individuals with ASD exhibit a deposition towards visual mental representation over verbal mental representation, referred to as the 'thinking in pictures' hypothesis. In the context of a number of cognitive tasks, experiment results strongly support the hypothesis that individuals with ASD tend to tap the visual mental presentation for completing these tasks. However, Kunda and

---

[1] https://tobiigaming.com/.

Goel urged researchers to take precautions in interpreting the data within the context of the tasks; and called for more in-depth studies at the behavioral and neurobiological levels.

3 Our Math Learning Application: Prototype Version

3.1 Application Design and Math Training Problem Presentation Styles

The application is running on a Windows Tablet (Win10), and consists of a "Training Material (TM)" module, a "Learning Materials (LM)" module and some audio files to (1) read out each question; (2) feedbacks on students' performance (praise or encouragement). Instead of providing a 'right' or 'wrong' feedback on accurate and inaccurate answers, we use more encouraging feedback for the child to engage. Hence, three presentation strategies were included: mathematical digit, pictures, and audio file (see Figs. 1, 2 and 3).

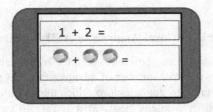

Fig. 1. The two presentation styles in the app: Digit (DIG) and Image (IMG)

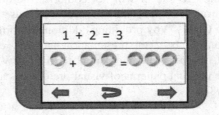

Fig. 2. The Application screen after the child answers the question where navigation buttons are shown

(IMG) 1+1 (correct)
(IMG) 1+2 (correct)
(SND) 2+1 (wrong)
(DIG) 1+2 (correct)
(DIG) 2+1 (correct)

Fig. 3. The child's performance record

Stage one—the training session. At the beginning, the TM module consists of short questions on addition, subtraction and multiplication. Figures 1, 2 and 3 shows the presentation styles and performance record for future analysis.

Meanwhile, the audio instruction of this math problem: "yi jia yi" (one plus one in Chinese) will be played. The app will then animate the arithmetic practice, as shown in Fig. 2 as an example.

Again, the audio instruction of the answer to this math question: "er" (two in Chinese) will be played, followed by a rewarding praise ('well done') will be played if the answer is accurate; a redirection sentence will be played to encourage the child to try it again if the answer is inaccurate. The user may choose to go back, repeat, or to the next item (Fig. 2). When the training session is over, a log data showing both the child's performance as well as the corresponding styles he/she had chosen will be recorded (Fig. 3).

The recorded data (as shown in Fig. 3) can then be saved and analyzed to offer valuable and objective information on the child's preferences, which then can be fed into the system for personalization.

Stage two—the training session. A learner can choose one of the presentation styles before each question is presented (as shown in Figs. 4, 5 and 6).

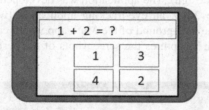

Fig. 4. The mathematical digit style during the training session

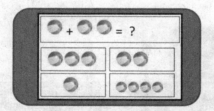

Fig. 5. The Picture Style during the training session

Again, all learners' in-application interaction as well as the performance will be recorded (see Fig. 3).

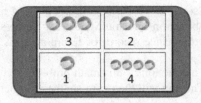

Fig. 6. The audio style where the question will be spoken out in Chinese

Feed-back from Participatory Design. The prototype of the application had been tested with three children with ASD in order to obtain feedbacks from both the children and their teachers who accompany them during the testing; interviews with teachers were also conducted. The results of their feedback had been incorporated into the design of next two versions of the application (v2.0 and v3.0).

4 Our Math Learning Application: Eye-Tracking Version (v2.0 and v3.0)

A second version of the application was designed in order to accommodate these feedbacks (participatory design). The application was developed using C# in Microsoft Visual Studio Enterprise 2015; an eye-tracking application (written in C# for Tobii EyeX^{TM}) is running at the background of the Math app which can be utilized to collect the eye-gaze data. Figure 7 captures the screenshots of the system.

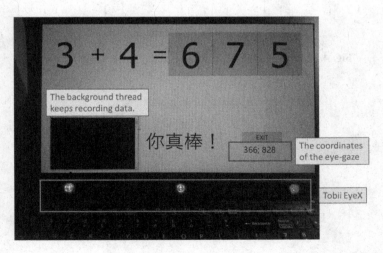

Fig. 7. The screenshot of the eye-tracker enabled learning application (v2.0) (Color figure online)

During the integration testing, we found out that since a working Tobii EyeX shows an array of three red lights right below the application (as highlighted in green in Fig. 7), it might pose a potential problem to the children who are not aware of an eye-tracking device before. Therefore, in the pilot testing, we adopted the third version of our application which uses a non-intrusive eye tracker Tobii Eye X2-60 (v3.0). Figure 8 shows a screenshot of the application while Fig. 9 shows the images used in the application (v3.0).

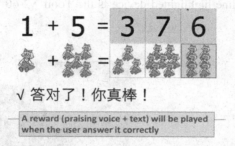

Fig. 8. A screenshot of the learning application used in the pilot study (v3.0)

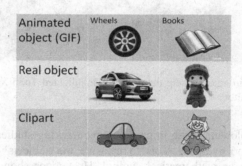

Fig. 9. Imagines used in the application (v3.0)

In order to assess our assumption of the possible link between presentation types and learning outcomes, we conducted a pilot study which will be described in details in the next section.

5   Study Results and Discussions

5.1   Participants, Apparatus and Study Procedure

Participants. One nine-year old child with low functioning ASD (LFASD) and one six-year old child with high functioning ASD (AFASD) participated in the pilot study.

Apparatus. A Dell workstation with 27 inches 4 K monitor with standard mouse and keyboard was used. A light and portable Tobii X2-60 eye-tracking device was mounted on the monitor.

Study procedure. Due to the high usability of the learning application and conversation with the teachers, no training was provided. Each child was asked to sit in front of the computer and use mouse to complete a total of twelve math questions (simple addition). The researcher demonstrated how to move the mouse and click a correct answer and asked the child to answer the rests. Figure 10 showed the study environment where the dash-line highlighted device is the Tobii X2-60 which was mounted below the monitor.

Fig. 10. The study environment where the dash-line highlighted Tobii X2-60 eye-tracker was mounted below the monitor

Study measures. Following those in previous eye-tracking studies [2–4, 18, 25], we adopted heat-maps and eye-gaze plots to measure the subjects' preferences of the screen objects: image or mathematical symbol. Heat maps show where the subject concentrated their eye-gaze and the duration of the gaze at a given point. A red spot over an area suggest that the subject (or group of subjects) focused on the given point for a longer period of time which could be inferred to demonstrate their interest on the visual spot over other spots (e.g. Fig. 11). Eye-gaze plots, on the other hand, do not combine more than one user in the screen; it visually shows the temporal movement of the user's fixation on the screen. The size of the dot denotes the duration of the eye-gaze time (Fig. 12).

5.2   Results and Discussions

Since each question has three optional answers, the chance of correctly answering it by random is 1/3, or 4 out of the total 12 questions. The child with LFASD failed to answer any question. In fact, he looked at the monitor for the first four seconds and then

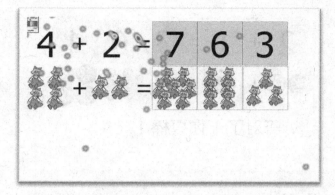

Fig. 11. The eye-gaze heat-map of the child with LFASD (Color figure online)

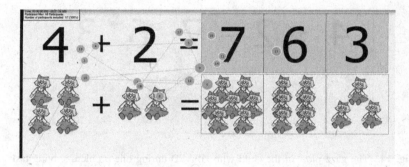

Fig. 12. The gaze plots of the child with LFASD

looking around (outside the monitor) for the next 70 s until he left. Figure 11 showed the heat-map of his eye-gaze data. The heat-map data showed no preferences towards either presentation styles.

Figure 12 present the gaze plots of the child where no preferences over either symbols were observed (size of the eye-gaze plot does not vary much). It was revealed that the child has not started to learn math, which provides clues to his eye-gaze patterns on the screen.

The child with HFASD solved 8 problems correctly (three wrongly). Out of 11 questions, he clicked pictures 5 times (once wrongly) and digits 6 times (twice wrongly). The selected pictures are clipart car (selected twice), and real doll, animated wheels, and animated book (once for each). His eye-gazing results are shown in Figs. 13 and 14.

The heat-map data suggested that the child focused more attention on the images (Fig. 13). The gaze plots data further supported it. Figures 14 and 15 showed two of them when he was solving two math question.

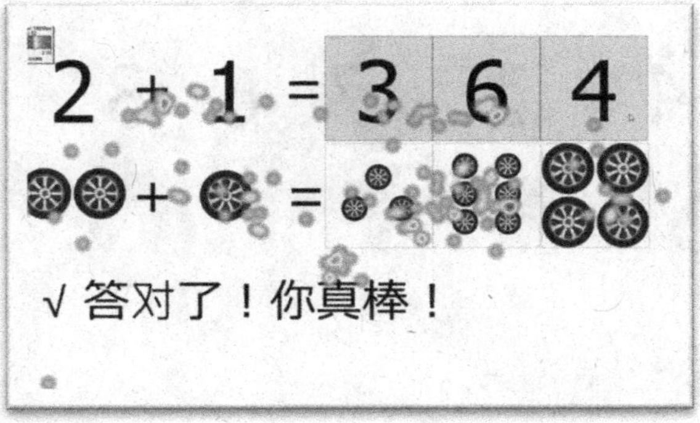

Fig. 13. The eye-gaze heat-map of the child with HFASD

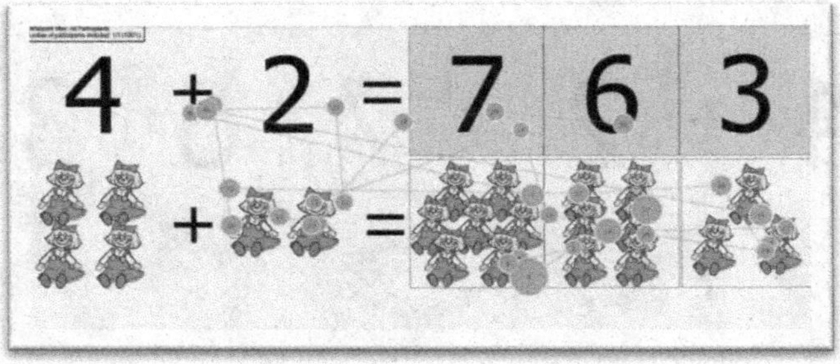

Fig. 14. The gaze plots of the child with HFASD during one problem-solving task

Fig. 15. The gaze plots of the child with HFASD during a successful problem-solving task

6 Concluding Remarks

In our present study, we aim to compare the effects of three different presentation styles during the training for children with ASD's mathematical skills (image-based, mathematical digit-based and audio-based ones) through the behavioral analysis and eye-tracking technology. Except for one LFASD child who has not officially started the math education, eye-tracking data indicated that the HFASD child show more interest in images.

Although it is still too early to draw conclusions on the preferences of images over mathematical symbols and the influences of appropriate and personalized design elements in math learning application on children's performance, our study nevertheless highlight the importance of tuning in such finer grained design elements so as to facilitate personalized learning.

In the future, more in-depth studies on viewing patterns could add to our understanding of the old question of whether individuals with ASD tend to 'think' in pictures. We are currently working on a prototype of adaptive math learning application that could react to the child's preferences over the screen objects (via observation of their eye-gaze patterns).

Acknowledgements. The authors acknowledge the financial support to this research by Wenzhou Municipal Science and Technology Bureau (温州市科技局, S20160012). Thanks also go to the children and their teachers at the Orange Wheat Field Children Support Center for participating in our study. Suggestion and constructive comments of the math questions by Dr. Lengleng Lim at Wenzhou-Kean University are also appreciated.

References

1. Benaron, L.D.: Biographies of Disease: Autism. Greenwood Press, London (2009)
2. de Gee, J.W., Knapen, T., Donner, T.H.: Decision-related pupil dilation reflects upcoming choice and individual bias. Proc. Natl. Acad. Sci. **111**(5), E618–E625 (2014)
3. Fiedler, S., Glockner, A., Johnson, J.G., Stewart, N., Krajbich, I.: The dynamics of decision making in risky choice: an eye-tracking analysis. Frontiers Psychol. **3**, 335 (2012)
4. Franco-Watkins, A.M., Johnson, J.G.: Applying the decision moving window to risky choice: comparison of eye-tracking and mouse-tracing methods. Judgment Decis. Making **6**(8), 740–749 (2011)
5. Geary, D.C.: Mathematical disorders: an overview for educators. Perspectives **26**, 6–9 (2000)
6. Geary, D.C.: Mathematics and learning disabilities. J. Learn. Disabil. **37**, 4–15 (2004)
7. Grandin, T.: Thinking in Pictures, Expanded Edition: My Life with Autism. Vintage Books, New York (2006)
8. Guillon, Q., Hadjikhani, N., Baduel, S., Roge, B.: Visual social attention in autism spectrum disorder: insights from eye tracking studies. Neurosci. Biobehav. Rev. **42**, 279–297 (2014)
9. Hansen, N., Jordan, N.C., Fernandez, E., Siegler, R.S., Fuchs, L., Gersten, R., Micklos, D.: General and math-specific predictors of sixth-graders' knowledge of fractions. Cogn. Dev. **35**, 34–49 (2015)

10. Holmqvist, K., Nyström, M., Andersson, R., Dewhurst, R., Jarodzka, H., van de Weijer, J.: Eye Tracking: A Comprehensive Guide to Methods and Measures. Oxford University Press, Oxford (2011)

11. Hurlburt, R., Happé, F., Frith, U.: Sampling the form of inner experience in three adults with Asperger syndrome. Psychol. Med. **24**, 385–396 (1994)

12. Jones, W., Klin, A.: Attention to eyes is present but in decline in 2–6 month old infants later diagnosed with autism. Nature **504**, 427–431 (2013)

13. Kim, H., Cameron, C.E.: Implications of visuospatial skills and executive functions for learning mathematics: evidence from children with autism and williams syndrome. AERA Open **2**(4), 1–16 (2016). SAGE Publications

14. Klin, A., Lin, D.J., Gorrindo, P., Ramsay, G., Jones, W.: Two-year-olds with autism orient to non-social contingencies rather than biological motion. Nature **459**(7244), 257–261 (2009)

15. Kunda, M., Goel, A.K.: Thinking in pictures as a cognitive account of autism. J. Autism Dev. Disord. **41**(9), 1157–1177 (2011)

16. Minshew, N.J., Goldstein, G., Taylor, H.G., Siegel, D.J.: Academic achievement in high functioning autistic individuals. J. Clin. Exp. Neuropsychol. **16**(2), 261–270 (1994)

17. Payne, J.W., Bettman, J.R., Johnson, E.J.: The Adaptive Decision Maker. Cambridge University Press, New York (1993)

18. Pierce, K., Marinero, S., Hazin, R., McKenna, B., Barnes, C.C., Maligea, A.: Eye tracking reveals abnormal visual preference for geometric images as an early biomarker of an autism spectrum disorder subtype associated with increased symptom severity. Biol. Psychiatry **79** (8), 657–666 (2016)

19. Preuschoff, K., 't Hart, B.M., Einhäuser, W.: Pupil dilation signals surprise: evidence for noradrenaline's role in decision making. Frontiers Neurosci. **5**, 115 (2011)

20. Szucs, D., Devine, A., Soltesz, F., Nobes, A., Gabriel, F.: Developmental dyscalculia is related to visuo-spatial memory and inhibition impairment. Cortex **49**(10), 2674–2688 (2013)

21. Tang, T., Flatla, D.: Autism awareness and technology-based intervention research in china: the good, the bad, and the challenging. In: Proceedings of Workshop on Autism and Technology - Beyond Assistance & Intervention, in conjunction with the 34th ACM International Conference on Human Factors in Computing Systems (CHI 2016), San Jose, CA, USA (2016)

22. Treffert, D.A.: The savant syndrome: an extraordinary condition. A synopsis: past, present, future. Philos. Trans. R. Soc. Lond. B Biol. Sci. **364**(1522), 1351–1357 (2009)

23. Wagner, M., Marder, C., Blackorby, J., Cameto, R., Newman, L., Levine, P., Davies-Mercier, E.: The Achievements of Youth with Disabilities During Secondary School: A Report from the National Longitudinal Transition Study-2. SRI International, Menlo Park (2003)

24. Whitby, P.J.S.: The effects of solve it! on the mathematical word problem solving ability of adolescents with autism spectrum disorders. Focus Autism Other Dev. Disabil. **28**(2), 78–88 (2013)

25. Zhou, J.L., Sun, J.J., Chen, F., Wang, Y., Taib, R., Khawaji, A., Li, Z.: Measurable decision making with GSR and pupillary analysis for intelligent user interface. ACM Trans. Comput.-Hum. Interact. (TOCHI) **21**(6), 33 (2015)

Learning Analytics

Dashboard for Actionable Feedback on Learning Skills: Scalability and Usefulness

Tom Broos[1,6](✉), Laurie Peeters[2], Katrien Verbert[3], Carolien Van Soom[4,6], Greet Langie[5,6], and Tinne De Laet[1,6]

[1] Faculty of Engineering Science, KU Leuven, Leuven, Belgium
tom.broos@kuleuven.be
[2] Leuven Statistics Research Centre, KU Leuven, Leuven, Belgium
[3] Department of Computer Science, KU Leuven, Leuven, Belgium
[4] Faculty of Science, KU Leuven, Leuven, Belgium
[5] Faculty of Engineering Technology, KU Leuven, Leuven, Belgium
[6] Leuven Engineering and Science Education Centre, KU Leuven, Leuven, Belgium

Abstract. In the transition from secondary to higher education, students are expected to develop a set of learning skills. This paper reports on a dashboard implemented and designed to support this development, hereby bridging the gap between Learning Analytics research and the daily practice of supporting students. To demonstrate the scalability and usefulness of the dashboard, this paper reports on an intervention with 1406 first-year students in 12 different programs. The results show that the dashboard is perceived as clear and useful. While students not accessing the dashboard have lower learning skills, they make more use of the extra remediation possibilities in the dashboard.

Keywords: Learning analytics · Scalable · Higher education · Learning skills

1 Introduction

This paper discusses the implementation and evaluation of a Learning Analytics (LA) intervention, which resulted in a student dashboard that provided 1406 first-year STEM (Science, Technology, Engineering, and Mathematics) students at the University of Leuven with actionable feedback on their learning skills. The study is an attempt to bridge the gap between LA research and the daily practice of supporting students in their first year of higher education. LA research is rigorous, open to scientific scrutiny, but studies are often limited to smaller groups of students or course settings favorable to the experiment. Massive Open Online Courses (MOOC's) and other born-digital forms of e-learning are attractive producers of data. Applying LA to the traditional context of higher education is challenging, as many interactions and learning activities are face-to-face, offline, and difficult to capture digitally. Therefore, the search for available digital traces to support personalized, actionable feedback to larger groups of students is of

© Springer International Publishing AG 2017
P. Zaphiris and A. Ioannou (Eds.): LCT 2017, Part II, LNCS 10296, pp. 229–241, 2017.
DOI: 10.1007/978-3-319-58515-4_18

particular interest. The digital traces used in the dashboard discussed in this paper build on the work of educational scientists related to the assessment and development of learning skills. More specifically, the experiment uses data gathered from the Learning and Study Strategies Inventory (LASSI), a questionnaire measuring learning skills [16].

2   Related Work

LA aims to improve learning and learning environments by collecting and analyzing the traces produced by learners [13]. Data from a wide variety of sources can be studied using statistical and data mining techniques. To deliver the insights derived therefrom back to these stakeholders, the data can be visualized using learning dashboards. First overviews of such LA Dashboards (LAD's) have been presented in [14,15]. Examples include Course Signals [1], SAM [4], and StepUp! [11]. Course Signals is a prominent example that predicts and visualizes learning outcomes based on three data sources: grades in the course so far, time on task, and past performance. If grades in the course so far are below a certain threshold specified by the teacher, a student will see a red color signal for the course. When they are above the threshold, past performance in other courses and time on task are used to calculate whether a student is on track (green light) or whether she may need to improve her activities for the course (orange light). As discussed in [15], research has shown that such a dashboard has an impact on student retention and drop-out, although this particular example is one of the few dashboards that has been thoroughly evaluated to assess the impact on learning effectiveness.

A first systematic review of LADs was conducted by Schwendimann, et al. [12]. The authors analyzed 53 articles. Their findings include that dashboards are mostly developed for instructors, and that impact on learning is rarely assessed. A recent systematic review of LADs has been presented by [2]. The authors have reviewed 94 papers that use LA to support students. A key outcome of this analysis is that "None of the studies included in the student use category broke down student use by demographic, learner characteristics, or student achievement levels. In order to better personalize recommendations and dashboards to students, we need to put more emphasis on understanding student use of these systems". In addition, while the majority information in LAD's is typically represented in a visual way, it has been noted [10] that complementary textual information can provide additional guidance. Leitner et al. [7] examined the state of the art of LA by analyzing 101 articles. One of the limitations they find in current research, is the limit in group size and the question if existing work has the potential to scale beyond small group sizes to a wider context.

3   Situation of This Study

The aim of this study is to learn about the use of a dashboard in a **realistic context** to provide **first-year students in higher education** with

actionable insight on their learning skills and possible actions to improve these skills. This is translated to the following objectives.

(1) To demonstrate and test the feasibility of a **scalable** approach to learning analytics, targeting a sizable group of students in STEM study programs.
(2) To construct a dashboard based on **information that is readily available** within the institution, but not yet shared with students.
(3) To collect user **metrics and feedback** to assess perceived usefulness and usability and to uncover areas for further research.

We apply the six critical dimensions of the LA framework of Greller and Draschler [5] to offer a shareable description of our intervention.

The **stakeholders**, both data clients and data subjects, are first-year students. The intervention uses two populations. Firstly, all students in the first year of a particular bachelor program, such that a student's learning skills can be compared to his/her peer students. Secondly, first-year students in previous academic years, such that the relation between a student's learning skills and first-year academic achievement (percentage of obtained study points) can be shown.

The **objective** of the dashboard is to unveil information on learning skills to students. The data was gathered for a study considering the relation between learning skills and study success, but was not offered to the data subjects, the students themselves. The dashboard combines reflection and prediction [5]. Concerning *reflection*, students receives feedback on their learning skills and the comparison with peers students (Fig. 1). Concerning *prediction*, the dashboard uses a "mild" form. To make students reflect on the importance of learning skills in their learning process, the study efficiency of the students of the previous year is shown in relation to their learning skills (Fig. 1).

This intervention takes advantage of linking the **data** of learning skills, gathered using paper-and-pencil questionnaires, and data from the university's data warehouse regarding the study points obtained by a student. Regarding **instruments**, the intervention does not rely on advanced *technology* and rather provides a *visualization* of the underlying raw data to students.

Now, we discuss **internal and external limitations**. Regarding *conventions*, both privacy and ethics are important. Students were asked to consent on the use of the learning skill questionnaire data for research, feedback, and the connection to their study results. The ethical soundness of the intervention was supported by the inclusion of study counselors and advisors in the development of the dashboard. Regarding *the time scale*, the intervention is just-in-time: students received feedback in the middle of the first semester. Regarding the *limitations* of the first-year students regarding interpreting LA data, the dashboard uses simple visualizations complemented with textual explanations.

4   Learning Skills Dashboard

4.1   Learning Skills

In the transition from secondary to higher education, students are expected to develop a set of learning skills that will help them in their learning path, as well as in their future professional career. Higher education institutions provide information and activities to support students to improve their learning skills, e.g. through coaching, counseling, or training sessions. To direct these efforts and to measure their effectiveness, institutions need to assess the level of learning skills of their students. The Learning and Study Strategies Inventory (LASSI) is a diagnostic instrument that can be used to measure a student's level of learning skills [6]. Based on a 60 (third edition) item questionnaire, a LASSI test reveals strengths an weaknesses of an individual, and relates this to the scores of other students. Being both a diagnostic and prescriptive instrument, LASSI does not focus on student characteristics that are invariable or difficult to change, such as gender, socioeconomic status, or ethnic background. Rather, it delivers indicators for areas that offer a perspective for growth and mitigation. Student's learning and study strategies are summarized in ten scales, each targeting a specific skill shown to be relevant to study success [16]. According to its publisher, the test is currently being used in over 3000 institutions worldwide [6].

This paper reports on an interactive dashboard that provides students with individualized feedback on their learning skills as measured through LASSI. The feedback targets five scales that were shown earlier to be best predictive for study success for our specific target group of STEM students: performance anxiety, concentration, motivation, the use of test strategies, and time management [9].

4.2   Dashboard Design

Figure 1 provides a screenshot of student's view on the dashboard. The main components of the dashboard are introduced below.

The dashboard is divided into six **tabs**. On access, the first tab shows an introductory text, explaining the purpose and components of the intervention and the origin of the data it is based on. The other five tabs, alphabetically ordered, provide a separate space for each of the five learning skills.

The dashboard contains a **visualization** of the data underlying the intervention that allows students to compare their learning skills with those of peers in the same program. A simple unit chart (Fig. 1) uses dots to represent the number of students within the respective norm scales for each of the five included learning skills. Each dot represents a single student and is attributed to one of five norm scales, ranging from very weak over weak, average and good to very good. The norm group that applies to the active student, is marked with a blue border and background hatching. For each skill, a second unit chart (Fig. 1) relates the skill level of previous year's students of the study program with their study success obtained in the first year. Again, each dot represents one student. In addition, the color of the dots represents the study success of these students using three

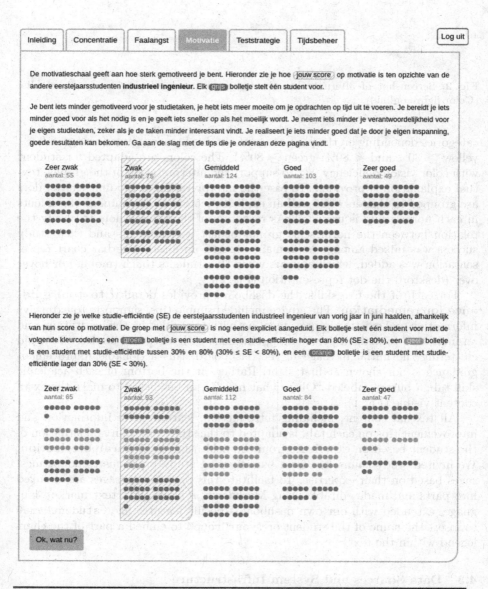

Fig. 1. Screenshot of a student's view on the dashboard. (Color figure online)

Fig. 2. Screenshot of alternate bar chart representation of previous year's results. (Color figure online)

categories depending on the percentage of obtained study points (orange < 30%, yellow ≥ 30% and < 80%; green ≥ 80%). The colors are adapted for student with color vision deficiency [8]. To support the interpretation of the graphs, textual explanation is provided. To ease the interpretation of the unit charts, dots are grouped in clusters of 25 and an explicit mention of the number of students in each norm group is provided. As reception of the colored dots to clarify the relation between the norm scale groups of last year students and their study success was mixed among the domain experts, an alternative bar chart representation was added, which appears when the students touch (mobile) or hover over (desktop) the dot representation (Fig. 2).

For each of the five skills, the dashboard provides detailed **textual guidance for remediation**. The advice included simple tips, signposts to extensive information and existing improvement activities provided by the institution, and an invitation to make a personal appointment with a student adviser. To avoid cluttering the initial message in the dashboard, this actionable improvement guidance is not shown at first sight. Rather, at the bottom of each academic skill tab, a button labeled "Okay, what now?" can be clicked to make the extra content visible (Fig. 1).

All textual content, including introduction, learning skill information and improvement tips on each tab, is adapted to the study program and situation of the student based on experience from the field using **text parameterization**. We invited study counselors from participating study programs to adapt messages based on their expertise. To facilitate this process, messages are chunked into parts and made editable using Markdown, a lightweight text markup language, extended with our own dashboard-specific features like @studentName@ to insert the name of the student or @yourGroup@ to embed a part of the chart legend within the text.

4.3 Data Sources and System Infrastructure

The central (SAP) ERP infrastructure is system of record for all official data on students, programs, courses, and results. The LASSI test data is collected and processed separately and was made available to the project in a comma-separated values (CSV) file. Data from these two sources was consolidated and loaded into a relational database using an Extract, Load, Transform (ELT) process.

The dashboard is accessible indirectly through the university's reverse proxy infrastructure, enforcing authentication by a central single sign-on system

(Shibboleth). This improves security and provides student with a familiar entry point, similar to other campus software. All data access requires invoking a database stored procedure that writes the request into an audit table. The dashboard was set up as a Single Page Application (SPA) that stands on its own once loaded. Each user action, like opening a tab or clicking a button, is transmitted back to the web server using a simple AJAX call with a dummy response. These events are stored into the web server's access log, to be handled by an extraction routine that operates outside busy hours.

5   Results

5.1   Target Group and Data Collection

1406 first year students in 12 different STEM programs received a personalized invitation by email to access the dashboard, stating that it provides actionable feedback on their learning skills based on a pen and paper questionnaire they earlier filled out in class. Students that did not complete the survey or did not consent to the usage of their data for research were excluded. Apart from the background recording of user activity, the dashboard contains a short feedback form with three questions: (1) I find this information *useful*; (2) I find this information *clear*; (3) I would like to receive *more* of this type of information.

5.2   Dashboard Interaction

1135 (80.7%) of the students clicked on the link in the invitation email and entered the dashboard. The click-through rate differs between study programs and ranges from 63.5% to 89.1% (Fig. 3). 67.7% of the students that did click through, did so within the 48 h after the dashboard was launched, 81.2% within 72 h and 98.1% within 168 h (Fig. 4).

Table 1. Number and percentage of students that go to the dashboard and provide feedback, depending on the device type.

	Total	Desktop	Smartphone	Tablet	Other
On platform	1135	847	260	21	7
	(100%)	(74.6%)	(22.9%)	(1.9%)	(0.6%)
Full feedback	167	148	15	2	2
	(14,7%)	(17.5%)	(5.8%)	-	-

Most students clicked through using a desktop browser (74.6%) or a smartphone (22.9%) (Table 1). The use of tablets and other media devices was limited. Students using a non-desktop device are clicking through faster, as indicated by the initial peak in their user share (Fig. 4).

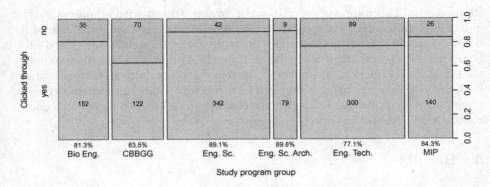

Fig. 3. Click-through per study program, expressed as the percentage of invited students. The 12 study programs are grouped as follows: Bio-Engineering; CBBGG (Chemistry, Biology, Biochemistry-Biotechnology, Geography, Geology), Engineering Science, Engineering Science: Architecture, Engineering Technology, and MIP (Mathematics, Informatics, Physics). The width of the bars is proportional to the number of students in the grouped study programs.

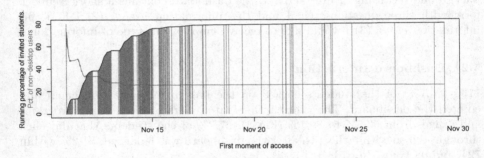

Fig. 4. Running percentage of invited students that clicked through to the dashboard. The vertical lines represent individual first access events. The blue line plots the share of non-desktop users. (Color figure online)

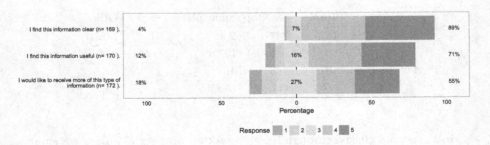

Fig. 5. Survey responses. Students were asked to provide feedback using the scale (−) 1-2-3-4-5 (+).

5.3   Feedback

Although the effort required to answer the three survey questions was minimal, only 14.7% of accessing students provided feedback on all three questions. Students using mobile devices such as smartphone and tablet are less tempted to provide feedback than desktop users (Table 1). Most of the students that provided feedback indicated that they find the dashboard useful (71%) and clear (89%). The preference for more information of the same type is also positive, but less pronounced (55%). Figure 5 summarizes the student feedback.

5.4   Student Profile and Behavior

On average, the 80.7% of the students clicking through to the dashboard, have a *higher score on the learning skill scores* (Fig. 6). This difference is significant for each of the learning skills as shown by a one-directional Mann-Whitney test (p-values 0.01921[*] for concentration, 0.01043[*] for anxiety, 0.00223[**] for motivation, 0.00001[****] for test strategy and 0.00104[**] for time management).

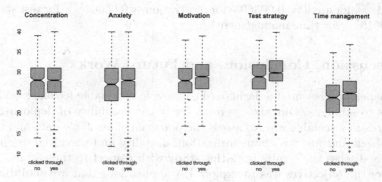

Fig. 6. Boxplots comparing the learning skill scores of students that did not (red) click through with those that did click through (green). (Color figure online)

Of the 1135 students that did click through to the dashboard, 399 (35.2%) clicked on 'Okay, what now?' to read the improvement tips on the concentration tab, 200 (17.6%) on the anxiety tab, 172 (15.2%) on the motivation tab, 173 (15.2%) on the test strategies tab and 229 (20.2%) on the time management tab. We compared the proportion of students viewing the tips for concentration (first tab) to every other learning skill using a Kruskal-Wallis test, applying a multiple comparison according to Dunn with a Bonferroni correction yielding p-values below 2e−16. Tips for concentration have significantly higher views compared to the other tips.

On average, students that read the improvement tips for a specific learning skill, tend to have a *lower corresponding learning skill score* (Fig. 7). This

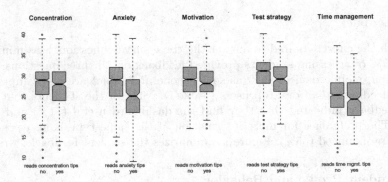

Fig. 7. Boxplots comparing the respective skill scores of students that did not (red) viewed the corresponding tips (by clicking 'Okay, what now?') with those that did view the tips (green). (Color figure online)

result is found to be significant for each of the learning skills when applying a one-directional Mann-Whitney test (p-values 0.01681[*] for concentration, <0.00001[****] for anxiety, 0.00360[**] for motivation, <0.00001[****] for test strategy and 0.00016[***] for time management).

6   Discussion, Conclusion, and Future Work

In this paper we presented a dashboard to provide actionable feedback on learning skills to students. Our aims were to study the feasibility of deploying such dashboards in a scalable way, to assess the potential of available data and to collect feedback and metrics about utilization, usability and perceived usefulness. Below, we discuss the results from this study with respect to these aims.

One of the objectives was to explore LA applications that are **scalable** and widely applicable. The dashboard demonstrates this ability, as it based on data that is already available in digital format within a typical higher-education institution (grades) or can easily become available (LASSI questionnaires). This data however, was not yet being fed back to students in a direct, coherent, and personalized way. From a technical perspective, we have chosen to avoid to reinvent the wheel and to rely on existing IT services within the organization when possible. We believe that this increases the acceptability of the solution. Potential scalability issues were avoided by keeping the transactional load limited by preparing most of the data in advance, while deferring the processing of event data until after the peak utilization.

We involved domain experts and practitioners early on in the process and relied on them for the preparation and distribution of the dashboard. We enabled student counselors to adapt the messages delivered to the student based on the study program and individual learning skills. We believe that this approach may enhance the acceptance of the dashboard within the institution, while at the same time improving its overall quality. We noticed that the click-through rate differs between study programs. Further involvement of stakeholders of the respective study programs may help to explain this difference in a follow-up study.

A simple visual representation using **unit charts** was chosen due to the limited statistical background in the target group of first-year students. For example, in some cases, the size of a norm group can be small. A typical representation with bar or column graph may be misleading, if the reader does not take the absence of statistical significance in consideration. In this case, a unit representation depicts a small number of dots (students) set against a larger population of peers. This should appeal to an intuitive caution not to rush into conclusions. However, the usefulness of unit charts is disputed. Some argue that the visualization, while appealing because of their conceptually simplicity, should be avoided in favor of bar chars, because the latter display the same information without slowing the reader down by encouraging [3] counting. The goal of our dashboard, however, is not to bring a message across as quickly as possible. We expect that the notion that each dot represents not just a number, but a real individual, a peer student, may contribute to the purpose of provoking self-reflection. The validation of this hypothesis is subject of future work.

The proportion of students providing **feedback** is limited. Although the questions had a prominent place in the dashboard design, there may be an underling usability problem that discourages students to provide feedback, especially for students accessing the dashboard using a mobile device as the feedback rate is even lower for these users. In a subsequent study, feedback gathered from focus groups may help to complement the embedded feedback instrument. In their feedback, students tend to appreciate the usefulness and clearness of the dashboard. When asked if they would like to receive similar (more) feedback however, the response is more moderately positive. The wording of the last question may have been ambiguous as it may refer to more feedback about learning skills in particular as much as it may refer to a more general interest in any type of learning related data, as was intended.

An **order effect** may explain the increased number of students reading the tips on the concentration tab. Students are likely to try out what happens when clicking on the first instance of the "Okay, what now?" button they encounter, regardless of their specific interest or profile. Based on this finding, which we initially did not intended to look into, we recommend study of an optimized order of the dashboard content by putting the variables that the student needs the most improvement for first.

An interesting finding, is that students that click through to the dashboard, have higher **learning skills scores** on average. LAD design should take into consideration that reaching different target groups may require different approaches and levels of effort, especially when targeting students with an at-risk profile. On the other hand, this observation may also point out that students with stronger profiles should not be overlooked in the design and that LA should not restrict itself to the at-risk profiles. On the other hand, once students clicked through to the dashboard, we noticed that those that engage more (view the improvement tips for a particular learning skill), are students with a higher "need" (lower scores for the corresponding learning skill on average). Therefore, we conclude from this study that the biggest challenge is to get at-risk students on the dashboard rather than to keep them engaged on the dashboard, which is subject of further research.

Acknowledgement. This research is co-funded by the Erasmus+ program of the European Union (562167-EPP-1-2015-1-BE-EPPKA3-PI-FORWARD). We thank Kurt De Wit, Tine Overloop and Maarten Pinxten for their assistance and advice and ICTS for providing the technical infrastructure to support the dashboard.

References

1. Arnold, K.E., Pistilli, M.D.: Course signals at Purdue: using learning analytics to increase student success. In: Proceedings of the 2nd International Conference on Learning Analytics and Knowledge, pp. 267–270. ACM (2012)
2. Bodily, R., Verbert, K.: Trends and issues in student-facing learning analytics reporting systems research. In: Proceedings of the 7th International Learning Analytics and Knowledge Conference, pp. 1–10 (2017)
3. Few, S.: Show me the Numbers: Designing Tables and Graphs to Enlighten. Analytics Press, Burlingame (2012)
4. Govaerts, S., Verbert, K., Duval, E., Pardo, A.: The student activity meter for awareness and self-reflection. In: CHI 2012 Extended Abstracts on Human Factors in Computing Systems, pp. 869–884. ACM (2012)
5. Greller, W., Drachsler, H.: Translating learning into numbers: a generic framework for learning analytics. Educ. Technol. Soc. **15**(3), 42–57 (2012)
6. H&H Publishing: LASSI, dutch version:© H&H Publishing Company, Inc., 1231 Kapp Drive, Clearwater, Florida 33765. Authors: Weinstein, Claire Ellen (1987-2002-2016). Dutch version: Lacante, Lens, Briers (1999, 2017). http://www.hhpublishing.com/_assessments/lassi
7. Leitner, P., Khalil, M., Ebner, M.: Learning analytics in higher education-a literature review. In: Peña-Ayala, A. (ed.) Learning Analytics: Fundaments, Applications, and Trends, vol. 94, pp. 1–23. Springer, Cham (2017). doi:10.1007/978-3-319-52977-6_1
8. Okabe, M., Ito, K.: How to make figures and presentations that are friendly to color blind people. University of Tokyo (2002)
9. Pinxten, M.: At-risk at the gate: prediction of study success of first-year science and engineering students in an open-admission university in Flanders. Any incremental validity of study strategies? (submitted for publication)
10. Ramos-Soto, A., Lama, M., Vazquez-Barreiros, B., Bugarin, A., Mucientes, M., Barro, S.: Towards textual reporting in learning analytics dashboards. In: 2015 IEEE 15th International Conference on Advanced Learning Technologies, pp. 260–264, July 2015
11. Santos, J.L., Govaerts, S., Verbert, K., Duval, E.: Goal-oriented visualizations of activity tracking: a case study with engineering students. In: Proceedings of the 2nd International Conference on Learning Analytics and Knowledge, pp. 143–152. ACM (2012)

12. Schwendimann, B.A., Rodríguez-Triana, M.J., Vozniuk, A., Prieto, L.P., Boroujeni, M.S., Holzer, A., Gillet, D., Dillenbourg, P.: Understanding learning at a glance: An overview of learning dashboard studies. In: Proceedings of the Sixth International Conference on Learning Analytics & Knowledge, pp. 532–533. ACM (2016)
13. Siemens, G., Long, P.: Penetrating the fog: analytics in learning and education. EDUCAUSE Rev. **46**(5), 30 (2011)
14. Verbert, K., Duval, E., Klerkx, J., Govaerts, S., Santos, J.L.: Learning analytics dashboard applications. Am. Behav. Sci. **57**(10), 1500–1509 (2013)
15. Verbert, K., Govaerts, S., Duval, E., Santos, J.L., Van Assche, F., Parra, G., Klerkx, J.: Learning dashboards: an overview and future research opportunities. Pers. Ubiquit. Comput. **18**(6), 1499–1514 (2014)
16. Weinstein, C.E., Zimmerman, S., Palmer, D.: Assessing learning strategies: the design and development of the LASSI. In: Learning and Study Strategies: Issues in Assessment, Instruction, and Evaluation, pp. 25–40 (1988)

Can We Apply Learning Analytics Tools in Challenge Based Learning Contexts?

Miguel Á. Conde[1(✉)], Francisco J. García-Peñalvo[2],
Ángel Fidalgo-Blanco[3], and María Luisa Sein-Echaluce[4]

[1] Robotics Group, Department of Mechanics, Computer Science
and Aerospace Engineering, University of León, Campus de Vegazana S/N,
24071 León, Spain
miguel.conde@unileon.es
[2] GRIAL research group, Computer Science Department, Faculty of Science,
Research Institute for Educational Sciences, University of Salamanca,
Plaza de los Caídos S/N, 37008 Salamanca, Spain
fgarcia@usal.es
[3] Laboratory of Innovation in Information Technologies,
Universidad Politécnica de Madrid, Calle de Ríos Rosas 21,
28003 Madrid, Spain
angel.fidalgo@upm.es
[4] Department of Applied Mathematics, University of Zaragoza,
Campus Rio Ebro, Calle de María de Luna 3, 50018 Zaragoza, Spain
mlsein@unizar.es

Abstract. The information and Communication Technologies changes how we interact with others and with the information. It can be really accessed at anytime and anywhere. Future professionals should be ready for this reality which requires changes in traditional teaching and learning methods. Challenge Based Learning is an example of them. This method poses challenges to students that they should solve employing the technology they use during their daily life. The evaluation of challenges solutions should take into account students' final outcomes but also the interactions that take place between them. This could be very hard given the wide choice of tools that students can apply. Learning analytics tools could be a solution.

This paper reviews and classifies the tools applied in several Challenge Based Learning experiments and describes different possibilities to apply Learning Analytics. From this research, it is possible to conclude that Learning Analytics can be applied in Challenge Based Learning contexts, but it is desirable to use a single platform to group the tools employed to solve the challenge.

Keywords: Challenge Based Learning · Tools · Learning Analytics · Learning evidences

1 Introduction

The society in which we live is continuously changing and we should be prepared for the opportunities that it brings to us. In the last 30 years, individuals have been involved in the digital revolution [1]. The emergence of new devices, new technologies, new

© Springer International Publishing AG 2017
P. Zaphiris and A. Ioannou (Eds.): LCT 2017, Part II, LNCS 10296, pp. 242–256, 2017.
DOI: 10.1007/978-3-319-58515-4_19

services, new business, even new interaction ways should be associated to changes in learning paradigms [2–4]. It is necessary to teach students to understand this digital society and help them to be active and efficient in this context. That is, students should acquire new competences related to their current landscape, where they should properly use technology, make decisions, work in teams, solve problems, etc.

In order to facilitate this, learning processes should be focused in learners and take into account that they are digital natives, and they are used to technology, to new media contents, etc. [5, 6]; and also that they are learning not only in institutional contexts [7–9]. Given this context it is necessary to find new educational approaches that increase students' motivation and engagement and help them to develop useful competences for the digital society.

One of these approaches is Challenge Based Learning (CBL). It encourages students to leverage the technology they use in their daily lives to solve real-world problems [10]. CBL is collaborative and involves not only students or teachers, but also other experts in specific fields. It works posing to students a big idea, they should discuss about it and define some main questions about this idea, from these questions a challenge is proposed. Students should address the challenge looking for a collaborative solution that involves their peers, teachers, experts, etc. After this, the solution, will be assessed [11].

The easiest way to assess a CBL project would be evaluating only the final result. However, in this way it is not possible to assess what each student involved in the project has done. Other relevant issues to analyze could be the partial results and the interaction among students and the other stakeholders of this project [12].

The analysis could be done by applying new educational disciplines, such as educational data mining, academic analytics or learning analytics, that offer different but convergent perspectives, methodologies, techniques and tools aiming to facilitate this transformation process [13]. But what is the aim of these disciplines? Educational data mining includes a series of techniques oriented to extraction of educational data through statistical machine learning and data-mining algorithms, for analysis and solution of educational research issues [14]. Academic analytics takes a different approach, focusing on the analysis of institutional data about students; therefore, it has a stronger focus on institutional policy decision making [15]. Finally, the main goal of learning analytics is "the measurement, collection, analysis and reporting of data about learners and their contexts, for purposes of understanding and optimizing learning and the environments in which it occurs" [16].

There is a wide choice of learning analytics (LA) tools with different aims and that can be applied in different context [17]. However, the tools employed in CBL approaches could be very heterogeneous. CBL could use a collaborative environment to facilitate the interaction between team members and also a great diversity of tools to solve the challenges [11]. Moreover, depending on the type of challenge the interaction can be carried out in different ways. For instance, the tools employed in a robotic challenge are not the same than the employed in a biology challenge. Given this context, the present paper aims to explore learning analytics tools and methodologies to be applied in CBL. The paper presents several possible scenarios and develop an example that uses a collaborative methodology to address the challenge and an ad-hoc defined LA tool to assess what has done each team member.

The rest of the paper is structured as follows: Sect. 2, describes the advantages and problems of CBL experiments and the tools employed; Sect. 3, presents what kind of tools can be applied depending on the experiments; Sect. 4 presents an example of application of a LA tool and finally (in Sect. 5) some conclusions are posed.

2 Challenge Based Learning Experiments

CBL has been applied successfully in different experiments [10, 11, 18–23] benefiting students in several ways such as [24]:

- Students achieve a deeper understanding of different topics, learn how to diagnose and define problems before proposing solutions, and how to develop their creativity.
- Students are involved in the definition of the addressed problem and in the solution process.
- Students are aware of the problem, they develop a research process and define and implement models to address it. In order to do so they work in a collaborative way in teams with peers from different disciplines.
- Students get closer to their community reality and contact and establish relationships with experts who may contribute to their professional development.
- Students strengthen the connection between what they learn in school and what they perceive of the world around them.
- Students develop high level communication skills through the use of social tools and media production techniques. With them they can create and share the solutions that they have developed.

However, previous experiments have also shown several limitations in the application of CBL:

- Global projects are often away from the specific contents of academic subjects [20].
- Traditional assessment systems can be a problem for students, because they may be more focused on assessments than on learning [25].
- Most of the CBL experiments cannot be easily associated to a specific subject in academic contexts. They used to be applied to CBL specific designed subjects or to master projects [22].
- Students' perception about this approach is not clear because not all the experiments have indicators to evaluate this [23].
- The participation of people with different roles may cause difficulties for students that should adapt their way to work to this situation [20].
- The results of the global projects are typically obtained when the academic year has finished [18].
- There is wide choice of tools to use in CBL experiences so evaluation is not easy [24].

We are going to explore this last limitation. CBL methodology is supported by the technology which helps student to develop their projects, contact with experts, public their results and maintain the level of engagement throughout the project [10]. From the review of previously mentioned CBL experiments it is possible to see that different tools can be employed during the experiments. These could be classified in:

- Tools for information access. One of the requirements in most of the reviewed experiments is that the students should be able to access to the Internet information both at the classroom and at home [10, 11].
- Tools for editing and publishing contents. In several of analyzed experiments students should generate outcomes such as video, or audio, HTML resources [10, 11], Power Points documents [21], etc. This means that students need tools that facilitate the production of that kind outcomes.
- Tools for publishing evidences of what was done. This is a possible way to facilitate formative assessment of students outcomes [10, 24], something necessary to know what each group has been doing. This means that tools that facilitate tracking the results achieved are necessary. There are several ways to do this, a ePortfolio may be applied so the student can publish their partial outcomes [24]; meetings with each group in several moments of the development of the challenge [10]; description of the work in a wiki [18], etc.
- Tools to facilitate the collaboration and communication of the stakeholders involved in the challenges. A shared working space is helpful for a successful challenge. The workspace should be available to students 24/7, include needed resources, access to activities, a calendar, and serve as a communication channel with the teacher and between team members. There are a wide variety of Web 2.0 resources available for project management and collaboration [11, 22, 24].
- Dedicated tools for specific fields. Some of the challenges are applied in very specific fields and they required that the students and teachers use ad-hoc defined tools, for instance an earthquake simulator or a robot. This means that they should have access to tools that help them to carry out so specific works.
- Learning environments or ecosystems. It is possible to group the above-mentioned tools in a single platform which would facilitate students access to the tools and teachers' assessment of learning evidences [18, 26–28].

3 Possible Applications of Learning Analytics Tools to CBL Experiences

Given the previous classification of tools applied in CBL experiments, and taking into account the information that can be stored and how it can be accessed, different possible LA tools could be considered.

Regarding the tools for accessing the information, there are many options. Students can use web browsers or other specific tools to access to information; they can also read tweets, blogs, forums, research papers, etc. There are tools that allow recording these actions. However, students may access to the information not only to learn but with other aims. Application of LA tools in this case is difficult. There are tools such as google analytics that can track students' interactions [29] for a specific web, something that cannot be enough in a CBL experiment where the students are using lot of different webs. It is also possible to analyze students' navigation through the browser [30, 31] but it is not easy to know who is navigating and if students are being accessed to the contents with learning proposes. Social networks can be also analyzed [32, 33], but again it is necessary an authentication process and to know what social networks are used and the with which aim. Taking this into account, it is clear that tracking students' information access can be very valuable; but in order to know how these activities impact learning processes it is necessary to channel them through a single platform (this will be described below).

It is also possible to analyze what students are doing for editing contents if they use a centralized online editing tool, a content repository [34] or a version control system [35]. This is because these systems provide monitoring capabilities. Depending on the tool applied it is possible to see what each student has been doing during a specific challenge (version control system, repository) or just the final outcome.

Regarding the tools for publishing outcomes, it is possible to apply different LA techniques, but the problem is again the variety of tools that the student can choose to do this. If there is not a centralized publication/learning tool, the students may use a forum, a blog, a wiki, a social network, a web, etc. In these cases, the best option is to define a specific tool to publish the outcomes and apply monitoring tools to it. In this way it would be possible to analyze students' interactions (when they have uploaded their works, the size, number of files, number of attempts) or even the contents uploaded (by applying, for instance, text mining techniques [36]).

The evaluation of students' interaction is easier in the collaboration tools. However, the problem is again the same than in previous samples, there are lot of tools for collaborating with peers. Most collaboration platforms provide tracking systems and dashboard. For instance Moodle provides forums, chats or messages to facilitate students interaction and Moodle analytics components facilitates tracking this activities [13]. However sometimes it is necessary to explore specific issues which requires the definition of ad-hoc LA tools [37, 38]. It would be desirable that all students use the same tools to collaborate in CBL projects.

The analysis of learning evidences when we apply tools for a specific context could also require of the development of specific tools. For instance if students use an ad-hoc defined simulator or a game [19] it would be necessary that this tool includes a monitoring systems. However, it should be noted that not all the activity that students carry out in a challenge can be easily monitored, especially when talking about ad-hoc defined tools. For instance, if students use Arduino kits during a challenge it could be possible to record with video cameras the building process and take this into account when evaluating the final, but the application of an LA tool in this case would be difficult.

Last but not least it is necessary to take into account learning platforms that groups a set of tools that can be applied during challenges. In this case, if we are using well known platforms it is easy to find different learning analytics tools with different goals. For instance, if we use Moodle in a CBL experiment we can use, the analytics component to obtain general information, GISMO component to check frequency of access to certain contents or activities, Moodle engagement module to check possible dropout, and Gephy or VeLA tool to explore how students interact [13, 38–40]. When using a centralized environment, it is possible to know who uses a tool and how, but the students could not choose the tools they want to work in the project.

In the following section, we are going to describe a CBL experiment that uses, among other tools Moodle as learning platform.

4 Application of a LA in a CBL Experiment

This section describes how a LA tool is applied in a CBL experiment carried out in a Spanish University. First subsection describes how CBL is adapted and implemented, after this we describe the tools employed and finally the results obtained.

4.1 How CBL Is Applied

This experiment applies a model based on the integration of CBL and Challenge Based Instruction (CBI) [18]. The model is implemented in 5 main stages:

- First stage consists of: (1a) the presentation of the model to explain where it is going to be applied and show results of previous experiments; (1b) the definition of the teams that will address a challenge; (1c) the description of general ideas and essential questions and the definition of the challenge; and (1d) the access to solutions defined in previous experiments.
- Second stage consists of: (2a) the development of activities to deal with the project (activities related to teamwork competence) such as: map of responsibilities, scheduling, working rules, etc.; and (2b) the access to examples of this kind of activities carried out in previous experiments.
- Third stage consists of: (3a) the execution of the work: doing research, working with external agents and handling technology (wikis, on-line storage, eLearning systems and editing and publishing videos); and (3b) the access to examples of the execution in previous experiments.
- Forth stage consists of: (4a) the completion of the service or product, usually in a wiki, blog, social network or web page; (4b) the organization of the used documentation; and (4c) the production of videos.
- Fifth stage consists of: (5a) the classification of existing repository resources and (5b) and the aggregation of new ones in the repository so they can be used in future experiments.

In parallel to the model stages formative and summative assessment are carried out.

Given this model an experiment was carried out with 169 of the 183 students enrolled in "Computer Science and Programming" of the Engineering of Energy Degree of the Technical University of Madrid. 28 teams were formed with an average number of 6 six members per team. Each team chooses a challenge in one of these four areas: academic life, learning, professional opportunities and knowledge about the degree. Each challenge aims to improve the subject or university context where it is develop [18].

The course duration is 60 h; 10 of them (distributed in 5 sessions) were employed to the application of the CBL&I model. During these sessions, the stages described above were developed including a formative assessment to evaluate the partial results were carried out in phases 3, 4 and 5.

A week after the last session, the teaching staff carried out a summative assessment that took into account the individual involvement of each team member, the results obtained and how they were developed. This assessment is carried out by applying CTMTC teamwork methodology [41]. It is supported by a LA system that allows individual tracking of team members' work [42, 43].

4.2 Tools Employed for the Implementation

During CBL experiment three tools were used in order to address the challenge and define the solution and one to assess how each member has developed teamwork competence when solving the challenge.

Regarding the tools used to address the problem the main platform is the LMS Moodle. This LMS is applied because it is very popular; it includes lot of learning apps that can be applied for collaboration and publication of contents; and because it is used by the university where the experiment is carried out. The following Moodle tools were used:

- The authentication system. Each student should have an associated user into Moodle. If they want to use the collaboration or publication tools the user should be first authenticated. In this way, all students' activity will be recorded and stored by Moodle and later can be analyzed
- Moodle Forums and Chats. These tools enable synchronous and asynchronous communication between the members of each team. Also in this case, all interaction will be stored so later may be analyzed. Figure 1 shows one of the groups with all the threads (personal information has been anonymized).

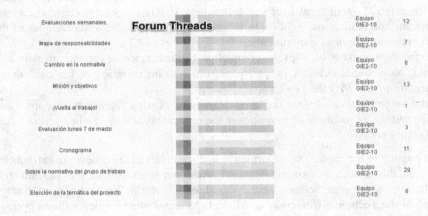

Fig. 1. Forum threads for group GIE2-10

- Moodle Wikis. This tool was used to publish the partial results of the activities carried out. Specially those related to the team competence acquisition. An example of a wiki is shown in Fig. 2. It presents the structure of the different pages that a team has defined in a Moodle to demonstrate how they develop the necessary phases to address a project as a team.

Challenge information

- ████ ███ ███████ (discussion thread)
- Team coordinator: ████████████ (discussion thread)

Goal and Aims

- Information
- Rules

Dynamic Scheduling

- Work distribution
- Chronogram

Development

- Challenge approach (discussion thread)
- Work distribution (discussion thread)
- Video Editing (discussion thread)

Results

- Link to the final result

Fig. 2. Moodle Wiki for group GIE1-15

For this CBL&I model a key issue is that students can access to the results of previous experiments and also classify and store their own outcomes. In order to do so a repository is used, the Collaborative Academic Resource Finder (Buscador de Recursos Académicos Colaborativos in Spanish) BRACO [44]. It consists of a Knowledge Management System (to which faculty and students can add content), an adaptive search engine (used by students and teachers to locate and identify resources) and a set of specific subsystems designed to support various academic activities. With this repository, each user can have her own distribution of contents and can choose the results shown. In addition, users can generate a portfolio with a selection of resources obtained during the search. Faculty can also organize the search outcomes as a list on a personalized webpage that students can see [34]. Figure 3 shows a searcher made in BRACO repository (http://www.e-braco.net/) that allows looking for contents by several criteria such as source, subject, area, thematic, author, etc.

In order to carry out the summative assessment it is necessary to take into account not only the final solution of the challenge but also the interaction between stakeholders that take place during the development of that solution. The final results can be easily reviewed because they can be available in a final deliverable, in the Internet, in the repository and/or in other online applications. However, the evaluation of the inter-actions is harder. Taking only into account the interactions related to teamwork development the analysis of the posts, threads and logs for all students in a group can last between 40 min and 1 h [37], without including the assessment. If we consider also the time for evaluation the estimated time per group could be around 3 h and 45 min [45]. If we think in a subject that has 8 students and 2 groups this is not critical. However, if the project, as in this case, has 28 groups, the work will last around 107 h. In order to solve this an ad-hoc Learning Analytics tool was developed and it is applied

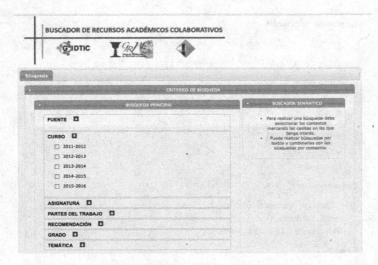

Fig. 3. BRACO educational resources repository

during assessment. The tool will allow to see the number of messages per forum, group or thread, and also the participation of each student, taking into account the number of short and long messages.

Finally, it is necessary to explore the tools used to produce the final result. In order to do this the students can freely choose what tools they use for editing videos, audios and publishing results, but the results should be accessible for all the involved stakeholders. A sample of these results is available on the following link: http://energytub.wixsite.com/energytub.

4.3   Results Obtained from the Application of the LA Tool

This section presents some of the results obtained during the application of CBL&I model, but it is specially focused in the results shown by the LA tool.

During the project 28 groups were involved, from them 24 were able to implement a real solution to the challenge, 4 failed because they do not carry out properly the tasks and due to a mismanagement of teamwork.

Regarding the interaction between team members there were a total 4684 messages for the 169 students, that is an average of 27.71 messages per user. In previous researches [42, 46], it is shown that a higher number of interactions is related to a better performance. Table 1 presents a summary of the interactions of each group and Fig. 4 shows a screenshot of the LA tool with the specific information for group GIE1-15.

The groups are organized in classes GIE1 and GIE2 and students can choose one of the available groups. This is the reason that some group numbers were not used. The first column shows the group name, the second the number of messages, the third the

Table 1. Distribution of messages by group

Group name	Messages num	Long messages	Short messages
Equipo GIE1-01	234 (10.87%)	62 (2.88%)	172 (7.99%)
Equipo GIE1-02	200 (9.29%)	57 (2.65%)	143 (6.64%)
Equipo GIE1-03	72 (3.35%)	26 (1.21%)	46 (2.14%)
Equipo GIE1-04	193 (8.97%)	60 (2.79%)	133 (6.18%)
Equipo GIE1-05	361 (16.78%)	146 (6.78%)	215 (9.99%)
Equipo GIE1-06	106 (4.93%)	47 (2.18%)	59 (2.74%)
Equipo GIE1-07	134 (6.23%)	42 (1.95%)	92 (4.28%)
Equipo GIE1-08	99 (4.6%)	19 (0.88%)	80 (3.72%)
Equipo GIE1-10	139 (6.46%)	55 (2.56%)	84 (3.9%)
Equipo GIE1-11	85 (3.95%)	26 (1.21%)	59 (2.74%)
Equipo GIE1-12	28 (1.3%)	7 (0.33%)	21 (0.98%)
Equipo GIE1-13	180 (8.36%)	109 (5.07%)	71 (3.3%)
Equipo GIE1-14	73 (3.39%)	26 (1.21%)	47 (2.18%)
Equipo GIE1-15	248 (11.52%)	72 (3.35%)	176 (8.18%)
Equipo GIE2-01	64 (2.53%)	13 (0.51%)	51 (2.01%)
Equipo GIE2-02	96 (3.79%)	19 (0.75%)	77 (3.04%)
Equipo GIE2-03	190 (7.5%)	64 (2.53%)	126 (4.98%)
Equipo GIE2-04	371 (14.65%)	94 (3.71%)	277 (10.94%)
Equipo GIE2-05	150 (5.92%)	25 (0.99%)	125 (4.94%)
Equipo GIE2-06	96 (3.79%)	18 (0.71%)	78 (3.08%)
Equipo GIE2-07	206 (8.14%)	19 (0.75%)	187 (7.39%)
Equipo GIE2-08	328 (12.95%)	55 (2.17%)	273 (10.78%)
Equipo GIE2-09	151 (5.96%)	16 (0.63%)	135 (5.33%)
Equipo GIE2-10	116 (4.58%)	48 (1.9%)	68 (2.69%)
Equipo GIE2-11	92 (3.63%)	23 (0.91%)	69 (2.73%)
Equipo GIE2-12	208 (8.21%)	26 (1.03%)	182 (7.19%)
Equipo GIE2-14	143 (5.65%)	54 (2.13%)	89 (3.52%)
Equipo GIE2-15	321 (12.68%)	30 (1.18%)	291 (11.49%)

number of long messages and the forth the number of short messages. These last two columns allow the teacher to have some knowledge about the quality of interactions, if in a group most of the messages are short this mean that the interaction is more assertive and there is not a real discussion. In the table, it is possible to see that groups that failed to define de solution for the challenge were those with a lower number of interactions GIE1-03, GIE1-12, GIE1-14 and GIE2-01. However, it is not possible to make general assumptions in this sense because the interactions are not the only issue evaluated during the challenge. But with this kind of tool it is possible to have knowledge about the level of participation and engagement of each members of the teams.

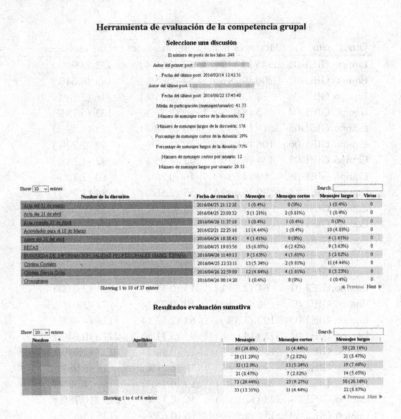

Fig. 4. Results of the LA tool for GIE1-15

5   Conclusions

CBL is a learning approach to teaching and learning that allows students use the technology they really use to solve real problems. This type of initiatives benefits students in different ways, making them closer to the real world and helping the acquisition of competences such as teamwork and communication skills.

The assessment of CBL should take into both the final results and the partial outcomes generated by the team members. However, evaluating only the results would mean to ignore other important issues that should be taken into account, such as the interaction between team members, or with other stakeholders implied in the development a solution to the challenge. The evaluation of this kind of interactions is usually difficult, because of it involves analyzing a great amount of information that is going to require a lot of time. In order to facilitate this analysis Learning Analytics tools could be applied. However, the question is if this kind of tools can be applied in CBL approaches, because CBL does not follow the typical structure of online learning courses and does not use the usual institutional tools.

In this paper, an analysis of the used tools in CBL is carried out. Taking into account these tools it is possible to assert that LA can be applied in CBL, although the way to do this and the performance of the LA techniques will depend on the tools choice to develop the challenge. After the analysis carried out it is possible to assert that it would be desirable to use a learning platform that groups the tools used by the student to develop the challenge. In this way, learning evidences can be easily recorded in a common place and with a defined data structure, which will facilitate further analysis.

As future works it would be desirable to replicate the experiment carried out in other contexts, with other learning platforms and learning analytics tools to support the conclusions obtained. In addition, it would be interesting the application of other learning tools during other stages of challenge solution development, for instance during the production of the final results.

References

1. García-Peñalvo, F.J., Seoane-Pardo, A.M.: An updated review of the concept of eLearning. Educ. Knowl. Soc. **16**, 119 (2015). Tenth anniversary
2. Conde, M.Á.: Personalización del aprendizaje: Framework de servicios para la integración de aplicaciones online en los sistemas de gestión del aprendizaje. Departamento de Informática y Automática, vol. Doctorado en Informática y Automática. Universidad de Salamanca, Salamanca (2012)
3. Conde, M.Á., García, F.J., Casany, M.J., Allier, M.: Open integrated personal learning environment: towards a new conception of the ICT-based learning processess. In: Lytras, M. D., Ordoñez-De-Pablos, P., Ziderman, A., Roulstone, A., Maurer, H., Imber, J.B. (eds.) Knowledge Management, Information Systems, E-Learning, and Sustainability Research. Communications in Computer and Information Science, pp. 115–124. Springer, Heidelberg (2010)
4. Punie, Y., Zinnbauer, D., Cabrera, M.: A Review of the Impact of ICT on Learning. European Commission Joint Research Centre - Institute for Prospective Technological Studies (2008)
5. Attwell, G.: The personal learning environments - the future of eLearning? eLearning Pap. **2**, 1–8 (2007)
6. Schaffert, R., Hilzensauer, W.: On the way towards personal learning environments: seven crucial aspects. eLearning Pap. **2**, 1–11 (2008)
7. Conde, M.Á., García-Peñalvo, F.J., Fernández-Llamas, C., García-Holgado, A.: The application of business process model notation to describe a methodology for the recognition, tagging and acknowledge of informal learning activities. Int. J. Eng. Educ. (IJEE) **31**, 884–892 (2015)
8. Halliday-Wynes, S., Beddie, F.: Informal Learning. At a Glance. National Centre for Vocational Education Research Ltd., Adelaide (2009)
9. Hager, P.: Recognition of informal learning: challenges and issues. J. Vocat. Educ. Training **50**, 521–535 (1998)
10. Johnson, L., Adams, S.: Challenge Based Learning: The Report from the Implementation Project. The New Media Consortium (2011)

11. Apple-Inc: Challenge Based Learning - Take action and make a difference. US (2009)
12. O'Mahony, T.K., Vye, N.J., Bransford, J.D., Sanders, E.A., Stevens, R., Stephens, R.D., Richey, M.C., Lin, K.Y., Soleiman, M.K.: A comparison of lecture-based and challenge-based learning in a workplace setting: Course designs, patterns of interactivity, and learning outcomes. J. Learn. Sci. **21**, 182–206 (2012)
13. Conde, M.Á., Hérnandez-García, Á., García-Peñalvo, F.J., Séin-Echaluce, M.L.: Exploring student interactions: learning analytics tools for student tracking. In: Zaphiris, P., Ioannou, A. (eds.) LCT 2015. LNCS, vol. 9192, pp. 50–61. Springer, Cham (2015). doi:10.1007/978-3-319-20609-7_6
14. Romero, C., Ventura, S.: Educational data mining: a review of the state of the art. IEEE Trans. Syst. Man Cybern. Part C Appl. Rev. **40**, 601–618 (2010)
15. Goldstein, P.J., Katz, R.N.: Academic analytics: the uses of management information and technology in higher education. Educase, Colo (2005)
16. Ferguson, R.: The State Of Learning Analytics in 2012: A Review and Future Challenges. The Open University (2012)
17. Hernández-García, Á., Conde, M.A.: Dealing with complexity: educational data and tools for learning analytics. In: Proceedings of the Second International Conference on Technological Ecosystems for Enhancing Multiculturality, Salamanca, Spain, pp. 263–268. ACM (2014)
18. Fidalgo-Blanco, Á., Sein-Echaluce, M.L., García-Peñalvo, F.J.: Integration of the methods CBL and CBI for their application in the management of cooperative academic resources. In: 2016 International Symposium on Computers in Education (SIIE), pp. 1–6 (2016)
19. Baloian, N., Hoeksema, K., Hoppe, U., Milrad, M.: Technologies and educational activities for supporting and implementing challenge-based learning. In: Kumar, D., Turner, J. (eds.) Education for the 21st Century — Impact of ICT and Digital Resources. IFIP International Federation for Information Processing, vol. 210, pp. 7–16. Springer, USA (2006)
20. Gaskins, W.B., Johnson, J., Maltbie, C., Kukreti, A.: Changing the learning environment in the college of engineering and applied science using challenge based learning. Int. J. Eng. Pedagogy **5**, 33–41 (2015)
21. Giorgio, T., Brophy, S.: Challenge-based learning in biomedical engineering: a legacy cycle for biotechnology. In: ASEE Annual Conference Proceedings (2001)
22. Malmqvist, J., Rådberg, K.K., Lundqvist, U.: Comparative analysis of challenge-based learning experiences. In: 11th International CDIO Conference, Chengdu, Sichuan, P.R. China (2015)
23. Marin, C., Hargis, J., Cavanaugh, C.: iPad learning ecosystem: developing challenge-based learning using design thinking. Turk. Online J. Distance Educ. **14**, 22–34 (2013)
24. OIE-TEC-Monterrey: Aprendizaje basado en retos. Tecnológico de Monterrey, Monterrey, Nuevo León, México (2016)
25. Savery, J.R., Duffy, T.M.: Problem-based learning: an instructional model and its constructivist framework. Educ. Technol. **35**, 31–38 (1995)
26. Conde, M.Á., García-Peñalvo, F.J., Alier, M., Mayol, E., Fernández-Llamas, C.: Implementation and design of a service-based framework to integrate personal and institutional learning environments. Sci. Comput. Program. **88**, 41–53 (2014)
27. García-Peñalvo, F.J., Hernández-García, Á., Conde, M.Á., Fidalgo-Blanco, Á., Sein-Echaluce, M.L., Alier, M., Llorens-Largo, F., Iglesias-Pradas, S.: Learning services-based technological ecosystems. In: Proceedings of the 3rd International Conference on Technological Ecosystems for Enhancing Multiculturality, Porto, Portugal, pp. 467–472. ACM (2015)

28. Conde, M.Á., García, F.J., Rodríguez-Conde, M.J., Alier, M., Casany, M.J., Piguillem, J.: An evolving learning management system for new educational environments using 2.0 tools. Interact. Learn. Environ. **22**, 188–204 (2014)
29. Amo-Filva, D., Casany-Guerrero, M.J., Alier-Forment, M.: Google analytics for time behavior measurement in moodle. In: 2014 9th Iberian Conference on Information Systems and Technologies (CISTI), pp. 1–6. IEEE (2014)
30. Fu, X., Budzik, J., Hammond, K.J.: Mining navigation history for recommendation. In: Proceedings of the 5th International Conference on Intelligent User Interfaces, New Orleans, Louisiana, USA, pp. 106–112. ACM (2000)
31. Mayer, J.R., Mitchell, J.C.: Third-party web tracking: policy and technology. In: 2012 IEEE Symposium on Security and Privacy, pp. 413–427 (2012)
32. Carrington, P.J., Scott, J., Wasserman, S.: Models and Methods in Social Network Analysis. Cambridge University Press, New York (2005)
33. Scott, J.: Social network analysis. Sociology **22**, 109–127 (1988)
34. Séin-Echaluce, M.L., Fidalgo Blanco, Á., García-Peñalvo, F.J., Conde, M.Á.: A knowledge management system to classify social educational resources within a subject using teamwork techniques. In: Zaphiris, P., Ioannou, A. (eds.) LCT 2015. LNCS, vol. 9192, pp. 510–519. Springer, Cham (2015). doi:10.1007/978-3-319-20609-7_48
35. Romero-Zaldivar, V.-A., Pardo, A., Burgos, D., Kloos, C.D.: Monitoring student progress using virtual appliances: a case study. Comput. Educ. **58**, 1058–1067 (2012)
36. Gašević, D., Dawson, S., Siemens, G.: Let's not forget: learning analytics are about learning. TechTrends **59**, 64–71 (2015)
37. Conde, M.Á., Hernández-García, Á., García-Peñalvo, F.J., Fidalgo-Blanco, Á., Sein-Echaluce, M.: Evaluation of the CTMTC methodology for assessment of teamwork competence development and acquisition in higher education. In: Zaphiris, P., Ioannou, A. (eds.) LCT 2016. LNCS, vol. 9753, pp. 201–212. Springer, Cham (2016). doi:10.1007/978-3-319-39483-1_19
38. Hernández-García, Á., Conde-González, M.Á.: Bridging the gap between LMS and social network learning analytics in online learning. J. Inf. Technol. Res. (JITR) **9**, 1–15 (2016)
39. Gómez-Aguilar, D.A., García-Peñalvo, F.J., Therón, R.: Analítica Visual en eLearning. El Profesional de la Información **23**, 236–245 (2014)
40. Gómez-Águilar, D.A., García-Peñalvo, F.J., Theron, R.: Tap into visual analysis of the customization of grouping of activities in eLearning. In: Proceedings of the First International Conference on Technological Ecosystem for Enhancing Multiculturality, Salamanca, Spain. ACM (2013)
41. Fidalgo-Blanco, Á., Lerís, D., Sein-Echaluce, M.L.: Monitoring indicators for CTMTC: comprehensive training model of the teamwork competence in engineering domain. Int. J. Eng. Educ. (IJEE) **31**, 829–838 (2015)
42. Fidalgo-Blanco, Á., Sein-Echaluce, M.L., García-Peñalvo, F.J., Conde, M.Á.: Using learning analytics to improve teamwork assessment. Comput. Hum. Behav. **47**, 149–156 (2015)
43. Conde-González, M.Á., Colomo-Palacios, R., García-Peñalvo, F.J., Larrueca, X.: Teamwork assessment in the educational web of data: a learning analytics approach towards ISO 10018. Telematics Inform. (2017, in press)
44. Fidalgo-Blanco, Á., García-Peñalvo, F.J., Sein-Echaluce, M.L., Conde-González, M.Á.: Learning content management systems for the definition of adaptive learning environments. In: 2014 International Symposium on Computers in Education (SIIE), Logrono, pp. 105–110 (2014). doi:10.1109/SIIE.2014.7017713

45. Fidalgo, Á., Conde, M.Á., Sein-Echaluce, M., García-Peñalvo, F.J.: Design and development of a learning analytics system to evaluate group work competence. In: 2014 9th Iberian Conference on Information Systems and Technologies (CISTI), pp. 1–6 (2014)
46. Agudo-Peregrina, Á.F., Iglesias-Pradas, S., Conde-González, M.Á., Hernández-García, Á.: Can we predict success from log data in VLEs? classification of interactions for learning analytics and their relation with performance in VLE-supported F2F and online learning. Comput. Hum. Behav. **31**, 542–550 (2014)

Learning Analytics and Spelling Acquisition in German – Proof of Concept

Markus Ebner[1(✉)], Konstanze Edtstadler[2], and Martin Ebner[3]

[1] Institute of Interactive Systems and Data Science,
Graz University of Technology, Graz, Austria
markus.ebner@tugraz.at
[2] Institute of Professionalization in Early Childhood and Primary
Teacher Education, University of Teacher Education Styria, Graz, Austria
konstanze.edtstadler@phst.at
[3] Department of Educational Technology,
Graz University of Technology, Graz, Austria
martin.ebner@tugraz.at

Abstract. German orthography is known to be quite difficult to master, especially for primary-school pupils in writing texts [cf. 1]. In order to support children with the acquisition of German orthography, we are developing a web-based platform for German-speaking users based on learning analytics techniques. Our goal is to motivate pupils age 8 to 12 to improve their spelling abilities by writing texts and by the possibility to publish them. Concerning spelling in combination with learning analytics the system provides - in case of an orthographic mistake - a specific feedback that encourages pupils to think about the spelling and to correct it. Based on occurred mistakes the teachers and the students are provided with a qualitative analysis of the mistakes. This analysis shows the problematic orthographic areas and gives suggestions for online and offline exercises as well as online courses that are explaining the orthographic phenomena. The aim of this article is to describe the architecture of the web-based system and a proof of concept by evaluating 60 essays. Furthermore, relevant background information is given in order to gain a better understanding in the complex interdisciplinary development.

Keywords: German orthography · Qualitative analysis of misspellings · Technology enhanced learning · Educational media

1 Introduction

This article presents a first proof of concept of the prototype platform from the project "IDeRBlog", which is an acronym of German *Individuell Differenziert Richtig schreiben mit Blogs*, which means translated literally to English "Individually differentiated correctly writing by using blogs". The project combines Technology Enhanced Learning (TEL) with Learning Analytics (LA) in the context of German orthography and spelling acquisition [2].

The IDeRBlog system provides a platform for children aged between 8 and 12 years. On this platform they can write and submit essays about their daily business or specified

© Springer International Publishing AG 2017
P. Zaphiris and A. Ioannou (Eds.): LCT 2017, Part II, LNCS 10296, pp. 257–268, 2017.
DOI: 10.1007/978-3-319-58515-4_20

topics, which are assigned or proposed by the teacher. Teachers then can review the texts on the platform, correct them, give feedback and hand it back to the students for further inspection. Before students hand in the text, the system offers the users the possibility to check their spelling with the help of our "*intelligent dictionary*". In case of a beforehand categorized mistake the systems gives a feedback that encourages the user to think about the spelling by applying a strategy in order to correct the mistake. In contrast to a conventional auto correction system which only provides information that the word is (possibly) wrong and may suggest the correct word - or a list of possibly words - our systems helps to gain deeper insight in the system of German orthography. The correct spelling of a word - without a strategy based feedback - is presented for only very few words. These are words that cannot be explained systematically by the system of the German orthography and need to be memorized. This way of supporting children by giving them a specific feedback when correcting texts is supposed to lead to a deeper understanding of the German orthography and its complex system.

The prototype is web-based due to the increasing use of devices such as computers and laptops as well as mobile devices with internet connection [3]. Thereby it is possible to trace interactions [4] between students and the learning platform for later analysis. Another benefit of this approach is the attractiveness of writing with computers for children [5]. The provided blog further gives reasons for writing because the pupils can publish their essays later on [6]. Therefore, we expect a higher motivation in formulating and revising a text in contrast to typical essay writing in a classroom [7].

Through this platform we suppose to gain insights into a learners' learning process [8] for early detection of learning issues. Teachers then can use this information to intervene [9, 10] and help pupils with the acquisition of German orthography. Therefore, the platform provides an area for teachers where they can correct and prepare the texts for publishing in the blog as well as write further feedback to the student.

1.1   Research Questions

In this article we will answer the following research questions to provide a proof of concept:

- Does this first test proof our concept of the system?
- How many spelling mistakes will be recognized by our *intelligent dictionary*?
- Which are the mistakes the system cannot identify?
- Which "teacher categories" are used most frequently?

1.2   Outline

The next section provides background about the German orthography, the intelligent dictionary and its system of categories. Further, the concept and the technology of the platform will be discussed. The third section will provide the results of the first test with texts provided by students. The last section discusses our findings, limitations and future work on this project.

2   Background

2.1   German Orthography

The German orthography is much more transparent than the English one, where "the alphabet contains just 26 letters [which] correspond to 44 phonemes associated with 102 functional spelling units" [11]. Nevertheless, it is not as transparent as, for example, the Turkish one. Therefore, a lot of words - but not all - cannot be spelled by relying on the phoneme-grapheme-correspondences since other orthographic principles are interfering. For example, the German word for *hat* <Hut> can be spelled correctly by relying on the phoneme-grapheme-correspondences, whereas the German word for *dog* <Hund> would be spelled incorrectly by purely relying on the correspondences. The reason for this is the so called phenomenon of terminal devoicing and the existence of the morphological principle. Because of these phenomena the word is pronounced as /hunt/which would lead to the incorrect spelling <*Hunt>. At the beginning of a syllable the obstruent is pronounced voiced, as in /hundə/. Consequently, the spelling of <Hund> is due to the morphological principle of the German orthography. Because of this principle morphemes and words are spelled the same way in all possible words (e.g. <Hund, Hunde, Hündin>, not <*Hunt, Hunde, Hündin>). Furthermore, the German orthography uses capitalization not only at the beginning of a sentence, but also within a sentence in order to mark substantives. Therefore, the reason for the correct spelling <Hund> in contrast to the incorrect spelling <*hund> lies in the syntactic principle.

The co-existence of these principles, which are described above in a very brief and superficial way (for a detailed description see e.g. [12]), often leads to the assumption that the German orthography is unsystematic and illogical. One possible consequence is, that children are confronted with an unsystematic way of instruction that focuses on learning by rote. Although the mastery of the orthography is rather important in German, since it is rather prestigious, students experience spelling instructions as boring and formal [13]. "In contrast to other areas of language learning, there is hardly space to argue about the correct or incorrect spelling of a word. This orthographical stiffness can probably serve as an explanation for its importance" [7].

2.2   Intelligent Dictionary

The main idea is to improve the orthographic competence of pupils by writing essays on a platform that provides a special feature - the intelligent dictionary - which gives a feedback in order to think about and consequently correct the misspelled word. It offers the correct spelling only in a few selected cases. Unlike a conventional auto correction system the intelligent dictionary in general does not offer the correctly spelled word straightaway in order to serve didactic purposes: First, students have to give attention to the feedback and have to process it by applying it on the misspelled word. Second, this approach is based on a wider definition of spelling competence that does not only include a person´s knowledge of the correct spelling of given words and the rules of orthography, but also being sensitive to misspelled words, knowing how to correct them, and applying strategies to prevent spelling errors in a long run [7, 14] Third, this system follows a modern approach of teaching and learning orthography, which considers the communicative aspect of writing (cf. e.g. [15]): The pupils work on their orthographic competence by writing essays which can also be published. Therefore, the motivation to correct the mistakes should be higher and it might be more attractive than doing conventional exercises that focus purely on orthography. Nevertheless, the platform offers online exercises and printable worksheets in order to work on a specific orthographic phenomenon. Although orthography is only one aspect among others of text writing skills, it is an important one to work on. This shows a big survey of various competences in German language including also reading and listening among others: The results indicate that 27% of the tested Austrian pupils in grade 4 did not reach the standards of the application of the correct orthography and punctuation in the task of producing texts (cf. [1]).

2.3 Categorization

In order to give a feedback for correcting the mistakes and in order to offer a qualitative analysis of the mistakes it is necessary to establish a complex system of categories. This system is developed on a linguistic and orthographic basis. Currently the systems covers 28 categories, separated into 143 phenomena and 58 feedbacks.

The reason for these unequal numbers lies in the different requirements: The categories are visible for the users in the qualitative analysis. Therefore, the number should be kept as small as possible, but as exact as necessary. These 28 categories are also labeled "teacher categories", since especially the teachers will work with them. Due to the complexity of German orthography the possible mistakes must be divided in different phenomena in order to categorize the misspelled words in an exact way for constructing the intelligent dictionary. In the system each phenomenon is connected with a category. For the feedback it is possible to merge two or even more phenomena. This helps to keep the amount of different feedbacks as small as possible in order that the users get familiar with the different hints. Considering the requirements of a scientific analysis the fine-grained phenomena allow a deep analysis in order to gain a better understanding of the acquisition process in a long run. Consequently, it could be necessary to add new phenomena or delete existing ones, which is easier to manage due to the level of phenomena.

To gain a better understanding of this system, an example of a category with its phenomena and feedback is given: The category "prefix" consists of 12 phenomena. Due to the morphological principle of German orthography a prefix is always spelled the same way in all possible words and word forms with this certain prefix. For example, the prefix *ver-* is always spelled as <ver> like in *verlaufen* (to lose ones ways), *verlieben* (to fall in love), *verreisen* (to go on a journey) and the prefix *ent-* is always spelled as <ent-> in *entdecken* (to discover) or *entfernen* (to remove). Each of the 12 phenomena of this category describe one prefix with its possible mistakes (e.g. <*fer> instead of <ver> in <*ferreisen> or <*end> instead of <ent> in <*end-decken>). Since spelling errors of this kind are very similar, the same feedback can be given for all 12 phenomena. Therefore, the pupils get the (literally translated) feedback

"Think about the spelling of the world building brick". This should guide the writer's attention towards the prefix and enable him/her to correct it.

The advantages of the linking of the different phenomena with one category are the following: First, this enables us to conduct analysis of each phenomenon separately in order to gain a better understanding of the use and frequency of spelling mistakes of each prefix. Second, we can add phenomena for prefixes that are not considered yet. Therefore, modifications concerning the phenomena can be undertaken without confusing the user.

Since the lexicon of a language is endless, it is not - and will never be - possible to consider all words of a language and all possible mistakes of a specific word. Therefore, the development of the intelligent dictionary is currently based on the words of the basic vocabulary of three federal states in Germany (for details see [7]). For these words all word forms are considered. This is challenging especially in the German language since it has quite a rich morphology. The number of word forms for one word varies from one word form (e.g. prepositions) up to 17 different word forms (e.g. adjectives).

Based on this word forms the possible mistakes are derived and assigned to a phenomenon. Therefore, one word form can be connected with different misspelled words in different phenomena.

2.4 Platform

With the IDeRBlog platform we try to combine the development of writing skills, acquisition of orthographic competence and improving the reading skills with modern means of communication and digital instruments [7].

Figure 1 shows the IDeRBlog system, which can be used after prior registration with a separate user management system. It is a web-based application with state of the art technology such as HTML5, responsive web design and web services for native Android or iOS applications (under development). The Application Server handles the communication from the students and the teachers and is implemented with the GRAILS web application framework for Java platforms. Grails is based on Groovy and uses different established frameworks such as Spring and Hibernate. To ensure a clean and manageable project the Model View Controller (MVC) Pattern is used.

The submitted text by the student is first analyzed automatically regarding spelling mistakes. Here we use the conventional system of dividing the text into sentences and further into tokens. After the part-of-speech tagging [16] the tokens are assigned to categories. Based on that information our intelligent dictionary will provide age-appropriate feedback, according to the detected spelling mistake in connection with its phenomenon. As described above, the feedback is designed to encourage students to reflect and think about the made spelling mistakes and become aware of the structure of the words [7, 20]. Additionally, spelling mistakes which have not been categorized by the intelligent dictionary will be marked as spelling mistakes without a specific feedback. Further, based on the occurred errors and its corresponding categories, the platform can recommend exercises from the provided training database [17]. In order to understand, how this systems works in practice, Fig. 2 shows the feedback for two different mistakes.

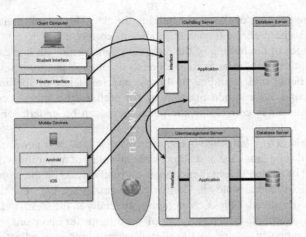

Fig. 1. Architecture.

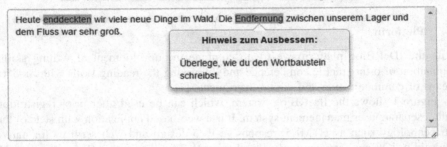

Fig. 2. Text correction example

Figure 2 shows a feedback example with the text, which means in English, „Today we discovered many new things in the woods. The distance between our camp and the river was very far". The student made two quite similar spelling mistakes: *enddeckten* ('(we) discovered') with <*end> instead of <ent> and *Endfernung* ('(the) distance') with <*End> instead of <Ent>, which are shown to him/her with the appropriate hint for correction: "Think about the spelling of the world building brick". As described in the background section, the writer's attention should be guided to the prefix and enable him/her to correct it. The headline serves as an instruction as it tells that pupils, that he/she can see his/her mistakes and that he/she gets hints for correcting them. The hints appear, when the pupils clicks on or hover over the highlighted word.

This intelligent dictionary is embedded in a platform that offers more features and has a specific workflow for pupils and teachers, as shown in Fig. 3 and described separately for pupils' and teachers' use.

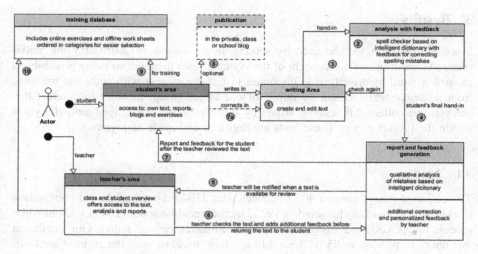

Fig. 3. Workflow for students and teachers.

Workflow for Pupils

After login the pupils have several possibilities: They can start to write a new text in the writing area (1) or access the reports of their previously submitted texts and the evaluation carried out by the teacher; they can access the private/class/school-blog, where they can find published texts of other pupils, or they can work on recommended exercises in the training database.

In case they start to write a new text, this text will be analyzed orthographically by the intelligent dictionary in a first step (2) [7]. Proper feedback, based on the spelling mistake and the category, will be displayed to the student - as shown in Fig. 2. In this phase, he/she can continue to correct the text (3) which supports the self-reflexivity of spelling mistakes by trying to correct them independently [18] and finally submit the text to the teacher (4). After the correction by the teacher, the student is informed about the report (7) or the necessity to redo the text writing (7a), then the process starts again (1). If the teacher has finished the review and correction of the essay, the pupil can blog the text in one of the three available blogs (8). Further, based on the evaluation of the texts, exercises are recommended to the student for self-learning (9).

Workflow for Teachers

As soon as the pupil submitted a text, the teacher gets a notification (5). The teacher can correct the submitted text within the platform concerning various aspects and add a personalized feedback. In the next step the teacher can either let the student edit the text according to the given feedback in order to resubmit his/her text again (7a) or make the final reviewed version available in the students' area (7). Concerning the orthographic competence of a specific pupil or the class in general, the teacher can inspect the performance according to the qualitative analysis and decide to assign spelling exercises to the pupil and/or class (10).

3 Results

Since the platform will be used by schools in the course of 2016/2017 our initial research aims to proof our concept of the system. Since there are so many possibilities to spell a word incorrectly it is important to test the system with authentic mistakes from authentic texts written by pupils of our target group. In order to conduct this analysis, we collected 60 essays written by students of 3rd grade, aged around 8 years within the project group. These texts are digitized and made anonymous.

3.1 Findings

The collected essays contain 405 sentences with 3792 tokens (words and punctuation marks). The amount of characters is 19237 including white space (15694 without white space). In the collected essays 549 spelling mistakes can be found. Our intelligent dictionary responded to 95 of these 549 spelling mistakes with the appropriate feedback. Currently our intelligent dictionary covers 17.3% of the total found spelling mistakes in the 60 essays.

The top 5 categories of the analysis based on the intelligent dictionary are (i) "gemination" (which means that only one consonant instead of two is spelled, e.g. <*gesamelt> instead of <gesammelt> 'collected'), (ii) "complex graphemes" (which means, that more than one letter is necessary for spelling one phoneme, e.g. <*speilen> instead of <spielen> 'to play'), (iii) "use of lower case letters instead of upper case letters" (e.g. <*buch> instead of <Buch> 'book'), (iv) "spelling of the s-sound" (e.g. <*weis> instead of <weiß> 'white'), "word to memorize" (this category contains words, that cannot be spelled correctly by applying a strategy, e.g. <*unt> instead of <und> 'and').

Table 1 shows the top 5 categories and the number of spelling mistake occurrences and percentage over all analyzed essays within the intelligent dictionary:

Table 1. Top 5 categories.

Category	Occurrence	%
Gemination	24	25.3
Complex graphemes	15	15.8
Use of lower case letters instead of upper case letters	13	13.7
Spelling of the s-sound	9	9.5
Word to memorize	8	8.4
Others	26	27.3

Those top 5 categories cover 72.7% of the found spelling mistakes from our *intelligent dictionary* (see Fig. 4). Since the category "complex graphemes" contains also missing dieresis (e.g. <u> instead of <ü>), which is a common mistake in handwriting, this category probably will not reach such a top place when children are typing on a keyboard because all German letters that require dieresis (<ä, ü, ö>) are

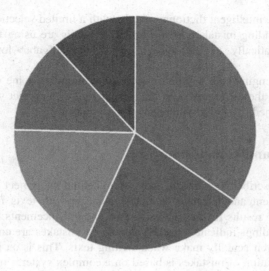

- germination
- complex graphemes
- use of lower case letters instead of upper case letters
- spelling of the s sound
- word to memorize

Fig. 4. Top 5 categories.

represented on the keyboard. Therefore, this phenomenon should not occur very often, whereas the phenomenona of <i.e.> instead of <ei> and/or <ei> instead of <i.e.>, that belong also to the same category are likely to happen. Problems in the field of capitalization are, like problems with spelling the different s-sounds, very common in the acquisition process.

Of course it was expected that not all mistakes are recognized by the *intelligent dictionary*. After the first proof of concept it is possible to describe these constraints closer:

First, some categories and/or phenomena are considered in the system, but the spelling mistakes need to be collected on basis of the written texts of the users. This is especially true for the use of English words in German texts (e.g. <*Capten> for <Captain>) and for names (e.g. <*Nickolaus> for <Nikolaus>).

Second, some spelling mistakes need to be analyzed by hand because mistakes concerning phoneme-grapheme-correspondences cannot be considered, since there are endless possibilities of disregarding the grapheme-phoneme-correspondences. As a consequence, the intended word is only recognizable due to the context because graphemes are for example either missing (e.g. <*Kunt> for <Kunst> 'art') or in the wrong position (e.g. <*Geschneke> for <Geschenke> 'presents'). This kind of mistakes will be collected, but it is not possible to systematically categorize them in advance in order to give a feedback.

Third, since the intelligent dictionary works with a limited selection of word forms and their corresponding mistakes, new words that pupils are using frequently should be added systematically to the system, e.g. <*hausaufgabe> for <Hausaufgabe> ('homework').

Fourth, a challenging task will be to teach the system that some words are spelled correctly, although the dictionary does not recognize it as a correct word, because the word is newly coined, e.g. <Partyhütchen> ('party hats').

4 Discussion and Conclusion

In this study we described the concept and system behind the project IDeRBlog and its workflow for student and teachers. A first evaluation with texts from students are showing promising results for future evaluations and enhancements for the intelligent dictionary. Our findings indicate that the categorized mistakes are corresponding with the mistakes children actually make when writing texts. This is an important finding since the categorization of mistakes is based on a complex systems of phenomena and categories. Due to the proven stability of the system, new words and mistakes can be added to the system in order to make the intelligent dictionary more powerful and to gain significant analysis in future.

The implementation of this system in schools has great advantages for teachers and pupils: First, the teacher gets easily a qualitative analysis of the spelling errors of his/her pupils. Until now qualitative analysis of spelling mistakes of essays need to be done by hand. This is a time consuming process that also requires a lot of knowledge (for details see [19]). Second, based on the results of the qualitative analysis the teachers know which orthographic areas are the most problematic ones of a specific pupil or of a whole group. By using the platform and the possibility of retrieving a qualitative analysis of the number and percentage of spelling mistakes per category the teachers are supported in planning their orthography classes. Furthermore, the system can be used for evaluating the progress of pupils in acquiring the German orthography in general or in acquiring specific categories of the German orthography. The advantage for the pupils is that they can improve their spelling in an attractive digital environment that is based on scientific finding. Therefore, the platform is a trend-setting development and application in the field of E-Learning and learning analytics with methodology in a certain subject - namely German orthography.

The system also has big advantages for researchers in spelling acquisition: It will be the first time that analysis of the used words and their spelling errors are possible. This can have a huge impact on understanding acquisition processes and consequently modifications of teaching and learning approaches.

Although there are many promising advantages, there is also a drawback: The advantages can only be considered if a big community is using the system frequently because analysis for pupils can only be carried out in case there are enough correctly and incorrectly spelled words. This aspect also affects the impact of the interpretation of this preliminary findings. The data basis is limited to 60 short texts from 3rd graders. Therefore, the presented findings show the possibilities of this system, but no real empirical evidence. Since our system is developed for pupils aged from 8 to 12 years, we should also add texts from 4th to 6th graders. The more schools and classes will use the system, the deeper will be the insight in the spelling process and orthographic competence of German speaking users. This is expected to happen in the course of 2016/17 when the whole systems is offered to the public.

In order to improve the *intelligent dictionary* for the users, the system should grow by adding words and their word forms as well as their possible mistakes based on the texts written by the pupils. Further we plan to predict the performance of students, make personalized recommendations for exercises provided by our platform and benchmark the performance of the student's progress in spelling acquisition.

Acknowledgments. This research project is supported by the European Commission Erasmus+ program in the framework of the project IDeRBlog under grant VG-SPS-SL-14-001616-3. For more information about the project IDeRBlog and its project partners: from Germany: Gros, M., Adolph, H., Steinhauer, N. (LPM Saarland[1]); Biermeier, S., Ankner, L. (Albert-Weisgerber-Schule, St. Ingbert[2]); from Belgium: Huppertz, A., Cormann, M. (GS Raeren[3]); from Austria: Ebner, M., Taraghi, B., Ebner, M. (TU Graz[4]); Gabriel, S., Wintschnig, M. (KPH Wien/Krems[5]); Aspalter, Ch., Martich, S., Ullmann, M. (PH Wien[6]); Edtstadler, K. (PH Steiermark[7], before: KPH Wien/Krems), please visit our homepage http://iderblog.eu/ (German language only).

References

1. Breit, S., Bruneforth, M., Schreiner, C. (eds.): Standardüberprüfung 2015 Deutsch, 4. Schulstufe. Bundesergebnisbericht, Salzburg (2016)
2. Ebner, M., Taraghi, B., Ebner, M., Aspalter, C., Biermeier, S., Edtstadler, K., Gabriel, S., Goor, G., Gros, M., Huppertz, A., Martich, S., Steinhauer, N., Ullmann, M., Ziegler, K.: Design für eine Plattform zum Schreibenlernen im Grundschulalter. In: Rathmayer, S., Pongratz, H. (eds.) Proceedings of DeLFI Workshops 2015 Co-located with 13th e-Learning Conference of the German Computer Society (DeLFI 2015), Munich, Germany, 1 September 2015, pp. 118–122 (2015)
3. Welche Geräte besitzt Du? In: Statista - Das Statistik-Portal (2016). http://de.statista.com/statistik/daten/studie/167839/umfrage/geraetebesitz-von-jugendlichen-in-deutschland/. Accessed 5 September 2016
4. Duval, E.: Attention Please! Learning analytics for visualization and recommendation. In: Proceedings of LAK11: 1st International Conference on Learning Analytics and Knowledge 2011 (2010)
5. Høien, T., Lundberg, I.: Dyslexia: From Theory to Intervention. Kluwer, Dordrecht (2000)

---

[1] LPM Saarland, Beethovenstraße 26, 66125 Saarbrücken, Germany.

[2] Albert-Weisgerber School St. Ingbert, Robert-Koch-Straße 4, 66386 St. Ingbert, Germany.

[3] School of Raeren, Hauptstraße 45, 4730 Raeren, Belgium.

[4] Graz University of Technology, Department Educational Technology, Münzgrabenstraße 35a, 8010 Graz, Austria.

[5] University College of Teacher Education Vienna/Krems, Mayerweckstraße 1, 1210 Vienna, Austria.

[6] University of Teacher Education Vienna, IBS/DiZeTIK, Grenzackerstraße 18, 1100 Vienna, Austria.

[7] University of Teacher Education Styria, Hasnerplatz 12, 8010 Graz, Austria.

6. Government of South Australia. Department for Education and Child Development, issuing body: Spelling: from beginnings to proficiency: a spelling resource for planning, teaching, assessing and reporting on progress. Department for Education and Child Development, Adelaide, South Australia (2011). http://www.decd.sa.gov.au/literacy/files/pages/Programs%20and%20Resources/Spelling_resource_FINAL.pdf. Accessed 8 September 2016

7. Edtstadler, K., Ebner, M., Ebner, M.: Improved German spelling acquisition through learning analytics. eLearn. Pap. **45**, 17–28 (2015)

8. Khalil, M., Ebner, M.: Learning analytics: principles and constraints. In: Proceedings of World Conference on Educational Multimedia, Hypermedia and Telecommunications, EdMedia 2015, AACE, Waynesville, NC, USA, pp. 1326–1336 (2015)

9. Siemens, G., Long, P.: Penetrating the fog: analytics in learning and education. EDUCAUSE Rev. **46**(5), 30 (2011)

10. Greller, W., Drachsler, H.: Translating learning into numbers: a generic framework for learning analytics. J. Educ. Technol. Soc. **15**(3), 42–57 (2012)

11. Snowling, M.J.: Developmental dyslexia: a cognitive developmental perspective. In: Aaron, P.G., Joshi, R.M. (eds.) Reading and Writing Disorders in Different Orthographic Systems, pp. 1–23. Kluwer Academic Publishers (1989)

12. Nerius, D.: Deutsche Orthographie. Georg Olms, Hildesheim (2007)

13. Küttel, H.: Probleme des Erwerbs der Orthographie. In: Nerius, D. (ed.) Deutsche Orthographie, pp. 417–451. Georg Olms, Hildesheim (2007)

14. Naumann, C.L.: Zur Rechtschreibkompetenz und ihrer Entwicklung. In: Bremerich-Vos, A., Granzer, D., Köller, O. (eds.) Lernstandbestimmung im Fach Deutsch, Beltz, pp. 134–159 (2008)

15. Mann, C.: Selbstbestimmtes Rechtschreiblernen: Rechtschreibunterricht als Strategievermittlung. Verlagsgruppe Beltz (1991)

16. Voutilainen, A.: Part-of-speech tagging. In: The Oxford Handbook of Computational Linguistics, pp. 219–232 (2003)

17. Ebner, M., Ebner, M., Edtstadler, K.: Learning analytics and spelling acquisition in German - a first prototype. In: Zaphiris, P., Ioannou, A. (eds.) LCT 2016. LNCS, vol. 9753, pp. 405–416. Springer, Cham (2016). doi:10.1007/978-3-319-39483-1_37

18. Bartnitzky, H.: Individuell fördern–Kompetenzen stärken. Grundschule aktuell **9**, 6–11 (2010)

19. Edtstadler, K.: Qualitative Fehleranalyse im Schriftspracherwerb. Kritik und Kriterien. In: Lindner, D., Beer, R., Gabriel, S., Krobath, T. (eds.) Dialog Forschung – Forschungsband 2015, pp. 169–178. Lit-Verlag, Vienna (2016)

20. Tsesmeli, S.N., Seymour, P.H.K.: Derivational morphology and spelling in dyslexia. Read. Writ. **19**(6), 587–625 (2006)

Data Analysis of Coaching and Advising
in Undergraduate Students.
An Analytic Approach

David Fonseca[1(✉)], José Antonio Montero[1], Mariluz Guenaga[2],
and Iratxe Mentxaka[2]

[1] La Salle, Universitat Ramon Llull, Barcelona, Spain
{fonsi,montero}@salle.url.edu
[2] University of Deusto, Bilbao, Spain
{mlguenanga,iratxe.mentxaka}@deusto.es

Abstract. This paper aims to analyze the data collected from a first approach at the process of applying coaching techniques in the advisor service of students in their first course of engineering. In this context, resources and techniques from the field of coaching can be very useful for the advisor, as those resources influence the student to reflect and be more aware of the situation he/she is living. This process should help prevent problems such as the frustration and insecurity that can appear among students, not only in the early stages of their studies, as we will show in the paper, and minimizing the number of student dropouts. Finally, we will discuss about whether the coaching process has improved the main objective of these types of approaches: that the student will be more qualified to take the appropriate decisions with greater discretion, motivation and responsibility in his/her engineering studies.

Keywords: Coaching · Advising · Educational guidance · Teaching support systems · Enhanced learning

1 Introduction

The engineering studies are often qualified as "difficult". Before getting to the specific subjects that usually attract the students (situated at the end of the studies), the first courses provide basics skills in more general and less motivating subjects. For these reasons (the difficulty of the studies and the unattractive initial subjects) and others such as the past crisis period, the number of engineering students in Spain has decreased, despite the recent upturn due to the high labor demand and progressively increasing salaries. In these years of "crisis", high dropout rate has been observed especially in the first courses due to their difficulty. Therefore, there is a clear need to accompany the student in this educational phase, since despite being adults; they are not prepared to pass the new difficulties. We can summarize the main objectives of the academic advisor (also known as tutor or academic supervisor) as:

- Accompany the student in his/her formation and advise him/her academically,
- Minimize the number of students dropping out of their studies,

© Springer International Publishing AG 2017
P. Zaphiris and A. Ioannou (Eds.): LCT 2017, Part II, LNCS 10296, pp. 269–280, 2017.
DOI: 10.1007/978-3-319-58515-4_21

- Improve the satisfaction of the students.

For these reasons, the faculty established the following principal functions of the tutor:

- Introduce him/herself personally at the beginning of the studies.
- Obtain teachers' collaboration to detect problems that can affect the students and inform about any situation concerning the student, to have in mind any academic situation to follow up.
- Regularly follow up with the student to identify any problems, even on a family level. Regarding this situation, report to the appropriate authorities responsible for that situation. Attend students, family and teachers quickly and effectively.
- Record and keep record of the results of interviews.
- Question him/herself after exams, especially in cases with high fail rate.
- Attend all academic councils to take care of all cases, as well as meetings referring to educational planning.
- Help the students with the subjects they choose and every question they may have.
- Study and analyze incompatibilities between subjects.
- Collaborate in the election of the delegate for each course and the representatives of the student council.
- Take care of complaints, claims and suggestions of the formation program as well as the services and the infrastructure.

This paper presents the experiences of an intervention carried out at Engineering La Salle Campus Barcelona-URL. In order to make the students more aware of their situation, some coaching resources are used in the university tutoring process. This way, students are able to make decisions with the right criteria, motivation, conviction and responsibility. This proposal deals with improving the acquisition of general skills in decision-making, critical capacity, self-motivation, initiative and self-knowledge. The aim of the experience is to assess the inclusion of coaching techniques in the advising services, and their evaluation for further uses using an analytic approach. The solutions and results will allow us to produce a shared system that will use specific techniques for specific problems according to their functionality in the past, suggested automatically by the system for any advisor and student.

This paper continues (Sect. 2) with a brief explanation of the current theoretical framework, concerning both the typical problems of academic supervision and the effects of coaching in the educational sector. In Sect. 3, the paper describes the design of the study performed in the Engineering studies, where coaching techniques were applied in certain cases of complex academic advising. In Sect. 4, we find the main results obtained, and finally (Sect. 5), we find the conclusions and the future lines of work.

2 Theoretical Framework

Academic tutoring is being established as a highly important [1] complementary activity to the student's evolution. In both pre-university (where the main aim is to avoid school drop-out [2, 3]) and university levels (where problems are usually more complex) we find an increasing number of educational centers that offer this service, especially in the first courses [4]. It appears almost certain that it is in the first university courses [5] that student's tutoring is most important.

The tutor reflects physically or digitally the information from every tutoring session, but this information is not proactive for future similar problems concerning other tutors. As we will see in next sections, in these cases the use of tutoring systems and learning analytics can improve the advising service with a more quickly identification of problems and solutions. In any case, a tutorial that effectively advises the student will generate a positive educational outcome, either causing a reduction in educational dropout rates and/or improving the student's academic results [6]. For this reason, and given the new educational panorama, it is vital to continue with the tutoring, and we must incorporate new resources, such as coaching [7].

2.1 Coaching and Self-regulated Learning

We can define the coaching as a way of enhancing people's consciousness. Coaching aims for people to be more aware of the reality they are living, in order to find a way of achieving one's objectives or solving one's problems [8]. We can find many works and experimental cases where coaching activities have been developed [8]. However, Bettinger and Baker from the National Bureau of Economic Research of Cambridge [9] carried out the most similar work within our framework. This work presents the effects of coaching among first-year university students in the fields of economics, education and sociology. Among other findings, the study quantifies a 5% reduction in dropout rates on the first year, as well as a 4% decrease in dropout after 24 months.

Whether a student engages in learning actively or chooses to disengage from the activity, completely or in part, he or she is lead by motivation, and in this context, it is a self-regulated choice. In terms of one widely cited model of self-regulated learning proposed by Winne and Hadwin [10, 11] learners exercise agency across four loosely sequenced phases: (1) They scan their environment to identify internal factors (cognitive, motivational, affective) and external features that may influence a task. (2) They frame goals and design plans to approach them. (3) They implement actions to animate their plans, monitor the match between a plan and its actualization and modestly adjust actions as they judge appropriate. And, (4) they re-examine aspects across these three prior phases to consider major, strategic revisions to understanding and action if progress toward goals is blocked, too slow or in some other way unsatisfactory.

Adapting this approach to a coaching strategy we are close to a GROW process [12, 13], defined by these phases:

- G (Goal): The student defines the objective he pursues, consistent with his own values.
- R (Reality): The student analyses, jointly with the tutor-coach, 'his reality'.
- O (Options): The student identifies the different ways of achieving the objective, and is advised about the benefits vs. costs of every option.
- W (Will): The student defines a plan of action: what, when, how, where...

On the other hand, and in accordance with the assumption that learners, as agents, will regulate their learning, Winne and Nesbit [14] recommended an approach that investigates "the way learners make things". This paradigm has three main components:

- Instruments should be developed to gather data that trace over time which information each learner operates on and how each learner operates on each of those selections.
- From the data obtained, temporally extended trajectories of engagement should be assembled for each learner.
- And finally, in exploring those trajectories and their relations to other "snapshot" data (e.g., responses to self-report questionnaires, measures of aptitude or end-of-course achievement), learners should be grouped into homogeneous groups based on data rather than pinning hope on random assignment to neutralize sources of unidentified variance.

2.2 Tutoring Systems and Learning Analytics

The first computer tutoring systems to be used in school classrooms [15, 16] showed the influence of the programmed instruction movement of the time: They presented instruction in short segments or frames, asked questions frequently during instruction, and provided immediate feedback on answers [17].

These systems guided learners through each step of a solution to a problem by creating hints and feedback as needed from expert-knowledge databases. The first-generation computer tutors have been given the retronym CAI tutors (Computer-Assisted Instruction tutors); the second-generation tutors are usually called Intelligent Tutoring Systems, or ITSs [18]. More recent reviews support conventional beliefs about CAI tutoring effects. For example, a 1994 review aggregated results from 12 separate meta-analyses on computer-based instruction carried out at eight different research centers [19]. Each of the analyses yielded the conclusion that computer-based instruction improves student learning to a moderate degree.

On the other hand, a learning analytic approach provides institutions with opportunities to support student progression and to enable personalized rich learning [30]. With the increased availability of large datasets, powerful analytics engines [31], and skillfully designed visualizations of analytics results [32], institutions may be able to use the experience of the past to create supportive, insightful models of primary (and perhaps real-time) learning processes [33].

A possible way to support teachers in monitoring and guiding student activities (including their collaboration), is by enhancing digital environments with learning analytics tools [20]. The traces left by student activities can be automatically collected, analyzed, and reported back to both students and teachers for optimizing learning [21]. Learning analytics that are specifically aimed at supporting the teacher may serve a number of functions. They can be placed on a continuum of how much control or choice is left to the teacher [22]: from providing overviews of data to suggesting particular actions to even undertaking those actions (for example, by automatically sending a message to a student).

We can find few proposals that have worked with the aim of creating interactive systems that allow for feedback from tutorials [23, 24], focusing on online student management [25], but not related with coaching methods in academic fields. For these reasons, our project is the first step in a process to define the main coaching variables and student situations in order to develop a system that can merge the tutoring systems, coaching approaches and learning analytics to predict both problems and solutions in the advising services.

3   Case Study and Method

3.1   Sample

For this study, 41 first year students from academic years 2014–15 and 2015–16 have been selected, belonging to the degrees of Telecommunications and Computer Engineering form La Salle, Universitat Ramon Llull. Students were selected based on their academic results of the first control point (first semester), where they have been evaluated in a total of 7 subjects.

From the 41 students, 21 have been assigned to the experimental group, and 20 to the control group. All of them, after the first basic tutoring, were identified as potential 'risky students', due to both personal and academic reasons. According to the available times for tutoring, 21 experimental cases were randomly selected, to which an intensive following was made based on coaching techniques.

3.2   Procedure

To obtain the initial profile of the students in the experimental group, an interview was carried out in order to identify the academic situation and personal problems regarding some of the following situations (which we will identify for the analysis of results as IS-#, corresponding with Initial Situation):

- IS-1: Frustration and demotivation due to bad results.
- IS-2: Existence of a limiting belief.
  - The degree is too difficult for the student.
  - The student is unable to study for a minimum of time.
  - …
- IS-3: Will to abandon their studies.
- IS-4: Incapacity to know how to face poor academic results:
  - What to do?
  - What to change?
  - …
- IS-5: Personal or family problems (non-academic).

According to the detected problems, coaching activities selected for application are (defined as CA#) [26–29]:

- CA-1: Visualization at ten years sight. This is a technique applied to achieve a desired emotional situation by imagining specific images. For example: when students are confused and do not know why they are studying their degree, they are asked to visualize how they would like their life to be in 10 years, both at professional and personal levels. This helps defining objectives at short and medium terms, since they have visualized and felt (at an emotional level) the future they desire.

- CA-2: Six thinking hats: Methodology that allows students to analyze the situation they are living from different points of view and not only theirs, in order to be aware of the different approaches that can be used to face their situation, creating new action alternatives.

- CA-3: Exposition to the concepts of reactivity and proactivity: Students are shown the difference between reactivity and proactivity. In most occasions, students become aware that their attitude towards their problem is reactive, and they complain without ever looking for alternatives to solve it. By asking about 'What one can do to improve the situation?', or 'What depends on oneself?' new alternatives emerge.

- CA-4: Use of tales as metaphors to help students discover what they need to discover. It is easier for students to become aware of what is happening if they see themselves reflected in the main character of a story. Tales can help students discern that their problems are limiting beliefs, their indecision, feelings of guilt, etc.

- CA-5: Helping to identify a clear objective through ponderous questions: Ponderous questions can make reflect, impact and even incommode. When students are not able to find an answer that satisfies them, then the process is started and they look for a change in their current situation, identifying a well-defined objective; achievable, relevant and bounded in the time period.

- CA-6: Question limiting beliefs with ponderous questions: Through the right questions, students are helped to identify data that justify some of their beliefs.

- CA-7: At an emotional level, identify the somatic triggers that allow awareness of an emotionally intense situation, in order to later define an escape behavior that breaks the blocking process: Through the use of the right questions, students are helped to identify the physiological indicators that warn of an incoming blocking situation. This way, before reaching an intense level leading to a block, they can define an escape behavior.

- CA-8: Exposition to the coherence triangle: think-do-feel. Students are shown the need of having coherence between what one thinks, does and feels.

- CA-9: Abdominal breathing that helps relaxing and regaining self-control: In some cases, students reach a level of anxiety and stress that prevents them from thinking with clarity. It is interesting, in these cases, to teach them to breath adequately.

- CA-10: The wheel of life adapted to students: It allows them to identify the areas in their lives they would want to improve. It is an interesting resource when the student is very confused and does not know the objective he/she desires.

With the aim of evaluating the followed method, we have accounted for two variables: academic and personal. Regarding the academic variable, we have identified he number of failed subjects at the end of the year and their variation with respect to the control point, and whether the student abandoned the course. The personal variables have been integrated in a subjective way, based on their tutor's evaluation of the process. The degree of satisfaction perceived by the tutor does not reflect the academic results, but the comments and feelings of students and their relatives. For example, a student may have failed several subjects, or even dropped out, and at the same time have a positive evaluation of the process from his tutor, because the student has evolved and became aware of the situation, taking decisions in a mature way once the situation is assimilated.

4   Main Results

As we can observe in Table 1, while in the control group the percentage of failed subjects between the exam and the end of the year has increased, this percentage has been reduced (from 4,86 to 4,14) in the experimental group. To estimate the probability that results are significantly similar, we used the Student's t-test, and tested a null hypothesis (Ho) that there are no differences in scores between variables. As P (T) = p two-tailed is 0.036, which is less than the threshold of 0.05, this means that there is a very high probability that the results are statically different. Comparing the homogeneity of the two groups, and therefore the possibility to continue with the experiment based on the academic results, the p two-tailed is 0.83, a value that confirms the initial academic similarity between the two working groups.

Table 1. Failed subjects

	Control group (n = 20)		Experimental group (n = 21)	
	Check point (7 subjects)	Final marks (7 subjects)	Check point (7 subjects)	Final marks (7 subjects)
Average of failed subjects	4,95	5,25	4,86	4,14
% with 6 or 7 failed subjects (High risk of drop out)	25,00	45,00	42,86	38,10
% with 5 or 4 failed subjects (Moderate risk of drop out)	75,00	30,00	38,10	14,29
% with 0 to 3 failed subjects (Medium/low risk)	0,00	25,00	19,05	47,62

Additionally, it was observed that while in the control Group (at the end of the course) there were 35% of drop outs (all of them from the high risk group identified at the beginning), in the experimental group the percentage of dropouts was reduced to 23,81%.

At the end of the academic year, students from the experimental group have managed to reduce the number of failed subjects significantly, as well as the percent-age of dropouts. In Table 2, we can observe the summary of problems identified at the beginning of the coaching process by the experimental group:

Table 2. Initial situation/problems detected (based on classification of Sect. 3.2)

Initial situation/problem	IS-1	IS-2	IS-3	IS-4	IS-5
Number of problems found	10	9	11	10	6
Percentage	47,62	42,86	52,38	47,62	28,57

Depending on the distribution of problems identified and their way of repeating, it was found that everyone shows an average of approximately two problems with a specific distribution of:

- 19% of the students show only one problem (with a 50% of predominance of IS-4),
- 47,6% shows two (with the most repeated template of IS-1 with IS-3, three repetitions, and the combination of IS-2 and IS-4, with two repetitions),
- 28,6% shows up to 3 problems all together (with 50% repetition of the problems IS-1, IS-2 and IS-3),
- Only one person (representing 4,8% of the sample) showed 4 initial problems (IS-[1–4]).

Analyzing the performed coaching sessions (an average of 3,76 with a maximum of 7 sessions and a minimum of 2), the summary of implemented activities can be found in Table 3:

Table 3. Coaching activities developed (based on classification described in Sect. 3.2)

Coaching activity	CA1	CA2	CA3	CA4	CA5	CA6	CA7	CA8	CA9	CA10
Times used	13	11	15	4	13	9	3	12	2	1
Percentage	61,90	52,38	71,43	19,04	61,90	42,85	14,28	57,14	9,52	4,76

We can summarize the situation with the experimental group like a sample of students with bad results at the intermediate point of the course (an average of 70%-failed subjects). A priori, this situation is the result of other three situations coming from the difficulty of the studies: feeling frustrated (47,62%), not knowing how to handle the complicated situation (47,62), and the desire to drop out (52,38%).

Based on such data, the most used coaching techniques (with an average of four techniques per student), always selected in function of every case are:

- Reactivity vs. proactivity (71,42%),
- Ten years personal situation visualization (61,94%),
- Identification of certain goals from fundamental and powerful questions (61,94%),
- Exposure of the coherence triangle: think-do-feel (57,14%).

Analyzing the existing individual correlation between the initial problems and the techniques implemented, there were no especially high factors found. For example, for the IS-1, the CA1 is the one that had the most use (positive correlation of 0,651); while for IS-2 we found 1 correlation with CA-6 and 0,763 for the CA-2. Another elevated amount we found is IS-3 with CA-1 (0,726 factor) but we didn't find another interrelation with index superior to 0,5 of use.

We have focused on two aspects for analyzing the effectiveness of the method: on one hand, and probably the most objective, is the continuity of the studies and the curriculum improvement of the student (Table 4). On the other hand, the subjective appreciation of the process by the tutor (Table 5).

Table 4. Efectiveness of the method based on the dropouts.

	Drop out = YES (n = 5)	Drop out = NO (n = 16)
Number of coaching sessions	3,83	3,73
Average of failed subjects (mid-term)	5,83	4,46
Average of failed subjects (final)	6,83	3,06
IS-3 (want to drop out)	80%	46,7%
Other initial main problem	IS-1 (50%)	IS-4 (53%)
Average of activities done	3,33	4,20
The main three techniques applied	CA-2 (60%)	CA-3 (86%)
	CA-8 (60%)	CA-5 (66%)
	CA-1 (40%)	CA-1 (66%)

Table 5. Efectiveness of the method based on the subjective assessment of the advisor/coach.

	Negative assessment (n = 5)	Neutral assessment (n = 9)	Positive assessment (n = 7)
Number of coaching sessions	3,40	3,33	4,57
Average of failed subjects (mid-term)	5,60	4,04	4,57
Average of failed subjects (final)	6,00	3,88	3,14
IS-3 (want to drop out)	40%	55%	57%
Finally drop out	60%	0%	14,2%
Other initial main problem	IS-1 (40%)	IS-1&2 (55%)	IS-4 (71,4%)
Average of activities done	3,20	3,66	4,85
The main three techniques applied	CA-3 (60%)	CA-3 (77%)	CA-1 (86%)
	CA-5 (60%)	CA-2 (66%)	CA-8 (86%)
	CA-1 (40%)	CA-1 (55%)	CA-5 (71%)

It is necessary to mention that the students that conform the sample analyzed in Table 5 were divided based on their results from the coaching process by their tutor. This way, the five students that were identified in the non-satisfactory process (first column), should not coincide with the five students that dropped out in Table 4.

These last results show us a series of interesting key concepts identified:

- The first idea of a large percentage of students when facing problems at the be-ginning of the course is to drop out (IS-3),
- Usually, students have more than one problem at a time, and all of them re-quire a different technique,
- The level of monitoring and motivation at the tutorial sessions influences directly on the rates of drop out and/or success of the coaching process that has been applied.

5 Conclusions and Future Work

One of the most interesting of the evaluated aspects is the comparison between the students' academic improvement of the control and experimental groups. If we calculate the difference between the number of failed subjects at the end of the course and on the first semester, the average result for a student in the experimental group is −0,62 (0,62 less failed subjects as the first semester, meaning there has been an improvement), while in the control group, the result is +0,3 (worsening by an average of 0,3 subjects). It can be observed that the improvement in academic performance of the experimental group with respect to the control group is of 0,92 subjects.

If we execute the same calculations excluding those students from both groups who dropped out of the degree, the results for the experimental group is −1,18, while for the control group it is −0,35. That is to say, if we only focus on the performance of those students who did not abandon their studies, there is a significant improvement in the experimental group's performance with respect to the control group. In this case, the difference is of 0,83 subjects.

On the other hand, the use of coaching as a work tool in academic tutoring has demonstrated its usability in the effective detection of problems in students. These problems are critical when they affect the student's performance, especially in the first courses, where the risk of dropping out is higher. As it has been demonstrated, the effective identification of problems and the adequate administration of solutions makes the student more aware of the situation and allows to remedy a complicated start.

Currently, there is work being done for correctly defining problem typologies, and for creating a system that automatically allows tutors to access solution proposals for registered problems based on coaching tools. The system must allow to facilitate and share experiences in the use of coaching that can be applied on tutor teams in heterogeneous environments such as Engineering, Architecture, Animation and Business Studies.

Acknowledgments. This research is being carried out through the Second ACM – Aristos Campus Mundus Research Grants Call – 2016 to fund the association's best projects of the ACM network. Project Code: ACM2016_07.

References

1. Powell, M.A: Academic tutoring and mentoring: a literature review. California Research Bureau, California State Library. CRB-97-01 (1997)
2. Allen, V.L.: Children as Teachers: Theory and Research on Tutoring. Academic Press, Cambridge (2013)
3. Coie, J.D., Krehbiel, G.: Effects of academic tutoring on the social status of low-achieving, socially rejected children. Child Dev. **55**(4), 1465–1478 (1984)
4. Álvarez, G.M., Rodríguez, S.: Manual de tutoría universitaria. Barcelona. Ed. Octaedro (2004)
5. Ross, J.A.: Teacher efficacy and the effects of coaching on student achievement. Can. J. Educ. Revue canadienne de l'education **17**, 51–65 (1992)
6. Cohen, P.A., Kulik, J.A., Kulik, C.L.C.: Educational outcomes of tutoring: a meta-analysis of findings. Am. Educ. Res. J. **19**(2), 237–248 (1982)
7. Carmel, R.G., Paul, M.W.: Mentoring and coaching in academia: Reflections on a mentoring/coaching relationship. Policy Futures Educ. **13**(4), 479–491 (2015)
8. Montero, J.A., Fonseca, D., Vicent, L., Climent, A., Canaleta, X., Villagrasa, S.: Technological needs calling for the application of coaching in university advising: functional proposal. In: Proceedings of Technological Ecosystems for Enhancing Multiculturality, Salamanca (Spain), vol. 1, pp. 665–670 (2016)
9. Bettinger, E., Baker, R.: The effects of student coaching in college: an evaluation of a randomized experiment in student mentoring (No. w16881). National Bureau of Economic Research (2011)
10. Winne, P.H., Hadwin, A.F.: Studying as self-regulated learning. In: Hacker, D.J., Dunlosky, J., Graesser, A.C. (eds.) Metacognition in Educational Theory and Practice, pp. 277–304. Mahwah, Lawrence Erlbaum Associates (1998)
11. Winne, P.H.: A cognitive and metacognitive analysis of self-regulated learning. In: Zimmerman, B.J., Schunk, D.H. (eds.) Handbook of Self-regulation of Learning and Performance, pp. 15–32. Routledge, New York (2011)
12. Grow, G.O.: Teaching learners to be self-directed. Adult Educ. Q. **41**(3), 125–149 (1991)
13. Dembkowski, S., Eldridge, F.: Beyond GROW: a new coaching model. Int. J. Mentor. Coaching **1**(1), 21 (2003)
14. Winne, P.H., Nesbit, J.C.: The psychology of academic achievement. Annu. Rev. Psychol. **61**, 653–678 (2010)
15. Atkinson, R.C.: Computerized instruction and the learning process. Am. Psychol. **23**, 225–239 (1968)
16. Suppes, P., Morningstar, M.: Computer-assisted instruction. Science **166**, 343–350 (1969)
17. Crowder, N.A.: Automatic tutoring by means of intrinsic programming. In: Galanter, E. (ed.) Automatic Teaching: The State of the Art, pp. 109–116. New York, Wiley (1959)
18. Van Lehn, K.: The relative effectiveness of human tutoring, intelligent tutoring systems, and other tutoring systems. Educ. Psychol. **46**, 197–221 (2011)
19. Kulik, J.A.: Meta-analytic studies of findings on computer-based instruction. In: Baker, E.L., O'Neil Jr., H.F. (eds.) Technology Assessment in Education and Training, pp. 9–33. Hillsdale, Erlbaum (1994)
20. Casamayor, A., Amandi, A., Campo, M.: Intelligent assistance for teachers in collaborative e-learning environments. Comput. Educ. **53**(4), 1147–1154 (2009)
21. Siemens, G., Gasevic, D.: Guest editorial e-learning and knowledge analytics. Educ. Technol. Soc. **15**(3), 1–2 (2012). http://www.ifets.info/journals/15_3/1.pdf

22. Duval, E.: Attention please! Learning analytics for visualization and recommendation. In: Proceedings of the 1st International Conference on Learning Analytics and Knowledge, pp. 9–17. ACM, New York (2011)
23. Bierema, L.L., Merriam, S.B.: E-mentoring: using computer mediated communication to enhance the mentoring process. Innov. High. Educ. **26**(3), 211–227 (2002)
24. Single, P.B., Single, R.M.: E-mentoring for social equity: review of research to inform program development. Mentor. Tutoring Partnersh. Learn. **13**(2), 301–320 (2005)
25. Freedman, R., Ali, S.S., McRoy, S.: Links: what is an intelligent tutoring system? Intelligence **11**(3), 15–16 (2000)
26. Callejas, A.: Técnicas cognitivo conductuales aplicadas a atletas de alto rendimiento. Lecturas: Educación física y deportes (89), 9 (2005)
27. De Bono, E.: Six Thinking Hats. Penguin, London (1989)
28. Suinn, R.M.: Visualization in Sports. In: Shelkh, A.A., Korn, E.R. (eds.) Imagery in Sports and Physical Performance, chap. 2. Baywood Publishing Company, Inc. (1994)
29. Adams, M.G.: Change Your Questions, Change Your Life: 12 Powerful Tools for Leadership, Coaching, and Life. Berrett-Koehler Publishers, Oakland (2016)
30. Bienkowski, M., Feng, M., Means, B.: Enhancing Teaching and Learning Through Educational Data Mining and Learning Analytics: An Issue Brief, pp. 1–57. US Department of Education, Office of Educational Technology (2012)
31. Tobarra, L., Robles-Gómez, A., Ros, S., Hernández, R., Caminero, A.C.: Analyzing the students' behavior and relevant topics in virtual learning communities. Comput. Hum. Behav. **31**, 659–669 (2014)
32. González-Torres, A., García-Peñalvo, F.J., Therón, R.: Human-computer interaction in evolutionary visual software analytics. Comput. Hum. Behav. **29**(2), 486–495 (2013)
33. Baker, R.: Data mining for education. Int. Encycl. Educ. **7**, 112–118 (2010)

Learning Analytics and Its Paternalistic Influences

Kyle M.L. Jones[✉]

Indiana University-Indianapolis (IUPUI), Indianapolis, USA
kmlj@iupui.edu

Abstract. Learning analytics is a technology that employs paternalistic nudging techniques and predictive measures. These techniques can limit student autonomy, may run counter to student interests and preferences, and do not always distribute benefits back to students—in fact some harms may actually accrue. The paper presents three cases of paternalism in learning analytics technologies, arguing that paternalism is an especially problematic concern for higher education institutions who espouse liberal education values. Three general recommendations are provided that work to promote student autonomy and choice making as a way to protect against risks to student academic freedom.

Keywords: Educational technology · Learning Analytics · Ethics · Autonomy · Paternalism · Student academic freedom · Liberal education

1 Introduction

Data-based educational technology systems increasingly include learning analytics (LA) tools, which present students personalized curricular materials and educational paths. LA proponents argue these things will lead to better outcomes for the student, the instructor, and the institution. However, the design of LA systems brings to the fore questions about whether or not designs of such systems are ethically above board. LA technologies, to varying degrees, make decisions for students, lead them to make particular decisions, or deny their choice for decision making altogether. By doing so, LA acts as a paternalistic technology. Herein, I address the paternalistic design of LA.

This paper will continue with four sections. First, I begin with a brief overview of LA. After this, I follow with a discussion of paternalism as a moral concept before addressing paternalism as it relates to technology. Next, I address prima facie cases against LA as a paternalistic technology. Finally, I consider how LA's paternalism runs counter to student academic freedom protections.

2 Learning Analytics

2.1 Learning Analytics Defined

LA is commonly defined as the "measurement, collection, analysis and reporting of data about learners and their contexts, for purposes of understanding and optimizing

© Springer International Publishing AG 2017
P. Zaphiris and A. Ioannou (Eds.): LCT 2017, Part II, LNCS 10296, pp. 281–292, 2017.
DOI: 10.1007/978-3-319-58515-4_22

learning and the environments in which it occurs." [1] In higher education, proponents of the technological practice employ data-driven systems to, inter alia, study student behaviors, inform students of their educational progress, and improve instructional methods. The practice aggregates a wide variety of data to support its analytic needs, mostly from on-campus sources like learning management systems and institutional student information systems. And while some of the information supporting LA students disclose to their institution, much of the valuable "digital breadcrumb" data is created as students interact with numerous types of information systems and sensors–from, among other things, wireless access points, RFID readers, e-mail servers, library databases, and student ID scanners.

2.2   Ethical Issues

Due to the variety, volume, and sensitivity of data institutions can aggregate, a lively conversation about ethics has emerged. But, to date little work has explicitly addressed LA's paternalistic design. Rubel and Jones [2] recognize that LA brings to fore important student autonomy issues. Similarly, Prinsloo and Slade [3] argue that the student vulnerabilities LA presents could decrease by improving student autonomy. And participants in Sclater's [4] study recognized that a code of practice for LA could counterbalance issues of institutional paternalism. While this literature and other works (see, for example, [5]) allude to paternalism as a form of negative liberty, they do not make explicit what, exactly, about LA is paternalistic; moreover, the current literature does not address how paternalism interferes with specific student rights or interests. Moving forward, I consider the philosophical foundations of paternalism and facets of technological paternalism in order to address this gap in the literature.

3   Paternalism

3.1   Soft/Hard and Weak/Strong Paternalism

Paternalism invokes liberty, for the purposeful limitation of one's liberty by another is, roughly, paternalistic behavior. Consider a close working relationship between two men, Jed and Charlie. When Jed restricts Charlie's ability to make a decision for himself, Jed reduces Charlie's capacity to make choices according to his own interests, values, and as a means to living a good life (however Charlie defines such a thing). This is a liberty-reducing action on Jed's part. However, what makes it paternalistic is Jed's intention, which is that he feels that his decision for Charlie will ultimately make Charlie better off. This is a fine start, but let us continue by considering Dworkin's [6, 7] formal views on paternalism.

According to Dworkin [7], "[p]aternalism is the interference of a state or an individual with another person, against their will, and defended or motivated by a claim that the person interfered with will be better off or protected from harm." Paternalism is codified in rules, policies and laws; it also manifests in social norms and technological design, as I will discuss later on. In each of these things, someone or something intercedes for an individual under the assumption that the individual's life will improve. Also important to note is that the target of paternalistic actions does not wish for such action to take place. Dworkin [6] provides the following as a formal definition:

P acts paternalistically towards Q if and only if:

(a) P acts with the intent of averting some harm or promoting some benefit for Q;
(b) P acts contrary to the current preferences, desires or dispositions of Q;
(c) P's act is a limitation on Q's autonomy.

(a), (b), and (c) occur in varying degrees depending on the intent of the paternalist. A soft paternalist justifies intrusion in an individual's life when the intrusion is simply to make sure the individual is informed about her decision–not to make the decision for her. Here, (a) is active, while (b) and (c) are not. On the other hand, a hard paternalist makes the decision for her, regardless of whether or not she's informed, which invokes (a), (b), and (c).

Paternalistic action is justified using a weak or strong explanation. A weak paternalist feels her interventions are justified when her actions allow the individual to accomplish her intended ends even though the individual's autonomy is compromised. Svendsen [8] clarifies this, writing, "[t]hat is to say that the weak paternalist focuses exclusively on the means an agent uses to meet their goals, though it is completely left to the agent to determine what those goals might be."

In contrast, a strong paternalist intervenes in a person's life because her goals/ends are wrong, irrational, or improperly prioritized, which justifies paternalistic behavior to stop the means used to achieve the incorrect ends. However, as Dworkin [7] argues, strong paternalists are only justified in their action when their interventions are fact-based, which is to say that they are intervening in an individual's life because the facts informing her actions are wrong; strong paternalism is not justified when paternalist interventions are enacted to change the values individuals use to inform their actions.

3.2 Libertarian Paternalism

A recent addition to the paternalism scholarship has come from Cass Sunstein and Richard Thaler's theory of libertarian paternalism. [9–11] According to the authors, their form of paternalism is a "relatively weak and nonintrusive type of paternalism because choices are not blocked or fenced off." [9] The essence of the theory is that the libertarian paternalist is justified in nudging, or suggesting particular choice options, to individuals when those choices maximize welfare and do not limit choosing other, non-nudged choice options.

Libertarian paternalism is built on a foundation of modern behavioral economics. Historically, humans were viewed as rational choice makers, but new theories suggest that rational choice making is not all that rational. There are too many competing interests or confusing in situ conditions that affect rational choosing. Instead, the liberal paternalist's interventions are justified because they present the individual with "good default rules [that] can neutralize and overcome" irrational choice making to yield "better overall choices" [8].

What makes "libertarian paternalism" seem like an oxymoron, as Sunstein and Thaler [9] point out, is the obvious fact that paternalism is not compatible with libertarian philosophy. To restrict freedom of choice–as an act of autonomy and a means to better welfare–is simply not libertarian. But, Sunstein and Thaler argue that the weak paternalism they suggest defends the theory against libertarian criticisms. Individuals still have free range to make their own choices regardless of the limited, but welfare-promoting "choice architecture."

Choice architecture refers to the options embedded in certain environments created by choice architects. Thaler, Sunstein, and their colleague John Balz [12] use the example of a school cafeteria to explain the concept. The cafeteria's choice architect, the cafeteria director, can use information about food choice to decide how to present options to students, such as:

1. Arrange the food to make the students best off, all things considered.
2. Choose the food order at random.
3. Try to arrange the food to get the kids to pick the same foods they would choose on .their own.
4. Maximize the sales of the items from the suppliers that are willing to offer the largest bribes.
5. Maximize profits, period.

Each of the options provide different outcomes for different parties, thus serving different interests. The choice architect has the "responsibility for organizing the context in which people make choices." [12] And these architects are not always neutral. Sometimes they have their own welfare in mind (e.g., they will setup conditions for choice making that financially benefits themselves); sometimes they are benevolent. Either way, it is important to note that choice architects have influence in (and power over) the lives of individuals for whom they are designing choice sets.

3.3   Moral Proxies and Choice Architects

Questions of technological paternalism stem from the moral influence embedded in technological systems, artifacts, and tools. Science and technology studies (STS) scholars, remarks, Millar [13], have long considered questions of technological determinism, momentum, and neutrality in order to delineate who or what has agency and moral responsibility: the human or the technology. Overall, STS scholarship argues that technology holds very little responsibility for embedded moral positions, but designers do. "Designers," writes Millar [13], "can intentionally embed moral norms into artifacts to achieve certain ends". The technology, then, takes on a proxy role: It simply represents the designer's moral position.

Designers epitomize the role of the choice architect and hold the power to create moral proxies. The communications they design into interfaces and the algorithms they embed in the architecture to inform and predict user behavior can mold or shift choice making in a paternalistic way. Their designs present individuals with particular courses of action and just-in-time information that can, among other things, limit or promote autonomy based on how they construct technology. Consider the common recommender system employed by Amazon.com. By suggesting "if you like this, buy this" options based on personalization algorithms, the designers have architected a choice set that did not exist before. And those choice options can be embedded with the designer's moral compass. For instance, a designer may believe that individuals who search for materials on gay culture should also be presented with specific religious literature as a moral counterweight, consequently the designer can code this perspective into the construction of the algorithm.

While personalized recommendations for books are by and large non-paternalistic, other types of recommendations or predictions are not. They may suggest, for instance, that users who interact with a system or behave in a particular way are more likely to be better off financially, professionally, or personally. Nudging users to act in a way that brings about these benefits highlights important questions. It is not always clear as to whether or not individuals are fully aware of why the technology is giving them recommendations and metrics, nor are they mindful of what is motivating and informing those nudges. The opaque nature of technologies, and the way that they conceal moral positions, should be concerning to users. Yet, the ubiquity of and reliance on highly complex technology in everyday life often leads individuals to unquestionably interact with systems and artifacts without a thought to paternalistic influences.

3.4   Four Facets of Technological Paternalism

With these things considered, Hoffmann [14] argues that technological paternalism is characterized by four facets. First, technological opacity makes it "incomprehensible" for individuals to make informed decisions about how to use technology and avoid paternalism. Individuals lack the intellectual capacity and skill set necessary to understand how technologies are interfering with their lives. Second, Big Data analytics embedded in technological design creates an air of objectivity or truth-by-data that subordinates (if not denies) personal subjectivity. People have confidence in data-driven systems, the predictive scores they present, and the recommendations they make because they seem to be neutral and based in fact. Third, aggregating massive datasets for analytic practices enables a wide array of actors to intervene in and craft strategies to direct the lives of individuals–often without their knowledge. And, finally, the ubiquity and interconnectedness of technologies and the datasets on which they rely allows for paternalistic intervention on a grand scale, allowing for targeted interventions for subsets of populations and individuals alike.

4   Learning Analytics and Prima Facie Cases of Paternalism

4.1   The Distribution of Benefits

In 2010, Colleen Carmean and Philip Mizzi [15] considered the role nudging techniques might play in LA technology. Motivated by the work done by Sunstein and Thaler, they argued for the creation of digital choice architecture that could "promote engagement, focus, and time-on-task behavior." Since then, LA technologies have matured with nudging at the core of their features.

Nudging works in a variety of ways in LA. For instance, one aim of nudging is to promote proven study strategies, while another is to encourage students to enroll in courses in which they are predicted to be academically successful. [16, 17] Other nudging techniques are embedded in learning management systems, where LA tools suggest to students just-in-time information. [18] Consider the University of Washington Tacoma, where students self-report academic behaviors. The institution's Persistence Plus LA system directed a student who reported math anxiety to stress management resources for math phobia, and at just the right moment–the student received the nudge to action before her next math quiz [19].

On the face of it, LA nudging purportedly yields good benefits. By providing assistance and direction when students are most likely to need it, nudging has the potential to increase performance, engagement, and persistence. [20, 21] And if students feel supported and successful, it is plausible that important metrics–like retention, time-to-degree, and graduation–will improve on campuses as students succeed year-to-year. Among LA advocates, these metrics are often the yardstick against which they judge the efficacy of the technology, for there is concern that higher education institutions are using too many resources and operating inefficiently without producing enough highly skilled and competitive students for the workforce. [22–24] However, the emergence of LA technology and the relative immaturity of related practices means that the allocation of benefits between and among students and their institution is still unclear.

Given that the ends to which proponents aim LA as a means are diverse, there is an open question as to whether or not the benefits (however they materialize) are justifiable, or will be distributed equally or equitably. About this, Rubel and Jones [2] write:

> Even if we suppose that the consequences of learning analytics are overall positive…there is a question as to who it benefits, and to what degree. It is certainly the case that learning analytics will be a benefit to institutions. And to the extent that institutions will use the information to further their mission of providing learning opportunities and helping ensure learning outcomes, some benefits would presumably accrue to students as well. But that does not mean that the distribution of benefits is good, or fair.

If we cannot assume that the benefits will redound to individual students, and if those benefits are more aligned with the interests of their institution, then there is a prima facie case against LA and nudging techniques. And when LA acts contrary to student preferences, it emboldens cases against LA. Furthermore, these cases only become stronger when they outright limit student autonomy.

The discussion that follows provides three examples of paternalism in LA technologies and practices with explanations as to why the paternalism is harmful.

4.2 Case One: eAdvising

For the first example, consider Austin Peay State University's implementation of Degree Compass, a homegrown eAdvising system. The system uses predictive analytics to pair students with courses that "fit their talents and their program of study."

[25] Among other things, course recommendations are weighted based on if they are relevant to the student's set degree path and whether or not the student will be academically successful in the course. Similarly, for students who have yet to choose a major, the system nudges them to consider majors in which they are likely to achieve academic success.

In this scenario, it may seem to a student that the institution is looking out for her well-being. The institution wants her to be academically successful and recommends to her degree paths and courses. Moreover, the system provides structure and just-in-time information that enables decision making during high-stress times, such as enrollment and course selection.

The problem with eAdvising systems, such as Degree Compass, is that their choice sets compromise a student's ability to make fully autonomous choices by presenting the path of least resistance to students. Simpler, they provide only those choices that are likely to lead to continued success. From an institutional perspective, there is little benefit to be had by showing students courses or programs they are predicted to do poor in. Due to financial burdens, it is best for institutions to guarantee, as much as possible, student success. For instance, getting students from admission to graduation as expediently as possible maximizes the financial resources spent on students while reaping the most financial benefit in terms of tuition and fees. It also improves metrics accreditors and the public use to judge the institution. Providing students options that run counter to these aims would not work in the institution's favor. The author has seen no evidence that suggests institutions would stop students from enrolling in particular courses and programs based on a predictive score alone, thus this type of LA system is a form of weak paternalism.

4.3 Case Two: Digital Fences

For a second example, consider the emerging use of "digital fencing" technology for attendance taking and enforcement. Systems, like Class120, draw digital fences using GPS technology around areas on campus, many of which are associated with a course and its assigned classroom. The Class120 app and geolocation tools in student smartphones work in tandem to report to professors, advisors, and–if permitted–even parents when a student is not within a class-associated fence on time. [26] Students, themselves, get nudged about the next time they need to be within a fence on campus before automatic messages are sent out noting their tardy or absence.

Many faculty members would agree that class attendance leads to academic success, and the literature is saturated with research that supports this correlation (for example, see [27–29]). So, it seems justifiable that institutions would create attendance policies enforceable by technologies to promote attendance and maximize related benefits. However, there is no guarantee that students will actually learn while attending class: the instruction could be poor, the course could be badly designed, or the students could be unengaged. Regardless, institutions are motivated to enforce attendance as a means to maximize "an efficient return on investment" in classroom infrastructure and instructional labor, as well as to address some stakeholder accountability arguments [30].

Class120 and related systems exemplify a form of strong paternalism. It may actually be in some students' best interests to use their time to attend to other needs, which, all things considered, make them better off. For instance, a student may have the intellectual capabilities to earn a satisfactory grade in a course regardless of lecture absences. Instead of attending class, she schedules more work hours to fulfill her financial obligations. But the justification for digital fencing rests on the argument that students should prioritize attending course sessions over other interests and ends. What plausibly happens is that the paternalism motivates students to attend class not to advance their education, but instead to prevent social repercussions and academic penalties.

4.4   Case Three: Libraries and Learning Analytics

As a final example, consider the University of Wollongong's foray into library resource use tracking for LA purposes. The library datasets keep track of the total number of student item loans and electronic usage information from proxy server logs, including access points, timestamps, duration data, and the specific electronic resources that students access. After analysis and reporting, the data informs teaching by disclosing to instructors whether or not their students are using library resources. [31] When resource usage was low–and academic risk levels were assumed to be high–instructors intervened by nudging students to use the library. As a result, instructors saw an immediate uptick in library usage by students.

Some librarians believe that participating in LA practices will prove their value to their institutions. Libraries are increasingly scrutinized for the costs of their physical and digital collections, not to mention the upkeep of their facilities. Stakeholders want data showing that such investments work towards and are aligned with institutional needs, such as improving learning outcomes. [32] And emerging research suggests that library usage does correlate with student success, engagement, and retention. [33, 34] While the intervention has good intentions to improve library usage and serve a secondary purpose of proving library value, there is a serious question about the peripheral harms that could accrue.

Any library action that borders on surveillance of intellectual behaviors brings up questions of intellectual freedom. In this example, the library observed intellectual behaviors as represented in the materials students reviewed (or did not review). The library's intent was well-meaning, but the act of surveillance was autonomy reducing. Library surveillance may have changed students' natural dispositions and preferences, in that they plausibly altered when they used the library and what materials they searched and engaged with in order to comport themselves in a way that would look positive in the analytics. Jantti [31] provides no explanation as to why students responded to the interventions to use library resources, nor does she explain if the interventions led to more selective and useful interactions with the library's collection. On the face of it, the paternalistic interventions could have harmed the conditions necessary for intellectual freedom.

5 Values at Risk and Recommendations

5.1 Liberal Education

When paternalistic actions inhibit student autonomy and put at risk the free pursuit of intellectual ideas and paths, a wider concern emerges related to student academic freedom. Most theories of liberal education posit that higher education institutions have a responsibility to promote student autonomy and put in place conditions for personal and intellectual flourishing. [35] Quoting Seneca, Nussbaum argues that liberal education "'liberates' students' minds from their bondage to mere habit and tradition, so that students can increasingly take responsibility for their own thought and speech." [36] Other theories also argue that university students, most of whom are the age of majority and have the capacity for autonomy, should be protected against paternalistic influence. [37] It is for these reasons that higher education has put in place academic freedom protections specifically for students and uniquely separate from faculty academic freedom.

5.2 Student Academic Freedom

At their best, universities maximize lernfreiheit–or student academic freedom–by developing students who can be their own person, follow their own interests and desires, and act authentically without undue institutional burdens. Working towards these ends requires universities to scaffold the expression of academic freedom by creating empowering circumstances and experiences that run counter to entrenched thinking and conformative being. To this point, Derek Bok [38] argues that institutions should expose students to a plurality of views, enable them to write and speak with purpose, develop their critical thinking capacities to carefully consider the information that informs their reasoning and ethical sense making, as well as prepare them to engage with a diverse citizenry and work in a global society.

The prima facie cases of paternalism against LA indicate that, to varying degrees, the conditions necessary for and the support of student academic freedom are at risk. Nudging students to academic paths of least resistance does not motivate them to consider yet to be discovered personal interests, nor does it engage them in a wider array of ideas. Moreover, the predictive measures employed by LA technologies puts at risk the things liberal education works to promote: critical thinking and autonomy. These metrics paternalistically convey what a student is predicted to be good at or do well in without fully informing students of what variables are included in the measures, the statistical error, or why the measures should be taken seriously at all. As a result, there is a serious concern that LA predictions will suppress choice making and, consequently, academic risk taking.

5.3 Recommendations

The technology and statistics that form the foundation of LA and the practices used to deploy LA insights are all still nascent. It is exactly because of this that the potential harms addressed herein can be limited. There is still ample time to consider long-standing values, such as liberal education and student academic freedom and determine if LA is designed in support of or runs counter to those values. Institutions should consider the following recommendations in order to respect these important values.

Justify the distribution of benefits: If LA's paternalism is to continue, colleges and universities must carefully consider whether or not the benefits or protections from harm the paternalistic action yields are in the best interests of the student. By and large, LA's paternalism seems aligned with institutional interests–not student interests. Arguably, institutions may claim that the benefits they receive from LA trickle down to students in one form or another. But this argument is indefensible given the ways in which the technology can direct student life and restrict choice making. Institutions must work to ensure that students will directly benefit from paternalistic technologies.

Optimize choice making: Institutions must make LA technologies and the algorithms that inform their design transparent. For students to make informed choices when considering specific choice sets or nudges to action, they need to understand what data or information supports LA in the first place. And they also need to understand the ends that their choice will work towards as a means. Doing these two things will work towards optimizing student autonomy while still allowing for the benefits based on LA's paternalism.

Hold designers accountable for good moral proxies: Student autonomy and academic freedom are moral proxies that designers can embed into LA technologies. But, LA vendors may not motivate their designers to consider these moral issues, and designers may not be sensitized to the harms their paternalistic designs can create. Institutions have a duty to hold LA designers accountable for building in good moral proxies into their designs, and should hold themselves accountable for carefully vetting systems to consider the harms that could accrue from poor designs.

6 Conclusion

I have argued that LA is a technology that employs paternalistic nudging techniques and predictive measures. These techniques can limit student autonomy, may run counter to student interests and preferences, and for sure do not always distribute benefits back to students–in fact some harms may actually accrue. The argument showed that paternalism in LA technologies is an especially problematic concern for higher education institutions who espouse liberal education values and promote student academic freedom. The paper ended with three general recommendations that work to promote student autonomy and choice making as a way to protect against risks to student academic freedom. Future research should consider developing particular information policy recommendations, and the literature would benefit from empirical work that analyzes how students perceive and respond to paternalistic LA designs.

References

1. Siemens, G.: Learning analytics: envisioning a research discipline and a domain of practice. In: Proceedings of the Second International Conference on Learning Analytics and Knowledge, USA, pp. 4–8 (2012)
2. Rubel, A., Jones, K.M.L.: Student privacy in learning analytics: an information ethics perspective. Inf. Soc. **32**(2), 143–159 (2016)
3. Prinsloo, P., Slade, S.: Student vulnerability, agency and learning analytics: an exploration. J. Learn. Analytics **3**(1), 159–182 (2016)
4. Sclater, N.: Developing a code of practice for learning analytics. J. Learn. Analytics **3**(1), 16–42 (2016)
5. Willis, J.E. III: Learning analytics and ethics: a framework beyond utilitarianism. EDUCAUSE Rev. (2014). http://er.educause.edu/articles/2014/8/learning-analytics-and-ethics-a-framework-beyond-utilitarianism. Accessed 11 Oct 2016
6. Dworkin, G.: Paternalism. Monist **56**, 64–84 (1972)
7. Dworkin, G.: Paternalism. Stanf. Encycl. Philos. http://plato.stanford.edu/entries/paternalism/. Accessed 11 Oct 2016
8. Svendsen, L.: A Philosophy of Freedom. Reaktion Books, London (2014)
9. Sunstein, C.R., Thaler, R.H.: Libertarian paternalism is not an oxymoron. Univ. Chic. Law Rev. **70**(4), 1159–1202 (2003)
10. Thaler, R.H., Sunstein, C.R.: Libertarian paternalism. Am. Econ. Rev. **93**(2), 175–179 (2003)
11. Thaler, R.H., Sunstein, C.R.: Nudge: Improving Decisions about Health, Wealth, and Happiness. Penguin, New York (2008)
12. Thaler, R.H., Sunstein, C.R., Balz, J.P.: Choice architecture. In: Shafir, E. (ed.) The Behavioral Foundations of Public Policy, pp. 428–439. Princeton University Press, Princeton (2012)
13. Millar, J.: Technology as moral proxy: autonomy and paternalism by design. IEEE Technol. Soc. Mag. **34**, 47–55 (2015)
14. Hofmann, B.: Technological paternalism: on how medicine has reformed ethics and how technology can refine moral theory. Sci. Eng. Ethics **9**(3), 343–352 (2003)
15. Carmen, C., Mizzi, P.J.: The case for nudge analytics. EDUCAUSE Rev. http://er.educause.edu/articles/2010/12/the-case-for-nudge-analytics. Accessed 12 Oct 2016
16. Parry, M.: Big data on campus. New York Times (2012). http://www.nytimes.com/2012/07/22/education/edlife/colleges-awakening-to-the-opportunities-of-data-mining.html. Accessed 12 Oct 2016
17. Slade, S., Prinsloo, P.: Learning analytics: ethical issues and dilemmas. Am. Behav. Sci. **57**(10), 1509–1528 (2013)
18. Ferguson, R.: Learning analytics: drivers, developments and challenges. Int. J. Technol. Enhanced Learn. **4**(5/6), 304–317 (2012)
19. Frankfort, J., Salim, K., Carmean, C.: Analytics, nudges, and learner persistence. EDUCAUSE Rev. http://www.educause.edu/ero/article/analytics-nudges-and-learner-persistenc. Accessed 12 Oct 2016
20. Goldstein, P.J., Katz, R.N.: Academic analytics: the uses of management information and technology in higher education. https://net.educause.edu/ir/library/pdf/ers0508/rs/ers0508w.pdf. Accessed 12 Oct 2016
21. Picciano, A.G.: The evolution of big data and learning analytics in American higher education. J. Asynchronous Learn. Netw. **16**(3), 9–20 (2012)

22. Bessen, J.: Employers aren't just whining – the "skills gap" is real. Harv. Bus. Rev. (2014). https://hbr.org/2014/08/employers-arent-just-whining-the-skills-gap-is-real/. Accessed 12 Oct 2016

23. Bienkowski, M., Feng, M., Means, B.: Enhancing teaching and learning through educational data mining and learning analytics: an issue brief (2012). http://tech.ed.gov/wp-content/uploads/2014/03/edm-la-brief.pdf. Accessed 12 Oct 2016

24. Bothwell, E.: US dominance in the World University Rankings 2015–16. Time High. Educ. (2015). https://www.timeshighereducation.com/news/big-beasts-strive-to-thrive-in-shifting-environment. Accessed 12 Oct 2016

25. Austin Peay State University: Degree Compass and my future. http://www.apsu.edu/academic-affairs/degree-compass-and-my-future. Accessed 12 Oct 2016

26. Belkin, D.: Cracking down on skipping class. Wall Street J. (2015). http://www.wsj.com/articles/cracking-down-on-skipping-class-1421196743

27. Chen, J., Lin, T.: Class attendance and exam performance: a randomized experiment. J. Econ. Educ. **39**(3), 213–227 (2008)

28. Donathan, D.A.: The correlation between attendance, grades, and the nontraditional student. Bus. Educ. Forum **58**(1), 45–47 (2003)

29. Moore, R.: Attendance and performance: how important is it for students to attend class? J. Coll. Sci. Teach. Teaching **32**(6), 367–371 (2003)

30. Macfarlane, B.: The surveillance of learning: a critical analysis of university attendance policies. High. Educ. Q. **67**(4), 358–373 (2013)

31. Jantti, M.: Libraries and big data: A new view on impact and affect. In: Atkinson, J. (ed.) Quality and the Academic Library: Reviewing, Assessing and Enhancing Service Provision, pp. 267–273. Chandos Publishing, Cambridge (2016)

32. Association of College and Research Libraries.: Standards for libraries in higher education. http://www.ala.org/acrl/sites/ala.org.acrl/files/content/standards/slhe.pdf. Accessed 12 Oct 2016

33. Soria, K., Fransen, J., Nackerud, S.: Library use and undergraduate student outcomes: new evidence for students' retention and academic success. Portal Libr. Acad. **13**(2), 147–164 (2013)

34. Wong, S.H.R., Webb, T.D.: Uncovering meaningful correlation between student academic performance and library material usage. Coll. Res. Libr. **72**(4), 361–370 (2011)

35. Aspin, D.: Autonomy and education: an integrated approach to knowledge, curriculum and learning in the democratic school. In: Bridges, D. (ed.) Education, Autonomy, and Democratic Citizenship: Philosophy in a Changing World, pp. 248–260. Routledge, New York (1997)

36. Nussbaum, M.: Liberal education and global community. Lib. Educ. **90**(1). https://www.aacu.org/publications-research/periodicals/liberal-education-global-community. Accessed 13 Oct 2016

37. Levinson, M.: The Demands of Liberal Education. Oxford University Press, Oxford (1999)

38. Bok, D.: Our Underachieving Colleges: A Candid Look at How Much Students Learn and Why they Should be Learning More. Princeton University Press, Princeton (2006)

Development of a Dashboard for Learning Analytics in Higher Education

Philipp Leitner[1(✉)] and Martin Ebner[2]

[1] Institute of Interactive Systems and Data Science,
Graz University of Technology, Graz, Austria
philipp.leitner@tugraz.at
[2] Department of Educational Technology,
Graz University of Technology, Graz, Austria
martin.ebner@tugraz.at

Abstract. In this paper, we discuss the design, development, and implementation of a Learning Analytics (LA) dashboard in the area of Higher Education (HE). The dashboard meets the demands of the different stakeholders, maximizes the mainstreaming potential and transferability to other contexts, and is developed in the path of Open Source. The research concentrates on developing an appropriate concept to fulfil its objectives and finding a suitable technology stack. Therefore, we determine the capabilities and functionalities of the dashboard for the different stakeholders. This is of significant importance as it identifies which data can be collected, which feedback can be given, and which functionalities are provided. A key approach in the development of the dashboard is the modularity. This leads us to a design with three modules: the data collection, the search and information processing, and the data presentation. Based on these modules, we present the steps of finding a fitting Open Source technology stack for our concept and discuss pros and cons trough out the process.

Keywords: Learning Analytics · Learning dashboard · Open Source · Technology enhanced learning · e-Learning

1 Introduction

A dashboard is a visual display of the most relevant information, which is consolidated and arranged on a single screen to be monitored at a glance and needed to achieve one or more objectives [1]. Siemens defined Learning Analytics (LA) as "the measurement, collection, analysis and reporting of data about learners and their contexts, for purposes of understanding and optimizing learning and the environments in which it occurs" [2]. Whereas, the main question addressed by Erik Duval is about what exactly should be measured to get a deeper understanding of how learning takes place [3].

Therefore, a Learning Analytics dashboard often present information to resources used, time spent, social interactions, artefacts produced, and exercise and test results [4]. Thus, the students are able to monitor their learning efforts for reaching their intended learning outcomes more easily [5].

© Springer International Publishing AG 2017
P. Zaphiris and A. Ioannou (Eds.): LCT 2017, Part II, LNCS 10296, pp. 293–301, 2017.
DOI: 10.1007/978-3-319-58515-4_23

In this paper we discuss the design and development of Learning Analytics dashboards in the area Higher Education (HE). Our objectives are:

1. cover the demands of the different stakeholders,
2. maximize the mainstreaming potential and transferability to other contexts, and
3. make it available for everyone by developing in the path of Open Source.

The research concentrates on developing an appropriate concept to fulfil these objectives and finding a suitable technology stack. Therefore, we determine the capabilities and functionalities of the dashboard for the different stakeholders. This is of significant importance as it identifies which data can be collected, which feedback can be given, and which functionalities are provided.

The main demands of the stakeholders are the support of different data-sources as well as different types of data-sources. Therefore, we searched for appropriate technologies which support various kinds of sources. During this search, we focused on technologies which are available under an Open Source licenses to cover our third objective.

Further, we wanted to easily combine different technologies, so we decided to go with a modular architecture. This ensures that the stakeholders can choose between different software modules (e.g. they can choose to use proprietary software) for easy adjustment to their needs. We decided to use a design with three layers: the data collection, the search and information processing, and the data presentation. Additionally, this approach helped us with our second objective, the transferability to other contexts and the maximization of the mainstreaming potential.

The next section provides background about Learning Analytics and dashboards. The third section explains the development of our Learning Analytics dashboard as well as improvements made throughout the different versions. The last section discusses the restrictions and remarks on future work.

2 Background

The purpose of Learning Analytics is the understanding and optimization of learning and the environment in which it occurs trough measurement, collection, analysis, and reporting of data [6, 7]. Since Learning Analytics was first mentioned in the New Media Consortium (NMC) Horizon Report 2012, it has gained an increasing relevance [8]. Further, the Horizon Report 2013 defined Learning Analytics as one of the most important trends in technology-enhanced learning and teaching [9]. Learning Analytics evaluates user's behavior in the context of teaching and learning. Further, it analysis and interprets this behavior to gain new insights to support stakeholders with models for improving learning and teaching, organization and decision making [2].

One of the main goals of Learning Analytics is the return of the gained knowledge to learners and teachers; thereby, optimizing their learning and teaching behavior, promoting the development of skills in the area, and to better understand education as well as the connected fields such as university business and marketing [10, 11].

The Learning Analytics Life Cycle, which was introduced in 2015 by Khalil and Ebner and shown in Fig. 1, consists of four parts. The learning environment, where stakeholders such as learner or teachers produce data. The big data, which consist of massive amounts of different datasets. The analytics, which include different analytical techniques. And the Act, where objectives are achieved to optimize the learning environment [12].

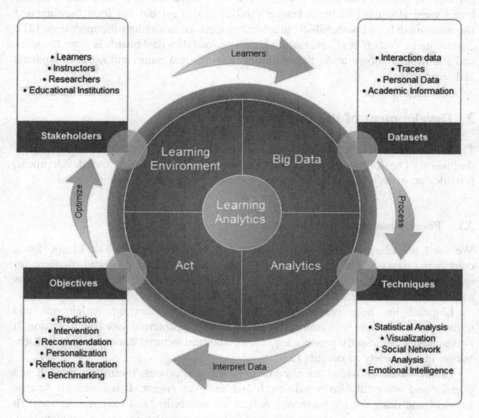

Fig. 1. Learning Analytics life cycle [12]

In Higher Education, Learning Analytics has been proven to help universities in strategic areas such as finance, resource allocation and student success [13]. Therefore, the universities are collecting more data than ever before to maximize the strategic outcomes [13]. Additionally, universities use methods of Learning Analytics to obtain findings on the progress of students, predict future behaviors and recognize problems at an early stage [10]. However, ethical and legal issues of collecting and processing the data of students are still seen as a barrier by the institutions [14, 15].

Learning analytics is applied in many adaptive learning systems such as MOOC-platforms [16, 17]. The results of such analysis are demonstrated on Learning Analytics Dashboards for better comprehension and further recognition of ongoing activities. An example of in detail analysis is the work on one-digit multiplication problems [18–20] or even beyond [21, 22]. Taraghi et al. analyzed at the first step the most prevalent error types and the statistical correlations between them in one-digit multiplication problems [23]. In a second step, they carried out a detailed analysis to highlight the misconceptions of students that are of higher relevance providing hints at probable reasons behind them [24, 25]. The discovered learning paths and difficulty levels were also used to build learner profiles [26]. Last but not least they applied Bayesian models and probabilistic graphical models for modeling misconceptions [27]. According to Verbert et al., evaluating Learning Analytics dashboards is often complex and still little is known about the usefulness to solve real issues and needs of students and teachers [4].

3   Development of the Dashboard

This section discusses the development and implementation of our Learning Analytics dashboard. The following subsection describes the foundation of our development, provides an overview, and gives a short explanation of the technologies used.

3.1   Foundation of the Development

We used the Elastic Stack[1] as foundation for our development. The Elastic Stack combines Logstash, Elasticsearch, and Kibana and provides a powerful platform for indexing, searching, and analyzing data. Additionally, each of these technologies is available under the Apache 2.0 Open Source License[2].

Logstash has been proven to be a powerful data collection, enrichment, and transportation pipeline with connectors to common infrastructure for easy integration. It is designed to efficiently process log, event, and unstructured data sources for distribution into a variety of outputs [28].

Elasticsearch[3] provided the abilities to search and process the information. It is a popular and powerful distributed search and analytics engine. It is based on Apache Lucene[4] and designed for horizontal scalability, reliability, and easy management. It combines the speed of search with the power of analytics via a sophisticated, developer-friendly query language covering structured, unstructured, and time-series data [29].

For the data presentation and visualization we used Kibana[5], an open source data visualization platform that allows interaction through powerful graphics. It provides various visualizations, such as histograms or geomaps, which can be combined into custom dashboards [30].

---

[1] https://www.elastic.co (last visited Feb. 25, 2017).

[2] https://www.apache.org/licenses/LICENSE-2.0 (last visited Feb. 25, 2017).

[3] https://www.elastic.co/products/elasticsearch (last visited Feb. 25, 2017).

[4] http://lucene.apache.org (last visited Feb. 25, 2017).

[5] https://www.elastic.co/products/kibana (last visited Feb. 25, 2017).

Unfortunately, Elastic Stack lacks security features, which forced us to add Search Guard[6] to our concept. This Elasticsearch plugin offers encryption, authentication, and authorization. It builds on Search Guard SSL and provides pluggable authentication modules. Search Guard is an alternative to ES Shield[7], and offers all basic security features for free. Search Guard is available under the Apache 2 Open Source License. An overview of the concept is shown in Fig. 2.

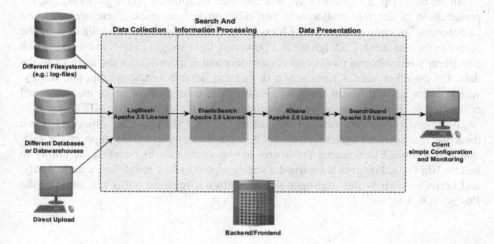

Fig. 2. Initial setup of our dashboard

This initial setup of the technology stack handles multiple data-sources very well, has a good scalability, and presents a custom and dynamic dashboard with good and easy visualizations. Unfortunately, there are problems with handling complex queries and despite Elasticsearch is able to handle minor data-relationships, it by design does not support them very well. As a result, executing queries costs more resources and take more time. Further, Kibana cannot handle data-relationships at all. A workaround for this problem is to combine the linked data-sources in Logstash and insert this combined-data into Elasticsearch, such as adding the user-data to each entry of a Learning Management System (LMS) actions). This might work for small settings, but is very resource intensive. Additionally, many-to-many relationships cannot be modelled this way!

3.2 The Final Concept

Because of our self-imposed requirements, it is essential for our dashboard to handle data-relationships, that's why we replaced the module for data presentation, Kibana with Grafana[8], which is able to handle relationships. Similar to Kibana, Grafana is most

---

[6] https://floragunn.com/searchguard (last visited Feb. 25, 2017).

[7] https://www.elastic.co/products/shield (last visited Feb. 25, 2017).

[8] http://grafana.org (last visited Feb. 25, 2017).

commonly used for visualizing time series data and provides a powerful and elegant way to create, explore, and share dashboards. Additionally, Grafana comes with an own authentication layer [31].

With this configuration the data presentation layer was able to handle relationships between data, but the problems with complex queries remain as well as the relation-limitations of Elasticsearch.

In the next step, we tried to solve this problems by splitting up the gathering and the presentation of the information into two different technologies. Therefore, we used CodeIgnitor[9] in combination with Charts.js[10] for the analysis and visualization of the data. On the one hand, CodeIgnitor is a powerful, light-weight PHP-framework, which consistently outperforms most of its competitors and responsible for the analysis of the data. On the other hand, Charts.js is a simple and flexible JavaScript charting library, which offers eight different ways to visualize the data, each of them animated and customizable. Both technologies are available under the open source MIT License[11].

Additionally, we extended our technology stack by the powerful, object-relational database management system PostgreSQL[12] (short Postgres). This support for relational data gives Elasticsearch the liberty to concentrate on its benefits, the ability to handle Big Data. Postgres has earned a strong reputation for reliability, data integrity, and correctness. It is free and open-source software, released under the terms of the PostgreSQL License[13] [32].

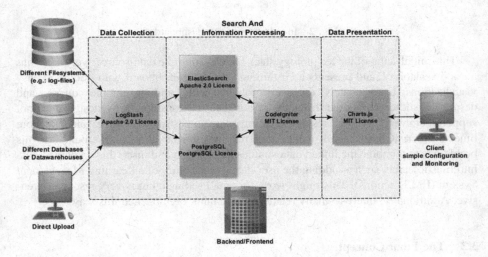

Fig. 3. Current/final setup of our dashboard

[9] https://www.codeigniter.com (last visited Feb. 25, 2017).

[10] http://www.chartjs.org (last visited Feb. 25, 2017).

[11] https://opensource.org/licenses/mit-license.php (last visited Feb. 25, 2017).

[12] https://www.postgresql.org (last visited Feb. 25, 2017).

[13] https://www.postgresql.org/about/licence (last visited Feb. 25, 2017).

After this step, the setup was able to handle all relationships. Additionally, the new created layer was able to combine the queries and taking of the complexity of the queries themselves. Despite that, we lost the ability of creating custom dashboards in the frontend. This concept of the dashboard, which is currently in use, is shown in Fig. 3.

4 Conclusion, Restrictions and Outlook

In this paper, we discussed the design and development of a Learning Analytics dashboard. We defined three objectives: the different demands of the stakeholders, the maximization of the mainstreaming potential, and the transferability to other contexts, and the development in the path of Open Source.

We fulfilled the demands of our stakeholders' trough supporting various types of data sources. Further, we kept the mainstreaming potential and the transferability to other context at a maximum by using a modular architecture. Thereby, it is possible to replace any of those modules with proprietary software already in use at the different universities. Finally, we achieved our last objective by introducing fitting Open Source technologies for our concept. Additionally, we described in detail our way of finding these technologies and explained the pros and cons of the different technology stacks.

Initial results show that the data and analytics layering allows the usage of multiple data sets and analytics techniques in a single interface for both, visualizing and analyzing. It should be mentioned that our final concept complies with our current requirements. Through future changes of those requirements, it might be necessary to adapt our concept. We are currently working on the proof of concept for our implementation of the Learning Analytics dashboard in the context of a Small Private Online Course (SPOC) which we are going to publish soon.

Acknowledgments. This research project is co-funded by the European Commission Erasmus +program, in the context of the project 562167-EPP-1-2015-1-BE-EPPKA3-PI-FORWARD. Please visit our website http://stela-project.eu.

References

1. Few, S.: Dashboard Confusion. Intelligent Enterprise (2004)
2. Siemens, G., Long, P.: Penetrating the fog: analytics in learning and education. EDUCAUSE Rev. **46**(5), 30 (2011)
3. Verbert, K., Govaerts, S., Duval, E., Santos, J.L., Van Assche, F., Parra, G., Klerkx, J.: Learning dashboards: an overview and future research opportunities. Pers. Ubiquit. Comput. **18**(6), 1499–1514 (2014)
4. Duval, E.: Attention please! Learning analytics for visualization and recommendation. In: Proceedings of LAK11: 1st International Conference on Learning Analytics and Knowledge 2011 (2010, to appear). https://lirias.kuleuven.be/bitstream/123456789/315113/1/la2.pdf. Accessed 25 Feb 2017

5. Charleer, S., Klerkx, J., Duval, E., Laet, T., Verbert, K.: Creating effective learning analytics dashboards: lessons learnt. In: Verbert, K., Sharples, M., Klobučar, T. (eds.) EC-TEL 2016. LNCS, vol. 9891, pp. 42–56. Springer, Cham (2016). doi:10.1007/978-3-319-45153-4_4

6. Elias, T.: Learning Analytics: Definitions, Processes and Potential (2011)

7. Khalil, M., Ebner, M.: When learning analytics meets MOOCs - a review on iMooX case studies. In: Fahrnberger, G., Eichler, G., Erfurth, C. (eds.) I4CS 2016. CCIS, vol. 648, pp. 3–19. Springer, Cham (2016). doi:10.1007/978-3-319-49466-1_1

8. Johnson, L., Adams, S., Cummins, M.: The NMC Horizon Report: 2012, Higher Education edn. The New Media Consortium, Austin (2012)

9. Johnson, L., Adams Becker, S., Cummins, M., Freeman, A., Ifenthaler, D., Vardaxis, N.: Technology Outlook for Australian Tertiary Education 2013–2018: An NMC Horizon Project Regional Analysis. New Media Consortium, Austin (2013)

10. Leitner, P., Khalil, M., Ebner, M.: Learning analytics in higher education—a literature review. In: Peña-Ayala, A. (ed.) Learning Analytics: Fundaments, Applications, and Trends. Studies in Systems, Decision and Control, vol. 94, pp. 1–23. Springer International Publishing, Heidelberg (2017)

11. Drachsler, H., Greller, W.: The pulse of learning analytics - understandings and expectations from the stakeholders. In: Buckingham Shum, S., Gasevic, D., Fergu-Son, R. (eds.) Proceedings of the 2nd International Conference on Learning Analytics and Knowledge (LAK 2012), pp. 120–129. ACM, New York (2012)

12. Khalil, M., Ebner, M.: Learning analytics: principles and constraints. In: Proceedings of World Conference on Educational Multimedia, Hypermedia and Telecommunications, pp. 1326–1336 (2015)

13. Bichsel, J.: Analytics in higher education: benefits, barriers, progress, and recommendations. EDUCAUSE Center for Applied Research (2012)

14. Sclater, N.: Code of practice "essential" for learning analytics (2014). http://analytics. jiscinvolve.org/wp/2014/09/18/code-of-practice-essential-for-learning-analytics.   Accessed 25 Feb 2017

15. Khalil, M., Ebner, M.: De-Identification in learning analytics. J. Learn. Anal. 3(1), 129–138 (2016)

16. Khalil, M., Taraghi, B., Ebner, M.: Engaging learning analytics in MOOCS: the good, the bad, and the ugly. In: International Conference on Education and New Developments, Ljublja-na, Slovenia, pp. 3–7 (2016)

17. Taraghi, B., Saranti, A., Ebner, M., Großmann, A., Müller, V.: Adaptive learner profiling provides the optimal sequence of posed basic mathematical problems. In: Rensing, C., Freitas, S., Ley, T., Muñoz-Merino, Pedro J. (eds.) EC-TEL 2014. LNCS, vol. 8719, pp. 592–593. Springer, Cham (2014). doi:10.1007/978-3-319-11200-8_85

18. Khalil, M., Ebner, M.: What massive open online course (MOOC) stakeholders can learn from learning analytics? In: Spector, M., Lockee, B., Childress, M. (eds.) Learning, Design, and Technology: An International Compendium of Theory, Research, Practice, and Policy, pp. 1–30. Springer International Publishing, Heidelberg (2016)

19. Taraghi, B., Frey, M., Saranti, A., Ebner, M., Müller, V., Großmann, A.: Determining the causing factors of errors for multiplication problems. In: Ebner, M., Erenli, K., Malaka, R., Pirker, J., Walsh, Aaron E. (eds.) EiED 2014. CCIS, vol. 486, pp. 27–38. Springer, Cham (2015). doi:10.1007/978-3-319-22017-8_3

20. Schön, M., Ebner, M., Kothmeier, G.: It's just about learning the multiplication table. In: Buckingham Shum, S., Gasevic, D., Ferguson, R. (eds.) Proceedings of the 2nd International Conference on Learning Analytics and Knowledge (LAK 2012), pp. 73–81. ACM, New York (2012)

21. Ebner, M., Schön, M.: Why learning analytics in primary education matters! Bull. Tech. Comm. Learn. Technol. **15**(2), 14–17 (2013). Karagiannidis, C., Graf, S. (ed.)

22. Ebner, M., Schön, M., Neuhold, B.: Learning analytics in basic math education – first results from the field. e-Learning Pap. **36**, 24–27 (2014)

23. Ebner, M., Schön, M., Taraghi, B., Steyrer, M.: Teachers little helper: multi-math-coach. IADIS Int. J. WWW/Internet **11**(3), 1–12 (2014)

24. Taraghi, B., Saranti, A., Ebner, M., Schön, M.: Markov chain and classification of difficulty levels enhances the learning path in one digit multiplication. In: Zaphiris, P., Ioannou, A. (eds.) LCT 2014. LNCS, vol. 8523, pp. 322–333. Springer, Cham (2014). doi:10.1007/978-3-319-07482-5_31

25. Taraghi, B., Saranti, A., Ebner, M., Schön, M.: On using Markov chain to evidence the learning structures and difficulty levels of one digit multiplication. In: Proceedings of the Fourth International Conference on Learning Analytics and Knowledge, pp. 68–72 (2014)

26. Taraghi, B., Saranti, A., Ebner, M., Müller, V., Großman, A.: Towards a learning-aware application guided by hierarchical classification of learner profiles. J. Univ. Comput. Sci. **21** (1), 93–109 (2015)

27. Taraghi, B., Saranti, A., Legenstein, R., Ebner, M.: Bayesian modelling of student misconceptions in the one-digit multiplication with probabilistic programming. In: Proceedings of the Sixth International Conference on Learning Analytics & Knowledge (LAK 2016). ACM, New York (2016)

28. Turnbull, J.: The Logstash Book. James Turnbull, USA (2013)

29. Gormley, C., Tong, Z.: Elasticsearch: The Definitive Guide. O'Reilly Media Inc., Sebastopol (2015)

30. Gupta, Y.: Kibana Essentials. Packt Publishing Ltd., Birmingham (2015)

31. Nabi, Z.: Pro Spark Streaming: The Zen of Real-Time Analytics Using Apache Spark. Apress, New York (2016)

32. Maymala, J.: PostgreSQL for Data Architects. Packt Publishing Ltd., Birmingham (2015)

Mixing and Matching Learning Design and Learning Analytics

Quan Nguyen[✉], Bart Rienties, and Lisette Toetenel

Institute of Educational Technology, The Open University, Milton Keynes, UK
{quan.nguyen, bart.rienties}@open.ac.uk,
lisette.toetenel@gmail.com

Abstract. In the last five years, learning analytics has proved its potential in predicting academic performance based on trace data of learning activities. However, the role of pedagogical context in learning analytics has not been fully understood. To date, it has been difficult to quantify learning in a way that can be measured and compared. By coding the design of e-learning courses, this study demonstrates how learning design is being implemented on a large scale at the Open University UK, and how learning analytics could support as well as benefit from learning design. Building on our previous work, our analysis was conducted longitudinally on 23 undergraduate distance learning modules and their 40,083 students. The innovative aspect of this study is the availability of fine-grained learning design data at individual task level, which allows us to consider the connections between learning activities, and the media used to produce the activities. Using a combination of visualizations and social network analysis, our findings revealed a diversity in how learning activities were designed within and between disciplines as well as individual learning activities. By reflecting on the learning design in an explicit manner, educators are empowered to compare and contrast their design using their own institutional data.

Keywords: Learning analytics · Learning design · Virtual learning environment · Learning media

1 Introduction

In the last decade, there is a growing body of literature [1–3] that seeks to develop a descriptive framework to capture teaching and learning activities so that teaching ideas can be shared and reused from one educator to another, so called Learning Design (LD) [4]. While the early work in LD has focused on transferring the design for learning from implicit to explicit, the relationship between LD and the actual learner response has been not fully understood. As the majority of feedback takes forms of assessments, and course's evaluations, which typically takes place after the learning process has finished (except for formative assessments), it prevents teachers from making in-time interventions. Recently, the advancement in technology has allowed us to capture the digital footprints of learning activities from Virtual Learning Environment (VLE). This rich and fine-grained data about the actual learners' behaviors offer educators potentially valuable insights on how students react to different LDs.

P. Zaphiris and A. Ioannou (Eds.): LCT 2017, Part II, LNCS 10296, pp. 302–316, 2017.
DOI: 10.1007/978-3-319-58515-4_24

Learning analytics (LA) has the potential to empower teachers and students by identifying patterns and trends from a wide variety of learners' data. Substantial progress has been made both in conceptual development [5, 6] as well as how to design appropriate predictive learning analytics to support students [7, 8]. Nonetheless, in line with [7, 9], findings from LA research in the past have been rather limited to delivering actionable feedback, while ignoring the context in which the learning data is situated. Thus, there is an increasing interest to align LA with LD, as the former facilitates the transfer of tacit educational practice to an explicit rendition, while the latter provides educators with pedagogical context for interpreting and translating LA findings to direct interventions [10–14]. While there are abundant discussions on the value and impact of integrating LD into LA to improve teacher inquiry [13, 14], only a few studies have empirically examined how teachers actually design their courses [15, 16] and whether LD influences satisfaction, VLE behavior, and retention [9, 17–19].

This study builds on previous work by [17, 19, 20] by dynamically investigating the use of learning design in 24 modules over 30 weeks at one of the largest distance higher education institutions in Europe using a combination of data visualizations and social network analysis. Our work contributes to the existing literature by capturing: (1) how learning activities interact with each other across modules, and (2) how teachers configure their course at activity level.

2 Learning Design at the Open University

2.1 Aligning Learning Analytics and Learning Design

In the last five years, LA has attracted a lot of attention from practitioners, management, and researchers in education by shedding light on a massive amount of (potentially) valuable data in education, as well as providing means to explicitly test existing pedagogical theories. Scholars in the field of LA have exploited various sources of data, such as activity logs of students [21], learning dispositions [22–24], or discussion forum [25]. While these studies provide important markers on the potential of LA in education, critics have indicated a gap between pedagogy and LA [26, 27]. Interesting patterns can be identified from student activities, such as number of clicks, discussion posts, or essays. However, these patterns alone are not sufficient to offer feedback that teachers can put into actions [8, 24]. Without a pedagogically sound approach to data, LA researchers may struggle with deciding which variables to attend to, how to generalize the results to other contexts, and how to translate their findings to actions [27]. Hence, LD can equip researchers with a narrative behind their numbers, and convert trends of data into meaningful understandings and opportunities to make sensible interventions.

Since the beginning of the 21st century, the term learning design has emerged as a "methodology for enabling teachers/designers to make more informed decisions in how they go about designing learning activities and interventions, which is pedagogically informed and makes effective use of appropriate resources and technologies" [1]. For more discussion on the origins of 'learning design' and 'instructional design', we refer readers to Persico, Pozzi [12]. Several approaches for designing learning have been proposed, yet, one common stage in almost every approach was the evaluation of the LD [12]. Persico, Pozzi [12] argued that the learning process should not only depend on experience, or best practices of colleagues but also pre-existing aggregated data on students' engagement, progression, and achievement. In a similar manner, Mor et al. [13] suggested that LA could facilitate teacher inquiry by transforming knowledge from tacit to explicit, and perceive students and teachers as participants of a reflective practice. For instance, in a study of 148 learning designs by Toetenel, Rienties [28], the introduction of a systematic LD initiative consisting of visualization of initial LDs and workshops helped educators to focus on the development of a range of skills and more balanced LDs. Feeding information on how students are engaged in a certain LD during or post-implementation can provide a more holistic perspective of the impact of learning activities [10].

Several conceptual frameworks aiming at connecting LA with LD have been proposed. For example, Persico, Pozzi [12] discussed three dimensions of LD that can be informed by LA: representations, tools, and approaches. Lockyer et al. [10] introduced two categories of analytics applications: checkpoint analytics to determine whether students have met the prerequisites for learning by assessing relevant learning resources, and process analytics to capture how learners are carrying out their tasks. In the recent LAK conference 2016, Bakharia et al. [14] proposed four types of analytics (temporal, tool specific, cohort, and comparative), and contingency and intervention support tools with the teacher playing a central role.

In this paper, we will use the conceptual framework developed by Conole [1] and further employed by Rienties, Toetenel [17]. Both conceptual and empirical research has found that the Open University Learning Design Initiative (OULDI) can accurately and reliably determine how teachers design courses, and how students are subsequently using these LDs [17, 19].

While there were numerous discussions in aligning LA with LD, the amount of empirical studies on the subject has been rather limited. For example, Gašević et al. [8] examined the extent to which instructional conditions influence the prediction of academic success in nine undergraduate courses offered in a blended learning model. The results suggested that it is imperative for LA to taking into account instructional conditions across disciplines and courses to avoid over-estimation or underestimation of the effect of LMS behavior on academic success. From our observation, most of the empirical studies attempting to connect LA and LD are derived from students activities [10], or differences in discipline [8], rather than how teachers actually design their course [29].

In our previous work, we have highlighted explicitly the role of LD in explaining LMS behavior, student satisfaction, retention, and differences in prediction of academic success [8, 9, 17–19]. For example, in our first study linking 40 LDs with VLE behavior and retention, we found that strongly assimilative designs (i.e., lots of passive reading and watching of materials) were negatively correlated with retention [18]. In a large-scale follow-up study using a larger sample of 151 modules and multiple regression analyses of 111,256 students at the Open University, UK, Rienties, Toetenel [17] revealed relations between LD activities and VLE behavior, student satisfaction, and retention. The findings showed that taking the context of LD into account could increase the predictive power by 10–20%. Furthermore, from a practitioner's perspective, the combination of a collaborative, networked approach at the initial design stage, augmented with visualizations, changed the way educators design their courses [28].

While these three studies at the Open University UK (OU) highlighted the potential affordances of marrying LD with LA on a large scale, two obvious limitations of these studies were the aggregation of learning activities in predicting behavior and performance (i.e., rather than their interaction), as well as the static rather than longitudinal perspective of LD. In these studies [9, 18], aggregate learning design data across the 40 weeks of each module were used, while in many instances teachers use different combinations of learning activities throughout the module [29]. To address this, in our recent study [20], we have dynamically investigated longitudinal learning design of 38 modules over 30 weeks and found that learning design could explain up to 60% of the students' time spent on VLE. While learning design at weekly level has revealed promising results, the design of individual learning tasks has not been examined due to the lack of data. Therefore, this study takes a further step by looking at the learning designs and the inter-relationships between learning activities at individual task level.

2.2   Research Questions

Our previous works have shown a diverse of learning designs across different disciplines over time. In this study, we take a further step by looking at the learning design at activity level.

- RQ1: How are different types of learning activities connected, both within the module and between modules?
- RQ2: What media were used to deliver the individual learning activities?

3   Methodology

3.1   Study Context

This study took place at the Open University UK, which is the largest distance education provider in Europe. Data in this study was generated from the OU Learning design initiative, which helps teams in defining their pedagogic approach, choosing and integrating an effective range of media and technologies, and enable sharing of good practice across the university [30]. When using data to compare module design across disciplines and modules, according to our previous work [17, 19] it is important to classify learning activities in an objective and consistent manner. In particular, each module goes through a mapping process by a module team which consists of a LD specialist, a LD manager, and faculty members. This process typically takes between 1 and 3 days for a single module, depending on the number of credits, structure, and quantity of learning resources. First, the learning outcomes specified by the module team were captured by a LD specialist. Each learning activity within the module's weeks, topics, or blocks was categorized under the LD taxonomy and stored in an 'activity planner' – a planning and design tool supporting the development, analysis, and sharing of learning designs. Next, the LD team manager reviews the resulting module map before the findings are forwarded to the faculty. This provides academics with an opportunity to give feedback on the data before the status of the design was finalized. To sum up, the mapping process is reviewed by at least three people to ensure the reliability and robustness of the data relating to a learning design. Even so, coding learning activities remains a subjective undertaking and efforts to increase the validity in coding instruments have to date resulted in lack of data which can provide context to analysis (Table 1).

Table 1. Learning design taxonomy

	Type of activity	Example
Assimilative	Attending to information	Read, Watch, Listen, Think about, Access
Finding and handling information	Searching for and processing information	List, Analyze, Collate, Plot, Find, Discover, Access, Use, Gather
Communication	Discussing module related content with at least one other person (student or tutor)	Communicate, Debate, Discuss, Argue, Share, Report, Collaborate, Present, Describe
Productive	Actively constructing an artefact	Create, Build, Make, Design, Construct, Contribute, Complete
Experiential	Applying learning in a real-world setting	Practice, Apply, Mimic, Experience, Explore, Investigate
Interactive/Adaptive	Applying learning in a simulated setting	Explore, Experiment, Trial, Improve, Model, Simulate
Assessment	All forms of assessment (summative, formative and self-assessment)	Write, Present, Report, Demonstrate, Critique

Source: Retrieved from Rienties, Toetenel [17]

3.2   Measurement of Learning Design

Seven categories of learning activities were measured in terms of workload, which is the number of hours that was allocated for each type of learning activities. Time spent on learning activities was restricted based on the size of the module, such as 30 credits equated to 300 h of learning, and 60 credits equated to 600 h of learning. However, the actual LD depends on individual teacher. Descriptive statistics of the seven types of learning activities can be found in Table 2, Appendix.

In addition, assimilative activities of five modules were decomposed into sub-categories such as: Words, Figures, Photos, Tables, Equations, Audios, Videos, and Others (Fig. 1). These represent different channels that students absorbed information. Due to limited space, we chose to report the results of an exemplar module in Social sciences. In this exemplar module, there were in total 267 individual learning activities that were decomposed, descriptive statistics can be found in Table 3, Appendix.

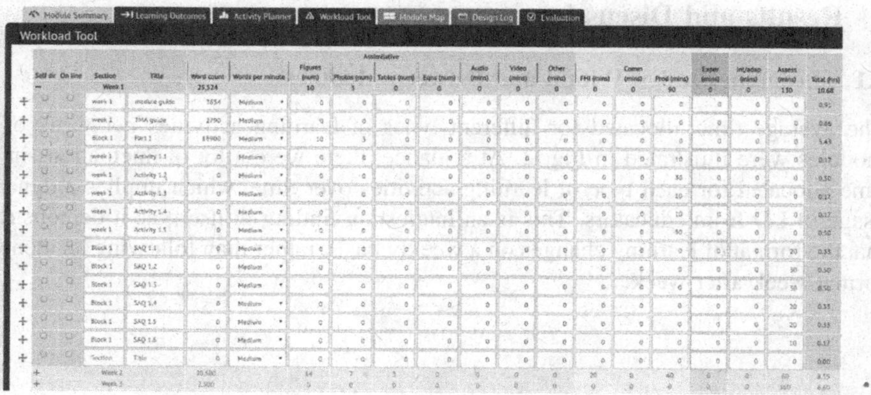

Fig. 1. Workload tool at individual task level of an exemplar module in the Social sciences

3.3 Data Analysis

Prior studies of Social Network Analysis (SNA) in e-learning, particularly in the improvement of LD have concentrated on examining patterns of learner communication and collaboration in various situations, such as when discussing, blogging and e-mailing [31]. Within the last three years in LA, SNA has been shown to be an effective tool to explore the relationships of learners in online discussion forum [29], as well as in face-to-face interactions, tracked for instance in eye tracking movements [32]. However, none has looked at the LD from a social network perspective, identifying connections between learning activities using 'big data'. Hora, Ferrare [29] suggested that teaching practice should be best viewed as situated in and distributed among features of particular settings. According to the systems-of-practice theory by Halverson [33], local practices are informed, constrained, and constituted by the dynamic interplay of artifact and tasks. Thus, in order to understand how teachers design their course, it is necessary to consider the inter-relationships among different learning activities, which is why we have employed a social networking analysis approach.

We used Tableau 10.1 to visualize the LD of 24 modules over 30 weeks of study time, and social network analysis (UCINET 6.627) to visualize the inter-relationships among learning activities. The LD dataset was a weighted two-mode network as it consisted of different learning activities across several weeks. Since we are primarily interested in the relationships among learning activities, the dataset was transformed to a one-mode network. We refer readers to our previous work [20] for more details of the data transformation process.

4 Results and Discussion

4.1 Learning Design Within and Between Modules

The average time allocated for different types of learning activities per week of 24 modules were illustrated in Fig. 2. At a glance, there were a lot of fluctuations in the time allocated for each type of learning activities over time, which implies a dynamic usage of LD from educators. This is an interesting finding in itself, as it demonstrates that the format of learning changes on a weekly basis, rather than following an identical format week after week.

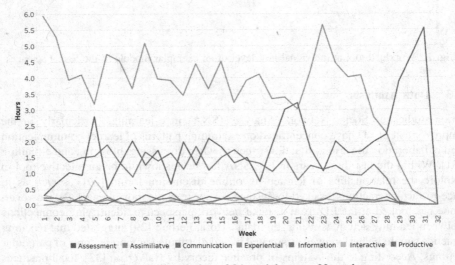

Fig. 2. Learning design of 24 modules over 32 weeks

In line with our previous findings [17, 19, 20], assimilative activities accounted for the majority of study time (M = 3.49, SD = 3.29), followed by assessment activities (M = 1.64, SD = 2.80), and productive activities (M = 1.16, SD = 1.49). Other types of learning activities such as communication, experiential, finding information, and interactive activities were underused on average. Assimilative activities and assessment activities seemed to follow opposite path, suggesting that where educators provide a lot of content, they do not provide assessment tasks and vice versa. In the beginning of a module, more assimilative activities were used to disseminate information to students whereas more assessment activities were used in the end of the module. The initial peak in assessment activities at the beginning of the module (week 5) suggests that many educators include an early assessment task to identify students that require additional support. Further correlational analysis (not included) suggested that assessment activities were negatively correlated with assimilative, information, communication, and productive activities. It was also interesting to see that many educators also included substantive time for productive tasks throughout their module, but the time allocation stops when students are due to prepare for their final assessment. Figure 2 shows, in line with our previous work [20], that educators had the tendency to reduce other learning activities when introducing assessments, in order to remain a balanced workload.

After capturing the dynamic picture of LD over time, we took a further step to examine how different learning activities are configured within each module. Due to the limited space, we only reported the LD of an exemplar module (60 credits) in Social sciences throughout the rest of the analysis. This module was selected based on the availability of LD data at individual task level, e.g. the time educators expected learners to spend on activities was mapped by minute on a weekly basis. A close look at the LD within modules (Fig. 3) revealed a combination of assimilative, assessment, productive, and finding information activities that were used. Similar to the overall trends shown in Fig. 2, this exemplar module allocated the majority of study time for assimilative activities (M = 3.29, SD = 2.38) with six formative assessments during the learning process and a final exam at the end.

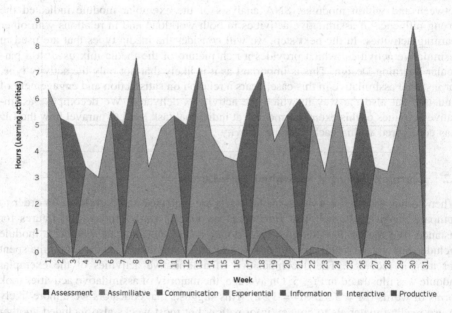

Fig. 3. Learning design and learning engagement of an exemplar module in Social sciences

Our social network analysis demonstrated the inter-relationships between different types of learning activities used in the exemplar module (Fig. 4). The network density was 14.3%, with 6 ties in total, and the average distance between pairs was 1. Productive and assimilative activities were strongly connected, implying that in this module educators combined productive and assimilative in the weekly LD. Assimilative activities had strong influences on both productive and finding information activities with the weight of 71.0 and 13.5 respectively. On the other hand, there was no connection between assessment activities and others, despite of its high frequency in

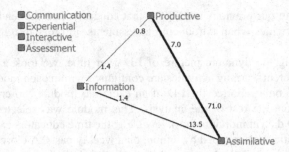

Fig. 4. Inter-relationships between learning activities of an exemplar module in Social sciences

the overall LD. This suggests that educators excluded other learning activities when introducing assessments, allowing learners to focus on their assessment task.

To sum up, our analysis at module level indicated a wide variety of learning design between and within modules. SNA analysis of the exemplar module indicated the strong influence of assimilative activities in both workload and in relations with other learning activities. In the next step, we will consider the media types that are used in assimilative activities, which provides a rich picture of the media mix used in a particular Learning Design. This is important as it is likely that not only the activity type, for instance assimilative in this case, bears a relation on satisfaction and engagement of students, but also the way in which the activity is delivered. We decompose assimilative activities of this exemplar module at individual task level to unravel how the LD was configured within each learning activity.

4.2   Learning Design at Individual Task Level

When coding learning activities, media assets are indicated at a high level, in order to compare the overall amount of time spent on video, words, photos and figures for instance. We accept that this high level notation does not indicate whether a module includes one video of half an hour or six videos of five minutes, as the total time spent per item is recorded. The decomposition of assimilative activities of the exemplar module was illustrated in Fig. 5. On average, the majority of assimilative activities took forms of words (M = 3.32, SD = 1.92). This suggests that educators were more likely to use reading materials to convey information, but most weeks also included another media element. Figure 5 also shows that figures and videos were also used overtime, but in less frequency compared to words.

Further SNA analysis demonstrates the inter-relationships between different types of assimilative activities and other learning activities. There were in total 40 ties in the network, with the density of 22% and the average distance between a pair of ties of 2.036. Firstly, there were strong connections between the use of words with photos, tables, and figures. These forms of assimilative activities often appeared together in reading materials. In line with the multi-media principle of Mayer [34], this module employed an integrated representation of graphics and words. Given the nature of this module, most of the graphics were representational (visuals that illustrate the

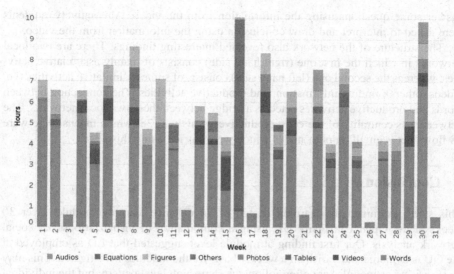

Fig. 5. Assimilative activities of an exemplar module in Social sciences.

appearance of an object), organizational (visuals that show qualitative relationships among content), and interpretive (visuals that make intangible phenomena visible and concrete) [34]. The use of words had a strong influence on photos, figures, and tables with the weight of 38.9, 16.4, 38.4 respectively (out-degree centrality = 118.541) (Fig. 6).

Secondly, videos were often used in combination with finding information activities and productive activities. For example, students were asked to watch a short video, and

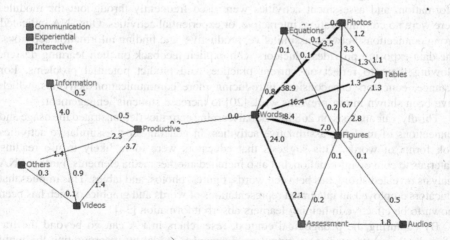

Fig. 6. Inter-relationships between assimilative activities and other activities of an exemplar module in Social sciences. **Note:** Blue nodes represent assimilative activities, red nodes represent other activities (Color figure online)

answer some questions using the information from the video. Alternatively, students were asked to interpret and draw conclusion using the information from the video.

The structure of the network also revealed interesting findings. There are two local networks in which the first one (right hand side) consists of mainly assimilative activities, whereas the second one (left hand side) consists of some assimilative activities (i.e. videos, others), finding information, and productive activities. The connection between words and productive activities acted as a bridge between these two local networks. The betweenness centrality of the edge productive-words was 28, which means there were 28 flows between all pairs of nodes which were carried using this edge.

5   Conclusion

This study examined the learning design of 24 distance learning modules over 30 weeks at the Open University UK using a combination of visualizations and social network analysis. Our first finding at module level suggested that LD as employed at the OU is dynamic and varies on a weekly basis for the modules investigated. This may be surprising as modules are often follow the same high level pattern, but the individual learning activities show a different visualization. In line with our previous findings [17, 19, 20], assimilative activities accounted for the majority of study time, followed by assessment activities, and productive activities. Assimilative activities and assessment activities seemed to follow opposite paths, suggesting that educators strategically reduced the time allocated for other learning activities when introducing assessments. Given the majority of OU's students were having either a full-time, or part-time job, ensuring a balance learning design is vital for students who are sensitive to sudden changes in the workload.

Our second finding from the analysis on an example module in social sciences revealed interesting pattern of learning activities. While assimilative, productive, finding information, and assessment activities were used frequently throughout the module, there were no communication, interactive, or experiential activities. Our SNA indicated strong connections between assimilative, productive, and finding information activities. The data exposure provides educators with explicit feedback on their learning design, allowing them to reflect on current practices and predict potential problems. For instance, educators can consider introducing more communication activities, which have been shown in our previous work [20] to increase students' engagement.

Thirdly, our analysis on 268 individual learning activities demonstrated the usage and connections of media in assimilative activities. In general, most assimilative activities took forms of words. This suggests that educators were more likely to use reading materials to convey information, but also included another media elements. Further SNA analysis revealed strong ties between words, figures, photos, and tables. This implies that educators employed an integrated representations of words and graphics, which has been shown to be effective in helping learners absorb information [34].

By capturing the pedagogical context, researchers in LA can go beyond the traditional process (trace data) – output (performance) model by incorporating the input (learning design). This will not only strengthen the predictive power but also empower educators to better translate LA findings into direct interventions.

Appendix

Table 2. Descriptive statistics of 23 learning designs over 32 weeks

Variable	N	Mean	SD	Min	Max
30 credits modules (13)					
Assimilative	397	2.89	2.46	0	12.44
Information	397	0.11	0.29	0	2.25
Communication	397	0.16	0.36	0	2.00
Productive	397	1.36	1.52	0	9.54
Experiential	397	0.15	0.76	0	9.00
Interactive	397	0.15	0.59	0	3.42
Assessment	397	1.27	2.25	0	10.5
Total	397	6.10	3.65	0	23.61
60 credits modules (10)					
Assimilative	337	4.17	4.00	0	15.00
Information	337	0.12	0.57	0	5.00
Communication	337	0.17	0.55	0	3.00
Productive	337	0.91	1.43	0	10.03
Experiential	337	0.04	0.20	0	1.75
Interactive	337	0.17	1.14	0	19.1
Assessment	337	2.13	3.33	0	15.00
Total	337	7.71	4.89	0	35.85

Note: Unit = hours. There were 23 modules with 774 weeks in total

Table 3. Descriptive statistics of a learning design at individual task level of an examplar module in Social sciences.

Variable	N	Mean	SD	Min	Max
Assimilative	267	0.58	1.60	0	9.00
Words	267	0.39	1.17	0	6.80
Figures	267	0.06	0.23	0	2.08
Photos	267	0.03	0.12	0	0.90
Tables	267	0.01	0.07	0	0.58
Equations	267	0.00	0.02	0	0.33
Audios	267	0.01	0.09	0	1.00
Videos	267	0.03	0.12	0	1.00
Others	267	0.04	0.56	0	9.00
Information	267	0.06	0.24	0	2.00
Productive	267	0.09	0.18	0	1.00
Experiential	267	0.00	0.00	0	0.00
Assessment	267	0.25	0.91	0	6.00
Total	267	0.98	1.75	0	9.00

Note: Unit = hours. There were 267 individual tasks in total

References

1. Conole, G.: Designing for Learning in an Open World, vol. 4. Springer Science & Business Media, New York (2012)
2. Dalziel, J.: Learning Design: Conceptualizing a Framework for Teaching and Learning Online. Routledge, New York (2015)
3. Lockyer, L., Bennett, S., Agostinho, S., Harper, B., Lockyer, L., Bennett, S., Agostinho, S., Harper, B.: Handbook of Research on Learning Design and Learning Objects: Issues, Applications and Technologies, vol. 1. IGI Global, New York (2008)
4. Dalziel, J., Conole, G., Wills, S., Walker, S., Bennett, S., Dobozy, E., Cameron, L., Badilescu-Buga, E., Bower, M.: The Larnaca declaration on learning design. J. Interact. Media Educ. **2016**(1), 1–24 (2016). doi:http://doi.org/10.5334/jime.407
5. Ferguson, R.: Learning analytics: drivers, developments and challenges. Int. J. Technol. Enhanced Learn. **4**(5–6), 304–317 (2012). doi:http://dx.doi.org/10.1504/IJTEL.2012.051816
6. Clow, D.: An overview of learning analytics. Teaching High. Educ. **18**(6), 683–695 (2013). doi:http://dx.doi.org/10.1080/13562517.2013.827653
7. Joksimović, S., Gašević, D., Loughin, T.M., Kovanović, V., Hatala, M.: Learning at distance: effects of interaction traces on academic achievement. Comput. Educ. **87**, 204–217 (2015). doi:http://dx.doi.org/10.1016/j.compedu.2015.07.002
8. Gašević, D., Dawson, S., Rogers, T., Gasevic, D.: Learning analytics should not promote one size fits all: the effects of instructional conditions in predicting academic success. Internet High. Educ. **28**, 68–84 (2016). doi:http://dx.doi.org/10.1016/j.iheduc.2015.10.002
9. Rienties, B., Toetenel, L.: The impact of 151 learning designs on student satisfaction and performance: social learning (analytics) matters. In: Proceedings of the Sixth International Conference on Learning Analytics & Knowledge, Edinburgh, United Kingdom 2016, pp. 339–343. ACM, New York (2016). doi:http://dx.doi.org/10.1145/2883851.2883875
10. Lockyer, L., Heathcote, E., Dawson, S.: Informing pedagogical action: Aligning learning analytics with learning design. Am. Behav. Sci. **57**(10), 1439–1459 (2013). doi:http://dx.doi.org/10.1177/0002764213479367
11. Lockyer, L., Dawson, S.: Learning designs and learning analytics. In: Proceedings of the 1st International Conference on Learning Analytics and Knowledge 2011, pp. 153–156. ACM, New York (2011). doi:http://dx.doi.org/10.1145/2090116.2090140
12. Persico, D., Pozzi, F.: Informing learning design with learning analytics to improve teacher inquiry. Br. J. Educ. Technol. **46**(2), 230–248 (2015). doi:http://dx.doi.org/10.1111/bjet.12207
13. Mor, Y., Ferguson, R., Wasson, B.: Editorial: learning design, teacher inquiry into student learning and learning analytics: a call for action. Br. J. Educ. Technol. **46**(2), 221–229 (2015). doi:http://dx.doi.org/10.1111/bjet.12273
14. Bakharia, A., Corrin, L., de Barba, P., Kennedy, G., Gašević, D., Mulder, R., Williams, D., Dawson, S., Lockyer, L.: A conceptual framework linking learning design with learning analytics. In: Proceedings of the Sixth International Conference on Learning Analytics & Knowledge 2016, pp. 329–338. ACM, New York (2016). doi:http://dx.doi.org/10.1145/2883851.2883944
15. Bennett, S., Agostinho, S., Lockyer, L.: Technology tools to support learning design: implications derived from an investigation of university teachers' design practices. Comput. Educ. **81**, 211–220 (2015). doi:http://dx.doi.org/10.1016/j.compedu.2014.10.016
16. Goodyear, P.: Teaching as design. HERDSA Rev. High. Educ. **2**, 27–50 (2015)

17. Rienties, B., Toetenel, L.: The impact of learning design on student behaviour, satisfaction and performance: a cross-institutional comparison across 151 modules. Comput. Hum. Behav. **60**, 333–341 (2016). doi:http://dx.doi.org/10.1016/j.chb.2016.02.074

18. Rienties, B., Toetenel, L., Bryan, A.: Scaling up learning design: impact of learning design activities on LMS behavior and performance. In: Proceedings of the Fifth International Conference on Learning Analytics and Knowledge 2015, pp. 315–319. ACM, New York (2015). doi:http://dx.doi.org/10.1145/2723576.2723600

19. Toetenel, L., Rienties, B.: Analysing 157 learning designs using learning analytic approaches as a means to evaluate the impact of pedagogical decision making. Br. J. Educ. Technol. **47**, 981–992 (2016). doi:http://dx.doi.org/10.1111/bjet.12423

20. Nguyen, Q., Rienties, B., Toetenel, L.: Unravelling the dynamics of instructional practice: a longitudinal study on learning design and VLE activities. In: the Seventh International Conference on Learning Analytics & Knowledge, Vancouver, BC, Canada. ACM, New York (2017)

21. Tempelaar, D., Rienties, B., Giesbers, B.: In search for the most informative data for feedback generation: learning analytics in a data-rich context. Comput. Hum. Behav. **47**, 157–167 (2015). doi:http://dx.doi.org/10.1016/j.chb.2014.05.038

22. Buckingham Shum, S., Crick, R.D.: Learning dispositions and transferable competencies: pedagogy, modelling and learning analytics. In: Proceedings of the 2nd International Conference on Learning Analytics and Knowledge 2012, pp. 92–101. ACM, New York (2012). doi:http://dx.doi.org/10.1145/2330601.2330629

23. Nguyen, Q., Tempelaar, D.T., Rienties, B., Giesbers, B.: What learning analytics based prediction models tell us about feedback preferences of students. Q. Rev. Distance Educ. **17**(3), 13–33 (2016)

24. Tempelaar, D.T., Rienties, B., Nguyen, Q.: Towards actionable learning analytics using dispositions. IEEE Trans. Learn. Technol. (2017, in press). doi:10.1109/TLT.2017.2662679

25. Wise, A.F., Cui, Y., Jin, W., Vytasek, J.: Mining for gold: identifying content-related MOOC discussion threads across domains through linguistic modeling. Internet High. Educ. **32**, 11–28 (2017). doi:http://dx.doi.org/10.1016/j.iheduc.2016.08.001

26. Gašević, D., Dawson, S., Siemens, G.: Let's not forget: learning analytics are about learning. TechTrends **59**(1), 64–71 (2015). doi:http://dx.doi.org/10.1007/s11528-014-0822-x

27. Kirschner, P.: Keynote: Learning Analytics: Utopia or Dystopia (2016). http://lak16.solaresearch.org/wp-content/uploads/2016/05/lak16keynotelearninganalytics-utopiaofdystopia-160428103734.pdf. Accessed 10 Oct 2016

28. Toetenel, L., Rienties, B.: Learning design–creative design to visualise learning activities. Open Learn. J. Open, Distance e-learn. **31**(3), 233–244 (2016). doi:http://dx.doi.org/10.1080/02680513.2016.1213626

29. Hora, M.T., Ferrare, J.J.: Instructional systems of practice: a multidimensional analysis of math and science undergraduate course planning and classroom teaching. J. Learn. Sci. **22**(2), 212–257 (2013). doi:http://dx.doi.org/10.1080/10508406.2012.729767

30. Cross, S., Galley, R., Brasher, A., Weller, M.: Final Project Report of the OULDI-JISC Project: Challenge and Change in Curriculum Design Process, Communities, Visualisation and Practice (2012). http://www.open.ac.uk/blogs/OULDI/wp-content/uploads/2010/11/OULDI_Final_Report_Final.pdf. Accessed 16 Oct 2016

31. Cela, K.L., Sicilia, M.Á., Sánchez, S.: Social network analysis in e-learning environments: a preliminary systematic review. Educ. Psychol. Rev. **27**(1), 219–246 (2015). doi:https://doi.org/10.1007/s10648-014-9276-0

32. Zhu, M., Feng, G.: An exploratory study using social network analysis to model eye movements in mathematics problem solving. In: Proceedings of the Fifth International Conference on Learning Analytics and Knowledge, pp. 383–387. ACM (2015)

33. Halverson, R.R.: Systems of practice: How leaders use artifacts to create professional community in schools. Educ. Policy Anal. Arch. **11**(37), 1–35 (2003). doi:http://dx.doi.org/10.14507/epaa.v11n37.2003
34. Mayer, R.E.: Multimedia learning. Psychol. Learn. Motiv. **41**, 85–139 (2002). doi:http://dx.doi.org/10.1016/S0079-7421(02)80005-6

Improving the Learning and Collaboration Experience

Attitudes Towards Mobile Devices in Estonian Basic Education: Using the Framework of the UTAUT Model

Liina Adov(✉), Olev Must, and Margus Pedaste

University of Tartu, Tartu, Estonia
Liina.adov@ut.ee

Abstract. Despite the use of mobile devices becoming more ubiquitous, and the possibilities they offer for learning becoming more recognized, research shows that mobile devices are not always used to their fullest potential. Previous studies have found that attitudes towards technology can influence whether, and in what way, mobile devices are used. At present, there have been few studies focusing on samples of basic school students and mobile device use. It was our aim, therefore, to test whether the widely used theoretical UTAUT model could also be applied to a sample of basic school students, or whether some changes would be required before it could be used for a study of attitudes towards mobile devices among basic education students. 3521 Estonian basic school students from 6th (n = 2673) and 9th (n = 848) grades participated in the study. From the results 4 attitude factors could be distinguished. These included: Self-efficacy, Social Influence, Anxiety and Performance Enjoyment. The attitudes towards mobile devices in learning explained approximately 43% of the variance of student's Behavioural Intention to use mobile devices, while Performance Enjoyment played a mediating role on the influence of Self-efficacy. Behavioural Intention explained 2% of the variance in the use of mobile devices for learning. The results suggest that some changes should be considered when researching students' attitudes towards mobile devices in basic education.

Keywords: UTAUT · Primary education · Students · Mobile devices · Attitudes

1 Introduction

Over the last two decades the accessibility and the use of technology has grown considerably, with things like information and communication technology (ICT), mobile devices becoming commonplace. This trend is evident in everyday life, as well as in learning environments. Teachers and educators are now encouraged to use mobile devices in educational settings. However, not all students take full advantage of the possibilities that mobile devices, such as smart phones and tablets, offer. There is a general concern as to how students will use these mobile devices and whether they will be used for educational purposes or simply for gaming. Several studies show that attitudes towards technology, such as ICT, can have an impact on whether the devices are used in an educational setting and how they are used [1, 2]. The DIGCOMP

© Springer International Publishing AG 2017
P. Zaphiris and A. Ioannou (Eds.): LCT 2017, Part II, LNCS 10296, pp. 319–329, 2017.
DOI: 10.1007/978-3-319-58515-4_25

(A Framework for Developing and Understanding Digital Competence in Europe) framework has also assisted in highlighting certain attitudes that are an important part of digital competencies [3]. It is therefore, necessary to examine the attitudes of students themselves towards mobile devices, as this can be instrumental in gaining an understanding of how mobile devices are actually used for learning. Furthermore, attitudes can give information on how to better develop interventions in order to help students use their mobile devices to their fullest potential. However, at present there has been a dearth of studies investigating students' attitudes and their relationships with mobile devices in a learning context. This is due to the fact that the vast majority of the existing research has only studied attitudes towards computers, such as ICT, and generally not focused on basic education [4, 5]. Portable devices, such as tablets and smart phones allow for more flexible possibilities in educational settings, as they can be used to support learning related activities more easily during the usual classes, and teachers no longer need to take students to a computer lab. Thus, mobile devices create new possibilities. Nevertheless, questions still arise as to the usefulness and usability of these devices. Therefore, it is important to test the existing theories and models that explain the relationship between attitudes towards the use of mobile devices within an educational context.

1.1 Measures of Attitude

There are several theoretical frameworks that allow researchers to measure the attitudes of people towards technology. Some of the most common of these include the technology acceptance model (TAM), the theory of planned behaviour (TPB), and the Unified Theory of Acceptance and Use of Technology (UTAUT) [2]. These models have proven useful for explaining the use of technology [6]. The UTAUT has become one of the most popular as it combines eight models and theories (e.g. TAM, TPB) in order to explain the factors that influence the acceptance of technology. Based on some of these pre existing theories, the authors utilized 7 attitudinal factors that have a direct influence on people's willingness to use technology, or as we term it Behavioural Intention, in different fields. They are as follows:

- Performance Expectancy – the degree to which an individual believes that using the technological system will help him or her to do a task more effectively;
- Effort Expectancy – the degree of ease or difficulty associated with the use of technology;
- Attitude Towards Technology Use/Enjoyment (ATUT) – the degree to which an individual experiences positive feelings (e.g. interest, enjoyment) towards the use of technology;
- Social Influence – the degree to which an individual perceives that it is important to others that he or she should use technology,
- Facilitating Conditions – the degree to which an individual believes that there is organizational infrastructure to support the use of technology;
- Self-efficacy – the belief in an individual's capability to successfully cope with using technology;

- Anxiety – the degree to which an individual experiences negative feelings (e.g. fear, doubt) about using technology.

The authors found that only Performance Expectancy, Effort Expectancy, Social Influence, and Facilitating Conditions actually had a direct influence on the intention to use, and the actual use of a certain technology (such as a computer or a specific program). Later research shows that all 6 categories in addition to Behavioural Intention (with the exception of Anxiety) could be differentiated in cross-cultural studies [7]. Furthermore, researchers have taken into account several variables that were not included in the original work of Venkatesh and colleagues in order to adapt the model into a different context (e.g. higher education [8]; computer based assessment [9]). The UTAUT is based on research made using ICT examples, and examines attitudes towards computers and other technological devices, but does not focus on mobile devices. However, in later studies, researchers adapted the theory and model to incorporate a more diverse array of technological applications in which case several additional variables were added, thereby demonstrating the effect on Behavioural Intention [10]. Based on this development, Venkatesh went back to the original model and made some modifications by adding the factors of Hedonic Motivation, Price Value and Habit (UTAUT2) [11]. The original model explained 77% of the variance in Behavioural Intention and 52% of the actual use of technology, while the percentages for the UTAUT2 were 74% and 52% respectively [10]. Based on previous results it is apparent that the addition of the three aforementioned variables does not affect how much of the dependent variable is explained. Despite criticism of the model in connection to whether the list of predictive variables is comprehensive enough, and conversely, whether there may be too many variables to make conclusions, as well as the question concerning the connection between Behavioural Intention and actual behaviour [12], the UTAUT is still a widely used model that has been validated by several empirical [10]. However, there is still a need to critically test the theory in new contexts.

Research using the UTAUT model shows it to be a useful framework for discerning attitudes towards technology. However, further research has also demonstrated the need for more flexibility in connection to the variables under observation. This is due to the fact that, depending on the context, other disparate attitudes can have a significant influence on the potential use of technology. As research on the use of mobile devices at the basic education level has been scarce, it raises the question of whether the UTAUT model can in fact be applied to the aforementioned context?

1.2 Attitudes Towards Technology in Educational Setting

The application of the UTAUT in an educational environment has been rather uncommon up to this point [10]. The vast majority of studies using the UTAUT have focused on organizations and work conditions, with few studies being conducted in educational settings. The studies that have focused on educational settings took place in universities [10]. This is somewhat surprising given the fact that the PISA results show that more and more basic school students have access to, and make use of technology in their everyday life [13]. The increasing importance of examining the factors that influence the attitudes towards technology, and the necessity of analysing of what technology is being used for among basic school students cannot be overstated. Experiences that are imprinted on students of that age can have impact on how they use their mobile devices later in life. Although the UTAUT has not been widely applied to this context, there are many independent studies showing that students' attitudes towards technology in learning plays an important role in peoples' willingness to use digital devices and whether the devices are in fact used for learning. Some examples of this will be given later.

In Terzis' and Economides's [9] study of university students' attitudes towards computer based assessment (CBA), they found that Perceived Ease of Use had a direct effect on behavioural intentions to use CBA's, whereas Self-efficacy had an indirect effect. Self-efficacy, or more specifically Computer Self-efficacy, has received a lot of attention in the field of technology acceptance and has been shown to play an important role in understanding how technology is used [14]. In the context of mobile learning (learning with mobile devices) among university students, it has been shown that Performance Expectancy, Effort Expectancy, Influence of Lecturers, Quality of Service, and Personal Innovativeness have a positive effect on behavioural intention [8]. It is also necessary to point out that in a university learning context, the Quality of Service, and Personal Innovativeness could be possible additions to the UTAUT model. [15] have also done research on the acceptance of tablets in an educational setting among university students. Using the UTAUT model they found that Effort and Performance Expectancy had a positive influence on Behavioural Intention through a more general positive attitude towards tablets. Social Influence and Facilitating conditions, on the other hand, had a direct positive effect on Behavioural Intention. But because past studies have focused on the university setting, it is difficult to say whether similar results could be expected from a sample of basic school students. Although, there has been research on basic school students indicating that attitudes towards ICT can determine whether technology is used for learning or not [16], this study was more descriptive in nature, and left many questions unanswered as far as the role of basic school students' attitudes towards the use of technology.

1.3   The Present Study

The aim of our study was to test whether the theoretical model of the UTAUT could be applied to the sample of basic school students, or whether some changes would be necessary before it could be used to research attitudes towards mobile devices in basic education.

We formulated the following research questions:

1. Can the factors of Performance Expectancy, Effort Expectancy, Enjoyment, Social Influence, and Anxiety of the UTAUT model be differentiated in the Estonian basic school student sample?
2. Which of the variables (Performance Expectancy, Effort Expectancy, Enjoyment, Social Influence, and Anxiety) predict students' Behavioural Intention, and can they be used to predict the use of mobile devices for learning?

2   Methods

2.1   Participants

In the spring of 2016 we conducted a large-scale study focusing on the use of mobile devices in an educational context among Estonian students. The study questioned 3521 students in the 6th (n = 2673) and 9th (n = 848) grades, from 147 schools with an average age of 13.3 (6th grade M = 12.6 and 9th M = 15.6). In total, 1824 girls and 1697 boys participated. Several criteria were used to select the schools from which the sample group was drawn. These criteria were: general education (the sample group did not include schools with special education); the use of Estonian as the basic teaching language; having more than 5 students in the target classes (6th and 9th), and a specific region (proportionally students from the city, the country side, bigger and smaller schools, etc.).

Parental consent in written form was gained before the questionnaires could be administered to the students. Only students' whose parents had agreed to the survey were requested to fill out a questionnaire. The questionnaires were administered in school, during class, using computers or tablets. The survey took approximately 45 min to fill out.

97% of the students who participated in the study reported owning a mobile device that could be used for learning. However, most of them primarily used their mobile devices for purposes other than learning. Our previous analysis of the same data showed that 49.9% of the students used their mobile devices for learning once a month or even less and only 4.9% of students use it for different learning tasks on a daily basis, such as for information searches, communication, and content creation [17]. However, 74.2% of students stated that they would be willing to use their mobile devices for learning, and only 9.3% of the students reported that they would be opposed to it.

2.2   The Instruments

Attitudes towards using mobile device for learning. The UTAUT was used as the theoretical basis to measure the student attitudes towards the use of mobile devices for learning. As mentioned in the introduction, the theory and the model have not been previously used in such a context, therefore we used a previously validated and reliable questionnaire to ask students about their attitude towards mobile devices in learning. However, as the previously mentioned the questionnaire did have some shortcomings (it did not have items regarding self-efficacy etc.). For this reason some constructs based on UTAUT were added.

The mobile device attitude questionnaire that we developed was based on a pre-existing questionnaire that had been developed by Pruet and colleagues [18]. It consisted of 20 items. Based on the theoretical background some additional items were added in order to measure Social Influence, Self-efficacy and Effort Expectancy [2]. The final questionnaire consisted of 31 items that were adapted into the Estonian language and a mobile device context. In addition, students reported on their willingness to use mobile devices for learning in STEM subjects (5-point scale).

Behavioural Intention and the use of mobile devices. Behavioural Intention to use mobile devices was measured via one item (with a 5-point scale): "I am willing to use mobile devices for learning".

Students answered questions related to how often they use mobile devices for information searches, communication, content creation and gaming in connection to learning; while they were in school; while they were outside of school, and how often they used mobile devices outside of school for other purposes. The activities were then grouped according to the nature and the location of the activity – in school for learning, outside of school for learning and outside of school for other purposes. The primary focus of the present study was on mobile device activities with a direct educational purpose.

2.3   Data Analysis

The statistical program Mplus (Version 7; [19]) was used for Confirmatory Factor Analysis and Structural Equation Modeling. In order to evaluate the models we used criteria for fit indexes proposed by Bowen and Guo [20], which are as follows: RMSEA: close fit: $\leq$ .05, reasonable fit: .05–.08, poor fit: $\geq$ .10; CFI: $\leq$ .95; TLI: $\leq$ .95.

3   Results

3.1   Attitude Factors for Students

Based on the confirmatory factor analysis (CFA) results, it was possible to discern 4 attitude factors from the student sample: Self-efficacy, Social Influence, Anxiety and Performance enjoyment ($\chi 2(143) = 1842.77$, p < .01, RMSEA = .058, CFI = 0.95, TLI = 0.94). The factor model is shown in Fig. 1. The Performance Enjoyment factor was formed by combining the Performance Expectancy and the Enjoyment factors. As seen in the Fig. 1 there was rather strong positive correlation between the Self-efficacy and the Performance Enjoyment factors (r = .79, p < .01) and a negative correlation between the Self-efficacy and the Anxiety factors (r = −.64, p < .01). One Effort Expectancy item (Eff2; "It is difficult to use mobile devices for learning") loaded onto the Anxiety factor, while another Effort Expectancy item (Eff1; "Using mobile devices for learning makes learning easier") loaded onto the Performance Enjoyment factor. Both of the items fit the description of the new factors and the changes were therefore acceptable. The model with Social Support and Effort Expectancy factors did not give satisfactory results ($\chi 2$ (174) = 3968.58, p < .01, RMSEA = .08, CFI = 0.90, TLI = 0.88).

3.2 Attitudes as Predictors of Behavioural Intention and the Use of Mobile Devices

Attitudes towards mobile devices in learning explained approximately 43% of the variance for the Behavioural Intention of students (Fig. 2). Behavioural Intention in turn explained 2% of the variance for the use in school and 2% of the use of mobile devices for learning at home respectively. Self-efficacy had an effect on Behavioural Intention through the mediation of Performance Enjoyment, with the former explaining 61% of the latter.

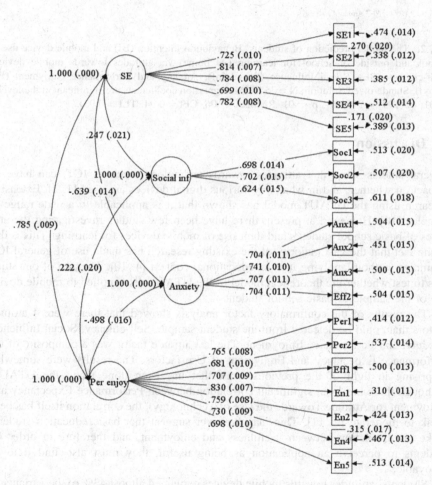

Fig. 1. The model of confirmatory factor analysis: students' attitudes towards using mobile devices for learning; standardized solution. All regression coefficients and correlations are significant at the level p < .01 (standard errors brought in parenthesis). SE – Self-efficacy; Social inf – Social Influence; Per enjoy – Performance enjoyment

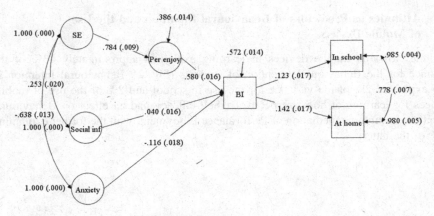

Fig. 2. The model prediction of students' Behavioural Intention (BI) and mobile device use in school and outside of school for learning (At home) via attitudes towards mobile devices (Self-efficacy (SE), Social Influence (Social inf), Anxiety and Performance enjoyment (Per enjoy)). Standardized Solution; N = 3527. All regression coefficients are significant at the level p < .01; χ2(199) = 2753.61, p < .01, RMSEA = .06, CFI = 0.94, TLI = 0.93.

4   Discussion

Several studies show that attitudes towards technology, such as ICT, can have an impact on whether, and in what way various digital devices are used [1, 2]. Extensive research using the UTAUT model has shown that it is applicable to a wide range of samples [10]. However, at present there have been few studies investigating the attitudes of basic school students and their use of mobile devices for learning. This is due to the fact that the vast majority of the existing research has made use of general ICT examples, without applying it to an educational context [4, 10]. The aim of our study was to test whether the theoretical model of the UTAUT also applied to mobile device use of the sample of basic school students.

The results of the confirmatory factor analysis showed that there were 4 attitude factors that could be detected from the student sample: Self-efficacy, Social Influence, Anxiety, and Performance Enjoyment. The last attitude factor was a composite of the Performance Expectancy and Enjoyment of Use factors. The results were somewhat surprising in light of the previous work that has been done using the UTAUT. Although there has been significant correlation between Performance Expectancy and Enjoyment (or Attitude Towards the Use of Technology), the correlation itself has been weak to moderate [2, 11]. This may however suggest that basic education students make no distinction between usefulness and enjoyment, and therefore in order for students to perceive an application as being useful, they must also find it to be enjoyable.

Students' attitudes towards mobile devices explained almost 43% of the variance in the Behavioural Intention of students use of mobile devices in learning. Whereas

Self-efficacy had an indirect effect on the Behavioural Intention through Performance enjoyment, with the former explaining 61% of the latter. These findings are in alignment with previous research showing that Self-efficacy has an indirect influence on Behavioural Intention [9]. Terzi and colleague however did not investigate the relationship between Self-efficacy and Performance Expectancy, although they were able to demonstrate a similar relationship with the mediation of Perceived Effort of Use [9]. The similar role of Self-efficacy has also been brought out in the Technology Acceptance Model [21], In that model Self-efficacy had an indirect influence on Behavioural Intention as well. The results from present study give us reason to believe that students who feel more confident using mobile devices may also find the activity to be enjoyable and useful. This in turn facilitates the use of mobile devices for learning and may help motivate students to use mobile devices for educational purposes. Furthermore, future studies should consider other possible mediating variables when investigating the influence of Self-efficacy on Behavioural Intention.

Behavioural intention explained 2% of the variance of the use of mobile devices for learning in school, and 2% of the use of mobile devices for learning outside of school respectively. This is much lower than the rates that have been found in previous studies (e.g. [10]). The results show that even if students have positive attitudes towards, and a willingness to use, mobile devices for learning, the behaviour may not actually become manifest. It could be that some characteristics which may be specific to a basic school context, and which we have not focused on in this study, also have an influence on students' behaviour. For example, several studies show that a teachers' own attitudes have an important influence on whether they are willing to use technology in teaching [22, 23]. Therefore, a teachers' own attitudes towards mobile devices and the willingness to use them may be one of the factors that influences the behaviour of students in basic school when it comes to the use of technology for learning. On the other hand, previous research has also brought to light similar results that show a weak relationship between BI and behaviour [24]. It is the relationship between these factors in the UTAUT model that has received the strongest critique [12]. As Bagozzi has mentioned, the singular link between Behavioural Intention and behaviour itself discounts the other possible factors that may influence whether individuals acts on their intentions [10]. The results from the present study also indicate that Behavioural Intention may be insufficient for predicting the usage of mobile devices for learning.

4.1   Limitations and Future Studies

Our sample was representative of the Estonian educational context, however, the proportion of 6th and 9th grade students was somewhat uneven, which may have had an influence on the applicability of the results among the two age groups. Therefore, the latter would be an important variable to take into account in future studies, especially when comparing the results for 6th and 9th grade students.

Future studies should also take into account teacher level variables, which may have a significant influence on students' behaviour when it comes to mobile device use for educational purposes. At present the UTAUT models have mostly been applied to adult samples where participants have more autonomy over their behaviour (than for example basic education students). This may be an important factor to take into account in future studies. It should also be mentioned that information on the students' behaviour was gathered through self-report questionnaires, which may be biased due to social-desirability. For this reason, the results of the questionnaires may not reflect the actual objective frequency of smart device use for learning by students. Future research should also make use of objective data on students mobile device use whenever possible.

Finally, it is important to consider the possible influence of the cultural context. Previous research has shown that the predictive power of the UTAUT model may vary across cultures [15]. More specifically, the research was done in the Estonian context, where it is very common for students to either have mobile devices at school, or for students to have the possibility of using their own mobile devices at school. Previous research does not provide direct information about how often mobile devices are actually used for learning, but rather has focused on mobile device availability. The habits of mobile device use may not apply to all cultures and should be taken into account when generalizing the results.

Future studies should also consider using the theoretical background of the renewed UTAUT models, and adding, for example, the additional factor of Habit to the list of predictive variables [11]. As was mentioned before in the discussion, the results are also in alignment with the TAM theoretical model, which gives us reason to believe that future studies may benefit from either combining several models together, or from developing an altogether different model that would suit the basic school context.

Acknowledgement. This study was funded by the Estonian Research Council through the institutional research funding project "Smart technologies and digital literacy in promoting a change of learning" (Grant Agreement No. IUT34-6).

References

1. Scherer, R., Siddiq, F., Teo, T.: Becoming more specific: measuring and modeling teachers' perceived usefulness of ICT in the context of teaching and learning. Comput. Educ. **88**, 202–214 (2015). https://doi.org/10.1016/j.compedu.2015.05.005
2. Venkatesh, V., Morris, M.G., Davis, G.B., Davis, F.D.: User acceptance of information technology: toward a unified view. MIS Q. **27**, 425–478 (2003)
3. Ferrari, A., Punie, Y., Brečko, B.N.: DIGCOMP: A Framework for Developing and Understanding Digital Competence in Europe. Luxembourg, Publications Office (2013). http://dx.publications.europa.eu10.2788/52966
4. Moos, D.C., Azevedo, R.: Learning with computer-based learning environments: a literature review of computer self-efficacy. Rev. Educ. Res. **79**(2), 576–600 (2009). https://doi.org/10.3102/0034654308326083
5. Pullen, D.: The influence of the home learning environment on middle school students' use of ICT at school. Australian Educ. Comput. **30**(1), pp. 1-25 (2015). http://journal.acce.edu.au/index.php/AEC/article/view/49
6. Ndubisi, N.: Factors of online learning adoption: a comparative juxtaposition of the theory of planned behaviour and the technology acceptance model. Int. J. E-Learn. **5**(4), 571–591 (2006)

7. Oshlyansky, L., Cairns, P., Thimbleby, H.: Validating the unified theory of acceptance and use of technology (UTAUT) tool cross-culturally. In: Proceedings of the 21st British HCI Group Annual Conference on People and Computers: HCI. but not as we know it, vol. 2, pp. 83–86. British Computer Society (2007). http://dl.acm.org/citation.cfm?id=1531429

8. Abu-Al-Aish, A., Love, S.: Factors influencing students' acceptance of m-learning: an investigation in higher education. Int. Rev. Res. Open Dist. Learn. **14**(5) (2013). http://www.irrodl.org/index.php/irrodl/article/view/1631

9. Terzis, V., Economides, A.A.: The acceptance and use of computer based assessment. Comput. Educ. **56**(4), 1032–1044 (2011). https://doi.org/10.1016/j.compedu.2010.11.017

10. Venkatesh, V., Thong, J.Y., Xu, X.: Unified theory of acceptance and use of technology: a synthesis and the road ahead (2016). https://papers.ssrn.com/sol3/papers.cfm?abstract_id=2800121

11. Venkatesh, V., Thong, J.Y., Xu, X.: Consumer acceptance and use of information technology: extending the unified theory of acceptance and use of technology. MIS Q. **36**(1), 157–178 (2012)

12. Bagozzi, R.P.: The legacy of the technology acceptance model and a proposal for a paradigm shift. J. Assoc. Inf. Syst. **8**(4), 244–254 (2007)

13. Students, Computers and Learning. OECD Publishing (2015). http://www.oecd-ilibrary.org/education/students-computers-and-learning_9789264239555-en

14. Marakas, G.M., Yi, M.Y., Johnson, R.D.: The multilevel and multifaceted character of computer self-efficacy: toward clarification of the construct and an integrative framework for research. Inf. Syst. Res. **9**(2), 126–163 (1998)

15. El-Gayar, O.F., Moran, M., Hawkes, M.: Students' acceptance of tablet PCs and implications for educational institutions. Educ. Technol. Soc. **14**(2), 58–70 (2011)

16. Hakkarainen, K., Ilomäki, L., Lipponen, L., Muukkonen, H., Rahikainen, M., Tuominen, T., Lehtinen, E.: Students' skills and practices of using ICT: results of a national assessment in Finland. Comput. Educ. **34**(2), 103–117 (2000). https://doi.org/10.1016/S0360-1315(00)00007-5

17. Pedaste, M., Must, O., Leijen, Ä., Mäeots, M., Siiman, L., Kori, K., Adov, L.: Nutiseadmete kasutamise profiilid loodusainete ja matemaatika õppimise kontekstis. Eesti Haridusteaduste Ajakiri, **5**(1), 99–129 (2017)

18. Pruet, P., Ang, C.S., Farzin, D.: Understanding tablet computer usage among primary school students in underdeveloped areas: students' technology experience, learning styles and attitudes. Comput. Hum. Behav. **55**, 1131–1144 (2016). https://doi.org/10.1016/j.chb.2014.09.063

19. Muthén, L.K., Muthén, B.O.: Mplus User's Guide, 7th edn. Muthén & Muthén, Los Angeles (1998–2015)

20. Bowen, N.K., Guo, S.: Structural Equation Modeling. Oxford University Press, New York (2012)

21. Venkatesh, V., Bala, H.: Technology acceptance model 3 and a research agenda on interventions. Decis. Sci. **39**(2), 273–315 (2008)

22. Oye, N.D., Iahad, N.A., Ab. Rahim, N.: The history of UTAUT model and its impact on ICT acceptance and usage by academicians. Educ. Inf. Technol. **19**(1), 251–270 (2014). https://doi.org/10.1007/s10639-012-9189-9

23. Pynoo, B., Tondeur, J., van Braak, J., Duyck, W., Sijnave, B., Duyck, P.: Teachers' acceptance and use of an educational portal. Comput. Educ. **58**(4), 1308–1317 (2012). https://doi.org/10.1016/j.compedu.2011.12.026

24. Taiwo, A.A., Downe, A.G.: The theory of user acceptance and use of technology (UTAUT): a meta-analytic review of empirical findings. J. Theor. Appl. Inf. Technol. **49**(1), 48–58 (2013)

25. Im, I., Hong, S., Kang, M.S.: An international comparison of technology adoption: testing the UTAUT model. Inf. Manag. **48**(1), 1–8 (2011). https://doi.org/10.1016/j.im.2010.09.001

A Guidance and Evaluation Approach for mHealth Education Applications

Tareq Aljaber$^{(\boxtimes)}$ and Neil Gordon

School of Engineering and Computer Science,
University of Hull, Hull HU6 7RX, UK
T.ALJABER@2013.hull.ac.uk, n.a.gordon@hull.ac.uk

Abstract. A growing number of mobile applications for health education are being utilized to support different stakeholders, from health professionals to software developers to patients and more general users. There is a lack of a critical evaluation framework to ensure the usability and reliability of these mobile health education applications (MHEAs). Such a framework would facilitate the saving of time and effort for the different user groups. This paper describes a framework for evaluating mobile applications for health education, including a guidance tool to help different stakeholders select the one most suitable for them. The framework is intended to meet the needs and requirements of the different user categories, as well as improving the development of MHEAs through software engineering approaches. A description of the evaluation framework is provided, with its efficient hybrid of selected heuristic evaluation (HE) and usability evaluation (UE) factors. Lastly, an account of the quantitative and qualitative results for the framework applied to the Medscape and other mobile apps is given. This proposed framework – an Evaluation Framework for Mobile Health Education Apps – consists of a hybrid of five metrics selected from a larger set during heuristic and usability evaluation, the choice being based on interviews with patients, software developers and health professionals.

Keywords: Heuristic evaluation · Usability evaluation · Evaluation framework · Stakeholders · Metrics

1 Introduction

Development of a wide range of applications has been enabled as a consequence of enhancements in mobile technology which can be utilized in numerous aspects of people's lives [1]. One example of these applications is mobile health education applications (MHEAs). These education applications have been utilized to improve the knowledge of different stakeholders, such as patients and health professionals, in addition to improving health [2, 3]. Patients need to develop their own health education to ensure corresponding improvement in their health, with support for their well-being coming through the use of MHEAs. Advances in mobile technology have led to significant growth in the number of mobile health (mHealth) applications and their use

© Springer International Publishing AG 2017
P. Zaphiris and A. Ioannou (Eds.): LCT 2017, Part II, LNCS 10296, pp. 330–340, 2017.
DOI: 10.1007/978-3-319-58515-4_26

by stakeholders. Concern from both the software development and health communities has been shown as an outcome of this technology revolution. In 2009, 800 people were involved in the inaugural mHealth Summit, a partnership between the National Institutes of Health, the Foundation for the National Institutes of Health, and the mHealth Alliance. One year later, the number of people joining the conference was extended to triple that figure [4], which is indicative of a significant growth in interest over a very short period of time.

Training and learning in health matters are increasingly significant issues, particularly as more people are living longer; this longevity increases the scale and complexity of the maintenance of health and well-being [5]. Health education reflects several areas, for instance learning how to manage health requirements without barriers, how to manage life in an acceptable way and how to receive appropriate treatment [6]. These requirements from the patients' side parallel those of the health professionals, who seek to update their medical knowledge and are looking for particular information. According to Istepanian and Lacal [7], "M-health was defined as wireless telemedicine involving the use of mobile telecommunications and multimedia technologies and their integration with mobile healthcare delivery systems". The small size of mobile phone devices leads, however, to various restrictions, such as limitations on resource storage and battery life, along with a limited screen size and available interface, which diminish the user experience and the quality of the service [8].

A recent study by the National Health Service (NHS) has noted that mobile health apps can create risks equivalent to the mechanical failure of supplementary medical devices, such as mechanical failure, poor manufacturing quality, faulty design, and user error, among other safety issues [9]. The main consequence of these faults is that many software developers of MHEAs do not utilize an appropriately particular framework/model in the evaluation of the usability of their apps to ensure that they meet certain requirements, such as health education for health professionals and patients. This highlights the significance of the lack of a framework to evaluate these apps to ensure they meet the requirements of the different stakeholders [2, 3]. The importance of using heuristic evaluation has been shown by the authors of recent work [10, 11].

2 Why Mobile Health Education Apps are Important

Mobile phone software is one of the central development areas in current computing [12]. According to Hernandez Munoz and Woolley [13], mobile phones are now common and essential devices for the general population, which shows that many people depend on them for a wide range of aspects of their daily lives, such as commerce, health education and transportation. People utilize mobile phones as flexible substitutes for desktop computers in order to meet their needs [14]. Through mobile phones, users can now access a wide range of types of information from anywhere, at any time [15].

There are two types of mobile phone device: one is the classic type, which contains two parts: a keyboard with a display screen above; the other has a touchscreen, and is split into either a half touchscreen controller above half a keyboard or a full touchscreen controller. The first touchscreen mobile phone was the Simon Personal Communicator, developed by IBM in 1992, although the first smart mobile phone on the market was the Ericsson R380, released in 2000 [16]. Moreover, seven years later, Apple released the iPhone. The iPhone was the first smartphone controlled predominantly by its touchscreen [16]. The Android operating system was released onto the market for touchscreen mobile phones one year later [16]. According to Leonardi et al. [17], a touchscreen set-up is a flexible and easy-to-utilize interface for novice users, better than a mouse set-up and keyboard, thus increasing the dependence on mobile phones. Moreover, recent research shows that one in every five people in the world uses a smartphone [18]. Recent estimates are that about 497 million mobile phones were in use in 2014 and that smart devices represented 26% of these [19]. This reflects the growing use of mobile phone devices, showing a vast intensification of the potential for having more applications installed and utilized. This highlights the importance of being able to rank and distinguish the useful apps from the not so useful.

3   Selected Usability Metrics for the Framework

A hybrid selection of metrics taken from heuristic evaluation (HE) and usability evaluation (UE) metrics was initially proposed and filtered by conducting 15 selected interviews with health professionals (HP), software developers (SD) and patients (P). With an initial selection of likely metrics, analysis of the data from the 15 interviews demonstrated the need to modify some of the metrics which had been selected, as these did not fully match the user requirements identified by the interviewees. The 15 interviews with health professionals, software developers and patients also reflected that some of the proposed hybrid metrics selected from HE and UE were not essential to their requirements, although some of the metrics needed to be complementary to our proposed hybrid selection. Furthermore, we systematized and categorized our hybrid selection of HE and UE metrics as: (A) Memorability, (B) Features, (C) Attractiveness, (D) Simplicity (containing learnability) and (E) Accuracy. The definitions of these metrics are illustrated in Fig. 1 [3].

4   Motivation for Constructing a Framework

We now consider the need to construct a framework for mobile health education apps. Firstly, in recent decades, several researchers have created UE metrics for general systems, although the principal part were by and large for web applications, not mobile applications, and not specifically for MHEAs [20, 21]. Secondly, usability is an increasingly important area of development for smartphones, as it is vital to avoid some of the problems mentioned in Sect. 2 and elsewhere [22]. Thirdly, as highlighted by

Constantinos and Kim [23], there is a lack of empirical research into the impact of the environment on mobile usability and the importance of user characteristics as a central point. They also specify in their paper that there has been no subjective research on the usability possibilities considered in such mobile studies [23]. This illustrates the lack of a structured approach to ranking, enhancing and measuring the usability of mobile applications in general, and mHealth education applications specifically. Fourthly, and most significantly, according to Constantinos and Kim [23], there is no suitable usability evaluation framework in the context of this type of mobile computing environment. This shows the need for our research, which includes building an evaluation framework for MHEAs. Moreover, as sales grow rapidly (by 10% during 2012/2013 [24]), this has seen the development and use of mHealth applications rising markedly since 2013: over 36% of all mHealth applications in 2014 had been released the previous year [25]. According to Dubey et al. [26], usability investigations benefit from a variety of methods, such as interviews, logging, and surveys. Finally, the number of mobile health apps is growing at a significant rate: more than doubling in the year between 2015 and 2016, by 57% to 259,000 apps [27].

5 Framework Design Stages

The framework passed through three design stages as the research progressed, as outlined in the following subsections.

5.1 First Design for the Framework

The initial design of our approach was in two parts: firstly, a data gathering exercise and analysis using a questionnaire, and then the development of a prototype system. We selected questionnaire questions from an analysis of possible metrics obtained from the literature: a selection of metrics creating a hybrid of heuristic evaluation and more general usability evaluation metrics. Figure 1 illustrates the first design for the framework [2].

As we progressed in this work, we found that the initial design was not going to provide an appropriate solution. The chosen hybrid selected metrics for using it in the questionnaire to measure the usability in MHEAs. These mobile health education apps already exist and are utilized regularly by different stakeholders. These different stakeholders use MHEAs for numerous aspects of their lives under the umbrella of health education. This highlighted the need to identify what the different stakeholders require, in order to be able to measure MHEAs. In order to address these requirements, we carried out a series of qualitative interviews to identify the different stakeholders' needs. This enabled us to design and finalize the hybrid of selected metrics depending on the requirements identified. This led to the second design for our evaluation framework.

5.2   Second Design for the Framework

The second design for our framework was an updated version of the first, and contained two parts from the first design: the questionnaire and the prototype. In addition, we considered the questionnaire questions developed from mapping between the different metrics that had been obtained from the literature from a hybrid of HE and more general UE metrics.

By conducting qualitative unstructured interviews with different stakeholders (HP, P and SD), we obtained an improved hybrid of five selected metrics: (A) Memorability, (B) Features, (C) Attractiveness, (D) Simplicity (containing learnability) and (E) Accuracy. Obtaining this accurate hybrid of selected metrics supported us in mapping between specific metrics and the actual questionnaire questions, the intention being to enable us to assess usability issues for MHEAs accurately. Moreover, these questions were designed for two outcomes: firstly, the ranking of existing MHEAs; secondly, as an aid to designing a prototype. Figure 2 presents the second design for the evaluation framework [3].

The above was then modified for the third design, as we aim to develop a tool to aid in selecting the most suitable mHealth apps for a given user. This is explained further in the next subsection.

5.3   Third Design for the Framework

The third design encompasses the first and second designs outlined above, changing the last part of the framework to a tool to guide the selection of mHealth apps based on usability criteria. This design reflects the first two experiments we conducted in our framework: firstly, unstructured interviews with different stakeholders (HP, P and SD), which led to obtaining a hybrid of selected metrics to meet their requirements; secondly, the questionnaire, which was based on mapping between the outcomes of the unstructured interviews and the questionnaire topics.

For the third design for the evaluation framework, the aims from the questionnaire were slightly modified to ranking existing MHEAs, along with the development of a tool to help different stakeholders choose between various MHEAs according to their needs. The selection tool is based on data from the analysis of the feedback to the questionnaire.

The third design for the evaluation framework is shown in Fig. 1.

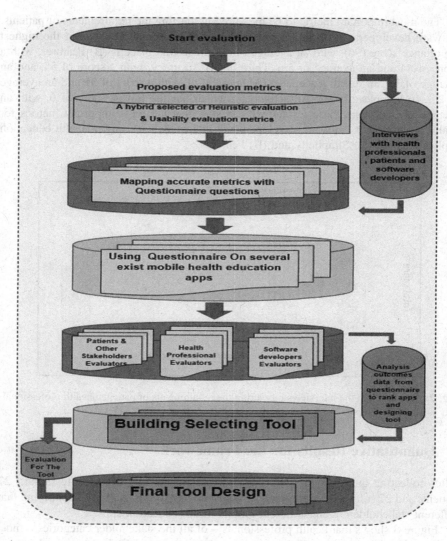

Fig. 1. Third proposed framework design

6   Qualitative Results for the Framework

After collecting data from 15 interviews (five interviews with health professionals, five with patients and five with software developers), we analyzed the feedback from all three sets of interviewees to identify their most important requirements when using mHealth education applications. Our results are shown in Fig. 2 and detailed below.

The most important metric to be measured in meeting the requirements of patients, software developers and health professionals is (D) Simplicity, showing the highest importance score (96), with an average of 6.4. In second place is (B) Features, with a score of 84 and an average of 5.6. Third is (E) Accuracy, with a score of 55, and an average of 3.7. In fourth place is (A) Memorability, with a score of 35 and an average of 2.3. In last place is (C) Attractiveness, which has the lowest score of 6, with an average of 0.4. From these results, we can state that the most important metrics for health professionals, software developers and patients when using mHealth education applications are (D) Simplicity and (B) Features.

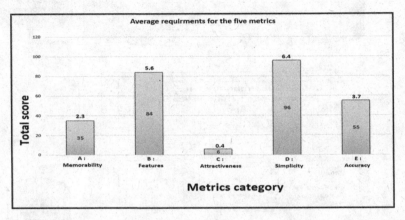

Fig. 2. Results from the interviews measuring the requirements of patients, health professionals and software developers

7 Quantitative Results for the Framework

After collecting questionnaire data from 81 participants (27 health professionals, 27 patients and 27 software developers), we analyzed the overall feedback, identifying that different stakeholders prefer different mobile health education apps.

Figure 3 shows that health professionals – of all the stakeholder categories – most prefer using Medscape, with average requirements of 4.1. In second place are patients/the general public with average requirements of 4. Last are software developers, with average requirements of 3.9. Moreover, there is no statistically significant difference within the group of professionals with Medscape, as the p-value in the statistical analysis is not less than 0.05.

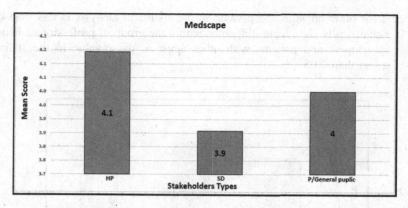

Fig. 3. Questionnaire results from measuring the requirements of patients, health professionals and software developers from Medscape

Figure 4 shows that patients/the general public most prefer using Epocrates, with average requirements of 4.5. In second place are health professionals, with average requirements of 3.3. Last are software developers, with average requirements of 3. Moreover, there is a statistically significant difference within the group of professionals between health professionals and patients with Epocrates, as the p-value in the statistical analysis is less than 0.05. There is a statistically significant difference within the group of professionals between software developers and patients with Epocrates, as the p-value in the statistical analysis is less than 0.05.

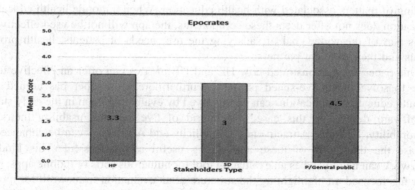

Fig. 4. Questionnaire results from measuring the requirements of patients, health professionals and software developers from Epocrates

Figure 5 shows that software developers most prefer other apps, such as WebMD and UpToDate, with average requirements of 4.5. In second place are health professionals, with average requirements of 3.7, and in last place are patients/the general public, with average requirements of 3.1. Moreover, there is a statistically significant difference within the group of professionals between health professionals and software developers for other apps, as the p-value in the statistical analysis is less than 0.05. There is a statistically significant difference within the group of professionals between software developers and patients with other apps, as the p-value in the statistical analysis is less than 0.05.

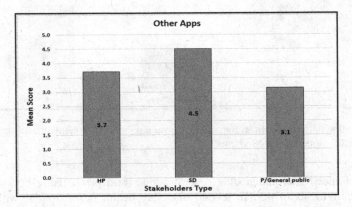

Fig. 5. Questionnaire results from measuring the requirements of patients, health professionals and software developers from other apps

8 Conclusion

mHealth education applications are utilized by a number of stakeholders for several critical reasons, which include saving effort and time, and simplifying their understanding of matters associated with health education. When a mobile health education application does not offer users these components, the app will not be used effectively; this is part of the wider goal of satisfying the user needs of patients, health professionals and their different partners.

This paper has demonstrated how HE and UE metrics can offer an effective technique to solve the above-stated problem. Furthermore, this paper has argued that mHealth education applications can be improved by evaluating them in the early stages of software design. In this case, our hybrid of five selected usability metrics - Memorability, Features, Attractiveness, Simplicity and Accuracy - can be enhanced to increase the likelihood of these apps being useful and successful. This kind of framework can be utilized as an evaluation tool for numerous sorts of mobile apps. This paper has focused on highlighting the structure of an evaluation framework for mobile health education applications that depends on a hybrid selection of metrics (HE and UE) and combines five metrics selected from a larger set of heuristic and usability evaluation factors, sifting them based on interviews with patients, health professionals and software developers. These five metrics correspond to specific aspects of usability acknowledged during a requirements analysis of typical users of mHealth apps. These five metrics were decomposed into 24 specific questionnaire questions. The aims of this project are to construct a set of tools for the evaluation of mHealth apps to enable them to be ranked, and thereby assist different stakeholders (such as health professionals, patients and others) to select apps that are suitable for them. Furthermore, our Evaluation Framework for Mobile Health Education Apps is proposed to offer guidance on system specifications and different user requirements for the software developers of mHealth apps.

References

1. Harrison, R., Flood, D., Duce, D.: Usability of mobile applications: literature review and rationale for a new usability model. J. Interact. Sci. **1**, 1–16 (2013)
2. Aljaber, T., Gordon, N., Kambhampati, C., Brayshaw, M.: An evaluation framework for mobile health education software. In: 2015 Science and Information Conference (SAI), pp. 786–790. IEEE, London (2015). doi:10.1109/SAI.2015.7237233
3. Aljaber, T., Gordon, N.A.: Evaluation of mobile health education applications for health professionals and patients. In: 8th International Conference on e-Health (EH 2016), pp. 107–114. IDIAS, Funchal (2016)
4. Qiang, C.Z., Yamamichi, M., Hausman, V., Altman, D.: Mobile Applications for the Health Sector. Technical report (2011)
5. Shareef, A.F.: Special issue on 'innovation in distance learning technologies in developing countries'. J. Learn. Technol. Newsl. **8**, 1–27 (2006)
6. Glanz, K., Rimer Barbara, K., Viswanath, K.: Health Behavior and Health Education: Theory, Research, and Practice. Jossey-Bass Wiley, San Francisco (2008)
7. Istepanian', R.S.H., Lacal', J.C.: Emerging mobile communication technologies for health: some imperative notes on m-health. In: 25th Annual International Conference of the IEEE EMBS, pp. 1414–1416. IEEE, Cancun (2003)
8. Silva, B.M.C., Rodrigues, J.J.P.C., Lopes, I.M.C., Machado, T.M.F., Zhou, L.: A novel cooperation strategy for mobile health applications. IEEE J. Sel. Areas Commun. **31**, 28–36 (2013)
9. Healthcare Applications: App Development: An NHS Guide for Developing Mobile NHS Innovations South East. Technical report (2014)
10. Gordon, N., Brayshaw, M., Aljaber, T.: Heuristic evaluation for serious immersive games and m-instruction. In: Zaphiris, P., Ioannou, A. (eds.) LCT 2016. LNCS, vol. 9753, pp. 310–319. Springer, Cham (2016). doi:10.1007/978-3-319-39483-1_29
11. Brayshaw, M., Gordon, N., Nganji, J., Wen, L., Butterfield, A.: Investigating heuristic evaluation as a methodology for evaluating pedagogical software: an analysis employing three case studies. In: Zaphiris, P., Ioannou, A. (eds.) LCT 2014. LNCS, vol. 8523, pp. 25–35. Springer, Cham (2014). doi:10.1007/978-3-319-07482-5_3
12. Zemliansky, P., St. Amant, K.: Handbook of Research on User Interface Design and Evaluation for Mobile Technology. Information Science Reference, New York (2008)
13. Hernandez Munoz, L.U., Woolley, S.I.: A user-centered mobile health device to manage life-threatening anaphylactic allergies and provide support in allergic reactions. In: 9th International Conference on Information Technology and Applications in Biomedicine (ITAB), pp. 1–4. IEEE, Larnaca (2009)
14. John, T.: Mobile Learning: Transforming the Delivery of Education and Training. Technical report, Edmonton (2009)
15. Ally, M.: Mobile Learning: Transforming the Delivery of Education and Training. Technical report, Edmonton (2009)
16. Lobo, D., Kaskaloglu, K., Kim, C., Herbert, S.: Web usability guidelines for smartphones: a synergic approach. Int. J. Inf. Electron. Eng. **1**, 33–37 (2011)

17. Leonardi, C., Albertini, A., Pianesi, F., Zancanaro, M.: An exploratory study of a touch-based gestural interface for elderly. In: 6th Nordic Conference on Human-Computer Interaction Extending Boundaries (NordiCHI 2010), pp. 845–850. ACM Press, New York (2010)

18. Heggestuen, J.: One in Every 5 People in the World Own a Smartphone, One in Every 17 Own a Tablet. http://www.businessinsider.com/smartphone-and-tablet-penetration-2013-10? IR=T

19. CISCO: Cisco Visual Networking Index: Global Mobile Data Traffic Forecast Update 2014–2019 White Paper. https://ec.europa.eu/futurium/en/content/cisco-visual-networking-index-global-mobile-data-traffic-forecast-update-2014-2019-white

20. Alva, M.E.O., Martínez P., A.B., Cueva L., J.M., Hernán Sagástegui Ch., T., López P., B.: Comparison of methods and existing tools for the measurement of usability in the web. In: Lovelle, J.M.C., Rodríguez, B.M.G., Gayo, J.E.L., Puerto Paule Ruiz, M., Aguilar, L.J. (eds.) ICWE 2003. LNCS, vol. 2722, pp. 386–389. Springer, Heidelberg (2003). doi:10.1007/3-540-45068-8_70

21. Ivory, M.Y., Hearst, M.A.: The state of the art in automating usability evaluation of user interfaces. J. ACM Comput. Surv. 33, 470–516 (2001)

22. Baharuddin, R., Singh, D., Razali, R.: Usability dimensions for mobile applications-a review. Res. J. Appl. Sci. Eng. Technol. 5, 2225–2231 (2013)

23. Coursaris, C.K., Kim, D.J.: A meta-analytical review of empirical mobile usability studies. J. Usability Stud. 6, 117–171 (2011)

24. Smith, A.: Smartphone Ownership – 2013 Update. Technical report, Washington (2013)

25. research2guidance 2014: mHealth App Developer Economics 2014. Technical report, Berlin (2014)

26. Kumar Dubey, S., Rana, A.: Analytical comparison of usability measurement method. Int. J. Comput. Appl. 39, 11–18 (2012)

27. research2guidance 2016: mHealth App Developer Economics 2016. Technical report, Berlin (2016)

Collaborative Hybrid Agent Provision of Learner Needs Using Ontology Based Semantic Technology

Mike Brayshaw[1](✉), Julius Nganji[2], and Neil Gordon[1]

[1] School of Engineering and Computer Science,
University of Hull, Hull HU6 7RX, UK
{m.brayshaw,n.a.gordon}@hull.ac.uk
[2] Information Technology, University of Ottawa,
1 Nicholas Street, Ottawa, ON K1N 7B7, Canada
jtanyung@uottawa.ca

Abstract. This paper describes the use of Intelligent Agents and Ontologies to implement knowledge navigation and learner choice when interacting with complex information locations. The paper is in two parts: the first looks at how Agent Based Semantic Technology can be used to give users a more personalised experience as an individual. The paper then looks to generalise this technology to allow users to work with agents in hybrid group scenarios. In the context of University Learners, the paper outlines how we employ an Ontology of Student Characteristics to personalise information retrieval specifically suited to an individual's needs. Choice is not a simple *"show me your hand and make me a match"* but a deliberative artificial intelligence (AI) that uses an ontologically informed agent society to consider the weighted solution paths before choosing the appropriate best. The aim is to enrich the student experience and significantly re-route the student's journey. The paper uses knowledge-level interoperation of agents to personalise the learning space of students and deliver to them the information and knowledge to suite them best. The aim is to personalise their learning in the presentation/format that is most appropriate for their needs. The paper then generalises this Semantic Technology Framework using shared vocabulary libraries that enable individuals to work in groups with other agents, which might be other people or actually be AIs. The task they undertake is a formal assessment but the interaction mode is one of informal collaboration. Pedagogically this addresses issues of ensuring fairness between students since we can ensure each has the same experience (as provided by the same set of Agents) as each other and an individual mark may be gained. This is achieved by forming a hybrid group of learner and AI Software Agents. Different agent architectures are discussed and a worked example presented. The work here thus aims at fulfilling the student's needs both in the context of matching their needs but also in allowing them to work in an Agent Based Synthetic Group. This in turn opens us new areas of potential collaborative technology.

Keywords: Collaborative technology · Serious games · M-Learning

© Springer International Publishing AG 2017
P. Zaphiris and A. Ioannou (Eds.): LCT 2017, Part II, LNCS 10296, pp. 341–351, 2017.
DOI: 10.1007/978-3-319-58515-4_27

1 Introduction

Universities can be thought of as huge information spaces and indeed one of the problems with things like embarking on the student voyage (e.g. Fresher's Week) is the amount of information the traveller has to deal with. All users face some aspect of this problem. In this paper we will deal with how we can personalise this choice mechanism. The first part of the paper represents a generalisation of work on personalisation for special needs [1–6] to employ an Ontology-Based Community of Agents for Personalisation of Services for students in general. The second part looks at how we can use same mechanisms to personalise group project undertakings and assessment. What this paper brings out to the fore is the AI Agent Based Deliberation mechanisms that underpin this retrieval and presentation process. The central aim of this work is to deliver a personalised service to students. One that works for individual needs but is flexible for individual desires.

The problem with the amount of information available to students is the classic "woods for the trees" dilemma. Potentially there is too much information out there – what we have to do is find the information that is needed and weed out the flotsam and jetsam of the sea of information. One way to do this is to offer better ways of personalising this information space so that users see only what is best suited to their needs, desires, and profile. In order to do this we can use AI as an editorial underpinning. Semantic Technology allows us to organise information in a smart way. At the heart of semantic technology is ontology based knowledge representation, and to utilise this we require a representation at a knowledge level [7]. However, merely representing your information in the right way is not enough - we need ways of operationalising this information. Then we can use a small society of agents to rationally operate and reason about this information. This paper will demonstrate how this can be achieved and give an example of it in use.

In the second half of this paper we will discuss how the above can be taken forward to achieve hybrid group working. We will discuss some of the important design issues and how we can bring this together into a proposed architecture that would allow mixed group working within the context of the formal academic assessment.

2 Knowledge Navigation

Clearly one thing that computers are good at is crunching data. The data/information versus knowledge/wisdom debate is played out elsewhere (e.g. [8]). Semantic Technology represents a new viewpoint for this discourse and focuses on a higher level of dialog of interface between users and technology. In this section we will discuss some knowledge ordering principles before going on to discuss technical solutions in the following sections. We consider in turn semantic knowledge representation, AI and Agency, and Individual perspectives of knowledge.

2.1   Semantic Knowledge Representation

The centre of this approach is the representation and use of knowledge and meaning. Into this we introduce the concept of knowledge engineering as a method of structuring and ordering this material. Ontologies provide ways of ordering, structuring, and storing knowledge. For knowledge engineers, they can then be used to drive problem solving. This historic approach naturally evolves into Semantic Technologies. The specific problem solving that we are concerned with here is how to customise and personalise information and services for general learner needs within a Domain Specific university context and the Ontologies developed reflect this.

2.2   Agency and AI

Having the knowledge is not enough; we need to do something with it. Agents (e.g. see [9]) provide autonomous ways to architect our AI that allows us to consider different aspects to our domain. What is actually an agent has a wide definition running from simple reflex devices as seen in animals and modellable by Finite State Machines, through to full cognitive architectures that can be an agency like the SOAR implemented in the QuakeBot [10, 11]. In the work presented here they are used both as architectural, structuring, elements in their own right and to provide beacons for knowledge navigation. They can thus be used both as order making devices within the semantic technology itself and also reflect important dialog players within a group context. In this way they have a dramatic effect on the team dynamics in the manor of playing a character – similar to Laird's use of agents above.

2.3   Personalisation and the Learning Space

In the context of providing an environment for learning, the enhancements that technology allow lie in the flexibility it can provide. Such flexibility can be in terms of the where, when and what of learning (see [12]). Computer based learning environments – whether a traditional virtual learning environment (VLE), or a fully immersive simulation of a learning space – can offer flexible and adaptive support for learning and assessment, from selecting and providing tailored content through to adaptive tasks and tests that respond to the apparent skills and capacity of the student user [13]. With flexibility comes the opportunity for the user to personalise. They may want to do this as a navigational device to deal with large volumes of data. This might involve varying the level of detail of view, compressing information, abstracting information or defining their own visualisations of the large domain data [14]. Brayshaw [15] extended this so that agents could be used as a basis for constructing customised views of a large search space which was the trace of a parallel program. At other times their need for personalisation may be driven by specific preferences to reflect taste. Other students may have specific needs like a disability (or disabilities) and need to tailor their services accordingly (e.g. [5]).

3   Using Ontologies and Agents to Personalise an Individual Student's Experience

On the web – given the vast array of information - users are more likely to interact with information that is personally tailored to their needs rather than general information that may not be of interest to them. Similarly, when learning online and searching information, time might be of the essence, especially when learners are trying to meet certain deadlines. Hence, in the e-learning domain, learners will benefit from personalised services as it will save time and will also be particularly helpful for learners with disabilities. In order to accomplish personalisation, some vital considerations include focusing on the following as depicted in Fig. 1, with the following components.

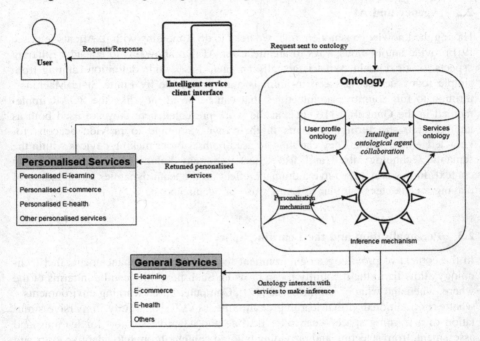

Fig. 1. Using ontologies and agents to personalise services for a single user.

3.1   Users

The users have various characteristics and needs. They could be users with special needs due to a disability, or they could have other needs brought about by their age or to represent learning styles. For users with disability, special accessibility considerations need to be made to ensure that they are fully included [16]. However, given that an ontology captures their needs, the method herein ensures that their needs are adequately met. In the e-learning domain, learners have specific goals which could be readily achieved by capturing their needs and preferences. When ontological design and development captures these needs and accurately represent the learner, it would facilitate personalisation of learning.

3.2   Client Interface

The users first interact with the ontology through an intelligent service interface through which they can manipulate the ontology such as directly making changes to it through updating or deleting information which is held about them. Indirectly, more information could be collected in the ontology based on user behaviour such as their interests over time which could also be inferred from their browsing patterns. If a disability-aware e-learning system for instance intelligently produces accessible formats of learning materials but the client interface is inaccessible, this could prevent most users with disabilities from accessing the content. Thus the client interface needs to also meet accessibility and usability standards in order to better respond to the needs of the user.

3.3   Ontologies

The semantic web offers a fantastic opportunity for collaborative provision of learner needs due to its ability to provide information to users in a meaningful way. The Web Ontology Language (OWL) can be used to produce ontologies that will capture vital information needed for provision of service. This information is collected about the users which includes their needs and preferences and the services that are available, which due to the explosion of information in this information age, is very vast; personalised services can be offered based on this information. Thus, a user profile ontology could be created to capture vital information about the user which could be updated as the user characteristics change probably due to age, an improvement in their situations (for those with disabilities) or a degeneration of their situation (such as acquiring other disabilities and thus having multiple disabilities; for those with disabilities).

An Agent based inference mechanism ensures that both the user and their requests are checked against existing services and the ontology to determine their existing needs and preferences and then transform the information into formats that meet the needs of the user. For a student who is completely blind for instance, audio and/or text-based formats of learning materials could be generated and presented to the learner.

3.4   Services

Users may need access to various services, again using an agent based model, which need to be personalised. Such services for instance could be e-learning, m-learning, e-commerce, etc. Due to the fact that most designers and developers of such services usually develop them without considering the needs of people with disabilities, some of these services might not be fully accessible to some users (such as those with disabilities). A learner for instance might want personalised course information from an e-learning service or personalised health information from an e-health service.

4   A Framework for Working in Hybrid Groups

We now demonstrate how to use agents and the technology described in Sect. 3 to personalise an individual's learning experience in a group working context. Learning can be a lonely experience, if it always has to be done in isolation. Working in groups has a long established didactic standing (e.g. [17]). There are some very pragmatic reasons motivating working in groups:

- We wish to simulate work as they will experience it when they leave education. For example, in Computer Science to prepare for working in a team of software developers.
- In such a team one person is not going to be able to write the whole of an app so team working is an inherent part of the process.
- Specialised expertise exists so groups can be more powerful than individuals.
- The power and importance of peer support and the encouragement that this may bring.

However working in groups has its downside for example:

- It is unfair when people get a very bad group and end up having to do all the work.
- It is unfair when people get a very good group and poor colleagues are carried by the collecting momentum.

Working in a group can be harder than working solo. There are personality issues, ego, politics, fallouts, relationships, and group dynamics going on. If you are very technically competent it can be very frustrating working in a mixed ability group. The eventual mark a student gets may not reflect their individual efforts or ability, or indeed their ability to work in a group, but may be the product of a particular social adventure. There are approaches to manage this scenario: with peer assessment of team work [18]. However, the motivation for the work reported here is to investigate how we could enrich the benefits of group working, by providing homogeneous groups that are all similar, allowing the candidate to interact, thus enabling the derivation of an individual mark. To interact like this we need other agents within the group. When we interact on the internet (e.g. via Facebook or Twitter) the assumption is that the agents we are talking to are other people – although this is an assumption that with the growth of Chatbots is not always the case. Here we will argue that if the degrees of freedom in the dialog is relatively constrained – say within the context of a technical design task or evaluation – then we can use software agents, and the same semantic technology as before, to participate in this process.

To achieve this we are going to turn to AI, and need to select an AI to use. For the purposes here we can take a liberal definition and define AI as anything that passes the Turing Test [19]. To be a partner in a group exercise one has to fulfil the role of a group member. Now the actual roles of these members may differ (e.g. [20]), so that the type of AI we might need to functionally implement may differ [21]. Considering a functional definition of AI from the Games context, it may vary from Finite State Machines approach to a full utilitarian AI (e.g. [22]). In the context of Game AI, as a minimum we require an interaction with a non-playing character (NPC) that is plausible and can convey the necessary narrative of the game. To do this it is not always necessary to have a full Knowledge based AI and we can instead utilise a look up table or Finite State Machine approach. This is how many chat bots or vreps actually work; they are not a fully functioning AI but are based on an Eliza like application [23]. Indeed, many of the chat bots that compete for the annual Loebner Prize [24] fall into this ilk. At other times a fully functional and reasoned AI is called for. Thus in this model, AI can be thought of as constituting a range of functionalities, depending on context, as illustrated in Fig. 2.

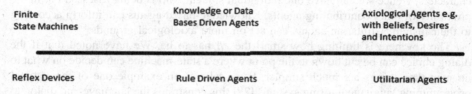

Finite State Machines	Knowledge or Data Bases Driven Agents	Axiological Agents e.g. with Beliefs, Desires and Intentions
Reflex Devices	Rule Driven Agents	Utilitarian Agents

Fig. 2. A range of agent based architectures

Here we adopt a black-box approach to the implementation of the AI and are concerned only how it resolves the function in the group. We propose three basic Agent Building Blocks. Reflex Devices are implemented as state machines. These are state agents and a state definition language is provided for them. Knowledge Agents have their own inference engine that provides forward and backward chaining productions, object-like permanent memory, truth maintenance, and uncertain reasoning systems. Axiological agents rather than just applying rules to a situation aim to reflect on the value of an action to an agent and purposely choose what to do next based on that judgement. This type of reflection is important in group dynamics.

4.1   Degrees of Freedom in Dialogs

So what are the reasons for a distinction between the types of agents required? Critical to this is the degree of freedom in the dialog. If the dialog itself is well constrained e.g. of a technical nature, then there are limited degrees of freedom about what can be asked and what responses a rationale correspondent can make. For example if we are in the context of configuration design there are a limited set of design choices that are available to the designer, the configurations, and the dialog is essentially one of enumerating these choices [25]. If we are in the context of teaching how to build a PC or design a local network we can start the dialog from a clear fixed point – for example from some requirements capture exercise which may be as basic as a questionnaire or hypertext dialog (which is another interface to the FSM mechanism above). Once we have our initial starting point then we can map out our dialog from here. This can be represented as essentially a decision tree and implemented as simple state machines.

However if we want a more intelligent collaboration then we need to consider our choice points in the dialog construction. To this end we propose two methods of doing this. One is essentially using a rule based system. For each choice point in the dialog a knowledge based inference can decide what to do next. The second method is a Utilitarian Agent mechanism. Each Software Agent can have their own agenda. In this manner from a pedagogical perspective they can be engineered to follow a particular role in the group ([26]). More specifically an agent can have characteristic beliefs, desire, and intentions that inform any particular dialog choice point. Equipping an agent with their desire and beliefs allows them to take their own attitudinal stance to dialog. We thus propose to enable agents to become character agents.

How does this affect working in groups? The above allows us to potentially construct hybrid groups of people and agents. It allows us to invest groups with particular characters. Hence we can have one individual student who is being assessed but in the proximity of other contributing agents. Knowledge-based agents can inform according to their insight. Utilitarian agents can act on more axiological grounds.

The key here is limiting how smart the AI has to be. We have noted that if the dialog choice can be cut down to the point where a state-machine can decide on what to do next then things are much simpler. If we take as an example one of the seminal programming language tutoring systems [27] this constrains the language and dialog to the core. A clear task was defined – to write a LISP program – but the names of all the functions and variables were prescribed by a fixed vocabulary. Whilst this at first sounds like a limiting constraint it places the task within the confines of current AI. Sacrificing vocabulary is a trade-off for greater interaction with AIs.

4.2 An Example

Let us take an example task. Say we are teaching an undergraduate HCI course. The assignment that we wish to set is a group project on Heuristic Evaluation where we wish to place our students in a group with a technical expert/specialist, a management expert, an implementer, and a developer. In the simplest form the student works through a dialog with each of their co-workers. The dialog can result in either a state transition based output or an inference based one. The output is an expert response to a final report. Based on their deliverables the student then has to edit their outputs into a coherent final report. The student thus has to reflect, synthesize, and enhance the contributions of their fellow workers. What they have to work on reflects on how they have interacted and worked with their fellow group workers. Furthermore their final deliverable is the sum of their interaction and their own contribution in the process of the group work. In this way we can give individual marks based on common groups. What each student had to work with is a common base. What they end up with is as a result of their interaction with common experts and their cut and interpretation of the group's interaction.

5 Conclusions and Future Work

In the work presented here we have discussed how we can use Agents and Semantic Technology to personalise individual student services. Secondly using the same approach we have shown a brief introduction to automating group assignments and assessment. With current trends in *ubicomp* [28] and the development of the MOOCs movement (e.g. EdX [29], Coursera [30], Canvas [31], or FutureLearn [32]), and criticisms thereof [33], how we deal with large numbers of students within a single cohort becomes a big issue. It is clearly desirable to give individual feedback where possible. At the same time we need to educate and prepare our students for the real world. Developing true scale software deliverables involves many person years of development effort. As such they will need to work in groups in order to achieve the above. As educationalists we therefore need to provide training for this type of working. However there is always frustration with group working in that we know individuals can carry a group and that the final mark derived may not always reflect an individual's contribution. By providing a common surface we here aim to let a single user interact with other agents and they together produce a group output. That we provide the same surface to multiple users means that an individual mark may be derived. In this paper the task has been heavily constrained and the degrees of freedom of dialog restricted. This is a realistic constraint within many educational contexts. For example if we wish to teach someone how to build a jet engine then there is a limit to the degrees of freedom in the task. Components fit in a certain way – there is a set way of engineering the task. In software engineering there are clearly more options although we may wish to steer our students in certain ways. Thus the choice of dialog options may be larger.

Where the degrees of freedom in dialog are limited then simple agents can meet our needs. A Finite-State Machine may resolve the issue. However if more reflection is required we provide a full knowledge based inference system and a utilitarian agent package.

Where we are going with this work is to address more discursive domains where the constraints on task are not so limited. Part of this wider range of functionalities could be to implement other characters e.g. the full range Belbin [24] proposed is Team Roles. Thus we could personalise the agent group further to give our learners scenarios that reflect on specific group make ups.

A Semantic Approach cannot only change the content of learning packages but can also change the culture of learning. The chalk and talk of a traditional lecture theatre centred campus is not going to satisfy an increasingly sophisticated clientele who are used to a rich media online world. Users interact with media in a flexible way and to be relevant in the future we have to change the gestalt of learning and the university experience. We can only do that by looking for a root and branch change to the user experience. What we have looked at here is how to use AI and Semantic Technologies to start to make this happen.

References

1. Nganji, J.T., Brayshaw, M.: Designing personalised learning resources for disabled students using an ontology-driven community of agents. In: Isaias, P., Nunes, M.B. (eds.) Information Systems Research and Exploring Social Artifacts: Approaches and Methodologies, Hershey, PA, USA, pp. 81–102. IGI Global (2013)
2. Nganji, J.T., Brayshaw, M., Tompsett, B.: Ontology-based e-learning personalisation for disabled students in higher education. ITALICS 10(1), 1–11 (2011)
3. Nganji, J.T., Brayshaw, M.: Towards an ontology-based community of agents for personalisation of services for disabled students. Presented at the IADIS Interfaces and Human Computer Interaction, Rome, Italy (2011)
4. Nganji, J.T., et al.: Describing and assessing image descriptions for visually impaired web users with IDAT. In: Proceeding of the Third International Conference on Intelligent Human Computer Interaction (IHCI 2011), vol. 179, pp. 27–37 (2013)
5. Nganji, J.T., Brayshaw, M., Tompsett, B.: Ontology-driven disability-aware e-learning personalisation with ONTODAPS. Campus-Wide Inf. Syst. 30(1), 17–34 (2013)
6. Nganji, J.T., Brayshaw, M.: Designing and reflecting on disability-aware e-learning systems: the case of ONTODAPS. In: 2014 14th IEEE International Conference on Advanced Learning Technologies (ICALT), pp. 571–575 (2014)
7. Newell, A.: The knowledge level. Artif. Intell. 18(1), 87–127 (1982)
8. Bellinger, G.: Systems thinking: knowledge management – emerging perspectives, 18 November 2004. http://www.systems-thinking.org/kmgmt/kmgmt.htm
9. Minsky, M.: The Society of Mind. Heninemann, London (1987)
10. Laird, J.E., Duchi, J.C.: Creating human-like synthetic characters with multiple skill levels: a case study using the SOAR Quakebot. Presented at the AAAI 2000 (2000)
11. Laird, J.E.: It knows what you're going to do: adding anticipation to a Quakebot. Presented at the AAAI 2000 Spring Symposium Series: Artificial Intelligence and Interactive Entertainment (2000)
12. Gordon, N.: Flexible pedagogies: technology-enhanced learning. In: Flexible Pedagogies: Preparing for the Future. The Higher Education Academy, York, United Kingdom (2014)
13. Gordon, N.: Enabling personalised learning through formative and summative assessment. In: Technology-Supported Environments for Personalized Learning: Methods and Case Studies, pp. 268–283. Information Science Publishing, Hershey (2009)
14. Brayshaw, M., Eisenstadt, M.: A practical graphical tracer for prolog (in English). Int. J. Man-Mach. Stud. Art. 35(5), 597–631 (1991)
15. Brayshaw, M.: A flexible and customisable program visualisation architecture. In: People and Computers, no. VIII. Cambridge University Press, Cambridge (1993)
16. Nganji, J.T.: The portable document format (PDF) accessibility practice of four journal publishers. Libr. Inf. Sci. Res. 35(3), 254–262 (2015)
17. Lewin, K.: Resolving Social Conflicts; Selected Papers on Group Dynamics. Harper & Row, New York (1948)
18. Gordon, N.A.: Group working and peer assessment—using WebPA to encourage student engagement and participation. Innov. Teach. Learn. Inf. Comput. Sci. 9(1), 20–31 (2010)
19. Turing, A.M.: Computing machinery and intelligence. Mind 59, 433–460 (1950)
20. Belbin, M.: Management Teams. Heinemann, London (1981)
21. Beranek, G., Zuser, W., Grechenig, T.: Functional group roles in software engineering teams. Presented at the HSSE 2005 Proceedings of the 2005 Workshop on Human and Social Factors of Software Engineering (2005)

22. Laird, J., Rosenbloom, P., Newell, A.: Chunking in soar: the anatomy of a general learning mechanism (in English). Mach. Learn. **1**(1), 11–46 (1986)
23. Weizenbaum, J.: ELIZA - a computer program for the study of natural language communication between man and machine. Commun. Assoc. Comput. Mach. **9**, 36–45 (1966)
24. The society for the study of artificial intelligence and simulation of behavior. In: The Loebner Prize, 10 February 2017. http://www.aisb.org.uk/events/loebner-prize
25. Watt, S., Zdrahal, Z., Brayshaw, M.: A multi-agent approach to configuration and design tasks. Presented at the Artificial Intelligence and Simulation of Behaviour Conference (1995)
26. Belbin, M.: Team Roles, 5 February 2017. http://www.belbin.com/about/belbin-team-roles
27. Anderson, J.R., Reiser, B.J.: The lisp tutor (in English). Byte Art. **10**(4), 159–160 (1985)
28. Weiser, M.: Some computer-science issues in ubiquitous computing. Commun. ACM **36**(7), 75–84 (1993)
29. EdX: EdX, 7 February 2017. https://www.edx.org
30. Coursera: Coursera, 7 February 2017. https://www.coursera.org
31. Canvas: Canvas Learning Management System, 1 September 2014. https://www.canvas.net/
32. FutureLearn: FutureLearn, 7 February 2017. https://www.futurelearn.com
33. Laurillard, D.: Five Myths about MOOCs, 16 January 2014. http://www.timeshigheredu cation.co.uk/comment/opinion/five-myths-about-moocs/2010480.article.   Accessed 9 February 2014

Improving Success/Completion Ratio in Large Surveys: A Proposal Based on Usability and Engagement

Juan Cruz-Benito[1]([✉]), Roberto Therón[1],
Francisco J. García-Peñalvo[1], José Carlos Sánchez-Prieto[1],
Andrea Vázquez-Ingelmo[1], Martín Martín-González[2],
and Jorge M. Martínez[2]

[1] GRIAL Research Group, Department of Computers
and Automatics, University of Salamanca, Salamanca, Spain
{juancb, theron, fgarcia, josecarlos.sp,
andreavazquez}@usal.es
[2] UNESCO Chair in University Management and Policy,
Technical University of Madrid, Madrid, Spain
{martin.martin, jorge.martinez}@upm.es

Abstract. This paper presents a research focused on improving the success/completion ratio in large surveys. In our case, the large survey is a questionnaire produced by the Spanish Observatory for University Employability and Employment (OEEU in the Spanish acronym). This questionnaire is composed by around 32 and 60 questions and between 86 and 181 variables to be measured. The research is based on the previous experience of a past questionnaire proposed by the OEEU composed also by a large amount of questions and variables to be measured (63–92 questions and 176–279 variables). After analyzing the target population of the questionnaire (with the target population of the previous questionnaire as reference) and reviewing the literature, we have designed 11 proposals for changes in the questionnaire that could improve users' completion and success ratios (changes that could improve the users' trust in the questionnaire, the questionnaire usability and user experience or the users' engagement to the questionnaire). These changes are planned to be applied in the questionnaire in two main different experiments based on A/B test methodologies that will allow researchers to measure the effect of the changes in different populations and in an incremental way. The proposed changes have been assessed by five experts through an evaluation questionnaire. In this questionnaire, researchers gathered the score of each expert regarding to the pertinence, relevance and clarity of each change proposed. Regarding the results of this evaluation questionnaire, the reviewers fully supported 8 out of the 11 changes proposals, so they could be introduced in the questionnaire with no variation. On the other hand, 3 of the proposed changes or improvements are not fully supported by the experts (they have not received a score in the top first quartile of the 1–7 Likert scale). These changes will not be discarded immediately, because despite they have not received a Q1 score, they received a score within the second quartile, so could be reviewed to be enhanced to fit the OEEU's context.

© Springer International Publishing AG 2017
P. Zaphiris and A. Ioannou (Eds.): LCT 2017, Part II, LNCS 10296, pp. 352–370, 2017.
DOI: 10.1007/978-3-319-58515-4_28

Keywords: Human-Computer Interaction · HCI · Online survey · Online questionnaire · Usability · User experience · Engagement · Trust · A/B test

1 Introduction

The collection of information by questionnaires and interviews is one of the most well-known and currently used methods to get users' opinions, both in the physical and digital environments.

It is common in many websites to have a form for entering information, either as a contact point, as part of the login for the system, as part of a payment process, etc. The forms are so integrated into the web user interaction, that their importance is relativized and it is assumed that the user will complete it by the mere fact that they are faced to them regularly. However, this is not so.

Indeed, the web forms pervasivity, in recent years have triggered certain trends and user behaviors towards such information entry tools. For example, it has been proven [1] the following regarding users' behavior towards forms:

- Users rely more on websites, even being more willing to perform complex actions (at all levels), such as purchases, payments, etc.
- They protect more their information, they are less willing to disclose personal information.
- They demand better products, are less tolerant to bad forms.

During the last years a lot of work has been carried out in relation to the questionnaires, establishing that users have some reluctance to complete a form from even before to begin filling it [1]. This poses certain problems regarding the achievement of information collection objectives intrinsic to any form.

Regarding the types of users who complete forms, different profiles can be set [1]:

1. Readers: Those who read the form carefully.
2. Rushers: These users rush in and begin completing fields, reading only when they think it is necessary.
3. Refusers: These users won't have anything to do with the form.

According to the literature, and intimately related to the Social Exchange Theory [2], some authors [1] distinguish three layers in the forms: relationship, conversation and appearance.

1. The relationship of a form is based on the relationship that who asks the questions has with whom responds.
2. The conversation of a form goes from the questions that are asked, to the instructions given or to the organization of the questions according to their topic.
3. The appearance of the form is the image it displays: placement of text, graphics, areas of data entry, color, etc.

Improving these factors, such as the relationship with the user, makes it easier for the user to participate and complete his task within the questionnaire.

This paper presents a research aimed at designing and validating different changes in the context of a very large questionnaire regarding users' trust, user experience, usability and engagement with the final goal of improving the users' completion/success ratios. These possible improvements are compared with another questionnaire previously developed for the same topics and context, by means of different methodologies and approaches. To present this research, the paper will have the following structure: Sect. 2 provides the needed context of the questionnaires and population study; Sect. 3 presents the research goals and experiments design; the fourth section comments on the proposed changes and improvements designed by the researchers; the fifth section presents the evaluation of the proposals carried out by experts. Finally, the sixth section presents the conclusions of the paper and outlines the future work to be done regarding this research.

2 Background: The Spanish Observatory for University Employability and Employment (OEEU)

During the months of June–July 2015, the Spanish Observatory for University Employability and Employment (OEEU) contacted several thousand Spanish university graduates (133588 individuals) through the universities (48, public and private institutions) where they got their degrees in the course 2009–2010 to invite them to fill out a questionnaire [3, 4].

This questionnaire had a common part with 60 questions and 167 variables measured, in addition to 3 specific itineraries depending on the users' previous responses. The first itinerary added 3 questions and 9 measured variables more. The second one, added 24 questions and 70 variables. Finally, the third itinerary added 32 more questions and 112 variables to the common part of the questionnaire.

Therefore, the questionnaire varies between 63–92 questions and 176–279 variables depending on the itinerary that the user follows. It can be stated without doubt that the questionnaire is very extensive.

The number of users who started the questionnaire was 13006 (9.74% of the total population), of which 9617 completed it (7.20% of the total population, 73.94% of the total started questionnaires).

The descriptive data regarding the age of the participants in the questionnaire were the following (the count of users is 12109 because the birthdate data was not mandatory and not all users filled it out):

```
count     12109.000000
mean         32.525972
std           7.018282
min          25.000000
25%          28.000000
50%          30.000000
75%          34.000000
max          80.000000
```

As for gender, 56.05% (7290) of the users who answered the questionnaire were women and 43.94% (5716) men. In relation to nationality, 98.54% (11672) of the users were Spanish and 1.46% (173) were foreigners.

About the users who dropped out of the questionnaire, the quartiles of the dropout rate based on the questionnaire screen where they left off were:

```
count     3389.000000
25%          4.000000
50%          5.000000
75%          7.000000
```

That is, 25% of the users left on screen 4 or before, another 25% left between screens 4 and 5 of the questionnaire, another 25% between screens 5 and 7 and another 25% between screen 7 and the end (depending on the itinerary).

Now, in 2017, a process of gathering information similar to the one carried out during 2015 will conducted again. In this case, the information to be collected is about graduates of masters studies that ended their studies during the 2013–2014 academic year. For this purpose, a questionnaire composed of between 32 and 60 questions and between 86 and 181 variables to be measured has been proposed (the questionnaire has again several itineraries depending on the user's answers). Without too much analysis in detail, it can be considered that despite the differences, it is a large questionnaire and shares some of the problems of the previous one in terms of difficulties or challenges that can appear during its completion by the users.

Before sending out the questionnaires to the students, the Observatory gathers some data about students from the participant universities. Currently, on February 2017, there are collected data from 28744 people coming from 32 public and private Spanish universities. About these former students, the Observatory have the following data:

Descriptive data regarding the age of the population to which the questionnaire will be addressed:

```
count    28744.000000
mean        35.854370
std         15.852381
min          5.000000
25%         28.000000
50%         31.000000
75%         38.000000
max        117.000000
```

Regarding the data about the age, obviously, the aging of the population with respect to the one of the previous questionnaire is noticed. This is normal taking into account that the required age to begin a master degree is higher than that required to access to a degree (at least on a regular basis).

Regarding the gender of the population to which the questionnaire will be addressed, 55.2% (16385) are women and 44.8% (13317) are men. In relation to nationality, this is the aspect in which the current population (graduates from master degree) is more differentiated from the study performed with degree graduates.

This time, the proportion of foreign students is greater, with 88.11% (25318) of Spanish students compared to 11.88% (3414) students with foreign nationality.

In general terms, it is possible to assume that populations (putting each of them in context) are not very different. In this sense, can be highlighted the main difference is in terms of nationality. This difference could lead to consider treating differently aspects of the questionnaire to adjust to possible cultural differences. In this case, there will be no cultural distinction when designing, presenting or performing the questionnaire. This could be considered a limitation of the study.

3   Research Goals and Experiments Proposal

3.1   Overall Research Goals

The main goals of the experiment that is being designed, and that will be presented below, are:

- Study how to improve the ratio participants actually starting the questionnaire (previously, close to 9.7% of the total population).
- Study how to improve the completion rate of the questionnaire (previously 73.94% completion rate).

In addition to these fundamental goals, another objective related to the second one can be proposed; namely, to grant that in case of dropout, users have completed all possible screens of the form (obtaining by this way more information even if they leave it).

3.2   Experiments Proposal

For the new version of the questionnaire, it is considered that several points can be improved compared to the questionnaire implemented in 2015 and to the ways of increasing users' participation.

To implement these improvements, it is proposed to carry out two experiments in parallel:

- A study on how to improve the invitation to graduates processes.
- A study on what improvements can be implemented in questionnaires to improve participation and completion ratios.

The key aspects of each of the studies will be discussed below, indicating the main changes to be implemented, etc.

Also, before implementing these changes to the questionnaires, in addition to being supported in part by the literature, they have been subject of experts validation through a questionnaire [5].

3.2.1   Study About How to Improve the Invitation Processes to Graduates

In the case of the questionnaires produced by the OEEU, it is necessary to consider a fundamental factor: the privacy of the user is a primary concern over above all else (among other reasons, due to sensitive data being handled). This project is respectful and complies to Spanish Personal Data Protection Act (LOPD), having registered the OEEU's database by the Spanish authorities to safeguard the data.

Due to the privacy restrictions imposed within the project, the Observatory does not keep data that would allow to relate a person with its information. That is, there is no information related to names, ID, exact date of birth, etc. The only exception is that the Observatory offers the option to users of including their email to get information about the investigations, or the results of the draw of some devices (Android tablets) held among the graduates who complete the questionnaire.

In view of these restrictions, and because of the e-mail -if it is obtained at all occurs at the end of the whole process- the universities are the responsible for contacting their graduates offering them to participate in the process of the questionnaires. In this contact message, universities tell graduates that there is a draw among those completing this form and provide a personal link to each student to complete the task. This invitation letter designed by the OEEU Observatory could be used or not by universities, being responsible each one of them of its use and modification.

The experiment proposal in this respect is based on sending two different invitation letters. One invitation letter will be an updated version of this text used for the previous questionnaires (updated to reflect the changes related to the new edition). The second invitation letter will change both in the textual content and visual appearance, applying some changes that will be explained in following sections of this paper (basically modifying the tone and textual content of the message, plus providing a different overall design to the message [6]).

The goal of these two different invitation letters is to send one (the old version) as invitation letter for most part of the universities. The second one (the new) will be used by universities that participated in the previous edition of the questionnaires phase to test if the changes lead to variations in the entrance and participation in the questionnaire changes over the previous edition. With this proposal, it is possible to see the effect of the changes in the invitation letter (using A/B test methodologies) considering several things:

- The context of each participating university is different (population, economic factors, etc.). Therefore, specific changes are made for universities participating in both calls for data collection.
- The population of the study has changed from the first edition of the data collection to this second (age, training, etc.). For this reason, the changes between different universities will be also validated within the same edition of the questionnaires for data collection.

In the following sections, the changes to be introduced will be discussed in depth. At any rate, these proposed changes that could be introduced in the questionnaires are limited by the various constraints of the project related to privacy (it is not possible to use external mailing platforms, etc.) and they focus fundamentally on the issues of improving trust and relationship between the user and the entity that proposes the questionnaire (the Observatory).

3.2.2   A Study About What Improvements Can Be Implemented
in Questionnaires to Improve Participation and Completion Ratios

Regarding the part of the study related to the changes in the questionnaire itself, several modifications are proposed at several levels [7].

The general approach of this study is to perform an A/B test with three variants (A/B/C). The proposal is composed by a main variant (A) that follows the outline of the previous edition questionnaire (available in Spanish in http://gredos.usal.es/jspui/bitstream/10366/127374/5/Anexos_OEEU_2015.pdf), from which we have some idea of efficiency, etc., along with two other variants (B and C) that change certain issues related to the Social Exchange Theory [2].

In general, variant B of the test refers to changes related to the relationship of the participant (who answers) and who proposes the questionnaire (first layer of theory) along with changes related to the appearance (third layer of the theory) [8, 9]. More broadly, this variant B is based on trust between the parties [10, 11], further improvements and changes with respect to user experience [12], usability [9] and interface design of the questionnaire [10, 13].

On the other hand, variant C of the test includes the proposed changes in variant B plus other changes related to the relationship between the stakeholders involved in the questionnaire (first layer of the theory) and to the conversation between them (second layer). From this point of view, variant C will focus more on issues related to user engagement [6].

In any case, the three versions of the questionnaire will maintain certain rewards offered in the previous process of data collection. For example, this time there will be again a draw of electronic devices (tablets) among those who complete the questionnaire. Also, the Observatory will continue maintaining communication with those users who want to receive the latest news of the Observatory and its research.

Regarding some factors such as age, disability, or other situations and personal contexts of users, in this case they will be obviated (except the application of general accessibility standards) because the experiment is not focused on specific aspects related to possible subgroups within the population of the study [9, 14]. It is assumed that this constitutes a limitation of the study.

The effect of the changes will be measured in two ways:

- Checking the data regarding the access ratio to the questionnaires, the completion of each part of the questionnaire and the completion ratio of the questionnaire (completed screens, dropout moments, etc.).
- Evaluating the *paradata* [15]. The *paradata* from a questionnaire are the auxiliary data that describe a process, such as response times, clicks, scroll processes, etc. In this case, the *paradata* will be related to the time it takes to the user completing the task of answering each page of questions, the time to complete the full questionnaire, the accesses to the questionnaire, etc. These *paradata* cannot be compared with similar data from the previous round of data collection about degree graduates, since nothing similar was done in that moment.

Usually, in this kind of research, users complete another questionnaire about their opinion about how they have felt about the questionnaire, how they have been able to solve the task, etc. In this case, due to the length of the questionnaire to be completed and the nature of the project, this research will not be carried out in this way. This is a limitation as to the richness of the results that can be obtained. What researchers plan to do is to invite the students, who decide to give their e-mail voluntarily at the end of the employability and employment questionnaire, to a new specialized questionnaire on these issues.

4 Proposed Improvements for the Questionnaire

In this section the different improvements designed for the questionnaire are described. The design process has been driven by a literature review. This literature review comprised about 650 books, papers and technical reports. The process for selecting the literature to be reviewed was:

- Making three different queries to the Web of Science and collect the results in order to iterate in reading the titles, abstracts and full content to select those papers really relevant for the topic of this research. The three queries performed were:
  - *(("form*") OR ("questionnaire*") OR ("survey*")) AND "usability" AND "factor*" AND (("web") OR ("online"))*
  - online forms usability
  - (("web" OR "online") AND ("questionnaire?" OR "form?") AND usability)

  This process and its results are gathered in the following spreadsheet https://docs. google.com/spreadsheets/d/1KbOCTVBqKh3Xz5nqqQY9-ywgZ2ggYNldb3O S6SasaXk/edit?usp=sharing. In the spreadsheet the 633 unique results retrieved from the Web of Science and their status regarding to their usage in the research regarding to each review stage are presented.
- Extracting the main references from these papers and books retrieved from the Web of Science and read them. This process lead to review another 15 papers, books, standards and technical reports. Most part of them were used in some way to design the proposals that are explained below.

Once the literature was reviewed, authors designed the improvements and changes for the questionnaire. These improvements and changes are mainly supported or inspired by the literature as well as by ISO usability guidelines and HSS (U.S. Department of Health and Human Services) guidelines [16–20]. The following sub-sections comment each change and measure, describing for each one its purpose, its goal, the identifier associated, etc.

The ID has been set for each proposed change related to the main application area of application within the HCI discipline; despite of that, most of them apply to more than one area, for that reason, researchers pick the main one as base for the identifier. Table 1 explains the relationship between each change/improvement (using the IDs explained in the subsections), its relationship with HCI knowledge areas or topics and with each layer of the Social Exchange Theory used as framework for the experiments design and the research in general. The main improvement areas of each change related to HCI topics are marked in red color and bigger size.

Table 1. Relationship between each change/improvement proposed, HCI application areas and layers of Social Exchange Theory

Layer of the Social Exchange Theory	Relationship	Conversation		Appearance
Improvement area regarding HCI	Trust	Engagement	Usability / User Experience (UX)	Design
TR1	X			X
TR2	X		X	X
TR3	X			
US/UX 1			X	X
US/UX 2			X	X
US/UX 3	X		X	
US/UX 4			X	X
TR4	X	X		
EN1		X		X
EN2		X		X
EN3		X		

4.1 Proposal for the Invitation Letter to the Questionnaires

Proposed change: *TR1. Modify the text and appearance from the invitation letter to the questionnaire.*

In the Fig. 1 the basic e-mail, designed by The Spanish Observatory for University Employability and Employment to invite the graduates in the previous edition of the data gathering process, is presented. In this edition of the data gathering process related to master graduates, the basic invitation letter text will be very similar, only changing the text to reflect the master degree of the graduates and specifying that two years ago there were another similar questionnaire that collected data from degree graduates (including also the results displayed in its web http://datos.oeeu.org).

Among the proposed changes are the inclusion of the university logo that sends the invitation, the inclusion of the OEEU logo, a change in design to make the questionnaire according to the colors and fonts used in other OEEU's products, and changes in the text to be perceived as a more personal invitation to the graduate. These changes are intended to improve user trust in the questionnaire and the activity of the Observatory [6, 11, 13, 21].

Figure 2 shows the proposed new design (visual and textual) for the invitation letter. As explained before, the new version will be used only by few universities to allow researchers the measuring of its effect in the graduates.

4.2 Proposal to Amend the Questionnaire for Variant B

Proposed change: *TR2. Adequacy of the image to the other digital products of the Observatory.*

Dear graduate (if the University wants, can personalize the email indicating the name of the graduate):

From the University (name of the University) we ask you to take 15 minutes of your time to answer a questionnaire, which for the first time applies to all Spanish universities, to know the employment status of university graduates.

The data entered will be processed anonymously by the University (name of the University) and The Spanish Observatory for University Employability and Employment (OEEU), complying with the Spanish Personal Data Protection Act (LOPD). The aggregated results will be available on the Observatory's website (www.oeeu.org).

Among the respondents to the survey will be drawn, during the month of June 2015, 10 tablets Samsung Galaxy Tab 4.

Click here to perform the survey: «URL»

Thank you for your cooperation!

A cordial greeting,
Name of University
Contact E-Mail
Contact telephone

Spanish Observatory for University Employability and Employment
udyc@oeeu.org
913364185

Fig. 1. Invitation letter proposed by the OEEU. Text translated by the authors from [5]

Dear graduate (if the university prefer, can send the mail personalized indicating the name of the graduate):

From the University (name of the University) and the Spanish Observatory for University Employability and Employment (OEEU, http://oeeu.org) we invite you to participate in a study to know the employment situation of the master graduates in Spain. To do this, we ask you to spend a little more than 15 minutes of your time in completing the questionnaire that we propose at the end of this email. In the questionnaire you will be asked about various aspects of your work, personal information (demographic data) and academic record to try to analyze how the master graduates in Spain get employment and what aspects affect their employability. The data you enter will be treated in an absolutely anonymous way and complying with the Spanish Personal Data Protection Act (LOPD).

As a consideration to your collaboration, we will raffle during the month of July 2017, 10 tablets Samsung Galaxy Tab 4. You will also be the first to know the results of those studies conducted with the questionnaire.

Click here to start the survey << Custom URL >>
Thank you very much for your collaboration!

A cordial greeting,
Name of University
Contact E-Mail
Contact telephone

Spanish Observatory for University Employability and Employment
udyc@oeeu.org
913364185

Fig. 2. Invitation letter with visual and textual changes proposed for the research. Adapted from [5]

This change is related to modifying colors, logotypes, typography, etc. to correspond the other products of the Observatory like its website http://datos.oeeu.org. This change is supported by the literature as a way to enhance the users' trust in the Observatory brand and products [1, 6, 8, 11, 13, 21].

Proposed change: *TR3. Inclusion of the Observatory's logo and university's logo.*

In the same way that previous proposal, the inclusion of the OEEU logo and the university logotype can reduce the distrust of the graduate to participate. In this case, the logotype of the university will help to build trust on the questionnaire website and the OEEU logotype will help him/her to associate the product with the institution that proposes it [1, 6, 21].

Proposed change: *US/UX1. Inclusion of a progress bar in the questionnaire.*

By observing a progress bar, the user can know its progress in the task of filling the questionnaire and estimate how much effort/time he/she will need to make to complete it. This can reduce the stress related to uncertainty about a task like an unknown questionnaire [1, 6].

Proposed change: *US/UX2. Present a visual focus animation on concrete actions.*

In this case, the web will provide a visual effect of focus to the user in that he will have always in the center of the screen the task to be solved (typically answering a question or filling an empty field), making also a defocused effect on the elements that are not fundamental to solve that task. This proposal is used in commercial questionnaire systems like http://typeform.com/.

The reader can access to the following URLs to check how this visual effect works: https://drive.google.com/file/d/0BwS7cZg3riXtajJtNGhkMnIzXzg/view?usp=sharing, https://drive.google.com/file/d/0BwS7cZg3riXtWGk1bmlvSVB5dDg/view?usp=sharing.

Proposed change: *US/UX3. Deactivation of control elements when an action is initiated.*

A typical example of this change is to deactivate a button in a website once it is pressed until its action is finished. This usability/user experience measure could make the user to trust on the sturdiness of the system and reduce stress situations like those where a button perform the same action several times after being pressed more than once [6].

Proposed change: *US/UX4. In related elements, instead of having smaller and more specific groupings, use some larger grouping, following the Gestalt principles on grouping.*

For example, following the proposal, the header of a table would be fixed while in the content can be scrolled up and down. It seeks to ensure that the large dimensions of analysis in some points of the questionnaire are grouped in an attempt to avoid user fatigue and reducing users' cognitive load when dealing with large tables or complex visual elements [1, 6, 22].

A visual explanation of this proposal can be observed in the following URL https://drive.google.com/file/d/0BwS7cZg3riXtdmZqQzBHZXJVcmM/view?usp=sharing.

4.3   Proposal to Amend the Questionnaire for Variant C

Proposed change: *TR4. Changes in the introduction text to the questionnaire.*

In this case, a change in the text will be sought in a similar way to the modification in the invitation letter to the users. The text changes to a more personal way of addressing the user and contributing important arguments to influence a better perception on what is going to be done and improving the confidence in the questionnaire and the entity that proposes it.

The text of the previous edition is presented in the Fig. 3 (the variant A will only update the data about the raffle in the text, etc.).

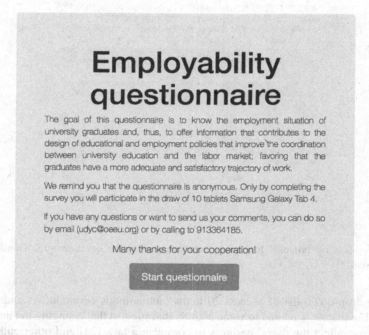

Fig. 3. Previous introduction text to the questionnaire. Translated and adapted from [4, 5]

In this case of variants B and C of the questionnaire, the introductory text would become (changing also the design and layout as commented in the proposal TR2) the displayed in the Fig. 4.

Proposed change: *EN1. In the questions related to the community in which they live, change the drop-down selector for a map with the autonomous communities of Spain.*

This will allow the user to select where the user lives through clicking the corresponding one. In this case, it is sought to have visual elements different from the usual ones that allow the user to interact in different ways during the completion of the questionnaire and avoiding to suffer so much fatigue on the repetition of actions. Also, the usage of a map tries to reduce the users' cognitive load that implies the activity of

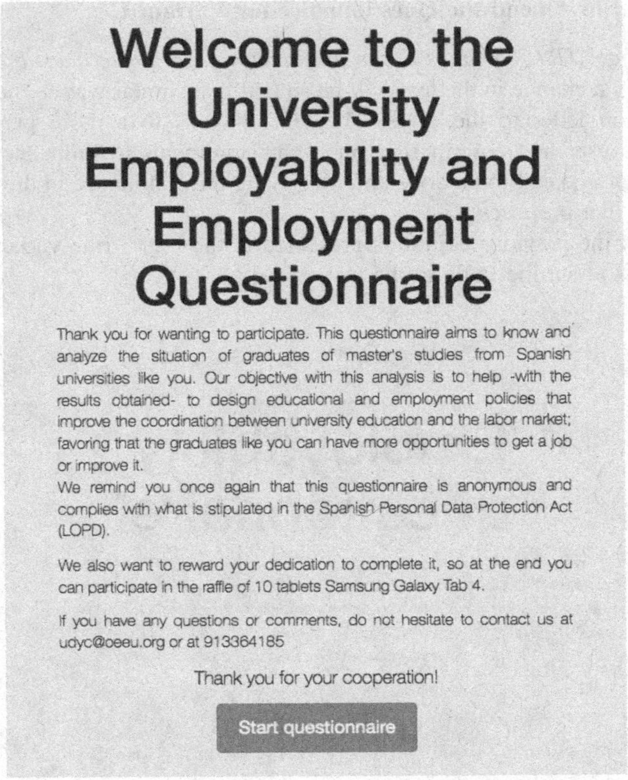

Welcome to the University Employability and Employment Questionnaire

Thank you for wanting to participate. This questionnaire aims to know and analyze the situation of graduates of master's studies from Spanish universities like you. Our objective with this analysis is to help -with the results obtained- to design educational and employment policies that improve the coordination between university education and the labor market; favoring that the graduates like you can have more opportunities to get a job or improve it.

We remind you once again that this questionnaire is anonymous and complies with what is stipulated in the Spanish Personal Data Protection Act (LOPD).

We also want to reward your dedication to complete it, so at the end you can participate in the raffle of 10 tablets Samsung Galaxy Tab 4.

If you have any questions or comments, do not hesitate to contact us at udyc@oeeu.org or at 913364185

Thank you for your cooperation!

Start questionnaire

Fig. 4. Modification proposal for the introduction text to the questionnaire. Translated and adapted from [5]

reading a drop-down list of at least 20 items (autonomous communities and cities in Spain). This change is related to some authors that suggest that changing the interaction elements can affect the users' easiness to complete a task [23] and other authors that explain that the time that an user interact with elements in the form is time that the users is not thinking in dropout [6].

Proposed change: *EN2. Inclusion of textual feedback related to user responses including information that may be relevant.*

This inclusion of textual feedback should be placed in at least three different moments of the questionnaire (i.e. after the demographic questions, after the enquiry about whether the graduated has been employed after the master degree or not, and in the final part of the chosen itinerary), regarding the different main dropout moments of the previous data collection process presented in the second section of this paper. This change requires introducing an intermediate screen between two pages of questions in the questionnaire. In this intermediate screen, information in relation to some of his/her answers enabling also comparison of their answers those provided by other users or official stats from other sources, will be provided to the user.

As an example of this kind of feedback, after the screen of the questionnaire where the user responds if he/she has ever worked and how many jobs he/she has had, in the questionnaire screen change (after pressing next), should be displayed a new screen, with only one the following questions, should be displayed:

- If the graduate answered that he/she did not have a previously a job: "Did you know that there are XX% of graduates in your promotion who have not been able to get a job?".
- If the graduate answered that he/she have had a job: "Do you know that the employment rate of master graduates in Spain is XX%?".
- If the graduate answered that he/she had several jobs: "Did you know what…? Like you there are XX% of people who have responded to this questionnaire that are in your same situation".

Proposed change: *EN3. Inclusion of web push notifications that allow Observatory to send messages to users in order to encourage them if they leave the questionnaire before finishing.*

These notifications can only be sent if the user explicitly accepts them. The notifications will be accompanied by the link to resume the questionnaire. From a technical point of view, the notifications will be sent to Chrome, Firefox and Safari browsers on Windows, Linux and Mac OS in desktop operative systems and to Android phones with any of those browsers (estimated total market share covered by a 61–77%).

This measure can help to increase the users' engagement as well as to try to improve the completion ratio of the questionnaires through the reinforcement.

Some examples of these kind of notifications are available (in Spanish) in [5].

Also, these web push notifications could help researchers to reach again the participants to invite them to another questionnaire to get feedback about the changes/improvements implemented finally in the form.

5   Evaluation by Experts

To validate the proposals designed to improve the questionnaire and reduce the dropout ratio and increase the participation ratio, five experts were invited to evaluate the proposed measures using questionnaire. These experts were selected because all of them work usually with questionnaires from different perspectives (some of them work with questionnaires focusing on improving their usability, use them for research in several contexts, or design questionnaires as part of their day by day work).

In the following subsections, details regarding the questionnaire will be commented, as well, the results and opinions gathered from that questionnaire will be presented and discussed.

5.1   Feedback Questionnaire

The assessment questionnaire completed by the experts is based on the proposal by Sánchez-Prieto et al. [24]. In it, the experts assess the relevance of each proposed change, its clarity and its importance, through a Likert scale (1–7 values). In addition the expert can comment on a qualitative way (typing comments in a textbox) any related issues to each question. Also, the questionnaire requires demographic data from the experts related to their gender, knowledge area, etc. [5] in order to characterize them.

5.2   Results and Discussion

First, in the validation questionnaire, the experts completed some answers about personal information. In this case, 4 out of 5 experts (80%) were men, 1 (20%) was woman. Regarding the age, 3 out of 5 (60%) are between 41 and 50 years old, while other 2 experts (40%) are between 31 and 40 years old. Regarding their knowledge areas, 3 out of 5 (60%) are related to Engineering and Architecture, while the other 2 (40%) are related to Social and Legal Sciences. Regarding their specialization field, 3 out of 5 (60%) are related to disciplines within Computer Sciences and the other 2 (40%) are related to disciplines within Economics.

Related to their responses about each proposal, as previously said, the expert had to assess the change proposal regarding the pertinence, relevance and clarity. Also in each question related to a proposal, the expert could introduce qualitative feedback through texting its opinion. Table 2 gathers the average mark, standard deviation and number of responses collected for each change/improvement proposal in terms of pertinence, relevance and clarity. Also, Table 3 gathers the same information but showing it in groupings related to the main topic associated to each change/improvement proposal (trust, usability/user experience and engagement) as well as the global average, standard deviation and number of responses collected in the assessment questionnaire. The calculations and original responses retrieved from the experts can be checked in the sheet 2 of the following spreadsheet https://docs.google.com/spreadsheets/d/1dO72Z iHTt83UI2_cfjSd5sO1M109TXdO5rysCqgIp94/edit?usp=sharing.

In general, the average mark of the assessment in each question and grouping topic could be considered as good: most of the results are in the Q1 (score 5.5).

This Q1 score is not achieved in the proposed change EN2 (*inclusion of textual feedback related to user responses including information that may be relevant*) pertinence and clarity, TR1 (*modify the text and appearance from the invitation letter to the questionnaire*) regarding its relevance and US/UX3 proposed change (*deactivation of control elements when an action is initiated*).

Regarding the qualitative comments introduced by the experts in their feedback, the following could be highlighted:

- Comments with recommendations about visual design and layout as well as minor changes in the text of the proposed invitation letter and proposed introduction text to the questionnaire.
- Comments about the fact that many users will not know previously the OEEU's visual brand, so many graduates would not develop positive feelings regarding to trust in TR2 proposal.

Table 2. Descriptive results from the experts' evaluation for each proposal regarding the pertinence, relevance and clarity

	Pertinence			Relevance			Clarity		
	Avg	Std	N	Avg	Std	N	Avg	Std	N
TR1	6.17	0.98	5	5.17	1.17	5	6.17	0.98	5
TR2	6.17	1.33	5	6.00	1.55	5	5.67	1.37	5
TR3	6.67	0.52	5	5.83	1.47	5	6.67	0.52	5
TR4	6.33	1.03	5	6.00	0.89	5	6.50	0.84	5
US/UX 1	6.50	1.22	5	6.83	0.41	5	6.50	1.22	5
US/UX 2	7.00	0.00	5	7.00	0.00	5	6.67	0.52	5
US/UX 3	5.67	2.42	5	6.00	2.45	5	5.33	2.42	5
US/UX 4	7.00	0.00	5	6.67	0.52	5	6.67	0.52	5
EN1	6.83	0.41	5	6.33	1.03	5	5.67	1.03	5
EN2	4.83	2.14	5	5.50	1.22	5	5.17	2.32	5
EN3	7.00	0.00	5	7.00	0.00	5	7.00	0.00	5

Table 3. Descriptive results from the experts' evaluation for each group of proposals and global assessment regarding the pertinence, relevance and clarity

	Pertinence			Relevance			Clarity		
	Avg	Std	N	Avg	Std	N	Avg	Std	N
TR	6.24	1.00	20	5.76	1.26	20	6.24	1.04	20
US/UX	6.48	1.47	20	6.62	1.32	20	6.24	1.51	20
EN	6.19	1.64	15	6.25	1.13	15	5.88	1.67	15
Global	6.27	1.30	55	6.22	1.30	55	6.11	1.42	55

- A comment regarding to US/UX3 (*deactivation of control elements when an action is initiated*) proposed change where the expert explains that he/she "is not aware about what implies this change".
- Very positive comments regarding the US/UX4 proposal (*in related elements, instead of having smaller and more specific groupings, use some larger grouping, following the Gestalt law on grouping*).
- Comments related to EN1 proposed improvement (in the questions related to the community in which they live, change the drop-down selector for a map with the autonomous communities of Spain) to include something similar for graduates that do not live now in Spain and live abroad (instead of selecting Spain autonomous communities, select countries, etc.).
- Two positive comments and another two expressing doubts about EN2 proposal (*inclusion of textual feedback related to user responses including information that may be relevant*). The positive comments explain that this change could lead to engage users by taking advantage of their curiosity. The other two explain that these extra screens and personalized feedback could break the users' trust in the data anonymization and introduce some distortions in the questionnaire.

- Some comments regarding little details that could improve the notifications. For example: the text to accept the reception of notifications should be "Yes, I accept" instead of "Ok, I accept" or introduce information about how much time will take to the user to complete the questionnaire if the he/she continues it.

In general terms, the feedback from the experts about the proposed changes/improvements for the questionnaire is very positive. Most part of the scores gathered by the experts are in the top first quartile of the scale (values 1–7), so can be accepted "as is" to be implemented in the questionnaire of course, after a final evaluation of the convenience with the project managers and OEEU coordinators.

On the other hand, the experts raised some doubts in other elements or certain assessment points, like the pertinence and clarity of EN2 proposal (textual feedback), the relevance of TR1 proposal (modifying the text and appearance of the invitation letter) or the relevance of the US/UX3 proposal (deactivation of control elements when an action is initiated). In these cases, all the evaluations exceeded the Q2 score (4.0 value), so still they can be considered as well perceived changes but, in any case, these should be reviewed again by the researchers, in order to improve them or discard certain proposals if there is no possible improvement for that.

Despite some of these changes that are not fully supported by experts usually are backed by other authors in the literature, researchers should follow a pragmatic approach that ensures the right application of this kind of changes/improvements for the specific case of the OEEU's questionnaire and its context.

Also, as previously commented, all these changes and improvement proposals will be validated again with the OEEU project coordinators and OEEU project managers before implementing them in the final version of the questionnaire that will be public in April 2017.

6   Conclusions

This paper presents a research focused on improving the success/completion ratio in large surveys. In this case, the large survey is the questionnaire produced by the Spanish Observatory for University Employability and Employment and that will be publicly available for graduates of master degree in April 2017. This questionnaire is composed by about 32 and 60 questions and between 86 and 181 variables to be measured. The research is based on the previous experience of a past questionnaire proposed also by the Observatory composed also by a large amount of questions and variables to be measured.

Analyzing the target population of the questionnaire (also comparing with the target population of the previous questionnaire) and reviewing the literature, the researchers have designed 11 proposals for changes related to the questionnaire that could improve the users' completion and success ratios (changes that could improve the users' trust in the questionnaire, the questionnaire usability and user experience or the users' engagement to the questionnaire). These changes are planned to be applied in the questionnaire in two main different experiments based on A/B test methodologies that will allow researchers to measure the effect of the changes in different populations and in an incremental way.

The proposed changes have been assessed by five experts through an evaluation questionnaire. In this questionnaire, researchers gathered the score of each expert regarding to the pertinence, relevance and clarity of each change proposed. Regarding the results of this evaluation questionnaire, the reviewers fully supported 8 out of the 11 changes proposals, so they could be introduced in the questionnaire with no variation. On the other hand, 3 of the proposed changes or improvements are not fully supported by the experts (they have not received a score in the top first quartile of the 1–7 Likert scale). These changes will not be discarded immediately, because despite they have not received a Q1 score, they received a score within the second quartile. Instead of being discarded, these changes will be reviewed again by the researchers and the Observatory staff in order to adequate them to the questionnaire. If there is no possibility to adequate them to the OEEU's questionnaire context, finally they will be finally rejected.

After all this work, research and validation processes, the future work is to implement all the accepted changes and variations in the OEEU's questionnaire for graduates of master studies and study what of these changes lead to a real improvement in the completion/success ratio related to the questionnaire.

Acknowledgments. The research leading to these results has received funding from "la Caixa" Foundation. Also, the author Juan Cruz-Benito would like to thank the European Social Fund and the *Consejería de Educación* of the *Junta de Castilla y León* (Spain) for funding his predoctoral fellow contract. This work has been partially funded by the Spanish Government Ministry of Economy and Competitiveness throughout the DEFINES project (Ref. TIN2016-80172-R).

References

1. Jarrett, C., Gaffney, G.: Forms that Work: Designing Web Forms for Usability. Morgan Kaufmann, Boston (2009)
2. Dillman, D.A.: Mail and Internet Surveys: The Tailored Design Method. Wiley, New York (2000)
3. Michavila, F., Martín-González, M., Martínez, J.M., García-Peñalvo, F.J., Cruz-Benito, J.: Analyzing the employability and employment factors of graduate students in Spain: the OEEU information system. In: Third International Conference on Technological Ecosystems for Enhancing Multiculturality (TEEM 2015). ACM Inc., Porto, Portugal (2015)
4. Michavila, F., Martínez, J.M., Martín-González, M., García-Peñalvo, F.J., Cruz-Benito, J.: Barómetro de Empleabilidad y Empleo de los Universitarios en España, 2015 (Primer informe de resultados) (2016)
5. Cruz-Benito, J., Therón, R., García-Peñalvo, F.J., Martín-González, M.: Herramienta para la validación de elementos de mejora UX/Engagement para los cuestionarios de recogida de información de egresados en el contexto del Observatorio de Empleabilidad y Empleo Universitarios (OEEU). GRIAL Research Group, University of Salamanca (2017)
6. Anderson, S.P.: Seductive Interaction Design: Creating Playful, Fun, and Effective User Experiences, Portable Document. Pearson Education (2011)
7. Kveton, P., Jelínek, M., Klimusová, H., Voboril, D.: Data collection on the internet: evaluation of web-based questionnaires. Studia Psychologica **49**, 81 (2007)
8. Flavián, C., Gurrea, R., Orús, C.: The effect of product presentation mode on the perceived content and continent quality of web sites. Online Inf. Rev. **33**, 1103–1128 (2009)

9. Huber, W., Vitouch, P.: Usability and accessibility on the internet: effects of accessible web design on usability. In: Miesenberger, K., Klaus, J., Zagler, W., Karshmer, A. (eds.) ICCHP 2008. LNCS, vol. 5105, pp. 482–489. Springer, Heidelberg (2008). doi:10.1007/978-3-540-70540-6_69

10. Seckler, M., Tuch, A.N., Opwis, K., Bargas-Avila, J.A.: User-friendly locations of error messages in web forms: put them on the right side of the erroneous input field. Interact. Comput. **24**, 107–118 (2012)

11. Shneiderman, B.: Designing trust into online experiences. Commun. ACM **43**, 57–59 (2000)

12. Recabarren, M., Nussbaum, M.: Exploring the feasibility of web form adaptation to users' cultural dimension scores. User Model. User-Adap. Inter. **20**, 87–108 (2010)

13. Pengnate, S.F., Sarathy, R.: An experimental investigation of the influence of website emotional design features on trust in unfamiliar online vendors. Comput. Hum. Behav. **67**, 49–60 (2017)

14. Sayago, S., Blat, J.: Some Aspects of Designing Accessible Online Forms for the Young Elderly. WEBIST **2**, 13–17 (2007)

15. Stieger, S., Reips, U.-D.: What are participants doing while filling in an online questionnaire: a paradata collection tool and an empirical study. Comput. Hum. Behav. **26**, 1488–1495 (2010)

16. ISO/DIS: Draft BS ENISO 9241-220 Ergonomics of human-computer interaction. Part 220: processes for enabling, executing and assessing human-centred design within organizations (2016)

17. ISO/DIS: Ergonomics of human-system interaction — Part 125: guidance on visual presentation of information (2013)

18. Bevan, N., Carter, J., Harker, S.: ISO 9241-11 revised: what have we learnt about usability since 1998? In: Kurosu, M. (ed.) HCI 2015. LNCS, vol. 9169, pp. 143–151. Springer, Cham (2015). doi:10.1007/978-3-319-20901-2_13

19. Bargas-Avila, J., Brenzikofer, O.: Simple but crucial user interfaces in the world wide web: introducing 20 guidelines for usable web form design (2011)

20. Bevan, N., Spinhof, L.: Are guidelines and standards for web usability comprehensive? In: Jacko, Julie A. (ed.) HCI 2007. LNCS, vol. 4550, pp. 407–419. Springer, Heidelberg (2007). doi:10.1007/978-3-540-73105-4_45

21. Seckler, M., Heinz, S., Forde, S., Tuch, A.N., Opwis, K.: Trust and distrust on the web: user experiences and website characteristics. Comput. Hum. Behav. **45**, 39–50 (2015)

22. Bargas-Avila, J.A., Brenzikofer, O., Tuch, A.N., Roth, S.P., Opwis, K.: Working towards usable forms on the worldwide web: optimizing multiple selection interface elements. Adv. Hum.-Comput. Interact. **2011**, 4 (2011)

23. Couper, M.P., Tourangeau, R., Conrad, F.G., Crawford, S.D.: What they see is what we get response options for web surveys. Soc. Sci. Comput. Rev. **22**, 111–127 (2004)

24. Sánchez-Prieto, J.C., Olmos-Migueláñez, S., García-Peñalvo, F.J.: Informal tools in formal contexts: development of a model to assess the acceptance of mobile technologies among teachers. Comput. Hum. Behav. **55**, 519–528 (2016)

Interaction Design Principles
in WYRED Platform

Francisco J. García-Peñalvo[(⊠)] and Jorge Durán-Escudero

GRIAL Research Group, Department of Computers and Automatics,
University of Salamanca, Salamanca, Spain
{fgarcia,jorge.d}@usal.es

Abstract. This paper presents the requirements elicitation phase for the
WYRED platform. WYRED (netWorked Youth Research for Empowerment in
the Digital society) is a European H2020 Project that aims to provide a
framework for research in which children and young people can express and
explore their perspectives and interests in relation to digital society, but also a
platform from which they can communicate their perspectives to other stakeholders effectively through innovative engagement processes. The requirement
elicitation is a basic step to design the interactive mechanism to build up the
needed social dialog among the involved stakeholders. In order to set up the
right interactive tasks, not only functional requirements are elicited, the
non-functional requirements play a key role in this project, specially regarding
to ensure the security and privacy of the underage people that will be presented
in the development of this project.

Keywords: WYRED · Social structure · Inequalities · Social mobility ·
Interethnic relations · Communication networks · Media · Information society ·
Innovation policy · Technological ecosystems · Requirement elicitation ·
Non-functional requirements · Privacy

1 Introduction

WYRED (netWorked Youth Research for Empowerment in the Digital society) [1, 2]
is a European H2020 Project that aims to provide a framework for research in which
children and young people can express and explore their perspectives and interests in
relation to digital society, but also a platform from which they can communicate their
perspectives to other stakeholders effectively through innovative engagement processes. It will do this by implementing a generative research cycle involving networking, dialogue, participatory research and interpretation phases centered around and
driven by children and young people, out of which a diverse range of outputs, critical
perspectives and other insights will emerge to inform policy and decision-making in
relation to children and young people's needs in relation to digital society.

WYRED aims to give young people a voice, and a space to explore their concerns
and interests in relation to digital society and share their perspectives and insights to
stakeholders with other strata of society.

© Springer International Publishing AG 2017
P. Zaphiris and A. Ioannou (Eds.): LCT 2017, Part II, LNCS 10296, pp. 371–381, 2017.
DOI: 10.1007/978-3-319-58515-4_29

To do that, WYRED should engage youngers in a process of social dialogue based on participatory research projects that allow them to surface and explore their concerns in ways defined by them. These projects may explore the issues chosen for investigation through a variety of approaches, including:

- Research projects where a social issue is addressed and solutions explored and discussed, surfacing attitudes and understandings through reflection in the process.
- Creative projects involving among others video, theatre, web publishing, comics, music, art, events of different kinds, that express attitudes and understanding though these media.
- Journalistic approaches, observing, documenting, recording and commenting on social phenomena, either online or off, producing documentary outputs in different media.
- Action research and ethnographic projects in which the participants explore their own perceptions as they play in their day-to-day lives, for example though journals or video blogging.
- Solidarity projects, where a specific problem is identified, and practical solutions implemented, where the output is a narrative of the process and the problems faced in solving them.

The central element in common to all the WYRED approach is that they will be driven by the young themselves. The projects will be self-directed, though supported by the WYRED project consortium; the research and youth partners have extensive experience in facilitating this range of different processes. The work will therefore generate a wide range of artefacts, and insights and recommendations grounded firmly in the concerns of the young themselves.

From a technological point of view, in order to fulfil WYRED goals successfully, a support platform should be developed that allows an easy interaction process among the involved stakeholders; high-level engagement conditions; a secure environment in which all the participants feel comfortable enough with the privacy issues, but with a special attention to the underage ones; and a suitable dashboard for data analytics. The development approach will be based on the ecosystem metaphor [3–9] in which one the users are an essential component of the resulting ecology [10, 11].

To define the technological platform, putting a special care in the requirements elicitation process is fully indispensable, for both obtaining the basic functional services, and, more important, gathering the non-functional requirements to allow the needed user experience and privacy conditions.

This paper summarizes the first iteration of this process under an Open Unified Process framework [12].

The rest of the papers is organized as follows. Section 2 includes the basic WYRED project information data-sheet; Sect. 3 introduces the technological background for WYRED project to understand better some defined non-functional requirements; Sect. 4 presents the most outstanding elicited requirements; Finally, Sect. 5 closes the paper with the most significant remarks.

2   WYRED Project Information Data-Sheet

WYRED (netWorked Youth Research for Empowerment in the Digital society) is a European Project (Ref. 727066.) funded by the Horizon 2020 Programme in its "Europe in a changing world – inclusive, innovative and reflective Societies (HORIZON 2020: REV-INEQUAL-10-2016: Multi-stakeholder platform for enhancing youth digital opportunities)" Call.

The project is coordinated by GRIAL research group [13] of the University of Salamanca (Spain), starting at November 2016 and ending at October 2019. The consortium is completed with the following partners:

- Oxfam Italia Onlus (Italy).
- PYE Global (United Kingdom).
- Asis Ogretim Kurumlari A.S. (Turkey).
- Early Years - The organization for young children LBG (United Kingdom).
- Youth for exchange and understanding international AISBL (Belgium).
- Zauchner - Studnicka Sabine (MOVES) (Austria).
- Boundaries Observatory CIC (United Kingdom).
- Tel Aviv University (Israel).

The total projects budget is 993,662.50€.

3   WYRED Platform Technological Base

WYRED platform will be based on a well-established technological ecosystem [14–17] that supports the interaction platform, taking into account that users are a component more in this ecosystem. This ecosystem must guarantee three main features in the project lifecycle: interaction facilitator, security and privacy supporter, and data analysis platform.

3.1   Interaction Facilitator

Most of the discussions will be done inside the platform. Given the importance of mobile online spaces [18–22], especially among children and young people, it is considered vital that the platform exist as a web-based platform and a mobile app with extensive integration with the social media in which the target groups are active. It will contain profiling functionalities, interaction spaces that facilitate and promote exchange of messages, videos and other artefacts in different formats, a repository for the artefacts generated in the research process, and a range of analytics instruments for the processing of the dialogue that takes place between WYRED participants.

3.2   Security and Privacy Supporter

The WYRED platform represents a safe space in which children and experts will be able to express their views and reflections on the influence of technology in their lives. As technology affects transversally all social areas and involves people of different nationalities and beliefs, the platform must make a double effort to preserve the space in which they will express personal opinions and monitor that will not be any type of abusive situation/cyber bullying among participants.

3.3   Data Analysis Platform

The social dialogue and participatory research activities in the project will generate heterogeneous data including transcripts, analysis, hypotheses, artefacts, workflows, narratives, quantitative and qualitative data related to perceptions and understandings around social change. The storage of this data will be based upon recent developments in Open Source grid-based Citizen Science platforms [23, 24] like MyExperiment (http://myexperiment.org) and open data formats including the Research Object standard (http://www.researchobject.org) and Linked Data (http://linkeddata.org). WYRED will exploit these and other standards and tools to provide flexibility in the ways the data can be managed, organized and made available in different formats and contexts. WYRED will actively engage a wide range of stakeholders by making the project platform a space where all can access the data and artefacts generated, explore and interpret them. The process of interpretation which will be managed by the consortium but open to all is expected to generate elements for potential new models and strategies for transitioning towards these models. These will permit automatic processing and analysis of the raw data from conversations and its visualization so that the user can interact with the visualizations in order to extract new knowledge or select data to be qualitatively analyzed [25–28] (as in the Keim cycle [29, 30] or VeLA model [31]). These visualizations will include word-cloud- based visualizations and social graph based visualizations [32].

4   WYRED Platform Requirements

The requirements elicitation is an indispensable task in order to define, design and implement the WYRED technological ecosystem as a highly interactive system. Three different kind of requirements are gathered and documented: information requirements, functional requirements and non-functional requirements [33].

Next subsections try to summarize the most important requirements of the WYRED platform, the full requirements catalog is available at [34].

4.1   Information Requirements

This category represents all the requirements about the information that the WYRED platform is going to manage. There is very important to set these requirements in order to know the data that is going to be managed in the proposed ecosystem.

4.1.1   Users' Visible Information

In WYRED one of the most important thing is to maximize the users' privacy. We are going to split the user's information between public and private in the platform.

The project partners answered a questionnaire about which should be the minimum required data to develop a right social dialogue. The selected data fields are: a nickname (no real names will be used in the interactive processes); the language; an avatar image, a localization (partners will have to agree which one: country, city, region, etc.); and a list of topics of interest.

4.1.2   Users' Private Information

The platform also has to manage more information about its users due to this can help us to extract patterns and get conclusions. However, this information will be private and nobody will see the private information of a specific user. Therefore, it will be treated anonymously in order to respect the users' privacy.

The information that we keep private is: the name; the surname; the country; the city; the sex; the age (birth date); the education level; and the email.

4.1.3   Platform Information

Data about the platform itself is needed to be managed. Two types of data will be distinguished:

- Documents shared in the platform, which can be editable, such as text documents, images, audios and videos.
- Usage statistics, where we can find information about how the users interact with WYRED system and data regarding the platform evolution.

The main problem to manage documents is that there are many formats that the platform has to support and they use many resources. For this reason, keeping them in a dedicate server to improve the platform performance has been decided.

The statistics save data about the number of publications for each user, her time in the platform, how many pages she has visited, in how many projects she is involved, etc.

4.2   Functional Requirements

This kind of requirements is related to the functions that the system has to support. A first questionnaire about services and functionality of the platform was sent to the project partners. This questionnaire allowed us to have a first approach to the core functionality of the platform, but we know more functional requirements will be included when other information requesting tasks will be performed such as stakeholders' questionnaires and a Delphi process.

4.2.1   Content Moderation

One of the aspect related to the privacy is how to keep the users' information private and avoid arguments in the platform. The solution that we have planned is to use an automatic system that checks all messages looking for a list of alert words. Although the intelligent system can find messages with marked words, these should be checked manually, for this reason we are going to develop a group of moderation tools for editing, deleting, moving, etc. messages. Moreover, we will put an option where the users can inform a moderator that there is a message that should be analyze.

4.2.2   Social Dialogue

The WYRED objective is that the youth people can interact themselves and speak things that are important for them, in some cases, they also can offer solutions for their own problems. For this reason, we have to allow that a user can register in WYRED. However, WYRED is not a chat but a platform where there should exist a structured social dialogue, so we are going to develop something like forum topics. This system helps the users answer questions and create discussion threads with their comments.

With the objective of having a good response, first of all, the users will fill a form where they can say in which things they are interested in. Therefore, a researcher or a user will create a project, this will be hidden for all that are not invited to participate; for achieving this, the creator will select what kind of users are going to be invited using the public user's information.

4.2.3   Engagement

One of the key elements to attracting young people is working on functionalities that improve the users' engagement. This helps to improve a lot of metrics such as page views, used time and social sharing.

The first requirement, which we have defined with this aim, is a translation system due to there are users from different countries that speak different languages. We have also thought that it would be interesting to use a gamification system to increase the users' engagement, due to it is one of the most common technique used right now. For improving the usability, we have planned to design custom styles for each age group, because of teenagers do not want to use a childish platform. We have also kept in mind that if a user likes our platform, she would like to share it with her friends, for this reason, we will develop an easy tool for social sharing.

4.2.4   Documents

In the social dialogue process, the researchers need to work with many kind of documents, such as text, audio, images and video. These documents are a relevant part in the WYRED project, so we have planned to develop tools for showing and sharing them. The researchers also suggested that they need an online editor and an easy way for adding annotation in audio and video files.

4.2.5   Research Area

The researchers are also an important part of the WYRED project, for this reason, they are going to have a private area. In this one, they will be able to monitor their own social dialogues, share information with other researchers and analyze their data.

In order to improve the data analysis process, we are going to develop visualization tools and a pattern matching system. The visualization tools will help the researchers to discover knowledge using charts, trees and other representations. The pattern matching system will use techniques such as datamining or natural language processing, in order to give to the researchers some patterns about the stored data.

4.3   Non-functional Requirements

These are very important for the effective use of a software system but also for the user experience. Besides, WYRED has to involve underage people, this means security and privacy requirements will be very important and significant for the success of the project goals.

So, these requirements group the restrictions and constraints related to the technical decisions and security issues.

The same as for the other requirements, a specific questionnaire was developed to inquiry the project partners.

4.3.1   Platform Design

When we planned how to design a platform for youth people, we checked that they use more their mobiles than other classic devices such as laptops or desktops. For this reason, we decided to use a responsive design that can work well in all kinds of devices. However, creating a platform where our users are going to use mainly mobiles has other problem, the performance. Usually mobiles have wireless connections and, depending on the country, they can be a bit slow, so we add a requirement about the platform performance.

We also would like to develop a mobile application for the more common mobile systems (Android and iOS), in order to get a better response from the user. However, this requirement is more a wish than an urgent necessity and for this reason, it will have a minor priority.

4.3.2   Platform Technologies

One of the objectives of WYRED is to develop a platform without spending money in non-relevant functions. Due to this, we have planned to use *Linux* servers and free technologies. *Linux* servers are cheaper than *Windows* servers and offer a solid base to develop a complete web platform, in the same way, there are free technologies/software such as *PHP* or *MySQL* that are widely used in web development and we can use them without a specific cost.

4.3.3   Security and Privacy Issues

Security and privacy are very important aspect to be tackled in an interactive platform with users from different profiles, nationalities, cultural backgrounds and so on, if we want to ensure the creation of a significant social dialogue. This is more relevant in WYRED ecosystem due to the most of the involved users are underage people.

These non-functional requirements have been presented in the definition of the information constraints and the functional requirements. Hidden data, restricted participation in the projects and activities, using of avatars instead of real personal information are some examples of what these requirements mean for the WYRED ecosystem.

Moreover, in order to ensure the privacy and keep the all the sensible content of the platform hidden for non-authorized and public users, all the content will not be indexed.

5   Conclusions

WYRED project has a very interesting challenge in order to aim its objectives regarding young people engagement into an interactive and creative process to know their opinion, expressed with their own voices, about the technological world they live including their relationships, experiences, believes and thoughts.

To do that, in an international and intercultural context, the technological ecosystem is an essential element. Without this platform, the project is non-viable, also with a wrong design of the interactive processes.

For this reason, one of the firsts tasks to be performed in this project has been the requirements elicitation process. It has been done in an iterative and incremental way, requesting information to every project partner regarding three areas: the data we need to manage, the services we have to offer and the non-functional aspects that cover the more technical issues of the system and, more in a more important way, the security and the privacy issues.

The requirement elicitation is not an easy task, especially if your stakeholders are geographically dispersed by seven countries, they have very different interests and cultural background and the most are not in habit to be involved in software requirements definition processes.

In order to manage these difficulties different elicitation techniques have been used, mainly based on online questionnaires, but this gathering method has been complemented with forum-based discussions and videoçonference sessions.

Finally, a first version of the WYRED requirement document is available with enough information to start the ecosystem development and deployment. We know, especially with regard to the system functionality, these requirements will evolve and grow, but the basis to the interaction design is yet defined.

Acknowledgments. With the support of the EU Horizon 2020 Programme in its "Europe in a changing world – inclusive, innovative and reflective Societies (HORIZON 2020: REV-INEQUAL-10-2016: Multi-stakeholder platform for enhancing youth digital opportunities)" Call. Project WYRED (netWorked Youth Research for Empowerment in the Digital society) (Grant agreement No 727066). The sole responsibility for the content of this webpage lies with the authors. It does not necessarily reflect the opinion of the European Union. The European Commission is not responsible for any use that may be made of the information contained therein.

This work has been partially funded also by the Spanish Government Ministry of Economy and Competitiveness throughout the DEFINES project (Ref. TIN2016-80172-R).

References

1. García-Peñalvo, F.J.: The WYRED project: a technological platform for a generative research and dialogue about youth perspectives and interests in digital society. J. Inf. Technol. Res. **9**, VI–X (2016)
2. García-Peñalvo, F.J., Kearney, N.A.: Networked youth research for empowerment in digital society. the WYRED project. In: García-Peñalvo, F.J. (ed.) Proceedings of the Fourth International Conference on Technological Ecosystems for Enhancing Multiculturality (TEEM 2016), Salamanca, Spain, 2–4 November 2016, pp. 3–9. ACM, New York (2016)
3. Dini, P., Darking, M., Rathbone, N., Vidal, M., Hernández, P., Ferronato, P., Briscoe, G., Hendryx, S.: The digital ecosystems research vision: 2010 and beyond. European Commission (2005)
4. European Commission: Digital Ecosystems: The New Global Commons for SMEs and local growth (2006)
5. García-Peñalvo, F.J.: Technological ecosystems. IEEE Rev. Iberoamericana de Tecnologias del Aprendizaje **11**, 31–32 (2016)
6. García-Peñalvo, F.J., García-Holgado, A. (eds.): Open Source Solutions for Knowledge Management and Technological Ecosystems. IGI Global, Hershey (2017)
7. García-Peñalvo, F.J., Hernández-García, Á., Conde-González, M.Á., Fidalgo-Blanco, Á., Sein-Echaluce, M.L., Alier-Forment, M., Llorens-Largo, F., Iglesias-Pradas, S.: Learning services-based technological ecosystems. In: Alves, G.R., Felgueiras, M.C. (eds.) Proceedings of the Third International Conference on Technological Ecosystems for Enhancing Multiculturality (TEEM 2015), Porto, Portugal, 7–9 October 2015, pp. 467–472. ACM, New York (2015)
8. Gustavsson, R., Fredriksson, M.: Sustainable information ecosystems. In: Garcia, A., Lucena, C., Zambonelli, F., Omicini, A., Castro, J. (eds.) SELMAS 2002. LNCS, vol. 2603, pp. 123–138. Springer, Heidelberg (2003). doi:10.1007/3-540-35828-5_8
9. Jansen, S., Finkelstein, A., Brinkkemper, S.: A sense of community: a research agenda for software ecosystems. In: 31st International Conference on Software Engineering - Companion Volume, ICSE-Companion 2009, Vancouver, BC, 16–24 May 2009, pp. 187–190. IEEE, USA (2009)
10. García-Peñalvo, F.J., Hernández-García, Á., Conde, M.Á., Fidalgo-Blanco, Á., Sein-Echaluce, M.L., Alier-Forment, M., Llorens-Largo, F., Iglesias-Pradas, S.: Enhancing education for the knowledge society era with learning ecosystems. In: García-Peñalvo, F.J., García-Holgado, A. (eds.) Open Source Solutions for Knowledge Management and Technological Ecosystems, pp. 1–24. IGI Global, Hershey (2017)
11. García-Peñalvo, F.J.: En clave de innovación educativa. Construyendo el nuevo ecosistema de aprendizaje. In: I Congreso Internacional de Tendencias en Innovación Educativa, CITIE 2016, Arequipa, Perú (2016)
12. Balduino, R.: Introduction to OpenUP (Open Unified Process). Eclipse Foundation (2007)
13. García-Peñalvo, F.J., Rodríguez-Conde, M.J., Seoane-Pardo, A.M., Conde-González, M.Á., Zangrando, V., García-Holgado, A.: GRIAL (GRupo de investigación en InterAcción y eLearning), USAL. IE Comun. Rev. Iberoamericana de Informática Educativa **15**, 85–94 (2012)
14. García-Holgado, A., García-Peñalvo, F.J.: The evolution of the technological ecosystems: an architectural proposal to enhancing learning processes. In: García-Peñalvo, F.J. (ed.) Proceedings of the First International Conference on Technological Ecosystems for Enhancing Multiculturality (TEEM 2013), Salamanca, Spain, 14–15 November 2013, pp. 565–571. ACM, New York (2013)

15. García-Holgado, A., García-Peñalvo, F.J.: Architectural pattern for the definition of eLearning ecosystems based on open source developments. In: Sierra-Rodríguez, J.L., Dodero-Beardo, J.M., Burgos, D. (eds.) Proceedings of 2014 International Symposium on Computers in Education (SIIE), Logrono, La Rioja, Spain, 12–14 November 2014, pp. 93–98. Institute of Electrical and Electronics Engineers, USA (2014)

16. García-Holgado, A., García-Peñalvo, F.J., Hernández-García, Á., Llorens-Largo, F.: Analysis and improvement of knowledge management processes in organizations using the business process model notation. In: Palacios-Marqués, D., Ribeiro Soriano, D., Huarng, K.H. (eds.) New Information and Communication Technologies for Knowledge Management in Organizations, pp. 93–101. Springer, Switzerland (2015)

17. García-Peñalvo, F.J., Johnson, M., Alves, G.R., Minovic, M., Conde-González, M.Á.: Informal learning recognition through a cloud ecosystem. Future Gener. Comput. Syst. **32**, 282–294 (2014)

18. Alonso de Castro, M.G.: Educational projects based on mobile learning. Educ. Knowl. Soc. **15**, 10–19 (2014)

19. Sánchez-Prieto, J.C., Olmos-Migueláñez, S., García-Peñalvo, F.J.: Understanding mobile learning: devices, pedagogical implications and research lines. Educ. Knowl. Soc. **15**, 20–42 (2014)

20. Sánchez-Prieto, J.C., Olmos-Migueláñez, S., García-Peñalvo, F.J.: ¿Utilizarán los futuros docentes las tecnologías móviles? Validación de una propuesta de modelo TAM extendido. RED. Revista de Educación a Distancia **52** (2017). Artículo 5

21. Sánchez-Prieto, J.C., Olmos-Migueláñez, S., García-Peñalvo, F.J.: A TAM based tool for the assessment of the acceptance of mobile technologies among teachers. GRIAL Research Group/University of Salamanca (2016)

22. Sánchez-Prieto, J.C., Olmos-Migueláñez, S., García-Peñalvo, F.J.: MLearning and pre-service teachers: an assessment of the behavioral intention using an expanded TAM model. Comput. Hum. Behav. (2017, in Press)

23. Blanke, T., Hedges, M.: Scholarly primitives: building institutional infrastructure for humanities e-Science. Future Gener. Comput. Syst. **29**, 654–661 (2013)

24. Florio, L., Reilly, S., Demchenko, Y., Varga, T., Harangi, G.: Advancing technologies and federating communities: a study on authentication and authorisation platforms for scientific resources in Europe. European Commission (2012)

25. García-Peñalvo, F.J.: Issue on visual analytics. J. Inf. Technol. Res. **8**, IV–VI (2015)

26. González-Torres, A., García-Peñalvo, F.J., Therón, R.: How evolutionary visual software analytics supports knowledge discovery. J. Inf. Sci. Eng. **29**, 17–34 (2013)

27. González-Torres, A., García-Peñalvo, F.J., Therón, R.: Human-computer interaction in evolutionary visual software analytics. Comput. Hum. Behav. **29**, 486–495 (2013)

28. García-Peñalvo, F.J., Colomo-Palacios, R., Hsu, J.Y.J.: Discovering knowledge through highly interactive information based systems foreword. J. Inf. Sci. Eng. **29** (2013)

29. Keim, D.A., Andrienko, G., Fekete, J.-D., Görg, C., Kohlhammer, J., Melançon, G.: Visual analytics: definition, process, and challenges. In: Kerren, A., Stasko, J.T., Fekete, J.-D., North, C. (eds.) Information Visualization. LNCS, vol. 4950, pp. 154–175. Springer, Heidelberg (2008). doi:10.1007/978-3-540-70956-5_7

30. Keim, D.A., Mansmann, F., Schneidewind, J., Ziegler, H.: Challenges in visual data analysis. In: Proceedings of the Tenth International Conference on Information Visualization, 2006, London, England, 5–7 July 2006, pp. 9–16. IEEE, USA (2006)

31. Gómez-Aguilar, D.A., García-Peñalvo, F.J., Therón, R.: Analítica Visual en eLearning. El Profesional de la Información **23**, 236–245 (2014)

32. Gómez-Aguilar, D.A., Hernández-García, Á., García-Peñalvo, F.J., Therón, R.: Tap into visual analysis of customization of grouping of activities in eLearning. Comput. Hum. Behav. **47**, 60–67 (2015)

33. Pohl, K.: Requirements engineering: an overview. In: Kent, A., Williams, J. (eds.) Encyclopedia of Computer Science and Technology, vol. 36. Marcel Dekker, New York (1997)

34. WYRED Consortium: Requirements Document. WYRED Consortium (2017)

Personal and Shared Perspectives on Knowledge Maps in Learning Environments

Anna Goy, Giovanna Petrone, and Claudia Picardi[(✉)]

Dipartimento di Informatica, Università di Torino, Torino, Italy
{annamaria.goy, giovanna.petrone,
claudia.picardi}@unito.it

Abstract. Knowledge maps are a powerful means to represent and share knowledge in both communication and learning. Collaborative knowledge mapping, in particular, enables comparing, discussing and bridging different perspectives on a topic. In this paper, we propose that it can be supported by providing users with multi-perspective maps, including one shared perspective and several individual ones. Building on our previous work about collaborative annotation of resources, we provide a formalization for multi-perspective concept maps, which we implemented in a proof-of-concept prototype. We then present the results of a formative qualitative evaluation performed on the prototype, where 12 participants, divided into 4 groups, performed a collaborative mapping task with two different versions of the tool: one in which only the shared perspective was available, and another in which the shared perspective was paired with a personal one. From the analysis of the observations gathered in the evaluation, as well as the subjective impressions of the participants collected by means of an electronic questionnaire, we draw requirements for an interaction model supporting multi-perspective concept maps. Such requirements can be summarized as follows: (1) the UI should overlay the personal and the shared perspective, to stress that they concern the same object (the map) and to enable comparison; (2) "shared" and "personal" should be supported by different work modalities, which should be explicitly enabled in the UI; (3) the UI should include a "revision of changes" mode to support users in evaluating changes by others, and relating their perspective to the work of others.

Keywords: Collaborative learning · Multi-perspective concept maps · Personal and shared perspectives

1 Introduction and Related Work

Knowledge maps – graphical representations aimed at *"describing intellectual landscapes"* [14] – are a powerful means to represent and share knowledge, with two major purposes:

- communicating/sharing knowledge with visual immediacy, making the relevant pieces of information and their connections easy to capture;

© Springer International Publishing AG 2017
P. Zaphiris and A. Ioannou (Eds.): LCT 2017, Part II, LNCS 10296, pp. 382–400, 2017.
DOI: 10.1007/978-3-319-58515-4_30

- learning/acquiring knowledge; knowledge maps are in fact a widely recognized learning aid.

These two tasks are not independent from each other:

- communication is core to learning: teachers and students share their knowledge, and researchers have investigated the use of knowledge maps [3, 5, 12], in particular in collaborative learning [9];
- communication both implies and works toward mutual understanding: the receiver learns something from its source – not always new information, but certainly her counterpart's perspective.

In both communication and learning, a knowledge map can be seen as a perspective on a topic. Therefore, comparing, discussing and bridging different knowledge maps becomes relevant to the tasks of acquiring and sharing knowledge, as it allows to become aware of one's own map as a perspective, to be constructively critical towards the subjective aspects of maps, and to work towards the definition of a common, shared perspective.

Moreover, the development of a *personal perspective* is an important formative goal: supporting the learner in relating her personal knowledge map to the shared one – and possibly to other learners' personal maps – can foster the development, recognition and meta-reflection on her own perspective [10].

In previous works, we have investigated how collaborative annotation of resources can be enhanced by keeping track of personal views [6, 7]. We found that the outcome of collaboration is perceived to be more satisfactory when each author is allowed to keep a personal view rather than sacrificing it to the common goal. Some users also reported that looking at the other participants' work on the shared view increased their awareness of their own perspective on the topic.

We have thus become convinced that the goal of collaboration is not necessarily to obtain an agreed-upon, univocal representation, but instead:

- to create awareness on the existence of different perspectives;
- to learn why, when and how one's own knowledge map represents a perspective rather than objective knowledge;
- to reach mutual understanding on the different perspectives;
- to learn from other people's perspectives, possibly modifying one's own as a result;
- to make available to others a multi-faceted, inclusive representation of "knowledge" on a given topic, which honors the different perspectives as well as the common grounds.

In order to implement this vision, and to be able to evaluate it, we applied it to a learning context characterized as: lifelong (a need that emerges from present-day knowledge-intensive and highly interconnected life styles [4]), ubiquitous (occurring anywhere, being open and loosely structured [8]), self-initiated and interest-driven (thus taking place outside formal education settings [2]).

Within this scenario, *Personal Learning Environments* (PLE) [1, 17] are emerging, allowing learners to build their own learning workspaces. Although PLEs often enable users to integrate shared and personal workspaces, the definition of models supporting these features is still an open issue [8].

The ultimate goal of our work is to define an interaction model, based on a formal representation of knowledge maps, coupled with automated techniques for comparing maps, highlighting similarities and differences with respect to different map features such as chosen concepts, types of connections and map topology [15].

In this paper, we take a first step in this direction, by drawing requirements, based on a formative qualitative evaluation, for an effective interaction model enabling users to handle both personal and shared perspectives within a web-based system for designing concept maps. Concept maps are a specific type of knowledge map [13], represented as connected graphs where nodes nodes represent ideas, thoughts, concepts, and edges represent connections between them.

In Sect. 2 we formally define multi-perspective concept maps; *personal* and *shared* perspectives are then characterized by the different actions that users can perform on them, along with the effects of such actions (Sect. 2.1). We then discuss the experimental scenario we envisioned (Sect. 2.2) and the proof-of-concept prototype we implemented in order to enable the evaluation (Sect. 2.3).

In Sect. 3 we present the results of a formative, qualitative evaluation of the interaction between users and multi-perspective concept maps; in Sect. 4 we discuss such results, outlining the lessons we learned from them, and drawing requirements for a novel proposal of interaction model. Section 5 concludes the paper highlighting future directions for research.

2   Multi-perspective Concept Maps

A concept map can be represented as a labelled graph $M = (C, R, l_c, l_r)$, where C is the set of concepts represented in the map, $R \subseteq C \times C$ is the set of relationships among them, $l_c:C \longrightarrow \Sigma^*$ is the set of labels (on an alphabet Σ) used for concepts, and $l_r: R \longrightarrow \Sigma^*$ is the set of labels used for relationships. Given such a map M:

- A *perspective* M' on M is a labelled subgraph (C', R', l_c', l_r'), where $C' \subseteq C$, R' is a subset of the projection of R on $C' \times C'$, l_c' is the projection of l_c on C', and l_r' is the projection of l_r on R'. In the following we will write $M' \subseteq M$ to denote M' is a subgraph of M.
- Given a concept map M collaboratively built by a group of users $\{u_1,...,u_n\}$, for each user u_i, $P(u_i) \subseteq M$ denotes her *personal perspective*, while P denotes the *shared* perspective.
- Each user u can view and manipulate (add, delete, modify) those elements of M (i.e., concept, relationships and labels) that belong to her $P(u)$. All users can view and manipulate elements of M belonging to P. Manipulations on $P(u)$ affect only $P(u)$ itself. Manipulations on P can affect also other $P(v)$s, with $v \neq u$. Available actions and their effects on the different perspectives are described in detail in Sect. 2.1.
- In addition, a user u can share elements belonging to her perspective $P(u)$, making them part of P as well, or decide she disagrees with elements belonging to the shared perspective P, removing them from her $P(u)$. The effects of these actions are also detailed in Sect. 2.1.

2.1 User Activities

The personal and shared perspectives are essentially characterized by (i) the actions that can be performed on them by the different users, and (ii) the effects these actions have on the other perspectives. These characterizations are an application of our previous work on collaborative tagging [6, 7] to multi-perspective concept maps.

A personal perspectives $P(u)$ can (and should) overlap with the shared perspective P: their intersection contains those shared elements user u agrees upon. On the other hand, the overlap between two personal perspectives $P(u)$ and $P(v)$ is contained in P; there cannot be common elements between two personal perspectives that are not shared among all. Of course, $P(u)$ and $P(v)$ can end up containing concepts or relationships with the same labels and connections, but they are regarded as different "objects" within the global map M.

A personal perspective $P(u)$ offers to its owner u, and only to her, the possibility to **Add**, **Remove**, **Edit**, **Move**, **Resize** and **Share** its "exclusive" elements, i.e. elements that belong *only* to $P(u)$. Of these actions, **Share** is the only one affecting other perspectives (namely, P). The shared perspective P offers all users the possibility to **Add**, **Remove**, **Edit**, **Move**, and **Resize** all of its elements, or **Disagree/Agree** with them. Most of these actions affect in different ways the personal perspective of the acting user, and the personal perspectives of the others (Fig. 1).

- *Add concept/relationship*: this action performed in $P(u)$ has no effect on other perspectives $P(v)s$ nor in P; if performed in P, the concept/relationship is added in $P(u)$ and to all the $P(v)$s of other users, as participants are assumed by default to agree with it.
- *Remove concept/relationship*: this action can be performed in $P(u)$ only on elements that do not also belong to P; it has no effect on other personal perspectives. If performed in P, the element is removed from P as well as from $P(u)$. Each $P(v)$, with $v \neq u$, containing the removed element, retains a *copy* of it belonging only to $P(v)$. In all cases, if the removed element is a concept/node, the action is applied in cascade to the relationships/edges connected to it in P or $P(u)$.
- *Edit concept/relationship* editing includes both changing the label a of concept or relationship, or changing how a relationship is connected. This activity, if performed in $P(u)$, has no effect on other perspectives. If the action is performed in P, it affects all the perspectives containing the modified concept/relationship.
- *Move/Resize concept*: this activity, if performed on elements belonging only to $P(u)$, has no effect on other perspectives. The position and size of elements belonging to P can be changed only in the shared perspective, even if they also belong to $P(u)$. When this happens, the action affects all the perspectives containing the moved/resized concept/relationship.
- *Share concept/*: this activity is available only in the personal perspective, on concepts/relationship belonging $P(u)$ but not to P; its effect is to add the map element to P. If the shared element is a relationship/edge, and one or both the concepts/nodes it connects do not belong to P, they are also added in P. When an element is shared from $P(u)$ to P, we assume that, by default, it is added to the

$P(v)s$ of other users $v \neq u$ too (in other words, we assume that other participants agree with it unless they explicitly disagree).

- **Disagree** *with concept/relationship*: this activity is available only in the shared perspective, and u can only disagree with elements in P that also belong to $P(u)$. The effect is to remove the element from $P(u)$; if the element is a concept also relationship/edges connected to it in $P(u)$ are removed.
- **Agree** *with concept/relationship*: this activity is available only in the shared perspective, and u can only agree with elements in P that do not belong to $P(u)$. The effect is to add the element to $P(u)$. If the element is a relationship, and one or both its connected concepts do not belong to $P(u)$, they are also added in $P(u)$, i.e. agreement is extended to them.

2.2   Usage Scenario and User Interface

The basic scenario we envision includes a small group of people (e.g., in our experiment, groups contain 3 users; see Sect. 3) collaborating in order to develop a shared concept map on a topic. Two variations can be devised (actually, two extremes in a spectrum of possibilities where the two situations are interleaved):

a. Users learn collaboratively by directly building a shared perspective. Personal perspectives essentially grow out of the shared one whenever there is a disagreement, i.e. a concept or relationship someone agrees with is removed by someone else.
b. Users learn first by themselves, building their personal perspectives, and only at a later stage, when they have reached a satisfactory conceptualization of what they have studied, they share their work. In this case the shared perspective emerges from a selective merge of the personal ones.

Here we focus on scenario (a), not because we deem irrelevant scenario (b), but in order not to broaden too much the scope of the study and risk creating confusion in the experimentation with users (see Sect. 3). In scenario (a) we therefore assume that users have the goal of building a final common map, and thus we expect the shared perspective to be their main focus. The characterization of user actions in the previous section takes into account the assumptions of scenario (a): whenever a user adds an element to the shared perspective, it is automatically added to the personal perspectives of all participants, and will be removed only if the will explicitly *disagree* with it.

2.3   Proof-of-Concept Prototype

Our proof-of-concept prototype, used in the evaluation described in Sect. 3, provides two versions of the tool for the collaborative management of concept maps: in the simpler version, named *onlyS*, users only interact with the shared perspective on the concept map; in the complete version, named *SplusP*, users can see and interact with both their personal perspectives and with the shared one, shown side-by -side on the screen (Fig. 1).

On the left, the user can see and interact with the personal perspective, while on the right she can see and act on the shared perspective. At any time, only one of the two is active, highlighted by a white background (the inactive one is grey). The user makes a perspective active by clicking on it.

In the personal perspective, white nodes represent exclusively personal concepts, while grey ones are shared nodes the user has agreed with. The former can thus be freely edited, moved or resized, while the latter can be edited, moved or resized only from the shared perspective. The current user interface does not make any graphical distinction between shared/non-shared agreed/non-agreed relations.

The user double clicks on the canvas to **Add** a new concept, while she double clicks on an existing element to **Edit** it (when this action is available). To **Add** a relationship between two concepts, the user selects a concept, clicks on "Aggiungi relazione" (*Add relationship*) button and then clicks on the second concept. Concepts can be **Removed** by first clicking on them and then pressing Backspace. A user can indeed do so with a shared concept in the personal perspective, but this triggers the **Disagree** action (the shared concept is removed from the personal perspective but retained in the shared one.

Concepts can be **Moved** or **Resized** by dragging either the concept itself or the resize handles, as in any shape drawing UI.

If the user in the personal perspective wants to **Share** a concept, she selects the concept and clicks on "Condividi con altri" (*Share with others*) button.

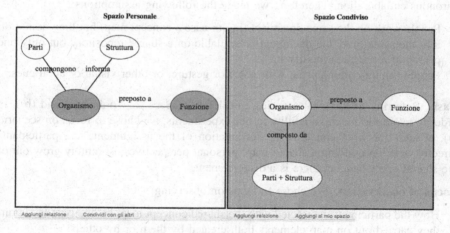

Fig. 1. Screenshot of the *SplusP* prototype

In the shared perspective, the user can also **Agree** again with a concept she had previously disagreed with, thereby re-adding it to her personal perspective; this can be obtained by selecting the concept and clicking on the button labelled "Aggiungi al mio spazio" (*Add to my space*).

The prototype has been built as a Web Application, exploiting in the front-end HTML5, JQuery and FabricJS, which is a specialized library to draw on canvas. The backend is implemented in PHP and MySQL. Our goal has been to quickly test the approach and be able to modify the user interaction, based on the user evaluation we performed on the current prototype.

3   Qualitative Evaluation

3.1   Assumptions

Type of collaboration. Our investigation broadly concerns collaboration in building concept maps. However, this includes a wide range of sub-tasks and situations involving different dynamics both in the user-to-user interaction and in the user-to-map interaction.

We can trace two major distinctions in collaborative work [11, 16]:

- *colocated* vs. *remote*
- *synchronous* vs. *asynchronous*

With respect to these distinctions, which result in four quite different types of collaborative activity, we narrowed down our study to the case of remote, asynchronous collaboration. Therefore, we made the following assumptions:

- People work on the same document (in our case a concept map) but they do not do it at the same time; the document is available on a shared repository but only one person at a time can modify it.
- People cannot communicate with voice or gesture, or other visual or aural cues.

Task. Referring to the two scenarios envisioned in Sect. 2.2 (points (a) and (b)), in order to avoid too much variability in our experiments, we chose to focus on scenario (a), at least for what concerns the formulation of the assignment, i.e., participants directly work on building a shared map; personal perspectives essentially grow out of the shared one whenever there is a disagreement.

Focus of observation. We chose to focus on observing:

- How the participants interacted with the shared concept map, i.e. the type of actions they carried out on map elements both created by them or by others.
- How the participants interacted with the personal perspective, when available.
- The participants' reactions to what happened during the collaboration.

We did not focus on the cognitive task of building the map *per-se*, and we did not observe nor address the *semantic content* of the resulting concept maps.

3.2   Experimental Setup

We recruited 12 participants[1] which were then divided into 4 groups (G1, G2, G3 and G4) of 3 people each. Each group received an initial briefing, describing the simulated task they had to carry out: "You are studying for an introductory psychology course, and you received a group assignment. You have to collaborate at building a concept map representing the relevant notions of a book section, and you need to do so using the digital tool we will provide you with."

In order to simulating a remote, asynchronous collaboration, users cannot communicate with each other during the task.

Each participant was provided with a short excerpt from an introductory psychology book; after reading it, each participant took two turns (lasting no more than ten minutes) at the computer.

Each group underwent the experiment twice, with two different text excerpts (X and Y), and with two different versions of the tool: *onlyS*, in which only the shared perspective was available, and *SplusP*, in which the shared perspective on the map was coupled with a personal one. Groups performed the experiment according to the following layout:

	First *onlyS* then *SplusP*	First *SplusP* then *onlyS*
First X then Y	G1	G3
First Y then X	G2	G4

One of us took notes recording the comments that the person using the tool voiced out loud while working, as well as their overall approach to the work, and any obstacle, difficulty or issue that could arise in the interaction. The recording of specific actions within the tool was carried out by the logging service of the application.

For each group, after both experiments were completed, we collected each participants' feedback by means of a computer-based questionnaire, described in the next section.

3.3   Results

Interaction Dynamics. We recorded (by taking notes and by logging user actions) the dynamics of the activity for each group (G1, G2, G3) with each tool (*onlyS* or *SplusP*). We also collected the comments of the users during the interaction, because it gives a better feel of the context where they were voiced. The dynamics of the activity as well as the users' comments are reported in Appendix A.

Table 1 shows the number of logged actions, by type, carried out across the whole experiment, either in the shared or in the personal space (when available).

---

[1] We recruited the participants among students in our university, with varied backgrounds either in computer science, or human studies.

Table 1. Action types across all groups

	tot azioni	add/edit/delete			layout	add	edit			delete			share own	copy to pers.
		tot	own	other			own	other	tot	own	other	tot		
onlyS	427	203	155	48	224	143	8	20	28	4	28	32	–	–
SplusP personal	186	118	–	–	68	54	–	–	1	–	–	63	–	–
SplusP shared	381	137	116	21	215	105	5	8	13	6	13	19	28	1
SplusP total	567	255	116	21	283	159	5	8	14	6	13	82	28	1

Questionnaire. The goal of the questionnaire was to obtain the subjective evaluation of the participants concerning the task we asked them to complete, and the tools they used to do so. The questionnaire was composed of 5 questions and a space for free final comments. We list here the 5 questions and provide histograms representing the participants' answers (Fig. 2). Free comments are fully listed in Appendix B; pertinent remarks are also quoted in the discussion (Sect. 5).

Q1: Given your previous experience (if any) and what you did today, how does it seem to you that drawing knowledge maps, either on paper or with a computer-based tool, as an aid to studying and learning, is easy/interesting/useful? *(answers on a 5-points rating scale)*

Q2: Which of the two tools you experimented with today was easier/more interesting/more useful for drawing knowledge maps as an aid to studying and learning? *(answers on a 5-points rating scale)*

Q3: Having a personal space in addition to the shared one was useful to you for... *(multiple choice with open option)*

Q4: According to the experience you had today, which of the following additional features could improve the tool(s)? *(multiple choice)*

Q5: Are there any other additional features or changes you would suggest for the *SplusP* tool? *(free text)*

4 Discussion and Requirements

SplusP was found by almost half the participants less easy to use than *onlyP*. The choice of tool did not seem to make the task more or less interesting; participants were divided on whether *SplusP* was more or less useful than *onlyP*. However, all participants but one put the personal perspective to use (see answers to questionnaire **Q3**). The overall analysis of the observations, including interaction dynamics, action log, and questionnaires, shows in our opinion that, in most cases, what the participants subjectively reported in the questionnaire is supported by our direct observation of their interaction.

In particular, our analysis shows that while users perceived the personal perspective feature as potentially interesting, the way it was implemented let their expectations

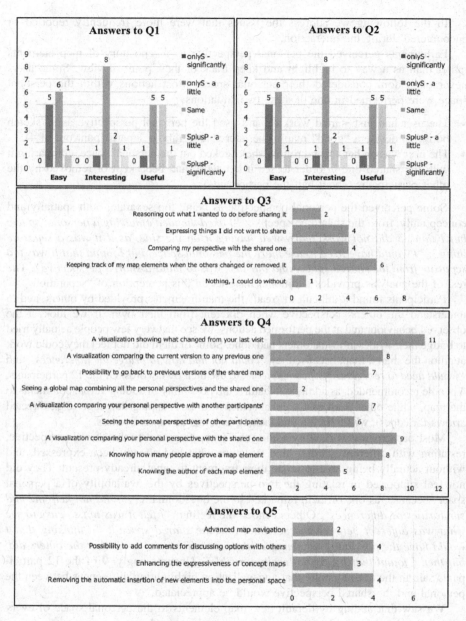

Fig. 2. Answers to questionnaire

down. Converging towards a shared perspective was deemed a difficult task in most difficulties attained to the task *per-se*, which were caused by interaction problems, and which could be eased by additional functionalities.

In the following we address the issues that were more frequently reported or encountered during the interaction.

Participants perceived the personal perspective as a repository of map elements rather than as a way to highlight and keep track of their point of view. Some users never or seldom considered their personal space. Most actions within the personal space were performed in one of these two situations:

- The user had just started working and used the personal perspective as a "sketch book" to devise a "good" map to be later shared (about 1 participant out of 4).
- The user was on her second round; she checked out the personal space, comparing it with the shared one in order to see if her work had been kept or removed by the other participants (about half the participants).

Some perceived the personal perspective as being too separate, both spatially and conceptually, from the shared perspective: *"I liked the idea of having a personal space, but I think it did not work really well having it on the side, as if it was a separate thing"*; *"I would have liked to use more the personal space, but I found that it was too separate from the shared space, and our task was to build a shared perspective"*. The rest of the analysis provides additional insights on this perception of "separation".

Participants found it difficult to "read" the map fragments provided by others, and to understand the others' perspective when different from their own. If we look at the observed behaviour and at the performed actions, we see that very few people actually tried to bridge their work with what others had done. Some of them did not feel they could work at all on the shared map, because they *"could not find how to bridge the differences"* and *"would need to reorganize [it] completely"*, to use their own words. Of the 12 participants, 4 people recommended, as additional feature, the possibility of adding verbal comments to the map, while other 3 asked for enhancements to the mapping language (e.g., directed arrows for edges), which they found lacking in terms of expressiveness.

Most participants worked by adding their map fragment to the shared perspective, restating with different wording and structure what had already been expressed, and without actually being able to relate their fragment to what already present. They did not feel supported in relating the two perspectives by the availability of a personal space, because, as one of them remarked in the questionnaire, *"it did not help me find similarities or differences"*. Others echoed the feeling: *"I felt it was not so easy to see what was different between the personal and the shared space"*, *"...thinking that I would have the possibility to compare [the personal space] with what the others did, but then I found that it was not really possible"*. Unsurprisingly, 9 of the 12 participants said in the questionnaire that a visualization highlighting differences between the personal and the shared perspective would be appreciated.

We saw that adding by default new map elements to the personal space of every participant, when such elements were added to the shared space, was a poor choice. Our idea was that, given the goal of a shared map, people would have tried to build upon the others' work, even in their personal space. Also, we thought that in this way everyone would be compelled to see what had been added from her last visit, and take a stance by either keeping it or discarding it from the personal perspective. However, most participants actually saw this as a defilement of their personal space: *"the shared space turned out a bit cluttered"*; *"[in the personal space] I had no means to* distinguish the others' work from mine"; "I was not interested in keeping what the others did in [my personal space]"; "I... did not look much at the personal [space]. Also because it got cluttered with the others' work".

All participants but one (11 people out of 12) said they would recommend, as an additional feature, the possibility of seeing changes with respect to their last visit. There seem to be two main reasons for this, according to their free remarks: on the one hand, to make clearer the proposed change, while still leaving room for undoing it: "I still had concerns about removing the others' work. ... if I removed what the others did, they maybe would not realize it"; "I was uncomfortable in removing things from the shared space, because it seemed to be rude. I would like to be able to suggest a removal, then let the others decide"; "I think it would be more useful for the collaboration to be able to see the changes proposed by each person". On the other hand, highlighting newly added elements allows to cherry pick what to add in one's own perspective and what to discard. As one participant put it: "I did not like the fact that the others' work was by default added to my personal space. I would have liked to be able to distinguish what was "new" from the last time I worked on it."

4.1 Improving the Interaction

Our present goal, given the above discussion of experimental results, is to propose a different interaction modality for supporting users in working with multi-perspective concept maps. However, the experiment showed that the focus should be shifted from the task of designing a shared concept map, to the task of comparing and reasoning on the different perspectives. Without achieving this goal, it is impossible for the group to build a shared perspective which honours the individual points of view.

The interaction modality implemented in the prototype was not up to this task: it brought users to see the personal perspective as a temporary, private repository, rather than as a way to clarify a participant's point of view. Nonetheless, the prototype allowed the participants to experiment interaction with both a personal and a shared perspective, which in turn provided us with insights on how such interaction could be improved.

There are two major points that the analysis of the experimental observations made clearer to us:

- **Perspectives arise when we look at the same object from different points of view. Even if we see different parts or aspects of the object, the object is the same.** Our participants reminded us of this when complaining about having two separate screen spaces, and when expressing the desire for a *differential* visualization.
- **"Personal" and "shared" do not only denote different perspectives on the same object, but also different work modalities on the same object.** Working *from* a given perspective is different than working *on* a different perspective. When a person works from a personal perspective, she acts on its elements, but her actions affect also the shared perspective. The opposite is also true. Our prototype did not clearly highlight this distinction, nor provide adequate feedback on the effects of users' actions, so that they could be supported in recognizing the distinction.

Based on these considerations, and on the analysis in Sect. 4, we propose that a novel interaction model for multi-perspective concept maps should take into account the following requirements:

1. The visualization should **overlay** the personal and the shared perspective. The visual cues communicating if a map element belongs or not to each perspective should be independent from each other: it should be immediately distinguishable if a map element belongs to the personal perspective, to the shared, or both.
2. The user should be able to choose between two **different editing modalities**, "personal" and "shared". It should be clear that in each modality the user essentially acts *from* the corresponding perspective, but her actions can affect also the other one (having both perspectives visible in overlay should help stressing this point). Strong visual cues should clearly communicate what modality is currently active.
3. **Changes since last visit** can be visualized too as an overlay between two (shared) perspectives: the last one the user worked with, and the new one that evolved while she was offline. This suggests that the "shared" modality mentioned in the previous point could include a "revision of changes" activity or work mode, supporting the possibility, mentioned by some of our participants, of expressing a vote or opinion on a suggested change. A revision of changes would also solve the problem of whether new elements added in the shared perspective should be automatically agreed with or not (as we saw, agreement by default was not appreciated by the evaluation participants). By specifically revising newly added concepts and relationships, the user would be supported in choosing what to do with each.

5   Conclusions

In this paper, we introduced *multi-perspective concept maps* as a tool for learning through collaboration in building concept maps for a given subject of study.

We defined the notion of *perspective* on a concept map, and we characterized what a *personal* and a *shared* perspective are in a group collaboration, by describing the different actions that each user can perform on the two types of perspectives, and the effects such actions have on the others' work. These definitions built upon our previous work on multiple perspectives in collaborative annotation of resources [6, 7].

We described a proof-of-concept prototype we implemented to test our proposal. We then presented the results of a formative qualitative evaluation, discussing them in order to draw principles and requirements for an effective interaction model for users to collaboratively work with both a shared and a personal perspective.

These principles and requirements also form the starting point for our future work on this topic. Our immediate goal is to design, and thoroughly evaluate, a new prototype incorporating the requirements emerged from the user study: *overlay* visualization of perspectives, multiple *editing modalities*, and a *"revision of changes"* feature. According to the users' feedback, the new prototype should also incorporate the possibility to discuss changes and choices with group members, by means of a *commenting* feature, and offer an *enriched concept mapping language* to allow for more expressiveness.

Appendix A

Here we fully describe the interaction dynamics observed during the evaluation.

P1, P2, P3 refer to the different participants in each group (Tables 2, 3, 4, 5, 6, 7, 8 and 9).

Table 2. Interaction dynamics for G1, Tool *onlyS*

All	Read text printed on paper
All	Sketch out a possible concept map on the text sheet
P1, round 1	Recreates the map sketched out on paper
P2, round 1	Does not touch what P1 did. Adds her own version of map *"The screen is small"*
P3, round 1	Essentially moves around the others' nodes, adding a few of her own *"I don't get it"* *"I would like to remove everything the others did, is that possible?"*
P1, round 2	Reorganizes the map, removing a few of the other participants' concepts *"Is there a scrollbar?"* (there is none: users have to drag the canvas in order to scroll)
P2, round 2	Works on what exists (deleting and modifying other participants' work) and adds a few concepts and relationships of her own
P3, round 2	Takes quite some time moving and removing concepts; adds a couple of relationships

Table 3. Interaction dynamics for G1, Tool *SplusP*

All	Read text printed on paper
All	Sketch out a possible concept map on the text sheet
P3, round 1	Recreates the map sketched out on paper **in the personal space**. Tries to share it all at once, failing (the tool does not allow it). Shares part of the map *"I will decide what to do with the rest after the others have done their part"*
P1, round 1	Works exclusively **in the shared space**, adding her own map to it
P2, round 1	Works a little bit (moving, adding) **in the personal space** but without sharing anything. Works a little bit (again moving, adding) **in the shared space** *"I would need to reorganize this completely"*
P3, round 2	Removes concepts **from the personal space**. Also, reorganizes **the shared space**, moving, editing and deleting what the others did
P1, round 2	Again, works exclusively **in the shared space**, and only adds concepts and relationships
P2, round 2	Works only **in the personal space**, removing concepts and relationships, and adding new ones

Table 4. Interaction dynamics for G2, Tool *onlyS*

All	Read text printed on paper
All	Take notes but do not sketch out the map on paper
P1, round 1	Starts to create her map directly on screen. Adds a few concepts and relationships. Appears uncertain
P2, round 1	Adds her own version of the map, without deleting anything. Edits a couple of P1's concepts *"If I had more time I would delete something"*
P3, round 1	Adds some concepts and relationships. and moves the existing ones. Deletes a few of the other participants' map elements
P1, round 2	Deletes some of the existing concepts and adds some other of her own
P2, round 2	Significantly edits the existing map (making changes and deleting). Also, adds a few elements
P3, round 2	Only edits and deletes a few elements, without reorganizing the space *"I would like to add a reflexive relationship"*

Table 5. Interaction dynamics for G2, Tool *SplusP*

All	Read text printed on paper
All	Take notes but do not sketch out the map on paper
P3, round 1	Adds a few concepts and relationships **in both personal and shared space**. Then edits and deletes some (from both spaces)
P1, round 1	Adds her own concepts and relationships **in the shared space**
P2, round 1	Works at reorganizing **the shared space** changing the map layout. Adds a few concepts/relationships of her own, and edits a couple of the existing ones
P3, round 2	Cleans out **the personal space** from concepts and relationships she is not interested in. Adds a few concepts/relationships in the shared space
P1, round 2	Works mostly at reorganizing **the personal space**, deleting unwanted concepts/relationships and adding new ones *"The shared space is a lot tidier than my own"*
P2, round 2	Again, reorganizes **the shared space**, adding a few map elements. Does not consider the personal space

Table 6. Interaction dynamics for G3, Tool *SplusP*

All	Read text printed on paper
All	P1 and P2 sketch out the map on paper. P3 underlines significant concepts or phrases in the text
P1, round 1	Recreates the map she sketched on paper **in the shared space** *"I would like to be able to add a one-to-many relationship"*
P2, round 1	Adds her own concepts and relationships **in the shared space** *"The personal space does not seem useful in the first round"*
P3, round 1	Adds her own concepts and relationships **in the shared space** *"I do not like that there is stuff in my personal space that I did not put there"*

(continued)

Table 6. (*continued*)

P1, round 2	Rearranges the layout **in the shared space** and adds a few concepts/relationships
P2-, round 2	Removes concepts/relationships **from both the spaces**. Adds a few elements **to the shared space**
P3, round 2	Adds a couple of elements **to the personal space** *"I do not really understand what the others did"*

Table 7. Interaction dynamics for G3, Tool *onlyS*

All	Read text printed on paper
All	P1 and P2 sketch out the map on paper. P3 underlines significant concepts or phrases in the text
P3, round 1	Adds a few concepts/relationships *"Before doing too much I want to see what the others do"*
P1, round 1	Edits all the existing elements and adds many of her own
P2, round 1	Slightly changes the layout of the map *"For me the map is ok as they did it"*
P3, round 2	Mostly changes the layout, adding only a couple of elements
P1, round 2	Mostly changes the layout
P2, round 2	Adds a couple of elements

Table 8. Interaction dynamics for G4, Tool *SplusP*

All	Read text printed on paper
All	Take notes but do not sketch out the map on paper
P1, round 1	Starts creating her map **in the personal space** *"I expected to be able to share it all at once"* (But it is not possible). She then chooses, given the time constraints, to wait for the next round
P2, round 1	Adds map elements to **the shared space**. Then adds some other elements also **to the personal space**
P3, round 1	Adds map elements to **the personal space**, then <u>shares</u> some of them to the **shared space** *"I would like to be able to express a one-to-many relationship"*
P1, round 2	Reorganizes the map layout **in the shared space**, without adding or deleting anything *"I would like to add a relationship between a concept and a relationship"*
P2, round 2	Mostly reorganizes the map layout **in the shared space**. Adds a couple of map elements **to the shared space**
P3, round 2	Moves a couple of concepts in the shared space. Then looks at the map(s) without changing anything *"My personal space is too messed up; I cannot compare my perspective to the shared one"*

Table 9. Interaction dynamics for G4, Tool *onlyS*

All	Read text printed on paper
All	Take notes but do not sketch out the map on paper
P3, round 1	Builds her own map, adding concepts and relationships
P1, round 1	Rearranges the map, editing a few elements. Adds a new concept
P2, round 1	Adds her own version of the map, without removing the existing elements
P3, round 2	Edits a few elements added by the others, and rearranges the layout
P1, round 2	Mostly rearranges the map layout, adding a couple of elements
P2, round 2	Adds several elements to the map, and rearranges the layout, without removing or editing anything

Appendix B

Here we report the complete free remarks the participants provided us with in the questionnaire (Table 10).

Table 10. Participants' answers to the final question (free comments)

a	I had problems with the position of the concepts on the screen. The other participants preferred to organize concepts in a star-shaped layout, with the most relevant concept in the centre, while I prefer a tree-like structure, with the most relevant concept at the top. I also had some difficulties with the interface, it was not so easy to arrange the map
b	I found it difficult to merge my own idea of concept map with the others; I could not read really well what the others had in mind, as if the map itself did not give me enough information. Also, I am not sure my perspective could really be bridged to the others, I felt the need to discuss my perspective with them before taking any actions, or we would end up bouncing between different perspectives depending on who had the last word. (*Did you take advantage of the personal space?*) I did not think the personal space would help me with this, because it did not help me find similarities or differences. And I thought that since our task was to build a shared perspective, working on my personal one would be a loss of time
c	I had difficulty to understand the reasons behind the others' actions, then when it was my turn I would have preferred to re-start from scratch. Having a personal space did not make it easier, I still had concerns about removing the others' work. Maybe because I felt it was not so easy to see what was different between the personal and the shared space. As a consequence, if I removed what the others did, they maybe would not realize it, and, in any case, they would not understand while I did it. I certainly felt so when they removed my work! I mean, I could not understand why
d	I did not like the fact that the others' work was by default added to my personal space. I would have liked to be able to distinguish what was "new" from the last time I worked on it. As it is, I spent a lot of time removing unwanted stuff from my personal space, which in the end did not turn out to be useful in building the shared perspective. At a certain point, I thought I would have preferred to work on my personal space alone, and then discuss with the others showing them my perspective and seeing theirs, before trying to come up with a shared version

(continued)

Table 10. (*continued*)

e	Honestly, I did not find the personal space to be really useful, and I almost did not use it. I think it would be more useful for the collaboration to be able to see the changes proposed by each person, like the different versions of the map
f	Every time I clearly saw the two perspective of the other two participants put together in the shared map, and I tried to sort them out, taking into account also my perspective. I liked the idea of having a personal space, but I think it did not work really well having it on the side, as if it was a separate thing
g	I think it may have been useful to be able to see the others' personal spaces, to better understand what they had in mind. The shared space turned out a bit cluttered
h	I was uncomfortable in removing things from the shared space, because it seemed to be rude. I would like to be able to suggest a removal, then let the others decide. In general I would have liked to be able to communicate with the other participants beyond the work we did on the map
i	My personal perspective was completely different from what the others expressed. I could not find how to bridge the differences. (*What about the personal space?*) It did not feel like the solution to this problem. Also, I did not like to find in it stuff before I had even accessed it once
j	It wasn't easy to understand the others' maps, this type of maps is too simple and leaves a lot of room to interpretations. Also, I spent a lot of time working on my personal perspective, thinking that I would have the possibility to compare it with what the others did, but then I found that it was not really possible, I had no means to distinguish the others' work from mine, it was a bit like those games where you have to find the differences between two quasi-identical images. It would be useful to be able to leave notes or suggestions for the others
k	I mostly put in the shared map my own version, without working on what the others did, apart from rearranging it. I used the personal space as a notebook for thinking, I was not interested in keeping what the others did in it
l	I would have liked to use more the personal space, but I found that it was too separate from the shared space, and our task was to build a shared perspective. So, I began by using the personal space, but then I moved to work on the shared space and did not look much at the personal one. Also, because it got cluttered with the others' work

References

1. Attwell, G.: Personal learning environments – the future of eLearning? eLearning Pap. **2**(1), 1–7 (2007)
2. Barron, B.: Interest and self-sustained learning as catalysts of development: a learning ecologies perspective. Hum. Dev. **49**, 193–224 (2006)
3. Basque, J., Paquette, G., Pudelko, B., Leonard, M.: Collaborative knowledge modelling with a graphical knowledge representation tool: a strategy to support the transfer of expertise in organisations. In: Okada, A., Buckingham Shum, S.J., Sherborne, T. (eds.) Knowledge Cartography. Advanced Information and Knowledge Processing, pp. 491–517. Springer, London (2014)
4. Billett, S.: The workplace as learning environment: introduction. Int. J. Educ. Res. **47**(4), 209–212 (2008)

5. Draper, D.C.: Collaborative instructional strategies to enhance knowledge convergence. Am. J. Distance Educ. **29**(2), 109–125 (2015)
6. Goy, A., Magro, D., Petrone, G., Picardi, C., Rovera, M., Segnan, M.: An integrated support to collaborative semantic annotation. Adv. Hum. Comput. Interact. **2017**, 12 (2017). doi:10.1155/2017/7219098. Article ID 7219098
7. Goy, A., Magro, D., Petrone, G., Picardi, C., Segnan, M.: Shared and personal views on collaborative semantic tables. In: Molli, P., Breslin, J.G., Vidal, M.-E. (eds.) SWCS 2013-2014. LNCS, vol. 9507, pp. 13–32. Springer, Cham (2016). doi:10.1007/978-3-319-32667-2_2
8. Häkkinen, P., Hämäläinen, R.: Shared and personal learning spaces: challenges for pedagogical design. Internet High. Educ. **15**, 231–236 (2012)
9. Hmelo-Silver, C.E., Chinn, C.A., Chan, C., O'Donnell, A.M.: The International Handbook of Collaborative Learning. Routledge, London (2013)
10. Kandiko, C., Hay, D., Weller, S.: Concept mapping in the humanities to facilitate reflection: externalizing the relationship between public and personal learning. Arts Humanit. High. Educ. **12**(1), 70–87 (2012)
11. Johansen, R.: GroupWare: Computer Support for Business Teams. The Free Press, New York (1988)
12. Molinari G.: From learners' concept maps of their similar or complementary prior knowledge to collaborative concept map: dual eye-tracking and concept map analyses. Psychologie française (2015). doi:10.1016/j.psfr.2015.11.001
13. Novak, J.D.: Learning, Creating and Using Knowledge: Concept Maps as Facilitative Tools in Schools and Corporations, 2nd edn. Routledge, London (2010)
14. Okada, A., Buckingham Shum, S.J., Sherborne, T.: Knowledge Cartography: Software Tools and Mapping Techniques, 2nd edn. Springer, London (2014)
15. Schwendimann, B.A.: Making Sense of Knowledge Integration Maps. In: Ifenthaler, D., Hanewald, R. (eds.) Digital Knowledge Maps in Education, pp. 17–40. Springer, New York (2014)
16. Skaf-Molli, H., Ignat, C., Rahhal, C., Molli, P.: New work modes for collaborative writing. In: Granville, B., Kutti, N.S., Missikoff, M., Nguyen, N.T. (eds.) Proceedings of International Conference on Enterprise Information Systems and Web Technologies, EISWT-2007, Orlando, United States, pp. 176–182 (2007)
17. Wilson, S., Liber, O., Johnson, M., Beauvoir, P., Sharples, P., Milligan, C.: Personal learning environments: challenging the dominant design of educational systems. J. e-Learn. Knowl. Soc. **3**(2), 27–38 (2007)

Designing a Peer Feedback Mobile Application as a Professional Development Tool

Evangelos Kapros[✉], Mirjam Neelen, and Eddie Walsh

Learnovate Centre, Trinity College Dublin, Unit 28,
Trinity Technology & Enterprise Campus Pearse Street, Dublin 2, Ireland
{evangelos.kapros,neelenm,eddie.walsh}@scss.tcd.ie
http://www.learnovatecentre.org/

Abstract. This paper describes a mobile application that functions as a professional development tool by leveraging peer feedback in corporate environments. Specifically, the focus has been on feedback about specific events where a behaviour around transversal competencies was evident. The design of the application and the analytics made the attempt to emphasise the professional development dimension of peer feedback, as opposed to merely a quantitative performance management one, and the appropriate aggregation of any analytics so as to avoid any inappropriate employee "surveillance" effects. Moreover, the paper presents results of three trials with employees and line managers in corporate environments. The trials confirmed the hypothesis that our method and application would function positively in combination with or as an improvement upon traditional performance management methods and tools, such as annual performance reviews or 360° feedback, assuming there is feedback culture and institutional support in the organisation.

Keywords: Informal social learning · Competencies · Feedback

1 Introduction

Contemporary organisations are changing and becoming more agile to address modern business needs. As a consequence, employees are also affected and respond to this change, thus becoming at the same time a vehicle for change. Transversal competencies, such as communication and collaboration are critical to move across this fast-paced and continuously evolving work environment. This change is ongoing and has been perceived already in 1999, when it was understood that training would need to reflect these changes, in what was called "21st Century Skills for 21st Century Jobs" [17]. While competency-based-education is not a new concept[1] [16], the reappearance of the need to explore it has created opportunities to re-surface much desirable student-centred pedagogies [13].

---

[1] Papers from the 70s go so far as mapping U.S. efforts to capture competencies during the 20s and 30s back to the operationalisation of WWI [5,6,11].

© Springer International Publishing AG 2017
P. Zaphiris and A. Ioannou (Eds.): LCT 2017, Part II, LNCS 10296, pp. 401–418, 2017.
DOI: 10.1007/978-3-319-58515-4_31

Our industry partners[2] have expressed the challenge to capture and objectively assess, analyse, and visualise employees transversal competencies as performed on the job. Previous research has demonstrated that current approaches, such as talent and performance management systems—standalone or integrated into LMSs—and 360° feedback generally lead to insufficiently accurate data about day-to-day employee performance [1,3,14].

Assessing transversal competencies is complex for many reasons. For example, in order to get accurate insight in these competencies, they need to be assessed through a process that is integrated in the natural workflow. Currently, that is commonly done through periodic self-rating and rating by others. One of the problems with rating is that it can be quite subjective. For example, a '3' on a 1–5 Likert scale, or labels such as 'Strongly Agree' or 'Seldom' are open to wide-ranging interpretations.

In addition, supporting employees in the development of their transversal competencies is complex as well as they are difficult to acquire and change. One reason is that transversal competencies mean different things depending on the context [12]. Furthermore, [7] points out that they cannot likely be learned in formal training settings.

We have designed, built, and evaluated a mobile application for peer feedback and analytics visualisations that try to address some of the above issues. The following sections of this paper describe the design process, the mobile application's functionality, and the evaluation as well as its results to date.

2   Design Considerations

2.1   Iterative Design Process

The design process was highly iterative, and we validated our design with approximately $n \approx 80$ participants in total. Various methods were used for validation, depending on the stage of the design or development. Throughout the design and development process we iteratively ran two functional tests (with 6 and 20 participants respectively) and four focus groups (varying from 2 to 8 participants each).

The team[3] has also conducted research using the Q methodology to evaluate an early version of the prototype (with 6 participants). The statements in the Q-set were formed by designers' intentions, in this case by the authors. End-users test the application and rank the statements, according how well they think the statement is realised in the corresponding feature. Results show different points of view. This methodology helped the team to understand which features were best—and worst—implemented and why, and also which features were seen as more critical by users. These insights facilitated prioritisation in following design iterations.

---

[2] http://www.learnovatecentre.org/membership/our-members/.

[3] The Q methodology team consisted of Stéphanie Gauttier in addition to the authors.

We have set up several trials to evaluate our designs and hypotheses. One functional trial (to ensure that everything is technically ready for full trials) and two full trials have been conducted so far (with approx. 12 participants each). Since our trials include human participants, our team completed a Research Ethics Approval process with the School of Computer Science and Statistics in Trinity College, the University of Dublin.

Process aside, the design was additionally informed by the limitations described below.

2.2 Limitations

Some limitations were imposed to the app during the implementation phase due to technical issues. For instance, since this was the first version of the software application, we decided to limit ourselves to a mobile app; however, we do plan to better integrate the tool with employees' workflows in the future, either as a browser plugin, or as an extension to collaboration software. Similarly, in this first version of the project we offer no calendar or contact-list integration. While these limitations may reduce the usability of the app, we anticipate that they do not affect the validation of the concept by our end users for the purposes of our trials.

Moreover, the application to date allows for feedback to/from one person at a time, about one competency at a time. While this may seem limiting with regard to the functionality and usability of the app, as it is not possible to send a common piece of feedback to a group about a specific event, it helped the researchers to evaluate the basic premises of the app. Allowing for multiple people or events would affect the app design in various ways which are described in the following section.

Another limitation concerned various ethics considerations around feedback in the workplace. These considerations are twofold: on the one hand the existence of the phenomenon of the "toxic worker" [10] who may use peer feedback opportunities to harm rather than improve their workplace, and the use of performance management as "surveillance" by abusive powerful roles within the organisation [2]. A feedback app could potentially facilitate such behaviours.

The following section describes design decisions which were made in response to the considerations in this and the previous section.

2.3 Design Decisions

The first main design decision that was made was to design and build our peer feedback professional development tool as a mobile software application (mobile app). While mobile phones are not always integrated in workplace workflows, they are practically ubiquitous in organisations where workers would typically undertake a periodic performance review or a 360° feedback process.

The app has two main user interaction paths: (*a*) send/receive feedback (unsolicited), (*b*) send/receive requests for feedback (solicited). In addition, it offers a view to analytics around the feedback.

Unsolicited Feedback

In what is the most straightforward usage scenario of the app, a peer should be able to send a piece of feedback to another peer.

To keep feedback actionable, it should be specific and timely, so the design decision was made that the peers should give feedback about a specific event to another peer. The recipient can acknowledge they received feedback or reply with another piece of feedback, but we avoided notes, comments, or any other type of bi-directional annotation of the feedback, as this feature might result in non-productive discussions around semantics rather than actual feedback. While there is room for discussion about semantics, there is no reason why our feedback app is a more appropriate place for such discussions than traditional organisational communications channels.

Solicited Feedback

Moreover, a peer has to be able to request a piece of feedback from another peer.

As above, in order to allow for actionable feedback, the requests are sent to a specific peer, and are about a specific event. In this version of our design, requests do not have a time-out window and can be acted upon anytime. Also, all requests are received and can be acted upon or not, but no ignoring mechanism is put in place either for an individual request or a sender.

Competencies Analytics

The feedback generated from the app is mapped by the peers with specific behavioural statements. To date we use anchors related to UC Berkeley Core Competencies[4]. We have fully deployed 5 Competencies and the corresponding behaviours and anchor statements, but in principle any equivalent framework could be used in our design.

Moreover, a different set of aggregated feedback analytics are visualised for team leads and managers; there is no requirement that these be in the mobile app: in our case, we developed a web-based application for these other roles. These roles do not have access to the peer feedback text itself, but they do have access to the competencies, behaviours, and anchor statements around said feedback.

Social Messaging Settings

In this version of the app we decided to exclude features such as blocking all feedback from a specific peer, or sending a piece of feedback anonymously. Our intention was to allow for accountability for and ownership of the sent feedback, and also observe if the social network of the feedback senders and receivers will isolate some individuals who may have been "toxic" in their feedback.

---

[4] http://hr.berkeley.edu/development/learning/uc-berkeley-competencies.

3   The Peer Feedback App

3.1   Use Within an Organisation

Our mobile peer feedback app facilitates an agile peer feedback process that allows for continuous formative peer assessment of transversal competencies based on near to real time on-the-job performance.

Table 1. Example of triads 'Competency-Behaviour-Anchor Statement' for a specific behaviour (Sharing information with others). These triads help describe behaviours objectively and can thus improve feedback.

Competency	Behaviour	Anchor statement
Communication	Sharing information with others	Shared accurate, timely information with appropriate colleagues in the right format
Communication	Sharing information with others	Did not share information with others when needed, which often created problems with the team

Fig. 1. High level use case diagram of the mobile peer feedback app.

The process fits into current workflows and supports more evidential feedback methods to reduce subjectivity in the data. This is achieved through a *flipped competency capture* process where one can map feedback about day-to-day activities to behaviours, which are then mapped to competencies. The app uses *behavioural anchors* instead of more subjective ratings, ensuring more objective peer assessment (see e.g. Table 1). More truthful data on transversal competencies are not only helpful for employees but also delivers more accurate data to organisations. Through the feedback, competency data is captured regularly, analysed and visualised and gives relevant, timely, and actionable insights to the employee (see Fig. 1).

Our mobile peer feedback app truly supports *informal social learning*, critical in todays agile workplace. It also acknowledges that this type of learning is highly contextualised [7, 8, 18] as the feedback is always event-based; for example it can be based on a meeting or presentation that just took place.

Peers can request feedback from and offer feedback to each other. The in-app feedback process acknowledges the many ways employees might (want to) develop their competencies. For example, they might want to focus on certain competencies for a certain period of time and request very focussed feedback on those. On the other hand, they might have strengths or weaknesses that they are not aware of. Peers can offer feedback at their own initiative to increase that awareness.

Peers explain what their team member did well or could improve in a free text field. This makes feedback more concrete and transparent. It supports an open learning culture. The app also includes a *scaffolding model* to support effective feedback. After all, feedback needs to be done 'right' to help someone learn and improve [9].

3.2   Benefits for Organisations

We have concluded thus far that a mobile peer feedback app used within functional and/or cross-functional teams supports employee transversal competency assessment and development and provides accurate business performance analytics.

A mobile peer feedback app recognises the social significance of learning from your peers in the workplace [7]. That is provided that an organisation supports an open feedback culture and allows the individual employee to own their feedback data so that they will be more open to improving their performance. This is a critical assumption for our trials.

Because this is not just about the individual's transversal competency assessment and development but also about business performance analytics, we have identified three user types with different needs. They will therefore receive different types of analytics.

Employees need to be able to improve their performance based on peer feedback. Therefore, they need detailed insights into the feedback they receive with regards to their behaviours. **Team leads** need to be able to act on identified competency gaps within their team and therefore need analytics on their teams competencies. The **business unit owner** (e.g. HR) needs to see organisational competency patterns and gaps.

The app also offers analytics to support conversations, for example between team members and their team lead. Because the feedback is highly contextualised, there should never be a focus on numbers only.

The quantity and quality of the data is increased by flipping competency capturing (feedback about day-to-day events or activities is mapped to behaviours, behaviours are mapped to competencies) which reduces subjectivity and acknowledges the context dependent nature of feedback. The app, within the limitations described in previous sections, wishes to deliver high quality UX/UI

Fig. 2. Analytics are tailored for each user type. The emphasis on usage statistics is intended to help the users focus on the context of their received feedback and, thus, on professional development, rather than on quantifying the results.

to support more continuous use as well as an in-app scaffolding model to support effective feedback. This model, as well as the open and transparent feedback process support an open learning culture (Figs. 2 and 3).

4 Impact and Results

Participants from the trials have completed a pre-trial survey, and we also conducted post-trial semi-structured interviews (4 team members, 4 team leads) with the completed-trial organisations. Preliminary findings around the impact of using the Feedback app were positive and favourable in regards to the design premise. More specific initial results on learning and performance improvement and feedback perception are outlined below.

4.1 Pre-trial

Learning and Performance Improvement. In the pre-trial surveys the majority of team members (2 different organisations) indicate that the current performance review process does not help them to understand their strengths and weaknesses. One of the team leads in the post-trial interview confirms this. He indicates that current performance reviews are basically salary reviews; there is no support for professional development or performance improvement. Both team leads see the feedback app as an opportunity to move from task- and results-oriented feedback to behaviour-focussed feedback. They believe that the app can function as a catalyst for conversations between peers on their competencies and that it will be an enabler for having accurate and focussed discussions

Fig. 3. Screenshot of the feedback app. The users select one person to give feedback to, about a specific event, and then they select an anchor statement that describes the behaviour through a slider UI component. Finally, through the open text the users can describe the behaviour, either positively or constructively. Scaffolded helpful information can assist users with how to give useful feedback.

on professional development opportunities. However, all interviewees interpret the feedback app more as a performance review tool than as a learning and development tool.

Feedback Perception. Both pre-trial surveys indicate that the current feedback process is perceived as unstructured and team members do not give each other focussed feedback. The majority of team members indicate that they feel capable giving peers feedback and almost everyone likes receiving it. All interviewees strongly felt that the feedback app would work in their culture of speaking up and helping each other. They also said that the app is very quick and easy to use so it will not distract for day-to-day activities. They indicated that the structure of the app made it easy to use and made them feel more comfortable giving the feedback.

The pre-trial surveys to the 3 participating organisations are presented below. Out of the 33 collected responses 32 were complete sets and were used in the analysis. A summarisation visualisation can be seen at Fig. 4 and a correlation matrix of the responses at Fig. 5.

The summary of the survey results clearly demonstrates a dissatisfaction with current feedback practices. Participants felt that in their organisations they either do not have a feedback process, or it is not very structured. In addition, the responses indicated that feedback is sparsely sought or given. However, the participants claimed to be capable of giving feedback to their peers, and even claimed that they would *like* to do so.

Concerning the correlations between the answers, the following were observed. The Pearson Coefficient r was calculated for the survey ($df = 30$,

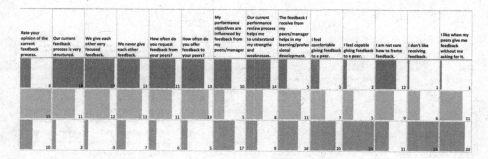

Fig. 4. Survey responses for all 3 organisations. Answers are on a Likert scale 1 – 5 where 1 are negative answers and 5 are positive answers. Here they are grouped into *negative*, *neutral*, and *positive* responses (top, middle, and bottom row, respectively). Positive answers here sometimes differ to *yes*, as in the negatively phrased question *I do not like receiving feedback* we take the positive answer to be *I like receiving feedback*. One can observe dissatisfaction with current feedback practices.

$\alpha = 0.5 : r = 0.349, \alpha = 0.1 : r = 0.449$) and statistically significant results were found for some pairs of questions. Specifically, the questions about the sentiment towards the existing processes present a statistically significant positive correlation, as do the ones about the comfort, capability, and desire to give/receive feedback.

There is a statistically significant negative correlation in the questions regarding the frequency of feedback as opposed to either the rating of the current processes, the focus of feedback, or the comfort in giving feedback. Moreover, the pair of questions regarding the opinion of the current process and liking unsolicited feedback similarly demonstrates a statistically significant negative correlation.

Apart from the correlation matrix for all the participants, individual matrices for each organisation were calculated (see Fig. 6). The organisation matrices yielded different patters than the overall matrix, notwithstanding their similarities as they contributed to the latter.

From these matrices one can clearly see that especially the bottom-right matrix is quite different in the correlations at replying the survey questions. The difference in correlation patterns, especially for this organisation is a clear indicator for **cultural differences** between organisations with regard to how they understand and treat feedback.

Envisaged Impact by Industry. We have asked our trial partners to share their vision on the envisaged impact of the peer feedback app on individual employees, organisational performance, and the learning culture.

– *What impact do you expect the mobile peer feedback app to have for individual employees?*

	C Rate your opinion of the current feedback process.	D Our current feedback process is very structured.	E We give each other very focused feedback.	F We never give each other feedback.	G How often do you request feedback from your peers?	H How often do you offer feedback to your peers?	I My performance objectives are influenced by feedback from my peers/manager	J Our current performance review process helps me to understand my strengths and weaknesses.	K The feedback I receive from my peers/manager helps in my learning/professional development.	L I feel comfortable giving feedback to a peer.	M I feel capable giving feedback to a peer.	N I am not sure how to frame feedback.	O I don't like receiving feedback.	P I like when my peers give me feedback without me asking for it.
C to everything		0.544013515	0.605144513	-0.364527475	0.181957449	0.0020536	0.113496667	0.520303025	0.230184221	-0.004132373	-0.158647728	-0.054181233	-0.257147817	-0.436074793
D to everything	0.544013515		0.390574804	-0.111623533	-0.075878215	-0.261585081	0.333014767	0.434079068	0.139033524	-0.250504791	-0.348865163	-0.305309711	-0.260141073	-0.265522445
E	0.605144515	0.390574808		-0.409379326	0.441187515	0.229426139	0.216109104	0.272169959	0.181959705	0.035624362	-0.160759927	0.031509198	-0.142373699	-0.231433792
F	-0.364527475	-0.111623533	-0.409379326		0.358180191	-0.320027444	-0.213793248	-0.242951776	-0.21841189	-0.444578954	-0.120047436	-0.057032375	0.040689423	-0.106135133
G	0.181957449	-0.075878215	0.441187515	-0.358180191		0.587692091	-0.093657123	-0.164918189	-0.331201477	0.341370048	0.03371127	0.374765448	0.149790762	-0.123623756
H	0.0020536	-0.261585081	0.229426139	-0.320227444	0.587692091		-0.173490197	-0.015437779	-0.025649459	0.3869726	0.233293458	0.10681593	0.051430285	0.203235695
I	0.113496667	0.333014767	0.216109104	-0.213793248	-0.093657123	-0.173490197		0.21158318	0.314867511	-0.059892319	0.059328106	-0.321719121	-0.017514236	-0.07349245
J	0.520303025	0.434079068	0.272169959	-0.242951776	-0.164918189	-0.015437779	0.21158318		0.446390939	0.084565252	-0.086894125	-0.226279542	-0.189884706	-0.221051208
K	0.230184221	0.139033524	0.181959705	-0.21841189	-0.331201477	-0.025649459	0.314867511	0.446390939		0.161670831	0.304911	-0.183851168	0.063902148	0.113538163
L	-0.004132373	-0.250504791	0.035624362	-0.444578954	0.341370048	0.3869726	-0.059892319	0.084565252	0.161670831		0.672149206	0.219967463	0.562968318	0.461126939
M	-0.158647728	-0.348865163	-0.160759927	-0.120047436	0.03371127	0.233293458	0.059328106	-0.086894125	0.304911	0.672149206		0.175328767	0.519040446	0.430637854
N	-0.054181233	-0.305309711	0.031509198	-0.057032375	0.374765448	0.10681593	-0.321719121	-0.226279542	-0.183851168	0.219967463	0.175328767		0.202870556	0.106670987
O	-0.257147817	-0.260141073	-0.142373699	0.040689423	0.149790762	0.051430285	-0.017514236	-0.189884706	0.063902148	0.562988818	0.519040446	0.202870556		0.652105174
P	-0.436074793	-0.265522445	-0.231433792	-0.106135133	-0.123623756	0.203235695	-0.07349245	-0.221051208	0.113538163	0.461126939	0.430637854	0.106670987	0.652105174	

Fig. 5. Survey response correlations for all organisations. Answers are on a Likert scale $1-5$ where 1 are negative answers and 5 are positive answers. Statistically significant values of the Pearson Coefficient r are highlighted ($df = 30, \alpha = .5 : r = .349$).

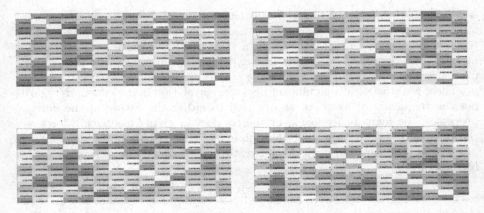

Fig. 6. Survey correlations matrices: (a) top left, all organisations. (b), (c), and (d), top-right and bottom, respectively, individual organisations. It is apparent how the individual correlations contribute to the aggregate ones. The difference in correlation patterns, especially for the bottom right organisation is a clear indicator for cultural differences between organisations.

"We want to move from results-oriented feedback to behaviour-focussed feedback so that we can have accurate conversations about performance." (*Team Lead 1*)

"We think this app can help create an open and honest feedback culture, which can increase an individual employees learning." (*Team Lead 2*)

– *What impact do you expect the mobile peer feedback app to have for organisational performance?*

"Instead of doing performance reviews that don't usually offer true data, you can spend less time on this app and get more accurate data. Win-win." (*Team Lead 1*)

"Using the feedback app, we expect to improve team communication, collaboration, and build leadership skills – all of which are essential in a fast-paced agile environment." (*Team Lead 2*)

– *How do you envision that the mobile peer feedback app will help to create or enhance the overall learning culture?*

"The continuous and seamless nature of the app will help the learning culture without putting strain on individuals." (*Team Lead 1*)

"With this app, we will have an implicit focus on professional development which will help us to have a learning culture without spending the time explicitly." (*Team Lead 2*)

4.2   Full Trials

Our full trials were conducted in authentic business environments, and lasted from 24 to 66 days, depending on the organisation. In addition to research on the app usability, the trials intend to determine temporal or usage patterns, or networking effects throughout the usage of the app. Furthermore, we want to explore if the app helps to gain more insight in behaviours/competencies and can support performance improvement. Last but not least, we research if team members perceptions on giving and receiving feedback change over time when they regularly use the feedback app.

We use a combination of qualitative (pre-trial competency assessment; pre-trial/post-trial surveys; and post-trial interviews) and quantitative (in-app usage) data methods to ensure a complete capturing of various aspects of the app usage.

Usage and Usability. The usage activity from trial 1 has shown that the team of 11 participants generated 89 items of feedback during the 66 working days, while trial 2 of 10 participants generated 19 items of feedback in 24 working days ($average_1 = 1.35$ and $average_2 = 0.8$, respectively; total $average = 1.2$ feedback items per day).

The breakdown of individual users show a wide distribution of activity between different team members. The 3 most active users sent 15 – 20 items of feedback, averaging approximately 1 – 2 times a week which is a significant increase of feedback frequency. The 3 least active users sent 6 or fewer items of feedback. As this was a trial in a real-world business setting, there was some change in roles and personnel within the team which will likely account for some of the least active users.

The overall amount of text feedback was weighted significantly in favour of positive over constructive with 56 positive statements and 10 constructive statements. The popularity of the competencies was as follows: *Communication* : 35.71%, *Collaboration* : 22.22%, *Problem Solving* : 19.84%, *Leadership* :

12.7%, *Service Focus* : 9.52%. With regard to the UC Berkeley anchors, even though they do not directly represent a progression on a scale, for the sake of simplicity we have coded them with values from 1 to 5; their usage popularity within the app was: $anchor_4$: 58.73%, $anchor_5$: 24.6%, $anchor_3$: 14.29%, $anchor_1$: 1.59%, and $anchor_2$: 0.79%.

Concerning usability, the team-lead analytics dashboard's SUPR-Q [15] score[5] is 78.5%, and the scores for the attributes represented by clusters of questions are: Usability 77.5%, Credibility 70%, Appearance 80% (Loyalty is out of scope in this context of a short-term trial). The SUS score for the app is 69.7, which, according to the adjective scale described in [4], is characterised as 'Good'.

Social Network Analysis. This usage was analysed with regard to its distribution and density per user. Since this is a peer-feedback tool, the first way this analysis was conducted was by analysing the networks that were formed when giving and receiving feedback. The density is 0.29, and the average clustering coefficient is 0.318, showing that the participant connections percentage and extent of interactions is approximately 1 out of every 3 possible interactions.

Three main findings can be reported from the network analysis. First, despite the small sample, there seems to be a clustering effect. Apart from the clustering coefficient value of 0.318 which, given that it is the global variable, shows a fair amount of clustering, one can see in Fig. 7 the existence of clusters. These can be either completely separate sub-groups, such as in the organisation labelled *team*3, or clusters that have no immediate neighbours, but are eventually separated after a degree of edge traversals. An example of the latter behaviour is the formation of separate groups with no immediate neighbours for nodes 110 and 127 in *team*6 (sub-groups circled in black in Fig. 7). This is a significant finding given that this is a peer feedback tool, therefore edge transversal does not necessarily imply carrying information: i.e., nodes 106 and 109 independently communicate with 107, but not necessarily about the same behaviour or attribute; in addition, these communications do not help node 110 and 127 to independently communicate.

Secondly, despite the popularity of some competencies against others, individual users can be seen to express different preferences in how they gave or requested feedback. Some focused on only a few competencies, while others had a more diverse range of feedback giving. For example, in Fig. 8 node 106 can be seen to have focused on only two competencies, while 107 on all of them. Similarly, 108 and 110 demonstrate the respective behaviours, thus showing that the diversity in behaviour is not specific to nodes with either high or low degree.

Finally, the same can be said about the anchor selections. Individual preference seems to be the main factor in the selection of anchor statements when giving feedback.

---

[5] As SUPR-Q is a percentile scoring system, these scores mean that the score is higher than the 78.5% of the benchmarked websites at [15].

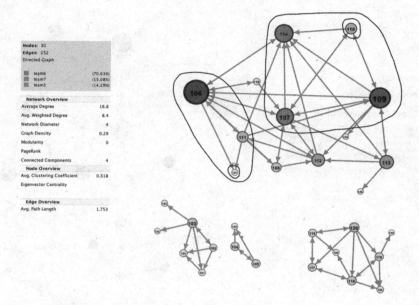

Fig. 7. Network analysis diagram of the mobile peer feedback app. Node size/colour show the degree. Even though the sample size was quite small, team6 and team3 formed clans, either strong ones in team3 or looser ones in team6 (i.e., nodes 110 and 127 have no common direct neighbours).

Text Analysis. With regard to the actual open text of the feedback, the following were observed. The feedback consists of 1379 words in 64 sentences, with an average of 12.7 words per sentence. It consists of 12% passive sentences, and it has an overall Flesch Reading Ease of 54.5 (out of 100), and a Flesch-Kincaid Grade Level of 8.8, which indicates that a ninth-grader should understand the text.

With regard to following the examples about how to give feedback, some did, i.e.:

- Positive Feedback: "You provided a lot of details through each stories which was great info for the team."
- Constructive Feedback: "You were going fairly fast and maybe allow a pause time for the listener to be able to digest the information you provided." While others did not:
- Positive Feedback: "Open badges integration"

The latter comment did not follow the examples, as beyond giving a status update on an item that the feedback giver appreciated, the nature of this appreciation is not explained, thus making it unclear to the feedback recipient if it was positive that the said integration even happened, or if it was masterfully executed, or if it was the process of it that was well done as opposed to just the final artefact.

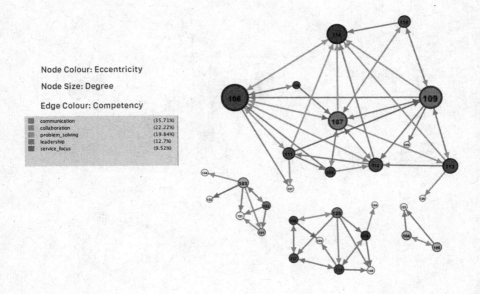

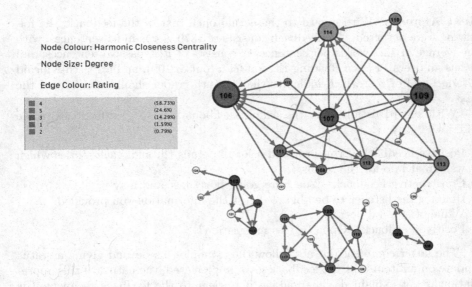

Fig. 8. Network diagram for different metrics of the mobile peer feedback app. Personal preference seems to affect the selection of competencies and anchor statements.

This ambivalence with regard to following the examples could be related to a playfulness that can be observed when using the feedback tool, as there were 7 occasions where emoticons (such as :-)) where used to display emotions.

After-Trial Interviews. The team also conducted interviews in all 3 organisations that participated in the pre-trial and the trial, after these were terminated. Interviews were taken from 8 individuals, from both roles of team member and team lead.

The interviews identified several common threads across teams and organisations.

Overall the app was usable and many users commented on it as being intuitive:

- "the whole layout and everything makes a lot of sense to me I mean it is very intuitive"
- "Easy enough to use - sliders very handy - picking the actual things you are giving feedback on or asking for feedback on different criteria like comms collab and all those; clear enough"

However, due to limitations of resources and as this is a trial software for a research project, there were also limitations, especially with having a mobile-only implementation:

- "mobile device is not the easiest thing to be jotting down long paragraphs on"
- "Asking contract engineers or employees... to implement and install applications on their own private hardware, that did come up... with more than one individual."

Concerning the actual feedback within the app, some indicative comments from the interviews were as follows:

- "Managers need to be trained in soft skills so that they know better how to give feedback. We are not prepared for some aspects of our role."
- "because of the behaviours you are not going to be overly hurtful or critical. You know, you do not feel like you are abusing somebody by giving feedback. It is constructive, so. There is nothing really stopping you in that regard."

With regard to how the tool compares to a traditional performance review, there was also a variety in responses:

- "I really think people would benefit from it (feedback app), because we do not sit down and talk about behaviour, and the annual review is not about behaviour, it is task driven."
- "So in terms of, was it evaluating me, I am not so sure, not within the trial period. I would not have felt that so much."
- "Not just the annual appraisals that it feeds into. In general you would have your set team 1-to-1s, weekly, bi-weekly or monthly, different teams do it differently. Those bits of information are also very useful for a manger of a resource going into those."

Finally, about the relation to professional development:
- "People saw value in learning competencies/skills, got team members learning that what they do relates to competencies/skills, helps me to change my language when I talk to my team about these things, do not think it was used to drive behaviour change"
- "Originally, it was to look at finding out which area I need to improve on but, with my ego talking, to tell other people what they are not doing right. It can be weapon as much as a tool for growth depending on the frame of mind you are at the time. None of us went back and asked questions about feedback, it was I have to do this, just tick the box and Ive done it. I gave a little bit of feedback about what went well but it was not really taken on board."

5   Discussion

Overall, the results presented above indicate an ambiguity around using feedback in an organisation: on the one hand some responses demonstrated great variation, but on the other hand some patterns do exist in replies and behaviours.

Firstly, the design of the app did not seem to affect the outcome of the trial, as the interviewees found it in general intuitive and the usability score it received was high. Therefore, despite the fact that some users were reluctant to install it on their mobile device (which was a known limitation of the trial as opposed to oversight), the ones who did install it did not report any serious issues.

Moreover, the usage was satisfactory, as there was more than one feedback item per day on average, and the reading level was adequate. This shows that the users were committed to this usage and did not take the tool lightly.

From the social network analysis and the interviews it can be seen that managers may require support in successfully setting up teams for feedback, as they often operate in an organisation with little to no prior feedback culture, and thus they may fail to motivate the team to use the tool, or strong clans may develop. However, the formation of clans in the network cannot be considered an outright negative outcome, as it may be the case that some teams are structured in a way that facilitates it. Moreover, the existence of clans is enhanced by our design decision to be able to give feedback to only one person at a time.

Having said that, the managers may not be the only ones who need support, as the team members often linked the current inadequate, in their opinion, feedback processes to their inability to effectively give feedback. A drop in the perceived comfort in and capability of giving feedback is noted between the pre-trial and after-trial periods. This is not to say that the app had a negative effect in feedback-giving, but rather that it increased awareness around peer rating and feedback as a vehicle for both performance management and professional development.

Finally, the diversity of opinion in the interviews and of behaviours in the social network analysis can be attributed to the lack of a unified organisational culture on these matters, a lack which allows for individual differences to flourish. This view is enhanced by the otherwise strong correlations we see in the survey results, where several statistically significant relations appear, despite the small sample. If the individual differences were not related to organisational culture, then they would have most likely also prevailed at the survey, and the identification of cultural patterns per organisation would have been impossible.

Thus, it is with the combination of the above points that it seems evident that *(a)* feedback can potentially support the performance management and professional development needs of an organisation, *(b)* but only given the appropriate institutional support, in both *cultivating and encouraging a feedback culture* overall and *supporting individuals in their learning and performance paths*, either as team members or as managers.

6   Conclusions

In conclusion, the original project objectives of creating a peer feedback application for professional development which also offers accurate performance data were met satisfactorily. We designed, built, and evaluated a mobile peer-feedback app that incorporated the principle of scaffolded feedback in order to achieve these objectives. The evaluation was conducted in real business environments.

Results demonstrate that team members and team leads alike perceive peer feedback as an improvement upon existing performance management methods, and perceive the app as also a professional development tool. However, there are conditions under which this approach functions successfully, and these lie within the organisation itself, as they need to actively pursue cultivating a feedback culture in order to avail the benefits in performance management and professional development.

Limitations in the evaluation to date give opportunities for further improvement of our approach. The communication of learning analytics related to the feedback to different stakeholders, and the exploration of different delivery mechanisms and platforms for the feedback and the analytics are some future steps for this project.

Acknowledgments. This research is supported by the Learnovate Centre at Trinity College, the University of Dublin. The Learnovate Centre is funded under the Technology Centre Programme through the Government of Ireland's state agencies Enterprise Ireland and IDA Ireland.

References

1. Aguinis, H., Gottfreson, R.K., Joo, H.: Using performance management to win the talent war. Bus. Horiz. **55**, 609–616 (2012)
2. Ajunwa, I., Crawford, K., Schultz, J.: Limitless worker surveillance. Calif. Law Rev. **105**, 3 (2017)
3. Akram, A.A., Cascio, W.F., Paauwe, J.: Talent management: current theories and future directions. J. World Bus. **49**, 173–179 (2014)
4. Bangor, A., Kortum, P., Miller, J.: Determining what individual SUS scores mean: adding an adjective rating scale. J. Usability Stud. **4**(3), 114–123 (2009)

5. Callaghan, R.E.: Education and the Cult of Efficiency. Chicago University, Chicago (1962)
6. Davies, I.: Objectives in Curriculum Design. McGraw Hill, New York (1976)
7. Eraut, M.: Informal learning in the workplace. Stud. Continuing Educ. **26**, 247–273 (2004)
8. Eraut, M., Hirsh, W.: The Significance of Workplace Learning for Individuals, Groups and Organisations, 9th edn. SKOPE, Oxford (2007)
9. Hattie, J., Timperley, H.: The power of feedback. Rev. Educ. Res. **77**, 81–112 (2007)
10. Housman, M., Minor, D.: Toxic Workers. Harvard Business School, Working Paper 16–057 (2015)
11. Neumann, W.: Educational responses to the concern of proficiency. In: Grant, G. (ed.) On Competence: A Critical Analysis of Competence Based Reform in Higher Education. Jossey Bass, San Francisco (1979)
12. Robles, M.M.: Executive perceptions of the top 10 soft skills needed in todays workplace. Bus. Commun. Q. **75**, 453–465 (2012)
13. Rotherham, A.J., Willingham, D.: 21st century skills the challenges ahead. Educ. Leadersh. **67**(1), 16–21 (2009). ASCD
14. Saba, J.: Winning Your Workforce: The Essential Guide to Improving Retention and Employee Performance. Saba eBook (2015)
15. Sauro, J.: SUPR-Q: a comprehensive measure of the quality of the website user experience. J. Usability Stud. **10**(2), 68–86 (2015)
16. Spady, W.G.: Competency based education: a bandwagon in search of a definition. Educ. Researcher **6**(1), 9–14 (1977)
17. Stuart, L.: 21st Century Skills for 21st Century Jobs. A Report of the U.S. Department of Commerce, U.S. Department of Education, U.S. Department of Labor, National Institute for Literacy and Small Business Administration. U.S. Government Printing Office (1999)
18. Tynjälä, P.: Perspectives into learning at the workplace. Educ. Res. Rev. **3**, 130–154 (2008)

The Influence of Trust on User Interactions in e-Transaction Platforms: The Context of a Developing Country

Godfrey O. Kingsley[✉], Sónia Sousa, and Abiodun Ogunyemi

School of Digital Technologies,
Tallinn University, Narva mnt 25, 10120 Tallinn, Estonia
{godfrey,scs,abnogn}@tlu.ee

Abstract. This paper reports recent findings which aims at informing design ideas and identifying characteristics that could help to develop e-transaction applications and systems that promotes perceived trust. To accomplish our goals, we employed the socio-technical model of trust by Sousa et al. [26], to on one hand determine if users' trust such e-payment system hosted by a third party company outside well known financial institutions (banks); then we further investigate how to incorporate trust into the platform. And on the other hand, as a design critique to establish bespoke visual clues that promotes perceived trust in the system and inform the system of potential pitfalls in their service design. A questionnaire was deployed to 500 current users of the platform and 106 valid responses were received. Our findings indicated that the trust features of concern to users are willingness, competency, predictability and benevolence with exception to honesty, reciprocity and motivation. Results presented are part of an ongoing research on trust related characteristics that should be tackled when designing and deploying e-transaction platforms in developing countries.

Keywords: e-Transaction · Human computer interaction for development · Trust in service design · User trust

1 Introduction

Various methods of e-transaction are continually transforming the way we do business over the Internet, including e-banking, e-ordering and online publishing/online retailing [17], by allowing the exchange of funds and data quickly, conveniently, and dependably than ever before. With e-transaction comes a number of benefits, such as cost reduction, flexibility, convenience, enhances productivity and efficiency, tracking individual spending, and it is now making handwritten signature on a paper document gradually a thing of the past, etc. Despite its advantages, a large number of users in developing countries are not willing to provide sensitive financial information over the web; the reluctance to entrust sensitive personal information like credit card numbers to businesses operating on the web is of a main concern in developing countries [12]. The cause of this has been mostly attributed to 'lack of trust' in various studies [1, 18, 19, 22, 25].

The concept of trust in the domain of Internet banking has received a significant rate of interest and was recognized by researchers as one of the key motives why a

© Springer International Publishing AG 2017
P. Zaphiris and A. Ioannou (Eds.): LCT 2017, Part II, LNCS 10296, pp. 419–434, 2017.
DOI: 10.1007/978-3-319-58515-4_32

large percentage of consumers are still reluctant to accept Internet banking, most especially in developing countries, and Nigeria in particular [21]. A lot of researchers have tried to study 'trust' in software applications (online or otherwise), because of its importance [5, 8, 13, 26, 29]. Several researchers have proposed design approaches, guidelines, patterns and characteristics to help promote trust in e-transaction platforms but it appears that in many developing countries, consumers source for information online but make purchases the traditional way [17, 18].

This study seeks to take a design approach in the context of Nigeria (a developing country) and employ the socio-technical model of trust [26] to explore the design characteristics that engender trust on a third party indigenous electronic payment service platform called 'Remita'.

The goal is to identify trust enhancing components in e-transaction service interface, to investigate the awareness of users of these components. The general aim is to analyze visual cues by evaluating certain variables that promotes or deter trust and thus propose heuristic design guidelines to foster trust in online.

Our contribution, therefore, is in providing insightful guidelines to designers by constructively informing design ideas and identifying characteristics that will help develop e-transaction applications and systems that promote perceived trust in developing countries. This is expected to encourage more patronage of users in e-transaction platforms and consequently contribute in narrowing the digital divide.

The paper is organized as follows. The next section situates the reader and gives a foundation of the work undertaken by providing a relevant literature review, short and clear definition of the terms and concepts being used in this paper. The Sect. 3 gives a description of the methodology. Section 4 presents the data analysis, findings and discussion. We provide limitations of the study, implications and future research directions and then conclude.

2 Related Studies

Individuals, from different cultures and backgrounds, are willing to trust software systems, as they trust other humans, knowing that there are potential risks, [10]. It is generally easier to develop trust between people in real life settings, face-to-face so to say, where people can see and "touch" each other, rather than online, where there are less (nonverbal) cues to take into consideration when developing trust, [30]. The theoretical reasoning behind this effect has been that trust helps people rule out undesirable, yet possible, opportunistic behaviors, and ultimately makes users more at ease regarding transactions [28]. Because of its importance in e-payment or software systems, a number of researchers have tried to tackle trust. Extant studies however, despite their merits have some limitations with regard to the approach and objective of this study.

Okoro et al. [15] investigated the issue of customer trust in mobile commerce to identify which factors had more influence on customers' trust during online shopping. The authors found that security design and content are the factors, which had the most influence on customers' trust. Fuzzy logic was applied for measuring trust level, uncovering hidden relationship between websites' features and trust level, solving the uncertainty problem and handling human reasoning where the reasoning processes behind customers' trust in mobile commerce transactions were taken into account.

Tsiakis and Sthephanides G. [27] explained that the fundamental prerequisite for e-payment systems adoption was that all participants ought to have absolute trust in the system that they participate. They discussed the contraction of trust in an electronic payment system which must take into consideration: data, identities and role behavior and that the adoption of e-commerce must consider trust and risk as important determinants of adoption behavior.

Kim et al. [11] in their study conducted in Korea, examined the effect of perceived trust, perceived security and their causes on intention to use electronic payments. They found that both perceived security and perceived trust affect current use of e-payment systems, and that the presence of security statement seal affects perceived security but it has no effect on perceived trust.

The study of Chellappa and Pavlou [3] on the other hand, propose mechanisms of encryption, protection, authentication, and verification as antecedents of perceived information security. These mechanisms are derived from technological solutions to security threats that are visible to consumers and hence contribute to actual consumer perceptions. A key empirical finding of the research was the relative strength of perceived security on trust in electronic transactions as opposed to retailer reputation and financial liability.

Pei Y. et al. [20] examined the factors influencing Chinese users' perception and adoption toward e-payment. Their results showed that perceived benefits and trust are significantly associated with consumers' use intention. Their findings suggested that users might value more on benefits (easy registration, learnability, convenience, fast processing and usability of the e-payment instead of financial benefits such as lower fees) of the e-payment system than trust on them. They inferred that the users are not concerned so much about the perceived risk when they select an e-payment system possibly because of good reputation and secure protection of e-payment systems in China and even so when they perceive the potential risks they still trust and would accept them.

Mukherjee and Nath [14] re-examine the commitment-trust theory (CTT) of relationship marketing in the online retailing context and sought to theorize the antecedents and consequences of commitment and trust in the online context. They identified five main antecedents to trust: (1) shared values; (2) communication; (3) opportunistic behavior; (4) privacy; and (5) security. In their findings, privacy and security features of the website along with shared values were identified as the key antecedents of trust, which in turn positively influences relationship commitment.

Grabner-Kräuter and Kaluscha [7] discussed the idea of a pattern language for trustworthy Internet storefronts to facilitate B2C electronic commerce. The authors argued that trust in e-commerce is influenced by several factors, person-specific (e.g. personality traits that influence trusting beliefs, intentions and behaviors) and contextual (such as technology and legal norms related to e-commerce) - that cannot be controlled by the online retailer. Yet, they believe that the idea of a pattern language for trustworthy Internet storefronts can be one promising element in building consumers' trust towards Internet merchants and in fostering B2C electronic commerce.

Mouratidis and Cofta P. [13] argued that successful online systems are those developed to also meet a number of non-functional requirements such as security, reliability and trust". Their paper emphasized the need to develop a field of study ("designing for trust") to improve software systems quality and eliminate cultural issues related to the inclusion of trust considerations into the development of software systems.

Sabi et al. [23] used a model based on Diffusion of Innovation (DOI) and Technology Acceptance Model (TAM) in investigating the contextual factors impacting adoption, implementation and usage of western designed software packages in developing countries using a case study of Cameroon. The aim was to explain user preference and trust in western designed banking software systems in developing countries. The findings from the study revealed that user engagement at an early stage in the implementation of a western designed software package in developing countries would greatly enhance user acceptance and usage of the system. However, this lack of engagement did not influence user preference of local systems or trust for imported western designed software systems. The statistical analysis of the influence of cultural and environmental factors showed that user preference of locally designed software systems over western designed systems was significant. However, trust in western designed systems was not significantly influenced by the cultural and environmental factors.

Past studies presented have indicated that trust is a major indicator that spurs the acceptance to use an electronic payment system. Most studies identified security and privacy issues as prerequisites for trust, [3, 11, 14]. Some studies tried to investigate trust from a design perspective [13, 15, 23]. However, past studies reviewed, did not critically consider the social and technical dimensions of examining trust with a design approach, from different lenses in other cultures, especially in the developing world to shed new light on its effect. Hence, this study seeks to look at the influence of perceived trust to use an electronic payment system from the perspective of users in a developing country context.

3   Theoretical Foundation

3.1   Trust in e-Transaction and Online Systems

e-transaction refers to electronic transaction and in this paper is simply defined as the use of electronic means to settle financial transactions among individuals, private and corporate [15]. Trust in electronic transactions was defined by Chellappa, R. and Pavlou, P. [3] as the subjective probability with which users believe that a particular transaction will occur in a manner consistent with their confident expectations.

3.2   The Socio-technical Model of Trust

The proposed model (Fig. 1.), which we advocate to be used as a design tool for informing the design of e-transaction platforms, depicts trust as a construct informed by 7 (seven) individual qualities. The model determines the extent to which one relates with one's social and technical environment. These constructs explain the individual qualities of trust: Motivation represents the degree to which an individual believes (even under conditions of vulnerability and dependence) he/she has the ability to perform specific beneficial actions when using a computer. Willingness reflects the positive or negative feeling about performing a given action while considering the risk and incentives. Competency reflects the degree of ease of use, when associated with the use of the system. Predictability represents the user's confidence that the system will help him perform a desired action in accordance with what is expected. Benevolence reflects the user's perception that most people share similar social behaviors and sharing values. Reciprocity represents the degree to which an individual sees oneself as part of a group. Honesty reflects an insurance quality when facing apprehension, or education setting. Qualities of trust as defined by Sousa et al. [26] are depicted in Fig. 1.

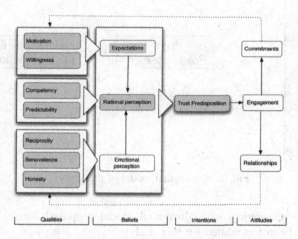

Fig. 1. Socio-technical model of trust (Sousa et al. [26])

3.3   The Case of Remita

One major recurring problem in Nigerian Banks is the overcrowding of banking halls, that had led to the movement of customers from one bank to the other, where they can obtain banking services without much delay, [2]. E-banking was adopted by banks in Nigeria so as to improve their service delivery, decongest queues in the banking hall, enable customers withdraw cash 24/7, aid international payment and remittance, track personal banking transaction, request for online statement, or even transfer deposit to a third party account, [9]. Payments of monthly salaries are delayed and often prone to fraudulent acts. The use of removable devices to store and move financial information around was also susceptible to fraud. The developers of Remita observed these procedures and the challenges that emanated through ethnographic investigations to come up with a solution they call Remita in order to meet both unmet and unidentified needs of the Nigerian financial market. Remita has the functionality to process third party cheques across different banks' platform through a process called e-cheque. The development company and other key members of the team brainstormed and brought multidisciplinary skills into conceptualizing Remita.

Remita is institutionalized in Nigeria having been endorsed by the Central Bank of Nigeria (CBN)[1] as the major gateway for moving funds across banks in Nigeria. The choice of Remita is therefore based on the perception that this study would gain useful insights into trust on e-service transactions from a widely used and an Institutionalised service. Using the socio-technical trust model (Fig. 2.), we examined Remita's platform for trust-enabling interactions.

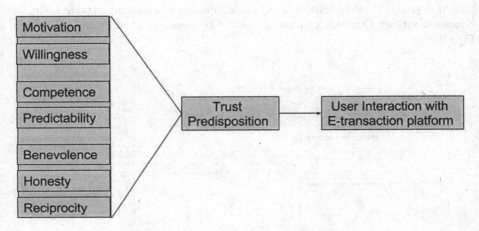

Fig. 2. Conceptual model of the study

Based on the theoretical and conceptual model proposed above, the following hypotheses have been formulated for this study:

H1:   Users are predisposed to use an e-transaction platform as trust is significantly enhanced by perceived motivation in the system

H_0:   Users are not predisposed to use an e-transaction platform, as trust is not significantly enhanced by perceived motivation in the system.

H2:   Users are predisposed to use an e-transaction platform as trust is significantly enhanced by perceived willingness in the system.

$H2_0$:   Users are not predisposed to use an e-transaction platform, as trust is not significantly enhanced by perceived willingness in the system.

H3:   Users are predisposed to use an e-transaction platform as trust is significantly enhanced by perceived competence in the system.

$H3_0$:   Users are not predisposed to use an e-transaction platform, as trust is not significantly enhanced by perceived competence in the system.

H4:   Users are predisposed to use an e-transaction platform as trust is significantly enhanced by perceived predictability in the system.

---

[1] https://www.cbn.gov.ng/out/2015/bpsd/circular%20on%20oagf%20revenue%20collection.pdf.

H4$_0$:   Users are not predisposed to use an e-transaction platform, as trust is not significantly enhanced by perceived predictability in the system.

H5:   Users are predisposed to use an e-transaction platform as trust is significantly enhanced by perceived benevolence in the system.

H5$_0$:   Users are not predisposed to use an e-transaction platform, as trust is not significantly enhanced by perceived benevolence in the system.

H6:   Users are predisposed to use an e-transaction platform as trust is significantly enhanced by perceived honesty in the system.

H6$_0$:   Users are not predisposed to use an e-transaction platform, as trust is not significantly enhanced by perceived honesty in the system.

H7:   Users are predisposed to use an e-transaction platform as trust is significantly enhanced by perceived reciprocity in the system.

H7$_0$:   Users are not predisposed to use an e-transaction platform, as trust is not significantly enhanced by perceived reciprocity in the system.

4   Methodology

This is an exploratory research using a case study of an e-payment service in Nigeria. We employed the socio-technical model of trust [26] to examine trust indicators on a third party indigenous electronic payment platform called 'Remita'. We partnered with the company that developed Remita in order to reach out to the actual users. The use of a survey method was adopted and online questionnaires were distributed to 500 current users of Remita using the LimeSurvey open source toll. A total of 106 responses were received and these respondents were from different states in Nigeria. Thus, the response rate was 21.2%.

We adopted the Analysis of Variance (ANOVA) statistical correlation coefficient method to analyze the relationship between the dependent and independent variables (trust indicators) where the core coefficient significant value $P \leq 0.01$.

This study is intended to determine on the one hand, why existing users are using the e-payment system? If it is because they trust such e-payment system hosted by a third party company outside well known financial institutions (banks), then we explore further with what trust components they see, use or feel. On the other hand, the trust enabling factors can be enhanced to attract others who are not users. Then we further investigate how to incorporate trust features into the e-payment platform to strengthen user trust.

5   Data Analysis, Findings and Discussions

This study has explored the role of trust in the context of a Nigerian e-payment service, Remita. To the best of our knowledge, this is the first study to systematically analyze user trust levels when they interact with online payment service. Secondly, based on well-established social psychological theories, we empirically contributed to refining the socio technical trust model proposed by [26]. The data from this study has helped in evaluating certain aspects of the model.

Regression analysis was carried out to evaluate the impact of the independent variables on the dependent variable. The items for the dependent variables were transformed using SPSS into a composite variable and it was carried out for the independent variables. The data from this study has helped us evaluate certain aspects of user trust in the developing country context.

Table 1. Model Summary

Model	R	R square	Adjusted R square	Std. error of the estimate
1	.967[a]	.935	.931	.25369

Model Summary, Table 1, displays the R .967 (the Multiple Correlation value representing the correlation between the actual scores of the dependent variable and the scores for the dependent variable predicted by the regression equation), the R squared .935 (the Multiple Squared Correlation value that if multiplied by 100 can be interpreted as a percentage to indicate that the independent variables account for 93.5% of the variability in the scores of the dependent variable), the Adjusted R square .931 and the Standard Error of the Estimate .254.

Table 2. Anova table (Dependent Variable: TRUST)

Model		Sum of squares	df	Mean square	F	Sig.
1	Regression	90.977	7	12.997	201.947	.000[a]
	Residual	6.307	98	.064		
	Total	97.283	105			

a. Predictors: (Constant), HONESTY, MOTIVATION, PREDICTABILITY, WILLINGNESS, RECIPROCITY, BENEVOLENCE, COMPETENCY

ANOVA, displays the Sum of Squares, df (degrees of freedom), Mean Square, F 201.947 which measure the size of the effects, $F(7,98) = 201.947$ and Sig. 0.000 where $P \leq 0.01$, shows the probability that the results are by random chance (Table 2).

The coefficient analysis in Table 3 shows the correlation between trust and trust indicators (motivation, willingness, reciprocity, competency, predictability, benevolence and honesty) using the socio technical model of trust by Sousa et al. [26]. Using a cutoff at $p \leq 0.01$ for the level of significance, with reference to Table 3, we can confidently infer the following:

As can be observed, the relationship between Motivation (operationalized through self-efficacy) and Trust is statistically not significant as $P = .885$ at $P \geq 0.01$. Therefore, the null hypothesis for H1 is accepted. Even though self-efficacy predicts motivation [24] and we hypothesized that trust is significantly associated with perceived

Table 3. Coefficients of the latent variables (Dependent Variable: TRUST)

Model	Unstandardized coefficients		Standardized coefficients	t	Sig.
	B	Std. error	Beta		
1 (Constant)	.027	.144		.184	.855
Motivation	−.012	.040	−.008	−.290	.772
Willingness	.161	.050	.140	3.189	.002
Reciprocity	.109	.057	.110	1.903	.060
Competency	.265	.075	.280	3.543	.001
Predictability	.182	.041	.209	4.475	.000
Benevolence	.180	.066	.191	2.709	.008
Honesty	.121	.069	.133	1.772	.079

motivation in the system, this was not the case in our research. Motivation features with regards to this e-payment system are insignificant to the trust levels of users.

There exists a statistical significant relationship between Willingness (operationalized through outcome expectations) and Trust. Here the null hypothesis for H2 is accepted as P = 0.002, at P $\geq$ 0.01. On similar lines, willingness was measured based on outcome expectations on a paper by Compeau and Higgins [4], as it appears from the responses, users already knew what to expect from the e-payment system and somewhat knew what the outcome of using the platform would be.

There exists a statistically non-significant relationship between Reciprocity and Trust. Where P = 0.060, at P $\geq$ 0.01. On similar lines, reciprocity in the information systems literature has been operationalized based on the premise of social capital. Social capital includes physical (e.g., driving a friend to the airport), emotional (e.g., giving a friend a hug), and informational (e.g., giving a friend advice about a big decision) resources, among others with expected returns at some future point; in other words, reciprocity is a key component of social capital [6]. In a user technology interaction such a scenario would not hold fit, as there does not exist social capital.

The relationship between Competency and Trust was statistically significantly as P = 0.001, at P $\geq$ 0.01. This was expected as high competency levels of the system was hypothesized to enhance trust.

As expected also, the relationship between Predictability and Trust was statistically significantly. P = 0.000, P $\geq$ 0.01. It appears that users of the platform are certain of what to expect from the platform with regards to their transactions.

The relationship between Benevolence and Trust is also statistically significant. P = 0.008, P $\geq$ 0.01. Therefore, a perception or experience of goodwill or kind consideration from the e-payment service heightens users trust.

On the contrary the relationship between Honesty and Trust is statistically non-significant. P = 0.079, Table 3. This implies that users perceived honesty of the e-payment system has no impact on their relation to trust in the system. In other words, it is of no relevance to user trust whether or not honesty hints are present in the system.

Therefore, what was important to the users was the functionalities, degree of ease of use and efficiency of the e-payment service (competence), if the e-payment service was designed with the user's best interest in mind and will always operate in such a way (benevolence), knowing that their expectations will be met (predictability) and finally knowing that the e-payment service will proffer expected outcomes which leads to a predisposition to interact with the system (willingness).

The results with regards to competency (which reflects the degree of ease of use and efficient functionalities) are consistent with the study of [20], which investigated the factors influencing Chinese users' perception and adoption toward e-payment. Their study revealed that the benefits users are most concerned about are the easy registration, learnability, convenience, fast processing and usability of the e-payment.

5.1   Design Reflections

Using the socio-technical trust model (Fig. 1.) as a design critique, we examined Remita platform for trust-enabling interactions to uncover opportunities for improvement. As a result of the evaluation, we found that the platform presents good design features, which should encourage meaningful user trust-enabling interactions but also points out some pitfalls to be considered.

Fig. 3. A screenshot of the welcome homepage of Remita (Color figure online)

The homepage (Fig. 3) has a well-balanced color scheme which includes warm and cool colors, the designs employs a good blend of color repetition which unifies the service and choice colors like grey in the background gives it some seriousness and professional feel. The cool colors give the platform an earnest, business-like ambience, creating an impression of seriousness and professionalism.

However, the address bar (Fig. 4) shows there is no Secure Sockets Layer (SSL) indicated, clearly stated, "Not secure". Perhaps the indication of a lack of security deters motivation to the existing users but however has no impact on their trust

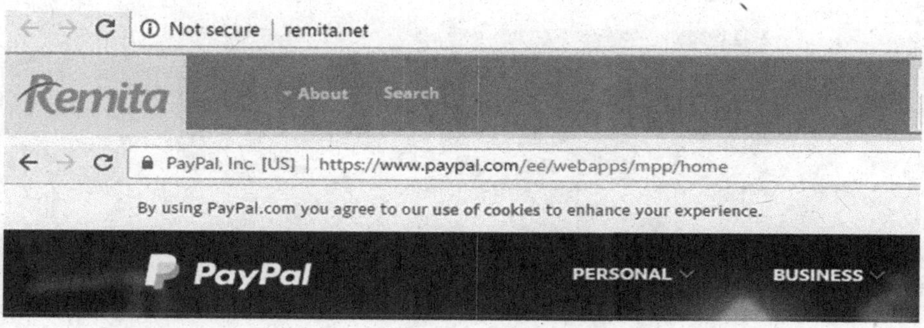

Fig. 4. Comparing Remita's address bar secure connection to PayPal's

Fig. 5. The pre signup page of Remita

to use the system according to our data analysis findings. On the contrary, this may likely hinder the trust of potential users and consequently their intention to use the service.

We believe a simple layout instead of a complex one is the key to keeping users interested. An effective use of white space (also referred to as negative space) commands attention to the intended actions/information for users to focus on. However, the positioning of the text fields and radio button as well as the header and footer design (See Fig. 5), employed in the use of white space by Remita, aesthetically does not achieve an appealing balanced to incite user's willingness to sign up.

In contrast to Remita, (Fig. 6) the PayPal signup page shows cheerful faces; indicating contented users of the platform, well-positioned information and a good use of white space. This creates somewhat of an 'halo effect' to trusting the information given in texts which collectively will most likely stimulate a users' willingness to go ahead with the sign up.

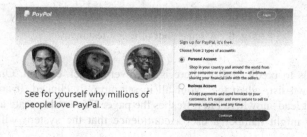

Fig. 6. The pre signup page of PayPal

Fig. 7. A screenshot of other parts of the Remita homepage

The webpage is responsive, which can be accessed on any internet enabled device, designed using bootstrap with nice visual flow and shows not only a variety of the uses of Remita, (See, Fig. 7) but provides a variety of prominent citizens' testimonials which depicts honesty (See, Fig. 8), proving to be a competent service to help users achieve their goals. With scrolling down the page a user finds even more motivation to sign up and an appeal to benevolence.

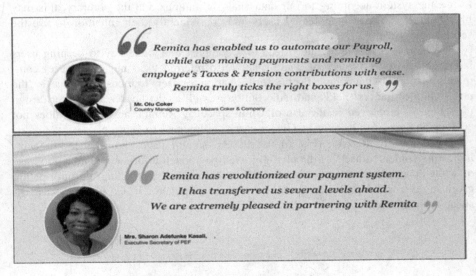

Fig. 8. A screenshot of users' testimony

With regards to predictability, there is however a slack evident. On the "About" button drop down list, when the "your all in one app" is clicked, it appears to be a broken link as it leads nowhere but refreshes the page. This could create a negative user experience and might hamper a user's confidence that the system will help him to perform a desired action in accordance with what is expected. Remita provides instant feedback through email on a customer service, which responds within 48 h and can be contacted via phone or on their social media platforms. A design recommendation to strengthen reciprocity would be to include a live chat in the system for onsite correspondence to provide real-time support to users as it applies with Transferwise as well as Cashenvoy (a Nigerian e-payment platform).

Furthermore, there is no means of a direct email messaging through the platform for a quick compose and send to the site as an easy option against a user sending through his/her email account.

We therefore, propose a redesign of the Remita platform to incorporate the missing visual clues and characteristics highlighted, which we propose might enhance user trust in the system. We also suggest a provision to a page showing the Remita partners e.g. the Central Bank of Nigeria, list of associated commercial banks, companies etc. and some well detailed user security/insurance information to boost users' trust perceptions and influence use of the platform.

5.2 Limitations

Our study is not without its own limitations, first, the online survey raises the problem of generalizability. This study selected certain socio-technical indicators but some latent factors may have an effect on trust in e-payment use. Furthermore, regarding why motivation (self-efficacy) was statistically non-significant to trust, we could argue that such a limitation might only be specific to our study. Since in the current study, data was collected from users who were tech savvy and in such a situation technological self-efficacy might not matter. Also, the current study focused only on existing users (employing the use of a survey), the exclusion of non-users may have had an effect on the research construct validity.

5.3 Implications and Future Work

The work undertaken and presented in this paper classified under the category of Human Computer Trust, presents an analysis of an indigenous e-payment service used in a developing country. The lessons derived from this study provide some implications. For the researchers, there is a need to look more closely into characteristics that engender trust in developing countries, and this outcome is consistent with a recent study in Nigeria [16], which drew a conclusion that trust is one of the challenges to developers because of failures to give attention to user experience considerations.

Apparently developers in developing countries fail to employ participatory design approaches, proper user testing, prototyping, and other Human Computer Interaction (HCI) techniques when designing services and most importantly e-payment platforms where users tend to be skeptical as evident in literature. We suggest for further studies; investigating non-users' awareness of e-payments services, here the question is 'why they do not use third party hosted e-payment service beside well known and insured financial institutions (banks)?' Is it trust-related? If yes, then how do we enhance trust? Else how do we address the reasons and trust alongside? This is to elicit clues, which may have been missed in the current study. We suggest also using a mix of questionnaires and interviews for richer data, to complement and expand the results found here. Also, data gathered revealed that over 90% of the users of the platform are proficient in navigating and using typical computer programs for a given task. This indicates that less tech savvy users are not using the platform; this leaves room for further investigation.

Furthermore, perceived motivation, reciprocity and honesty have no significant influence on users' predisposition to trust deserve further study in the future. This however, suggests that online payment providers should enhance user experience and design their platforms by strengthening the significant trust indicators investigated in this study and including users in the design process to clearly see and understand features to engender trust.

6   Conclusions

In the current study, we employed the socio-technical model of trust [26] to investigate the influence of trust predictors on users of on an e-payment platform in the context of a developing country. There are two fundamental questions raised in this study, formulated as; first, what are the design considerations for promoting the trust appeal when designing e-payment systems? And secondly, what are users' perceptions regarding trust enabling indicators with interactions on e-payment platforms? To achieve the answer to these questions, online questionnaires were administered to current users of the platform and a critical evaluation of the e-payment service was carried out.

Our study revealed that users are attentive to competency, benevolence, predictability and willingness features in the design of trust-enabling e-services as opposed to motivation, honesty and reciprocity. The implication is that design features incorporating the latter factors in order to foster and enhance the trust appeal of an e-payment system and engender the trust of users are not being supported and this provides some opportunities for future research.

Finally, this study provides a basic framework to explore e-transaction service models in developing countries. We encourage a trust-enabling evaluation carried out by a UX specialist to investigate trust concerns "with users" to proffer design directions on e-transaction platforms. Therefore, trust evaluation and redesign should be a continuous process on an e-transaction platform.

Acknowledgments. The authors would like to thank all the participants in this study as well as the developers of Remita.

References

1. Akintola, K.G., Akinyede, R.O., Agbonifo, C.O.: Appraising Nigeria readiness for e-commerce towards achieving vision 20:20. Int. J. Res. Rev. Appl. Sci. **9**(2), 330–340 (2011)
2. Augustine, N.A.: Queuing model as a technique of queue solution in Nigeria banking industry. Developing Countries Study **3**(8) (2013). ISSN 2224-607X (Paper) ISSN 2225-0565 (Online)
3. Chellappa, R.K., Pavlou, P.A.: Perceived information security, financial liability and consumer trust in electronic commerce transactions. Logistics Inf. Manag. **15**(5/6), 358–368 (2002)
4. Compeau, D.R., Higgins, C.A.: Computer self-efficacy: development of a measure and initial test. MIS Q. **19**(2), 189–211 (1995)
5. Cyr, D.: Website design, trust and culture: an eight country investigation. Electron. Commer. Res. Appl. **12**(6), 373–385 (2013)
6. Fred, S., Jessica, V., Nicole, B., Rebecca, G., Cliff, L.: Privacy in interaction: exploring disclosure and social capital in facebook. Association for the Advancement of Artificial Intelligence (2012). (www.aaai.org)
7. Grabner-Kräuter, S., Kaluscha, E.A.: Engendering consumer trust in e-commerce: conceptual clarification and empirical findings. In: Petrovic, O., et al. (eds.) Trust in the Network Economy, pp. 55–69. Springer, Wien New York (2003)
8. Lacohée, H., Cofta, P., Phippen, A., Furnell, S.: Understanding Public Perceptions: Trust and Engagement in ICT Mediated Services. International Engineering Consortium, Chicago (2008)
9. John, A.O., Rotimi, O.: Analysis of electronic banking and customer satisfaction in Nigeria. Eur. J. Bus. Soc. Sci. **3**(3), 14–27 (2014). http://www.ejbss.com/recent.aspx. ISSN: 2235-767X
10. Jøsang, A., Marsh, S., Pope, S.: Exploring different types of trust propagation. In: Stølen, K., Winsborough, William H., Martinelli, F., Massacci, F. (eds.) iTrust 2006. LNCS, vol. 3986, pp. 179–192. Springer, Heidelberg (2006). doi:10.1007/11755593_14
11. Kim, C., Mirusmonov, M., Lee, I.: An empirical examination of factors influencing the intention to use mobile payment. Comput. Hum. Behav. **26**(3), 310–322 (2010)
12. Lawrence, J., Tar, U.: Barriers to e-commerce in developing countries. Inf. Soc. Justice **3**(1), 23–35 (2010)
13. Mouratidis, H., Cofta, P.: Practitioner's challenges in designing trust into online systems. J. Theor. Appl. Electron. Comm. Res. **5**(3), 65–77 (2010). doi:10.4067/S0718-18762010000300007
14. Mukherjee, A., Nath, P.: Role of electronic trust in online retailing a re-examination of the commitment-trust theory. Eur. J. Mark. **41**(9/10), 1173–1202 (2007)
15. Nilashi, M., Ibrahim, O., Mirabi, V.R., Ebrahimi, L., Zare, M.: The role of security design and content factors on customer trust in mobile commerce. J. Retail. Consum. Serv. **26**, 57–69 (2015)
16. Ogunyemi, A., Lamas, D., Adagunodo, E.R., Rosa, I.B.: HCI practices in the Nigerian software industry. In: Abascal, J., Barbosa, S., Fetter, M., Gross, T., Palanque, P., Winckler, M. (eds.) INTERACT 2015. LNCS, vol. 9297, pp. 479–488. Springer, Cham (2015). doi:10.1007/978-3-319-22668-2_37
17. Okoro, E.G., Kigho, K.E.: The problems and prospects of e-transaction: the Nigerian perspective. J. Res. Int. Bus. Manag. **3**(1), 10–16 (2013)

18. Oreku, G., Mtenzi, F., Ali, A.: A viewpoint of Tanzania e-commerce and implementation barriers: ComSIS. Comput. Sci. Inf. Syst. **10**(1), 263–281 (2013). doi:10.2298/CSIS110725002O

19. Oseni, K., Dingley, K.: Challenges of e-service adoption and implementation in Nigeria: lessons from Asia. World Acad. Sci. Eng. Technol. Int. Sci. Index Inf. Eng. **2**(9), 135 (2014)

20. Pei, Y., Wang, S., Fan, J., Zhang, M.: An empirical study on the impact of perceived benefit, risk and trust on e-payment adoption: comparing quick pay and union pay in China. In: 7th International Conference on Intelligent Human-Machine Systems and Cybernetics (2015). doi:10.1109/IHMSC.2015.148

21. Naimat, P.F.: The effect of trust in adoption of internet banking: a case study of Nigeria. Int. J. Econ Bus. Manag. **1**(2), 19–24 (2013)

22. Popoola Naimat, F., Arshad, B.R.: Strategic approach to build customers trust in adoption of internet banking in Nigeria. J. Internet Bank. Comm. **20**(1) (2015). http://www.arraydev.com/commerce/jibc/JIBC

23. Sabi, H.M., Mlay, S.V., Tsuma, C.K., Bang, H.N.: Conceptualizing user preference and trust in western designed banking software systems in developing countries. J. Internet Bank. Comm. **20**, 126 (2015)

24. Schunk, D.H.: Self-efficacy and academic motivation. Educ. Psychol. **26**(3&4), 207–231 (1991). Copyright @ !1991, Lawrence Erlbaum Associates, Inc.

25. Seckler, M., Heinz, S., Forde, S., Tuch, A., Opwis, K.: Trust and distrust on the web: user experiences and u characteristics. Comput. Hum. Behav. **45**, 39–50 (2015)

26. Sousa, S., Dias, P., Lamas, D.: A model for human-computer trust: a key contribution for leveraging trustful interactions. In: 2014 9th Iberian Conference on Information Systems and Technologies (CISTI), pp. 1–6. IEEE (2014)

27. Tsiakis, T., Sthephanides, G.: The concept of security and trust in electronic payments. Comput. Secur. **24**(1), 10–15 (2005)

28. Turel, O., Gefen, D.: The dual role of trust in system use. J. Comput. Inf. Syst. **54**(1), 2–10 (2013)

29. Yousafzai, S., Pallister, J.G., Foxall, G.R.: Multidimensional role of trust in internet banking adoption. Serv. Indus. J. **29**(5), 591–605 (2009)

30. Zheng, J., Veinott, E., Bos, N., Olson, J.S., Olson, G.M.: Trust without touch: jumpstarting long-distance trust with initial social activities. In: Proceedings of the SIGCHI Conference on Human Factors in Computing Systems, pp. 141–146. ACM (2002)

Integration of Estonian Higher Education Information Technology Students and Its Effect on Graduation-Related Self-efficacy

Külli Kori[✉], Margus Pedaste, and Olev Must

University of Tartu, Tartu, Estonia
kulli.kori@ut.ee

Abstract. Low graduation rates in higher education are problem in many countries. This study investigates Estonian higher education IT studies, where focus is on interaction with computers, but first-year dropout rates are very high. The aim of the study was to establish which factors influencing dropout based on the literature are associated with each other, and according to Tinto's dropout model, to investigate the role of academic experience and social work-related experience in first-year IT students' graduation-related self-efficacy. Data were collected from 509 Estonian first-year IT students. The initial model shows that bivariate association found in the literature give a simplified impression of the graduation-related self-efficacy. Although Tinto's model can be implemented in first-year IT studies, IT work experience has a much greater effect on the graduation-related self-efficacy than academic experience. This means that working in IT field is very important for students in Estonian IT curricula and universities should take this into account.

Keywords: Academic experience · Graduation-related self-efficacy · Information Technology · Social experience · Work experience

1 Introduction

1.1 Dropout Rates

Substantial dropout rates in higher education are a problem worldwide. This study focuses on the graduation in Information Technology (IT) related curricula in higher education. The curricula focus on interaction with computers, which requires digital competence from the students. The European average dropout rate in higher education is 19% in the IT field [1]. However, in Estonia about two thirds of undergraduate IT students do not finish their studies (authors' calculations based on [2]). This exceeds the European average dropout rate in IT as well as other fields of studies in Estonia, where 46.1% of the students drop out (authors' calculations based on [2]).

In general, dropout rates are the highest during the first year of studies [3]. Among the students who entered undergraduate IT studies in Estonia in 2013, the first-year dropout rate was 32% [4]. The authors' calculations based on data from the Estonian Education Information System [2] show that the general first-year dropout rate in IT studies is 29.8%. This means that half of the students who drop out during their three years of

P. Zaphiris and A. Ioannou (Eds.): LCT 2017, Part II, LNCS 10296, pp. 435–448, 2017.
DOI: 10.1007/978-3-319-58515-4_33

undergraduate studies do so during the first year. Figure 1 demonstrates that dropout rates in the Estonian IT curricula are higher than in other curricula. The first-year dropout rate in other fields of studies is only 18% in Estonia (authors' calculations based on [2]). The first year of studies is crucial for students, and it is therefore important to investigate first-year dropout in IT curricula.

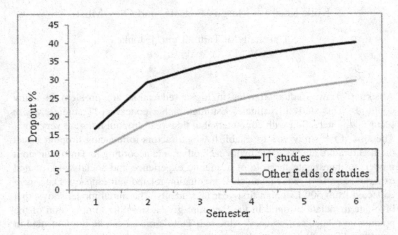

Fig. 1. Comparison of cumulative dropout rates during three years of undergraduate studies between IT curricula and other curricula in Estonia (authors' calculations based on EHIS, 2015).

1.2 Dropout as a Process

According to Tinto [5], dropout can be defined in two ways: (1) referring to students who leave the higher education institution in which they are currently studying and it is not known if they continue studies later in a different curriculum or different institution; or (2) referring to students who leave the higher education institution and will never receive any degree. A study in Australia revealed that if they followed the first definition then after the first study year 20% of the students were not studying in the same university, but the rate of students who actually did not study on the higher education level (the second definition) was less than 10% [6]. So, many students who drop out of a particular higher education curriculum probably continue their studies later in a different institution or different curriculum.

High dropout rates become a problem if the insufficient proportion of graduates with digital competence fails to meet the needs of the labor market. This is happening right now in the IT field: the number of IT graduates has been decreasing since 2006 in the European Union [7], and forecasts suggest that the unmet demand for IT practitioners keeps rising. According to different scenarios 913,000–1,300,000 IT workers could be missing by the year 2020 [7]. Thus, more IT graduates are needed in the labor market.

There is a demand for people with good digital competence not only in the Information and Communication Technology (ICT) sector, but in other fields, as well.

In Estonia about half of the IT workers are working in the ICT sector and half in other fields [8]. Also, IT companies in Estonia sometimes hire people who do not have an IT degree. It has been found that only half of Estonian IT workers have a higher education degree [8]. Thus, both those students who are studying IT and those who drop out of their IT studies can apply for a variety of jobs that require digital competence.

During past decades research on dropout has moved from the psychological viewpoint (students' individual attributes, skills, and motivation) towards a more complicated viewpoint that takes into account the role of the environment in the institution [9]. Larsen et al. [10] divided theories about dropout into four groups: economically, psychologically, organizationally and sociologically grounded theories. According to the economically grounded theory dropout is a rational decision based on the relationship between students' estimated investment in education and estimated return on education. The psychologically grounded theory tries to describe a typical dropout and focuses on factors like study behavior, perception of and attitude towards studying. The organizationally grounded theory explain dropout by focusing on participation, communication and membership in academic communities within the university. Last but not least, the sociologically grounded theory considers social and institutional structures as most important in understanding dropout.

Although the reasons for students dropping out cumulate individually [11], many studies have investigated dropout reasons in higher education. Based on a systematic review above all the previously mentioned theories, Larsen et al. [10] differentiated between eleven factors influencing dropout: (1) sociodemographic background of students, (2) academic competencies/pre-requisites for studying, (3) preparation for studying, (4) motivation for studying, (5) learning strategies, (6) study conditions, (7) social and/or academic integration within university/adaptation to university life, (8) overall evaluation of university life, (9) outside opportunities for dropouts (e.g., favorable business cycles), (10) economic situation of students, and (11) living conditions including housing, family and personal situation or support and student jobs. Firstly, the current study investigates how the factors concluded by Larsen et al. [10] relate to each other and affect first-year IT students' retention.

Secondly, the current study investigates IT students' retention following one of the most often used dropout models which is developed by Vincent Tinto and which follows sociologically grounded theory. Tinto's [12] complex model of students' departure includes some of the factors that Larsen et al. [10] found with the systematic literature review: sociodemographic background, academic competencies/pre-requisites for studying, preparation for studying and academic and social integration. The model shows that the following aspects are an important influence on students' dropout decision: pre-entry attributes (family background, skills and abilities, prior schooling), goals/commitments, institutional experiences that can be divided into academic and social, and academic and social interaction. Academic experiences are divided into formal academic performance and informal interactions with faculty and staff. So, grades and collected credit points can be seen as part of a formal academic experience that could influence students' dropout decision. Other studies have also shown that students with lower academic achievement exhibit a higher probability of dropping out [13–15]. This can be explained by the rules set by universities – if a student does not pass enough courses during a year he or she will be expelled.

Dropout is a process – a period when students are thinking about dropping out, which may lead to either actually dropping out or continuing their studies. During that period it is still possible to change students' minds and support them in order for them to opt for continuing the studies. Students' uncertainty about their graduation refers to their low graduation-related self-efficacy. Self-efficacy is defined as people's belief about their ability to perform successfully in a certain activity or task [16] and the results of previous studies [17, 18] indicate that if students have higher graduation-related self-efficacy, they are more likely to actually graduate. Because the IT students who participated in the current study were still studying in the university, actual graduation rates were not available and first-year IT students' graduation-related self-efficacy is under investigation.

1.3   Integration of IT Students

In Tinto's model social experiences are divided into formal extracurricular activities and informal peer group interactions. Social integration includes feeling part of a group, being satisfied with introductory courses, feeling able to question lecturers, and socializing outside university hours [19]; this may influence a student's decision to continue studying or drop out. Such ways of communication have also been found important already in the process of students choosing the university [20]. However, social experiences are also interactions outside university with other IT students or people in the IT field, e.g., in the IT work environment.

Students work during their studies mainly for two reasons: earning money or getting work experience, which is valued in the labor market [21]. Students can work in different areas if the goal is earning money, but if IT students want work experience then they need to work in the IT field. So, in addition to interacting with computers and developing digital competence in their studies, IT students may also experience this at work. Working in the IT field engages the students in the community of IT workers, which could influence their decision to graduate. This means that working in IT field can be seen as part of social integration of the students. Therefore, the current study focuses only IT-related work (not any work that IT students might do). However, it has been found that working during studies can have a negative effect on studies owing to less time for studying, increasing the likelihood of dropout [22, 23]. In Estonia it has been found that already at the beginning of the first semester 8% of IT students report working in IT field, and other students are also considering work [24]. It can be concluded that working during studies is an important part of the social experience that could influence the graduation in IT curricula.

1.4   The Aim

A number of bivariate relations between variables that influence dropout or retention can be found in the literature (e.g. [10]); however, it is not known if combining them into one multivariate model gives a better overview of what influences the graduation-related self-efficacy. Therefore, the first aim of this study was to establish which factors that influence dropout based on [10] are related to one another and based on that create the first model of graduation-related self-efficacy for first-year IT studies.

The second aim was to take a well-known dropout theory (Tinto's dropout model [12]) and implement it in first-year IT studies. Thus, the second model can be created that shows the role of academic experiences and social work-related experiences in graduation-related self-efficacy.

2 Methods

2.1 Participants

The participants of this study were 509 higher education IT students who started their studies in 2013 and 2014 in three higher education institutions in Estonia and eight different IT related curricula. 71.5% of them were male and 28.5% female. This is similar to the gender distribution in IT studies in Estonia, where about 75% of the students are male [24]. The students responded to questionnaires twice: at the beginning of the first semester and at the beginning of the second semester. In addition, data about students' academic achievement – average grade and collected credit points (in ECTS, i.e. European Credit Transfer and Accumulation System, 1 ECTS means 26 h of work) – was collected from the universities' study information systems.

2.2 The Instruments

The questionnaires were designed based on the factors that could influence dropout, differentiated by Larsen et al. [10] (see variables and constructs in Table 1). While designing the questionnaires expert discussions were held with people teaching IT students to increase the validity of the instruments. The questionnaire included the following blocks of questions in the following order: background information, multiple choice questions (questions about knowledge of job opportunities, prior experience with studying IT, curricula, and studying in the university), open-ended questions that required a short answer (questions about the probability of graduation, working in IT field during and after studies, communicating with other people in the IT field), and additional questions (e.g., about prior work in IT field). To learn about students' motivation the Academic Motivation Scale (AMS-C 28) College (CEGEP) version [25] was added to the end of the questionnaire. The scale contained 28 items that students had to evaluate on a 7-point scale. The Academic Motivation Scale helps to determine 7 constructs of motivation: intrinsic and extrinsic motivations are both divided into three subcategories, a motivation being the seventh category [25]. While analysing the data, the average score was calculated for all of the 7 constructs of motivation as well as for intrinsic motivation (includes three constructs) and extrinsic motivation (includes three constructs).

The IT students that participated in the current study still have some time until graduation. Therefore, the data about actual graduation rates was not available and students' graduation-related self-efficacy was the focus of this study. Graduation-related self-efficacy was measured by one question: "How strong is the probability of you

Table 1. Variables and constructs that were used in this study

Factors	Questions
Sociodemographic background	Age
	Gender
	Native language
Preparation for studies, academic competencies and pre-requisites for studying	When did you start to learn programming?
	How long did you learn IT in school?
	Have you worked in the IT field before?
	Average grade in the first and second semester
	Collected credit points in the first and second semester
Overall evaluation of university life, study conditions and learning strategies	How informed are you about your curriculum?
	How well does the curriculum meet your expectations?
	How complicated are your university studies compared to your high school studies?
	How pleasant are your university studies compared to your high school studies?
	How does a negative grade (failure) influence your motivation to continue your studies and graduate?
Motivation for studying	Academic Motivation Scale (AMS-C 28) College (CEGEP) version
Social integration within university	How many of your friends are also IT students?
	How many of your friends work in the IT field?
	With how many of your course mates do you communicate regularly after school?
Outside opportunities for dropout, living conditions, economic situation of students	Do you work in the IT field?
	How informed are you about job opportunities in the IT field?
	How strong is the probability that you will start working (or continue working) in the IT field during your studies?
	How strong is the probability that you will work in the IT field after graduation?

finishing your studies?", and the students answered by giving a percentage. The graduation-related self-efficacy was the focus of this study as students' perceptions of their graduation or dropout may lead to actual dropout if bad experiences or dropout reasons cumulate. Also, it has been found before that those IT students who will drop out estimate the probability of their graduation as being lower than those who will not drop out [4]. This suggests that graduation-related self-efficacy is related to students' actual behavior.

2.3 Data Analysis

Structural Equation Modelling (SEM) with the Mplus 7.31 program [26] was used for creating the models. The statistical indices used to evaluate the models were the following: comparative fit index (CFI) [27], standardized root mean square residual (SRMR) [28] and root mean square error of approximation (RMSEA) [29]. The following cut-off values of goodness-of-fit values were used: for CFI 0.95 or above, for SMRM 0.08 or below [30], and for RMSEA 0.1 or below [31].

3 Results

3.1 Initial Model of the Graduation-Related Self-efficacy

An initial multivariate model was created based on bivariate associations found in the literature. The model, shown in Fig. 2, is able to describe 78.4% of the graduation-related self-efficacy (R^2 = 0.784) and was the best model that came out with the SEM. However, the model is quite complicated, with rather poor fit indexes. For the first model, the CFI was 0.649 (below 0.95, which is the cut-off value [30]), SMRM 0.155 (greater than 0.08, which is the cut-off value [30]), and RMSEA 0.214 (greater than 0.1, which is the cut-off value [31]).

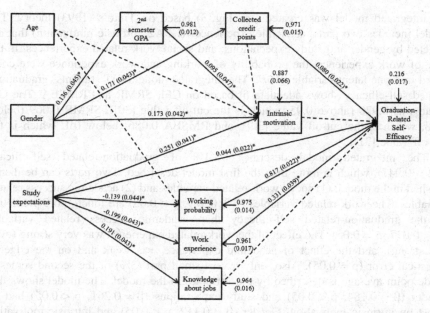

Fig. 2. The initial model of the graduation-related self-efficacy. Standardized coefficients are presented. Fit indexes: CFI = 0.649, SMRM = 0.155 and RMSEA = 0.214. * marks statistically significant (p < 0.05) associations; - - - - > marks associations that were not statistically significant.

The following variables were included in the model: age, gender, study expectations, second semester GPA, collected credit points, intrinsic motivation, probability of working, work experience and knowledge of job opportunities. Whereas some of the associations were statistically significant, some were not. The following is an overview of the statistically significant associations. Study expectations had an effect on the probability of working ($\beta = -0.139$, $p < 0.05$), work experience ($\beta = -0.199$, $p < 0.05$), knowledge of job opportunities ($\beta = 0.191$, $p < 0.05$), intrinsic motivation ($\beta = 0.251$, $p < 0.05$), and the graduation-related self-efficacy ($\beta = 0.044$, $p < 0.05$). The probability of working ($\beta = 0.817$, $p < 0.05$) and work experience ($\beta = 0.331$, $p < 0.05$) had an effect on the graduation-related self-efficacy. Gender had an effect on intrinsic motivation ($\beta = 0.173$, $p < 0.05$), collected credit points ($\beta = 0.171$, $p < 0.05$) and second semester GPA ($\beta = 0.136$, $p < 0.05$). Second semester GPA had an effect on intrinsic motivation ($\beta = 0.095$, $p < 0.05$). Finally, the collected credit points had an effect on the graduation-related self-efficacy ($\beta = 0.080$, $p < 0.05$). The other effects were not statistically significant. Still, the model is presented in the current paper to show that even if the associations between the variables were reasonable based on the literature, the multivariate model seems overly complicated, and not all the associations are important.

3.2   Integrated Model of the Graduation-Related Self-efficacy

An integrated model was created (see Fig. 3) based on Tinto's (1993) theory. The model includes two parts: academic experiences (GPA2, intrinsic motivation) that are affected by gender and study expectations; and social work-related experiences. In the case of work experience, the probability of working and work experience were combined into one latent variable, *Work*. The integrated model of IT students' graduation-related self-efficacy shows adequate fit based on CFI, SRMR and RMSEA. The CFI value was 0.970 (above 0.95, which is the cut-off value [30]), SRMR 0.069 (below 0.08, which is the cut-off value [30]), and RMSEA 0.086 (below 0.1, which is the cut-off value [31]).

The integrated model describes 94.1% of graduation-related self-efficacy ($R^2 = 0.941$), which is more than the first model described. Two parts can be distinguished in the model: (1) social work-related variables and (2) academic success related variables. The work-related variables ($\beta = 0.969$, $p < 0.05$) are much more predictive of the graduation-related self-efficacy than academic success related variables ($\beta = 0.037$, $p = 0.05$). The effect of the work-related experience was very strong (even too strong), and the effect of academic experience was weak and on the edge of statistical error ($p = 0.05$). Also, only a very small part (3%) of the second semester grade point average is described by the variables in the model. The model shows that gender ($\beta = 0.184$, $p < 0.05$) and study expectations ($\beta = 0.261$, $p < 0.05$) had an effect on intrinsic motivation. Gender ($\beta = 0.112$, $p < 0.05$) and intrinsic motivation ($\beta = 0.111$, $p < 0.05$) had an effect on the second semester GPA.

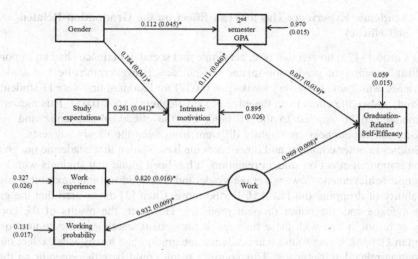

Fig. 3. The integrated model of graduation-related self-efficacy. Standardized coefficients are presented. Fit indexes: CFI = 0.970, SRMR = 0.069 and RMSEA = 0.086. * marks statistically significant (p < 0.05) associations.

4 Discussion

4.1 Bivariate Associations Give a Simplified Impression of the Graduation-Related Self-efficacy

The initial multivariate model was created based on bivariate relations found in the literature [10]. However, the model may be misleading as it includes, in addition to statistically significant associations, some statistically not significant associations between the variables and the fit indexes showed inadequate fit.

Other studies have detected bivariate associations between age and motivation (e.g., in the context of language learning [32]), as well as academic achievement and motivation [33]. In the context of the IT field it has been found that older students are more interested in working during their studies [24] and that knowledge of job opportunities may lead to work during studies, and from there, to dropout [22, 23]. However, these associations between the variables were not statistically significant in the model created. The associations between the variables are actually more complicated than the model shows, and it can be concluded that the initial multivariate model gives an incomplete impression of the graduation-related self-efficacy. Investigating graduation-related self-efficacy based on a more complex model (e.g., Tinto's dropout model [12]), not bivariate associations as presented by Larsen et al. [10], convey a better impression of what influences it.

4.2   Academic Experience Has a Weak Effect on the Graduation-Related Self-efficacy

Tinto's model [12] showed that both academic and social experiences had an important role in influencing the graduation-related self-efficacy. However, the effect of academic experience was found to be very weak ($\beta = 0.037$) for Estonian first-year IT students in this study. Also, the effect is on the edge of statistical error ($p = 0.05$). This means that the model can be applied to the IT field, but the effects of academic and social work-related experiences are slightly different from what the theory suggests.

Studies in other countries and other curricula have shown that academic integration has an important effect on student retention. It has been found that students with lower academic achievement (lower average grade and less credit points) exhibit a higher probability of dropping out [13–15]. Furthermore, Chen [3] discovered that the grade point average was the major dropout predictor. However, the results of the current study were not in line with these findings of previous research – in the context of the Estonian IT field, it was found that academic integration had a very weak effect on the graduation-related self-efficacy. This contrary result could be either specific to the IT field or the Estonian context. The IT field has its specificity, but the national culture and policy may also influence students' reasons for dropping out of higher education [19].

4.3   Social Work-Related Experience has a Major Effect on the Graduation-Related Self-efficacy

Based on the results of this study it can be concluded that social work-related integration is much more important in predicting the graduation-related self-efficacy than academic integration in the context of first-year IT studies in Estonia. A majority of the graduation-related self-efficacy can be described by work experience, which includes both the probability of working and prior work experience. So, social integration is important in the process of deciding to drop out or not.

Other studies have also revealed that social integration influences dropout in higher education. For example, Duque [34] found that student involvement (includes energy devoted to studies, time spent on campus, active participation in student organizations as well as interaction with faculty members and other students) influenced dropout. Working in IT field during studies could be similar social integration as students interact with people who work in the field of their studies. The negative side of working during studies is less time for studying, which may cause dropout [22, 23] or have a negative effect on students' academic progress [35]. Also, students may lose their motivation to study if the university teaches something that students do not need in their work. Therefore, IT students may choose to bring their digital competence labor market.

Other studies have also highlighted that there is a gap between employers' expectations and the skills of university graduates. It has been found in both engineering education and information systems curricula that in addition to technical skills (e.g., programming), employers expect students to have softer skills, such as communication and problem solving [36, 37]. Working IT students have also been found to have less motivation to study than those students who do not work [38]. This suggests that the skills and knowledge taught in university are not what students who are working in IT field need in their workplace. Therefore, universities should collaborate more with IT companies and offer studies that meet the needs of their students' future jobs. Currently IT companies value prior work experience, but if university graduates have the knowledge and skills needed at work then prior work experience may become less important. This means that IT students will not have to work during their studies.

4.4 Limitations and Further Studies

This study had some limitations. The results could be problematic because the effect of the latent variable *work* on the graduation-related self-efficacy is very strong and the regression residual is low. This result seems too good. It might be that for students the work variable is almost the same as graduation-related self-efficacy. Also, the results may be influenced by the questionnaire that was used – the question about the graduation-related self-efficacy was located in the questionnaire next to questions about starting work in the IT field. However, the *work* variable included work experience, which was not located in the questionnaires next to questions about working and graduation-related self-efficacy. For further studies, several different questions should be asked about probabilities of work to prevent such problems.

The result could also be influenced by response rate. It could be that those who did not respond to the questionnaire were already dropping out and the ones who responded had higher confidence about their graduation.

The results suggest that the work aspect needs further investigation. In this study only working in the IT field was under investigation, but working in other fields during studies may also affect the graduation-related self-efficacy. Further investigation is required to understand why working in the IT field has such a strong effect on the graduation-related self-efficacy. However, it is difficult to investigate working students as there are no official statistics on this and self-reports is the only data collection method.

Further investigation is also necessary to see if the graduation-related self-efficacy is similar to the actual graduation. Longitudinal data collection from IT students in Estonia is currently planned. After the additional data collection all three study years can be included in developing a model for undergraduate IT studies.

5 Conclusions

The first aim of this study was to investigate the bivariate associations between the factors that influence dropout and to create a multivariate model of graduation-related self-efficacy for first-year IT studies. The results show that creating a multivariate model based on bivariate association does not give a good overview of the graduation-related self-efficacy because the associations between different factors are overly complicated in the model and statistical errors may occur.

The second aim was to implement Tinto's [12] dropout model for first-year IT students in Estonia and investigate the role of academic and social work-related experiences in graduation-related self-efficacy. An integrated model was created showing that both academic and social experiences have a statistically significant effect on the graduation-related self-efficacy. However, working in the IT field, which is part of social integration, has a major effect on students' graduation-related self-efficacy, and the effect of academic integration is quite weak. The reason why working is so important for the students might be that university studies do not meet the expectations of IT companies, who therefore demand work experience from IT graduates. The issue of dropout remains, but it can be recommended that universities offer students better preparation for entering the labor market in order to retain their students.

Acknowledgement. This research was supported by the European Union through the European Regional Development Fund. It is financed within the project "Conceptual Framework for Increasing Society's Commitment in ICT: Approaches in General and Higher Education for Motivating ICT-Related Career Choices and Improving Competences for Applying and Developing ICT".

References

1. Hüsing, T., Korte, W.B., Fonstad, N., Lanvin, B., van Welsum, D., Cattaneo, G., Kolding, M., Lifonti, R.: e-Leadership. e-Skills for competitiveness and innovation vision, roadmap and foresight scenarios final report (2013). http://eskills-vision.eu/fileadmin/eSkillsVision/documents/VISION%20Final%20Report.pdf. Accessed 14 Dec 2015
2. Estonian Education Information System (EHIS): Estonian ministry of education and research (2015). http://www.ehis.ee/. Accessed 4 Mar 2016
3. Chen, R.: Institutional characteristics and college student dropout risks: a multilevel event history analysis. Res. High. Educ. **53**, 487–505 (2012)
4. Kori, K., Pedaste, M., Tõnisson, E., Palts, T., Altin, H., Rantsus, R., Sell, R., Murtazin, K., Rüütmann, T.: First-year dropout in ICT studies. In: Proceedings of IEEE Global Engineering Education Conference in Tallinn, Estonia EDUCON 2015, pp. 444–452 (2015)
5. Tinto, V.: Dropout from higher education: a theoretical synthesis of recent research. Rev. Educ. Res. **45**(1), 89–125 (1975)
6. Long, M., Ferrier, F., Heagney, M.: Stay, play or give it away? Students continuing, changing or leaving university study in first year. Centre for the Economics of Education and Training, Monash University (2006)
7. Gareis, K., Hüsing, T., Birov, S., Bludova, I., Schulz, C., Korte, W.B.: e-Skills for jobs in Europe: measuring progress and moving ahead. Final report, Bonn, Germany (2014)
8. Jürgenson, A., Mägi, E., Pihor, K., Batueva, V., Rozeik, H., Arukaev, R.: Eesti IKT kompetentsidega tööjõu hetkeseisu ja vajaduse kaardistamine [Mapping the current situation and needs of Estonian labour with ICT competencies]. Poliitikauuringute Keskus Praxis, Tallinn (2013). http://www.kutsekoda.ee/fwk/contenthelper/10373139/10493921/IKT_uuringu_lyhikokkuv6te.pdf. Accessed 14 Dec 2015
9. Tinto, V.: Research and practice of student retention: what next? J. Coll. Stud. Retent. Res. Theor. Pract. **8**(1), 1–19 (2006)

10. Larsen, M.S., Kornbeck, K.P., Kristensen, R.M., Larsen, M.R., Sommerseol, H.B.: Dropout phenomena at universities: what is dropout? Why does dropout occur? What can be done by the universities to prevent or reduce it? Education **45**, 1111–1120 (2013)
11. Kinnunen, P., Malmi, L.: Why students drop out CS1 course? In: Proceedings of the Second International Workshop on Computing Education Research, pp. 97–108. ACM (2006)
12. Tinto, V.: Leaving College: Rethinking the Causes and Cures of Student Attrition. University of Chicago Press, Chicago (1993). 5801 S. Ellis Avenue, IL 60637
13. Belloc, F., Maruotti, A., Petrella, L.: How individual characteristics affect university students drop-out: a semiparametric mixed-effects model for an Italian case study. J. Appl. Stat. **38**(10), 2225–2239 (2011)
14. Araque, F., Roldan, C., Salaguero, A.: Factors influencing university drop out rates. Comput. Educ. **53**, 563–574 (2009)
15. Stratton, L.S., O'Toole, D.M., Wetzel, J.N.: A multinomial logit model of college stopout and dropout behaviour. Econ. Educ. Rev. **27**, 319–331 (2008)
16. Bandura, A.: Self-efficacy. In: Ramachaudran, V.S. (ed.) Encyclopedia of Human Behavior, vol. 4, pp. 71–81. Academic Press, New York (1994)
17. Bandura, A., Barbaranelli, C., Caprara, G.V., Pastorelli, C.: Multifaceted impact of self-efficacy beliefs on academic functioning. Child Dev. **67**, 1206–1222 (1996)
18. Alivernini, F., Lucidi, F.: Relationship between social context, self-efficacy, motivation, academic achievement, and intention to drop out of high school: a longitudinal study. J. Educ. Res. **104**(4), 241–252 (2011)
19. Troelsen, R., Laursen, P.F.: Is drop-out from university dependent on national culture and policy? The case of Denmark. Eur. J. Educ. **49**(44), 484–496 (2014)
20. Dao, M.T.N., Thorpe, A.: What factors influence Vietnamese students' choice of university? Int. J. Educ. Manag. **29**(5), 666–681 (2015)
21. Kivinen, O., Nurmi, J.: Labour market relevance of European university education. From enrolment to professional employment in 12 countries. Eur. J. Educ. **49**(4), 558–574 (2014)
22. Taylor, G., Lekes, N., Gagnon, H., Kwan, L., Koestner, R.: Need satisfaction, work–school interference and school dropout: an application of self-determination theory. Br. J. Educ. Psychol. **82**, 622–646 (2012)
23. Polidano, C., Zakirova, R.: Outcomes from combining work and tertiary study. A national vocational education and training research and evaluation program report. National Centre for Vocational Education Research Ltd., PO Box 8288, Stational Arcade, Adelaide, SA 5000, Australia (2011)
24. Kori, K., Altin, H., Pedaste, M., Palts, T., Tõnisson, E.: What influences students to study information and communication technology? In: Gómez Chova, L., López Martínez, A., Candel Torres, I. (eds.) INTED2014 Proceedings, IATED Academy, pp. 1477–1486 (2014)
25. Vallerand, R.J., Blais, M.R., Briére, N.M., Pelletier, L.G.: Construction et Validation de l'Échelle de Motivation en Éducation (EME) (Construction and validation of the learning motivation scale). Revue Canadienne des Sciences du Comportement **21**, 323–349 (1989)
26. Muthén, L.K., Muthén, B.O.: Mplus user's guide. 7th edn. Muthén & Muthén, Los Angeles (1998–2012)
27. Bentler, P.M.: Comparative fit indexes in structural models. Psychol. Bull. **107**, 238–246 (1990)
28. Jöreskog, K., Sörbom, D.: LISREL 7 – A Guide to the Program and Applications, 2nd edn. SPSS, Chicago (1989)
29. Browne, M.W., Cudeck, R.: Alternate ways of assessing model fit. In: Bollen, K.A., Long, J.S. (eds.) Testing Structural Equation models, pp. 136–162. Sage, Newbury Park (1993)
30. Hooper, D., Coughlan, J., Mullen, M.: Structural equation modelling: guidelines for determining model fit. Articles: 2 (2008)

31. Maccallum, R.C., Browne, M.W., Sugawara, H.M.: Power analysis and determination of sample size for covariance structure modelling. Psychol. Methods **1**(2), 130–149 (1996)
32. Macintyre, P.D., Baker, S.C., Clément, R., Donovan, L.A.: Sex and age effects on willingness to communicate, anxiety, perceived competence, and L2 motivation among junior high school French immersion students. Lang. Learn. **52**(3), 537–564 (2002)
33. Bruinsma, M.: Motivation, cognitive processing and achievement in higher education. Learn. Instruction **14**(6), 549–568 (2004)
34. Duque, L.C.: A framework for analysing higher education performance: students' satisfaction, perceived learning outcomes, and dropout intentions. Total Qual. Manag. **25**(1), 1–21 (2014)
35. Beerkens, M., Mägi, E., Lill, L.: University studies as a side job: causes and consequences of massive student employment in Estonia. High. Educ. **61**(6), 679–692 (2011)
36. Woratschek, C.R., Lenox, T.L.: Information systems entry-level job skills: a survey of employers. In: Proceedings of the Information Systems Educators Conference, San Antonio, vol. 19 (2002)
37. Zaharim, A., Omar, M.Z., Basri, H., Muhamad, N., Isa, F.L.M.: A gap study between employers' perception and expectation of engineering graduates in Malaysia. Education **6**(11), 409–419 (2009)
38. Kori, K., Pedaste, M., Leijen, Ä., Tõnisson, E.: The role of programming experience in ICT students' learning motivation and academic achievement. Int. J. Inf. Educ. Technol. **6**(5), 331–337 (2016)

discuss: Embedding Dialog-Based Discussions into Websites

Christian Meter[✉], Tobias Krauthoff, and Martin Mauve

Department of Computer Science,
Heinrich-Heine-University Düsseldorf, Düsseldorf, Germany
{meter,krauthoff,mauve}@cs.uni-duesseldorf.de
http://cn.hhu.de

Abstract. In this paper we present the web application *discuss*, which provides a novel approach to embed structured discussions into any website. These discussions employ a formal argumentation system in their backend and can be used in addition to or replace existing comment sections. By interacting with the content of the website, we allow to include this content in the discussion. Furthermore, the same discussions can be accessed from multiple websites to bring their audiences together and create a single large discussion. To form a combined audience, it is necessary to use a common backend and we present an exemplary implementation of this scenario.

Keywords: Online argumentation · Collaborative work · Discussions · Dialog-based approach · Web technologies · Computer science

1 Introduction

Many websites and online news media provide their readers with the opportunity to comment and discuss their content. In fact, the ability to participate in such a discussion or to read what others think about an article is a major reason to prefer online content over offline media. While current solutions are quite suitable to provide simple feedback, they do a rather poor job at fostering meaningful discussions among the readers. This is especially true in those cases where this would be most needed: for articles that receive a lot of reader-feedback due to their popularity or controversial nature.

Commonly, comment sections are located below online articles. They provide a vertical-oriented discussion, where one comment follows the other, often combined with the possibility to directly reply to an individual comment. This is the same design used, for example, by Facebook or Twitter or, in fact, in most forum systems. It is well known, that this design has significant flaws when used for discussions and argumentation rather than simple feedback [1,2], for example redundant comments, lack of structure or simply missing scalability when large numbers of users try to express their opinions. Some online editorials, e.g. The Guardian, are really interested in the comments from the users to enrich the

© Springer International Publishing AG 2017
P. Zaphiris and A. Ioannou (Eds.): LCT 2017, Part II, LNCS 10296, pp. 449–460, 2017.
DOI: 10.1007/978-3-319-58515-4_34

journalism, but often they are abusive, violate their community standards and the journalists are confronted with huge numbers of comments, which they have to moderate [3]. In general, online editorials show keen interest in the discussions in the comments and are interested in the user's opinions.

To solve these problems and allow for meaningful online argumentation regarding issues raised in an online news media article, we propose to integrate *dialog-based online argumentation* in the website hosting the article. In dialog-based online argumentation the user performs a time-shifted dialog with those users who previously participated in the discussion. The new user can then react to statements from those other users and provide her own statements. This dialog is performed in natural language and the user does not need any specific skill other than being able to read and write. This concept has been implemented in the argumentation system *D-BAS* [4], which is a public accessible web-application. The system also provides an application programming interface to use its backend to remotely perform steps in the argumentation.

In this paper, we present *discuss*, which uses the interface of D-BAS to embed structured discussions in arbitrary websites. discuss is a JavaScript-based extension, which can seamless integrate dialog-based discussions into websites. This tool can be used to enhance or replace existing comment sections whenever a discussion is intended to be held with or among the readers. It gives users that participate in the discussion the option to add references to parts of the online article to their statements. Those parts are then marked in the article, so that other readers can jump right into the ongoing discussion. Furthermore, it is possible to browse and search for those arguments in the discussion that reference the current website.

Our main contributions in this paper are: (1) integrating the interface for dialog-based online argumentation into regular web-content, (2) allowing for references between the argumentation and the content of the website, (3) navigating the argumentation by means of links and search requests and (4) providing a way to use the same discussion across multiple websites.

The paper is structured as follows: Sect. 2 contains the related work to compare our approach to existing established technologies in the Web. Section 3 is about the prototype D-BAS and the concept of dialog-based argumentation. Section 4 describes the functionality of discuss, while Sect. 5 focuses on our implementation. The last Sects. 6 and 7 conclude the paper and give an outlook to future work.

2   Related Work

The most popular tools to provide reader feedback are simple comment sections in form of a linear list of user statements or the use of forum-based systems. Both display all the negative aspects mentioned above. There are three specific systems that we want to discuss in more detail:

The first system is *Disqus*, which enables discussions on arbitrary websites [5]. In fact, Disqus is a JavaScript application, which needs to be installed by webmasters and brings a hosted alternative to self-hosted comment sections. One unique characteristic is that instances from different websites can discuss about a global topic. Disqus does not introduce new techniques to enhance discussions and, in general, provides the same functionality as normal comment sections, i.e. add, reply to and vote on comments. This tool is popular for its simplicity and is therefore used quite frequently. It does not address the common problems of comment sections, though. Enabling a global discussion, however, is quite interesting and will also be used in our application.

rbutr [6] is a browser extension which gives the users the ability to link several websites sharing a common topic. These links can then be combined with arguments to introduce information from website *B*, which might support or rebut the article presented on website *A*. When a user then visits website A, she is presented a small popup showing that B provides arguments against the contents of A. Therefore, rbutr can be used to link contents from different websites to adjust false information presented on another website. The general idea of using contents from the Internet to support one's own statement is also used in discuss.

ArguBlogging from ARG-tech [7] can be installed as a bookmarklet[1], which needs no further configuration and can directly be used by interested users. The main concept of this tool is to select arbitrary text passages from websites and post them with a reference to the original source on one of the supported blogging sites, currently *tumblr* and *Blogger*. ArguBlogging then creates a post on the user's personal blog and gives her the ability to discuss about this text passage. A popup is presented to other users, who use ArguBlogging, when they arrive on a website, where another user already has selected some text and discussed it on her blog. These other users can then react to this statement and join the discussion. The idea behind the text-selection feature from ArguBlogging is also used in discuss, but in our case it will be directly integrated into a dialog-based discussion.

3   Dialog-Based Online Argumention

The goal of dialog-based online argumentation is to enable any user to participate efficiently in a large-scale online argumentation. At the same time it avoids, or at the very least reduces, the problems that occur in unstructured online argumentation such as a high level of redundancy, balkanization, and logical fallacies.

In the following, we briefly describe terms that will be used to explain the main aspects of dialog-based online argumentation. Based on these terms, we then introduce the main concepts of dialog-based online argumentation.

Each discussion is a set of *statements*, which are the most basic primitives used in an online discussion. The negation of a statement is itself a statement. Individual participants might consider a given statement to be true or false.

---

[1] http://www.bookmarklets.com/about/.

A *position* is a prescriptive statement, i.e., a statement which recommends or demands that a certain action can be taken. Further on we need to distinguish between first-order and second-order *arguments*. A first-order argument consists out of a premise group—a set of at least one statement—and a conclusion, i.e. a statement. Both are connected by an inference, which is either supporting or attacking, so that the premise group is a reason for or against the conclusion. A second-order argument has the same kind of premise group, but the conclusion is the inference of an argument. With this we can argue about the validity of another reason-relation. Together, the arguments of a debate form a (partially connected) *web of reasons*.

The core idea of dialog-based online argumentation is a loop consisting of three steps: (1) presenting a single argument; (2) gather feedback from the user based on a list of alternatives and (3) the system selecting the next argument that is shown to the user based on the response and, possibly, the data gathered from the responses of other participants [4]. In this way the user and the system perform a *dialog* where the system selects arguments that are likely to be of interest to the user and then the user provides feedback on those arguments.

A first thing that the system needs to do when a new user wants to participate in the online discussion is to choose an initial argument. This is challenging since the system has no information on the user, yet. One fairly straightforward solution is to simply ask the participant for an initial position she is interested in. After she has chosen or provided her position, she is asked to select or provide a statement explaining her choice. This statement is used as the premise, whereas the position forms the conclusion.

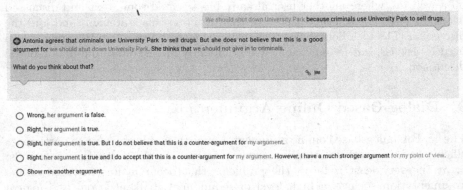

Fig. 1. Gathering feedback during a confrontation in D-BAS.

Once a user is confronted with an argument (see Fig. 1), she can provide feedback on the argument, as shown in Figs. 1 and 2. Based on the feedback the system then selects the next argument that is shown to the user. A first prototype implementing this idea is the dialog-based argumentation system (D-BAS) which is available for testing[2].

---

[2] https://dbas.cs.uni-duesseldorf.de.

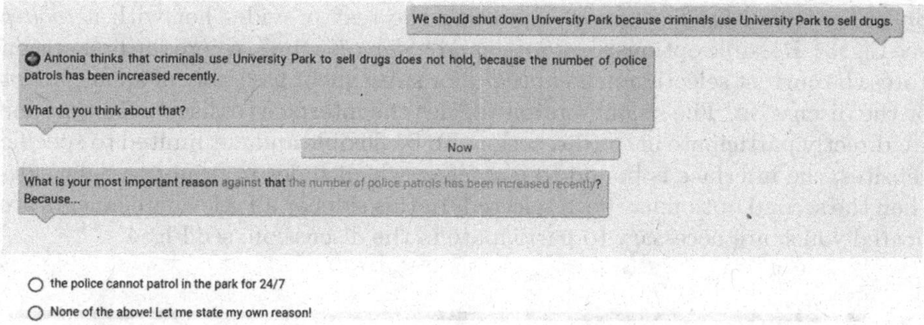

We should shut down University Park because criminals use University Park to sell drugs.

🔵 Antonia thinks that criminals use University Park to sell drugs does not hold, because the number of police patrols has been increased recently.

What do you think about that?

Now

What is your most important reason against that the number of police patrols has been increased recently? Because...

○ the police cannot patrol in the park for 24/7

○ None of the above! Let me state my own reason!

Fig. 2. Justification of the opinion in D-BAS.

4 Functionality of Discuss

The idea of discuss is to embed dialog-based online argumentation into regular website content. To describe our implementation in more detail, we use an example where a city wants to reduce its spending and asks the citizen to propose some actions (positions) and to discuss them in detail. A user provided the position "We should shut down University Park" and other users started to discuss this position. This is the current state and we will show through this example how discuss works.

4.1 Embedding Discuss into Online Articles

Imagine we have a discuss-powered website and have an article about the situation of the University Park. This article contains facts about the future of the University Park, which other users have proposed to close to cut spending of the city. As an example we assume that the article contains information about an investor, who is going to bear the costs of the park for the next years. We also assume, that our exemplary reader already has knowledge about the ongoing discussion and therefore knows some arguments in it. This is not absolutely necessary, but simplifies the explanation of our contribution.

The user starts reading this article. On her way through, she finds an interesting fact, which she wants to integrate in the discussion about closing University Park. To this end, she selects the appropriate text from the article, e.g. *"But apparently there is an anonymous investor ensuring to pay the running costs*

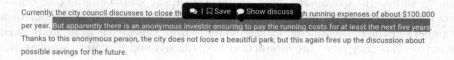

Currently, the city council discusses to close th 💬 | 🔖Save 💬Show discuss h running expenses of about $100.000 per year. But apparently there is an anonymous investor ensuring to pay the running costs for at least the next five years. Thanks to this anonymous person, the city does not loose a beautiful park, but this again fires up the discussion about possible savings for the future.

Fig. 3. Tooltip pops up when the user selects a text passage in the article.

for at least the next five years". Selecting the text provides her with a *tooltip* (see Fig. 3). Possible options are *"Save"* and *"Show discuss"*, where the first option stores the current selection in a *clipboard* for subsequent assembly of an argument for the discussion. The second option toggles the interface to discuss, so that she can directly participate in the discussion. To be flexible and not limited to specific websites, the interface is bound to a *sidebar*, which slides in from the right side, when the second option has been selected. In this sidebar all relevant elements are located which are necessary to participate in the discussion, see Fig. 4.

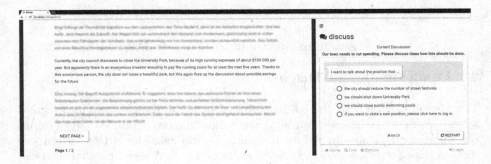

Fig. 4. Side-by-side integration of discuss into an online article.

Now, she can use the selected text and the interface of discuss to participate in the discussion and to create a direct citation of the text passage to her choice. We call these citations *text references* and the user can connect them with any statement in the discussion. With the knowledge the reader gained with this article, she is able to form a counter argument against closing the park and add a suitable reference to her statement. In this case her selection from above, pictured in Fig. 3, seems to be best-fitting, because it describes the future of the University Park in one sentence. These new facts are relevant and can stop the discussion about closing the University Park (if the sources of this article are trustworthy and the contents are true).

As a last step, the reader needs to add her argument to the correct location in the discussion. Since we are assuming, that she already has knowledge about the discussion, she can use the *search engine* for navigation. When the user now wants to add the fact that the investor is going to bear the costs, she needs to find the correct argument from the other user, e.g. *"We should shut down University Park, because shutting down University Park will save $100.000 a year"*. Adding the exemplary input "$100.000" in the search engine (see Fig. 5) provides the statement we are looking for and we can now formulate our own argument against it supported by the reference from this article as it can be seen in Fig. 6. This completes the interaction with discuss and the user can close the sidebar to continue reading the article.

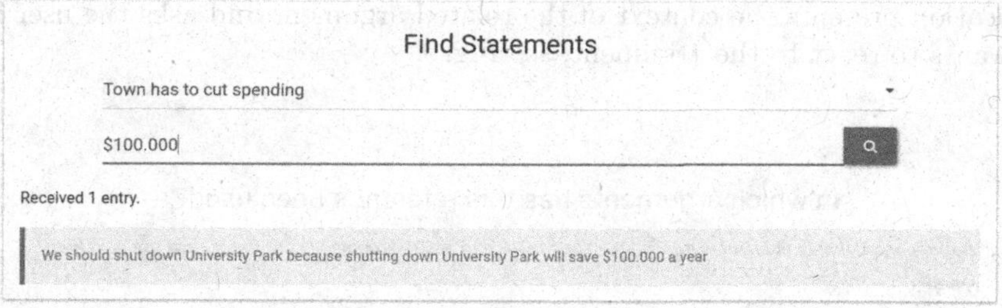

Find Statements

Town has to cut spending   ▾

$100.000| 🔍

Received 1 entry.

We should shut down University Park because shutting down University Park will save $100.000 a year

Fig. 5. Find position in the discussion, where the high costs of University Park is discussed.

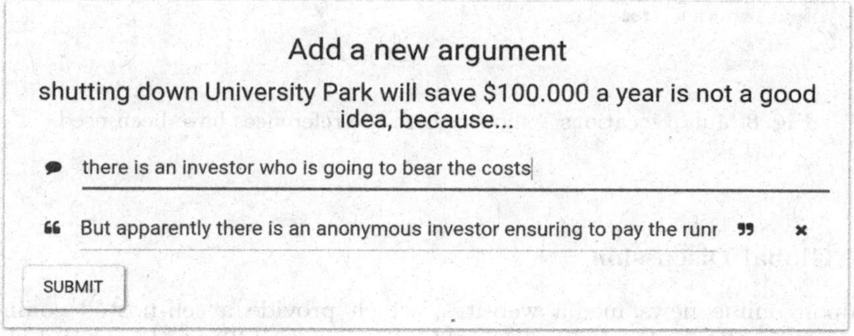

Add a new argument

shutting down University Park will save $100.000 a year is not a good idea, because...

💬 there is an investor who is going to bear the costs|
_____

❝ But apparently there is an anonymous investor ensuring to pay the runr ❞   ✖

SUBMIT

Fig. 6. Constructing a new argument with a text reference.

Arguments, references and their relations are stored in a common backend. All references from this article, which have been used in the discussion, are then highlighted in green color and appear in the text (see Fig. 7). Returning users or new readers of this article can easily see, that these text passages have been used in the discussion, and can interact with them by clicking on a reference. This click again toggles the sidebar and offers a simple interface with all linked locations in the discussion, where this reference has been used (see Fig. 8). Multiple locations are possible, since many users could use the same reference in their arguments.

Text references provide the easiest way to jump to a relevant position in the discussion and to directly start to discuss, because through a reference, our

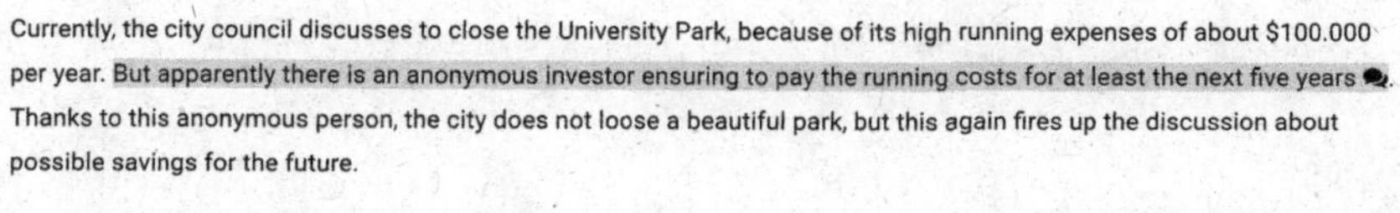

Currently, the city council discusses to close the University Park, because of its high running expenses of about $100.000 per year. But apparently there is an anonymous investor ensuring to pay the running costs for at least the next five years 💬. Thanks to this anonymous person, the city does not loose a beautiful park, but this again fires up the discussion about possible savings for the future.

Fig. 7. Highlighted text reference which was previously used by a user (Color figure online).

application presents the context of the related argument and asks the user how she wants to react to the argument, see Fig. 9.

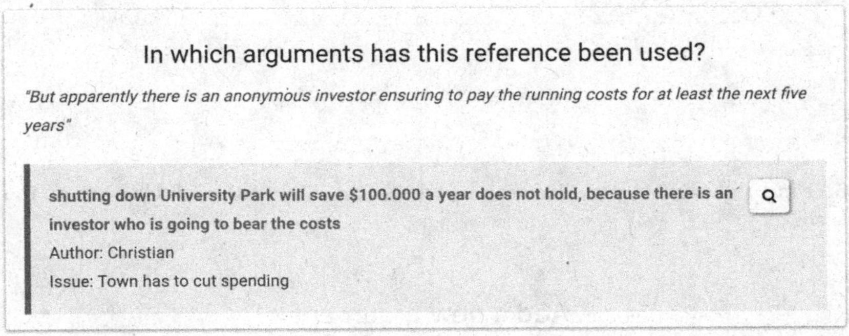

Fig. 8. Jump locations – shows where the references have been used.

4.2 Global Discussion

Common online news media websites, which provide a self-hosted comment section, only allow a local discussion. There is no possibility to leave the borders of this website to interact with users from other news media websites. Disqus [5] provides a feature for inter-website discussions, which we also included in discuss. To realize global discussions, we use one D-BAS instance as a common backend for websites that integrate discuss.

With these global discussions, a more heterogeneous peer group can be reached. Studies showed, that heterogeneous groups have a positive impact on the outcome of a discussion, i.e. solutions emerging from these discussions have a significantly higher quality and those solutions from homogeneous groups were never better compared to the heterogeneous group [8]. Therefore, enabling discussions among users from different online news media, with various levels of education and contrasting opinions, mutually support the discussion. Online news media are often known to have different audiences or specific political orientations and it could be very interesting to analyze discussions between those divergent peer groups, but this leaves the scope of this publication.

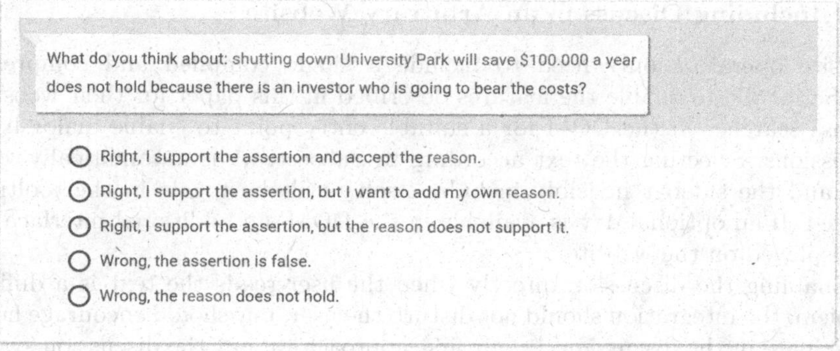

> What do you think about: shutting down University Park will save $100.000 a year
> does not hold because there is an investor who is going to bear the costs?

○ Right, I support the assertion and accept the reason.

○ Right, I support the assertion, but I want to add my own reason.

○ Right, I support the assertion, but the reason does not support it.

○ Wrong, the assertion is false.

○ Wrong, the reason does not hold.

Fig. 9. Jump options – giving the user multiple options how she wants to react to the related argument.

5 Implementation

While implementing discuss we encountered a number of challenges that we outline in the following sections.

5.1 Technical Foundation

To create an application, which does not slow down existing websites and can pick any desired position in the *document object model* (DOM) of the website, we need to have powerful programming techniques and languages fitting our needs. The first prototype was implemented in pure JavaScript, but after few weeks the application became too complex and it was clear that we needed a framework to keep clean code and to reduce complexity. We were also unsatisfied with state-handling and the general language design of JavaScript, which is why we switched to the functional programming language *ClojureScript*[3] and re-implemented the functionality of the first prototype with just a few lines. ClojureScript compiles down to optimized JavaScript code with the *Google Closure Compiler*[4], which results in much faster code than we could manually develop. Using this compiler collection produces also much smaller production files thanks to advanced optimizations and dead code elimination. For dynamic user-interface handling, we chose Facebook's *React.js*[5].

These components allowed us to implement a stable and small web-application without disturbing or conflicting the website it has been embedded into. Since discuss adds many features and DOM manipulations as seen in the previous section, it is very important to choose the best-fitting components, because otherwise it would result in a slow or crowded application.

---

[3] https://clojurescript.org/.

[4] https://developers.google.com/closure/compiler/.

[5] https://facebook.github.io/react/.

5.2   Including Discuss in an Arbitrary Website

Website operators only need to include a single compiled and compressed JavaScript file to enable the features described in this paper for their websites. discuss searches in the DOM for a suitable entry point to enable dialog-based discussions. Selecting the text according to Subsect. 4.1 is automatically available and the sidebar invisibly includes itself until the toggle in the tooltip is pressed. If an optional `div` is available in the DOM, an additional interface will be displayed on the website.

Enabling the discussion directly when the user reads the text is a difficult problem: the integration should not disturb the user, but should encourage her to participate in the discussion. In our first approach we put the discussion system directly between the lines of the article and split the text when the user toggled discuss with a switch. But this slide effect was very confusing and is possibly not usable in most kinds of websites. We then experimented with including the interface below the article. This also proved to be a bad choice since the reader then has to jump to the bottom of the article to participate in a discussion triggered by a statement in the article. In our final version, we used the sidebar to interact with discuss. Optionally, the webmaster can include a second interface by simply adding a `div` with a specific ID.

Using a tooltip can be seen on several websites, like Medium [9]. We added listeners to the article to activate the tooltip, when a text passage has been selected. This provides an unobtrusive method to interact with our application.

The clipboard temporarily stores the user's text selections for later usage. This has been implemented to provide the possibility to read the text, store interesting passages and keep on reading, see Fig. 10. In the end, the user can pick her favorite selection to add it to her argument via drag and drop.

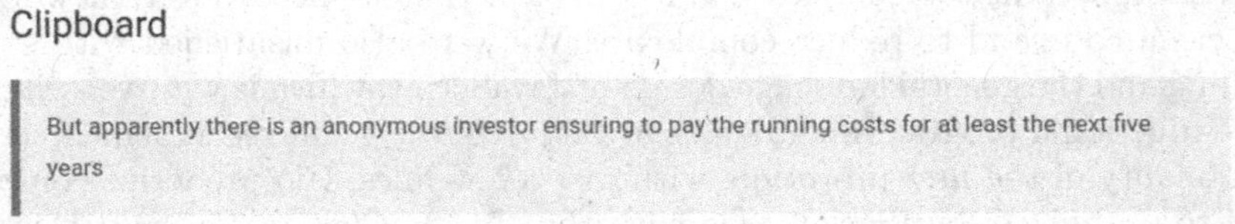

Clipboard

> But apparently there is an anonymous investor ensuring to pay the running costs for at least the next five years

Fig. 10. Using a clipboard to locally store text references.

It is not possible to directly modify the contents of a reference. Our idea is that it should be a direct quotation of the article which is also technically required to find the same text passage in the article. Otherwise, new users will not be able to see the colored reference in the text. We are aware that it is currently still possible to modify the DOM to add a reference of your own desires or to use the browser console for modifications. This would create an untruthful reference, which could lead to false information and false trust in an argument. A server-side verification that the provided string can exactly be found in the article is thinkable, but is currently not implemented.

5.3   Execution Platform

For first testing purposes, we set up a D-BAS instance at our university. As the default configuration uses discuss this backend to directly demonstrate a fully functional application with global discussions enabled. It is possible to use its own backend, which is conform to our application. Therefore, it is not necessarily needed, that the backend is a D-BAS instance – it just needs to provide a suitable interface so that discuss can interact with it.

We are following common best-practices in web development and implemented a RESTful API in D-BAS to expose an interface for external applications, who want to use this dialog-based backend for their applications, whilst discuss is the first project using this interface. This approach for discussion software has already been described in [10] and it presents the general approach how to achieve reusable components in software development, which is why we are also following this structure. Furthermore, [10] proposes the idea to encapsulate the core argumentation logic into an own platform called *Dialog Game Execution Platform* to develop a reusable argumentation core and make it accessible for other applications. In our examples from this paper are we using D-BAS as our default execution platform.

6   Conclusion

Asking the readers to leave a comment below an online news media article is common practice on most websites. But with state-of-the-art comment sections, crowded masses of comments are a typical result. discuss helps to structure discussions and to conduct more productive discourses.

In this paper we used techniques from dialog-based online argumentation to enable our idea of more structured discussions in arbitrary contexts. To achieve this, we implemented discuss as a web application, which follows basic principles of our dialog-based approach and extends discussions by enabling references, global discussions and flexible inclusions into websites.

Feel free to test discuss under http://cn.hhu.de/discuss and you are welcome to provide us your feedback.

7   Future Work

We are currently working on more use cases of dialog-based discussions and are evaluating, where our approach could enhance the discourse experience on the Internet. Next, we will extend discuss to support more functions from our backend, e.g. premise groups. In addition, we will evaluate our application in real-world applications and try to cooperate with well-known online news media providers.

Since many people are actively participating in discussions in social networks like Facebook, we will investigate how we can integrate structured discussions into this context. Conceivable are solutions as social bots, which interact with the users based on text messages.

References

1. Klein, M.: Using metrics to enable large-scale deliberation. In: Collective Intelligence in Organizations: A Workshop of the ACM Group 2010 Conference, pp. 103–233 (2010)
2. Spada, P., Klein, M., Calabretta, R., Iandoli, L., Quinto, I.: A First Step toward Scaling-up Deliberation: Optimizing Large Group E-Deliberation using Argument Maps (2014). doi:10.13140/RG.2.1.3863.5688
3. The Guardian: The dark side of guardian comments (2016). https://www.theguardian.com/technology/2016/apr/12/the-dark-side-of-guardian-comments. Accessed 14 Oct 2016
4. Krauthoff, T., Baurmann, M., Betz, G., Mauve, M.: Dialog-based online argumentation. In: Proceedings of the 2016 Conference on Computational Models of Argument (COMMA 2016) (2016). doi:10.3233/978-1-61499-686-6-33
5. Disqus Inc: Disqus - the no.1 way to build an audience on your website (2016). https://disqus.com. Accessed 14 Oct 2016
6. rbutr: rbutls, debunkings and counter arguments to misinformation on the internet - think again (2016). https://rbutr.com. Accessed 14 Oct 2016
7. Bex, F., Snaith, M., Lawrence, J., Reed, C.: ArguBlogging: an application for the argument web. Web Semant. Sci. Serv. Agents World Wide Web **25**, 9–15 (2014). doi:10.1016/j.websem.2014.02.002. http://linkinghub.elsevier.com/retrieve/pii/S1570826814000079
8. Hoffman, L.R., Maier, N.R.: Quality and acceptance of problem solutions by members of homogeneous and heterogeneous groups. J. Abnorm. Soc. Psychol. **62**(2), 401 (1961). doi:10.1037/h0044025
9. A Medium Corporation: Medium (2016). https://medium.com. Accessed 16 Oct 2016
10. Bex, F., Lawrence, J., Reed, C.: Generalising argument dialogue with the dialogue game execution platform. In: Proceedings of the 2014 Conference on Computational Models of Argument (COMMA 2014), pp. 141–152 (2014). doi:10.3233/978-1-61499-436-7-141

Design and Development of Intelligent Learning Companion for Primary School Students Based on the Tour of Well-Known Scenic Spots in Beijing

Yujun Wang[1], Haotian Ma[1], Chengyu Li[1],
and Feng-Kuang Chiang[1,2(✉)]

[1] School of Educational Technology, Beijing Normal University, Beijing, China
fkchiang@bnu.edu.cn
[2] Beijing Advanced Innovation Center for Future Education,
Beijing Normal University, Beijing, China

Abstract. Nowadays intelligent phones can realize more and more functions, and the multi-point touch screen multiplies the interactions between user and phone. With the development and spread of intelligent phones, mobile learning has enjoyed an ever-increasing popularity. In the process of educational reform, the concepts of learning by playing and self-study have been encouraged. Meanwhile it is discovered that primary schools students in China have a great demand in travelling every year to the extent that travelling, has been recognized as a means of informal learning. For it can offer a new way of learning by playing and edutainment, especially when it is related to textbook knowledge. Based on the situation above, the article argues about the feasibility and necessity of designing an intelligent learning companion app to help primary school students study through the process of travelling, and give a set of design scheme of the app.

Keywords: Mobile learning · Intelligent learning companion · Travelling · Primary school students · Scenic spots in Beijing

1 Introduction

Plenty of fields have been influenced by the great and rapid development of technology, and education is among the fields being influenced most. Through the last decade different scientific disciplines, including pedagogy, have explored the educational possibilities of technologies such as elearning [1] and iPad in classroom [2]. Under this context, ICT in education has appeared much more frequently. With people's in-depth studies of elearning, the notion of elearning has also been branching out, giving rise to new methodologies that try to get the most of certain technologies [3], and concepts like mlearning, which is the short for "mobile learning", emerge.

The existing definitions of mobile learning very much. One closest definition to the meaning of mlearning in this article is *"mLearning can be understood as an evolution of eLearning which allows students to take advantage of the advantages afforded by*

P. Zaphiris and A. Ioannou (Eds.): LCT 2017, Part II, LNCS 10296, pp. 461–472, 2017.
DOI: 10.1007/978-3-319-58515-4_35

mobile technologies to support their learning process and constitutes the first step towards the creation of ubiquitous learning" [4], which means studying anywhere and anytime. Mlearning constitutes one of the most popular fields and it is becoming a new and efficient way for knowledge accumulation and transmission. Mobile terminals offer many possibilities to students regarding communication and autonomous work, being an important resource when it comes to develop Personal Learning Environments [5]. Mobile terminals mentioned above mainly include smartphone and tablet, and smartphone owns a larger number of users and is more suitable for people of all ages, so this article will consider smartphone only.

Smartphones are small size devices that combine the features of the conventional mobile phones and extra advantages like flexibility, a wide range of functionalities and Internet connectivity. When it comes to the use in learning, smartphones can be used in a broad set of mobile learning experiences, from game based learning activities [6] to the distribution of eLearning content [7]. The ways of utilizing smartphone to study are various and the applicable age is also quite extensive. Parnell and Bartlett [8] point out their use as a tool to prepare eportfolios with Pre-primary students' works. The work of Mandula, Meda, Muralidharam and Parupalli [9] explores the possibilities of sending lesson videos to the student's terminals, and that of Kamaruzaman and Zainol [10] about the possibilities of the M-Language application for smartphones. Both articles prove that studying by smartphones is suitable for secondary education students. Jarvela, Naykki, Laru together with Luokkanen [11] and Lum [12] find that an increasing number of universities integrate smartphones in everyday activities, whether they are used as a communication tool, a content delivering tool or a basis for collaborative learning activities.

One most obvious advantage of studying by smartphones is the individualization, no matter in ways of study or study contents. Traxler said that the individual nature of the devices contributes to the customization of the contents and their adaptation to the needs of the individuals and their environment [13].

And another concept-intelligent learning companion, is also pretty important. "Intelligent learning companion" is a creative combination of artificial intelligence technology and learning companion. It can be understood as, through algorithms in artificial intelligence and computer simulation, designing and developing a virtual learning companion in system, which can communicate and interact with learners. It can also help and lead learners to study and record their study process as well as growth process [14]. As we all know, peers play a quite essential role in a person's school-days. They can provide assistance and affect his or her study efficiency, effectiveness, motivation and so on. Interestingly, researchers find that virtual learning companions can do the same. Bailenson and Yee [15] have shown that non-verbal mirroring in the form of behavioral mimicry can increase the likeability and persuasive effect of a virtual agent. Bickmore and Picard [16] have developed interaction and evaluation strategies to increase empathetic and caring relationships between agents and participants. Providing the participants a choice, in terms of the ethnicity and gender of an agent-tutor, has also been shown to have beneficial impacts on learners' impressions of the agent and on their own performance; similarly, matching learners' gender and ethnicity also leads to more positive impressions and performance [17]. Intelligent learning companion is the improved version of virtual learning companion, because it can remember individual characteristics and provide personalized study contents, plans and assistance.

2 Demand Analysis

First, we conducted a questionnaire survey in order to make sure whether an Intelligent Learning Companion app is needed by primary school students when they visit famous scenic spots in Beijing. We divided primary education students into three groups according to their grades. Junior group (Grade 1 and Grade 2), intermediate group (Grade 3 and Grade 4), and senior group (Grade 5 and Grade 6). Then, we chose The Forbidden City as an example. We went there, randomly picked families with primary education students on the spot, and requested parents and their children to finish our questionnaire on their phone (the first ten students of each age group become our samples, so thirty samples in total; if a family has more than one child, it is still regarded as one sample).

Question 1 to 3 are for parents. Question 1 is "How often do you take your child/children to travel every year?" As in shown in Fig. 1, among thirty samples, half of parents say they take child/children to travel about 1 to 3 times a year; 40% do that more than 4 times; only 10% do not do that at all. Question 2 asks about whether parents will consider taking children to educational scenic spots. 76.7% of the parents usually will consider that, 20% hardly think about that, and only one sample says it won't give it a shot as Fig. 2. Question 3 is "Will you intend to teach your child/children knowledge or principles?" As is shown in Fig. 3, 73.3% give a positive answer, 26.7% consider less, no parents do not think about that at all. From above, we can conclude that most parents take their children out for travelling and have the will to provide children opportunities to obtain something during the processes.

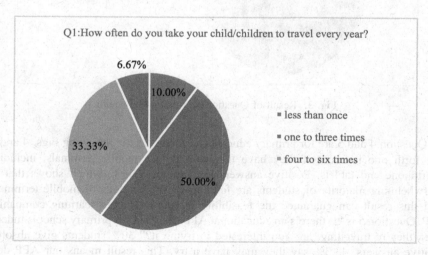

Fig. 1. Result of Question 1 in the questionnaire

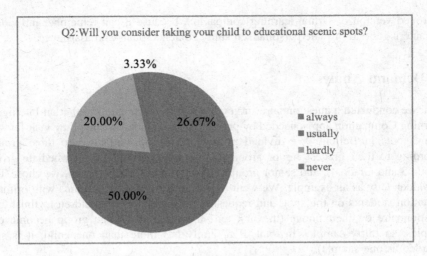

Fig. 2. Result of Question 2 in the questionnaire

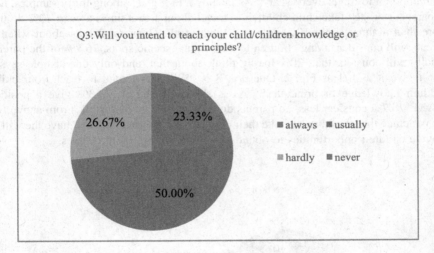

Fig. 3. Result of Question 3 in the questionnaire

Question 4 and 5 are for primary education students, as the following Figs. 4 and 5. The forth one is about if they have the habit to use mobile terminals, including smartphone and tablets. Positive answers account for 93.3%, which shows that an overwhelming majority of students are familiar with operations of mobile terminals. And this result can guarantee the feasibility of our intelligent learning companion APP. Question 5 is "If there's an educational APP designed for primary school students when they're travelling, are you interested in trying it?" 30% students give absolute positive answers, 43.3% say they may have a try. This result means our APP does appeal to our objective users, so it has implications.

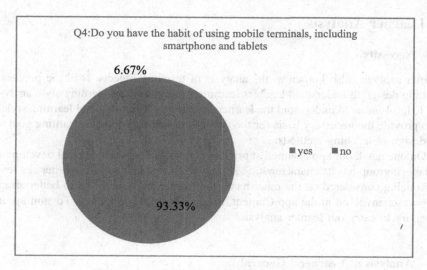

Fig. 4. Result of Question 4 in the questionnaire

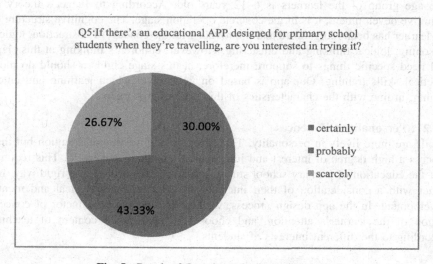

Fig. 5. Result of Question 1 in the questionnaire

Question 6 is about expectations for this APP. It's an open-ended question for both parents and students and we got 22 answers for this question. After we review these answers, expectations in descending order are: helpful for obtaining knowledge and senses, easy-to-use, both educational and entertaining, appealing to children, with delighting interfaces and route planning function, free of charge, interactive, innovative and power-saving. All these expectations will be taken in to consideration when we develop this APP.

3 Learner Analysis

3.1 Necessity

Learner analysis, also known as the analysis of teaching objects, is in the process of teaching design to understand learners learning preparation and learning style analysis. It is helpful for us to understand the learners' learning preparation and learning style so as to provide the necessary basis for the analysis of learning content, learning goal and the design of teaching methods.

On one hand, our app is aimed at primary school students. The mental development of the age group has its characteristics, so they must be separated from other age levels when being considered on the other hand, the learner analysis for us to better arrange the courses involved in the app Content, improve learning efficiency. To sum up, it is necessary to carry out learner analysis.

3.2 Analysis of Learners' General

3.2.1 Age

The age group of the learners is 6–12 years old. According to Piaget's theory of cognitive development, it is in the concrete operation stage. The cognitive structure of the learner has been reorganized and improved, with the concept of abstraction, logical reasoning, logical thinking and clustering. However, children's thinking at this stage still need specific things to support, therefore, at this stage children should do more practical skills training. Our app is based on field travel which learning and entertaining, in line with the characteristics of this age-group learners.

3.2.2 Personality Differences

Pupils are more lively in personality. They usually lack a focus of attention but they process a high degree of interest and imagination, energetic and lively. This requires that the education of primary school students is not be conducted in a rigid way, but rather with a consideration of their interests, to cater to their physical and mental development. In the app design process, we take into account the factor of concentration of the learner's attention, and choose the appropriate content of teaching according to the different interests of students.

4 Research Objective and Content

4.1 Research Objective

- Design an app based on the constructivism learning theory and the theory of psychological theory such as partnership theory.
- Conduct case study on the effect of primary students learning through travelling with the help of mobile application software.
- Explore the feasibility and validity of mobile learning terminal assisting primary school students in gaining knowledge during the journey.

4.2　App Function

Based on the result of demand analysis and learner analysis above, we would like to design an app, which can assist primary school students in Beijing in learning through the whole travelling process. The whole travelling process includes the period before visiting a scenic spot, during visiting a scenic spot and after visiting a scenic spot. Before travelling, the app can recommend the tourist attractions or tourist routes that are more convenient for users. During the journey the app can guide the user and offer some information about the scenic spot they are visiting which is related to textbook knowledge, while after the journey it can provide with extensive information about the scenic spot as well as some games and tests to make sure that the users grasp the textbook knowledge.

Considering the interactivity, we expect to design a learning companion. Users can choose the image of the companion according to their preference. Besides providing information, the learning companion can also make daily communication and simple interaction with the users based on the feature information reserved when the users register.

4.3　Research Content

Selection of attractions. In our app, we hope to design several tourist routes that contain three or four scenic spots each. During the app concept design phase, we decided to choose one route for instance to test the efficiency of the app. The tourist route we choose is the historical route, which consists of the Forbidden City, the Great Wall and Yuanmingyuan Imperial Garden (the Old Summer Palace). Among the above three spots we prepare to choose the Forbidden City as a sample. We will collect the data based on the Forbidden City.

Find the relation between the scenic spots and textbook knowledge. We classify the textbook knowledge by subjects and grades, and find the relationship between the scenic spots. Take the historical route as a sample, we list the textbook knowledge related to the scenic spots as the following Table 1.

Table 1. Relative textbook knowledge about the scenic spots in the historical route

Historical route	Relative textbook knowledge	Text version	Function of intelligent learning companion
The Great Wall	1. Common sense: history of the Great Wall 2. Culture :function of the Great Wall	People's education press The national primary school Chinese (S version) Shandong education press	Phonetic explanation, text introduce, stories

(*continued*)

Table 1. (*continued*)

Historical route	Relative textbook knowledge	Text version	Function of intelligent learning companion
The Forbidden City	1. Common sense: history of the Forbidden City 2. Culture :anecdote of the Forbidden City 3. Technology : palace architecture	People's education press The national primary school Chinese (S version) Shandong education press	Phonetic explanation, text introduce, stories, videos
Yuanmingyuan Imperial Garden(the Old Summer Palace)	1. Common sense: history of Yuanmingyuan Imperial Garden 2. Culture:Chinese modern history	People's education press The national primary school Chinese (S version)	Phonetic explanation, text introduce, stories, instructional games

Design UI. After completing data collection and finding relative textbook knowledge of scenic spots, we need to design the image of the intelligent learning companion and software interface. The intelligent learning companion will appear in the middle of the main interface. During the learning process the intelligent learning companion will interact with the user from time to time, reminding the user of the remaining learning tasks, instructing the user to start a new scenic spot, or helping the user to complete travel diary or take a rest properly. Figure 6 has shown an example of our ideal interface. The four buttons at the bottom of the interface will lead user to the main interface, to choose travelling route or spot, to continue studying tasks and to check personal data on after another. The sample image shows the process of choosing travelling route and spots.

Survey and Evaluation

(1) Questionnaire survey
   After completing the prototype of the app, we need to compile questionnaire and scale, and choose some students in our experimental primary school. Evaluate the learning effect of the examinees through the questionnaire and scale to find out whether the app has aroused students interest in learning during travelling and improve students' mastery of the corresponding knowledge.

(2) Behavior observation
   After obtaining the permission of students, parents, and teachers, we will record the using procedure of some students by video, and analyze the video under the guidance of psychologist and educational experts to find the efficiency of the app from the perspective of behavioral science.

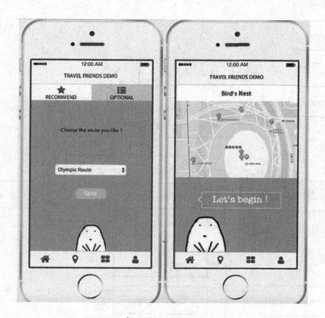

Fig. 6. Sample interface image

5   Technical Route

The Fig. 7 shows the process of design a phone app. It's explained that all the steps in this figure are not in a strict order. We decided to consult this model and determine our technical route.

5.1   Collect and Clarify the Relationship Between the Knowledge in Secondary School Textbook and Certain Scenic Spots

According to the scenic spots chosen before, we will choose relative knowledge of different subjects and different grades, so we can establish the knowledge database of the app.

5.2   Develop the Incentive Mechanism

In line with the characteristics of secondary school students' attention, develop the incentive mechanism following the law of reinforcement.

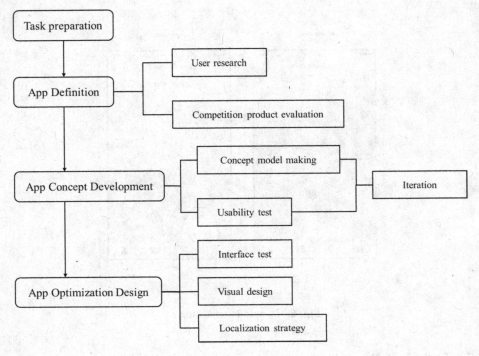

Fig. 7. Design flow

5.3   Making Electronic Resources

This includes designing the image of virtual learning partner, proper UI and other pictures. In some cases, this involves audio and video, we will choose different resources according to the specific topics.

5.4   Program Writing

Write the program of app and pay attention to the interactivity.

5.5   Test and Improve the App

After developing the app, we will test it in the experiment school. We will judge the effect of the app through questionnaire and interview. We will also invite secondary school teachers to use and evaluate the app. After collecting the opinions, we will improve the app.

5.6   Analyze Data and Write Paper

After the whole research process, we will write a paper and promote our research results.

6   Expected Outcomes and Effect

- Strengthen the elementary students' passion for learning and sense of autonomy, which can also help promote the educational reform.
- Offer a form of entertainment, and help students gain the awareness of learning by playing.
- We expect the app can improve student's learning ability and help students form the habit of self-study.
- Increase student's interest in visiting traditional Chinese scenic spots and inheriting traditional culture.

References

1. José, C.S.P., Susana, O.M., Francisco, J.G.: Understanding mobile learning: devices, pedagogical implications and research lines. Teoría de la Educ. Educ. y Cultura en la Soc. de la Información **15**(1), 24–42 (2014)
2. Chiang, F.K., Jiang, S., Sun, M.G., Jiang, Y.: E-schoolbag use in Chinese primary school: teachers' perspectives. In: Niemi, H., Jia, J. (eds.) New Ways to Teach and Learn in China and Finland- Crossing Boundaries with Technology, pp. 105–122. Peter Lang, Frankfurt am Main (2016)
3. Prieto, J.C.S., Miguelá ñez, S.O., Garcíapeñalvo, F.J.: Understanding mobile learning: devices, pedagogical implications and research lines. Teoría De La Educ. Educ. Y Cultura En La Soc. De La Información **15**(1), 20–42 (2014)
4. Conde, M.Á., Muñoz, C., García, F.J.: mLearning, the first step in the learning process revolution. Int. J. Interact. Mob. Technol. (iJIM) **2**(4), 62–64 (2008)
5. Ramos, P.H., García Peñalvo, F.J.: Contribution of virtual classrooms to the personal learning environments (PLE) of the students of the career of informatics applied to education of national university of Chimborazo. In: Proceedings of the First International Conference on Technological Ecosystem for Enhancing Multiculturality, Salamanca, Spain, pp. 507–513 (2013). doi:10.1145/2536536.2536614
6. Camargo, M., Bary, R., Boly, V., Rees, M., Smith, R.: Exploring the implications and impact of smartphones on learning dynamics: the role of self-directed learning. In: 2011 17th International Conference on Concurrent Enterprising (ICE), pp. 1–7 (2011)
7. Gopalan, A., Karavanis, S., Payne, T., Sloman, M.: Smartphone based e-learning. In: Proceedings of the 3rd International Conference on Computer Supported Education, Noordwijkerhout, Netherlands, vol. 2, pp. 1–12 (2011)
8. Parnell, W., Bartlett, J.: iDocument: how smartphones and tablets are changing documentation in preschool and primary classrooms. Young Child. **67**(3), 50–57 (2012)

9. Mandula, K., Meday, S.R., Muralidharan, V., Parupalli, R.: A student centric approach for mobile learning video content development and instruction design. In: 2013 15th International Conference On Advanced Communication Technology (ICACT), pp. 386–390 (2013)

10. Kamaruzaman, M.F., Zainol, I.H.: Behavior response among secondary school students development towards mobile learning application. In: 2012 IEEE Colloquium On Humanities, Science and Engineering (CHUSER), pp. 589–592 (2012). doi:10.1109/CHUSER.2012.6504381

11. Jarvela, S., Naykki, P., Laru, J., Luokkanen, T.: Structuring and regulating collaborative learning in higher education with wireless networks and mobile tools. Educ. Technol. Soc. 10(4), 71–79 (2007)

12. Lum, L.: The move to mobile: where is a campus's place in the mobile space? Currents 38(4), 18–20 (2012)

13. Traxler, J.: Current state of mobile learning. In: Ally, M. (ed.) Mobile Learning: Transforming the Delivery of Education and Training, pp. 9–25. AU Press, Edmonton (2009)

14. Zhang, P.F., Xun, S., Ji, L.X.: Affective interaction strategies "smart partners" in the primary game of learning communities. China Educ. Technol. 10, 123–128 (2014)

15. Bailenson, J.N., Yee, N.: Digital chameleons: automatic assimilation of nonverbal gestures in immersive virtual environments. Psychol. Sci. 16, 814–819 (2005)

16. Bickmore, T., Picard, R.W.: Establishing and Maintaining Long-Term Human-Computer Relationships. Trans. Comput. Hum. Interact. 12(2), 293–327 (2004)

17. Baylor, A.L., Shen, E., Huang, X.: "Which pedagogical agent do learners choose? the effects of gender and ethnicity." In: E-Learn World Conference on E-Learning in Corporate, Government, Healthcare, & Higher Education, Phoenix, Arizona (2003)

The Evaluation on the Usability of Digital Storytelling Teaching System in Teaching

Pei-Fen Wu[1], Hui-Jiun Hu[2], Feng-Chu Wu[3], and Kuang-Yi Fan[4(✉)]

[1] National Changhua University of Education, Changhua 50007, Taiwan
pfwu@cc.ncue.edu.tw
[2] National Chiayi University, Chiayi 621, Chiayi County, Taiwan
[3] National Ilan University, Yilan 26047, Taiwan
[4] National University of Tainan, Tainan 70005, Taiwan
kuangyi@mail.nutn.edu.tw

Abstract. In the conception of stories, most beginners create stories at their will, which would result in a poor architecture. At present, few digital story-telling systems have been developed to lead beginners to stories featuring a complete structure. With emphasis on story structure, this study aims to develop a digital storytelling system, Digital Storytelling Teaching System-University (DSTS-U). With the system, learners will be able to quickly create stories with a structural architecture and enhance the variation of the contents of stories through different story structures. Moreover, this study probes into the usability of the system from three dimensions, namely, teaching environment assessment, system features evaluation, and self-story assessment. The subjects of this study were 40 college students who were all beginners, including 21 males and 19 females. The experiment lasted for four weeks. According to the research findings, the experts made positive comments on the teaching environment the DSTS-U system provided for learners. This indicates that learners can create a structural story and acquire more knowledge of story concept with the DSTS-U system. Additionally, positive comments were also made on user's system function features evaluation as well as on self-story satisfaction. For users, the DSTS-U system is an efficient tool to develop stories in a profound way. Therefore, this study has come to the conclusion that the story structure-led teaching model is necessary. By acquiring the knowledge of the structural story concept, learners can generate a structural story from a basic structural archi-tecture with the help of different variation-oriented structures, so as to enrich the contents of stories.

Keywords: Digital storytelling · Story structure · Usability evaluation · Teaching environment assessment · System features evaluation · Self-story assessment

1 Introduction

In the human history, most events were narrated in a written or spoken form. Complicated ideas, concepts or information will become more comprehensible if they are explained in the form of storytelling (Chung 2006). According to Porter (2005), it is

© Springer International Publishing AG 2017
P. Zaphiris and A. Ioannou (Eds.): LCT 2017, Part II, LNCS 10296, pp. 473–487, 2017.
DOI: 10.1007/978-3-319-58515-4_36

important for students to communicate with each other through digital media; students should have strong communication ability and be equipped with diverse ideas and different communication skills; aside from expressing their ideas in a written form, they should be able to create and share their stories in diverse ways. Stories can be constructed in the combination of various media, including picture, sound, music, film, transition, subtitle, and action (Skinner and Hagood 2008). With the rapid technological advancement, digital storytelling has come into being. Based on technology, it will become an efficient tool for improvement in teaching and learning (Ibanez et al. 2003; Mello 2001; Sadik 2008). Hence, the educational application of digital storytelling has been attracting the attention from a vast number of educators (Chung 2006; Robin 2008; Sadik 2008; Shin and Park 2008). Many studies have shown that digital storytelling can strengthen students' capabilities, including narration, writing, creativity, critical thinking, and problem solving (Mou et al. 2013; Sylla et al. 2015; Xu et al. 2011; Yang and Wu 2012). The factors for story development can be integrated into the conceptual diagram to improve learners' thinking on story construction (Liu et al. 2011); according to the element, a story can be created in four stages. By developing the stories about their life, students can enhance their learning effectiveness, critical thinking, and learning motivation (Yang and Wu 2012).

The digital storytelling system can be applied to teaching in various forms, and it can strengthen the capabilities of students. But in terms of story development, there hasn't been a digital storytelling system which can lead beginners to a story featuring a complete structure and a progressive story development architecture. For that reason, this study developed a system with a structural story architecture to help beginners create structurally complete stories with digital media. Meanwhile, the variation-oriented structural function teaching was adopted to help learners create different stories.

To assist college students obtaining the knowledge of story concept and developing diverse capabilities, this study added different concepts of story structure into the digital storytelling system. Therefore, the research purposes of this study are as follows: (1) to develop a storytelling structure system featuring complete creation for college students; (2) to assess the teaching environment and features usability of the digital storytelling system.

2 Literature Review

2.1 Development of the Application of Digital Storytelling to Teaching

Jonassen and Hernandez-Serrano (2002) argued that stories could promote learning and help students solve problems. Robin (2005) believed that digital storytelling encouraged learners to organize and express their views and knowledge as well as help them with study in a unique and meaningful way. Robin and Pierson (2005) pointed it out that digital storytelling could sustain students' and teachers' imagination and facilitate significant story creation to improve the experience of students and teachers. According to Tsou et al. (2006), storytelling is a pragmatic and efficient teaching tool; combining digital storytelling with linguistic courses was a creative learning method which could improve students' reading, writing, speaking and listening. Renda (2010) encouraged teachers to adopt digital storytelling because it could facilitate the instruction in class (Robin 2008) and help students turn a complex and chaotic world into an orderly and rational one in the plot development of stories (Bruner 1990; Gils 2005).

Gils (2005) believed that the educational application of digital storytelling had the following advantages: (1) it offered more variation than the traditional teaching; (2) it provided personalized learning experience; (3) it gave more attractive explanation; (4) it facilitated the creation of stories about realities; (5) it enhanced students' participation in learning. Padilla-Zea et al. (2013) developed instructive games with the storytelling system. In the research, they emphasized that story architecture, constituent, the definition of relevant attributes, and the sequence of events could improve writing. Di Blas (2009, 2010) also argued that digital storytelling could accelerate the team work among students in education; apart from contributing to a closer tie among peers, it could fuel the interaction between students and teachers; as far as digital quality was concerned, students could develop many information abilities through storytelling. Storytelling is a path leading to innovation and more efficient learning; it motivates learners to review and construct their knowledge (Liu et al. 2011).

To date, scholars in different areas have applied digital storytelling to teaching. On top of enhancing basic learning motivation and effectiveness as well as writing, it also improves cooperative participation and critical thinking. Therefore, it can help students develop various abilities. With the creative and unique teaching, students can make use of their imagination and think about problems from diverse perspectives and develop the problem-solving ability. Driven by technological advancement, digital storytelling has been rigorously developed (Miller 2004). An official digital storytelling pattern can be presented through more complicated media. Therefore, digital storytelling is a word with broad meaning which includes various storytelling methods (Pierotti 2006).

Porer (2005) regarded digital storytelling as "an old art featuring verbal storytelling where images, pictures, music, sound effects and the stories of authors are combined to form a movie". Digital storytelling is highly modifiable, and the works can be shared through the Internet (Susono 2007; Laura 2015; Russell 2010).

This study aims to develop a storytelling system to help students create highly structural stories with much variation. It is hoped that the system will not only enrich students' knowledge of story concept but also improve their capabilities.

2.2 Usability Evaluation of the System

Teaching Environment Assessment

Nokeleinen (2006) proposed the model of empirical assessment of teaching environment where the following factors were adopted to measure the teaching materials of digital learning: learner control, learner action, cooperative/collaborative learning, objective orientation, adaptability, additional value, motivation, background knowledge assessment, flexibility and feedback. Psomos and Kordaki (2011) believed that the educational digital storytelling environments (EDSE) included the basic teaching criterion concepts of the constructivist learning, so they proposed 16 factors for an overall assessment of the EDSE in education, including collaborative learning, creativity and innovation, multiple representations, motivation, cultural sensitivity, gender equality, cognitive effort, feedback, learner control, flexibility, learner activity, value of previous knowledge, sharply-focused goal orientation, experiential value, knowledge organization and metacognition.

Usability Evaluation

As for the system usability evaluation, Schafer (2004) proposed five dimensions, namely, comprise, construction, presentation, interactivity, and appeal, which were included in the DS application software evaluation model with 12 criteria: concreteness, involvement, conceptual structure, coherence, continuity, cognitive effort, virtuality, spatiality, collaboration, control, interactivity and immersion.

According to the theory by Schafer, Psomos and Kordaki (2012) believed that the digital storytelling system had some common features. For instance, the materials of digital stories are preset or created by the user and can present the contents of stories; the story architecture usually follows a conceptual structure, and the storytelling of the structure is related to the literal definition of certain story; the conceptual structure would influence the cohesion and consistence of the meaning of the story. Moreover, the spatial application of story factors also influences the cognitive effort to make a story, while the image presentation is dependent on the degree of virtuality and spatiality. Spatiality means that objects can develop in several directions with the contents of stories in any space, while virtuality indicates the degree to which stories are presented in a virtual way. Additionally, the degree of the collaboration in the creation of a story, the degree to which the user controls the plot development of the story, and the degree of interaction allowed by software all influence the degree to which the user is immersed in the creation of stories. Hence, the common features of the above systems were adopted to establish an assessment model of the digital storytelling system.

Norms of Self-evaluation

The seven factors of digital story proposed by Matthews-DeNatale (2008) were adopted to develop the norms of story evaluation:

- View (self/audience): self-view means that one sets an objective early and is clear about the focus throughout the process; view of audience indicates that the creator can clearly explain why the selected text, music and pictures are suitable for the target audience.
- The sound is clear, and the music fits the plot.
- Rhythm: an appropriate rhythm (development and textual segment) can help audience become involved in the story.
- Emotion: Emotional change needs to be consistent with the plot, and audience wants to get acquainted with the motif, figure and creators.
- Image: Image building matches the unique atmosphere and tone in different stages of a story and delivers the meaning or metaphor of symbols.
- Economy: Details are well made, and the story is neither too long nor too short.
- Source citation: The owners, organizations, citations, ideas, music sources and sponsors are clearly marked, and the pictures or sound which is not created by self can also be accepted.

According to the DS application software evaluation model first proposed by Schafer (2004), this study developed a digital storytelling system with 5 dimensions and 12 criteria (concreteness, involvement, conceptual structure, coherence, continuity, cognitive effort, virtuality, spatiality, collaboration, control, interactivity and immersion), so as to evaluate the features of the stories created by learners. According to the analytical results of the reliability and validity of the trial test on the system, the composition layer and the construction layer were combined to form the "fundamental layer". As Schafer employed the 4-point scale, only positive and negative views could be stated, and there wasn't the item of "Neutral". To avoid the problem of relevance, the system features scale of this study is based on the Likert's 5-point scale.

According to what has been mentioned above, technological development has contributed to an increasing number of digital storytelling creations, so that most people can edit their personal stories and share them with others through diverse digital media at any time. In general, digital stories are created in the form of picture and photo, and the plot is developed through text or illustration. Some stories are filmed and edited before they are told; some stories are published on blogs, rich in text and picture. There are special websites and systems for the user to make digital stories, but existing software and systems are unable to help the user create stories with story structure or develop plots with different structures. Therefore, this study used the Pure MVC design system architecture, Flash, and the ActionScript to develop a digital storytelling system, presenting the plots of all scenes created by the user through the storyboard of a linear story structure. Moreover, the process of the user's storytelling was transcribed and recorded with a microphone.

To strengthen the capabilities of students, digital storytelling has been applied to a wide range of courses. In this study, the story setting and the story creation theory proposed by McKee (1997) were taken as the basis of the system construction; they were combined with story review to lead the user to make digital stories, so that learners can develop stories with the basic linear structure. Moreover, the four variation-oriented structures (the paralleled structure, the Z-shaped structure, the bus station structure, and the ring structure) put forward by Sullivan et al. (2012) were added into this digital storytelling system, so that the user can create stories with diverse structures. Finally, the application and usability of the digital storytelling system in teaching were evaluated, so as to explore the role of the system in helping learners create structurally complete stories and develop stories with different variation-oriented structures.

3   Research Method

The digitalized storytelling system is developed in this study by diverse structures that confer on the issue of the structural integrity of the story. The usability evaluations of teaching environment assessment, system features evaluation and self-story assessment are completed by the experts (investigation of teaching environment), user's operation (features of digital storytelling system) and user's satisfaction (of created storytelling). There are three stages in assessment framework to evaluate as shown in Fig. 1.

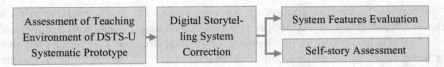

Fig. 1. The Assessment framework

In the first stage, three experts were invited to evaluate the teaching environment of DSTS-U systematic prototype (Psomos and Kordaki 2011) by 16 factors to confirm its effectiveness.

In the second stage, the digital storytelling system was operated by the user and then evaluated the characteristics of the usability of system when effects on learns to create a story. The software of Digital Storytelling Application Evaluation, proposed by Schafer's (2004), is used on evaluating. It is divided into four levels of a total of 12 factors to measure the advantages and disadvantages of the DSTS-U system.

In the third stage, the user assesses the story setting, creation and overall satisfaction of their created story to determine the effect of DSTS-U system on the benefits of the story structure development.

3.1 Experimental Tools

The research tool of DSTS-U system is based on elements of digital storytelling, procedure and related literature. It combined with Pure MVC framework, Flash tool, compiled in the ActionScript language to complete the SWF file, and then executed by the Flash Player on different platforms.

The experiment is carried on the process of story set, story creation and story review bases on the DSTS-U system, and then analyze the results. The story creation model of DSTS-U including 1. Freestyle creation; 2. Structured creation; and 3. Variant structure. The framework of system as shown in Fig. 2.

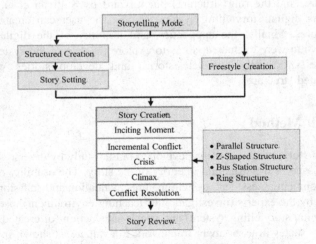

Fig. 2. The framework of DSTS-U system

The DSTS-U system provides learners with a quick and structured storytelling approach that enrich story content through story setting, story creation and story review. There are four different variations in the stage of story structure to enhance and to plenty the story content. Additionally, the DSTS-U system provides a freestyle mode where one could play creative freely. The operation process of system is shown in Fig. 3.

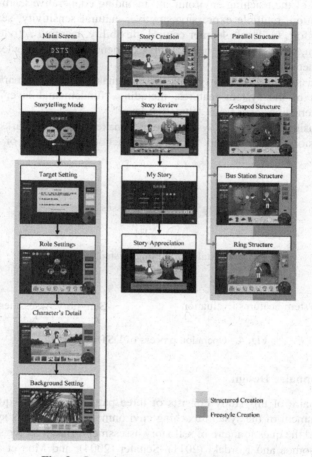

Fig. 3. Operation process of DSTS-U system

3.2 Research Subjects

The DSTS-U system, a storytelling system guides creative story with variation and complete structure, is developed for college students. There were 40 sophomores, 21 males and 19 females, as subjects who have no prior knowledge or similar experiment of digitized storytelling system. According to the teaching of the digital storytelling system, the experiment is planned to last for four weeks. Each experiment was repeated for four times (including the pretest), and each time lasted for 90 min.

3.3 Research Hypotheses

According to the research architecture, the first step is to assess the teaching environment of the system, which is followed by the system features evaluation and the self-storytelling, as is shown in Fig. 4.

H1: After using the DSTS-U system, the user makes positive remarks on the 16 dimensions of the teaching environment, including cooperative learning, creativity and innovation, multiple expression, motive, cultural sensitivity, sexual equality, cognitive effort, feedback, learner control, flexibility, learning activity, knowledge organization, clear objective orientation, experiential value, knowledge organization, and meta-cognition.

H2: After using the DSTS-U system, the user makes positive remarks on the four dimensions of the system features, including "fundamental layer", "expression layer", "interaction layer" and "attraction layer".

H3: After using the DSTS-U system, the user makes positive remarks on the "story setting", "story creation" and "overall satisfaction with story" of the self-story assessment.

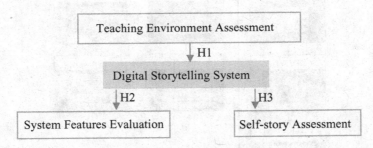

Fig. 4. Operation process of DSTS-U system

3.4 Questionnaire Design

The questionnaire of this study consists of three parts, namely, the questionnaire of expert's assessment of the system teaching environment, the subject's system features evaluation, and the questionnaire of self-story assessment. Based on the studies of such scholars as Psomos and Kordaki (2011), Schafer (2004), and Mou et al. (2013), the items and sentences of the scales were slightly modified to meet the direction of discussion. There were altogether 42 items.

Before the official experiment, 12 copies of the questionnaire were used for the trial test, where Cronbach's Alpha was taken as the test standard to modify the items which were semantically unclear or impractical, so that the Cronbach's Alpha of all the dimensions stayed between 0.553 and 1.000, which was above the 0.5 suggested by the scholars (Fornell et al. 1981). In this way, the questionnaire was reliable.

3.5 Data Analysis Tool

In this study, SPSS 20.0 was taken as the data analysis tool of the questionnaire items and used to explore the relevance between the items and the dimensions. Additionally, the qualitative view was adopted for a deeper analysis to demonstrate the results of this study.

4 Analysis and Discussion

4.1 Analysis of the Reliability and Validity of the Questionnaire

The Cronbach's α of the dimensions of the system features assessment of the scale stayed between 0.674 and 1.000, and the overall Cronbach's α was 0.899. The Cronbach's α of the dimensions of self-story assessment ranged from 0.677 to 0.732, and the overall Cronbach's α was 0.869, which was higher than the 0.7 mentioned by Nunnally (1978), indicating a high level of reliability. According to Fornell and Larker (1981), the combined reliability should be higher than 0.6, and a higher value indicates that the items are more capable of detecting potential variables. The combined reliability of the dimensions was between 0.821 and 1.000, which is consistent with the level suggested by the scholars. The average variance extracted (AVE) of the dimensions stayed between 0.553 and 1.000, higher than the 0.5 suggested by the scholars (Fornell et al. 1981). According to Table 1, both the combined reliability and the AVE reached the standard level, which means that this study has a high level of dimensional reliability.

Table 1. Analysis of reliability of the scale

Content	Dimension	Cronbach's alpha	Composite reliability	AVE
System features assessment	Fundamental layer	0.822	0.881	0.649
	Presentation	0.674	0.860	0.754
	Interactivity	0.694	0.831	0.621
	Appeal	1.000	1.000	1.000
Cronbach's alpha = 0.899				
Self-story assessment	Story setting	0.677	0.821	0.605
	Story creation	0.799	0.862	0.558
	Overall satisfaction with story	0.732	0.831	0.553
Cronbach's alpha = 0.869				

Tables 2 and 3 show the matrix of relevant coefficients among the dimensions, and diagonal shows the AVE square roots of the conceptual variables. It reveals that the variables of the dimensions in the model indeed varied from each other, which means that the questionnaire of this study has a high level of discriminant validity.

Table 2. Discriminant validity of the dimensions of the system features evaluation

Dimension	Construction layer	Presentation	Interactivity	Appeal
Construction layer	0.806			
Presentation	0.722	0.868		
Interactivity	0.784	0.570	0.788	
Appeal	0.669	0.493	0.696	1.000

Table 3. Discriminant validity of the dimensions of the self-story assessment

Dimension	Story setting	Story creation	Overall satisfaction with story
Story setting	0.778		
Story creation	0.577	0.747	
Overall satisfaction with story	0.452	0.724	0.744

4.2   Analysis of Usability

The DSTS-U system is something new for beginners, so it takes them some time to get used to it. In terms of difficulty, the story system is suitable for beginners (Table 4).

Table 4. Analysis of the difficulty of the story system

Difficulty	Number of subjects	Percentage
Very easy	2	5%
Easy	17	43%
Average	21	52%

In the Experimental Group, 38 subjects believed that the hints offered in the story creation were very clear or clear, accounting for 98% of the samples (Table 5). Hence, it is possible to make the conclusion that the instructions in the hint column on the left side of the DSTS-U system interface are clear enough for learners to follow the steps of story creation (Table 5).

Table 5. Analysis of the clarity of the hints offered in the story creation

Clarity	Number of subjects	Percentage
Very clear	7	17%
Clear	31	78%
Average	2	5%

37 subjects were very clear or clear that structure was needed for story design, accounting for 92% of the samples. Therefore, it is possible to make the conclusion that the user follows the story architecture of the DSTS-U system and is clear that structure is needed for story design (Table 6).

Table 6. Analysis of the degree of being clear that structure is needed for story design

Degree of clarity	Number of subjects	Percentage
Very clear	5	12%
Clear	32	80%
Average	3	8%

12 subjects agreed to continue to use the system to tell stories, taking up 30% of the samples; 28 subjects showed the attitude of "Average", accounting for 70%. Therefore, most of subjects showed the attitude of "Average" when asked to continue to tell stories with this system (Table 7).

Table 7. Analysis of the intention to continue to tell stories with this system

Degree of agreement	Number of subjects	Percentage
Agreeable	12	30%
Average	28	70%

Analysis of the Standards of the DSTS-U Digital Storytelling Teaching Environment

This study aims to develop a storytelling system featuring complete creation. To evaluate the usability of this system in a prudent way, the questionnaire was made according to relevant academic papers, and three experts were invited to analyze the teaching environment of the digital storytelling system. On the whole, the average of the three experts' scores for such dimensions as collaborative learning, creativity and innovation, motive, cultural sensitivity, feedback, flexibility, learning activity, knowledge organization, clear objective orientation, and experiential value was high. In terms of cognitive effort, the average of the scores by the experts was low; as for learner control, it was "Average"; when it comes to sexual equality and meta-cognition, the average of the scores by the experts was very high (Table 8).

Analysis of Difference in the System Features Dimension

In the system features evaluation, the average score of the fundamental layer, the expression layer, the interaction layer, and the attraction layer was 4.03, 4.05, 4.06 and 4.15 respectively. It is estimated that the DSTS-U system combined with different virtual materials can facilitate the creation of story board of different visual effects. The scores of the operation of whole system, the story creation progress, the flexibility of modification, the collaborative creation, and the degree of immersion were positive.

Analysis of Self-story Assessment

There was no significant difference in gender among the dimensions of the self-story assessment, which indicates that gender would not affect the use of the digital story-telling system. This study adopted the ANOVA and the Post-Hoc test to explore if the difference in the degree of being clear that structure is needed for story design would influence the variable of continuing to use the system. The significance of the "Levene test with equal variables" was lower than .05, which implied heterogeneity. In the

Table 8. Experts' scores for the digital storytelling teaching environment

Standard	T1	T2	T3	Total average
Collaborative learning	4	4	4	4
Creativity and innovation	3	4	5	4
Multiple representations	4	4	4	4
Motivation	4	4	4	4
	4	4	4	
Cultural sensitivity	4	4	4	4
Gender equality	4	5	5	4.67
Cognitive effort	2	3	2	2.33
Learner control	3	3	4	3.33
Feedback	4	3	4	3.67
Flexibility	5	4	5	4.33
	4	4	4	
Learner activity	4	3	5	4
Value of previous knowledge	5	4	4	3.92
	4	4	4	
	4	3	4	
Sharply-focused goal orientation	4	3	4	3.67
Experiential value	3	4	4	3.67
Knowledge organization	4	4	5	4.33
Metacognition	5	4	5	4.67

Games-Howell test, p was .002 (which was .000, lower than .05), showing significant difference between "those who are averagely clear that structure is needed for story design" and "those who are clear that structure is needed for story design"; "those who are clear that structure is needed for story design" showed a stronger intention of continuing to use this system. It is deduced that the user find it difficult to the DSTS-U system in the first use and that it takes him/her some time to get used to it; however, after he/she becomes clear that structure is needed for story design, he/she is willing to continue to use the DSTS-U system.

With the DSTS-U system, the user can adopt several story factors to establish story board quickly and try the combination of different materials with the hints of different scenes. The different image presentation, along with the written description, indeed enables the user to create a structurally complete story.

In the experiment, the subjects needed to discuss the setting of story objective, role, role's preference, and spatial and temporal background to become familiar with and apply the concepts of different variation-oriented structures. After that, they entered the stage of story creation directly and developed stories through such scenes of triggering event, progressive conflict, crises, climax and ending. In this stage, it is possible to enrich the contents of stories through the variation-oriented structures. In the final story review, the stories were reviewed and slightly modified, so that the subjects would be able to create a story with a complete structure and much variation in content.

Research results: H1: After using the DSTS-U system, the user made positive remarks on the 16 dimensions of the teaching environment.

H2: After using the DSTS-U system, the user made positive remarks on the 4 dimensions of the system features.

H3: After using the DSTS-U system, the user made positive remarks on the 3 dimensions of the self-story assessment.

As a whole, the digital storytelling system developed in this study enables learners to present stories in forms of text, picture and recording; moreover, learners are clear about their direction and the objectives to achieve with the hints; the structural concept enables learners to immediately acquire knowledge; the use of the system meets the need of cultural diversity and sexual equality, and the mental loading is low; learners can master the system in a flexible way. If they encounter any problems in the use, they can receive immediate response. With the assistance of teachers, students will indulge themselves in the creation, enhance their awareness of story structure, and feel willing to use the system again. Therefore, learners can create a story with a complete structure and obtain the knowledge of story concept with the help of the DSTS-U system.

5   Conclusion

With story structure as the basis, this study attempts to develop a digital storytelling system called Digital Storytelling Teaching System-University (DSTS-U). With the system, learners can quickly create stories with structural architecture and increase the variation in stories with different story structures. Also, the usability of this system was evaluated from three perspectives, namely, teaching environment assessment, system features evaluation, and self-story assessment.

The results show that the experts provide a positive evaluation for the DSTS-U on learner's teaching environment. It is sure that the DSTS-U system achieves the purpose of this study with positive evaluation of the characteristics and self-story satisfaction. The user could create a structured story and prompted the knowledge of story concept by using the DSTS-U system. The user would complete a structured digital story through the tips to guide when familiar with the DSTS-U system. In additional, DSTS-U system provides a good creative tool for users to create an in-depth story. In the process of DSTS-U, knowledge construction of structural stories concepts would be learned when the user starts the variant structure story creation based on the basic structural formula. It would enrich the story deeply.

References

Bruner, J.: Acts of Meaning. Harvard University Press, Cambridge (1990)

Chung, S.K.: Digital storytelling in integrated arts education. Int. J. Arts Educ. **4**(1), 33–50 (2006)

Di Blas, N., Paolini, P., Sabiescu, A.: Collective digital storytelling at school as a whole-class interaction. In: Proceedings of the 9th International Conference on Interaction Design and Children, pp. 11–19 (2010). doi:10.1145/1810543.1810546

Di Blas, N., Boretti, B.: Interactive storytelling in pre-school: a case-study. In:Proceedings of the 8th International Conference on Interaction Design and Children, pp. 44–51 (2009). doi:10. 1145/1551788.1551797

Fornell, C.R., Larcker, F.F.: Evaluating structural equation models with unobservable variables and measurement error. J. Mark. Res. 18(1), 39–51 (1981)

Gils, F.: Potential applications of digital storytelling in education. In: 3rd Twente Student Conference on IT, University of Twente, Faculty of Electrical Engineering, Mathematics and Computer Science, Enschede, 17–18 February 2005

Padilla-Zea, N., Gutiérrez, F.L., López-Arcos, J.R., Abad-Arranz, A., Paderewski, P.: Modeling storytelling to be used in educational video games. Comput. Hum. Behav. 31, 461–474 (2013). 10.1016/j.chb.2013.04.020

Ibanez, J., Aylett, R., Ruiz-Rodarte, R.: Storytelling in virtual environments from a virtual guide perspective. Virtual Reality 7(1), 30–42 (2003)

Laura, G.: Teaching techniques: using "Storybird" in young learners' creative writing class. Engl. Teach. Forum 53(4), 35–37 (2015)

Liu, C.C., Holly, S.L., Shih, J.-L., Huang, G.-T., Liu, B.-J.: An enhanced concept map approach to improving children's storytelling ability. Comput. Educ. 56(3), 873–884 (2011)

Jonassen, D.H., Hernandez-Serrano, J.: Case-based reasoning and instructional design using stories to support problem solving. Educ. Tech. Res. Dev. 50(2), 65–77 (2002)

Matthews-DeNatale, G.: Digital Storytelling Tips and Resources. Simmons College, Boston (2008)

McKee, R.: Style, Structure, Substance, and the Principles of Screenwriting. HarperCollins Press, New York (1997)

Mello, R.: The power of storytelling: how oral narrative influences children's relationships in classrooms. Int. J. Educ. Arts 2(1) (2001). http://www.ijea.org/v2n1/

Miller, C.H.: Digital Storytelling: A Creator's Guide to Interactive Entertainment. Focal Press, Burlington (2004)

Mou, T.Y., Jeng, T.S., Chen, C.H.: From storyboard to story: animation content development. Glob. Sci. Res. J. 1(1), 18–33 (2013)

Nokeleinen, P.: An empirical assessment of pedagogical usability criteria for digital learning material with elementary school students. Educ. Technol. Soc. 9(2), 178–197 (2006)

Nunnally, J.C.: Psychometric Theory (2nd ed.). McGraw-Hill Press, New York (1978)

Pierotti, K.E.: Digital Storytelling: an application of vichian theory. Master thesis, Brigham Young University (2006)

Porter, B.: Digitales: The Art of Telling Digital Stories. Bernajean Porter Consulting, Denver, Colorado, USA (2005)

Psomos, P., Kordaki, M.: A novel pedagogical evaluation model for educational digital storytelling environments. In: Proceedings of E-Learn 2011, Honolulu, Hawaii, USA, 17–21 October 2011, pp. 842–851. AACE, Chesapeake (2011)

Psomos, P., Kordaki, M.: Analysis of educational digital storytelling software using the "Dimension Star" model. Int. J. Knowl. Soc. Res. 3(4), 22–32 (2012). doi:10.4018/jksr. 2012100103

Renda, C.: Beyond journals: using digital storytelling to encourage meaningful teacher reflection. In: Gibson, D., Dodge, B. (eds.) Proceedings of Society for Information Technology & Teacher Education International Conference 2010, pp. 1165–1170 (2010)

Robin, B.: Digital storytelling: a powerful technology tool for the 21st century classroom. Theory Pract. 47, 220–228 (2008)

Robin, B.: The educational uses of digital storytelling (2005). https://digitalliteracyinthe classroom.pbworks.com/f/Educ-Uses-DS.pdf

Robin, B., Pierson, M.: A multilevel approach to using digital storytelling in the classroom. In: Crawford, C., Carlsen, R., Gibson, I., McFerrin, K., Price, J., Weber, R., Willis, D. (eds.) Proceedings of Society for Information Technology & Teacher Education International Conference 2005, pp. 708–716. Association for the Advancement of Computing in Education (AACE), Chesapeake (2005)

Russell, A.: Toontastic: a global storytelling network for kids, by Kids. In: TEI 2010, pp. 271–274 (2010). doi:10.1145/1709886.1709942

Sadik, A.: Digital storytelling: a meaningful technology-integrated approach for engaged student learning. Educ. Technol. Res. Dev. 56(4), 487–506 (2008)

Schafer, L.: Models for digital storytelling and interactive narratives. In: 4th International Conference on Computational Semiotics for Games and New Media, Split, pp. 148–155 (2004)

Shin, B.J., Park, H.S.: The effect of digital storytelling type on the learner's fun and comprehension in virtual reality. J. Korean Assoc. Inf. Educ. 12(4), 417–425 (2008)

Skinner, E.N., Hagood, M.C.: Developing literate identities with English language learners through digital storytelling. Read. Matrix 8(2), 12–38 (2008)

Sullivan, K., Schumer, G., Alexander, K.: Ideas for the Animated Short with DVD Finding and Building Stories. Taylor & Francis (2012)

Susono, H., Simomura T., Oda, K., Ono, E.: Production of storytelling by college students using Kamishibai, video-camera and computer. In: Research Report of JSET Conferences, JSET07-2, pp. 23–28 (2007)

Sylla, C., Coutinho, C., Branco, P.: Play platforms for children's creativity. Creativity Digit. Age 12, 223–243 (2015). doi:10.1007/978-1-4471-6681-8_12

Tsou, W., Wang, W., Tzeng, Y.: Applying a multimedia storytelling website in foreign language learning. Comput. Educ. 47(1), 17–28 (2006)

Xu, Y., Park, H., Baek, Y.: A new approach toward digital storytelling: an activity focused on writing self efficacy in a virtual learning environment. Educ. Technol. Soc. 14(4), 181–191 (2011)

Yang, Y.T.C., Wu, W.C.I.: Digital storytelling for enhancing student academic achievement, critical thinking, and learning motivation: a year-long experimental study. Comput. Educ. 59, 339–352 (2012). doi:10.1016/j.compedu.2011.12.012

Nellodee 2.0: A Quantified Self Reading App for Tracking Reading Goals

Sanghyun Yoo[(⊠)], Jonatan Lemos, and Ed Finn

School of Arts, Media and Engineering, Arizona State University,
Tempe, AZ, USA
{cooperyoo, jlemoszu, edfinn}@asu.edu

Abstract. Many readers nowadays struggle with finishing the books that they set out to read. To find a solution to this issue, we performed a design exercise which resulted in the development of a reading app that uses a quantified self (QS) approach to track reading goals, called Nellodee. This app allows readers to estimate the number of pages they would have to read to reach a daily reading goal and tracks their progress over time enabling them to reflect on their reading performance. In this paper, we present the design and implementation of our system and the results of an early pilot test are discussed.

Keywords: Reading · Quantified self · Self-monitoring · Self-tracking · Goal-setting · Personal informatics · Digital reading app · Reading goals

1 Introduction

In the digital era, there are boundless possibilities for using computational interfaces and ubiquitous computing to enhance reading practices. E-readers such as the Kindle, Nook, Kobo, and iBook allow readers to read e-books across different platforms. Additionally, many readers these days perform their reading sessions in digital devices due to their abundance and availability [3, 20], enabling the use of digital reading strategies, especially self-regulation and self-monitoring [1].

Self-knowledge through numbers or Quantified Self (QS) is a movement that is based on incorporating technology and data acquisition on different aspects of a person's daily life. QS promotes self-tracking of various kinds of personal information, ranging from physical activities to environmental information [11, 12]. Commonly, QS users utilize their tracked data to see how they are or are not reaching the goals they set for themselves [9] and this type of systems also help people collect personally relevant information for the purpose of self-reflection and gaining self-knowledge [8].

Studies have shown that when readers set goals for themselves they tend to positively change their behavior [10, 21], and when they meet their reading goals their confidence and sense of achievement increases [17]. Thus this work in progress presents a study which is an attempt to have insights into how reading habits can be improved through a quantified approach, by allowing participants to set reading goals for themselves, while at the same time allowing them to track their reading performance to reflect upon it.

© Springer International Publishing AG 2017
P. Zaphiris and A. Ioannou (Eds.): LCT 2017, Part II, LNCS 10296, pp. 488–496, 2017.
DOI: 10.1007/978-3-319-58515-4_37

The goal of this study is to investigate if providing readers with access to their progress data makes them more likely to reach reading goals. The design of a prototype quantified-self reading app called Nellodee will be presented, and the pilot study that was carried out to try to answer our research questions will be described.

2 Related Work

Recent developments in the field of ambient sensors and wearable tracking devices have led to an interest in self-tracking and self-monitoring. Effectiveness on increased awareness and behavior change has led to the development of various quantified tools for daily life and work [2]. Health and physical activities are the most tracked events in QS interventions. Within the health domain, researchers and companies have designed technologies for tracking physical fitness, sleep, diet, and stress [12].

Several attempts have been made to integrate self-monitoring and QS into the design of learning environments. Rivera-Pelayo et al.'s research shows how QS approaches can support evaluating past experiences in order to promote continuous learning [15]. Other studies have found that frameworks for the application of QS applications to support reflective learning have a potential higher impact on self-awareness and student learning [7, 16]. The act of reading has also become more quantified with the development of e-readers and self-tracking technologies. Mobile eye tracking technology has also been used to determine how much people read, what type of documents they read, and how much they understand of what they are reading [4, 5]. Systems such as the Wordometer, estimate the number of words a person reads which is similar to the counting of steps using a pedometer [6].

Although reading metrics have already been used to analyze reading performance, few attempts to allow deep self-reflection in digital reading have been made. Thus, we see an opportunity to help readers who struggle with finishing their assigned book readings to achieve their reading goals by providing them with a mobile application that allows them to track their reading performance and reflect upon it.

The following section of this paper presents Nellodee, which is a digital reading app that uses QS techniques to track the reading progress of its users. The readers can set reading goals for themselves and reflect on their performance. It constitutes an initial approach to test if digital readers can benefit from a QS approach.

3 Nellodee

Nellodee started as a design fiction exercise inspired by some of the features found in the Primer device from Neal Stephenson's sci-fi novel "The Diamond Age" [19] and it is named after one of its characters. The result of this design exercise is a digital reading app which uses QS techniques to track the reading progress of its users. The prototype is a standalone application for iOS that enables readers to set personal reading goals and reflect on their performance. It aims at providing a unique reading experience of providing reading metrics to audiences of all age groups who are enthusiastic about reading.

4   Design and Implementation

4.1   Reading Page

The landing page of the app is similar to other reading apps for the iPad, such as Kobo, Nook, Kindle, and iBooks (See Fig. 1). The unique feature of the design of Nellodee's reading page, is that it shows the page the reader started reading on a given day and the target page that was set as the daily reading goal for that day. The bottom bar shows the page the user is reading at the moment, and the "running silhouette" icon also indicates the current page. The bar is used to show how far the user is from completing the daily goal. The completion rate of the goal is also shown to allow the reader to be self-aware of her performance.

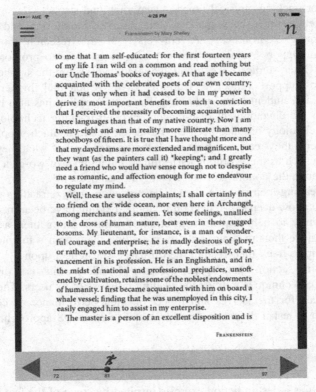

Fig. 1. Reading page. The reader started her daily reading session from page 72, and the target daily goal is page 97

4.2   Goals Page and Trends Page

Nellodee has a 'goals page' where readers can monitor their daily reading metrics. Readers can set daily goals for how many pages they want to read each day. They can choose to set their personal goal by pages per day or by the date they want to finish reading the book by (See Fig. 2). Based on the reader's goal-setting, the 'daily goal' graph shows the goal of each day in grey bars. Readers can also compare their daily goal (grey bar) and the number of pages they have actually read each day (brown bar).

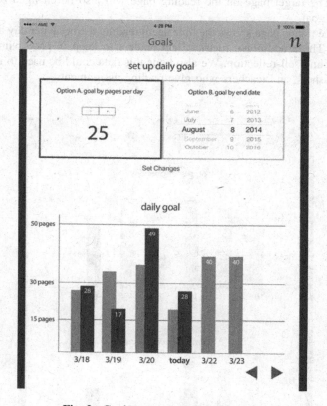

Fig. 2. Goals page (Color figure online)

According to Steel's research [14], procrastination is defined as a "prevalent and pernicious form of self-regulatory failure". Often when readers want to reduce procrastination, they make short-term or long-term plans to meet their goals later [18]. We designed two different ways to update the goals of upcoming days based on the missed pages. For the long-term option, the system adapts the goals to spread the missed pages over the remaining days. For example, if the daily goal is 25 pages and the user only read 20 pages, the updated daily goal will be "(25 − 20)/(days left) + 25". In the short-term option, the missed pages will be carried forward to the next day. So the updated goal for the next day is "25 + 5", and the goal of the rest of the days is still "25".

Li et al. found that if a user has been tracking an activity for a long period of time, they are more likely to allow themselves to miss the goals [9]. When designing Nellodee, we saw that a long-term plan may fail to stimulate readers to achieve daily goals in the early days and end up adding too many pages to updated daily goals when the end date is getting close. Thus, we decided to apply the short-term plan and allow readers to change their goals at any time. Readers can self-monitor their achievement rate and reset the goal to an achievable level, especially when they see the next day goal is too high. The target page on the reading page will also be changed based on the revised daily goal.

Finally, the trends page shows the time spent reading the book per day and per page (See Fig. 3). These additional metrics help readers to keep in pace with time, contributing enabling self-reflection. We also hope this data could be used to inform book authors, publishers, and teachers who give reading assignments.

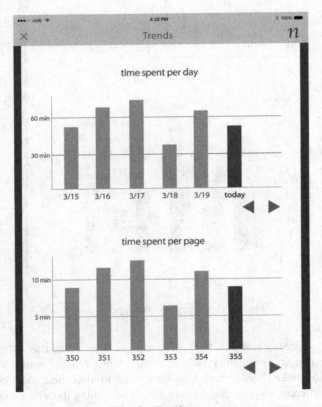

Fig. 3. Trends page

5 Study Design Overview

This project aims to answer the following research question: "Does providing readers with access to their reading data makes them more self-aware of their reading performance and more likely to reach daily reading goals?"

The working hypothesis of this research is that quantified-self features in a digital reading app will support students to achieve their reading goals. To increase our understanding of the way self-reflection affects reading performance, the following goals were to be reached:

- Identify the context where the digital reading sessions occur.
- Identify the way readers perceive quantified-self features as useful.

5.1 Procedure

Four graduate student participants (N = 4, 3 = female, 1 = male) pilot tested the Nellodee app installed in four iPad Air2 devices over the course of a two-week period while reading a book of their choice. There were two conditions: (1) NLD-Experiment: The Nellodee app which contained reading metrics that the participants could see and, (2) NLD-Control: The Nellodee app with a control condition without these metrics. Participants were randomly assigned to two groups of two students in each group. In the first week (session 1), group A read the book with NLD-Experiment, while group B read the same book with NLD-Control. In the second week (session 2), groups A and B switched roles. The reason why we had two different groups was to minimize the possibility of the two conditions variating over the two time periods, independent of the use of Nellodee.

5.2 Measures

The main source of data was the information collected through the app from each reading session. This data contained the number of pages, time and log information of each participant. The following are the metrics that were collected:

- Achievement rate of reading goals
- Number of pages read per day
- Number of pages read per week
- Time spent per page
- Frequency of looking at the Trends Page
- Frequency of looking at the Goals page
- Frequency of changing daily goals

The effectiveness of the app in helping users meet their goals was also assessed by gathering data from a post-study interview, which surveyed the perceived usefulness of its features and its context of use.

5.3 Interviews

After completing the two weeks of reading sessions, participants were asked to come to our lab for a short interview to acquire better insights on how the participants were using the app. Every interview lasted on average 15 min including questions about the features of the app, about how useful it was in helping them or not to meet the reading goals they set for themselves and about potential future uses.

6 Early Findings

During the two-week pilot study, we collected data from the reading sessions and found out that the app is robust and user-friendly. However, there were no significant differences between the two groups of readers. Since our study sample was relatively small, we focused more on the qualitative feedback from the participants at this stage.

The most interesting feature about Nellodee for the participants was goal tracking. P1 said "when I reached my goal, I was motivated to read more". P3 said "I think the goals and the history of your reading with the number of pages is a good feature to have". Some readers suggested notifications upon goal completion, P1 said "when someone completes a goal, giving notifications such as 'congratulations' or 'you reached your goal' can motivate the reader".

When asked about their reading behavior some participants felt that reflecting on their performance was useful, P1 said: "when I reached my goal, I was motivated to read more", the user also said "if you see your performance, you feel like you are engaged with the book and you want to improve more". On the other hand, other readers did not find it necessary to set goals for themselves, P2 said "if I read more pages is because I am interested in the content". By reflecting upon the types of readers who would set goals for themselves, P4 said: "the whole concept of having feedback on performance and setting goals for yourself depends on the personality of the participant".

The interviewees also let us know that the app had good usability. P2 said "I think it was easy to use." Some of the readers wanted to have features that are present in other e-readers. If some of these features are to be implemented, for example P1 suggested push notifications to remind readers to continue their reading sessions; we would need to perform further tests to assess their efficacy.

Indeed, the collected data shows that all the participants lost interest in the app after one week. We found that app usage was significantly lower for week two than for week one. It is certainly plausible that in addition to self-tracking and self-monitoring, there are plenty of other general factors which affects user's reading performance. P4 said "I was traveling this week, so I didn't have much time to read", and P2 said "the book isn't interesting enough for me". Another potential explanation is that quantified self features may encourage and motivate the existing readers to read more, but are less interesting for occasional readers to resume reading. For future iterations, we are considering adding features to keep readers interested in using it. Adding additional features such as rewards, feedback messages about their performance and notifications are also considered.

When participants were asked about the possibility of using Nellodee to read for leisure purposes, P1 said "I would, since it as the features that other PDF readers have.". However, some did not find it appealing, P2 said "I don't think it would help me to read for pleasure (…) it kind of makes me feel pressure not pleasure". From these responses, we infer that different types of reading goals [13] might influence the way participants perceive our app.

7 Conclusion

In this paper, we presented the first iteration of the development process of the Nellodee reading app. We developed this system to have more insights into reading habits and see how allowing readers to set reading goals for themselves and track their reading performance can support them in the completion of readings tasks. This early pilot test helped us refine our approach to use QS features in reading apps that are gear towards motivating users to read more and complete reading assignments.

In the pilot test, we found that even for a small group of testers, there were different motivations towards their chosen reading materials, some chose their books to read for leisure others for learning purposes. Taking into account these motivations might inform us better in selecting the population that could benefit more from the use of our system, college students for example.

In the future, we plan to conduct a field study in a classroom with participants from courses where there are books that are assigned throughout a long period such as an entire semester. One of our future goals will be to compare how they perform against digital readers that do not track their reading progress. We argue that by providing readers with QS features such as goal-setting and goal-tracking, we can help them improve their reading performance.

Acknowledgments. This study was reviewed and approved by Arizona State University's Internal Review Board (STUDY00004066) and was made possible with support from the National Science Foundation (NSF #CRS0496).

References

1. ChanLin, L.J.: Reading strategy and the need of e-book features. Electron. Libr. **31**(3), 329–344 (2013)
2. Choe, E.K., Lee, N.B., Lee, B., Pratt, W., Kientz, J.A.: Understanding quantified-selfers' practices in collecting and exploring personal data. In: Proceedings of the 32nd Annual ACM Conference on Human Factors in Computing Systems, pp. 1143–1152 (2014)
3. Hupfeld, A., Sellen, A., O'Hara, K., Rodden, T.: Leisure-Based Reading and the Place of E-Books in Everyday Life. In: Kotzé, P., Marsden, G., Lindgaard, G., Wesson, J., Winckler, M. (eds.) INTERACT 2013. LNCS, vol. 8118, pp. 1–18. Springer, Heidelberg (2013). doi:10.1007/978-3-642-40480-1_1
4. Kunze, K., Masai, K., Inami, M., Sacakli, Ö., Liwicki, M., Dengel, A., Ishimaru, S., Kise, K.: Quantifying reading habits: counting how many words you read. In: Proceedings of the 2015 ACM International Joint Conference on Pervasive and Ubiquitous Computing, pp. 87–96 (2015)
5. Kunze, K., Iwamura, M., Kise, K., Uchida, S., Omachi, S.: Activity recognition for the mind: toward a cognitive "quantified self". Comput. **46**(10), 105–108 (2013)
6. Kunze, K., Kawaichi, H., Yoshimura, K., Kise, K.: The wordometer–estimating the number of words read using document image retrieval and mobile eye tracking. In: 12th International Conference on Document Analysis and Recognition, pp. 25–29 (2013)
7. Lee, V.R: "What's happening in the "quantified self" movement?". In: ICLS 2014 Proceedings, pp. 1032–1036 (2014)

8. Li, I., Dey, A., Forlizzi, J.: A stage-based model of personal informatics systems. In: Proceedings of the SIGCHI Conference on Human Factors in Computing Systems, pp. 557–566 (2010)
9. Li, I., Dey, A., Forlizzi, J.: Understanding my data, myself: supporting self-reflection with ubicomp technologies. In: Proceedings of the 13th International Conference on Ubiquitous Computing, pp. 405–414 (2011)
10. Locke, E.A., Latham, G.P.: Building a practically useful theory of goal setting and task motivation: a 35-year odyssey. Am. Psychol. **57**(9), 705 (2002)
11. Mathur, A., Van den Broeck, M., Vanderhulst, G., Mashhadi, A., Kawsar, F.: Tiny habits in the giant enterprise: understanding the dynamics of a quantified workplace. In: Proceedings of the 2015 ACM International Joint Conference on Pervasive and Ubiquitous Computing, pp. 577–588 (2015)
12. Oh, J., Lee, U.: Exploring user experience issues in quantified self technologies. Eighth International Conference on Mobile Computing and Ubiquitous Networking (ICMU), pp. 53–59 (2015)
13. O'Hara, K.: Towards a Typology of Reading Goals (1996)
14. Steel, P.: The nature of procrastination: a meta-analytic and theoretical review of quintessential self-regulatory failure. Psychol. Bull. **133**(1), 65 (2007)
15. Rivera-Pelayo, V., Zacharias, V., Müller, L., Braun, S.: Applying quantified self approaches to support reflective learning. In: Proceedings of the 2nd International Conference on Learning Analytics and Knowledge, pp. 111–114 (2012)
16. Santos, J.L, Verbert, K., Govaerts, S., Duval, E.: Addressing learner issues with StepUp!: an evaluation. In: Proceedings of the Third International Conference on Learning Analytics and Knowledge, pp. 14–22 (2013)
17. Schoep, M., Wood, E.: Motivating Students to Read Extensively. ISSN 1756-509X 1: 16 (2015)
18. Sjöklint, M., Constantiou, I.D., Trier, M.: The Complexities of Self-Tracking-An Inquiry into User Reactions and Goal Attainment (2015). Available at SSRN 2611193
19. Stephenson, N.: The Diamond Age, Or, A Young Lady's Illustrated Primer. Bantam-Random, New York (1995)
20. Thayer, A., Lee, C.P, Hwang L.H., Sales, H., Sen, P., Dalal, N.: The imposition and superimposition of digital reading technology: the academic potential of e-readers. In: Proceedings of the SIGCHI Conference on Human Factors in Computing Systems, pp. 2917–2926 (2011)
21. Zimmerman, B.J., Bandura, A., Martinez-Pons, M.: Self-motivation for academic attainment: the role of self-efficacy beliefs and personal goal setting. Am. Educ. Res. J. **29**(3), 663–676 (1992)

Author Index

Printed in the United States
By Bookmasters